EDINBURGH UNIVERSITY PUBLICATIONS
History, Philosophy and Economics
No. 16

The Governance of
MEDIAEVAL ENGLAND
from the Conquest to Magna Carta

H.G. RICHARDSON F.B.A. AND G.O. SAYLES F.B.A.

EDINBURGH
at the University Press

© 1963
H.G. Richardson and G.O. Sayles
EDINBURGH UNIVERSITY PRESS
22 George Square Edinburgh
North America
Aldine Publishing Company
529 South Wabash Avenue, Chicago

ISBN 0 85224 102 X
First Published 1963
Reprinted 1964, 1974

Printed in Great Britain by
Lewis Reprints Ltd.
(member of The Brown, Knight & Truscott Group)
London & Tonbridge

APOLOGIA PRO LIBELLO SUO

THE form and content of this book may seem to require an explanation. Its aim is both critical and constructive. While seeking to clear from the path of the historian much that seems to us worthless and misleading, a mere clog upon learning, we also endeavour to put in its place teaching founded upon a scrupulous examination of the sources and, to our utmost endeavour, free from bias and preconception. Why, then, it may be asked, does the name of William Stubbs come so persistently into the book? We have been assured that his *magnum opus* is not read now or, if read at all, not by the rising generation of historians. But how much was the *Constitutional History* ever read by undergraduates? Maybe it was on their shelves, but what does that tell us? Could it not be said of Stubbs, as it has been said of his contemporaries of equal authority, 'the happiest hours of my life were those I ought to have spent with you'? Yet, even if undergraduates were deaf to all advice—and the *Constitutional History* has never ceased to be commended to history students[1]—they could not escape Stubbs's teaching. It has come to them in ever repeated lectures; it is to be found in every textbook.

For all that concerns the constitutional history of mediaeval England, the teaching of William Stubbs has been inexpugnably dominant in English and American universities for more than eighty years. As a very recent American commentator has said, 'revision of the political and constitutional history of the later Middle Ages has meant, in the main, revision of Stubbs's *Constitutional History*'.[2] If his teaching has been questioned in this field or that, the questionings have not greatly disturbed historians. They may concede that, here and there, Stubbs's views need to be revised, but they still feel able to commend the body of his work as authentic and reliable history. The *Constitutional History*, says Mr A. L. Poole, 'remains, in spite of its date, the best and most authoritative starting point for a detailed study of mediaeval institutions'.[3] And it has, it would appear, the quality of a prophylactic. It is described by the late Director of the Institute of Historical Research 'as a sovereign antidote' against the tendency which young historians have (so it is alleged) to proceed 'from one novelty to another, from the latest periodical to the latest

---

[1] See *Handbook for History Teachers*, ed. W. H. Burston and C. W. Green (London, 1962), p. 448: 'Once familiar with the rudiments [students] should certainly read W. Stubbs, *Constitutional History of England*, the most influential single book on medieval English history.'

[2] *Speculum*, xxxvi (1961), 228.

[3] *From Domesday Book to Magna Carta* (1951), p. 500.

Festschrift' and to become in the process ' "up-to-date" without being well grounded'.[1]

Those who have had the *Constitutional History* constantly at hand know how many current views originated with Stubbs. His beliefs have been passed on almost without scrutiny: echoes are to be found everywhere. Let us cite but one example, that of Stephen Langton's supposititious part in shaping Magna Carta. It is difficult to imagine that so many historians should have arrived independently at conclusions that are so questionable, so remote from probability, so incompatible with the available evidence. It matters not, however, whether appearances are deceptive, whether this strange consensus is or is not the result of unbiased and individual enquiry. It may save much argument if, without express reference to later writers, we go direct to the fountain head and expose Stubbs's errors. The one criticism will serve for all, and the reader will be able to apply it to the same story wherever he finds it. Our book then is devised not merely for those who have actually read the *Constitutional History* but also, and indeed principally, for that large majority who have lacked the courage or the leisure to do so. For Stubbs's doctrines and Stubbs's misconceptions will be found repeated, it may well be almost unawares, not only in textbooks—those homes of superseded learning—but in books that purport to be the fruit of original research. Though Stubbs be unmentioned and unacknowledged, he stands in the background, and the persistence of his errors makes our task doubly necessary. Nor do we seek to address British and American historians only. We trust that this book may find its way into the hands of our continental colleagues lest, as too often in the past, they accept the *Constitutional History* as of final authority and thereby confuse some not unimportant issues in the history of their own countries.[2]

It may be well to add that, though the reader may not find among our references some recent (as well as older) books and articles that bear upon the period covered by this volume, he must not infer that we have not read them or considered them carefully. No object, however, would be served either by expressing a dissent which is plain enough from our text as it stands or by citing the views of those whose conclusions agree with our own: their support may comfort us, but it does not add to the weight of the evidence. Over many years now we have gone to the sources, and our chapters have been written and re-written in the light afforded by contemporary witnesses of the events, dimly as this light may sometimes shine in the pages of later mediaeval writers. We say this in no disparagement of our fellow historians, whose changing opinions—it goes without saying—have influenced ours, though more often through the medium of an

[1] Sir Goronwy Edwards, *William Stubbs* (1952), p. 20.
[2] Cf. the comment of the editor of the *English Historical Review* (lxxvii.355) in April 1962: 'The shadow of Stubbs lies as heavily across French constitutional history as it does across English.'

article, even a review, than of a book. If we have inadvertently failed to acknowledge such guidance, let us here express our sincere appreciation of those in especial who have drawn our attention to sources we might otherwise have overlooked.

We have, of course, written in order to convince. We have selected our facts and arranged them in patterns to convey as nearly as possible the realities of life as it seems to us they would have appeared to a detached observer. We have endeavoured to draw with a firm outline and we have presented our conclusions as persuasively as our craftsmanship permitted. All this the reader has a right to demand. But it is to the sources, to a representative assembly of texts at the very least—not, we may emphasise, a selection carefully chosen to bolster up some foregone conclusion—that we would direct the reader who would know the truth. And we shall have failed in our aim if we do not persuade some of our readers to look, or look again, at the sources. If with the aid of texts unknown to us or perchance misunderstood by us, they are able to confute us, none could more willingly submit to correction. We would, however, be spared the censure of those who may be moved to contradict without examining the texts we have cited in our notes.

Goudhurst,   H. G. R.
Kent

Institute of Advanced Legal Studies,   G. O. S.
University of London

CONTENTS

I

WILLIAM STUBBS
THE MAN AND THE HISTORIAN

Lᴇᴛ it be said at the beginning: Stubbs had eminent virtues. He
was erudite, industrious, by his lights conscientious. He deserved the rewards of his calling: a canonry at fifty-three, the
episcopate at fifty-eight. Nor had he to complain of want of recognition for his scholarship. In his own lifetime he loomed pre-eminent
among English historians. There were contemporaries with greater
abilities and finer minds—Green, Maitland, Gardiner—but they
lay within his shadow. Never was prophet more honoured in his own
country and among his own people. The successor in his chair at
Oxford proclaimed him 'the one man among living scholars .to
whom one may most freely go as to an oracle'.[1] To Gladstone he was
'the first historical authority of the day'.[2] And when men praised the
historian, they had in mind the *Constitutional History*, with its adjunct
the *Select Charters*. There were those who viewed this reverence, this
adulation, with a twinkling eye.

To read the first volume of Stubbs was necessary to salvation; to read the
second was greatly to be desired; the third was reserved for the ambitious
student who sought to accumulate merit by unnatural austerities. The
lecturer lectured on Stubbs; the commentator elucidated him; the
crammer boiled him down. Within those covers was to be found the final
word in every controversy, and in this faith the student moved serene.[3]

But doubters or scoffers have always been few. The cult of Stubbs
has persisted wherever Oxford historians abide, and even at Cambridge 'his great book' has been placed in 'a category in which no
other secondary history book is to be found'.[4]

We believe this respect for Stubbs's teaching to be not merely
exaggerated but mistaken, and the succeeding chapters will give
solid reasons for our dissent. In the first place, however, we must endeavour to provide a background, to tell what manner of man
Stubbs was and to say a little of his work as an editor of historical
texts, work which is likely to give him a securer, if humbler, title to

---

[1] Freeman, *Methods of Historical Study* (1886), p. 11.
[2] *Letters of William Stubbs*, ed. Hutton, p. 231.
[3] Tanner, 'The teaching of Constitutional History', in *The Teaching of History* (ed.
Archbold), p. 54.
[4] Cam, 'Stubbs Seventy Years After', in *Cambridge Historical Journal*, ix (1948), p. 129

fame than the work for which he is most celebrated. And, as historians should, we must remember some dates. They will at least save us from advancing the thesis that Stubbs wrote good history because, as a bishop, he was in touch with life.[1]

Stubbs was born in 1825, the same year as Huxley; Darwin's *Origin of Species* was published in 1859, Stubbs's own *Constitutional History* over the years 1874-8; he was bishop of Chester in 1884, and he died bishop of Oxford in 1901. With his elevation to the episcopate his historical publications shortly reached their end: his working career as a historian covered little more than thirty years.[2]

Stubbs entered Christ Church in April 1844. He came to a university still ecclesiastical in outlook and organisation, a university in turmoil. Newman resigned his fellowship at Oriel in October 1845 and was received into the Roman Church. The echoes of the religious controversies, which then reached their climax and had, as Stubbs said, engrossed 'all the thinking men of the university',[3] reverberated loudly for a few years until, in the furore created by the first University Commission appointed in August 1850, Oxford forgot religion to fight reform. But before this, Stubbs had vacated his fellowship at Trinity on his presentation to the living of Navestock. The Oxford he knew as a young man was, then, Oxford unreformed: its spirit was his spirit. Looking back, at a time when the university had already suffered radical change, while he could see that the disputants of his early days had been handicapped by their lack of historical training, Stubbs did not question the importance of the subjects of disputation. He thought it fitting that his predecessor in the chair of Modern History, Goldwin Smith, should employ his 'learning, acuteness, earnestness and eloquence . . . on the behalf of Christian Truth against philosophic sciolism'.[4] A moral purpose underlay his own historical studies: history must justify the ways of God to man. 'Modern civilization', he said, 'is the work of Christianity and has inherited nothing from ancient civilization except what Christianity has gathered up into itself and preserved.'[5] Nor did he see any reason to modify in 1886 the belief he had expressed in 1867 that Modern History and Natural Science could be equated because each aroused 'a consciousness . . . that we are growing able to justify the Eternal Wisdom . . . that we are coming to see . . . a hand of justice and mercy, a hand of progress and order, a kind and wise disposition, ever leading the world on to the better'.[6] Without any sense of incongruity, Stubbs the historian dons the mantle of the Hebrew

---

[1] Rowse, *The Use of History* (1946), p. 68.
[2] The first edition of the *Registrum Sacrum Anglicanum* was published in 1858. The two volumes of *William of Malmesbury* appeared in the Rolls Series in 1887 and 1889. A complete list of Stubbs's publications will be found in the Appendix to *William Stubbs, Bishop of Oxford*, ed. Hutton: this is based, in a revised and abbreviated form, on the *Letters of William Stubbs*.   [3] *Seventeen Lectures on the Study of Medieval and Modern History*, p. 8.
[4] *Ibid.*   [5] *Lectures on Early English History*, p. 207; *Seventeen Lectures*, p. 27.
[6] *Seventeen Lectures*, p. 27.

prophet. 'The constitutional effects of the Conquest are not worked out', he says, 'in William's reign, but in that of Henry I. The moral training of the nation does not as yet go beyond castigation: the lowest depth of humiliation has yet to be reached, but even that yields necessary lessons of its own.'[1] From first to last his intellectual position did not sensibly alter: to all seeming his ideas were mature and set, his path determined, by the time he was a servitor at Christ Church. The truth that is to be approached without presupposition was not for him. The New Learning of the nineteenth century pursued a course remote from the channels of his own thought. The fierce currents that stirred and tormented the minds of his contemporaries passed him by and left him unmoved. He stood *super antiquas vias* and was content.

He made no secret of the fact that he was, in his own words, 'steeped in clerical and conservative principles'.[2] He was a High Churchman, except in the matter of ritual at one with Pusey and the Tractarians, and such he remained. His obvious dislike of the Puritan cause; his refusal to believe that a dissenter could write a history of England; his strenuous objection to any participation by Oxford in a commemoration of Luther; his studious avoidance of a Unitarian minister 'from whose opinions he differed so profoundly'; his detestation of the 'higher criticism' and his burning of a book by Herbert Spencer: all such things make plain the inflexible cast of his mind.[3] It is not surprising that Stubbs impressed one of his Oxford colleagues as thinking 'that church affairs should not be fully discussed in history—something about "touching the Ark" '.[4] And let an Oxford historian, who knew him well, give his impression of Stubbs in later life.

Stubbs [says Dr Grundy] was a great historian. He also had the reputation of being a great humorist. Some years' experience of him made one think that bishops might gain that reputation somewhat easily. But humorist or not, you could not help liking him. . . . I had known him for several years before he suggested to me that I should take Holy Orders and asked me to come to Cuddesdon to discuss the question with him. I went there very unwillingly. I had always supposed that he was rather a broad churchman. I found him one of the most rigid high churchmen that I ever met. Towards the close of the interview he asked me to name some churchman with whose views I was in sympathy. I named Charles Kingsley. The interview came to an end very shortly afterwards.[5]

Other Oxford historians, whose memories went back to Stubbs, have borne witness to his affability, especially to the young.[6] Yet, at bottom, there was this rigidity, this *parti pris*, of Oxford in the 1840's.

---

[1] *Constitutional History*, i.313.   [2] *Seventeen Lectures*, p. 32.
[3] *Letters*, pp. 75, 126, 144, 283, 335; Gooch, *History and Historians in the Nineteenth Century*, p. 321; Maitland in *E.H.R.*, xvi.425.
[4] *F. Y. Powell*, ed. Elton, p. 212.   [5] Grundy, *Fifty-five Years at Oxford*, p. 92.
[6] Oman, *Memories of Victorian Oxford*, p. 105.

Stubbs has, however, spoken on this point for himself. There is an unforgettable passage in his last statutory lecture, delivered in 1884 on the eve of his departure for Chester. He tells of his first meeting with John Richard Green:

I knew by description the sort of man I was to meet: I recognised him as he got into the Wells carriage, holding in his hand a volume of Renan. I said to myself, 'if I can hinder, he shall not read that book'. We sat opposite and fell immediately into conversation. . . . He came to me at Navestock afterwards, and that volume of Renan found its way into my waste-paper basket.[1]

Stubbs met Green in 1863. On 24 June in that year there had been published in Paris Renan's *Vie de Jésus* and before the end of August it had passed through six editions. It had loosed in France the most bitter controversy.[2] Stubbs had heard of the book; open-minded Green had bought it. Stubbs had condemned it and this—it can hardly be doubted—without reading it and, more than twenty years later, he looked back upon the incident with satisfaction. And yet never was *odium theologicum* more misplaced. Truth and learning have never had a more disinterested and devoted servant than Renan nor one more tolerant of the ideas he had abandoned. To historians, in especial, Renan's life and work should have a peculiar significance as they contemplate the detachment of his mind from old habits of thought, the growing determination to test premises and, by a rigid logic, to follow the argument to the end. Renan may have fallen short of his aim, to recount without bias the history of Israel and Christendom. His mind was perhaps less critical than he himself perceived. His immediate results, like Darwin's, may be superseded. But both he and Darwin were principal creators of the New Learning, which is as much the foundation of the modern study of history as it is of the modern study of natural science. Stubbs knew not Renan the historian: he saw only Renan the heresiarch.

Stubbs's approach to truth was not that of Renan or of Darwin, and this was equally apparent in religion, in politics and in history. He was convinced that a historian could not write without party bias. He knew that, in politics at least, he was a partisan and that his sentiments were deeply rooted. In a charming fragment of autobiography he recalls the influences that had formed his character, the *genius loci* and the family tradition of yeoman farmers. 'True blue Tory' that he was, he had, as a tiny boy, waved the party flag in the face of Henry Brougham, and he felt it impossible to disengage himself from his past.[3] As he grew older, his private comments on the contemporary scene lacked nothing in forthrightness: 'I like the Austrians as Germans'; 'I cannot bear the French . . . the French are

[1] *Seventeen Lectures*, p. 433.
[2] For details, see Henriette Psichari, *Renan d'après lui-même* (1937), pp. 230-42.
[3] *Seventeen Lectures*, pp. 474-5.

liars . . . I have none of your penchant for the French as a nation';
'those horrid Poles'; 'extreme contempt for Victor Emmanuel . . .
that Garibaldi'. For Bright he had 'lost all respect', for Russell he
'never had any respect'.[1] How then was a man, who knew himself
so prejudiced, to justify himself? Salvation lay in honesty, to be an
honest Tory or an honest Whig, but still a party man, in writing
history as in politics.[2]

In choosing mediaeval history as his field Stubbs was happily
inspired. Here the strength of his political and religious convictions
was the least handicap; they were irrelevant. His claim that his
Constitutional History scarcely betrays ecclesiastical prejudice or political bias was one hardly necessary for any historian to assert,[3] even
in jest, and it was a poor compliment to pay him to declare, as
Maitland did, that 'it was possible to know the *Constitutional History*
fairly well and yet not know how its author would vote at a parliamentary election'.[4] No one thinks so ill of Stubbs as to put him on
the level of those who write Marxist morphology or Fascist philology.
Prejudiced as he may have been, he was neither fool nor rogue.
Nor were such illusions as he had about the constitution of mediaeval
society and the structure of mediaeval politics the result of donning
'the spectacles of Victorian Liberalism'[5]: his illusions were the
current historical anachronisms from which he failed to free himself,
the consequence, not of political bias, but of insufficient critical dis-
cernment. It is, indeed, evident that he had little capacity for thinking clearly about the nature of historical truth and of its attainment.
Six statutory lectures, his first in 1867, his last in 1884, with two in
1876 and two in 1877, show that Stubbs pondered long over the
methods and teaching of his chosen study.[6] There is in these lectures
a deal of good sense that every historian will recognise, with some
amusing tilting at windmills; there is more than a suggestion of the
petulance that statutory lecturing always excited in Stubbs; there
are mistakes, such as his incomprehension of ancient history and his
underestimate of its future[7]; but there is very little to indicate that
Stubbs had worked out the methods and processes which should
govern the writing of the major work he had on hand in these years.
Doubtless we must remember that these were public lectures, given
against the grain, that technicalities were perhaps best avoided—
though there are many details in them that only those in touch with

[1] *Letters*, pp. 71, 73, 97, 98.
[2] *Seventeen Lectures*, pp. 22-3, 34-5, 125-7, 467.   [3] *Ibid.*, p. 32.
[4] Maitland in *E.H.R.*, xvi (1901), p. 424. It is possible that there is here an echo of
Paul Guiraud's testimony a few years earlier to Fustel de Coulanges: 'il serait malaisé de
deviner, en le lisant, s'il était monarchiste ou républicain, libéral ou autoritaire' (Guiraud,
Fustel de Coulanges (1896), p. 176).
[5] Ernest Barker, 'Maitland as a Sociologist', in *Sociological Review*, xxix.123: '[Stubbs]
wrote his *Constitutional History of England* in spectacles—the spectacles of Victorian Liberalism—which are all the more curious on his nose when one remembers that he was a
natural Tory.'
[6] *Seventeen Lectures*, pp. 1-131, 427-43.   [7] *Ibid.*, pp. 88-9.

current historical literature would appreciate. Yet here was an opportunity to explain how a historian approaches his material, the
rationale of his inferences, how historical knowledge advances; and
all is vague, imprecise, buried in irrelevancies.

Stubbs was disabled by the weakness he had for approaching a
problem with the solution already in his mind. It is not disputed that
his ideas on early Germanic society were merely the notions fashionable in German academic circles; and his leading ideas on parliamentary history were borrowed from the *Lords' Reports on the Dignity
of a Peer*.[1] Having adopted his conclusions, Stubbs found that the
facts fitted: it was with him, as we have said, in history as in politics
and religion. All might have been well if the conclusions had, by
chance, been sustained; but the major conclusions, those that stand
out in the *Constitutional History*, are gross anachronisms. A French
critic has said of Stubbs:

He projected into the past the image of the constitutional monarchy
which he saw working under his own eyes and to which he attributed the
greatness of his country.[2]

And, despite the exaggeration in this cruel charge, there remains a
substratum of truth: Stubbs too often failed to view mediaeval men
and mediaeval institutions operating in a mediaeval setting.

Not only the rigidity of his mind but his very industry was a
handicap in the pursuit of truth. For ever turning to fresh tasks, he
was reluctant to revise anything he had already written. Little given
to self-criticism, he was impatient of the criticism of others.[3] Though
he claimed for history 'a special dignity of its own, the dignity of
being able to accept new lights and correct old prejudices',[4] the
pressure on his time and the constitution of his mind did not permit
him to apply the principles he professed. For the same reasons there
are discrepancies and inconsistencies in his teaching: he is often in-
decisive. His admirers regard these failings with indulgence, if not
as manifestations of his judicial mind and his 'remarkable impartiality'.[5] But Stubbs was neither eminently judicial nor remarkably impartial and was, at times, among the most incautious and

---

[1] Richardson and Sayles, *Parliaments and Great Councils in Medieval England*, pp. 6-7.
We deal at greater length with Stubbs's obligations in a later volume.

[2] Petit-Dutaillis, *Studies supplementary to Stubbs' Constitutional History*, p. 307. We should
perhaps give the original French text: 'Malgré des réticences que lui commandait sa
probité d'historien, il projetait dans le passé l'image de la royauté constitutionelle qu'il
voyait fonctionner sous ses yeux et à laquelle il attribuait la grandeur de son pays' (*Histoire
constitutionelle*, édition française, iii.vi).

[3] Witness his reproofs to Green: *Letters*, pp. 157-9: 'As to your pert criticism on
[the Select Charters] allow me to say. . . . On the other points you glance at, you know
our ideas are at variance fundamentally' (1871); p. 171: 'please in reviewing me . . .
withdraw your mind from the points on which we differ and concentrate on those on
which we agree. I do not like people to say "Here is a serious mistake", when it is a
radical difference in view'; 'if you will tread on my toes about Charles I and Laud, you
cannot expect me to trust your views of George III implicitly' (1875).

[4] *Seventeen Lectures*, p. 465.

[5] Gooch, *History and Historians in the Nineteenth Century*, pp. 319-21.

dogmatic of historians.[1] And the fact remains that, whatever the excuse, the alterations he made in successive editions of the *Constitutional History* were slight and that he made scarcely any effort to adjust his thought to fresh arguments—whether those of Vinogradoff on folkland or Round on knight-service or Maitland on parliament —which called for the revision or reappraisal of his previous conclusions.

The *Constitutional History* we may, however, leave on one side for the moment, and turn to other fields in which Stubbs was once accorded pre-eminence. His exposition of the historical independence of the Church of England from the Church of Rome affords a clear demonstration, in a field apart from constitutional history, of the way in which he fell victim to traditional interpretations of the past and followed tradition blindly. Let us set out the problem. The Reformers of the sixteenth century had come to look upon the pope as a usurper. The extreme form in which such a view could be put is seen in Prynne's *Exact History of the Pope's Intolerable Usurpations upon the Liberties of the Kings and Subjects of England and Ireland*, as one of the alternative titles of his vast collection of records runs. Coke agreed with Prynne in this, if in little else, and, though he wrote more soberly, he strove to show by historical proofs that royal jurisdiction in ecclesiastical matters antedated the Reformation. We must, however, do justice to the common lawyers. From their point of view the Reformation had made very little difference. They were impressed, as must be also any dispassionate observer, by the truth that, like many other revolutions, the religious revolution of the sixteenth century had left the current of ideas and the stream of practice flowing on with little obvious change. Certainly, so far as ecclesiastical jurisdiction impinged upon the common law, the differences were almost imperceptible. Take a sentence from Coke where his mind is turning on conflicts of jurisdiction. 'And certain it is', he writes, 'that this kingdom hath been best governed, and peace and quiet preserved, when both parties, that is, when the justices of the temporal courts and the ecclesiastical judges, have kept themselves within their proper jurisdiction, without encroaching or usurping one upon another: and where such encroachments or usurpations have been made, they have been the seeds of great trouble and inconvenience'.[2] His mind is travelling beyond Henry VIII: his authorities and instances go back to Bede and Saint Augustine. There is no discontinuity. In the general pattern of the ecclesiastical courts, the slight adjustments necessary after the breach with Rome were of very little account, as we see from his exposition.

---

[1] As a brief example, take this sentence from a lecture in 1878: '[The Crusades] were the first great effort of mediaeval life to go beyond the pursuit of selfish and isolated ambitions; they were the trial-feat of the young world essaying to use, to the glory of God and the benefit of man, the arms of its new knighthood' (*Seventeen Lectures*, p. 180).
[2] *Institutes*, iv.321.

Had Coke been a historian or a philosopher, he might have drawn a parallel: from time to time the general pattern of secular courts had been subjected to even greater adjustments. The Common Bench had been absorbed by the court *coram rege* under John, to revive in the early years of Henry III, and to find a place in a tripartite division of the courts of common law in 1234, with the King's Bench as the supreme tribunal. Parliament had later arisen to correct the inadequacies of the courts of common law and, when it had changed its character, equity had found a refuge in the court of chancery. The jurisdiction of the council had burgeoned into the court of Star Chamber, and there had been more recent developments of which Coke was a living witness. But all these changes, for good or ill, had been adaptations of an ancient stock to meet the supposed needs of the State or the subject and to achieve the ends of justice, justice which changes its complexion to satisfy the caprices of man and his rulers. Had the changes in the ecclesiastical courts meant more than this?

If, however, the history of the conflicting jurisdictions of the civil and ecclesiastical courts is approached from the standpoint of the ecclesiastical lawyer and not from that of the common lawyer, it presents a different aspect. In pre-Reformation England litigants in courts Christian were continually being thwarted; ecclesiastical judges were continually being prohibited, under penalty, from hearing causes; in parliament the lords spiritual were not infrequently protesting or washing their hands when proposals were afoot for limiting the authority of the Curia in England. All these trammels and inhibitions were regarded by churchmen as usurpations on the part of the secular power. But in practice the Church had come to an accommodation with the State and, since each was useful to the other, quarrels were never pushed too far and neither side, at least after the pontificate of Innocent III, advanced claims that left no possibility of retreat. We may think that the winning cards were in the hands of the secular rulers, and certainly, when it came to extremes, history was to show that a king was mightier than a pope. But for three centuries there was no quarrel that was worth the inconvenience of a total breakdown. When the final breakdown came, the English Church became Erastian. The judges sitting in courts Christian became the king's ecclesiastical judges and the ancient canon law became the king's ecclesiastical laws.[1] Little was changed except this; but this, from the ecclesiastical lawyer's point of view, was fundamental. His authority derived now, not from the pope, but from the king.

Doubtless the Reformation was more than a matter of jurisdiction. But it is for reasons other than historical that men minimise or exaggerate the differences in doctrine and religious observance that the breach with Rome brought in its train, and excuse or condemn

---

[1] Statutes, 37 Henry VIII, c. 7; 2 and 3 Edward VI, c. 23, section 2.

the changes. In the light of their prejudices many views are possible, and these views have been apt to colour the thoughts of historians and to obscure their understanding of the Middle Ages. For it is undeniably true that their views on the rectitude or depravity of the mediaeval Church have affected their judgement of the part played by the pope and the Curia in plain matters of historical fact which should be beyond dispute. Seemingly, as with others of like mind before him, Stubbs's prejudices, his presumptions (if that be the better word), prevented him from seeing that there is more than one approach to the history of ecclesiastical jurisdiction in pre-Reformation England and that the truth may wear different aspects according to the avenue of approach. Evidently, to appreciate the problem duly, we must look at it from more than one angle, and we must, above all, avoid the twin fallacies of interpreting the past in the light of the present and of importing theological prepossessions into a historical argument. Otherwise we may burlesque, as indeed Prynne blatantly burlesqued, the conflicts of the Middle Ages.

Stubbs, whatever he was, was not, like Prynne, an Erastian, but his general conclusion in this matter was very much the same: the pope (in Prynne's language) had been an intolerable usurper. Except in this conclusion, Stubbs was no companion of Prynne's, but this conclusion was vital to his position. Nevertheless he attributed great significance to apostolic succession—a consideration to which an Erastian would be indifferent—and not the least important of his historical works, one involving much original research, was the *Registrum Sacrum Anglicanum*.[1] Here he presented the evidence for uninterrupted continuity in the consecration of English bishops by consecrated bishops. This continuity seemed to him of the utmost consequence. On this ground, if not on this ground alone, the English Church remained what it had always been, a part of the catholic church, though not of the Roman Catholic Church. Though the link with Rome was snapped, the link with the church universal was unsevered. But, however real this distinction may be, however true may be its historical basis, the argument that the Church of England has had a continuous and uninterrupted life has something of a metaphysical air. Historically it is at least equally true that in the life of the Church of England there have been interruption and discontinuity. From this aspect of truth Stubbs shrank. He shared the not uncommon belief that the English Church had had a continuous and self-contained existence and had successfully resisted all attempts by the mediaeval papacy to encroach upon its primitive and native authority.

Stubbs's interest in the history of ecclesiastical jurisdiction in England was deepened and sharpened by his appointment to the Royal Commission to enquire into the constitution and working of

[1] First published 1858; revised edition, 1897.

ecclesiastical courts. As the historical authority upon whom his colleagues depended, Stubbs took his duties seriously, attended every
one of the seventy-five sessions, and contributed, as an appendix to
the Report, a historical survey of canon law as it seemed to him to
have operated in England in pre-Reformation days and later.[1] He
assured his fellow Commissioners that 'attempts to force on the
Church and the Nation the complete canon law of the Middle Ages
were always unsuccessful', that the collections of papal decrees,
which had been officially recognised by the papacy as containing
the whole law of the Church, 'were not authoritative' in England,
where an 'independent and imperfect system' prevailed until the
sixteenth century.[2] The final statement of his views, incorporated in
the Report itself, declared that 'the canon law of Rome, though
always regarded as of great authority in England, was not held to be
binding on the courts. . . . The laws of the Church of England from
the Conquest onwards were, as before, the traditional Church law
developed by the legal and scientific ability of its administrators and
occasionally amended by the constitutions of successive archbishops,
the canons of national councils, and the sentences or authoritative
answers to questions delivered by the popes.'[3] To put the position
briefly, in the words used by Stubbs's biographer and apologist, the
English Church in the Middle Ages was not 'in bondage to the legal
system of the Papacy'.[4] This view, Stubbs claimed, was 'true history'.[5]

The Report of the Royal Commission appeared in 1883 and
Stubbs's conclusions were generally accepted until 1896,[6] when the
question was re-opened by Maitland.[7] He read, as Stubbs had read
before him, the *Provinciale* of William Lyndwood, the one outstanding
English canonist, who in, or shortly after, 1430 had completed and
published a commentary upon the provincial constitutions of the
archbishops of Canterbury. As he read, Maitland realised that
Stubbs's conclusions were in direct conflict with the evidence on
which they were ostensibly founded. For Lyndwood spoke without
equivocation: because an inferior cannot annul the law of a superior,
therefore an archbishop cannot annul the decrees that have been
duly promulgated by a papal legate; it is possible for an archbishop
to make additions to papal law, provided he does not alter its substance, for what an inferior does will not hold good if in any way it
restricts that law.[8] There could be no doubt that Lyndwood regarded papal law as valid and binding in England and quite immune

---

[1] Ecclesiastical Courts Commission, *Report*, Historical Appendix (I).
[2] *Ibid.*, i.25a.   [3] *Ibid.*, p. xviii.
[4] *Letters*, p. 206.   [5] *Seventeen Lectures*, p. 335.
[6] Stubbs's contributions to the Commission's Report were, however, attacked at the
time and some amusing instances of inconsistent pronouncements on his part were given
in a pamphlet by J. T. Tomlinson, *The 'Legal History' by Canon Stubbs . . . reviewed* (1884).
But the author's purpose was polemical and he did not anticipate Maitland's criticism.
[7] In the *E.H.R.*, xi.446-78.
[8] Lyndwood, *Provinciale* (1679), lib. iii, tit. 6 (p. 137, note *o*); lib. iii, tit. 9 (p. 154,
note *f*).

from any alteration in essentials by an English provincial council. Of purely English canon law, of local rules that were allowed to stand because they obeyed each of two conditions, first, that they did not run counter to the basic principles of the law of the Western Church and, second, that they had been in force for a reasonable length of time, Maitland could find only occasional traces. That Maitland's reading of Lyndwood is correct, no one now ventures to dispute. That Lyndwood is both representative of canonist opinion and represents historical facts, there is equally no question. Why then did Stubbs err? It was because, as Maitland said, he, like others, had confused two propositions: (i) that in England the State did not suffer the Church to appropriate certain considerable portions of that wide field of jurisdiction which the canonists claimed as the heritage of ecclesiastical law; (ii) that the English courts Christian held themselves free to accept or reject, and did in some cases reject, the canon law of Rome.[1] These are two distinct propositions, of which the first is true and the second untrue, and the first lends no support to the other. And when Stubbs wrote that 'attempts to force on the Church and the Nation the complete canon law of the Middle Ages were always unsuccessful', he was asserting not one proposition but two. If we omit the Church from this sentence, it is unexceptionable: if we omit the nation, it is worse than false, for it is meaningless. The identification of Church and nation, in the sense implied by Stubbs's words—a mediaeval lawyer would have written of *sacerdotium* and *regnum*—is valid after the Reformation but is without validity at any earlier time. However many were the strands that connected the two ages of the English Church, there had, in fact, been a revolution. Its consequences were the creation of a national church and, in matters of jurisdiction, the substitution of the king for the pope. Doubtless it is permissible to welcome the one consequence while deploring the other, but it is idle to pretend that the two consequences are not historically and inexorably linked or that one of the consequences existed before the cause.

Maitland's cool and courteous demonstration, written by one who, as he said, was a dissenter from both English and Roman churches, was unanswerable. Yet some of Stubbs's friends and disciples attempted his defence, not perhaps an altogether ingenuous defence.[2] Stubbs had, in fact, done far more than 'minimise unduly'—the words are Tout's—the authority of the pope. He had accepted with-

[1] *Roman Canon Law in the Church of England* (1898), p. 51. In this book Maitland collected the paper mentioned on p. 10, n. 7, and five later essays. It should be emphasised that Maitland was not concerned with the details of procedure any more than Stubbs had been, but simply with the truth of a general proposition.

[2] We have already referred to Hutton's apology in *Letters*, p. 206. An elaborate defence of Stubbs and attack on Maitland was written by Ogle, *The Canon Law in Mediaeval England* (1912): this was examined and refuted by H. W. C. Davis, 'The Canon Law in England', reprinted in *Davis Papers*, pp. 123-43. The force of Maitland's criticisms is attenuated in Tout's biographical notice of Stubbs in *Dictionary of National Biography*, Supp. 2, volume 3.

out question, and then set out to prove, that the Reformation had not broken in an essential the continuity of the Church of England. He wished that continuity had been preserved. He projected his bias into the Middle Ages and, interpreting the evidence in the light of a cherished doctrine, he failed to see the real problem. Had he expressed his views in the fifteenth century, he would, it has been said, have exposed himself to a charge of heresy.[1] If heresy be the denial of truth, the charge still lies. Unwitting heresy, for Stubbs seems never to have appreciated to the full the force of Maitland's argument. He had the opportunity to reconsider and restate his case when in 1900 he published the third edition of his *Seventeen Lectures* which contained two lectures on 'The History of the Canon Law in England'. However, he modified the text no more than by substituting grudgingly here and there indefinite for precise phraseology.[2] In a prefatory note he referred to Maitland's criticisms but without abandoning his own views, leaving the issue to be determined by 'competent authority, gladly submitting to be set right'.[3]

The lasting reputation Stubbs has earned rests, we believe, upon his work as the editor of historical texts. Among so much that is mediocre and too much that is positively bad, nearly all the volumes he contributed to the *Rolls Series* stand out by reason of their sound and solid scholarship. If no volume of his has the originality and importance of Maitland's sole contribution, the *Memoranda de Parliamento* of 1305, all, or nearly all, of Stubbs's work, with one regrettable exception, is learned and sensible. The introductions are perhaps too diffuse and not always strictly relevant, despite the restrictions imposed by the Master of the Rolls upon unnecessary embellishments. But Stubbs departed from the straight path, and tried the patience of the reader, no farther than his brother editors: the Victorian age could sometimes afford to dally. And if he was, now and again, somewhat long in coming to the point, he made few positive mistakes. It would, however, pass the wit of his most devoted admirers to defend the portrait of King John which he prefixed to the second volume of the *Memoriale* of Walter of Coventry.[4] This is no serious contribution to history but the commination of a predestined sinner, the gathering of rumour and scandal, little tempered by the copious records of the reign.[5] Not much more than an expansion of what he had already written and published in the following year (1874) in the first volume of the *Constitutional History*, it affords a curious sidelight on Stubbs's critical standards. He had

[1] Fisher, *F. W. Maitland* (1910), p. 102.
[2] For example, the words 'not received as having any authority' became 'not formally and explicitly received'. The original text and the revisions are set out in parallel columns in the *Quarterly Review*, vol. 217 (October 1912), p. 425.
[3] *Seventeen Lectures*, pp. 335-6.   [4] *Memoriale*, ii.xi-lxxx.
[5] Even Mr A. L. Poole admits that in this instance 'the great historian's work' is 'affected by conscious bias and preconceived ideas' (*From Domesday Book to Magna Carta*, p. 425, n. 3).

first turned to Matthew Paris as his principal source for John's reign, and in the *Constitutional History* it is Matthew who is cited. But by the time that he was engaged upon Walter of Coventry's *Memoriale*, Stubbs had discovered that Matthew was merely repeating or, as Stubbs put it, 'interpreting' Roger of Wendover.[1] Consequently the citations in his introduction to Walter of Coventry are from Roger as well as from Matthew; but he did not trouble to adjust, in any of the later editions, his citations in the *Constitutional History*, where there is not a single reference to the primary source.[2] The fact is—and we shall give some further illustrations—that Stubbs was little concerned with testing the authenticity of his sources: he needs must be superficial in this matter or the tasks in hand would never be completed. It was the inadequate attention he could spare for detail that led him to attempt the identification of the *Gesta Regis Henrici II* with the lost *Tri-Columnis* of Richard of Ely.[3] Though Liebermann politely called this identification a 'brilliant hypothesis',[4] it was a guess that will not stand scrutiny. To the possibility that the *Gesta* might be an earlier version of the *Chronica* of Roger of Howden Stubbs gave considerable thought, but he was finally led to reject it.[5] That the relation between the two texts is, in fact, precisely this has been demonstrated by Lady Stenton, inspired by the chance discovery of a charter in which Howden is named.[6] If the identity of authorship now seems certain, it needed not only the flash of intuition but the assurance provided by the charter, confirmed by the evidence of the texts. It is hardly to Stubbs's discredit, therefore, that the light did not come to him. Nevertheless it must lower the esteem in which an editor is held, that he did not appreciate the relationship between two of his major texts, a relationship that becomes the more obvious as the texts are examined in detail.

Commonly, however, Stubbs was blessed with better fortune. He rarely undertook to edit a text that demanded protracted research, but, within his limitations, he was acute and painstaking, and the texts as they left his hands (with an exception we shall remark) were critical and trustworthy. Those that had been printed before, and these were the majority, were substantially better edited than the older editions, a compliment that cannot be paid to all the editors of other re-edited texts in the *Rolls Series*. And whether Stubbs had or had not the benefit of the labours of earlier editors, his texts were always faithful to the manuscripts, discriminating in noting variants, and generally reliable.[7] But what is perhaps most impressive is the rapidity with which volume succeeded volume, each attaining the

---

[1] *Memoriale*, ii.lxxxii.

[2] *Constitutional History*, vol. 1 (1st ed.: 1873), pp. 515-42; (6th edition: 1897), pp. 554-83. The references are, however, altered from Wats's edition to Luard's in the Rolls Series.   [3] 'Benedict of Peterborough', i.lvii-lxiii.   [4] *Letters*, p. 141.

[5] 'Benedict', i.liii-liv; a more elaborate argument is in Howden, i.li-lxv.

[6] *E.H.R.*, lxviii.574-82.

[7] His lapses, as, for example, his treatment of Henry II's assizes, were largely due to

same respectable standard. There were other copious editors in those days—Dr John Allen Giles, for example, who has earned our grudging gratitude for his *Patres Ecclesiae Anglicanae*—but none who did so much and did it so well. The unremitting labour demanded stern self-discipline. It is no wonder that he wrote in 1871: 'I have been so busy with Lectures and the fourth volume of Hoveden that I have been quite a recluse'.[1] And in a statutory lecture, delivered in 1876, it was with justifiable pride that he pointed to his record of published work in the ten years during which he had occupied his chair.

I have [he said] completed ten volumes, and nearly an eleventh volume, of the English Historians published by the Master of the Rolls; I have edited the whole of the third volume and assisted in the first and second volumes of the Councils of the English Church: I have published the volume of Select Charters, which has now passed into a third edition, and two volumes of the Constitutional History of England, besides other work edited or passed through the press for practical aid in historical study.[2]

It was a wonderful achievement; but its volume and speed allowed little time for the minutiae of scholarship and the maturation of judgement that we look for in the greatest of editors. And when the test came, when Stubbs undertook a task outside the field with which he was familiar, he fell far short of what lesser men have accomplished. The familiar field lay among the mediaeval chronicles of the earlier Middle Ages, chronicles which afford our primary knowledge of events and documents; documents of which there are rarely other texts; events which are little documented otherwise. Some of the chronicles rested on earlier chronicles, but it is the exception to find Stubbs at fault in identifying an earlier chronicle upon which the text before him was based.[3] Apart from chronicles, the material Stubbs edited did not present serious textual problems. The supplementary matter, such as the *Epistolae Cantuarienses* (the second volume of the *Chronicles and Memorials of Richard I*), the similar collection of correspondence prefixed to *Gervase of Canterbury*, with some lesser texts elsewhere, depended upon single manuscripts.

Experience of this kind was of but limited value when it came to editing the *Chronicles of the Reigns of Edward I and Edward II*, which lay outside his accustomed field. Nothing could make this collection of jejune annals important, unless it were the destruction of the voluminous records of the two reigns, or rather of the reign of Edward II, for actually such interest as the annals have lies there.

his lack of training. He learnt as he went along, and he never mastered the science of diplomatic. We deal with the assizes of Henry II in Appendix IV: below, pp. 438-49.

[1] *Letters*, p. 159.   [2] *Seventeen Lectures*, pp. 1-2.

[3] He was unquestionably at fault, as he himself acknowledged, in asserting that the *Itinerarium Regis Ricardi* could not have been translated from a French original (*Seventeen Lectures*, p. 177). The 'poem of Ambrose' is not now accepted, however, as the French source of the *Itinerarium* (Edwards in *Tait Essays*, pp. 59-77).

But if they were to be edited, since they have no merit as literature, express no really personal view, and depend upon contemporary documents, eked out with contemporary news, the editor's task consisted primarily in identifying the underlying sources. It is true that, once these sources are identified, the historian need hardly notice the narrative, just as a chronicle which reproduces an earlier chronicle is valueless except for any additional matter it contains; but it is an editor's duty to jettison all useless lumber or at least to indicate what is mere repetition. Herein, the earlier mediaeval chronicles differ generally from the later mediaeval chronicles, because, with the earlier compilations, it is rarely that we can get back to the source of the source, though we may disentangle elements that have been imperfectly fused. For earlier times documents have rarely been preserved or transmitted independently of narrative sources; this form of control is therefore almost always lacking. But from the thirteenth century onwards the reverse is true.

Now let us see how Stubbs approached his editorial duties in this instance. One of the crucial documents for the reign of Edward II is that which is alleged to have set in motion the process against Gavaston. The articles are said to have been presented to the king by the earl of Lincoln at the Easter parliament of 1308. The document was known to the compilers of two of the chronicles edited by Stubbs—the Bridlington writer and the author of the *Annales Londonienses*.[1] The former gives an inaccurate Latin translation, and the latter reproduces only the first of three articles. The full French text exists in a manuscript that has long been in the British Museum, that should have been known to Stubbs and was not. He could check the text of the Bridlington writer by the *Annales Londonienses*, but the comparison seems to have led him to the conclusion that the Latin rendering of the second and third articles was not derived from the original document but was part of the narrative. The original text, which we reproduce in an appendix, has not been printed hitherto and has been ignored by those who have written of Edward II.[2] It may be remarked that the document is highly suspicious and was probably concocted after the Ordinances and perhaps after Gavaston's death; but when it was circulated, it was accepted in good faith by contemporaries, though its falsity was suggested when later it was foisted upon Hugh Despenser by the king's enemies.[3] But whatever the case against the authenticity of the document, there is no question of its importance, and a competent editor of two chronicles in which it appeared would at least have established the true text and might have been expected to discuss in his introduction its origin

---

[1] *Chronicles of the Reigns of Edward I and Edward II*, i.153-4, ii.33-4.

[2] There is a bare reference to the manuscript in Dimitresco, *Pierre de Gavaston*, p. 38. See also *Speculum*, vol. xxiv, p. 66.

[3] According to the *Historia Roffensis* it was Hamon of Hythe, then bishop of Rochester, who exposed the fraud (Vesp. E. xxi, fo. 33b-5).

and influence. Later historians might thus have been saved from some ludicrous mistakes. Another capital document of Edward II's reign is the sentence of excommunication against Gavaston. Little more than half of the lengthy text was copied by the compiler of the *Annales Londonienses*, and Stubbs printed this fraction with no indication that it was incomplete.[1] The full text is available, however, in several manuscripts, two of which Stubbs had, presumably, at one time used.[2]

These are but two examples, out of many, of his cursory methods of editing. Further examples may be spared, for we can refer to a critical examination, already published, of the text of the *Annales Paulini*[3] which, together with the *Annales Londonienses*, make up the first volume of the *Chronicles of the Reigns of Edward I and Edward II*. It is clear that Stubbs paid insufficient attention to the textual problems presented by the *Annales Paulini* and that obvious indications of multiple authorship escaped his notice. But what was worse, his failure to check the narrative in detail led him to express a high opinion of its merits as a whole, whereas only one section of it has any substantial value and that chiefly for local history. It is almost needless to add that the most worthless and misleading section of the *Annales Paulini* has been accepted by later writers at Stubbs's high valuation. Following faithfully in the footsteps of the master, they have given currency to its picturesque, but wildly inaccurate, account of the coronation of Edward II and have drawn the appropriate deductions.

As with a number of other publications in the *Rolls Series*, it may be doubted whether it was worth while to print in their entirety the contents of the *Chronicles of the Reigns of Edward I and Edward II*, but there is no question of the manner in which the texts should have been edited, once the decision had been taken. The editing of these chronicles plainly demanded the collation of the texts with contemporary sources of embarrassing complexity, those sources behind the source which are the only true historical evidence. But Stubbs's rapid methods were not suited to such a task, and the last historical work he published whilst still at Oxford falls far below his reputation, falls to the depressing level of the minor works in the Rolls Series.

Of the *Constitutional History*, which is the principal object of our criticism, we have as yet said little. What may to-day seem surprising is that, not only its errors and misconceptions, but its large deficiencies for so long escaped remark. How far the constitutional historian should concern himself with the history of administration must depend upon the scale of his narrative, but it should never be

---

[1] *Chronicles of the Reigns of Edward I and Edward II*, i.154-5.
[2] The Registers of Simon of Ghent and Henry Woodlock. A variant text is in Cambridge University Library, MS. Dd. vii.14, p. 228. The full text is printed in *Registrum Simonis de Gandavo* (Canterbury and York Society) i.237-40: see also *Registrum Henrici Woodlock*, i.293.   [3] Richardson in *Speculum*, vol. xxiii, pp. 630-40.

far from his thoughts. A constitution, even a paper one or an imaginary one, has no meaning apart from administrative practice. Stubbs, for the most part, ignored administration. The pages he devoted to the practice of the exchequer in the twelfth century[1] are not matched by any account of the control of the revenue in other centuries.[2] Nor does he concern himself with the control of expenditure in the twelfth century, and his only references to the matter in later centuries occur at those points when it becomes the subject of controversy[3]: the background, which might make the controversies intelligible, is never supplied. If he pays some attention to the practice of the exchequer, he pays practically none to the practice of the chancery. The evolution of the equitable jurisdiction of the chancellor, which is linked with the evolution of parliament, lies almost beyond his horizon.[4] The rise of the king's secretary does not interest him. He knows but fragments of the history of the courts of common law and those fragments of dubious value: he enumerates the measures by which, as he supposed, the judicial machinery received its final form under Edward I, but, this done, he concludes that 'from henceforth they cease to have any special bearing on our main subject'.[5] That main subject is, of course, parliament, but his approach to this, as to the whole mechanism of government, is falsified by his 'idea of a constitution'. That the council, of which parliament was an emanation, should be the fundamental element in the working constitution of England from the thirteenth to the fifteenth century, was a concept irreconcilable with the constitution imagined by Stubbs, nor did he conceive that it was the council that lay at the centre of the administration. So he passed it over with incomprehension and inadequate references.[6]

It is plain that Stubbs did not sit down to the task of discovering how, in practice, the country was governed in the Middle Ages. He had, it must be remembered, no experience of administration and seemingly no intuitive perception of administrative processes. An Oxford fellowship and a country parsonage were no preparation for the study of English government, and a hundred years ago the study of public administration was hardly conceivable as an academic discipline.[7] Educated Englishmen, and Stubbs was no exception, took administration for granted. Just as a historian's battles were fought without regard to commissariat and transport, so government was carried on, as far as historians were concerned, without a thought for the civil service. Had Stubbs undertaken his investigations seriously —perhaps a kinder adverb is intensively—he would have had to go

[1] *Constitutional History*, i.407-15. [2] Cf. *ibid.*, ii.288-90.
[3] *Ibid.*, ii.594-9. [4] *Ibid.*, ii.267, 281-2.
[5] *Ibid.*, ii.279. [6] *Ibid.*, ii.267-74, iii.254-62.
[7] This is true of England, though at Glasgow John Millar, professor of Civil Law, 1761-1801, had lectured on the 'principles of government', including 'the present state of the English government' (*Juridical Review*, N.S. vi (1961), pp. 218-33).

beyond the *Lords' Reports*, beyond the *Rotuli Parliamentorum* and the *Statutes of the Realm*, beyond Prynne, beyond Nicolas and his *Acts of the Privy Council*. He would have been led to investigate unprinted sources, in his day difficult, though not impossible, of access, and the *Constitutional History* would have been longer in the making and constructed on a different plan. Even as it was, when he had come to the end of his story, he found himself cumbered with a mass of historical detail that could not be fitted into his narrative, that related ill to his 'idea of a constitution' or clogged its exposition. This matter he consigned as 'Parliamentary Antiquities' to a final chapter, an appendix, almost an irrelevance. Here is to be found some of the material out of which critical historians are striving to reconstruct the English parliament as it was known to mediaeval Englishmen.

The *Constitutional History* has been described as 'virtually a history of England from Julius Caesar to the accession of the Tudors, the first authoritative survey of our national life . . . it embraces Church and State, law and justice, administration and finance'.[1] That this is an exaggeration the preceding paragraphs sufficiently indicate. But the book does contain much political history and something of the personal history of English kings. Inevitably and rightly, the constitutional historian must study the principal characters who contrived and adapted the means of government and the circumstances in which they acted. Nor is it easy to distinguish between the king's private life and his public deeds: his idiosyncracies have a political import. But, filled with preconceptions and prejudices, Stubbs had difficulty in regarding Henry II, John, Edward I and Edward II, as men of their day; he saw them rather as figures appropriate to the parts he allotted to them in his imaginary drama of the constitution. Stubbs's Edward I is fictitious: the others suffer not only from the artificial environment in which they play their parts, but from Stubbs's weakness, the weakness of his times, for moralising out of season. If there are kings who do not suffer so badly as these at his hands, he is no safe guide to character or to motive. Yet Stubbs's principles were almost impeccable.

The man who would rightly learn the lesson that the seventeenth century has to teach, must not only know what Charles thought of Cromwell and what Cromwell thought of Charles, but must try to understand the real questions at issue, not by reference to an ideal standard only, but by tracing the historical growth of the circumstances in which those circumstances arose: he must try to look at them as it might be supposed that the great actors would have looked at them, if Cromwell had succeeded to the burden which Charles inherited, or if Charles had taken up the part of the hero of reform. In such an attitude it is quite unnecessary to exclude party feeling or personal feeling. Whichever way the sentiment may incline, the truth, the whole truth and nothing but the truth, is what

[1] Gooch, *History and Historians in the Nineteenth Century*, p. 319.

history would extract from her witnesses: the truth which leaves no pitfall for unwary advocates, and which is in the end the fairest measure of equity to all.[1]

'Not by reference to an ideal standard only'! Alas! how that ideal standard—of the constitution, of conduct—constantly prevented Stubbs from seeing men and events 'as it might be supposed that the great actors would have looked at them'.

The *Constitutional History* met with immediate and tremendous success and received the unstinted praise of those who appeared best qualified to judge its merits. The first and second volumes reached Freeman as he was approaching the end of his prolonged labours upon the *History of the Norman Conquest*. He hailed these volumes as 'the greatest monument of English historical scholarship'. 'Much that I had meant to say', he went on, 'much that it had never occurred to me to say, I found said already as no man but the master of English history could have said it.'[2] Even Maitland, who cast the first stone, and had a better right than any of us to do so, was loud in his appreciation of the *Constitutional History*. 'We have no wish', he wrote in the introduction to the *History of English Law*, 'to say over again what the Bishop of Oxford has admirably said, no hope of being able to say with any truth what he has left unsaid.'[3] This praise we can understand only in its historical context. No book quite like Stubbs's had ever before appeared in England. Its faults were largely unperceived because they were the faults of Victorian scholarship. If now we mistrust his judgement and regret his failures to distinguish between fancy and fact; if we wax impatient at his facile moralising and his conventional homilies; yet, as a mere feat of compilation, the *Constitutional History* still extorts our respect and admiration. Here was, or seemed to be, an unequalled, representative assemblage of recorded facts, industriously sorted and arranged. None, at the time, perceived that the facts had sometimes been ill-arranged, that the pattern was often misconceived. Few, if any, readers guessed that the ground had been inadequately surveyed, that much more, which was highly relevant to the history of the English constitution, lay undisturbed in manuscript, sometimes, indeed, in neglected printed books. Few, if any, readers could have guessed that the facts of life and law in the Middle Ages would come to be regarded with eyes that had been opened to a new vision.

For this new vision many scholars were responsible. In England two men were especially prominent, Maitland and Round. Our esteem for Maitland could be expressed only in words that approached extravagance. For Round we have no unqualified regard. Even by contemporary English standards he was overvalued in his lifetime: by the side of a Felix Liebermann or a Léopold Delisle he

---

[1] *Constitutional History*, iii.637.   [2] *History of the Norman Conquest*, v, p. vi.
[3] *History of English Law*, i, p. xxxvi.

was amateurish and undisciplined. Often hasty and muddled, he fouled the wells of truth as much as any of his fellows who were made to feel the lash of his criticism. But he taught by precept, if not always by example, the importance of minor and subsidiary documentary sources and the necessity for the most scrupulous accuracy in dating, collating and interpreting them. Round had been a pupil of Stubbs and as a young man unto old age he never wearied of singing his teacher's praises. But towards the end of his life doubts began to assail him, and in an essay he had left unpublished at his death he wrote these words:

No one, I think, will suspect me of imperfect appreciation where our great historian is concerned, but his work occasionally betrays a certain vagueness of conception, a lack of clearness in definition, which perhaps is sometimes met with in the work of English scholars.[1]

None but those well acquainted with Round's writings, his reiterated, obsequious, adulation of Stubbs, his venomous, unceasing denigration of Freeman and Hubert Hall, can appreciate the delicate meiosis of this criticism. He realised at long last the failings of his master: vagueness of conception; lack of clearness in definition. But if Round had been so long blind to Stubbs's faults, the rest of the world had been nearly as slow in casting off their blindness.

There is no gainsaying that, if it is approached as we would approach a massive piece of historical scholarship, for which indeed it has for so long passed current, the *Constitutional History* is an inadequate and misleading book. And we have Sir Charles Firth's word for it that in his conversation Stubbs himself 'clearly indicated . . . that many of the conclusions stated in his *Constitutional History* must be regarded as hypotheses rather than facts'.[2] Perhaps the book would have been weakened as a pedagogic instrument if it had been framed in frank recognition of this truth, and certainly the mode of expression gave no hint to countless readers that what had the appearance of rock was nothing but mirage and shifting sand. This may be said of most textbooks; and what more could be expected of the *Constitutional History*? Projected in 1868, Stubbs wrote rapidly, with 'all his impetuous passions in full freshness',[3] and the last of the three volumes appeared in 1878. During these ten years Stubbs was busy with much other work and, extraordinary as his powers were, these three large volumes could not be the fruit of great original research, and what original thought there was in the exposition was straitly conditioned by the outlook of Stubbs's own epoch. The mischief is that the *Constitutional History* outlived, and still outlives, its day; and this mischief was wrought not by Stubbs, but by those who expounded and commended the book without seriously examining it and who failed to perceive that it was written to be speedily

[1] *Family Origins*, p. 223.   [2] *Modern History in Oxford*, p. 24, n. 4.
[3] *Letters*, p. 305.

and happily superseded, that the learning it reproduced and summarised was already antiquated, as must be all textbook learning in
a progressive science. *Habent fata sua libelli*: unluckily the *Constitutional
History* escaped its allotted destiny. Even if it had been a much better
book, it would be foolish to expect a textbook, now more than eighty
years old, to stand up to serious criticism, as foolish as to expect the
hasty textbook writer to do more than take his facts and fancies
where he could most easily find them.[1] The wonder is perhaps that,
scattered here and there in the *Constitutional History*, good honest
compiling from the sources is to be found, dealing quite adequately
with incidents, isolated problems: wheat among the chaff. But in
the mountain of chaff the wheat is now of little account, and the chaff
is fit only to be thrown away.

[1] Stubbs did not conceal from his friends that it was hack work: as he said to Freeman,
when he was planning it in 1868, 'the principal part is *cash*' (*Letters*, p. 154).

II

THE PROBLEM OF THE NORMAN CONQUEST

No competent student of Anglo-Saxon England is likely to maintain that Stubbs's treatment of pre-Conquest history has retained any substantial value. He had at his command very nearly all the sources of information available at the present time, and some of his best work was done in this period, for the three volumes of the *Councils and Ecclesiastical Documents*, which he edited with A. W. Haddan, left little to be desired. And yet the first eight chapters of the *Constitutional History*, which take the story from the dim beginnings to the Norman Conquest, are worse than worthless to the uninstructed. So far as constitutional history in the stricter sense is concerned, Stubbs's errors arose largely because he accepted without question the notions of his learned contemporaries on the early institutions of the Germanic peoples, which are typified in what has been called the mark theory. This was a hypothetical reconstruction of primitive Germanic society that bore very little relation to such scanty historical facts as were supposed to justify it, and none at all to the very considerable body of laws and charters which have happily survived to illuminate the story of the English people. It postulated a primitive society of free and self-governing communities existing from a remote past and, despite the attrition of time and circumstance, emerging ever and anon in popular assemblies and popular elections. This belief in the continuity of free and, as it were, spontaneously organised institutions permitted Stubbs to recognise the sheriff in the laws of Ine of the early eighth century and to speculate that the sheriff was chosen in the folkmoot. So far as historical evidence went, he knew that there was no proof of election in the folkmoot and that the sheriff was a royal officer nominated by the king, but he could not forbear to provide a background to English institutions that accorded with the temper of his own age.[1] In the same spirit he asserted that the ealdorman 'was originally elected in the general assembly of the nation',[2] and that 'in theory' election belonged to the king and witan conjointly,[3] although in practice election 'was regulated more by the king's favour and by hereditary claims than by a substantive selection'.[4] Nor did Stubbs find any difficulty in accepting Kemble's 'canon' that the Old English king

---

[1] *Constitutional History*, i.126-7. [2] *Ibid.*, p. 125.
[3] *Ibid.*, p. 149. [4] *Ibid.*, p. 157.

was elected. 'Of all elections', he said, 'the most important was no
doubt that of the kings; and this belonged both in form and substance to the witan.'[1] If he baulked at the corollary, that the witan
had the power to depose the king, he did so with reluctance and found
some instances of 'regular and formal' depositions.[2] It followed, of
course, that the king 'was hedged in by constitutional forms', though,
oddly enough, 'they were very easy to break through'. When England
became united under West Saxon kings, 'their power of increasing
the witenagemot by nomination being admitted, they could at any
time command a majority in favour of their own policy'. Consequently the witenagemot threatened to become 'simply the council
of the king, instead of the council of the nation'.[3]

At every turn Stubbs is haunted by two ghosts: the ghost of a
mythical Germanic past of free institutions, and the ghost of an
imaginary constitution which the king is required to respect. These
ghosts, in varied disguises, haunted him to the end. They prevented
him from considering the facts objectively and, by their obtrusions,
they prevented him from setting down a plain history of institutions
such as they appeared in contemporary documents. But his first
eight chapters were, after all, no more than a curtain-raiser. However
interesting in themselves the institutions of Anglo-Saxon England
may be, they are of importance to the constitutional historian only
in so far as they affected the fabric of government in later centuries.

Nothing can be more certain than that the century before the
Norman Conquest had seen great changes in the English polity, so
that the England of the time of the last English kings presents a great
contrast to the England of Athelstan (924-39). It is the England of
Edward the Confessor and of Harold that is significant, because
upon that foundation Norman and Angevin England was built. And
if we confuse the conditions of the mid-tenth century with the conditions of the mid-eleventh century, if we accept as evidence for the
one period what is evidence for the other, we shall not be likely to
understand at all clearly what happened thereafter.

When Edward came to the throne in 1043, the shire system, the
basis of mediaeval administration, was new and incomplete. Obviously no such system could begin to apply to the whole country
until it was under a single ruler, that is from the time of Edgar
(959-75); but the control exercised by Edgar and his successors over
the north was markedly less than their hold over the south. It is in
the outh that the shire system begins. The Burghal Hidage of the
early tenth century (if that date may be accepted, at least provisionally) shows that for purposes of defence southern England was

[1] *Ibid.*, p. 150.
[2] *Ibid.*, p. 155. For a careful examination of the evidence and consequent destruction
of Kemble's thesis see Chadwick, *Studies in Anglo-Saxon Institutions*, pp. 355-66.
[3] *Constitutional History*, i.157. Need we warn the reader that a bare majority vote is a
conception alien to the early Middle Ages?

organised round a series of fortresses or fortified towns.[1] It has been denied that the districts assigned to the fortresses were administrative units,[2] but, however that may be, their existence is difficult to reconcile with the existence of an organised system of shires such as we find in the eleventh century. And when we advance from the period of the Burghal Hidage to the reign of Athelstan, we learn something of the administrative district of which London was the centre. It is quite plain that the district extends both south and north of the river Thames and that the authority of the rulers of London must cover a good part of Surrey as well as of Middlesex[3] and, indeed, extends into modern Kent and Essex. It is within these boundaries that later barons of London will claim to have the privilege of hunting[4] and that the rural manors are found which have dependent 'town-haws' or burgages in London.[5] The inference is irresistible that, within the boundaries formed on the east by the Lea and the Darent, on the north by the Chilterns, on the west by the Wey and on the south by the Downs—boundaries of marsh, woodland and waste—we must see an administrative unit of the middle of the tenth century. In the eleventh century these boundaries have gone for the purpose of administration. A separate shire of Surrey (literally, the southern region) is in existence.[6] The southern part of the London district has been detached, and London is also administratively separate from Middlesex. In the later eleventh century, London has its own portreeves and Middlesex its own sheriffs.[7] The London dis-

[1] For the text and commentary see Robertson, *Anglo-Saxon Charters*, pp. 246-9, 494-6. A rather earlier date than that suggested by Chadwick is perhaps possible.

[2] Stenton, *Anglo-Saxon England*, p. 262 *n*. Previous writers have assumed the contrary: e.g. Chadwick, *op. cit.*, pp. 219-27; Morris, *The Mediaeval English Sheriff*, pp. 17-22. James Tait, while rejecting the idea of burghal district courts in the shires of the South, nevertheless accepted a London district court (*Medieval English Borough*, pp. 23-4, 36).

[3] VI Athelstan, 5, 8.4. We adopt Liebermann's interpretation that the southern boundary must be south of the Thames and therefore includes part of modern Surrey (*Einleitung zum Statut der Londoner Friedensgilde*, p. 10; *Gesetze der Angelsachsen*, iii.119). There is much evidence to support this view, not least the number of Surrey manors with haws in London and Southwark: see n. 5 below. A full discussion of the problem must, however, be reserved for another occasion.   [4] *Gesetze*, i.526.

[5] There are haws or men in London and Southwark, belonging to manors in Essex, Kent, Middlesex and Surrey, shown in Domesday Book. They are particularly numerous in Surrey, not because this was a peculiarity of the county but because they were noted more frequently. They are found at Banstead, Battersea, Beddington, Bermondsey, Bletchingley, Chirington, Ditton, Kingston, Lambeth, Merton, Mortlake, Oxted, Walkhampstead, Walton. The grouping of London and Southwark for this purpose is the strongest possible confirmatory evidence for their administrative unity in the tenth century. The Essex manors connected with London are Barking, Waltham and West Thurrock. There is evidence for similar connexions with Fulham and Staines in Middlesex and Dartford and Lewisham in Kent. The evidence is, however, too complex to be discussed in a footnote.

[6] The name goes back to the eighth century (*Place Names of Surrey*, p. 1). The region would retain this name whatever the administrative connexion with the lands on the north bank of the Thames.

[7] The line of portreeves is well represented by Ulf, Wulfgar, Swetman, Leofstan, Ælfsige, under the Confessor (Robertson, *Anglo-Saxon Charters*, pp. 211, 234, 342, 370-1) and by Geoffrey (de Mandeville) under the Conqueror (*Gesetze*, i.486). The sheriff of Middlesex is mentioned in Domesday Book and his name is also given, Roger (i.127 a.1, 2). He had pre-Conquest predecessors in Ælfgæt (Robertson, *op. cit.*, pp. 353, 546) and Ulf, who seems to be identical with Ulf the portreeve (*ibid.*, pp. 344, 576).

trict may not be typical of burghal districts in southern England: it may have been exceptionally large, and its later subdivision was certainly exceptional. Elsewhere we may see a pre-Conquest shire in the process of formation when Eadric Streona unites Winchcomb-shire with Gloucestershire.[1] There was, it would seem, no uniform plan, no uniform evolution. Local circumstances had determined which areas should form a burghal district: local circumstances determined which areas should form a shire. But before the Conquest nearly all England, except the extreme north, was shired ground, with shires of all shapes and sizes, from the puny Middlesex to the vast Yorkshire with its three ridings, each as big as a shire elsewhere. The smallest county of all, Rutland, is a post-Conquest creation, as are Lancashire, Westmorland, Cumberland, Durham and North-umberland. They are extensions of the pre-Conquest system.

The important attributes of the shire are the sheriff and the shire-moot or county court. Sheriffs and shire courts, as they were known in the eleventh century, do not go back beyond Edgar, if so far, and they are devices of royal government.[2] Doubtless in their invention old material was used and old ideas, but they were essentially new creations. So, too, were those divisions of the shires, the hundreds or wapentakes with their courts, though in origin these courts may be older than those of the shires.[3] What ancient materials, what ancient ideas, are represented in shire and hundred are matters of specula-tion rather than of evidence. The essential fact is that they were there in 1066, new and efficient instruments of government to be used and extended as the king thought fit.

Beyond extending the system, the Norman kings left what they had found practically unchanged. After some experience a local justice (or justiciar) seems usually to have been appointed as a con-troller or a colleague of the sheriff, and these appointments were made until the early years of Henry II. The brief history of this insti-tution we discuss later and we need say no more at this point. We must, however, spare some words for the earl. In the Old English state he had wielded great power. Known originally as the ealdor-man, he became known in the eleventh century as the earl,[4] and by the Normans he was equated with the count. That at one time he participated in local administration and, in particular, in the ad-ministration of justice is testified by his customary rights to the 'third

---

[1] Heming, *Chartularium*, p. 280.

[2] The evidence is assembled by Harmer, *Anglo-Saxon Writs*, pp. 45-54.

[3] The direct evidence for hundred courts is no older than Edgar (I Edg. 1, III Edg. 5: *Gesetze*, i.192, 202), though it seems incontestable that the hundred is older than the shire of his laws (Cam, *Liberties and Communities in Mediaeval England*, pp. 64-90). The best arguments for the relative antiquity of the hundred court are that, up to the Conquest, its business was more extensive than that of the county court and that it was not sub-ordinate to the county court.

[4] The change in style is indicated in the poem on the battle of Maldon (991). Byrthnoth the ealdorman of A.S. Chronicle E, *s.a.* 991, and A, *s.a.* 993, is called earl (lines 6, 28), while Ælfwine calls his grandfather ealdorman (line 219).

penny' of the revenue of the shire and of boroughs.[1] But since in the eleventh century, if not before, the earl had been given charge of several shires, his direct participation in administration must have been limited. That he sat regularly in the 'folkmoot' with the sheriff and bishop, as Stubbs supposed, is no more than conjecture, derived from a law of Edgar and the addresses of early writs.[2] Neither bishops of extensive dioceses nor earls of extensive earldoms are likely to have found time for the detailed business of the courts, though on special occasions they may have been present,[3] and as important land-owners they were likely always to be represented there.[4] Under the Norman kings no baron was given so extensive an earldom as is found under the last English kings. The Norman earls were identified with particular shires, but their power derived from the extent of their territorial possessions and not from any territorial functions. Their title was one of honour and not of office. Nothing could illus-trate this more clearly than their acceptance of the office of local justice or of sheriff,[5] and in this fact lies one of the greatest contrasts between the Old English and the Norman régimes. So far as it went, the suppression of the greater earldoms destroyed any tendency there may have been towards provincial autonomy and promoted central-ised administration. But mediaeval government was always replete with incongruities, and the unification of English administration never went so far as to suppress palatinates and marcher lordships, where the king's writ did not run. Consequently we must not read too much into this or any other contrast between the Old English and the Norman state. The Normans had little statecraft and little foresight. They came as conquerors, not as reformers: if they had no mind to mend their own habits and customs, they had little mind to mend the habits and customs of the conquered.

The persistence into the early twelfth century, and occasionally into the reign of Henry II, of English charters and English writs[6]

---

[1] This customary payment may be due to Scandinavian influences. It is, in any case, noteworthy that, in the account by Snorri Sturlasson of Harold Fairhair's administration of those parts of Norway brought under his control, the earl received a third of the revenue of his shire (*Heimskringla*, Harald Haarfayre's Saga, ch. 6: Jónsson, pp. 44-5; Monsen, p. 46). The custom cannot very well be earlier in England than the second half of the tenth century when the shire system seems to have superseded the burghal districts.

[2] *Constitutional History*, i.128-9. The documentation is, in any case, inadequate and, such as it is, extends from Edgar to Edward I.

[3] In one case, where both earl and bishop are present, it is evidently an important meeting where the king is represented, and in another case, where the bishop is present, he is personally interested: both occasions are in the reign of Cnut (Robertson, *Anglo-Saxon Charters*, pp. 150-2, 162-4).

[4] Nothing, however, is known of the frequency with which the shire court met in the eleventh century, though the inference is that for some purposes it was being summoned more frequently than the two meetings in the year of Edgar's law. When in the thirteenth century we learn something in detail, the courts are monthly or six-weekly according to local custom (Morris, *Early English County Court*, pp. 190-1).

[5] For appointments as local justice see below, pp. 173-4. For the earl-sheriffs under Stephen see Morris, *The Mediaeval English Sheriff*, p. 107.

[6] No systematic collection of post-Conquest documents in English has been made. For charters and writs see *Regesta Regum Anglo-Normannorum*; but the editorial discussion

should indicate to us, as surely as the persistence of English institutions, that for half a century or so from 1066 the English way of
life was not sensibly altered. The Normans had very little to teach,
even in the art of war,[1] and they had very much to learn. They were
barbarians who were becoming conscious of their insufficiency.
'Under William the Conqueror nearly all the dioceses, nearly all the
larger abbeys of Normandy, had at their head an Italian or a Lothar-
ingian.'[2] If the Normans were more aware of their deficiencies in
the Church than in the State, it was not because they were skilled
in the arts of government. They were not great administrators: in
their small barbaric province they had never been seriously confronted with the problems of administration. They made shift with
the relics of earlier systems of government and some later improvisa-
tions.[3] In a sense this is true of all mediaeval states, but the English
state of the eleventh century was, by contrast with them, an ordered
polity, and an ordered polity, unless it is completely disrupted by an
invader, is likely, as so many historical examples testify, to persist,
to survive the dislocation of foreign and civil war. And despite his
barbaric devastation of much of his new kingdom, Duke William was
of a mind to preserve what he regarded as his inheritance. We may
add that, if the Conqueror's will had prevailed and the dukedom of
Normandy had gone to his eldest son and his line and the kingdom
of England to his second son and his line,[4] the Norman Conquest
would have been a transitory episode and the foreign element it had
introduced would, we make bold to say, have been absorbed into
English society almost without trace. The Scandinavian conquest,
earlier in the eleventh century, is a telling parallel.

That the Normans had little statecraft and little foresight, that
they had very little to teach and very much to learn, seems to us the
obvious conclusion from their history; but so to declare is, we recognise, to fly in the face of the settled convictions of successive generations of historians to whom the Conqueror has appeared as a heroic
figure of almost superhuman proportions. Nor did he lack panegy-
rists of his own time, not least the Peterborough monk who had
resided for a while at his court and to whom he seemed exceedingly

of them is disappointingly brief (i.xvi; ii.xxviii). Other documents have been printed by
Thorpe, *Diplomatarium*, pp. 436-40, 599-600, 633-8, 645-9; Earle, *Land Charters*, pp. 257-
77, 346-7; Robertson, *Anglo-Saxon Charters*, pp. 230-42; and they are scattered elsewhere,
e.g. Somner, *Antiquities of Canterbury*, 1.179; Liebermann, 'Drei nordhumbrische Urkunden
um 1100' in *Archiv für das Studium der neueren Sprachen*, cxi.275-84; Hist. MSS. Comm.,
Ninth Report, appendix, pp. 62*b*, 65*a*.

[1] Below, p. 61.

[2] We adapt a sentence of Marc Bloch's, *La société féodale: la formation des liens de dépendance*, p. 102: Sous Guillaume le Conquérant, presque tous les diocèses, presque
toutes les grandes abbayes de la Normandie . . . avaient à leur tête des Italiens ou des
Lorrains.

[3] Haskins, *Norman Institutions*, chapter 1 (pp. 3-61). The evidence is scanty. Here, as
elsewhere, Haskins seems to overrate the achievements of the Normans, as he certainly
underrated the maturity of Old English institutions.

[4] Ordericus Vitalis, *Historia Ecclesiastica*, iii.242-3, 256.

wise and of great nobility, more worshipful and commanding than
any of his predecessors. But these praises are outweighed by the
catalogue of the king's faults, his egotism, his cruelty, his greed and
his avarice, the very negation of ideal kingship.[1] William, indeed,
seems to have been astute without wisdom, resolute without foresight, powerful without ultimate purpose, a man of very limited aims
and very limited vision, narrow, ignorant and superstitious. Of the
pattern of his Norse ancestors, he was inferior to the greater among
them and—to draw a particular comparison—he was morally and
intellectually on a much lower plane than Cnut. His reputation has
been greatly enhanced among historians by the lucky survival of
Domesday Book, an inestimable boon to a learned posterity, but a
vast administrative mistake. Devised, as the Domesday survey obviously was, to augment the king's already swollen revenue,[2] we
cannot guess to what practical purpose its findings could have been
put had he survived. In the event he died before the plan could be
carried to completion, and it was never thought necessary to make
the effort required to check the details and to supply the lacunae.[3]
The survey seems to have been the fruit of a personal whim of the
king, who could have had little conception of the work entailed and
the drain upon the clerkly skill available, a drain extending greatly
beyond the staff attached to the king's chapel or his court. The more
closely the texts are examined, the more complex appear to be the
processes involved in the execution of the plan. We may admire the
ingenuity of the unknown planner behind the scheme while deploring
his inability to concentrate his attention upon a practical objective.[4]
There is nothing to suggest that the collection of any item of revenue
was materially affected for good or ill by the results of the survey.
The collection of geld, the principal item, continued with much the
same simple documents as before.[5] Within a generation Domesday

[1] A.S. Chronicle, s.a. 1086 (Plummer, pp. 119-21; Thorpe, pp. 354-6). The passage
we have paraphrased runs: Se cyng Willelm þe we embe specað wæs swiðe wisman 7
swiðe rice 7 wurðfulre and strengere þonne ænig his foregenga wære. Just as a 'rich'
knight was a noble knight (below, pp. 127-9), so here 'rice' must have the same meaning.
The catalogue of the king's faults is in verse and seems to be by another hand, but the
chronicler accepts it as true.

[2] This is quite specifically stated in the final article of enquiry, 'et si potest plus haberi
quam habeatur' (Select Charters, p. 101).

[3] Some omissions, e.g. particulars relating to London (which it is important to remember formed no part of Middlesex) may possibly be explained by the loss or delayed
arrival of the relative particulars before volume 1 of Domesday Book came to be bound.
But we cannot explain in this way the omission of particulars relating to a substantial
part of Kent on the Sussex border. For the omission of particulars regarding county
boroughs see Jenkinson, Domesday Re-bound, p. 28. Elsewhere such details as the number
of plough-teams are missing. No single explanation will cover every omission, and we are
not convinced by Mr Galbraith's suggestions (Making of Domesday Book, pp. 80, 195-6).

[4] Mr Galbraith (op. cit., pp. 28-44) has attempted a hypothetical reconstruction of
the procedure. This may perhaps suggest rather greater elaboration than was actually
necessary; but it gives a good idea of the complexities the commissioners had to face.

[5] We may compare the Northampton geld roll, which appears to belong to the 1070's
(Robertson, Anglo-Saxon Charters, pp. 230-6, 481), with the post-Domesday Middlesex
hidage, which apparently served the purpose of collection (Weinbaum, London unter
Eduard I und II, pp. 85-7).

Book itself had become a historical monument, respected but un-used.[1] If the greater churches obtained, as they seem to have done, copies of the entries or the underlying returns that affected them, they obtained nothing else than the information they themselves had supplied, if in a rather different form.[2] True, Domesday Book ultimately proved useful in checking claims that land was ancient demesne of the Crown[3]; but consultations were so infrequent that the centuries have left upon its leaves but little trace of wear and tear. Domesday Book does not seem to be an example of that prac-tical genius which historians have somewhat overgenerously attri-buted to the Normans. Indeed, the world had to wait until the col-laboration of Henry I and Roger of Salisbury before seeing much tangible evidence of it, and then it was speedily lost to view under Stephen. But we must not anticipate what we have to say hereafter.

If we stress the essential continuity between political institutions before and after the Conquest, we are not unmindful of the differ-ences between the conditions of 1066 and 1166; but though in the twelfth century there were new elements in the political structure, elements that were to be of great significance for the future, we doubt whether the differences were any greater than those between 966 and 1066. In this light it seems open to question whether the changes which are manifest in the England of Henry II, as con-trasted with the England of Edward the Confessor, were in any large measure due, at least directly, to the change in the rulers of the country which resulted from the duke of Normandy's victory at Hastings. We endeavour in later chapters to explain what were the forces that made for change and determined its direction, but it will be well to begin by reviewing briefly the explanations given by Stubbs. We need hardly recite at length his teaching on 'the effect of the Norman Conquest on the character and constitution of the

---

[1] In the years immediately succeeding the Domesday survey reference was occasionally made to the returns or to Domesday Book to establish titles (*Domesday Re-bound*, pp. 47-50; Galbraith, *op. cit.*, pp. 207-9). But the latest known occasion of this kind appears to have been in 1111 when the question at issue was the hundred in which the manor of Lewknor lay (*Chron. Mon. de Abingdon*, ii.116; *Regesta*, ii, no. 1000). It is possible, as Mr Galbraith supposes, that the particulars in Domesday Book were summarised in a smaller volume in the twelfth century, and this might explain the excellent state of preservation of the original volumes; but there appears to be no contemporary reference to such a breviate. An elaborate *abbreviatio*, written in the thirteenth century, which may possibly be a copy of an earlier volume, does not seem to have been put to any practical use (*Domesday Re-bound*, p. 47; Galbraith, *op. cit.*, pp. 213-4).

[2] It seems impossible to resist the conclusion that most of the detail in Domesday Book came from the landowners themselves. This is Mr Galbraith's argument (*ibid.*, pp. 38, 221); but we ourselves would go much further in admitting that such details were fur-nished in writing, very much as particulars of knight service were furnished in 1166 and other particulars in reply to the Inquest of Sheriffs in 1170. We can see no other plausible explanation of the composite records of holdings in the five counties covered by the Exon Domesday. Mr Galbraith thinks that these were the end product of the commissioners' enquiries (*ibid.*, pp. 115-6); but why should they go to the trouble of sorting out and aggregating particulars which could be obtained for the asking from the tenants-in-chief at the outset of their enquiry?

[3] Hoyt, *Royal Demesne*, pp. 173-8. For this and other appeals to Domesday, see also *Domesday Re-bound*. pp. 48-50.

English': it is—dare we say, characteristically?—dogmatic and perverse. But no one, we imagine, now supposes that the Conquest
'stimulated the growth of freedom and the sense of unity' or that 'the
powers which it called forth were largely exercised in counter-acting
its own influence'—a dark saying, indeed—though there may be
some who still share the belief that to the Conquest were due 'the
importation of new systems of administration, and the development
of new expedients, in every department of government'.[1] These
questions we defer and, to begin with, we propose to examine a
proposition that is perhaps more fundamental, that of feudalism.
'Feudalism', said Stubbs, 'in both tenure and government was, so
far as it existed in England, brought full-grown from France.'[2] This
is a view that still has its advocates among those with a deeper
knowledge than Stubbs possessed, a view we must treat with respect,
though perhaps those who share this view might not agree with the
qualifications which Stubbs introduced elsewhere. 'The reign of
Henry II', he said, 'saw the end of feudalism, so far as it had ever
prevailed in England, as a system of government. . . . Feudalism
continued to exist as the machinery of land tenure, and morally in
its more wholesome results as a principle of national cohesion and
the principle of loyalty.'[3]

As a preliminary, however, let us say a little of the words 'feudal'
and 'feudalism', the most regrettable coinages ever put into circulation to debase the language of historians. We would, if we could,
avoid using them, for they have been given so many and such imprecise meanings. But since we cannot rid ourselves of the words and
must live with them, let us endeavour, when we use them, to do so
without ambiguity. And first let us recall that of recent years there
has come into use among English historians the term 'bastard
feudalism', coined to denote the relationship between great lords
and their retainers in the later Middle Ages.[4] This relationship, so
the argument goes, was based, not upon a fief that passed by inheritance, but upon a contract of service, an 'indenture'. It is implied that this was a development of the later fourteenth and
fifteenth centuries and brought with it a change in the social structure. The troops employed on each side in the Wars of the Roses
were recruited under indenture: they were 'retainers' in the popular
sense of the word as contrasted presumably with the vassals of earlier
centuries. 'Bastard feudalism' is obviously a comparative term. At
some time, it is implied, there was a feudalism without prefix, and
this feudalism entered into a union with some other body of law or

---

[1] *Constitutional History*, i.269-70.   [2] *Ibid.*, p. 273 *n.*
[3] 'Benedict of Peterborough', ii.xxxvii.
[4] The term has been traced back to Charles Plummer who used it, without any
technical significance, in his introduction to Fortescue's *Governance of England* (1885),
p. 15. For its recent use see Dunham, *Lord Hastings' Indentured Retainers*, pp. 7-8, where there
is a useful bibliography.

social practice to give birth to a debased offspring, something hybrid, with mixed characteristics. Now, it is true that, however we define feudalism, there are elements other than feudal in the law and social structure of the fifteenth century. But what seems very doubtful is whether this is any less true of the fourteenth or thirteenth or twelfth century; whether English feudalism was not bastardised (if that unpleasant word is admissible) at its very birth.

Among historians there is, as we have said, a wide range of notions as to what should be termed feudal. Some would see feudalism, or at least strong feudal tendencies, in pre-Conquest England,[1] while others hold, with Stubbs, that feudalism came into England with the Conqueror.[2] Again, while some would see the approaching end of feudalism in England in the employment by the king of mercenary troops and professional ministers,[3] others find in England and Normandy 'the strongest and most unified feudal states', precisely because there the power and control of the central government were greatest.[4] *Vox et praeterea nihil!* The word has been so bandied about by historians that we can hardly reproach those sociologists who would see feudalism in the most diverse institutions in the most remote periods and places, those 'exotic feudalisms with which universal history appears everywhere to be strewn', to use Marc Bloch's words.[5] But if the concept and the term are to be in the least useful, there must be precise definition. We cannot at one and the same time hold that feudal institutions were introduced into England in 1066 and that they existed among the Anglo-Saxons, nor that they reached both their zenith and nadir under Henry II. What seems abundantly evident is that the origins of feudalism, however restricted a meaning we give the word, cannot have been the same in every country and that, however much feudal practices tended to assimilate, no single cause can be postulated. And let us, above all, avoid such a baseless notion as 'feudal system', for systematic is the last adjective we should apply to the aimless, spontaneous product of hazard and circumstance. The feudalism—we apologise even for repeating the abstract noun—the feudal institutions of each country must be regarded, in the words of Montesquieu, as 'an event that happened only once in the world and is never likely to be repeated',[6] something *sui generis*, the nature of which is sadly obscured by at-

---

[1] To cite a current textbook: 'Feudal elements and inchoate feudal arrangements were certainly present in Edwardian England. . . . England was not so feudal as Gaul. But she was probably developing in the same direction . . .' (Barlow, *Feudal Kingdom of England*, p. 11).
  [2] This is the classical view: cf. Stenton, *Anglo-Saxon England*, p. 672. It is the view advisedly accepted by the distinguished Belgian scholar, F. L. Ganshof, whose words are cited below. [3] Carl Stephenson in *A.H.R.*, xlviii.265.
  [4] Strayer, 'The Development of Feudal Institutions' in *Twelfth-Century Europe and the Foundations of Modern Society*, pp. 77-88: our citation is from p. 87.
  [5] *La société féodale: les classes et le gouvernement des hommes*, p. 242.
  [6] *De l'esprit des lois*, livre xxx, ch. i (ed. Truc, ii.296): 'un événement arrivé une fois dans le monde et qui n'arrivera peut-être jamais'.

tempted generalisation or synthesis. About such an institution, a singular phenomenon, the historian can ask precise questions and expect definite answers, supported by exact evidence.

Let us then take as the text of our discussion a sentence of M. Ganshof's, even more precisely phrased than the sentence we have cited from Stubbs: 'la conquête de l'Angleterre par le duc de Normandie en 1066 a introduit la féodalité en Angleterre'.[1] And since William the Conqueror—though he may have known the adjective *féodal* as applied to the tenant of a *fief*, a feudum[2]—knew no such word as *féodalité* and would not have understood such an abstraction as feudalism, let us ask what exactly he, and those who came with him, did introduce into England.

The Norman king regarded himself as the legitimate successor of Edward the Confessor. Though we call him the Conqueror, in his own eyes he was the legitimate heir. His was no foreign monarchy. If he introduced some new fashions, he was not perhaps conscious that they were new. And even the ceremony of crown-wearing at the principal feasts of the Christian year—a ceremony at which the *laudes* were sung, undoubtedly a Frankish custom in origin—which, by reason of the notice taken of it by the Peterborough Chronicler,[3] has been thought to be a characteristically foreign introduction, seems, on the contrary, to have been observed, not only by Edward the Confessor, but by his predecessors in the tenth century.[4] But if the Conqueror considered himself to be the true heir of the Old English kings, he could not conceive of himself as king in any other sort than a Frankish king, the king at Paris to whom he owed a vague allegiance and whom he and his ancestors had looked upon as a model, a model by which they regulated their own courts. And so dignitaries with foreign names were introduced into the English king's court: the seneschal (steward), the butler, the chamberlain, the constable, the marshal, though these dignitaries had had their counterparts in pre-Conquest England and might be given in Latin the same title.[5] When, however, we come to learn something of these offices in the twelfth century, it is clear that they are more honorific than functional and, if the titular dignitaries exercised any great influence in the post-Conquest English state, it was not by reason of any court office they held.[6] And, as we shall see, almost immediately after Henry I had conquered Normandy, the reins of government were passed to a minister unknown to the Franks, the justiciar

---

[1] *Qu'est-ce que la féodalité?* (1947), pp. 83-4.

[2] Since it was with the Conqueror's licence that Peter, one of the king's knights, became the *feodalis homo* of Abbot Baldwin of Bury, we may presume that he was acquainted with the French equivalent *homme féodal* (Douglas, *Feudal Documents*, p. 151).

[3] A.S. Chronicle, *s.a.* 1086 (Thorpe, p. 355; Plummer, pp. 219-20).

[4] Appendix I: below, pp. 397-412.

[5] Larson, *The King's Household in England before the Norman Conquest*, pp. 125-36, 195-6. See also Round in *E.H.R.*, xix.90-2.

[6] Cf. Round, *The King's Serjeants*, chapter 4. We deal later (p. 224) with the position of court dignitaries at the exchequer.

—the king's *alter ego*, the principal minister when the king was present in the kingdom, his representative and the viceroy when the king was absent.

Foreign influences, therefore, were more apparent than real in modifying the character of the English monarchy, while below the seat of power the changes at first were few or none[1]; and when change did come, it was not the result of foreign influence but as a response to the needs of good government. Thus, the county and hundred courts continued and so, it would seem, did the courts it is convenient to call manorial, although 'manor' is not a term to be found in England before 1066.[2] If the post-Conquest earls lose the extensive powers of pre-Conquest earls, the sheriff remains the local representative of the central government. The revenues of the English kings become the revenues of the Norman kings, although they are supplemented by revenues arising out of feudal incidents. The witan continues, if with an altered complexion, as the king's council. The structure of the state remains essentially as it was, modified perhaps, but not changed in any fundamental element, to accommodate any new ideas of the relationship between lord and vassal which the Normans brought with them.

Before we pass on, however, let us justify the assertion that manorial courts continued pre-Conquest courts. The connexion is well illustrated by a private charter issued within two generations of the Conquest, between 1108 and 1122, though probably nearer the latter year.[3] This is the grant of two villages, one in Huntingdonshire and one in Shropshire, by William Peverel of Dover to his steward Thurstan. These villages are granted 'in feodo et hereditate et sacha et socha et tol et theam et infangenethef', and they are to be held 'pro servicio dimidii militis'. These last words we must look at again, but here we should consider the conditions on which Thurstan receives his lord's gift. To hold in fee and inheritance gives him no jurisdiction over his tenants; but extensive jurisdiction is given him when he is granted sac and soc, toll and team and infangentheof, for, put briefly, these rights enable him to try both civil and criminal causes. For these rights, the Norman conquerors have no equivalent term, and the inference must be that, in acquiring

---

[1] We are not concerned with questions of status. We doubt, however, whether convincing evidence could be produced for the prevailing belief that there was a general debasement of the peasantry after the Conquest or that slaves were generally enfranchised by their new Norman lords (cf. Stenton, *Anglo-Saxon England*, pp. 463-73; Poole, *Obligations of Society*, pp. 12-13). As we point out later (pp. 121-2), the slave trade persisted in England well into the twelfth century, and penal slavery may have lingered on thereafter in Wales and the Marches (*Placita de Quo Warranto*, pp. 818-9). So far as freemen were concerned the Conquest must have resulted in many individual cases of hardship; but the machinery of local government, which depended upon them, was to all appearances kept running unimpaired. And it is with administration that we are concerned.   [2] Cf. Stenton, *op. cit.*, 473-95.

[3] There are two versions of this charter, in *Curia Regis Rolls*, xii.309-10, and in *Cartae Antiquae* (Pipe Roll Soc.), ii, no. 478. It is printed also by Eyton, *Antiquities of Shropshire*, xi.35, and Stenton, *First Century*, p. 274.

these rights, they are acquiring what their English predecessors had.[1] These rights, as many charters and the Hundred Rolls testify, are widespread and, if under Edward I the Old English words were obscure and if they required a gloss even in the twelfth century,[2] in the early years after the Conquest there could be no doubt of their meaning, even though their meaning may have differed in detail from place to place. We do not lack a contemporary commentary: the *Leges Henrici*. In principle, jurisdiction belongs to the king, but he has partly divested himself of it by grant to archbishops, bishops, earls and other great men who have sac and soc, toll and team and infangentheof in their own lands and sometimes elsewhere. The king retains capital pleas in his own hand, and barons who have soke are still subject to royal judges, who see that the law is observed. That this was the rule under Old English kings and that this rule has not been abrogated, the compiler of the *Leges* makes clear.[3] And it is because such jurisdiction as the barons possess is regarded as subordinated and delegated that, with the evolution of royal justice, baronial jurisdiction will gradually be eroded. The point of view expressed in the *Leges* is very much that of Bracton, though in his exposition Bracton draws his inspiration from Tancred.[4] A baron has no inherent right that can be asserted against the king. He has a minor jurisdiction over his own men, with which the king will not interfere, but more than this he can have only by royal grant.

The king may grant wide immunities, franchises, and there are notable instances before the Conquest as after[5]: of the most famous among them, that of Oswaldslow, we shall have occasion to speak later. But all these franchises are by royal grant and are subject to royal control. It may be that there are ancient cities which have privileges and customs that go back beyond the memory of man, before kings made written grants to urban communities. And it may be that these communities themselves are no deliberate creation, but have resulted from the play of common interest, the need for a polity within city walls that will give coherence to the townhaws and sokes that depend upon intramural and extramural lords, lay and ecclesiastical.[6] But just as the franchises are not independent states, so

---

[1] Stenton, *Anglo-Saxon England*, pp. 485-93. The continuity of this jurisdiction is well illustrated by the charter of Henry I confirming to the canons of York their pre-Conquest privileges (*Historians of the Church of York*, iii.34-6). The existing text is grossly inflated but is based upon a genuine document: cf. *Regesta Regum Anglo-Normannorum*, no. 1083. In any case, the charter represents the canons' claims.

[2] A gloss is provided in the 'Leges Edwardi Confessoris', 22-22.4 (*Gesetze*, i.647-8), the original version of which can be no later than the closing years of Henry I's reign.

[3] 'Leges Henrici', 20-20(3), 24 (*Gesetze*, i.560-1).

[4] *Traditio*, vi.67-8.   [5] Stenton, *Anglo-Saxon England*, pp. 486-93.

[6] This is one of the darkest problems of the centuries before and, indeed, for some time after the Conquest. London is the outstanding example, and by reason of its size and importance may be exceptional; though similar problems, if on a smaller scale, must have presented themselves in other towns. Cf. Maitland, *Domesday Book and Beyond*, pp. 181-2. Before the middle of the eleventh century London must have had a corporate existence, as the addresses of the writs of the Confessor and the Conqueror show (Harmer, *Anglo-Saxon Writs*, pp. 211, 234; *Gesetze*, i.486); but it is difficult to conceive how soke

these cities are not city states. They lie within the king's hand, and many of them will acknowledge the king as their direct lord. The royal boroughs form part of the king's demesne, every bit as much as the royal manors that are scattered up and down the country; and the citizens and burgesses, as the dwellers upon the king's manors one day will be, are privileged folk precisely because they depend upon the king.[1] The dwellers in seignorial and monastic boroughs, like the dwellers in baronial and monastic manors, are less fortunate, less privileged folk. An illustration may not be amiss. If there was one town that approached the level of a city state—and in other circumstances, such as those prevailing in Italy or Germany, might have become one—it was London. Its importance and the power of its citizens are manifest even in the scattered notices of the tenth and eleventh centuries[2]; and in the reign of Stephen the Londoners took a hand in king-making.[3] But they did not treat with William the Conqueror as sovereign with sovereign, but as suppliants, doubtless as suppliants it was well to placate, but still suppliants, and the Conqueror confirmed the customs (*laga*) they had enjoyed under the Confessor.[4] What these customs were we learn from the charter that Henry I granted them, and from that charter we see that they bought other privileges from the king.[5] Yet from time to time in the twelfth century, the king could deal very arbitrarily with the Londoners. Under Stephen they could be placed, first by the Empress and then by the king, in the power of a turbulent baron whose support the rivals to the throne wished to purchase, Geoffrey de Mandeville.[6] Whether or not they accounted under

jurisdiction could have arisen had not the soke preceded the communal courts (cf. Page, *London*, pp. 127-58). Doubtless the presence of the king's representative, the portreeve, tended to unify administration; but there is no indication of the existence of such an officer in London under Athelstan ('Judicia Civitatis Lundoniae' in *Gesetze*, i.173-83). There are bishops who have some measure of jurisdiction, and there are reeves, who presumably represent lay lords. Together they have united in a frithgild. This may be the beginning of incorporation, but the area over which authority is exercised is much wider than the city walls or any banlieu. That there was a king's reeve, a *wic-gerefa*, in London in the seventh century (*Gesetze*, i.11) we may well believe without believing in the uninterrupted continuation of such an office.

[1] It has been argued that royal boroughs became assimilated to royal manors and that they were not primitively regarded as part of the royal demesne (Hoyt, *Royal Demesne*, pp. 115-20); but this argument seems to overlook the history of pre-Conquest boroughs which were founded on royal estates or were fortified by the king's order. The king's interest was both administrative and financial and the burgesses were of necessity privileged (Stenton, *op. cit.*, pp. 521-31). We agree, however, with Mr Hoyt that the privileges of the sokemen on ancient demesne gradually evolved in the twelfth and thirteenth centuries (*op. cit.*, pp. 180-207). These privileges were later than those of citizens and burgesses.

[2] Particularly in the A.S. Chronicle, to which Plummer's index (ii.406-7) is an adequate guide.

[3] The sole authority for Stephen's 'election' by the Londoners is *Gesta Stephani* (ed. Potter), pp. 3-4; but, at best, this implies the recognition of his claims (cf. Round, *Geoffrey de Mandeville*, pp. 2-3, 247-9). For their conduct towards the Empress see *ibid.*, pp. 69, 84, 115-6. A rather different view is taken by Miss McKisack in *Powicke Essays*, pp. 78-9.

[4] *Gesetze*, i.486; *Select Charters*, p. 97.

[5] *Gesetze*, i.524-6; *Select Charters*, pp. 128-30: for correction of text see *E.H.R.*, xlii.80-7.

[6] Round, *Geoffrey de Mandeville*, pp. 92, 105-11, 141-3, 150, 153, 373.

Henry II for the city ferm was a matter for the king's decision.[1] Under Richard I their liberties were apparently forfeited for a while when they were bargaining for a reduced ferm.[2] But if, shortly afterwards, in a period as near anarchy as ever was known in England, they aspired to be a commune on the continental model, it was a dream soon forgotten.[3]

In the Norman kings' political relations with ecclesiastics, nobles and urban communities, we can see no breach with the past. There are inevitable changes, but nothing that cannot be fairly regarded as evolutionary. In the twelfth century, it is true, other conceptions were at work besides those of the Old English polity. The principal barons held lands on both sides of the Channel and their ideas were deeply coloured by their country of origin. Of certain of these foreign introductions discussion is best reserved—of homage and of 'feudal incidents'—but here we must mention the honour, the aggregation of manors possessed by one lord, for which a central court, the honour court, was held. These manors might be scattered, but the vassal was under an obligation, when summoned, to attend the honour court. This rule must have been established not very long after the Conquest, before the consequences of marriages, grants and inheritance had put the lordship of two or more honours into the hands of a single baron, for under Henry I a vassal could not be compelled in law to attend the court of an honour of which he was not tenant, even though that other honour belonged to the same lord.[4] Only important tenants-in-chief ever held honours, and

---

[1] The intricacies of pipe-roll accounting were not quite mastered by Tait and his summary for the reign of Henry II must be treated with caution (*Medieval English Borough*, pp. 163-9). The ferm throughout the reign was £500 in blanched money and £22 *numero*, that is £547 in current coin. On the meaning of these terms, see below, p. 233, n. 12. Any suggestions that the ferm varied in amount and any consequent inferences appear to be illusory. From Michaelmas 1157 to Michaelmas 1163 the citizens were directly responsible for the ferm: thereafter sheriffs appointed by the Crown from among the citizens were responsible, though the change may have been technical rather than substantial. There was, however, one interval, between Michaelmas 1174 and Michaelmas 1176, when the Crown appointed *custodes*, the reason presumably being that the king needed to keep a tighter grip upon the city. The details and arguments cannot be compressed into a footnote and must be given elsewhere.

[2] Three *custodes* account for the twelvemonth from Michaelmas 1189. In the following twelvemonth the ferm was reduced to £300 in blanched money (£315 in current coin), but for one month in this year the city had been taken into the custody of the constable of the Tower of London. The citizens did not account directly for the ferm until Michaelmas 1194 (*Pipe Roll, 2 Richard I*, p. 156; *3 Richard I*, pp. 135-7; *7 Richard I*, pp. 113-4). Great difficulty is presented by the statement that it was Earl William (de Mandeville) who had custody of the city, as constable of the Tower, for thirty days in 1190-1, for he was certainly dead the previous year. However, there can be little doubt that he was in some way represented by Gilbert Carbunel, who managed to transfer the debt for his share in the ferm to Geoffrey fitz Peter, who succeeded to Earl William's estates. But Geoffrey, who was then justiciar, persuaded the barons of the exchequer in 1205 that he had been charged by mistake (*Pipe Roll, 7 John*, p. 6).

[3] The most elaborate, but not very trustworthy, account is that by Round, *Commune of London*, pp. 219-51. For more balanced statements see Petit-Dutaillis, *Studies*, pp. 96-106, and Tait, *op. cit.*, pp. 251-2. None of these writers notes that the *commune* of London is mentioned in chancery documents of 1200 and the thirteenth century (*Rot. Chartarum*, p. 60b; *Rot. Litt. Claus.*, ii.45b). There are a good many other references in the thirteenth century to the *commune* of London and of other towns. But to discuss this matter further would take us far from our immediate subject.   [4] 'Leges Henrici', 1 b (*Gesetze*, i.575).

honour courts were never numerous in England.[1] We know very little of them until centuries after the Conquest, when their significance was small. If their existence in the reigns of the early Norman kings has the importance that has been claimed for them, it must be because they mark a new conception of the relationship between tenants and their lords. The tenant owes suit to his lord's court, wherever that court may be held, and there is laid upon him the duty of counselling his lord as well as of fighting for him. But is this relationship tenurial or personal? Does it not spring from the fact that, before the original post-Conquest tenant acquired land in England, he was already tied by a personal bond to his lord, who had been his leader in the duke of Normandy's victorious expedition and was subsequently his leader in the army of occupation during the duke's uneasy reign as king of England? Or, it may be, the tenant was a relative of his lord. Tenurial and personal bonds, even in the eleventh century, were still two facets of the same relationship, though already their unity was disturbed. Even in the pages of 'Glanville' and Bracton we find reminiscences of an older order of society when the grant of lands was the reward of service and their acceptance the promise of service, the expression of a personal, enduring, almost sacred, relationship between lord and man. Of these matters we shall say more. We raise the issue here because we question whether the relations of a lesser thegn or freeman, thegn and earl differed fundamentally from the relations of vavassor, baron and count: these designations are treated as equivalent in the translations of Cnut's laws.[2] And while there is doubtless a parallel between the court of an honour and the king's court, it is surely an exaggeration to say that 'every important honour was a state in miniature governed, as was the kingdom, by its lord with the help of tenants whom he convened to form a court'.[3] For though a common principle gave rise to the honour court and played its part in the evolution of the king's court, the similarities do not extend very far. Honour courts seem speedily to have decayed as the jurisdiction of the king's court advanced and widened. If they ever were of importance in comparison with the hundred and county courts and the courts held by the king's justices, their importance was transitory, and even for this brief period of their history direct evidence can hardly be said to exist.[4] Still, the principle that the tenant, in this case the tenant-in-chief, owed his lord counsel may have played its part in determining the form that parliament and council were to take in the later Middle Ages; and the course of English history might possibly have been somewhat different if the principle had not been recognised under Norman kings and reinforced, we may add,

---

[1] Stenton, *First Century*, pp. 41-60; *Anglo-Saxon England*, p. 619.
[2] II Cnut, 71.1-5; 'Leis Willelme', 20.1-2a (*Gesetze*, i.358-9, 506-7).
[3] Stenton, *Anglo-Saxon England*, p. 628.   [4] Stenton, *First Century*, *loc. cit.*

by centuries-long contact with French traditions and French institutions. Yet outwardly after the Conquest there seems to have been
little change. The Old English witan was not noticeably different
from the Norman king's council. The Peterborough Chronicle uses
the same word to describe both[1]; and already under Edgar the
bishops and abbots, the ealdormen, thegns and sheriffs, came to
reverence and counsel the king at the principal feasts of the year as
the bishops and abbots, the earls, barons and ministers came to
reverence and counsel Norman kings.[2] Nor could an honour court
under the Normans have looked very different from the gathering
of thegns who attended an English earl. But while the king's council
went from strength to strength, modifying its composition as it grew,
and reached its apogee in the fifteenth century, honour courts have
left but the slightest mark on English history. The vitality of the
king's council and the decay of honour courts—and we are ourselves
in doubt whether 'decay' is an appropriate word—are phenomena
which help us to appreciate correctly the influence of 'feudalism' in
England.

If we may spare yet a few more words for English towns, we
should remark that, while they were not uninfluenced by French
ideas and nomenclature, they yet appear obstinately English. The
circumstance that seignorial boroughs were dependent upon French
lords did lead to the introduction of some French notions, as the
widespread grant of the customs of the obscure Norman town of
Breteuil testifies.[3] But far more powerful, because more important
towns were concerned, was the influence of the customs of London,
the privileges of which were sought by such towns as Exeter, Gloucester and Oxford.[4] Towards the end of the twelfth century, the
influence of French ideas is again to be seen in the adoption of the
title of mayor for the chief municipal officer of London[5]; but though
the usage spread through the country in the thirteenth century, it
seems to have signified little more than a change of name and perhaps
a little added dignity.[6] The narrow circle of citizens or burgesses who
governed English towns were French-speaking and the Old English
title of portreeve had ceased to have a meaning for them, even if it
were still remembered. In London the portreeve had given place to
the 'justice' within a generation or so after the Conquest,[7] and if,

---

[1] For witan and witenagemot before and after 1066 see Plummer, i.159, 173-4, 185,
216-7, 233, 236, 251.   [2] Appendix I: below, p. 406.
[3] This was the discovery of Mary Bateson (E.H.R. xv.73-8, 302-18, 496-523, 754-7;
xvi.92-110, 332-45). Subsequent research has led to some correction in detail (Tait,
English Medieval Borough, pp. 350-2).   [4] Ballard, British Borough Charters, pp. 12-15.
[5] Howden (iii.212) mentions the mayor in April 1193. A deed (B.M. Add. Charter
1046) mentioning Henry fitz Ailwin as mayor may be late in 1192, since the second in
rank, Roger fitz Alan, appears to be the sheriff.
[6] The earliest instance known is Winchester in 1200 (Rot. Chartarum, p. 60b); but this
points to an earlier adoption of the title. For later instances see Tait, Medieval English
Borough, p. 291 n.
[7] For the local justice, see below, pp. 173-4. That there was a local justice in London
in the eleventh century, at latest under William II, is clear from Stephen's charter to

after the decay of that office early in Henry II's reign, there was a city officer, superior to the sheriffs, who bore a specific title, it seems not to have been preserved.[1] In what circumstances under Richard I a chief officer was elected who bore the name of mayor we are very imperfectly informed, though the adoption of the title appears to be connected with the adoption of the title of *commune* for the community of citizens.[2] If, however, there was an urge to imitate continental institutions, this was a very transient phase, and the strength and persistence of older ideas are seen in the survival of the title of alderman given to the councillors, who might well have been entitled *échevins*, had French influences on English civic institutions been more than superficial and intermittent.[3] If, upon the Continent, the *commune* can be fitted into a theoretical scheme of feudal institutions—and, for the most part, it fits but ill[4]—English towns remained obdurately immune from such feudal concepts as gained a foothold in the country at large.

English 'feudalism' we must think of, not in terms of the conditions bordering on anarchy of much of Stephen's reign, not in terms of the Barons' Wars under John or Henry III, but in terms of England at peace, under the strong hand of Henry I or Henry II or the ordered rule of the great justiciars, Ranulf Glanville, Hubert Walter or Geoffrey fitz Peter. The men we have named symbolise centralised government, an organised state, justice administered by the king's court at Westminster or locally by royal judges itinerating throughout the country. This is the achievement of the twelfth century in what has been called 'Feudal England'. But is this form of government, this kind of justice, feudal? Could the answer to this question possibly be affirmative without inverting any intelligible meaning that can be attached to 'feudal'? 'Feudalism' in England is rather some part—and by no means the most prominent feature—of the background of a state which, to all appearance, is not feudal. After the office of justiciar has passed into history, the English state will evolve for hundreds of years on the lines established in the thirteenth century, while feudal tenures will lose their meaning and feudal

Geoffrey de Mandeville II (Round, *Geoffrey de Mandeville*, p. 141). Geoffrey had previously been portreeve: see p. 24, n. 7; above.

[1] In 1180-7 (the date is uncertain) we find the constable of the Tower of London, Osbert de Glanville, presiding over the Husting (St. Paul's MS. 15/839). About 1190 Ralf of Cornhill appears to be president of the court, with the future mayor, Henry fitz Ailwin, second in rank: Ralf is given no title (*Cartularium S. Iohannis Baptiste de Colecestria*, p. 296). On 25 March 1192 Henry of Cornhill appears to preside, and again Henry fitz Ailwin is second in rank (P.R.O., Ancient Deeds A.2383).

[2] See p. 36, n. 3, and p. 38, n. 5, above. The gap, of apparently at least a year, between the recognition of the 'commune' and the adoption of the title of 'mayor' has not been explained. It would seem that at first 'commune' and 'mayor' were not associated.

[3] The word, in the Latin form *skivine*, seems to occur once only, in the oath of 1193 (Round, *Commune of London*, pp. 235-6; M. Weinbaum, *London unter Eduard I und II*, ii.57: cf. Tait, *Medieval English Borough*, pp. 266-7, 292).

[4] Luchaire's definition of a commune as a *seigneurie collective populaire* is classical (*Les communes françaises*, p. 97). But the most important city of France, Paris, could not be brought within that definition.

GME D

incidents survive merely as fiscal instruments. The state is independent of feudalism and if, perforce, its organisation must at some
points be accommodated to certain feudal ideas and forms, it cannot
at any period be justly termed a feudal state. This conclusion is at
variance with the picture commonly presented to us. 'England after
the Conquest', we are told, 'displays equally [with Germany] the
French type [of feudalism]: the lords who were enfeoffed with
honours there, as doubtless also lords of lower rank, held their
courts, composed of their vassals, and adjudged tenurial and feudal
actions as well as some others.'[1] This picture is presented to us as
true only for the first century after the Conquest, a period for which
we have relatively little information and when conjecture is least
controlled and most dangerous. Evidently the picture is not true of
any later period; and it remains for those who hold these views to
show that the division of jurisdiction between king and barons, as
we find it under Henry II and his sons, differed radically from the
division of jurisdiction under Henry I. In some respects the form of
jurisdiction, the organisation of justice, may have changed; but had
the king usurped powers and rights that the barons had formerly
possessed? The twelfth-century legal texts that have come down to us
do not convey this suggestion: and, as we shall see, the surviving
royal records from Henry I's reign appear to contradict it.

In any case, as our information accumulates in the later twelfth
and the thirteenth centuries, it is plain that the number of actions
coming before seignorial courts, which might strictly be called
'feudal', was, in fact, negligible—in England such feudal actions
were tried in the king's court—while the tenurial and other actions
that came before seignorial courts were, in all human probability,
such as would have come before them, had there been no Norman
Conquest. Between England and France there is, indeed, in this
matter at least, not likeness but contrast. Take any volume of the
printed *Curia Regis Rolls* and read it side by side with any volume of
the *Olim*, the records of the French king's court a century or so later.
Both mirror a French society and, in a sense, a feudal society: but in
England actions in the king's court, so far as they can be called
feudal, are essentially proprietary; in France such actions in the
king's court are essentially jurisdictional.[2] The difference goes deep.
If in France feudal laws produced 'la régle avec une inclinaison à
l'anarchie et l'anarchie avec une tendance à l'ordre et à l'harmonie',[3]
such words would be grotesquely inept to describe the effect of
feudal ideas in England. It was no light matter always to preserve

[1] Ganshof, *Qu'est-ce que la féodalité?*, pp. 181-2.
[2] Evidently a full demonstration is impossible in a brief space; but the essential nature
of the jurisdiction of the parliament of Paris is illustrated by the actions in which the
English king was involved as duke of Guyenne. A convenient summary will be found in
Ducoudray, *Les origines du parlement de Paris*, pp. 1005-12. See also the paper by P. Chaplais,
'The Chancery of Guienne' in *Jenkinson Studies*, pp. 61-80.
[3] Montesquieu, *De l'esprit des lois*, livre xxx, ch. 1 (ed. Truc, ii.296).

the king's peace, but wherever English law prevailed, not only in England itself but in Scotland and Ireland in the thirteenth century, there the king was supreme, his authority beyond challenge. Every jurisdiction was subject to his jurisdiction; every local law was dominated by the common law.

III

THE OLD ENGLISH MILITARY SYSTEM

DISCUSSIONS of the consequences of the Norman Conquest have been largely focused upon the question whether the military service demanded of a tenant-in-chief under the Norman kings was in any way derived or developed from the tenurial obligations of pre-Conquest landowners. There seem to us to be larger and more important questions involved in the transition from the Old English state to the Anglo-Norman state. But since the issue cannot be escaped, it may be well to set down what can be learned of the Old English military organisation. Nothing like a complete account is possible. What we can learn is made up of glimpses and fragments, glimpses that may deceive, fragments that have been fitted into more than one speculative pattern.

There is some measure of agreement that the hundred, a territorial unit older than the shire and enduring almost within living memory, had as its ultimate basis the provision of a hundred fighting men. However that may be, by the time we come to know anything very definite about it, the hundred, with the related five-hide unit, had been adapted, if it had not been devised, to provide an expeditionary force. Its members were called up when the king led an *expeditio*, an *exercitus*. The nature of the force is singularly well illustrated by its adaptation to provide ship's crews: three hundreds, not necessarily maritime, were combined to furnish a complement of sixty men and, apparently, the ship also.[1] This was not, it is true, the only basis of recruitment for the navy: it might, for example, be varied or supplemented by imposing upon the estates of a cathedral church the obligation of finding a ship's crew.[2] Such an expedient may not, however, have been introduced until the days of the renewed Danish invasions under Ethelred, while the hundredal system, in its main lines, must, we think, go back at least to the reign of Edgar, and it may have been introduced by him. The authority upon

---

[1] Canon Isaac Taylor seems to have been the first to have studied the groupings of hundreds in threes (*Domesday Studies*, i.72-6). The inflated charter of Edgar (*Cart. Saxonicum*, no. 1135) is the earliest evidence for the liability of a three-hundred group: the substance of this charter cannot very well be a later invention. The widespread imposition of this type of liability in the tenth and eleventh centuries is not open to dispute: see, *inter alia*, Plummer, *Saxon Chronicles*, ii.185-6; Cam in *Tait Essays*, pp. 14-22; Harmer, *Anglo-Saxon Writs*, pp. 266-7; John, *Land Tenure in Early England*, pp. 116-21.

[2] Robertson, *Anglo-Saxon Charters*, p. 164: the date appears to be 1023 (*ibid.*, p. 412). It is to be inferred also from bequests of ships that bishops were charged with the duty of providing them (Whitelock, *Anglo-Saxon Wills*, p. 53).

whom we rely is a panegyrist who seems undoubtedly to have written before the end of the tenth century. What remains of this source is to be found in the pages of Florence of Worcester and (we think, at second hand) William of Malmesbury. Among much else in Edgar's praise, it is told how he organised three squadrons of warships to patrol the British seas and keep the island safe from invasion.[1] The complement of each squadron appears to have been 1200 men, which would be sufficient for twenty ships, making a total fleet of sixty.[2] A fleet of this size would exhaust the contributions of 180 hundreds, representing perhaps a quarter of the organised forces of the country,[3] and its maintenance may have been possible under this system only while the country enjoyed the long and profound peace which earned for Edgar the title of *pacificus*, though remnants of the system are still observable after the Conquest. There is much we would like to know of Edgar's fleet. We might suppose that each ship was navigated by a professional seaman, and it is a little perplexing to find that the only steersmen of whom we have knowledge in the Confessor's day lived in inland counties, two in Worcestershire and one in Bedfordshire.[4] Now the steersman was at the time the master of the ship,[5] and the steersman of the bishop of Worcester's ship, Edric of Hindlip,[6] was also the commander of the bishop's

---

[1] Florence of Worcester, *Chronicon,* i.143-4; William of Malmesbury, *Gesta Regum,* i.177-8. We agree with W. H. Stevenson that, for what there is in common between them, Malmesbury was the borrower (Asser, *Life of Alfred,* pp. lx-lxiii), though the relation between the two chronicles as they stand is complex (*ibid.,* p. 109 *n*). Curiously enough, Stevenson, like Stubbs before him (Malmesbury, *op. cit.,* ii.cxxviii-cxxxi), overlooked these passages when making his comparison between the texts; they seem to put completely out of court the suggestion by Professor Darlington that Florence had Malmesbury before him (*Vita Wulfstani,* p. xviii *n*). There would seem no doubt, however, that Ælfric had the panegyric before him when he composed his homily on St. Swithun (*Lives of the Saints,* i.440-71). Stevenson saw in this homily a confirmation of the story in Florence and Malmesbury of the eight kings who swore fealty to Edgar at Chester (Florence, i.142; Malmesbury, i.165; *E.H.R.,* xiii.505-7). But Ælfric was paraphrasing Latin sources, in this homily chiefly Landferth (below, p. 121, n. 3), and, though there are touches of his own, there can hardly be any question, that, in the conclusion of the homily when he is eulogising Edgar (ll. 444-53), he is drawing upon the panegyrist. Since this homily cannot well be dated later than 997, it follows that the panegyrist was writing before then. Florence's text (pp. 143-4) refers to 'iii.DC.robustas . . . naues', where it would seem evident that *nautas* is the true reading.

[2] A number of references to fleets in the A.S. Chronicles suggests that they were organised in squadrons of twenty. The most significant entry is *s.a.* 1009, which tells how Wulfnoth enticed the crews of the fleet assembled at Sandwich until he had twenty ships and how Brihtric went in pursuit with eighty ships (Thorpe, pp. 260-1; Plummer, p. 138). Other entries refer to forty ships, *s.a.* 1015, 1018; 60 ships, *s.a.* 1040; 160 ships, *s.a.* 1016 (Thorpe, pp. 276-7, 284-5, 296; Plummer, pp. 146, 154-5, 160). Similar numbers, 20, 40, 60, are given in the *Heimskringla* (Jónsson, pp. 129, 131-2; Monsen, pp. 141, 143, 145). This reckoning by scores was probably conventional: more precise figures are given elsewhere.

[3] We assume that under Edgar there was not a double liability for the *landfyrd* and *scipfyrd.* The number of hundreds under Edgar's sovereignty is, of course, uncertain. A convenient table, showing the number of hundreds in the country covered by the Domesday Survey, will be found in Stubbs, *Constitutional History,* i.107.

[4] D.B., i.173 b 1 (Edric), 174 b 1 (Turchil stirmannus regis Edwardi), 217 b 1 (Vlfech stirman regis Edwardi).

[5] See the gloss in 'Quadripartitus' to *steoresman,* 'id est gubernator' (*Gesetze,* i.222).

[6] Round in *V.C.H., Worcester,* i.248-9.

troops when they served in the king's host.[1] The duties must have alternated. The crews, too, were not only seamen but warriors also, and they were provided with coats of mail.[2] We need not, however, suppose that a crew was composed of landsmen, for there is good reason to believe that service with the king's ships had commonly been commuted for a money payment,[3] and that the seamen were in large part mercenaries.[4] It is probable, however, that the higher command was provided by high-born thegns, very much as in the days of the Tudors, not, of course, that we need call them amateur seamen, for they were probably as skilled in fighting by sea as by land. In this way we can explain the story of Wulfnoth, who in 1009 suborned a squadron of the king's ships and was pursued by four other squadrons under the command of Brihtric,[5] as well as later references to the ships of Osgod Clapa and of Earl Godwin and his sons.[6] The Mercian ships which King Edward dismissed in 1049[7] were doubtless those controlled or commanded by Earl Leofric, and we hear in 1055 of the ships of Earl Ælfgar, Leofric's son.[8] The principle of lordship clearly operated as much on sea as on land, though it is hard to suppose that there was not a stricter discipline in the navy than is likely to have obtained in mediaeval armies. But whatever may have been the position in Edgar's day, under the Confessor the loyalty of the crews seems to have been given, not to the king, but to their lord. Even when Godwin's son Swein had been declared a traitor (*nithing*), two ship's crews still adhered to him,[9] and it is ominous to read in 1052 of Earl Godwin's ships and the king's ships in rival fleets.[10] In some way, as we shall see was the case with the army, there seem to have been combined personal followers of the king and of the nobles, mercenaries, and seamen recruited on the basis of one man from every five hides. Whether service with the fleet discharged liability for service with the host is a question to which no certain answer seems possible: land in the eleventh century

[1] 'Edricus qui fuit tempore regis Edwardi stermannus navis episcopi et ductor exercitus eiusdem episcopi ad servitium regis' (Heming, *Chartularium*, i.81).

[2] Conclusive evidence is provided by the will of Archbishop Ælfric. He bequeaths to the king his best ship and sixty helmets and coats of mail for the crew (Whitelock, *Anglo-Saxon Wills*, p. 53). Compare A.S. Chronicle, *s.a.* 1008, 'of viii hidum helm] byrnan, (Thorpe, pp. 258-9; Plummer, i.138).

[3] The phrase 'geldum acceptum fuit ad navigium faciendum' can hardly have any other meaning (Heming, *Chartularium*, i.78), and the same inference must be drawn from the liability of Malmesbury to find 'xx solidos ad pascendos suos buzecarlos' (D.B. 1.64 b). So also *nauigia* in D.B., i.173 a 1 seems to imply a money payment (see p. 45, n. 1, below).

[4] Besides the reference to the butsecarls in the preceding note, the references to them and to lithsmen in the Chronicle can be understood only in this sense: cf. Plummer, ii.239-40.

[5] Above, p. 43, n. 2.

[6] For Osgod Clapa's ships see A.S. Chronicle, C,D, *s.a.* 1049-50 (Thorpe, p. 308; Plummer, pp. 166-7). For Godwin and his sons see below.

[7] A.S. Chronicle, *s.a.* 1049 (Thorpe, p. 308; Plummer, p. 168).

[8] A.S. Chronicle, C, *s.a.* 1055 (Thorpe, p. 326; Plummer, p. 186). The crews were clearly in Ælfgar's pay.

[9] A.S. Chronicle, C, D, *s.a.* 1049-50 (Thorpe, p. 310; Plummer, pp. 170-1).

[10] A.S. Chronicle, *s.a.* 1052 (Thorpe, pp. 318-9; Plummer, pp. 180-1).

may have been charged with the double burden.[1] The nature of the service certainly seems to have differed, for while service with the host was occasional, service with the fleet, at least in Edgar's day, was an annual routine which, starting soon after Easter, demanded a good many weeks' duty that would take a man from the Channel to the Western Isles and back again. After Edgar's death this system must have lapsed, for it was sought to revive it on a larger scale in 1008.[2] The great fleet thus assembled in 1009, however, suffered disaster[3] and, though a fleet of some sort was maintained until the end of the Old English kingdom,[4] it is uncertain to what extent Edgar's system survived.

Although the land force appears to have been organised on the basis of the shire and not on any grouping of hundreds, save in quite exceptional circumstances, as in Oswaldslow,[5] the ultimate unit of assessment, whether in terms of men or money, appears to have been the same as for the fleet. In southern England this was the five-hide unit. Just as a ship's crew of sixty was drawn from, or assessed upon, three hundreds—that is, in principle, three hundred hides—so five hides furnished, in principle, one warrior for service with the king's army.[6] Whatever unit was adopted in the rest of the country, there is no reason to suppose that the conception was not everywhere the same. But, as with the navy, the system was not incompatible with the principle of lordship, and, indeed, the effective use of the armed forces from the shires would depend upon the leadership of the local ealdorman. He himself would have his own followers, his thegns and the fighting men of his household, his *hiredcnihtas* and his *hiredmen*, his *heorðgeneatas*, his *heorðwerod*—the names are many.[7] In an emergency it would be upon them that he would rely, as the ealdorman Byrthnoth did when he led his men to oppose a Danish raid.[8] Under

---

[1] This appears to be the inference from the entry in Domesday Book under Worcester (Bishampton): Quatuor liberi homines tenebant de episcopo T.R.E. reddentes . . . expeditiones et nauigia (D.B. 1.173 a 1).

[2] A.S. Chronicle, *s.a.* 1008 (Thorpe, pp. 258-9; Plummer, p. 138); *Gesetze*, i.242-3 (V Ethelred 27). As under Edgar the ships were to be assembled immediately after Easter for an annual cruise.

[3] A.S. Chronicle, *s.a.* 1009 (Thorpe, pp. 259-61; Plummer, pp. 138-9).

[4] It is desirable to challenge such statements as that Edward 'dispersed his own standing force of warships' in 1050 (Stenton, *Anglo-Saxon England*, pp. 424-6) or 'wholly disbanded his fleet' (Blair, *Introduction to Anglo-Saxon England*, p. 105). Our only authorities are A.S. Chronicle C and E, and it is clear that the ships paid off were those of mercenaries (lithsmen) which had been engaged to augment the fleet. Since the king's ships are mentioned *s.a.* 1052 in A.S. Chronicle, C, D, E, there can be no doubt on the matter (Thorpe, pp. 309-10, 318-9; Plummer, pp. 168-9, 178-9).

[5] It is evident that in Oswaldslow the bishop of Worcester's contingent was separately organised and commanded (Heming, *Chartularium*, i.81: above, p. 44, n. 1).

[6] Maitland, *Domesday Book and Beyond*, pp. 156-9.

[7] For *hiredcniht* see Whitelock, *Anglo-Saxon Wills*, p. 23, and *Crawford Charters*, p. 23, where a distinction is made between them and *hiredmen*. Most *cnihtas* in charters and wills could equally well be called *hiredcnihtas*: cf. Miss Whitelock's note, *op. cit.*, p. 127. References to literary sources will be found in Bosworth-Toller, but the military significance of *hiredcniht* is not realised: see the following note.

[8] All the three words *hiredmen*, *heorðgeneatas* and *heorðwerod* occur in the *Battle of Maldon*, lines 24, 204, 261. There seems little difference in meaning between them.

a king whose hold upon the throne was uncertain an ealdorman's forces would be virtually independent, and the well-known story of Eadric Streona's changes of side illustrates the strength of his authority over the Mercians and his freedom from control.[1] The story was repeated with little variation by Geoffrey de Mandeville under Stephen[2]: and it is worth recalling that so close was the parallel between Ethelred's reign and Stephen's that there was a recrudescence of viking raids.[3] The story is hardly different under Edward the Confessor, except that the house of Godwin proved more powerful than any combination that could be brought against it. Whether before or after the Conquest only a strong king could overcome personal and local loyalties or keep the land free from invasion.

It is hard to realise that behind the anarchic, fissiparous tendencies of society in the tenth and eleventh centuries, there was an enduring conception of order, based upon the duty of the subject to the king and involving the contribution of armed forces to his fyrd, whether by land or sea. And here we come to the difficult and obscure problem of the relationship of a great man's personal following to his tenurial obligations. It seems obvious that there would be overlapping. From the freeholder's standpoint there might be a double obligation, a divided allegiance, though in England there were not the complications there were in Normandy, where, for example, a tenant of the bishop of Bayeux might be bound by his tenure to serve the bishop or the duke or the king of France.[4] In England, however, in the eleventh century there was the complication caused by the employment of butsecarls, lithsmen and housecarls, if indeed these mercenaries were new, except in name.[5]

---

[1] A.S. Chronicle, s.a. 1009, 1015, 1016 (Thorpe, pp. 262-3, 274-83; Plummer, pp. 139, 145-7, 150-3).   [2] Round, *Geoffrey de Mandeville*, chapters 2-9.

[3] That there was a raid by the Norwegian king, Eystein Haroldson, late in the reign, perhaps in 1151, does not admit of doubt. There is a detailed account in the Heimskringla and parallel sources (*Heimskringla*, ed. Jónsson, pp. 584-5: for translation, with useful identification of place names, see Anderson, *Early Sources of Scottish History*, ii.215-8). Nor do we see any ground for doubting the substantial accuracy of the Continuator of Sigebert of Gembloux who records, s.a. 1138, an invasion or raid by the Danish king, Eric the Lamb (*M.H.G., Scriptores*, vi.386). The claim to the English throne attributed to him is not so fantastic as has been suggested, for he was descended from Estrid, the sister of Cnut the Great, and his great-grandfather, Swein, had been a formidable rival to William the Conqueror. Was Stephen's title so much better? Freeman supposed, quite improbably, that the chronicler confused the Danish king with the Scottish king David, defeated at the battle of the Standard in 1138 (*Norman Conquest*, v.860-2), and he was later supported by J. Steenstrup, on the ground that Eric had the by-name of David (*Historisk Tidsskrift*, 10th series (1933), ii.290-2). To allege that the chronicler confused may be a convenient way of getting rid of his evidence, but there is no reason to suppose that he knew either the name of the king of Scots or Eric's by-name, for he mentions neither.

[4] The inquest of 1133 into the services due from the tenants of the bishop of Bayeux reflects the conditions of the eleventh century (Round, *Family Origins*, pp. 201-5). An amended text of the inquest has been established by Navel, 'L'enquête de 1133 sur les fiefs de l'évêché de Bayeux', in *Bulletin de la Société des Antiquaires de Normandie*, xlii.5-80: see especially pp. 14-15.

[5] For all these see Plummer, ii.239-40. The housecarls have been elaborately studied by Larson, *King's Household in England*, pp. 152-71; see also *Crawford Charters*, pp. 139-41. Danish in origin, they appear to have remained Danish, or mainly so, until the end of the Old English kingdom. That some received grants of land (Stenton, *First Century*, pp.

Like many other problems of military organisation in the Middle Ages, the method by which troops, recruited under more than one system, were integrated into a single force can be but a matter of speculation. The same kind of question arises in connexion with Harold's army at Hastings and the many later occasions when mercenaries fought side by side with men holding military fiefs who served in person. And then there were local forces, which are generally known to historians as the 'fyrd', and there were, too, the garrisons of boroughs, the burghal knights, the fighting burgesses, who somehow were integrated with more mobile forces. We have little more than the details of the battle of the Standard[1] to guide us in our speculations upon pre-Conquest conditions, though some vague words of the Saxon Chronicles tell us how in 893 Alfred divided his fyrd into two divisions, one of which took the field while the other remained at home, apart from those men who defended the boroughs. Later in the same year the Chronicles tell us how the Londoners joined the king's army that came from the West in an attack upon the Danish fortress at Benfleet[2]: since the English won a complete victory, they can have been no untrained local levies nor, when the West Saxon kingdom was fighting for its very existence, is recruitment likely to have been adjusted with a nice regard for five-hide units. But, again, the expedients of a time of 'total' warfare are not likely to have been the expedients of a land at peace, of England, let us say, under Edgar; nor were the conditions and practices under Edgar likely to be found under his son Ethelred. It seems safe to suppose that, if in origin the hundredal organisation was simple and uniform over southern England, by the end of the tenth century the military system had become complex, and its complexity was increased by the employment of mercenaries. We may recall the well-known fact that Alfred engaged Frisian mercenaries to man his ships,[3] and if there were mercenaries in his *scipfyrd*, there were likely enough to be mercenaries in his *landfyrd* also. Mercenaries were not first known in England in the eleventh century. Still, the impression we get is that, while under mounting pressure over the centuries expedients had been devised to supplement the armed forces, original tenurial obligations had been left, if not intact, at most modified in detail. We cannot otherwise account for the many relics of the five-hide system that are to be found not only in Domesday Book but in much later documents.[4]

But if the fyrd is to be equated, as is the modern convention, with

120-2) does not mean that the bulk of them did not remain mercenaries. Their numbers it is impossible to estimate, but we must guard against reckoning them in thousands as the very questionable sources for their history suggest.

[1] Richard of Hexham and Ailred of Rievaulx, both in *Chronicles of the Reigns of Stephen, Henry II and Richard I*, iii.159-64, 181-99. Upon the details we comment later, p. 75.

[2] A.S. Chronicle, *s.a.* 894 (Thorpe, pp. 164-9; Plummer, pp. 84-6).

[3] A.S. Chronicle, *s.a.* 897 (Thorpe, pp. 176-7; Plummer, p. 91).

[4] Vinogradoff, *English Society in Eleventh Century*, p. 55; Hollings in *E.H.R.*, lxiii.453-87.

the local defence forces, such as those who fought in the battle of the
Standard, we must not delude ourselves by imagining that we are
echoing the thoughts or the language of pre-Conquest England. On
the contrary we are departing a long way from the normal Old
English usage. And at this point let us ask the difficult question,
'What was the fyrd?' We shall get little help from recent writers,
who seem to employ the word ambiguously, if not erroneously, in
contexts where certainty and clarity are especially desirable. Do the
writers of an older generation help? No one spoke of the fyrd more
confidently, nor used the word more consistently, than E. A. Freeman.[1] He equated the fyrd, unqualified by any adjective, with 'the
landfyrd, the militia of the shires'.[2] And we must remember what
'militia' meant in Freeman's own day: a force, raised by county
quotas, required to assemble for twenty-eight days' training in every
year, that could be embodied at any time for compulsory military
service within the kingdom. No man between the ages of eighteen
and thirty-five was in law exempt, though the necessary quotas were
in practice recruited voluntarily. This, then, is the model Freeman
had in mind. 'Harold, or Eadmund, or any other chief in whom
men put trust', he went on, 'could easily raise an army of this kind,
an army patriotic and brave after its own fashion, an army perfectly
ready to fight a battle, but which, after either winning or losing a
battle, was always eager to go home again.'[3] He speaks later of 'the
fyrd, the legal English levy',[4] and he assumes that after the Conquest
there were in England two parallel military organisations. 'The
king as king', he said, 'could summon the fyrd of the nation; as
lord he could summon his military tenants'[5]; while Stubbs seems to
put the same concept in rather different words when he speaks of
'the maintenance of the national force of defence, over and above
the feudal army'.[6] But if we ask what was the nature of this fyrd, by
what process was it recruited, assembled, armed, organised and paid,
Freeman seems to give no answer, scan his pages as we may. It
would appear that such knowledge is so commonplace that we
should know without telling. Regretfully we must confess our ignorance. But, after all, dictionaries are there to help us. Let us
consult Bosworth-Toller.

'Fyrd', we learn, has a number of possible meanings, but one
definition stands in the forefront: 'the military array of the whole
country'.[7] This seems evidently to be Freeman's fyrd. We have but
to look up the authorities for this definition and our ignorance will
be remedied. We glance down the column and are a little taken
aback, for instead of references to ancient texts, the only authority

---

[1] Besides the references in the following notes, see *Norman Conquest*, iv.150, 276;
v.371, 385.   [2] *Ibid.*, iii.337.   [3] *Ibid.*, iii.337-8.
   [4] *Ibid.*, iii.338.   [5] *Ibid.*, v.864-5.   [6] *Constitutional History*, i.291.
   [7] Bosworth-Toller, *Anglo-Saxon Dictionary*, *s.v.* fyrd; Supplement, *s.v.* fird. See also
N.E.D. s.v. ferd, fyrd.

upon which the lexicographers rely is Stubbs's *Constitutional History*. We must then turn to Stubbs. He is verbose and not very explicit. Still, of one thing he seems certain: 'military service became . . . a personal duty that practically depended upon the tenure of land'. Perhaps we misunderstand either Freeman or Stubbs, for they do not seem to have identical conceptions of the fyrd. But Stubbs, at least, gives his authorities.[1] These are, in the first place, a few references to continental authorities which we may pass over, and then some references to English sources covering a wide period of years. One of these English sources is the well-known law of Ine which prescribes the penalties for deserting the king's host.[2] Two ranks of society are named, gesiths and ceorls. Not all gesiths are subject to quite the same penalty. There is a mulct of 120 shillings in every case, but if the gesith has land he will lose that as well, while if he is landless . . . We stop short. It is at once apparent that, in the seventh century, either the obligation to serve with the fyrd did not run with tenure, with the possession of land, or the king's host was not the fyrd in the sense in which Stubbs uses the word. The next reference that Stubbs cites in full is again well known: it comes from the first Worcestershire entries in Domesday Book.[3] We may doubt whether a text of the eleventh century can shed much light upon conditions in the seventh; but, for what it is worth, the later text tells us that, if a man is so free that he has soc and sac and can go where he will with his land, he will be liable to forfeiture if he fails to answer the summons to the host, while if the defaulter is a freeman who has a lord, he is mulcted in forty shillings. Nothing is said to imply that this freeman must necessarily own land, nothing of losing it if he does: the implication is that it is the lord who determines which of his retainers shall accompany him to war, for if one fails he may bring another.[4] Stubbs then does not seem to prove his case: the evidence he is able to adduce does not fit his conception— a preconception perhaps—of the fyrd. He leaves the whole question in the air.

We turn therefore to a more recent historian, who tells us that 'it is only reasonable to assume that all able-bodied freemen would fight, or attempt to fight, when their country was invaded', but who suggests no ground for this assumption.[5] Remembering Wulfstan's *Sermo ad Anglos*, we are in doubt whether this assumption is reasonable.[6] But it is not seriously contended that this *levée en masse*, this militia, to use Freeman's phrase, is the fyrd of recorded history. For this fyrd we are referred to 'the one text which illustrates the com-

---

[1] *Constitutional History*, i.209.   [2] Ine, 51 (*Gesetze*, i.112).
[3] D.B., i.172 a 1.   [4] Cf. Maitland, *Domesday Book and Beyond*, p. 159.
[5] Stenton, *Anglo-Saxon England*, p. 287. The same writer asserts elsewhere (*First Century*, pp. 117-9) that 'fyrd service . . . is plainly the duty of peasants, not of nobles'; but the texts he cites do not seem to us to bear this interpretation.
[6] *Sermo Lupi ad Anglos* (ed. Whitelock), pp. 34-6.

position of the fyrd in the time before the Danish wars'.[1] This text is a charter of about the year 800 which shows Cenwulf of Mercia agreeing 'that an estate of thirty hides should furnish only five men when the fyrd is called out'. The transaction was, in fact, a complicated one, the object seemingly being to free the land from all burdens except the three universal customary obligations—burhbot, brigbot and fyrdfare—and even service with the host, *expeditionis necessitas*, was to be limited to five men.[2] This number appears clearly to be a reduction; but was the reduction from twenty or thirty (or whatever the number of free tenants on the thirty hides might be) or was the liability, now limited to five men, a mere reduction from the six that would be demanded on the basis of the five-hide unit? The latter alternative seems to us the more probable.[3] It may well be that the charter reflects a recent change from an obligation to provide one warrior for every six hides to an obligation to provide one warrior for every five hides. The grantee, one Pilheard, is excepted from the new rule.

What then was meant by *expeditio*? There is abundant evidence, in vocabularies and Latin renderings of Old English texts, that *expeditio* translates fyrd.[4] But a fyrd might be a select force. Clearly a *scipfyrd* or naval expedition, whether based upon the five-hide unit or in any other way, did not involve calling out all the freeholders in the land. It would seem to follow that a *landfyrd*, based upon the five-hide unit or in some other way, might also be select. Doubtless calling up twenty men from every hundred would mean assembling a respectable force in most shires, but something much more limited than 'the military array of the whole country'. Moreover, if 'it is clearly unusual for the fyrd of any particular shire to serve beyond its borders',[5] fyrd in this sense can bear little relation to the *expeditio*, the *exercitus*, which the king leads against his enemies. Nor need we suppose that, because ceorls and landless gesiths served in Ine's fyrd, what was in view was something else than a royal *expeditio*. Ine's law will fit very well a body of men who had taken service under the king's standard, not because of any tenurial obligations but for reward, an army that, in terms of the later Middle Ages, would consist of landed knights, landless knights and serjeants. Though Ine's army is a fyrd, it is not Stubbs's fyrd or Freeman's fyrd, not the general body of freemen who in Henry II's reign were required to provide themselves with appropriate arms, an obligation which, it is believed, has had a continuous history from remote ages.

---

[1] Stenton, *Anglo-Saxon England*, p. 288.
[2] Birch, *Cartularium Saxonicum*, no. 201.
[3] Cf. Chadwick, *Origin of English Nation*, p. 160.
[4] Wülcker-Wright, *Vocabularies*, col. 20, 232, 393; *Gesetze*, i.112-3, 316-7; Bosworth-Toller, *Supplement*, s.v. fird.
[5] Stenton, *op. cit.*, p. 287. This is said of the ninth century; but if there was a local fyrd as distinct from the king's fyrd, presumably the same law or custom would apply in the tenth and eleventh centuries.

We are prepared to accept as a historical fact a universal obligation upon freemen, by custom or from necessity, to bear arms for the purpose of local defence. Yet the frequent contemporary references to fyrd, *expeditio, exercitus*, are not to such a 'fyrd' at all, but to smaller, better armed, better disciplined, mobile bodies, of no uniform composition, indifferently the retainers, the household troops, of king or great noble, landowners under obligation to follow the king in person or troops provided by such landowners, mercenaries. In this sense 'fyrd' or its Latin equivalents, when unqualified, will tell us nothing of the basis of recruitment, whether the troops are mounted or not, whether they wage war by land or sea, just as a modern phrase, such as 'expeditionary force', of itself tells us nothing of like details.

We have said that we are prepared to accept as a historical fact a universal obligation upon freemen to bear arms for local defence, but the difficulty we have to face is that this obligation has been assumed rather than proved. We look in vain in the Laws for any hint of this obligation. The texts that have been supposed to give some such indication prove to be evidence for a very different kind of military force. Nevertheless it is, as we have already suggested, difficult to believe that, when under Alfred the kingdom of Wessex was fighting for its very existence, there was any nice regard for the limitations placed upon the obligation of landowners to furnish men for the king's fyrd. But on this matter our only authority, the Anglo-Saxon Chronicle, could hardly be less informative.[1] It is not until the time of Edmund that we find in the Chronicle language that gives at least some indication that, in circumstances which closely resembled those that confronted Alfred, there was a form of general conscription. Edmund, we are told, raised five armies. Of the first we are told that he summoned all able-bodied men to the fyrd under the threat that failure to obey would be visited with the full penalty. The reason for this threat appears clearly to be that, shortly before, a summons had been issued and an army assembled, but the troops mutinied and dispersed because King Ethelred had not assumed command and the Londoners had not sent their contingent.[2] There is nothing in what we are told to suggest that the army had been recruited on any other basis than the legal liability resting upon landowners to furnish one man for every five hides for the king's fyrd. We must also infer—and this explains the threat in the second summons—that the mutiny had remained unpunished. Fearful of treason, however, the king abandoned the resummoned army (that is Edmund's first army), and it was presumably dismissed. Shortly afterwards Ethelred died and Edmund became king and raised an army (his second) in Wessex. Of the summons of this army we have

---

[1] A.S. Chronicle, *s.a.* 894: see above, p. 47.
[2] *Ibid., s.a.* 1016 (Plummer, p. 147; Thorpe, pp. 276-7).

no details. It fought an inconclusive battle with the Danes and suffered heavy casualties: presumably the survivors made their way home. Almost immediately Edmund summoned his third army and relieved London: again we are not told the terms of the summons.[1] It is when we are told of the fourth and fifth armies that we get a hint that for these there was a wider basis of recruitment than that normal for summoning the fyrd, for it is said that all the English people were summoned.[2] We must not take these words too literally: they could have applied only to freemen. Slaves were not reliable in the face of the enemy, since they could count upon their freedom by deserting to the Danes.[3] Even if we suppose that all freemen capable of bearing arms were summoned, we may still have to make reservations. Doubtless the implication is that these armies included more men than would normally obey the summons to the king's fyrd, but the additional numbers may not have been great. Even in the direst necessity kings do not throw untrained, unarmed men against seasoned professional soldiers such as Cnut commanded.[4] In any case, it seems obvious that so wide a summons was quite exceptional.

After 1016, when Edmund's brief reign came to an end, we catch no further glimpse of any similar call to the general body of freemen until 1138 when the battle of the Standard was fought. Of this battle we shall have more to say, but here we may note that it derives its name from the standards of the town forces in the English army.[5] This is an element we must not overlook. Scanty though our information regarding Alfred's campaigns may be, one fact is made plain—the town forces played an important part in them[6]; and we may infer that the Londoners, at least, played an important part in Edmund's campaigns.[7] No reference, however, seems to be made in any account of Harold's battles either to town forces or to any forces other than Harold's personal following, his mercenaries and the knights furnished in the customary way for the king's fyrd.[8] We cannot argue from the silence of our authorities, but it is hazardous to supplement their silence by conjecture. Of one thing we may be sure, that the forces engaged either in the Danish wars or in Harold's

[1] Plummer, pp. 147-51; Thorpe, pp. 277-81.

[2] ealle Engla þeode (Plummer, pp. 150-1; Thorpe, pp. 282-3).

[3] This is clear from Wulfstan's Sermo ad Anglos, preached a year or two earlier (ed. Whitelock, pp. 34-5, lines 104-8, 120-1).

[4] Thurkil and his Jómsvikings were with Cnut, having left Ethelred's service in 1013 (A.S. Chronicle, s.a. 1013, 1017: Thorpe, pp. 270-3, 284-5; Plummer, pp. 143-4, 154-5). Some account of the Jómsvikings will be found in Blair, Introduction to Anglo-Saxon England, pp. 93-6. The story in the Jómsvikinga Saga is romance, but it is founded on fact (Ashdown, English and Norse Documents, pp. 184-7).

[5] Below, p. 75.   [6] Above, p. 47.

[7] A.S. Chronicle, s.a. 1016 (Plummer, pp. 147-53; Thorpe, pp. 276-85).

[8] The only definite statement appears to be that of William of Malmesbury, Gesta Regum, i.282: 'praeter stipendarios et mercenarios milites, paucos admodum ex provincialibus habuit', where the stipendarii seem to be household troops. In stressing the fact that a large part of Harold's army had not arrived at the battlefield, the Chronicles lend credibility to this statement (Plummer, pp. 198-9; Thorpe, pp. 337-9). Florence of Worcester (i.227) speaks to the same effect.

two campaigns were, by modern standards, insignificant. Large mediaeval armies never existed except in the imagination of historians, contemporary or modern.[1] The limitations imposed by supplies of arms and food, by discipline and, above all, by distance were inescapable and insuperable. Throughout the Middle Ages arms and armour, except the most primitive, were scarce and dear.[2] Food could not be transported in any quantity, and troops lived on the country. Apart from the town forces, of which we know little, the only discipline possible was that afforded by the tie between lord and man or that between the mercenary and his paymaster. Mobility was possible only for a small, well-armed, mounted, disciplined force: even so, the name of herestreet[3] indicates that the mobility of the fyrd depended upon such relatively good roads as existed. It follows that, whatever the potential reserves of manpower, no effective means existed for equipping, feeding, drilling or organising a large army.

The supposititious 'fyrd' of historians has sometimes been compared to the armies raised in France by the *arrière-ban*. This was known in Normandy in the eleventh century and is well illustrated by the inquest into the fiefs of the bishopric of Bayeux.[4] On the lands of the bishopric there were 120 knight's fees, divided between knights and, to a small extent, vavassors. The bishop owed, however, the service of no more than twenty knights to the duke in the ordinary way. It was only when the *arrière-ban* was proclaimed that the whole military service due from the bishop's tenants was mobilised. The point to remark is that there was no question, even in an emergency, of calling up all freemen, but merely those who were bound by their tenure to render military service. The relation between the duke and the tenant-in-chief was maintained, but instead of furnishing twenty knights the bishop had, on this occasion, to furnish six times the number. There is no evidence that in pre-Conquest England there was any institution, any legal obligation, parallel to the *arrière-ban*. At the same time there is nothing to suggest that, when armies were recruited beyond the numbers furnished by normal tenurial obligations, the recruits were other than mercenaries or the personal followers or tenants of king, ealdormen and thegns. The idea of a 'national' army[5] lay in the remote future.

It will be apparent that we are not disposed to accept the post-Conquest 'fyrd' which figures prominently in the pages of recent

[1] On the subject generally see Lot, *L'art militaire et les armées au moyen âge*, i.278-364: for the battle of Hastings see *ibid.*, pp. 282-7.
[2] It is hardly necessary to cite further evidence than the Assize of Arms (*Select Charters*, p. 183, cc. 4-8).
[3] See Bosworth-Toller, *Dictionary* and *Supplement*, s.v. herestræt: cf. firdstræt, herepaþ. Such roads not infrequently figure in charters as notable landmarks.
[4] Navel, *L'enquête de* 1133, pp. 14-15, 43-4.
[5] Cf. Plummer, *Two Saxon Chronicles*, i.338: 'and so the (national) army or militia'. See also Stenton, *First Century*, p. 118: 'in the eleventh century the fyrd was still a true national levy'.

historians, and we ask whence comes this unquestioning belief in an institution for whose existence we have sought unavailingly in contemporary sources. Though the source for this belief seems never to be acknowledged, it appears undoubtedly to be none other than E. A. Freeman, for while Freeman's teaching is now generally discredited, his thesis of two parallel military organisations after the Conquest, a feudal army and the 'fyrd',[1] dies very hard. Any reference to the employment of Englishmen as soldiers after 1066 is apt to be construed as a reference to the 'fyrd', although this word is not used in the contemporary source. For this curious error Stubbs must share the responsibility with Freeman. He regarded the oath contained in the apocryphal 'Ten Articles of William I', binding all freemen in England to bear arms in the king's service at home or abroad, as a reference to the 'fyrd',[2] and he asserted that 'on one occasion Ranulf [Flambard] brought down a great force of the fyrd to Hastings'.[3] The word 'fyrd' is, we need hardly remark, not to be found in either of the authorities for this incident that have come down to us, and it is at least doubtful whether this force, which is absurdly magnified to 20,000 men, was composed of Englishmen, though there may have been Englishmen among them.[4] Later writers have found no difficulty in accepting Stubbs's misinterpretation and embroidering upon it; and they have discovered the 'fyrd' constantly in action under the two Williams, employed especially in putting down risings of 'rebellious Norman barons'.[5] 'To the English fyrd', we are solemnly assured, 'was due in the main the success of the royal cause' when Rufus came into conflict with Odo of Bayeux.[6] It is but a step, preposterous though it may seem, to identifying the *pedones* (infantry) who, according to Florence of Worcester, assembled at Hastings in 1094, with the *milites* (cavalry) who, on the evidence of Domesday Book, were assessed on every five hides in Berkshire.[7]

The stages by which the liability of landowners to provide knights for the king's army, assessed on the basis of hidage, gave way to an arbitrary quota or *servitium debitum* are obscure. We shall examine the problem later,[8] but we may say this, here and now, that it seems manifestly impossible that the two assessments should have existed simultaneously or that the tenants of the 'rebellious Norman barons' should, at one and the same time, be following their lords and 'flocking to the king's standard'.[9] The difficulty is not resolved by

---

[1] *Norman Conquest*, v.864-5; above, p. 48.
[2] *Constitutional History*, i.285-91, 469.   [3] *Ibid.*, p. 327.
[4] A.S. Chronicle, E, *s.a.* 1094 (Thorpe, pp. 360-1; Plummer, p. 229); Florence, ii.35. Note that, though the Peterborough Chronicle says that the king sent for 20,000 Englishmen, Florence says that he sent for foot-soldiers, *pedones*.
[5] Poole, *From Domesday Book to Magna Carta*, p. 102.   [6] *Ibid.*, p. 106.
[7] Ramsay, *Foundations of England*, ii.192. There is nothing in the sources to show that the men, however numerous they were, had been provided with money by the shires. The most probable explanation is that they had been paid an advance of ten shillings for wages and that, when their passage overseas was cancelled, they were required to refund.   [8] Below, pp. 85-91.   [9] Poole, *op. cit.*, p. 102.

identifying the post-Conquest 'fyrd' with Freeman's 'militia' or a 'national' army which, had it existed, would nevertheless have necessarily been composed of the tenants of Norman barons, though tenants, presumably, who did not hold their land by knight service. The alternative conception of a free native population, existing apart from the English tenants of Norman lords and drafted into a 'militia' that acted as a counterpoise to foreign feudal knights, is a fantasy which those who speak of a post-Conquest 'fyrd' would doubtless repudiate, so contrary is such a conception to all historical evidence. But whence is this imaginary 'fyrd' to be drawn? The point is that neither Freeman nor Stubbs nor all those who have accepted their ideas and, indeed, their very phrases,[1] have thought out the problems involved. The obvious explanation of the references to the employment of English soldiers by Norman kings after the Conquest, beginning, it may be remarked, as early as 1074,[2] is that they were mercenaries who served the Normans for pay, just as they had doubtless served King Harold and King Edward and their earls and thegns for pay, and just as Thurkil the Tall and his Jómsvikings had served King Ethelred for pay.[3]

The 'fyrd' of Freeman and Stubbs and their followers is an imaginary institution, a wishful illusion. It cannot be too strongly stressed that normally 'fyrd', as used in Old English texts, means nothing more than an armed force, whether by sea or by land, and, moreover, that it is synonymous with 'here'.[4] Both words are colourless; and, despite the philologists, 'fyrd' no more means 'levies' than 'here' means a 'band of marauders'.[5]

We have described in outline, and doubtlessly inadequately, the military organisation of the Old English state, with as few conjectures as possible of our own. We now come to describe the men who formed the principal part of the *landfyrd*, the expeditionary force which the king led to battle. These men were knights, the most appropriate rendering that can be found for the Old English word *cnihtas*. Knights, we have been told, 'are the principal element in the feudal conception of society'.[6] What, then, was meant by a knight?

[1] Cf. Stenton, *Anglo-Saxon England*, p. 424: William Rufus called out the militia; *ibid.*, p. 580: the militiamen were sent home; *ibid.*, p. 581: such elements of the militia as he could collect.

[2] A.S. Chronicle, D, E, *s.a.* 1074 (Thorpe, pp. 346-7; Plummer, p. 209). Note that the force is definitely stated to be English and French. Florence (ii.10) implies that it was mainly English. [3] Above, p. 52, n. 4.

[4] See, for example, A.S. Chronicle, E, *s.a.* 1016: 'Heron þissum geare cum Cnut cyning mid his here clx. scipa', where D reads simply 'mid his here' (Thorpe, pp. 276-7; Plummer, pp. 146-7): E, *s.a.* 1073, has 'Engliscne here' where D, *s.a.* 1074, has 'Englisce fyrde'. So also the writers will alternate *scipfyrd* and *sciphere*, *landfyrd* and *landhere* (Plummer, i.367, 388). Perhaps the best evidence that *fyrd*, *here*, and, we may add, *werod* were all synonyms is to be found in Ælfric's paraphrase of the Book of Maccabees in *Lives of Saints*, ii.84-98, lines 281, 290, 302, 330, 332, 350, 352, 432, 483, 485.

[5] Professor Garmonsway, who gives these definitions in his translation of the Anglo-Saxon Chronicle (pp. 273-4), has been misled by the historians, whom Professor Bruce Dickins reproves for their ignorance of Anglo-Saxon (p. ix).

[6] Poole, *Obligations of Society*, p. 36.

'Knight' is one of those native words that inform us what were the common objects of the English countryside at the period of the Conquest. Just as the words 'beef', 'mutton', 'pork', 'veal', 'poultry', when contrasted with 'bread' and 'cheese', tell us, without need for research, a great deal about the diet of the higher and lower classes of mediaeval society in England, so the fact that a knight was not called *chivaler* in native speech in the Middle Ages tells us that he is English of the English. When an Englishman saw a mounted soldier after the Conquest, he did not need to be told what the object was, even though it might be French: he had seen plenty of the kind before and he had a word for it. Nor need we look far beyond the Peterborough Chronicle for proof. Of William the Conqueror it relates that at his crown-wearings 'there were with him all the great men from all England, archbishops and bishops, abbots and earls, thegns and knights'; in 1088 'there were within the castle [of Tonbridge] Bishop Odo's knights and many others who would hold it against the king'; in 1094, Roger the Poitevin 'had seven hundred of the king's knights with him' in the castle of Argentan.[1] In the Old English kingdom there had been gilds of knights in London, Canterbury and Winchester, and knights had been members of gilds in Cambridge and Exeter.[2] The poverty of our sources does not permit us to make positive assertions about other English boroughs, but we can have little doubt that every borough had its knights, for every borough needed fighting men. At Cambridge, indeed, the knights seem to have been thought rather too ready with their weapons, and the rules of the gild made special provision for those occasions when they committed outrages.[3] The knights of London and Canterbury, whose gilds survived the Conquest, were well-to-do men and their gilds held valuable property.[4] At Cambridge and Exeter, on the other hand, the knights appear to have been of inferior status, if not greatly inferior, to the thegnly class: they were probably not numerous, for these boroughs were small, and the knights did not form gilds of their own.[5] We stress the military character of these burghal knights,[6] for historians have been too ready to follow the ancient

---

[1] A.S. Chronicle, *s.a.* 1086, 1088, 1094 (Thorpe, pp. 355, 357, 360; Plummer, pp. 220, 224, 229).

[2] For the London Cnihtengild see Harmer, *Anglo-Saxon Writs*, pp. 231-5; for that at Canterbury see Somner, *Antiquities of Canterbury* (1703), i.179; for that at Winchester see D.B., iv.531, 533; for those at Cambridge and Exeter see Thorpe, *Diplomatarium*, pp. 610-4. See also Gross, *Gild Merchant*, i.183-8; Tait, *Medieval English Borough*, pp. 119-23.

[3] Thorpe, *op. cit.*, p. 612.

[4] The London gild transferred their property to Holy Trinity, Aldgate. The Canterbury gild exchanged property with the monks of Christchurch during Anselm's episcopate (1093-1109).

[5] The knights at Cambridge were responsible to their lords, presumably thegnly members of the gild. The membership of the Exeter gild is obscure, but it is evident that the knights were not of the highest status (Thorpe, *ut supra*).

[6] This has been questioned (Stenton, *First Century*, pp. 134-5), but Maitland seems to have had no doubt (*Domesday Book and Beyond*, pp. 190-1). The knights at Canterbury, however, were in the late eleventh century the ruling members of the chapmen's gild, but this does not exclude military duties.

tradition of the philologists in translating *cniht* as youth or servant or retainer or disciple, even where the obvious and better meaning is plainly knight.[1] Doubtless in some contexts, and particularly in early texts, the word may bear another meaning, although already in the ninth century it can mean a fighting man, a member of a gild of knights,[2] surely not a gild of youths or servants or retainers or disciples. The word is as incapable of bearing such a meaning here as it is in a charter that tells us how 'many a good knight' was present in the shiremoot of Worcester in the early eleventh century.[3] And, to take an example in a different context, we cannot give any sensible meaning to the word, other than knight, when we are told that Bishop Oswald of Worcester granted land to a *cniht* named Osulf because of their kinship.[4] We shall adduce further evidence, but let us forthwith introduce a witness, than whom we could have no better for the century before the Conquest, Abbot Ælfric, who translates *Non sine causa miles portat gladium* as 'Ne byrð na se cniht butan intingan his swurd.' Ælfric's knight is God's thegn, the typical *bellator*, who provides, with the *laborator* and the *orator*, the three pillars which sustain the state.[5] Elsewhere Ælfric says in a similar context that '*bellatores* are they who defend our boroughs',[6] and we have here a very neat proof that these gilds of burghal knights were, indeed, gilds of warriors.

By Ælfric's time the words *cniht* and *miles* had both had a long history in England. To Bede, or at least to the men who came to translate Bede into English, *miles* meant a king's thegn: alternatively, the same man might be called *minister*. The employment of the former or latter word depended upon whether the writer was considering the thegn in his military or his civil capacity. He was, it would seem, as a rule a young man, unmarried and of noble birth, in the service of the king or the royal family, corresponding almost exactly to the landless knight of good birth under the Angevin kings,

[1] Benjamin Thorpe translated 'cniht' by 'boy' or 'follower' or 'page' in pre-Conquest documents, and by 'knight' in post-Conquest documents, except once, when he translated 'cnihtan' by 'young ones' (*Diplomatarium*, pp. 559, 561, 612-3, 633; *Anglo-Saxon Chronicle*, ii.71, 185, 189, 192-3, 197, 220). Sweet in his *Student's Dictionary of Anglo-Saxon* gives 'boy; attendant, servant, retainer' as the only meanings, and it is no matter for surprise that later translators have hesitated, even in the most obvious instances, to venture to translate *cniht* as 'knight'. The result has been to make bathos of lines 9 and 152 of the *Battle of Maldon*, where 'knight', in the sense of a young warrior, seems obviously to be required. English knights out hawking on horseback are to be seen depicted on the Bayeux Tapestry, exactly as Offa's kinsman, the *cniht* of line 9, was doing before the battle: manners and the meaning of words had not changed significantly in the seventy-five years separating Maldon from Hastings.

[2] Birch, *Cartularium Saxonicum*, no. 515: 'Ego Æðelhelm 7 cniahta gegildan': others read *gealdan* or *geoldan*. It is to be noted that the knights of the gild are distinguished from the townsmen, the 'ingan burgpare'.

[3] Robertson, *Anglo-Saxon Charters*, p. 164. A similar phrase occurs in the testing clause to an agreement of much the same date (*ibid.*, p. 154). [4] *Ibid.*, p. 96.

[5] Ælfric, 'On the Old and the New Testament' in *The Old English Version of the Heptateuch* (ed. Crawford: E.E.T.S.), pp. 71-2. Ælfric is professedly citing Rom. xiii.4; but *miles* does not occur in the *textus receptus*.

[6] *Ælfric's Lives of the Saints* (ed. Skeat: E.E.T.S.), i.120-2, line 817: 'bellatores synd þa ðe ure burga healdað'.

of whom William Marshal is the supreme example. Like William, the young *miles* might gain advancement, acquire an estate, and become a *comes*, a *gesith*.[1] By the end of the tenth century *miles* had come to be applied not only to the young thegn, but to mature, landed men of great authority. The author of the *Vita Oswaldi* seems to recognise two ranks of noble only, the *dux* or ealdorman and the *miles* or thegn: *comites*, as a class, have disappeared.[2] At the same time *miles* is used to translate the English word *cempa*, a warrior, who is presumably a freeman but need not be of distinguished birth.[3] *Miles* then had much the same range of meaning before the Conquest as after.[4] *Cniht* was a description that became restricted only slowly and gradually to the high born. Again Ælfric provides our best illustrations. For him and for the hearers of his homilies *cniht* might mean one of the king's courtiers[5]; in combination with *bur* (chamber), *burcniht* might mean a knight charged with keeping the gate of the king's palace[6]—the exact equivalent of the *hostiarii milites* of the *Constitutio Domus Regis*[7]—or a knight in attendance on the king, a chamberlain,[8] a minister who is elsewhere called a *burthegn*;[9] on the other hand, a *horscniht* is plainly a groom.[10] However, it is clear that, by the late tenth century, a knight might be a king's thegn and that the word is associated with dignified, and especially with military, service, although it might not yet be free from association with menial service. The old English king then, like his Norman and Angevin successors, has his domestic knights, his *hiredcnihtas*, as they are elsewhere described[11]: and for *hiredcniht* we have surely an exact translation in the Latin of Domesday Book, the *miles regis domesticus* who owes the relief due from a thegn.[12] And just as the king's thegns might be knights, so an abbot's thegns might be. We have the names of six of the knights of the abbot of Ramsey—Toki, Leofwine, Brichmar, Osbern, Wlwine, Leiwulf—who, about the year 1055, accompanied Abbot Ælfwine to the arbitration which determined the boundaries in the fenland between Ramsey and Thorney.[13] There

---

[1] Chadwick, *Studies on Anglo-Saxon Institutions*, pp. 333-40; Guilhiermoz, *Essai sur l'origine de la noblesse*, pp. 87-91.

[2] *Vita Oswaldi*, pp. 427-8, 436, 444-50. These passages will sufficiently indicate the author's vocabulary.

[3] Wülcker-Wright, *Vocabularies*, i.309, 450, 539; *Ælfric's Colloquy* (ed. Garmonsway), p. 41, line 241.

[4] Vinogradoff, *English Society in the Eleventh Century*, pp. 74-9. The suggestion that it was only the landless knight who was identified with the *cniht* of Old English society (Stenton, *First Century*, p. 145) seems to us to be quite untenable.

[5] *Be Hester* in Grein, *Bibliothek der Angelsächsischen Prosa*, iii.98, lines 216, 219.

[6] *Ibid.*, line 213. Ælfric is paraphrasing from line 208 onwards Esther VI, and the *burcnihtas* are the 'duo eunuchi regis qui janitores erant' of Esther II.21 in the Latin text. In line 110 they are called 'twegen his burðena'.

[7] *Dialogus de Scaccario*, p. 134.   [8] *Be Hester*, p. 100, l. 278.

[9] See Bosworth-Toller and Supplement, *s.v.* burthegen and n. 6, above.

[10] *Be Hester*, p. 99, l. 242.

[11] Whitelock, *Anglo-Saxon Wills*, p. 127.   [12] D.B., i.56 b 1.

[13] *Cartularium Mon. de Rameseia*, i.188; iii.36. The transcripts do not preserve the original forms, but there is no reason for doubting the authenticity of the document (Harmer, *Anglo-Saxon Writs*, pp. 253-6).

is no need to avoid calling these men knights by translating the word as 'retainers', or to imagine that they were essentially different from the tenants holding by knight service who figure in the abbot of Ramsey's *carta* of 1166.[1] There was no magic in the year 1066 which changed the meaning of *cniht* from one day to the next, so that, whereas in the evening it had meant anything but knight, on the morrow this was its only meaning. Nor is it possible that Anselm was in error when he asserted that there were *milites*, holding of the church of Canterbury, of exactly the same kind before the Conquest as there were after it.[2] The monks of Christ Church are not likely to have been in ignorance of conditions before 1066, of which some were living witnesses, nor is there any reason why they should mislead the archbishop.

It is perhaps from the laws of Cnut[3] that we derive our most convincing evidence of the manner of man an English knight might be —not that Cnut's legislation was, at least in this respect, original.[4] Here we learn that the upper classes of pre-Conquest society were composed of men who, when they succeeded to their father's lands, were expected, and were rich enough, to pay a heriot (or relief) of armour and arms, warhorses and substantial sums in gold. And it may be said in passing that, while many words have been wasted on the distinction between Anglo-Saxon and Norman tenures, the institution of heriots plainly implies heritable estates, just as the nature of these heriots implies military service. Nor did the men of the twelfth century, when they studied Cnut's laws, imagine that these were concerned with a different form of society and different tenures from the society and tenures of their own day. It is true that the laws do not speak of knights, but—leaving earls apart—of thegns and freemen. Equally, the twelfth-century French and Latin adaptations of Cnut's laws have no word corresponding to 'knight': the earl becomes a count; the thegns and freemen become barons and vavassors.[5] The reason appears obvious. The laws are concerned with ranks, while the word 'knight' is still descriptive of an occupation which is common to several ranks of society. The laws are not concerned with men who were landless or so near that condition as to merit no special mention. Such poor landless knights were doubtless plentiful, as well before the Conquest as after, men who sold their services and lived on their pay and perquisites, and it may be well to remark that, when we read in the Peterborough Chronicle of the seven hundred knights who were with Roger the Poitevin at

---

[1] *Red Book of the Exchequer*, i.370-2.
[2] Anselm, *Opera* (ed. Schmitt), iv.59 (no. 176): written in 1094.
[3] II Cnut 71 (*Gesetze*, i.356-8).
[4] As shown by the will of Æthelmær (971-83), whose heriot is evidently the equivalent of the equipment of four knights of high rank, each with a gold bracelet, sword, helmet, coat of mail, two spears, two shields, two horses (Whitelock, *Anglo-Saxon Wills*, pp. 26, 127). See also the will of Ælfhelm, probably later (*ibid.*, pp. 30, 134), and of Bishop Alfwold, 1008-12 (*Crawford Charters*, p. 23).   [5] *Gesetze*, i.356-9, 506-7.

Argentan, while we may reasonably doubt whether there was a seventh of this number in the castle, we cannot doubt that among the garrison there were a good many mercenaries.[1] Landed knights, who were men of substance, were never thick upon the ground, and in the whole of Normandy not more than fifteen hundred knights are known to have been enfeoffed, and these fifteen hundred included many men of very little consequence.[2]

Landed or not, the knight, before and after the Conquest, was a mounted soldier, more or less effectively armoured. The richer he was, the better mounted, the better armed, the better armoured. As time went on, it was the richer men to whom the title of knight was exclusively given, men, that is, who were rich in land. Indeed, it became obligatory on such men to become knights or to pay for the privilege of freedom from the onerous duties that gradually accumulated upon landed knights.[3] But at the time of the Conquest the distinction between an English *cniht* and a Norman *chivaler* was not that the latter was richer or better mounted or armed: they were not different in much else than speech and culture. 'Harold dux Anglorum et milites sui' figure prominently at the beginning of the Bayeux Tapestry. If these English knights—as we do not hesitate so to translate the Latin—had not been labelled, we might excusably have mistaken them for Norman *chivalers*. The designer of the tapestry, who is credibly believed to have lived within living memory of the events it depicts, failed to see the sharp distinction that has become apparent to modern historians. If he were blind, we prefer to share his blindness. And then, as it seems to us, other contemporary witnesses failed equally to distinguish, except in the matter of race and speech, between English and French, and even here they stumbled occasionally. *Milites* are to be found widely scattered over Domesday Book. There we find a good many English *milites*,[4] just as we find French thegns in the Exon Domesday,[5] though men of the same class are apt to be called thegns without qualification if they are English and *milites* if they are French.[6] Though all are freemen, these French knights are of all social grades, from substantial landowners, the equivalent of the English five-hide thegns, to men who had to be content with a small holding that put them on a level with the English peasant.[7] French knights were no class apart: they fitted into the vacant places, high and low, among the defeated and dispossessed English people. And it is desirable at this point to em-

---

[1] A.S. Chronicle, E, *s.a.* 1094 (Thorpe, p. 360; Plummer, p. 229). In the Latin version of Florence of Worcester (*Chronicon*, ii.34), 1400 serjeants (*scutarii*) are added to the 700 knights: the numbers are absurd, but the proportion of knights to serjeants is reasonable.
[2] The figure of 1500 is given as the approximate total of knights owing service to the barons in Normandy in 1172 (*Historiens de la France*, xxiii.698, no. 434). Of these the duke could count on rather more than half (*Red Book of the Exchequer*, ii.647: but compare *Historiens de la France*, xxiii.698 where a total of 581 is given for imperfect returns). The rest were available in the event of an *arrière-ban*.   [3] Below, p. 131-4.
[4] D.B., i.62 b, 130 a 1, 241 b 2.   [5] D.B., iv.428.
[6] Vinogradoff, *English Society*, pp. 80-7.   [7] *Ibid.*, pp. 74-9.

phasise that, so far as the evidence goes, the Norman Conquest introduced no new conceptions of warfare, no new ranks of society. It is because of their implications that it is necessary to deny such statements, made by historians of repute, as that 'Harold's army was confined by its nature to a type of warfare which was already obsolete in the greater part of Western Europe'[1] or that 'the battle of Hastings was in essence the defeat of infantry by a composite force, where the cavalry manoeuvred in support of the foot-soldiers'.[2] To argue thus is to argue against the evidence. There was no revolution in the art of war[3] and no consequent social revolution. Evidently the Conquest brought with it an almost complete displacement in the higher ranks of society: in the course of the Conqueror's reign the Old English nobility practically disappeared and were replaced by foreigners.[4] But the process was literally a replacement: estates were not thrown into hotch-potch and then redistributed. In landholding as in government, there was continuity. What was new was a foreign system of tenure which was gradually imposed upon the old native system. It is this gradual development, not any catastrophic change, that would justify us in speaking of English feudalism.

[1] Stenton, *Anglo-Saxon England*, p. 576.

[2] Bloch, *La Société féodale: les liens de dépendance*, p. 284.

[3] The older view has been shown to be untenable by Glover, 'English Warfare in 1066' in *E.H.R.*, lxviii.1-18. It was based on the belief that on the Continent knights practised 'the art of fighting on horseback', but there is much evidence that knights commonly fought on foot. A good deal of information was collected by Drummond, *Studien zur Kriegesgeschichte Englands im 12 Jahrhundert* (Berlin: 1905), pp. 34-96. Later writers have also drawn attention to particular occasions when the knights were dismounted. Carl Stephenson believed that the Normans employed 'heavy-armed cavalry' and that this was rendered possible by 'the introduction of the thoroughbred charger or *destrier*'. He regretted that he had 'no positive evidence to offer' (*A.H.R.*, xlviii.259-60). He need have looked no further than the Bayeux Tapestry for evidence destructive of his thesis. Here, if anywhere, the superiority of the Norman (and French) horses should be depicted. The artist has failed to observe it. French and English knights are mounted on horses of the same type.

[4] Corbett in *Cambridge Medieval History*, v.508. 'Some dozen pre-Conquest landowners and their men' had lands valued at about £4000 a year, or rather more than a fourteenth in value of the lands held by laymen outside the towns. These figures contrast with the lands valued at over £30,000 a year held by about 170 Norman and French barons. The under-tenants present a much greater problem, but there seems little doubt that among the mesne tenants at the time of the Domesday survey the French greatly preponderated in wealth and power, if not in numbers.

IV

THE SHADOW OF FEUDALISM

IF we are to attempt a rational account of the settlement that followed the Norman Conquest, we must begin by dissipating a myth, the myth that almost immediately after his coronation King William introduced 'feudalism' into England and that he did this by allotting quotas of knight service to the estates of his tenants-in-chief. So rapid was his work, we are assured, that it was accomplished before the end of 1070. The details of this remarkable feat are unfortunately wrapped in almost complete obscurity, and the belief that it was performed at all rests, not upon any contemporary authority, but solely upon an obviously erroneous assertion, more than a century later, by Roger of Wendover and the assumptions of J. H. Round.[1] Since Round's whole thesis, which has won general acceptance, turns upon his interpretation of Wendover's words, we may give a little space to an examination of this piece of evidence.

The passage in Wendover's annal for 1070[2] upon which Round seized states that the Conqueror gave orders that all bishoprics and abbeys which held baronies and had hitherto been exempt from secular burdens should render knight service and that the quota, fixed arbitrarily, should be enrolled. Taken out of its setting this passage might seem worthy of serious consideration, if it could be shown to be drawn substantially from an early source. But Wendover's annal, as a whole, is nonsensical, and any statement in any part of it needs ample corroboration before it is to be believed. Among other improbabilities he states that in this year Archbishop Stigand and (the yet unborn) Alexander, bishop of Lincoln, fled to Scotland: and this is no unfair measure of Wendover's historicity. Round, it may be explained, knew Wendover's annal only through Matthew Paris's *Historia Anglorum* and, although the editor of this chronicle had given the clearest indication that Paris was merely reproducing Wendover with some embellishments,[3] Round surmised that the passage upon which he relied 'perhaps represented the St. Alban's tradition'—whatever that might mean—and it is with this feeble evidence, if evidence it can be called, that he claimed to have verified his 'simple and obvious inference' that 'just as

---

[1] *Feudal England*, pp. 295-308. [2] *Flores Historiarum*, ii.7-8.
[3] *Historia Anglorum* (ed. Madden), pp. 12-13: see also *Chronica Maiora* (ed. Luard), ii.6-7.

Henry II granted out the provinces of Ireland to be held as fiefs by the familiar service of a round number of knights, so'—in the year 1070—'Duke William granted out the fiefs he formed in England'.[1]

Neither Round nor, indeed, very recent writers have thought it necessary to go behind Paris to Wendover or to enquire what truth may lie behind Wendover's extravagances: for all of them, whether supporters or critics of Round, Paris is the ultimate authority.[2] And it may perhaps be thought pedantic on our part to object to reliance upon what is, at best, secondary authority when the primary authority is available; after all, Round was but following the example of Stubbs. But Round should at least have known, and his supporters should know, that the lands of bishops and abbots were not exempt from secular burdens before the Conquest, though some favoured abbeys may have been exempt, as favoured abbeys were after the Conquest. Before therefore trusting Paris, or, in turn, trusting Round, every historian who addressed his mind to the subject was in duty bound to investigate Paris's credentials, which means examining Wendover's.

There is no evident reason why this statement of Wendover's regarding knight service should be thought more worthy of credence than the rest of the annal in which it occurs. Nevertheless, let it be admitted, Wendover, though he tampered freely with his authorities and embroidered to his fancy, had some basis for his stories. His nonsense is in some way related to genuine accounts of the harrying of monasteries in 1070 and of the council in which Stigand was deposed.[3] There are traces of indebtedness to Florence, whom elsewhere he follows closely, and also to some such source as the Abingdon chronicle.[4] Even the story of Stigand's flight to Scotland was known to William of Malmesbury and, rather astonishingly, was believed by him, though he gave the archbishop more chronologically possible companions.[5] Wendover's story of the enrolment of the services due from bishops and abbots is, again, very like the Abingdon story of their enrolment 'in annalibus', which apparently means in the pipe rolls.[6] But the Abingdon writer, though he places this happening before the death of Abbot Athelhelm in 1084, does not connect it with the harrying of the monasteries in 1070: this was done by Wendover, and the date, at least, lacks all authority. And, again, the Abingdon writer is no authority for the Conqueror's allotting quotas of knights service on tenants-in-chief in general: nor, indeed, did Wendover suppose that his source (if it were not the

[1] *Feudal England*, pp. 260, 298.
[2] Chew, *Ecclesiastical Tenants in Chief*, pp. 3, 8; Douglas and Greenaway, *English Historical Documents*, ii.894-5; John, *Land Tenure in Early England*, p. 153.
[3] A.S. Chronicle, D, *s.a.* 1071, E, *s.a.* 1070 (Thorpe, pp. 344-5; Plummer, pp. 204-5); Florence of Worcester, ii.4-5.
[4] *Chron. Mon. de Abingdon*, i.483.
[5] *Gesta Regum*, ii.309.
[6] *Chron. Mon. de Abingdon*, ii.3; cf. *Dialogus de Scaccario*, pp. 107, 115, 124.

Abingdon chronicle) had said any such thing. Both speak only of bishops and abbots and say no word of lay barons. Some support for the Abingdon story may, perhaps, appear to be found in the Ely chronicler, who speaks of the *obsequia debita*, which were demanded from abbots and bishops in 1072 for the Scottish war, and of the *debitum servitium* which had been imposed by the Conqueror, apparently universally, but which was exacted wrongfully (*violenter*) from churches.[1] There can, however, be little doubt that these stories from Abingdon and Ely, whatever truth may lie behind them, are coloured by the writers' knowledge of their own age. Hence the references to annual rolls and to *servitium debitum*, which are phrases of the later twelfth century. But here for the moment we may leave them, merely noting that it is only the Ely writer who makes a vague reference to the general imposition of *servitia debita* by the Conqueror.

Apart from the witness of late monastic chroniclers which will not stand examination, the only support that Round could bring forward for his assumptions was a writ addressed to Abbot Æthelwig of Evesham, summoning to Clarendon all the knights due from all men within his bailwick and specifying in particular the five knights due from the abbot himself.[2] There is, however, no more reason to suppose that the Conqueror had fixed the quota due from the abbot of Evesham than to suppose that he had fixed the quota due from the archbishop of Canterbury, whose service, as Anselm implies, appears to have been determined before 1066.[3] Nor is there any reason to suppose that the secular obligations of bishops and abbots had at this early date been increased or decreased. What the obligations of other landowners were within the seven shires administered by Æthelwig we can but surmise, but to guess that they were the quotas reflected in the *servitia debita* ascertained in 1166 is to guess wildly. We do not, in sober fact, know the purpose of the writ of summons; we do not know who were summoned or their numbers; we are not even certain of the year of the summons. The only certain fact, beyond those in the writ itself, is that it was issued before Æthelwig's death in 1077. It seems unlikely, however, that the purpose of the writ was to assemble the French knights who were in the service of the king's French barons.[4] If, as is believed, the Conqueror's hold on England was precarious and 'for nearly twenty years after the battle of Hastings the chances were against the survival of the Anglo-Norman monarchy' and if in 1085 King William had to bring into England an unprecedented number of French mercenaries in

[1] *Historia Eliensis*, pp. 216-18.

[2] *Feudal England*, p. 304. Round did not discover this writ as he claimed, a 'discovery with which H. W. C. Davis credited him (*Select Charters*, p. 96): a better text had been printed by Ellis in his *Introduction to Domesday Book*, ii.447-8.

[3] Letter to Hugh, archbishop of Lyons, in *Opera* (ed. Schmitt), iv.59, no. 176; above, p. 59, n. 2.

[4] If the meaning is that the customary pre-Conquest service is to be rendered, the writ, of course, tells against Round.

order to meet the threat of invasion,[1] then it seems unlikely that the French knights resident in England, even the relatively few who could have been enfeoffed with English lands before 1077, would be permitted during Abbot Æthelwig's lifetime to stay for long quietly at home. If they constituted, as they seem to have done, an army of occupation, they were likely to be in a state of continuous mobilisation. Why it should be supposed that Æthelwig was required to summon these French knights or any of them to Clarendon is not self-evident. He seems, on the contrary, to be a most improbable agent for the purpose. And if, instead of surmising with Round that the date of the writ is 1072, we surmise that its date lies between 1067 and 1070, which seems equally possible, how then do we interpret it and what becomes of Round's thesis? We cannot build upon such flimsy foundations.

In any case, there appear to be very cogent arguments against the assumption that quotas of knight service were determined in 1070. Need it be recalled that Earl Waltheof was not convicted until 1076 and that his great estates could hardly have been divided among King William's French followers at any earlier date? Would it not have been extraordinary if, within four years of William's coronation, all the land in England, whether escheated or not, had been surveyed and newly charged with quotas of military service, with not a whisper of this tremendous operation in any contemporary chronicle, in any surviving document? And would it not have been singular, if this survey had taken place, that no trace of it should be found in the book which records the greater survey of 1086? For reasons that appear later, 1070, a year of internal strife and foreign invasion, seems a most unlucky year to pitch upon for what we venture to describe as an imaginary administrative act of major proportions. But we attach no particular significance to the year: the same objections attach to any year within Æthelwig's lifetime. The difficulty is not to find arguments against Round's assumptions but to find arguments for them. Truth to tell, his were not the usual methods of historical investigation. He scorned 'the anticataclysmic tendencies of modern thought ... the theory of gradual development and growth'.[2] His mind would not adapt itself to scientific processes. He guessed, sometimes brilliantly rightly, but as often woefully wrongly. He was at his, almost incredible, worst on this occasion.

Let us, if possible, get away from assumption and endeavour to base our conclusions upon fact. One fact stands out, that by the year 1086 the Normans were settled in England, foreign counts and barons had displaced English earls and thegns and, though there were a good many disputed titles to the lands of dispossessed English owners, the settlement was all but complete. Apart from bishoprics and abbeys, but a small minority of English owners had retained

[1] Stenton, *First Century*, pp. 149-50. [2] Round, *op. cit.*, p. 225.

their lands and, while the estates of the churches were almost intact and had, indeed, in some cases increased, English bishops and English abbots had been replaced by foreigners. A record of the changed ownerships over the greater part of England was in course of preparation, and that record we still possess. Though it often mentions knights, it does not, however, except in the most incidental way, say anything of knight service, and we certainly cannot deduce from Domesday Book that any record of quotas of knight service had yet been made. Not only has no such record survived, but it is quite certain that no record of the kind was known in the reign of Henry II. And when in 1166 it was desired to make such a record, there was no thought that quotas of knight service had been established in the eleventh century. The king's ministers did not seek to look beyond the days of the king's grandfather, Henry I. His reign was the starting-point, the period which determined the *servitium debitum*: the service a man's ancestors owed in respect of a fief in the reign of Henry I was owed in 1166.[1] But even so, the king's ministers had no knowledge of any record made earlier in the century nor, although tenants-in-chief were required to make returns of the service due from them, does any one of them seem to have had any document to which he could refer, any charter from any king setting down the service due from any of his lands. This does not mean that there was no understanding by tenants-in-chief of their obligations, no conventional figures accepted by the exchequer upon which demands for scutage were based—the pipe rolls show that such figures, if not complete figures, existed[2]—but, even so, there were disputes which could have been settled in the simplest possible way if there had been an authoritative record, just as disputes of another kind were settled by reference to Domesday Book. The only possible conclusion is that there was no survey and no written evidence of knight's fees in the eleventh century or at any time before 1166. Even Round, who could accept the word of Matthew Paris for the enrolment of quotas of knight's fees in 1070, could not believe in charters of enfeoffment specifying the service due from the Conqueror's followers. It may be well to quote his words. 'It is impossible to resist the inference, from such evidence as we have, that the amount of the *servitium debitum* was a matter of custom and tradition, and could not usually be determined by reference to written grants or charters.'[3]

How then did quotas of knight service arise? The best evidence we have comes from some of the great churches and, imprecise as it is, we may get some guidance from it. But before we discuss this evidence there are certain associated problems to face. In the first place, it will be well to clear away a misconception that has arisen,

[1] *Ibid.*, pp. 237-9.
[2] *Ibid.*, pp. 249-56: the footnotes give particulars from the pipe rolls. See, for ecclesiastical tenants-in-chief, Chew, *English Ecclesiastical Tenants in Chief*, pp. 19-20.
[3] Round, *op. cit.*, p. 257.

as a result of Round's acceptance of the Wendover-Paris story, that bishoprics and abbeys before the Conquest were not burdened with secular obligations.[1] It would follow—to quote the words of a recent writer—that 'the size of the feudal army was much increased by the imposition of knight service on bishoprics and abbeys'.[2] Whether it is not misleading to speak of 'the feudal army' is a matter we shall shortly discuss: the immediate question is whether, whatever the manner in which quotas of knight service were determined, an additional burden was placed upon ecclesiastical estates. Such evidence as we have seems to point in a contrary direction. Let us take an example. In the time of the Confessor, Abingdon Abbey had possessed some 500 hides in Berkshire[3] and, unless we are to take it upon ourselves to contradict the express statement in Domesday Book that there the rule had been for every five hides, without exception, to provide one knight for the king's host,[4] then we must deduce that from the abbey lands there came a hundred knights. After the Conquest not only was the assessment of the abbey for geld reduced to 300 hides, but by 1166 the abbey's quota of service was no more than thirty knights in respect of all the abbey's estates, whether in Berkshire or elsewhere.[5] Let us dismiss any quibble that the pre-Conquest army was not 'feudal' or that the abbot's obligation in 1166 was personal, whereas in 1066 the burden had apparently rested directly upon the tenants of the abbey. In law such a distinction is important; but in plain fact the number of knights furnished from abbey lands, so far from being increased, had been reduced by more than two-thirds. Abingdon does not stand alone. Hyde Abbey, which upon the five-hide basis might have been charged with the service of sixty knights, escaped with the service of twenty,[6] while Shaftesbury Abbey, with a *servitium debitum* of seven knights, had estates with a hidage of over 340.[7] The greater number of religious houses founded before 1066 had, moreover, a *servitium debitum* of five knights or less and a good many were totally exempt.[8] We shall suggest that the way in which they were assessed to knight service reflects not the caprice of the Conqueror or any Norman king but pre-Conquest conditions, and we shall support this suggestion by an examination of the evidence relating to Ramsey Abbey. But before we turn to Ramsey, we may mention another case, which has been much discussed, that of the bishop of Worcester, who managed to limit his obligation to fifty knights, although this represents less than the pre-Conquest burden upon the three hundreds of Oswaldslow and not the full burden that pre-

---

[1] *Ibid.*, pp. 298-9.   [2] Stenton, *Anglo-Saxon England*, p. 626.

[3] From the particulars in D.B., i.58 b 1-59 b 1, the assessment T.R.E. appears to have been 493 hides and in 1086 no more than 302¼ hides.

[4] Si rex mittebat alicubi exercitum, de v. hidis tantum unus miles ibat. We think the words 'T.R.E. communiter per totam Berchesciram' of the preceding sentence governs this sentence also (D.B., 1.56 b 1).   [5] Chew, *op. cit.*, p. 20.

[6] *Ibid.*, pp. 6, 20.   [7] *Loc. cit.*   [8] *Ibid.*, pp. 5, 8.

sumably had fallen upon the whole of the episcopal estates, which were assessed at between 500 and 600 hides.[1]

Ramsey Abbey was successful in limiting its obligation to the provision of four knights for the king's service, although its lands had been assessed at over 300 hides and although many more than four knights are found enfeoffed with monastic lands,[2] just as there had been many more knights holding monastic lands before the Conquest. We assert this, not only because we have the names of six of the abbot's knights in 1055,[3] but also because in the closing years of the century Abbot Aldwin was released from the obligation to bring a retinue of ten knights with him when he attended the king's court on the principal feasts. The charter that tells us this is important because the reason why a retinue of three knights was substituted for ten is stated to be that three knights had been the extent of the service rendered by the abbot's predecessors.[4] Of course, this service has nothing to do with knight service in the ordinary sense, service in war, but is what is known as a coronation service. We have independent evidence that not only the Conqueror but the Old English kings liked to be surrounded by prelates and nobles, with thegns and knights in their train, on the great feasts when the king wore his crown.[5] This royal magnificence could easily become a burden upon those who were required to attend, a burden to be lightened or escaped, just as the burden of military service was. Now, by Abbot Aldwin's predecessors must be meant at least some who had held office before the Conquest,[6] and the charter therefore is evidence not only for pre-Conquest crown-wearings but for pre-Conquest remissions of knight service, though not of military service. When, therefore, we find Ramsey Abbey's military service reduced to four knights, it seems reasonable to infer that this reduction too had a pre-Conquest origin and that the concession was successfully maintained. If this is a reasonable inference, it seems reasonable also to infer that the Old English foundations that are exempted from knight service after the Conquest, such as Burton, Croyland, Gloucester, Thorney and Waltham,[7] had enjoyed exemption before the Conquest. No other explanation is apparent. Doubtless the Norman kings were as inclined to benevolence towards religious foundations as their predecessors had been: none of their own foundations in England appears to have been burdened with knight service or, if they had been burdened for a time, they were soon relieved. But this makes it all the more probable that the Norman kings respected any conces-

---

[1] Chew, op. cit., pp. 6-7, 19. Maitland's suggestion of continuity in the amount of knight service due from the bishop (Domesday Book and Beyond, pp. 159-60) and Round's criticism (E.H.R., xii.493) are irrelevant to the present issue, for both seem to have misunderstood the problems.   [2] Chew, op. cit., pp. 6, 123.   [3] Above, p. 58.
[4] Cart. Mon. de Rameseia, i.235.   [5] Appendix I: below, pp. 405-6.
[6] The preceding abbots were Herbert (1087-91), Ailsin (1080-7), Ælfwin (1043-80): see Cart. Mon. de Rameseia, iii.174-5.
[7] Chew, op. cit., p. 8; Knowles, Monastic Order in England, p. 609.

sions that had been made to religious houses before the Conquest.

Whatever may be the inferences to be drawn from the facts we have recited, the bare facts themselves suffice to refute any idea that the exaction of knight service from bishoprics and abbeys after the Conquest increased the 'feudal army'; and not only this, for the facts should destroy finally the credibility both of Wendover's fables and of the more sober assertions of the Abington and Ely chroniclers that knight service was imposed generally upon bishoprics and abbeys by the arbitrary act of the Conqueror, if, indeed, it is necessary to read so much into their words. We must not, however, leave the impression that all religious houses were treated with the same benevolence as those we have named. Very few, it is true, were charged with a high *servitium debitum*, but there is the anomalous case of Tavistock Abbey with estates assessed at thirty hides and a *servitium* of sixteen knights,[1] and there is the equally anomalous case of Peterborough Abbey with a *servitium* of sixty knights, the same number as that with which the bishoprics of Canterbury, Lincoln and Winchester were charged.[2] It is possible, therefore, that in isolated instances some arbitrary act may have given rise to the unacceptable generalisations of the Abingdon and Ely chroniclers.[3] Both of them, indeed, have stories relating to their own houses which we are disposed to believe, even though we may have to qualify them. We need not repeat these stories in detail. What appears to have happened is that troops of French knights were quartered upon reluctant abbots and that in course of time these unwelcome guests, or some of them, were settled upon monastic lands, in part perhaps by compulsion from the king, in part perhaps as the lesser of two evils, for their presence within the abbey precincts could not be tolerated for long. The abbot of Westminster appears to have suffered a similar visitation.[4] There is, however, no evidence that these visitations were at all general, and in each of the three cases of which we have knowledge there seem to have been special circumstances. The Abingdon chronicler himself associates this quartering of French knights upon the abbey, firstly with the need to provide a garrison for Windsor Castle, and secondly with a threatened invasion by the Danes.[5] Ely was a centre of disaffection and the scene of Hereward's defiance of the Conqueror. A force of French knights was evidently required near the capital, and Westminster Abbey was a convenient place in which to house them; and it is by no means unlikely that other religious houses in the neighbourhood of London had to afford accommodation also. But there is nothing to suggest that, however serious the inconvenience at the time, any of the three houses was in the long run prejudiced.

[1] Chew, *op. cit.*, pp. 5, 9, 20-1.   [2] *Ibid.*, pp. 4-5, 19-20.
[3] *Historia Eliensis*, p. 216; *Chron. Mon. de Abingdon*, ii.3.
[4] As suggested by Dean Armitage Robinson, *Gilbert Crispin*, p. 41.
[5] *Chron. Mon. de Abingdon*, ii.3.

We have said enough to show that no generalisation can hold true for every abbey charged with knight service, for there is no consistent pattern. No satisfactory explanation has been advanced for the relatively heavy burden upon Tavistock Abbey, and we certainly cannot attempt one.[1] The suggestion has been made that the undoubtedly exceptional burden upon Peterborough Abbey may in some way be connected with the appointment of the warlike Turold of Fécamp as abbot, who, beside his spiritual mission, had for a time to hold the abbey against any threat from Hereward and the Danes at Ely.[2] The equally heavy burden upon the see of Lincoln may be associated with its greatly increased endowment since the Conquest.[3] In both these cases we may have examples of a quota settled during the reign of the Conqueror; but elsewhere and in the great majority of cases it seems as though, behind the determination of the quota of service, there was a long history in which favour and chance had played their part, but no arbitrary act of any Norman king.

It may be thought that we have said over-much of ecclesiastical tenants-in-chief, especially if we dismiss any idea that they made a significant contribution to the 'feudal army'. But the difficulty is that, in approaching the problem of lay fees, we are handicapped by the absence of any such scraps of evidence as are available for ecclesiastical estates. Nevertheless, even with these scanty, and just barely relevant, items of information, we can, we think, form a reasonably accurate picture of the situation in England in the reign of the Conqueror. In 1070 Abbot Turold rode into Peterborough with a troop of eight score mercenaries at his heels. He found there the charred ruins of a monastery devastated by the English rebels.[4] There was no place to house the men, except by billeting them wherever accommodation could be found. There was no money to pay them, except what the abbot might have brought with him. Early in that year there had been a general harrying of monasteries by the Normans on the excuse that the English had, as the custom was, placed their valuables for safe-keeping there; and the raiders took not only these deposits but such precious things as they could find and safely carry away, not sparing the chalices and ornaments of the church.[5] In the following year the king himself, at the head of other bands of mercenaries, reduced the Isle of Ely, where he enriched himself with a great sum of money.[6] The Conqueror's barons

---

[1] Professor Knowles suggests one (*op. cit.*, pp. 610-11). We ourselves suspect that the heavy burden has a pre-Conquest origin.   [2] Knowles, *op. cit.*, p. 610.

[3] For the charters of William I and William II, which set out the additional endowments but do not, of course, mention knight service, see *Registrum Antiquissimum*, i.2-17.

[4] A.S. Chronicle, E, *s.a.* (Thorpe, p. 345; Plummer, p. 207).

[5] A.S. Chronicle, D, *s.a.* 1071, E, *s.a.* 1070 (Thorpe, pp. 344-5; Plummer, pp. 204-5); Florence, ii.4-5; *Chron. Mon. de Abingdon*, i.486.

[6] A.S. Chronicle, D, *s.a.* 1072, E, *s.a.* 1071 (Thorpe, pp. 346-7; Plummer, p. 208). We infer that the true date is 1071, but this is perhaps open to question: in any case, the event was subsequent to the harrying of the monasteries. Florence describes the king's forces as consisting of butsecarls (ii.9). The 'sceattas manega' presumably belonged to

did not differ greatly from Turold or William himself: they too were leaders of bands of mercenaries. They were mercenaries, too, who were the enforced guests at Abingdon, Ely and Westminster. Nor did conditions sensibly alter in the latter part of the reign. Large troops of mercenaries were engaged by the bishops, even by the saintly Englishman, Wulfstan, either for vainglory or perhaps, on the king's orders, as a precaution in the event of a Danish invasion.[1] These stipendiary knights, riotous and drunken, formed part of the household even of bishops, until their presence proved impossible to support. Provision for some was made by enfeoffments on ecclesiastical estates, as doubtless upon lay fees, though the more numerous and better rewarded beneficiaries from sub-infeudation appear to have been men of a superior class.[2] Other stipendiary knights, as at Westminster, may have been provided with separate houses,[3] while some remained in their lord's household. Yet others doubtless were discharged to ply their trade elsewhere.[4] Their numbers appear to have been greatly in excess of the *servitia* due from tenants-in-chief in the twelfth century, for England was a land held down by force, ruled by an army of occupation. What, above all, we must dismiss from our minds is any idea that after a few years of turmoil peace reigned in the land and there was a neat progress to a new order, nicely documented at each stage. The transition was violent, bloody and disorderly. Any attempt at reconstructing the process of transformation—a very partial, imperfect, even fractional, transformation—of the Old English into the Anglo-Norman state must take as its first postulates hazard and gradualness. We can dismiss any idea of grand designs or well devised plans, and we must think rather of fearful men seeking to control a rebellious land under the threat of hostile invasion, men ruthless and rapacious, driven to repressions and barbarous cruelties, conquerors in many ways inferior to the conquered, certainly with no better contrivances in the arts of government, no superior learning, no better skills in the crafts or in agriculture, learners rather than teachers.

It seems generally to be supposed that infeudation and sub-infeudation, knight service and service in arms, were all facets of one

the English notables who had taken refuge in the Isle, but were placed for safe-keeping in the church.

[1] *Vita Wulfstani*, pp. 55-6; *Historia Eliensis*, p. 217. In his *Gesta Pontificum* (p. 281) William of Malmesbury explains that Wulfstan's troop of stipendiary knights—'pompam militum secum ducens'—was in imitation of the Norman custom.

[2] The tenants of Abingdon Abbey afford an outstanding example (*Chron. Mon. de Abingdon*, ii.4-5), and the same favour to men of superior status is indicated by the *Historia Eliensis*, *loc. cit.* Cf. Chew, *op. cit.*, pp. 118-9.

[3] There are mentioned in D.B., i.128 a 1 the twenty-five houses near the abbey provided for knights and others. The knights appear to be distinct from those enfeoffed with abbey lands.

[4] It is expressly stated by the Abingdon chronicler that the second troop of knights quartered on the abbey were paid off and returned home (*Chron. Mon. de Abingdon*, ii.11); but, if William of Malmesbury is to be believed, this is not what happened at Worcester (*Vita Wulfstani*, p. 56).

problem, the problem of getting an armed force into the field. In fact three distinct, if related, questions fall to be considered. Infeudation and sub-infeudation are legal and social questions; knight service, the determination of *servitia debita*, is a question of revenue; the constitution of the armed forces—let us be forgiven a truism— is a military question. We approach the last question first. Military tenures and actual military service were two very different things, and enfeoffment bore little relation to the effective military force at the disposal of the king. To speak of 'the feudal army', as is commonly done, is to disguise the truth, which was that the forces employed by English kings were, necessarily, for the most part professional and mercenary.[1]

Robert of Torigni, writing of Henry II's preparations for the war of Toulouse, tells us that the king did not bother landed knights, townsmen and country folk, but that his force was composed of his tenants-in-chief with a few of their vassals and 'innumerable stipendiary knights'.[2] The truth of Robert's statement has been disputed, Round arguing that the pipe roll of 1159 'presents proof to the contrary'.[3] It is plain that Round assumed that the barons who accompanied the king were themselves accompanied by their tenants who held fiefs by knight service, although, as he himself stated, the fiefs which were in the king's hands paid scutage. In other words, the king did not require mesne tenants to fight but preferred their money wherewith to engage mercenaries. Why the king's tenants-in-chief should not be of a like mind, Round did not explain. Of course, no major baron was ever likely to be followed by the number of knights represented by his enfeoffments—by the sick, the maimed, the aged, the minors, the heiresses; and the full number had to be made up in some other way, the most obvious way being the engagement of mercenaries. The evident difficulty experienced by monasteries in getting their tenants to go on active service is sufficient indication that no tenant-in-chief could count upon a satisfactory call to arms.[4] It was simpler and more profitable to collect scutage and take household knights or mercenaries into the field. As is not infrequently the case, Round's 'proof to the contrary' proves to be a questionable assumption. Nor is Robert of Torigni without the best of contemporary corroboration. No less a witness than Richard of Ely, Henry II's treasurer, declares that the king preferred to expose mercenaries to the hazards of war.[5] Richard did not explain that Henry's preference was grounded in experience and that his reliance upon professional soldiers gives the clue to his military effectiveness.

---

[1] For the employment of mercenaries by the Norman kings see J. O. Prestwich, 'War and Finance in the Anglo-Norman State' in *Trans. R. Hist. Soc.*, 5th Series, iv.19-43.
[2] Robert of Torigni (ed. Howlett), p. 202.   [3] *Feudal England*, p. 280.
[4] Chew, *op. cit.*, pp. 147-56; Sanders, *Feudal Military Service in England*, p. 55.
[5] *Dialogus de Scaccario*, p. 52.

The story of the professional soldier goes back many years. We have seen that there is reason to believe that mercenaries were commonly employed in the Old English kingdom. Of post-Conquest mercenaries the most prominent in England in the century after the Conquest were the stipendiary knights who came from Flanders. Whether they were always the most numerous is another matter, but of them we have the fullest information. A significant fact about them is that they served the English king under contract, a contract that was clothed in contemporary terms, but which is nevertheless the direct ancestor of the contracts of service of the later Middle Ages.[1] The knight who served under contract was well known on the Continent before 1066, but he first appears with certainty in English history in 1101 when Henry I entered into a contract with Robert count of Flanders under which, in return for an annual payment of £500, the latter undertook to provide on demand 1000 knights for service in England or Henry's French dominions. This contract, frequently renewed by successive kings and counts, is happily known to us in the original text.[2] On its first renewal nine years later the contract provided for a smaller contingent of 500 knights and for a reduced payment of 400 marks,[3] but this does not mean that the king was less dependent upon mercenaries, for the Flemish knights formed but a part of the band of foreign mercenaries who found employment with the English king. John, for example, had in his service knights not only from Flanders but from Brabant and Hainaut[4] as well as from his own continental dominions, men such as Fawkes of Bréauté, Gerard of Athée and Engelard of Cigogné who were prominent in his contest with his English barons.[5] Naturally enough, we know much less of English mercenary knights and our knowledge is chiefly from financial records, but we see them defending the coastal counties and the Welsh march, garrisoning castles and guarding the king's treasure.[6] The civil war of Stephen's reign offered a golden opportunity to these soldiers of fortune, of low social status and indifferent morals.[7] We are told that a minor baron

---

[1] For these see Lyon, *From Fief to Indenture*, pp. 251-4, and Appendix VI: below, pp. 466-9.

[2] *Foedera*, i.7; Vercauteren, *Actes des Comtes de Flandres*, no. 30, pp. 88-95. For the date, 10 March 1101, see *Regesta*, no. 515.

[3] *Foedera*, i.6; Vercauteren, no. 41, pp. 109-16; *Regesta*, no. 941.

[4] Dept, *Les influences anglaise et française dans le comté de Flandre*, pp. 54-68, 157-62.

[5] For Fawkes de Bréauté and his family see Norgate, *Minority of Henry III*, pp. 223-33, and our *Select Cases of Procedure without Writ*, pp. xxx-xxxii. For Gerard of Athée and Engelard of Cigogné see Maitland, *Pleas of the Crown for the County of Gloucester*, pp. xiii-xvi.

[6] Excellent examples of the employment of stipendiary knights on the coast and on the Welsh march are to be found in *Pipe Roll, 13 Henry II*, p. 201; *14 Henry II*, pp. 198-9: upon these entries see *E.H.R.*, lxix.603. For the garrisoning of castles see the particulars collected by Round, *Feudal England*, pp. 270-2. For guarding treasure in transit see *Pipe Roll, 5 Henry II*, p. 45. These are, of course, but a fraction of the references that might be cited.

[7] Witness the worthy wandering knight who, after 1154, could no longer rob as he was wont and fell into poverty, so turned highwayman and was hanged (*Rolls of the Justices in Eyre for Gloucestershire etc.*, ed. D. M. Stenton, p. 167).

of this time, John fitz Gilbert, the marshal, had three hundred knights in his household[1]: the number is a poetic exaggeration, but the fact that a man of so little consequence could retain in his service a troop of knights is significant. Those in the service of Henry II after peace had been restored to the land were doubtless of the better sort, but even so they were of lowly status and were hardly to be distinguished from serjeants, the common men-at-arms who were the typical professional soldiers of the later Middle Ages.[2] To complete the picture, mention should be made of two other classes of mercenaries in the service of the king, the Welsh infantry, an irregular ill-armed force,[3] and the highly skilled crossbowmen, engaged primarily, it would seem, for the defence of castles but employed also in the field.[4] The English do not appear to have used the crossbow; but it was well known in the eleventh century on the Continent and many crossbowmen must have come to England after the Conquest,[5] even though the weapon may not have been used at Hastings.[6] It does not seem to have been very effective at that date and does not appear to have become a formidable weapon until the technical advances of a century or so made the crossbowman the most mechanically skilled of contemporary soldiers.[7]

[1] *Histoire de Guillaume le Maréchal*, i.3, lines 52-8.

[2] This is well illustrated by the change in the description of the soldiers guarding treasure in transit: see *Trans. R. Hist. Soc.*, 4th Series, xv.77-8. Flemish knights are called serjeants, *servientes*, in *Pipe Roll, 9 Henry II*, p. 71: £100 is paid to William Cade, the great money-lender of St. Omer, for bringing them from Flanders.

[3] A troop, stated to number 1000, was taken to France by Henry II in 1174 ('Benedict of Peterborough', i.74; Robert of Torigni, p. 265). Payments to Welsh serjeants are occasionally noted in the pipe rolls (e.g. *Pipe Roll, 32 Henry II*, pp. 29, 55; *33 Henry II*, pp. 40, 45), and such notices are more numerous under Richard I: cf. p. 84, n. 4, below.

[4] For the technical aspect see Payne-Gallwey, *The Crossbow* (1904); pp. 44-7 relate particularly to England, but are inadequately documented.

[5] Crossbowmen, *arbalisterii, balisterii*, appear in Domesday Book, but they do not seem to be mentioned except in Gloucestershire, Lincolnshire, Norfolk, Suffolk and Sussex (D.B., i.18 b 1, 162 a 1, 338 a 2; ii.110 a, 117 a, 118 a, 320 a, 324 a, 382 b). This does not mean that they were unknown elsewhere, and there were doubtless a good number not provided with land.

[6] The Bayeux Tapestry depicts only the short bow. Either we cannot rely upon the tapestry on such matters or we must reject the statement of William of Poitiers (ed. Foreville, p. 184) that the Conqueror 'pedites in fronte locavit sagittis armatos et balistis', unless indeed we give some other than the normal meaning to *balista*. Guy of Amiens, *De Bello Hastingensi*, lines 337-8, says:

Praemisit pedites committere bella sagittis
Et balistantes miserit in medio.

But in any case, it would seem that the crossbow cannot have been prominent in the battle.

[7] In the early years of Henry II crossbowmen appear to have been paid at the rate of 4d. a day as compared with the knight's 8d. and the serjeant's 1d. (*Pipe Roll, 8 Henry II*, p. 53; *9 Henry II*, p. 69; Round, *Feudal England*, pp. 270-2). By the early years of John the standard rate for a crossbowman was 12d. a day, with an allowance of 3d. if he had three horses. At that time serjeants were receiving 2d. a day. The clearest statement will be found in *Pipe Roll, 7 John*, p. 14. The editor has collected a good deal of material from other sources in his introduction, pp. xxi-xxv, but this is not always easy to interpret. However, the superiority of the crossbowman and his mobility are evident. His importance under Henry II is illustrated by the example of a grant, given in 'Glanville': per liberum servicium inveniendi tibi unum arbelastarium in exercitu domini regis per quadraginta dies (lib. xii, c. 3: ed. Woodbine, p. 150). It may be added that the long bow largely ousted the crossbow, as well as the short bow, as a military weapon in England later in the Middle Ages, and consequently its further mechanical perfection (e.g. the

What then of the soldiers who were neither 'feudal' nor mercenary, those local forces which modern historians have been pleased to term the 'militia' or the 'fyrd'. We have already questioned such confused anachronisms, and we have said that between the time of Edmund Ironsides and the battle of the Standard we have found no evidence of the employment in the field of any other troops than those of the household of kings and nobles, mercenaries, burghal knights and burgesses, and those who were called upon to serve by reason of their, or their lord's, tenure.[1] There is, however, one piece of evidence for the reign of Henry I that suggests an ancient obligation falling upon both townsmen—for which, indeed, we have much other evidence—and countrymen. This is a charter (much inflated in the form in which it has come down to us) issued by Henry I in favour of the church of York. The canons were confirmed in the privilege they had enjoyed before the Conquest of discharging any military obligation falling upon their land by providing a standard-bearer, with the banner of Saint Peter, whose duty it was to lead the burgesses into battle.[2] This charter explains, better than any other document, the constitution of the force which won the battle of the Standard in 1138. In that force there was not only the banner of Saint Peter, but the banners of Saint John of Beverley and Saint Wilfrid of Ripon, and we may be sure that the burgesses of the three towns were with the banners. The knights and the able-bodied men of the countryside were there too. The unusual feature appears to have been the presence of the parish priests. But the little army consisted of more than local levies: the backbone seems to have been provided by mercenaries under the command of the count of Aumale and Walter of Ghent and a troop of knights sent by the king under the command of Bernard of Bailleul. Without this stiffening the local forces might not have proved very effective, although the decisive stroke seems to have been given by the archers early in the battle. These archers who, following the normal tactics of the day, would constitute the front line, were presumably local men, so numerous were they. The knights on both sides, we may remark, fought, as was not uncommon, on foot.[3] The contrast between the facts of this battle, upon which we are singularly well informed, and the conventional, but quite illusory, picture of 'feudal' warfare drawn by modern historians is one to be kept in mind.

But to return to these local forces, who spring suddenly into the light of history in 1138. Though Henry II's Assize of Arms is the

use of steel) has little direct interest. The crossbow still held its own under Edward I, but towards the end of his reign it may have been in its decline (Morris, *Welsh Wars of Edward I*, pp. 87-92, 302).   [1] Above, pp. 51-2.
[2] *Historians of the Church of York*, iii.34-6; *Regesta*, no. 1083.
[3] Richard of Hexham, pp. 159-64; *Relatio de Standardo*, pp. 181-99, in Howlett, *Chronicles of Stephen*, vol. iii.

earliest legislation known to us that attempted to regulate the obligation falling upon able-bodied freemen to bear arms, we possess in the so-called 'Laws of Edward the Confessor' a description of the local forces as they existed in the early years of Henry's reign and, we may suppose, in previous reigns.[1] They are, however, not in the least like a 'militia'. Prior to the Assize the organisation, it seems clear, was based upon lordship. The Assize itself, it will be remembered, provided that a lord should have ready arms and armour for his household knights: and it is an eloquent commentary upon the military effectiveness of 'feudalism' that he was strictly prohibited from disposing of this equipment. Some measure of organisation—perhaps it is no more than wishful thinking on the part of the author—is, however, suggested by the statement in the 'Laws' that annually, on the morrow of Candlemas (3 February), there was to be a view of arms in cities, boroughs, castles, hundreds and wapentakes, though the jurisdiction of barons, within their own franchises, was to be respected. The Assize, which might have been more clearly worded, appears to change the date of the view of arms to the feast of St. Hilary (13 January), and it certainly provided for its enforcement by the justices itinerant. More significantly still, it required all those who bore arms to swear fealty to the king. The purpose of the Assize seems clearly to have been to break the link between lord and man, to take out of the hands of disloyal barons a potential armed force they had shown their capacity to abuse. Its effect, though this is not specifically stated, was to transfer the control of the local forces from the freeman's lord to the sheriff. In other respects the changes introduced by the Assize were small: matters of definition and regulation.[2] Neither the Assize nor later legislation, while imposing compulsory military equipment and training, created a conscript army or converted the local levies into an effective striking force.[3] But this is equally true of the system of military tenures. Of the two institutions the system of local levies, as reorganised, was perhaps more likely to provide a reserve of fighting men, raw and untrained as they inevitably would be. The real reserve was provided by the professional soldier.

The realities of the situation at the end of the twelfth and the beginning of the thirteenth century are well illustrated by the arrangements for repelling a feared invasion by the French in 1205.[4] One-tenth of the number of knights who in theory owed service to the king were summoned to London, a force of perhaps fewer than 500 mounted men, to supplement the mercenaries already at the king's

---

[1] *Gesetze*, i.656. We cannot accept Liebermann's view that this passage is derived from or, indeed, owes anything to the Assize of Arms: see *Traditio*, xvi.166-7. For the date of the Assize itself see Appendix IV: below, p. 439, n. 3.

[2] Text in *Select Charters*, pp. 183-4. The introductory matter should be disregarded.

[3] To the orders of 1205, 1230 and 1242 we refer below. Permanent legislation, the Statute of Winchester, c. vi, was passed in 1285: the text is conveniently reprinted in *Select Charters*, p. 466.   [4] *Ibid.*, pp. 276-7, from *Rot. Litt. Pat.*, p. 55.

disposal. In this way a striking force would be provided to meet the enemy after they had landed. But more than this was needed. The sheriffs, therefore, on hearing tidings of a landing, were on their own responsibility to assemble all the able-bodied men of the shire, knights, serjeants and others, landed and landless, the latter being promised their keep while serving. Behind these directions lies the assumption that all men liable to bear arms will be equipped as the assize directed. But there is no pre-conceived organisation: everything is to be improvised by the sheriff.[1] There is, let us note in particular, no suggestion that lords are to lead their men to battle. There are to be proclamations in markets and at fairs and wherever else the sheriff thinks proper: all is left to him. It would have required a military genius in every shire to turn this armed mob into the semblance of an army. At best it might, at great sacrifice, have delayed the enemy a little. Fortunately the enemy did not come. But it was not until afterwards that a rudimentary organisation was devised.[2] And here we may leave, for the moment, the discussion of local levies and mercenaries and the other constituents of mediaeval armies and turn back to the question of tenures, of knight's fees, with which this chapter began.

When the Conqueror granted military fiefs in England and directed in some measure their sub-infeudation, he can have had no illusion that he was in this way raising an army. We want no better proof of this than his insistence that the Norman abbot of Abingdon should enfeoff a stipendiary knight who had been captured at sea and maimed by Danish 'pirates', leaving him without his hands, a useless mouth, if ever there was one. The abbot provided him with an estate from the abbey demesne.[3] What the king did, and what his tenants-in-chief did, was to grant land on conditions familiar to them, the conditions upon which French fiefs were held: no alternative was readily conceivable by men of such limited knowledge and such limited experience. They were military tenures, but they might be military only in name. Therefore, relying as they did upon mercenary troops, the problem confronting Norman and Angevin kings was to make the best use of the resources provided by military tenures, without counting upon them to furnish more than a modicum of effective soldiers. In the end the problem defeated them, and military tenures ultimately became no more than a means of raising money in oppressive ways. But a brief examination of the efforts to make military tenures serve a directly military end may be salutary

[1] For the text, preserved by Gervase of Canterbury or his continuator, providing for an organisation with a hierarchy of constables (*Historical Works*, ii.96-7), see below, p. 113: it cannot possibly be an order issued on this occasion.   [2] Below, p. 113.
[3] *Chron. Mon. de Abingdon*, ii.6-7. The knight, named Hermer, seems to have been granted a life tenancy, but it resulted in a permanent diminution of the demesne. The extent of the land granted is not stated, but another knight, named Hubert, mentioned in the same paragraph and apparently similarly enfeoffed at the order of the king, had a grant of five hides of land in villeinage (see also *ibid.*, p. 4).

in removing any illusions that may remain about 'feudal armies'. To begin with, we must distinguish between tenants-in-chief and mesne tenants. Quite irrespective of the conditions of their tenure, the greater barons would inevitably have been among the leaders of any royal army. We need spare no further words for them. Even the humbler knights who held in chief of the king—there were not many of them—were likely to obey a writ summoning them to join the host. We may leave out of consideration the ecclesiastical tenants-in-chief, representing perhaps a seventh of the services nominally due to the king, for after the eleventh century it was unusual for them to discharge their obligations except in money.[1] But tenants-in-chief were a small minority. The bulk of the 'feudal army' was composed of mesne tenants, and let us reiterate—for the point must be driven home—just as subject to the ordinary incidents of life as tenants-in-chief, to age, disease and death: at any time there were among them minors and heiresses, the sick, the maimed, the infirm. And it is well to remember that, when we talk of knight's fees, we are not talking of men but of land and the obligations attached to land, and that 5000 or 6000 knight's fees, or whatever other figure we like to substitute for that number,[2] may represent a good many more tenants; and the more the number was increased the greater would be the opportunity for evasion, the less the ability of the tenant to perform military service. Whether the greater number of tenants was produced by direct division of the lord's demesne or land held in villeinage or by sub-infeudation on the part of the tenants themselves, the result would be the same. It is true that, on the one hand, a number of knight's fees might be held by one mesne tenant, not necessarily of the same lord, or a tenant-in-chief might be the mesne tenant of other lords—and such a state of affairs obviously did not simplify personal service—but, on the other hand, a single knight's fee might be divided into several parts, all held directly of a tenant-in-chief. Let us take an actual example. Three knight's fees belonging to Abingdon Abbey were divided unequally between twelve tenants and seem to have been so divided in the eleventh century.[3] The tenants do not appear to have been expected to serve in the field, though they may have been expected at one time to perform castle-guard: but, as we shall see, by the reign of Henry I their value to the abbot was that they made payments to his chamber. As other particulars furnished by the list of the abbey's tenants show, this was by no means the end of the complications. Widely separated units and parts might be combined in the owner-

---

[1] Chew, *op. cit.*, pp. 37-74. Under Henry III, however, personal service seems usually to have been rendered for a much reduced quota (*ibid.*, pp. 52-3).

[2] For various estimates see Round, *Feudal England*, p. 292; Inman, *Domesday and Feudal Statistics*, p. 50; Drummond, *Studien zur Kriegsgeschichte Englands*, pp. 20-33.

[3] *Chron. Mon. de Abingdon*, ii.5-6. These are the portions of fees belonging to the abbot's chamber. Two tenants hold half a knight's fee each; five hold one-fifth each; five hold varying portions of another fee.

ship of one tenant to make up a knight's fee.[1] This was a common practice. But since the mesne tenant had little difficulty in alienating parts of his fee, fresh permutations and combinations were constantly occurring. Since, however, the king looked to the tenant-in-chief to discharge the obligations attached to the whole of the fief, neither the division and subdivision of its parts nor changes in ownership were any concern of the king's ministers, unless the fief fell into the king's hands. Then the ministers, in the event of war, did not attempt to exact personal service from the tenants, but demanded scutage. This was, at least, the state of affairs under Henry II, when the survival of the pipe rolls means that we can see the system at work.[2] But there is no reason to suppose that the systematic conversion of knight service into money payments was then an innovation, for the evidence of scutage can be traced back many years.

One of the earliest references to scutage is found in a royal charter of 1100, exempting Lewes Priory from this among other burdens.[3] Lewes was one of the Conqueror's foundations and this reference to scutage is puzzling, for it suggests that religious houses founded by the Norman kings had not originally been immune, as is believed, from knight service.[4] But at least we have here evidence that scutage was already known in the eleventh century, commuting not merely fractional services or obligations otherwise difficult to discharge but the multiple services to which a well-endowed monastery might otherwise be liable. The best evidence for the early commutation of fractional services is afforded by the list of military tenants of Abingdon Abbey which includes details of the three knight's fees we have already mentioned. This list cannot be much later, if it is not earlier, than the year 1100. The fractional services form a group apart: they are, as we have said, appropriated to the abbot's chamber doubtless because they were a source of revenue, although it is possible that originally all the tenants had performed castle-guard at Windsor on the basis of a forty days' spell of duty for a complete knight's fee. But already it is noted against the names of two tenants, who hold a fifth and a sixth part of a knight's fee, that they 'dant scuagium et non faciunt wardam', while the two co-heiresses of another tenant, who held a fifth part of a knight's fee, obviously could not perform castle-guard.[5] Here scutage is not a payment by

---

[1] Thus two tenants of the abbey had each a knight's fee of five hides made up of distant portions (*ibid.*, p. 5).   [2] Above, p. 72.

[3] Morris in *E.H.R.*, xxxvi.45; *Regesta*, no. 510.

[4] Pre-Conquest foundations in Normandy had not been exempt (*Historiens de la France*, xxiii.694; *Red Book of the Exchequer*, ii.625-6), and it may well be that the Conqueror imitated the practice of his English predecessor in granting freedom from military service. For a list of Norman foundations see Knowles, *Monastic Order in England*, p. 701; cf. *ibid.*, pp. 607-8.

[5] *Chron. Mon. de Abingdon*, ii.5-6. The list, as it stands, contains the names of a number of men living under Henry I: Hugh of Buckland, Herbert fitz Herbert and Gilbert Marshal (below p. 82). An entry 'Sueting avus Matthie' indicates that, in its original form, the list went back some years, and a reference to 'tempore huius abbatis' seems to mean in the time of Abbot Athelhelm (1071-84).

a tenant-in-chief to the king, but by the mesne tenant to his lord. Thus we have already the two aspects of scutage familiar in the twelfth and thirteenth centuries, and this suggests that the institution may have had a long history by 1100. It had not, however, yet become the general practice for ecclesiastical tenants-in-chief to commute their obligations in this way, for Archbishop Anselm had found himself in trouble with William Rufus in 1097 because the knights he had furnished for service against the Welsh were personally unsatisfactory and ill-equipped.[1] There is no reason to suppose, however, that these were enfeoffed knights. Had they been, then some of them, if we can rely upon Domesday Book, were also tenants-in-chief, while others were knights who had been enfeoffed very recently by the king himself during the voidance of the see, much to Anselm's indignation.[2] History has its ironies, but this jest we may regretfully dismiss. The probability is that the archbishop's obligation had been discharged, in whole or in part, by engaging mercenaries as cheaply as possible. Certainly the abbot of Abingdon discharged his obligation to the Conqueror by sending stipendiary knights to Normandy.[3] But the story of Anselm's knights does suggest that the king would be well advised to accept a money payment and engage mercenaries of his own choice.

Such a solution was, however, far ahead of the thought of the times. Knight service continued for long to be discharged in one of three ways: by a money payment; by providing a substitute; by personal service. Let us give some actual examples, and first that of a minor tenant-in-chief, William of Semilly. He told the court in 1226 how, all through the barons' war with King John, he had served *nomine illius servitii* in Oxford Castle and that afterwards he had been at the siege of Bedford Castle, while at the moment he was maintaining a knight in Gascony in the king's service with Richard of Cornwall.[4] It seems evident that William of Semilly, though he held a knight's fee, could not inaptly be called a professional soldier. During his long service under John, he must have been in the king's

---

[1] Eadmer, *Historia Novorum*, p. 78: cf. *Vita Anselmi, ibid.*, p. 377. In the light of the not inconsiderable amount of evidence regarding the knights enfeoffed with lands of the see of Canterbury, it is difficult to understand the comments on this passage in Stenton, *First Century*, pp. 148-9. Nor does it seem helpful to relate Eadmer's story to the absurd inventions of the Christ Church monks in 1188, who stated that in England generally knights took the place of 'threngs' (*Epistolae Cantuarienses*, p. 225). They made no specific reference to Kent and the misspelt word would seem an obvious mistake for 'thegns'. The word 'dreng' was known in southern England, as the poem on the Battle of Maldon testifies (line 149); but it does not seem to have the meaning that Sir Frank Stenton attributes to it in Kent (*op. cit.*, pp. 146-8).

[2] The list of archbishop's knights in D.B., i.4 includes Hamon the steward (*dapifer*), the count of Eu and Hugh de Montfort, all important tenants-in-chief with lands in several counties. In Anselm's letter to Hugh, archbishop of Lyons, he says that the king is treating lands formerly held by English knights as escheats and 'militibus partim daret, partim dare disponat' (*Opera*, ed. Schmitt, iv.59). According to Eadmer (*Historia Novorum*, p. 40), the king asked Anselm to condone these enfeoffments.

[3] *Chron. Mon. de Abingdon*, ii.5.

[4] *Curia Regis Rolls*, xii.465-6 (no. 2323); also in *Bracton's Note Book*, iii.570-1 (no. 1734).

pay, and presumably it was at no loss to himself that he was maintaining a knight in the king's service in Gascony. Tenurial obligations and professional services might be conjoined. We may contrast William with a mesne tenant of an earlier date, Henry de Neville, who had been enfeoffed by Earl Hugh Bigod with a knight's fee and who was, of a verity, no professional soldier. Between 1166 and 1170, there appear to have been seven occasions when he might have undertaken service in the field, five expeditions to Wales and two in France. In respect of the expeditions to Wales he paid four marks and two shillings. It is not clear that he received a summons to join these expeditions; but he seems undoubtedly to have been summoned, at least formally, to join the host for service oversea. On both occasions he pleaded that he was unfit. On the first occasion he paid scutage of two marks; on the second occasion he paid a knight to go in his place.[1]

When Hugh de Neville had been enfeoffed there was presumably an expectation that he would actually serve in arms, and it is possible that his failure to do so was due to age or infirmity. But our next example will be of a fief deliberately created, within two generations of the Conquest, where there could hardly have been such an expectation. The motive behind the enfeoffment may have been to reward faithful service, but the return to the lord could only be occasional cash payments, together with the usual 'incidents' arising from military tenure. When William Peverel of Dover enfeoffed his steward Thurstan with the manors of Gidding in Huntingdonshire and of Daywell in Shropshire for the service of half a knight, nothing can be more certain than that he did not add to the number of his vassals or increase the armed force at his command. The honour of Peverel escheated to the Crown and, while the Huntingdonshire fief remained with Thurstan's successors, the Engain family, the king granted the Shropshire fief to Mereduc son of Rhys of Powis. The Engains claimed that, in consequence, their liability was halved, and it was finally admitted that their service was no more than that of a quarter of a knight. Now it is quite clear that, when it was recorded in the exchequer in 1166 that Garnier Engain answered for half a knight, the meaning was that he was assessed to scutage on half a knight's fee, while his son Richard claimed that, in consequence of his loss of the Shropshire fief, his assessment to scutage should be halved.[2] Here we have an interesting case of mesne tenants who became tenants-in-chief, but without altering the nature of their service. Had the fee not been fractional, the king might have gained an armed knight when the honour escheated: all he actually gained was a small amount of scutage and

[1] *Red Book of the Exchequer*, i.396; ii.cclxxix-cclxxx.
[2] For the original charter see above, p. 33. For the later history see *ibid.*, i.372; *Pipe Roll, 14 Henry II*, p. 103; *33 Henry II*, p. 81; *6 Richard I*, p. 77.

the right to relief and wardship. Let our final example be one where, though the mesne tenants suffered from no disability, it was impossible that they should render personal service to the king on behalf of the tenant-in-chief. Among the tenants of the abbot of Abingdon under Henry I were Hugh of Buckland, Herbert fitz Herbert and Gilbert Marshal.[1] The first was a heavily engaged minister, at one time the sheriff of eight counties[2]; the second was one of the king's chamberlains[3]; the third was the king's marshal.[4] In each case the ministerial duties of the mesne tenant to the king, quite apart from any other circumstance, were incompatible with the duties of a tenant by knight service towards the abbot, unless their service was performed by delegating it to knightly members of their households, or by themselves enfeoffing knights who would perform the service on their behalf, or by engaging stipendiary knights. The final alternative was to pay scutage to the abbot, and since it became customary for the abbot himself to discharge his liability by paying scutage, there can be little doubt that in such cases knight service meant money payments.

Before we pass on, let us make it abundantly clear that such in-compatibilities as we find at Abingdon were not a gradual develop-ment—if indeed the adjective is appropriate for the brief interval of time between the reign of the Conqueror and the reign of Henry I— but were inherent in the form of 'feudalism' introduced into England. No one, we might imagine, could give serious consideration to the particulars for any county in Domesday Book and retain the illusion that there was any necessary obligation on mesne tenants to serve their lord as knights in the field. Few passages can be better known than the list of Lanfranc's knights entered under Kent; and the first question that any student of the 'feudal army' might be expected to put to himself is how such of the archbishop's knights as Hamon the steward, the count of Eu and Hugh de Montfort contrived to dis-charge their duties at once as tenants-in-chief and as mesne tenants.[5] What could possibly be gained, in a military sense, either by the king or by the archbishop, from such enfeoffments? It is easy to understand the material gain to those insatiable Norman barons who were avid to add estate to estate, fief to fief, or the social gain to an archbishop who wished to add to his retinue barons who, if not of the most exalted rank, were men of no little consequence. But what conceivable relation can such considerations bear to military efficiency?

We have given enough examples to show how highly artificial the conception of knight service was in England and how remote it was from furnishing the king with a 'feudal army'. Not, of course, that

---

[1] *Chron. Mon. de Abingdon*, ii.5.   [2] Morris, *Mediaeval English Sheriff*, pp. 77-9.
[3] Below, pp. 217-18.   [4] *Complete Peerage*, X, app., pp. 91-2.
[5] See p. 80, n. 2, above.

the king had any desire for such an army and, indeed, he would have been highly embarrassed, had it been incumbent upon him in time of war to call up the sub-tenants from every military fee into which the fiefs of his tenants-in-chief were divided. Doubtless among the mesne tenants there were a considerable number skilled in arms and some who, like William of Semilly, were soldiers by profession; but a large proportion were incapable of bearing arms or were unskilled and had no taste for warfare. If mesne tenants were to be employed at all, there had to be some measure of selection. We have seen that in 1205 the king called up only one in ten of the knights upon whose services he was, in principle, entitled to draw.[1] The method of selection is quite obscure—it might quite well have meant the substitution of a mercenary—but presumably selection was left to the tenants-in-chief, who would also enforce the obligation upon the remaining mesne tenants to find two shillings a day for the support of the selected knights. This conjecture leaves many points unresolved; but since selection was no new device, there was presumably a traditional way in which details were worked out. Richard I had resorted to some measure of selection. The chroniclers talk vaguely of the summoning of every third knight, but this is probably a conventional expression for a small part of the knights owing military service,[2] and there is every reason to suppose that the fraction was much smaller than one-third. We could have no better evidence than a letter of Richard's written in April 1196.[3] He asks Hubert Walter to summon all those owing knight service to be in Normandy by the second of June following, prepared for a long campaign, but no baron is to bring with him more than seven knights at most, and some are entirely excused because their services are required elsewhere. Bishops and abbots are expected to make a generous contribution, in money or possibly in hired knights. The long lists of those charged in respect of scutage for this expedition are testimony to the light incidence of personal service and the heavy incidence of monetary contributions.[4] The story cannot have been very different on previous occasions.[5] It is probable, however, that the king desired personal service less and less, and the chronicler's statement that in 1197 he asked for no more than three hundred knights, though these were to serve for a year, must be very near the

---

[1] Above, p. 76.

[2] Howden (iii.242) states that in 1194 the king called up one-third of the service due from each fief. The pipe roll shows that many tenants-in-chief did not cross into Normandy (for references see the index to *Pipe Roll, 6 Richard I*, p. 360, *s.v.* scutagium), though it is impossible to arrive at a figure representing a proportion of the total services due. That the one-third is conventional is suggested by the statement of Richard of Devizes that Longchamp in 1191 summoned 'tertium . . . totius Anglie militem' (ed. Howlett, p. 409): and see p. 84, n. 2, below. [3] Ralf de Diceto, *Opera*, ii.lxxx.

[4] *Chancellor's Roll, 8 Richard I*, p. 422, *s.v.* scutagium. The campaign in question is the 'tertius exercitus Normannie'.

[5] The evidence of the earlier pipe rolls is similar: *Pipe Roll, 6 Richard I*, p. 360; *7 Richard I*, pp. 382-3. It must be remembered that not all payments would be brought to account in the pipe rolls.

truth.[1] Richard was but following the practice of his father. Very early in his reign Henry II is credited with calling up the conventional one-third of the knights due to serve,[2] and we may be sure that, where personal service was rendered, only a small fraction of the mesne tenants served in the field. If we are asked why we dismiss even one-third as a grossly exaggerated proportion of the services nominally due, we must reply that, quite apart from Henry's well attested preference for mercenaries,[3] it is impossible to conceive how any force of knights in number approaching two thousand could be transported across the Channel and maintained in a state of efficiency.[4]

A restricted 'call-up', if this is an appropriate designation for a system we understand so imperfectly, must have been an unsatisfactory and clumsy device, and early in the reign of Henry III it had been abandoned in favour of individual bargains struck with tenants-in-chief.[5] The effect of this new system is not without its bearing upon any conclusions we would otherwise draw regarding personal service in the twelfth century, for we must suppose that the Crown did not give very much away, though there are some obvious instances of favouritism. Those tenants-in-chief whose service was that of a single knight or some small number up to ten could not hope to benefit from the new scheme,[6] but at the highest points in the scale the effect is striking: a baron whose service ran nominally into hundreds might be able to bargain for a mere handful of knights. The reductions were made upon no evident principle, though it has been suggested that the value of the fief was taken into consideration. Favour, as we have said, played its part, and it is difficult to believe that the reduction of the king's brother's service from 315 knights to eight was anything but a form of beneficial enfeoffment.[7] Such a reduction was, of course, exceptional, but every-

---

[1] Howden, iv.40. It is presumably upon this rather poetical passage and the relevant passage in the *Vita Sancti Hugonis* by Gerald the Welshman (*Opera*, vii.103-6) that Adam of Eynsham embroidered in his *Magna Vita sancti Hugonis*, pp. 248-52, where he tells the story of Hugh of Lincoln's resistance to the king's demand. This story is incredible, as Sir James Ramsay long ago pointed out (*Angevin Empire*, pp. 355-7), and disbelief is strengthened by the details of the 'donum pro militibus' in the pipe roll (*Pipe Roll, 10 Richard I*, pp. xix-xxiv). The story is entirely spoilt by the recorded fact that the saintly bishop had paid the previous scutages in respect of Norman expeditions and claimed the appropriate allowances like any other accountant (*Chancellor's Roll, 8 Richard I*, pp. 109-10).

[2] Robert of Torigni, *s.a.* 1157 (ed. Howlett, p. 193): 'ita ut duo milites de tota Anglia tertium pararent'. The pipe rolls do not assist in elucidating the actual arrangements.

[3] See above, p. 72. Boussard has collected the references in the chronicles: his thesis would have been strengthened if he had collected the many details from the pipe rolls ('Henry II Plantagenet et les origines de l'armée de métier' in *Bibliothèque de l'École des Chartes*, cvi.189-224).

[4] The position regarding foot soldiers was different: 2000 Welsh might be transported over a number of months (*Chancellor's Roll, 8 Richard I*, p. xvii). Very few mounted constables and serjeants were attached to them as officers, and presumably the men lived upon the country.

[5] Sanders, *Feudal Military Service*, pp. 56-67.

[6] This is implied by the 'Unknown Charter of Liberties', c. 7: si aliquis debet inde servitium decem militum, consilio baronum meorum alleviabitur (McKechnie, *Magna Carta*, p. 486).   [7] Sanders, *op. cit.*, pp. 66, 71-84.

where, save in the lowest range, there was a marked scaling down.[1] Recognised quotas gradually established themselves and new *servitia debita* replaced the old.[2] The new system was, however, linked with the past through the insistence by the Crown that the tenant-in-chief should serve in person and, provided he did so, by the preservation of his right to demand scutage from his tenants on the ancient basis, whatever reduction had been made in his quota.[3] The practical result in the number of enfeoffed knights serving in the field was much the same as that which Henry II had achieved by different methods, leaving undisturbed the financial liability of mesne tenants who held nominally by knight service.

And now, having, as we hope, come nearer to the military realities of the twelfth century and rid ourselves of the illusion of a 'feudal army', we may return to the problem of *servitia debita*. The conception is, we believe, in origin fiscal, though plainly it is linked with real or notional quotas of military service. When we find knight service grouped with gelds and scots and other accustomed charges (*consuetudines*) in a writ of William Rufus, directing that all these are to be assessed on the most favourable basis, we can hardly doubt that it is the financial incidence of knight service that is uppermost.[4] Curiously enough, the only known writ in which this grouping occurs is in favour of Thorney Abbey, which was exempt from knight service, and the inference is that we have here a common formula which was incorporated in writs sought by ecclesiastical or lay tenants-in-chief who believed themselves to be overcharged: for quite clearly the abbot of Thorney could not in this respect be *melius admensuratus* than any honour anywhere in England. It should be noted also that the writ does not refer to scutage, as some few years later a charter in favour of Lewes Priory will do,[5] but to *servitium militum*. Like Archbishop Anselm, ecclesiastical tenants-in-chief may hire knights,[6] but it is not yet customary for them to commute their liability by a payment to the king. The Thorney writ appears then to mark an intermediate stage. It is not, we surmise, until scutage had become not merely an occasional alternative to military service but an important source of revenue, that the king's ministers concerned themselves with the liability of tenants-in-chief and, in particular, ecclesiastical tenants-in-chief. We can be sure that this stage had been reached when Roger of Salisbury was justiciar, that is from 1109 onwards. Had it been reached earlier? There is no evidence and we must be content to begin our enquiries at this point. In 1127 the church of Ely, at the cost of a large fine to the king, obtained a charter remitting £40 of the £100 with which it had been the custom to charge its estates when scutage ran through

---

[1] *Ibid.*, pp. 84-8.   [2] *Ibid.*, pp. 136-160.
[3] There is a good summary of the position by Powicke, *The Thirteenth Century*, pp. 556-9, which we need not elaborate.   [4] *Regesta*, i.136, no. lxxii (dated 1093-9).
[5] Above, p. 79.   [6] Above, p. 80.

England, so that its liability was in future to be limited to £60.[1]
Earlier in Henry I's reign the bishop of Norwich had been complaining to Roger of Salisbury that £60 had been exacted from him for
'knights', in terms which certainly do not suggest that this was a
customary payment.[2] The impression with which we are left is that
the barons of the exchequer are as yet only in the initial stages of
determining liabilities for scutage. There is no word in either case
of *servitium debitum*, nor is there any phrase resembling it or suggesting
that such a conception existed.

The impression we gain from these documents is, we think, amply
confirmed by the pipe roll of 1130. In that roll, it is true, there is no
mention of scutage, but there are a number of entries relating to an
auxilium militum.[3] The purpose for which it was levied we do not
know: perhaps *auxilium militum* is merely an alternative name for
scutage but, in any case, this levy, whatever its justification, seems
evidently to have been assessed upon knight's fees. It was paid by
both churchmen and laymen, and the rate appears to have been
uniformly twenty shillings a fee in the shires administered directly
by the king's ministers.[4] We use this guarded language, because the
tax was demanded in respect of knight's fees outside these boundaries,
from Carmarthen and from the bishopric of Durham[5] and perhaps
from elsewhere, and in these outlying areas the rate appears to have
been one mark a fee. We cannot speak more definitely because the
bulk of the entries concerning this aid must have been on the pipe
roll of 1129, which is lost, and on the roll of 1130 the entries relate
only to unpaid balances carried forward and amounts which, for
some reason or other, were in dispute. The levy, we have said, is
described as *auxilium militum*, but it is also qualified as *vetus*. The
adjective evidently distinguishes this aid from one more recent, and
we are safe in inferring that the latter had been demanded in 1130
and had not been brought to account by Michaelmas of that year,
because otherwise it would have left its mark on the pipe roll. When
then was the 'old knights' aid' demanded? The reply seems to be
that it was put in collection after the death of Ranulf Flambard on
5 September 1128, for it is only by reason of the voidance of the see
that an account for Durham figures on the pipe roll.[6] The knights
of the bishopric are now liable directly to the Crown and it is the
keeper of the temporalities who accounts at the exchequer. It is
noticeable that the Durham knights are said to make a *donum*,[7] but,

---

[1] Round, *Feudal England*, pp. 268-9 (*Regesta*, no. 1499); *Pipe Roll, 31 Henry I*, p. 44.
[2] Below, pp. 160-2.
[3] *Pipe Roll, 31 Henry I*, pp. 49, 84, 89, 132, 153-4.
[4] This is to be inferred from the common factor in the round figures for debts, no part
of which had apparently been paid in 1129, namely 60s., 100s and £25 (*ibid.*, pp. 49,
84, 154).
[5] *Ibid.*, pp. 89, 132. For the Carmarthenshire items see Lloyd, *History of Wales*, p. 428.
[6] Below, pp. 225-6.
[7] *Ibid.*, p. 132: 'de dono militum episcopatus'.

as students of the pipe rolls will be aware, a *donum* differs from an *auxilium* only in name and it may be synonymous with scutage.[1]

The interest of these entries as a whole for the history of taxation does not seem to have been appreciated; but to discuss most of them further would lead us far afield. Here we are concerned particularly with only two of them: £25 demanded of the bishop of Exeter and 100 shillings demanded of the abbot of Croyland. Now the *servitium debitum* of the bishop under Henry II seems to have been assessed at 17½ fees, though he appears to have admitted to no more than 15½; but in addition he seems to have been assessed at 7½ fees in respect of the chapelry of Bosham in Sussex, an assessment which he also contested and from which he was ultimately relieved.[2] It appears evident that in 1128 a demand was made on him on the basis of twenty-five fees and that he disputed the liability. Against the abbot of Croyland, on the other hand, no *servitium debitum* was charged under Henry II: he was regarded as exempt.[3] In this light it does not seem remarkable that after two years neither the bishop nor the abbot had made any payment. Is not the most probable explanation this, that, when the demands were made, the bishop demurred that the sum demanded of him was excessive and that the abbot protested that he was not liable? We submit that we are justified in adducing these two entries as further evidence that under Henry I the barons of the exchequer were as yet in the initial stages of determining liabilities for scutage.

We may now revert to the cases of the bishops of Ely and Norwich. There can be no reasonable doubt that the rate of scutage under Henry I was sometimes a mark and sometimes twenty shillings, although we do not know the circumstances in which the lower rate was charged: our inferences from the pipe roll of 1130 are confirmed by a private charter of the reign of Stephen which mentions these two rates.[4] The same rates, we may add, were still regarded as customary in 1166.[5] It follows that, assuming the higher rate, the bishops were each charged upon the basis of sixty fees: at the lower rate, which seems unlikely, the number of fees would be ninety. Even if we were to assume, as, indeed, has been done,[6] that an exception-

---

[1] Round, *Feudal England*, pp. 275-6; *Red Book of the Exchequer*, i.415-8; *Pipe Roll, 5 Henry II*, pp. 31-2.

[2] The facts are complicated (Chew, *op. cit.*, pp. 4-5, 19). Miss Chew, following Round, gives another explanation of the bishop's assessment, but she does not seem to have known of the entry in the pipe roll of 1130.

[3] Chew, *op. cit.*, p. 10. If under Henry I Evesham and Wilton were assessed at five knight's fees as they were later (*ibid.*, pp. 5, 20), then the barons of the exchequer were in 1128-9 attempting to bring Croyland into line. The abbot did pay at this rate, very exceptionally, in 1159 as a contribution to the scutage of Toulouse (*Pipe Roll, 5 Henry II* p. 65).

[4] Charter of Gilbert, earl of Pembroke (1138-48/9), in favour of the church of St. Mary, Southwark, printed by Round, *Studies in the Red Book of the Exchequer*, pp. 8-9, from Nero C iii, fo. 228.

[5] *Red Book of the Exchequer*, i.193. These rates appear to have been exceeded only once in Henry II's reign: see the table in Ramsay, *Revenues of the Kings of England*, i.195.

[6] Stenton, *First Century*, pp. 181-3.

ally high rate was on occasion charged, we could hardly suppose that it exceeded the highest rate.quite exceptionally levied under Henry II, namely two marks a fee. But if we divide £60 by this rate, we shall not obtain as the answer to our sum the number of fees recognised as the assessment of both churches in Henry II's reign, namely forty.[1] It is then quite evident that, whatever rate of scutage we can assume to have been imposed under Henry I, the known demands upon these two churches in his reign are inconsistent with their *servitium debitum* under Henry II. And not only was the liability of churches evidently uncertain under Henry I but so also was the liability of lay barons. On the occasion of one of Henry I's expeditions against the Welsh there had been a dispute regarding the services due from the honour of Arundel, and it had been necessary to make enquiry by the oath of four of the oldest and most trustworthy knights of the honour, from whose verdict there was no appeal.[2]

There are many other signs of uncertainty even in 1166. The most striking instance is that of Westminster Abbey which was charged with scutage upon seventy-five fees in 1156, an assessment subsequently reduced to fifteen on the abbot's protest.[3] On the other hand the bishops of Ely and Norwich were assessed, if not at the beginning of the reign, very shortly afterwards, at forty fees.[4] How this reduction from the assessment under Henry I was effected we can but conjecture, though we may perhaps reflect that the bishop of Ely was Nigel, the all-powerful finance minister of Henry II. If the assessment of ecclesiastical tenants-in-chief, who seem usually to have commuted their liability, was a matter of uncertainty, it is likely that the assessment of lay barons would be even more uncertain, and this is evident from the returns they made in 1166. If a few alleged that their service had been fixed from the Conquest, which could be no more than tradition,[5] there is a more general air of doubt.[6] The explanation would appear to be that, just as in the thirteenth century new *servitia debita* were established, not by any single administrative act, but gradually by the acceptance of bargains and compromises that hardened into custom, so in much the same way *servitia debita* were established in the twelfth century.

What does need explanation is how it came about that, when firm figures were arrived at in 1166, both ecclesiastical and lay fiefs alike followed a certain pattern. Though there are a number of fiefs that are rated at fifty or twenty-five knight's fees, the prevailing pattern is a rate of sixty or forty fees or some precise fraction of these figures, thirty, twenty, fifteen and ten. There are two or three large fiefs

---

[1] Round, *Feudal England*, p. 249; Chew, *op. cit.*, pp. 4, 19.
[2] *Red Book of the Exchequer*, i.200-1; Round, *op. cit.*, p. 245.
[3] *Pipe Roll, 2 Henry II*, pp. 63-4; Chew, *op. cit.*, pp. 5, 20.
[4] *Ibid.*, p. 19.   [5] *Red Book of the Exchequer*, i.382, 400.
[5] See the particulars collected by Round, *op. cit.*, pp. 244-5, 257-8.

that do not fall into this pattern and a number of small fiefs with odd numbers of fees which could well be the result of bargaining or the division of estates.[1] The puzzle is to account not for these but for those that conform to a pattern. Now it would seem obvious that a round number like sixty, fifty and so on would be very easy to re-member and very simple to record. Every time a summons was addressed to a tenant-in-chief, he would, one would have thought, assemble his troops, arranged in six, five or four constabularies down to a single constabulary, and by constant repetition this arrangement would have impressed itself upon the minds of tenants-in-chief, mesne tenants, household knights and everyone else concerned. Why then should it come about that those making a return in 1166 of the assessment of their fiefs under Henry I should have had to resort to the memories of the ancients (*antiqui*) or be obliged to say 'non sumus certi' or 'secundum quod scire possumus'?[2] Can it be that the disturbances of Stephen's reign had so dislocated ancient practices that after less than twenty years the memory of them was effaced? This seems improbable. The reason why reference was made to the position in Henry I's reign was not because of any such un-certainty but because Henry II, in this as in other matters, refused to acknowledge the legitimacy of any arrangements in the usurper's reign and insisted that his rights were founded upon the rights en-joyed by his grandfather. But if *servitia debita* had been generally or universally established in Henry I's reign, it is notable that the writ calling for the returns of 1166 makes no reference to any such thing and does not call for a statement of the *servitium debitum* from each tenant-in chief, but instead asks for (*a*) the number of knights en-feoffed on the day Henry I died, (*b*) the number enfeoffed since then and (*c*) the number of knight's fees in the tenant's demesne, which seems to have been understood to mean the number of knights in the tenant's household.[3] Now it is remarkable that, despite the un-certainties in the minds of those making the returns, the figures under the first and third heads should in so many cases add up exactly to sixty, fifty, forty and so on, and it would seem evident that those concerned had not infrequently put their heads together and devised a common formula for their replies, aided perhaps by suggestions from above, for as a rule everything seems to have been arranged between the exchequer and the sheriffs on the one hand and the barons upon the other.[4] Doubtless there were exceptions where the return is the original composition of the baron, but these were rela-tively few. It is remarkable, too, that ecclesiastical tenants-in-chief should conform to the same pattern, although, as we have seen, there could have been no certainty as to their obligations even late

---

[1] Round, *op. cit.*, pp. 253-7.   [2] As Round pointed out, *op. cit.*, pp. 244-5, 257-8.
[3] Round, *op. cit.*, pp. 238-9.
[4] Cf. *ibid.*, p. 240. For introductory clauses on a common model see *Red Book of the Exchequer*, i.270, 275, 276, 277; for concluding formulas, *ibid.*, pp. 347, 348, 351.

in Henry I's reign: here again the maximum figure is sixty, with all the larger fiefs to pattern, apart, that is, from those privileged houses, either exempt or with a very low rating.[1]

If, as seems to us most probable, the neat figures of the *servitium debitum* are not as a rule historical but are arranged according to a formula, whence was this formula derived? To that question no certain answer can be given, although we can rule out Normandy which presents a very different picture in 1172, a picture which cannot have changed essentially since the days of Henry I. We cannot speak with certainty of the days of the Conqueror, for there is no written evidence; but there is no probability that the marked characteristics of knight service in the twelfth century were not already present in the duchy. In Normandy the quotas of knight service were much smaller than in England, and though there are some as high as twenty, the general run is much less.[2] The only point in common is the recurrence of the factor of five; but that factor is to be found just as prominently in the military obligations of hundreds and estates in pre-Conquest England. A more suggestive parallel may perhaps be drawn from the saga of Harold Fairhair, a younger contemporary of Alfred the Great, of whom it is related that, when he had conquered those parts of Norway not yet under his control, he required every earl (*jarl*) to furnish the royal army with sixty warriors and every *herse*—a rank that can be roughly equated with baron —with twenty warriors.[3] Even if it be objected that saga history is not veridical, yet the tradition is significant, and it may be more than a coincidence that the same figure of sixty knights was the quota required from the barons to whom Henry II granted the kingdoms of Cork and Limerick.[4]

The suggestion we have to make is that *servitia debita*, far from having been introduced at the Conquest, were gradually established, first by the occasional settlement of disputes, as at Arundel, and thereafter by reducing those of uncertain amount to something approaching a uniform standard, beginning with ecclesiastical fiefs and culminating in the general review of 1166. This uniform standard was not derived from Norman practice, but appears to be associated with a widespread, traditional convention.[5] The exact point on the scale at which a quota was fixed would doubtless be a matter of

---

[1] Chew, *op. cit.*, pp. 4-5, 19-20; above, p. 68.

[2] For the whole of Normandy we have figures only for 1172 (*Red Book of the Exchequer*, ii.624-45; *Historiens de la France*, xxiii.693-8), but the figures for that year in respect of the bishopric of Bayeux are substantially the same as those revealed by the inquest of 1133, and the figures of 1133 reflect those of the eleventh century.

[3] *Heimskringla*, Harald Haarfayre's Saga, ch. 6 (Jónsson, pp. 44-5; Monsen, p. 46). Note, too, another parallel: the earls have the third penny of the revenue of the shire.

[4] 'Benedict of Peterborough', i.163. Hugh de Lacy had the grant of Meath for the service of 100 knights.

[5] Round himself drew attention to a late parallel (1322-8) in Navarre which is cited in Ducange, without a precise reference, *s.v.* 'barones' (*Feudal England*, p. 288). Since he was ignorant of the Scandinavian parallel, he did not appreciate the significance of the widespread occurrence of the same range of figures.

individual negotiation, in which the circumstances of each fief and any earlier arrangement would enter into consideration. In this way it is possible to account not only for the regular quotas (if we may so term them), but also for occasional irregularities and the quotas of fifty and twenty-five. But conjecture cannot be driven too far, and no purpose is to be served by substituting one insubstantial hypothesis for another. The points we would stress are, firstly, that the organisation of troops in multiples of five or ten was no more 'feudal' than the employment of mounted soldiers in warfare, and, secondly, that there is no evidence for the general determination of *servitia debita* before the reign of Henry II and that such evidence as we have for the reign of Henry I points, not to any settled system, but to uncertainty. Above all, we would stress that no deductions regarding the size, composition, organisation or disposition of the armed forces of the Norman and Angevin kings can be based upon the *servitia debita*, whether those conventionally ascribed to Henry I or those determined in 1166 which increased those conventional figures by the number of knight's fees created since 1135. And one last word: when we speak of the armies of this period, the one adjective we should above all avoid is 'feudal'.

V

CONQUEST AND SETTLEMENT

IN the preceding chapters we have endeavoured to remove misconceptions which have, in our view, led to much exaggeration of
the effect of the Norman Conquest on English society. As we shall
show, it was the conquest of Normandy by the English king that had
consequences in every respect more momentous and lasting. This
was, it is true, an indirect consequence of the battle of Hastings, yet
no necessary consequence but the chance result of the incapacity of
Duke Robert and the unscrupulous ability of Henry I. But the substitution of a dynasty of foreign kings and a foreign aristocracy, the
subordination of the native speech in favour of a foreign tongue, the
introduction of foreign conceptions of law: these are no light matters.
Yet how far was the current of English life diverted; how far were
the invaders absorbed into English society; how far did they desire
or endeavour to change or to mould it?

And here perhaps we may cite some words of Edward Freeman's.
Freeman has long been under a cloud, but it seems to us that, of all
the historians during the last hundred years, he wrote the wisest
words on the consequences of the Conquest. 'The chief points to be
borne in mind', he said, 'are that there was no one moment when a
"Feudal System" was introduced into England; that the feudal
tenures of land were developed gradually; that in England they were
merely a system of land tenure, and had not the political results
which they had in other countries; lastly, that they had nothing to
do with any formal distinction between men of Norman and men of
English birth.'[1] He might have added that this was because such
changes as there were operated within the framework of the Old
English polity and institutions. 'Feudalism', if it was ever more than
an arbitrary pattern imposed by modern writers upon men long
dead and events long since past, was never more than a shadow of
itself in England. There was no cataclysmic change. And so, despite
the spilt blood, the cruelties, the injustices, the hatreds; despite all
there was to divide the conquered from the conquerors, intensified
by the difference in language; despite the constant pull of Normandy
which ensured that the barons remained French in speech and
thought: before Henry II's reign was at an end the two peoples had
effected some kind of union. If there were rulers and ruled, lords

[1] *Norman Conquest*, v.864.

and men, French-speaking superiors and English-speaking in-
feriors, there were no longer conquerors and conquered. But while
there was a unified English polity, there was at the same time an
Anglo-Norman state with so much in common, in organisation and
law, that it stood distinct and apart from the congeries of states
which made up the misnamed Angevin empire. There were differences between the organisation and law of the two countries, most
markedly in their distinctive local administrations which retained,
largely unmodified, their pre-Conquest character. But these differences were slight in comparison with the differences between
England and Normandy on the one hand and Anjou, Poitou
and Aquitaine on the other. The central administration of both
England and Normandy had evolved upon a common pattern,
a pattern not native to either, but imposed from above. This, as we
shall show, is the cardinal factor in twelfth-century history; but, let
us emphasise, it was not a necessary consequence of the Conquest
of 1066.

In the early days of the Conquest, tentative attempts had been
made to utilise and continue the services and authority of the Old
English aristocracy,[1] but after the revolts of 1069 and 1075 the
juxtaposition of English and French, with very few exceptions, did
not take place at the highest levels but at lower levels, in the towns
and in the countryside. Scattered handfuls of foreigners, outnum-
bered and unwelcome, thrust themselves, or were thrust, among
vengeful natives. Frenchmen were so frequently slain by undiscover-
able assailants that any unidentifiable murdered man was presumed
not to be English, and the consequences were visited upon the
neighbourhood.[2] For a century a smouldering hostility continued.
Yet co-operation was essential to ensure the continuance of an
organised state of any sort. If the king's court and the king's council,
the baronial honour courts, could function though they were exclusively French, the courts of the shire, the hundred, the manor,
were, of necessity, mainly English. It is at this level that continuity
was assured. The interpenetration of the two societies left, it is true,
the lowest levels untouched, the mass of the people, the peasants, the
poorer townsmen. But French became the gentlemanly language for
men of English as of French descent; French culture, the culture of
the Île de France, became fashionable. This, however, was the work
of the twelfth century. The stratification of languages continued
until the fifteenth century; and just as the English language emerged
profoundly modified in vocabulary and structure, so the English

[1] For the employment of Englishmen see Stenton, *Anglo-Saxon England*, pp. 615-7.
The known facts are, however, very few. We need not give references to the original
authorities, which are sufficiently indicated in Freeman, *Norman Conquest*, iv.233-318,
573-85, and Ramsay, *Foundations of England*, ii.66-73, 102-5.
[2] 'Leges Henrici', 92.6. For the murder fine see 'Articuli', x, 3; 'Leis Willelme', 22;
'Leges Edwardi Confessoris', 15, 16 (*Gesetze*, i.487, 510, 608, 641-2). See also below,
pp. 178-80.

polity emerged as a blend of French and English elements, with much that was as original as any invention of man can be.

Assimilation then was the work of centuries, but accommodation, an uneasy accommodation doubtless, had to be almost immediate. Let us look at the position from the village level. In the manor in the days of the Conqueror, the new tenant, whether he was lord of it or a sub-tenant, was the heir of some dead or dispossessed Englishman. In a sense an English tenure was transformed into a Norman tenure, but, as a matter of law, the transformation cannot have presented great difficulty nor, so far as we can discern, did the position of an incoming Frenchman differ materially from that of an Englishman who was fortunate enough to be left undisturbed. The very words of the charters that have come down to us attest, as we have seen, the persistence of native principles of tenure. Of the incidents of tenure as they were affected by the Conquest we shall speak shortly, but in the first place it seems desirable to say something of the public duties which fell upon all freeholders, whether French or English, because this was a factor of the greatest importance in the absorption of the newcomers into English society. So far as the French intruder was concerned here was a new experience, an additional burden arising out of the tenure of his English fief. In Normandy there were no shire courts or hundred courts; but English local administration depended upon their efficient working and, since the intruding tenant of English land succeeded not only to the profits but also to the burdens attached to it, he owed suit to the local courts. It is notable that, when we come to learn of these courts after half a century of Norman rule, we are told nothing to suggest that Frenchmen played any different part from that of Englishmen. Such divisions as we can perceive are between large landowners and small landowners, between the *barones comitatus* and the lesser freemen. These barons of the shire are the men whom Bracton will call *buzones*, the leading men who in the thirteenth, as in the twelfth, century determined what the judgement of the court should be.[1] The small men followed their lead: indeed, they did not dare pass a judgement without them.[2] Now doubtless the barons of the shire were predominantly Frenchmen; but the English suitors were at first in a strong position because they alone knew the customary law and the ancient procedure. The local court of necessity became bilingual and, while the pre-Conquest practice of addressing writs to the county court in English was continued for some time,[3] it was found simpler to trans-

---

[1] Below, pp. 181-5. We may note here that *buzo* is a latinisation of *bouzon*, the almost exact equivalent of modern slang 'big shot', for the word means an arrow or crossbow bolt of larger size than that normally used: see Godefroy, *Dictionnaire*, s.v. *boujon*, and Tobler-Lammatsch, *Altfranzösische Wörterbuch*, s.v. *bouzon*.   [2] Below, p. 183.

[3] Five only of Henry I are catalogued in volume ii of the *Regesta*, nos. 506, 532, 840, 1055, 1388, the latest being conjecturally dated 1123. But writs of transitory importance are much less likely to be preserved than formal charters, and we must remember that the muniments of laymen, especially of the twelfth century, have rarely survived.

mit writs in Latin which, until the end of the thirteenth century and perhaps later, were translated into the two vernaculars.[1] We guess, and we do not think that we guess wildly, that the stratification we perceive elsewhere in the twelfth and thirteenth centuries was early established in the local courts. The poorer suitors spoke English and had little influence, though the ancestors of some of them may well have come over· with the Conqueror. The well-to-do, whether French or English in origin, spoke French and took the leading part: they were the county aristocracy. But this superiority was not all gain: as time went on, these French-speaking aristocrats had heavier and heavier burdens laid upon them as the king's justice became better organised and all-pervading. Of this development we shall, however, speak a little later. Here we would emphasise how it was that suit to the local courts forced the newcomers to play their part in maintaining Old English institutions and how in this way the distinction between conqueror and conquered came to be blurred and French speech came gradually to mean no more than social superiority.

The French intruders, let us repeat, replaced Englishmen— Englishmen of many social grades. The manner in which this was done has been obscured by an absurd controversy regarding the size or value of a knight's fee. Determined to assert the discontinuity between the Old English and Norman society and to combat 'the anticataclysmic tendencies of modern thought', J. H. Round found it a necessary conclusion 'that the knight's fee held by an under-tenant consisted normally of an estate worth £20 a year and was not based on the "five hides" of the Anglo-Saxon system'.[2] There is, it need hardly be said, no evidence that anyone in the eleventh century connected knight's fees with a standard annual revenue. Such conceptions belong to an age when knighthood had become identified with an elevated social class, the county aristocracy, and this, as we shall show, was the gradual work of the twelfth century. Round, however, was merely echoing, without verification, one of Stubbs's varying opinions: 'the value of the knight's fee must already [in the time of Lanfranc] have been fixed at twenty pounds a year'.[3] But the only evidence Stubbs adduced was a wild invention by the monks of Christ Church in the year 1188.[4] Nor are Round's ingenuous

[1] See Morris, *Early English County Court*, p. 173, no. 34. We have here the explanation of the French and English 'proclamations' of 1258 (*Foedera*, i.377-8; *Select Charters*, pp. 387-8).

[2] *Feudal England*, p. 295. Round is here continuing a discussion begun at pp. 225-35.

[3] *Constitutional History* (1st ed.), i.262; (6th ed.), i.285.

[4] *Epistolae Cantuarienses*, p. 225. We have already commented upon this fiction: above, p. 80, n. 1. When a value was put upon a knight's fee in the latter part of the reign of Henry II, the minimum was an annual value of 15 marks: the 16 marks of the received text of the Assize of Arms is an obvious scribal error (*Select Charters*, p. 183). We can thus account for the £10 valuation (15 ms.) which is found elsewhere (Stenton, *First Century* pp. 166-9). This is the valuation of the fee of a knight *cum plenis armis*; the half fee, that is the fee of a knight *cum planis armis*, was reckoned at 10 marks: for the distinction between fully armed and lightly armed knights see Guilhiermoz, *Essai sur l'origine de la noblesse*,

statistical enquiries more helpful.[1] One of the most valuable pieces of evidence for the persistence of the five-hide unit is provided by the list of tenants of Abingdon Abbey, dating (in the form we have it) from early in the reign of Henry I, that was thrust by a continuator into the chronicle of the abbey. Round drew figures from that list in order to demonstrate that there were many fees departing from a five-hide standard; but we have only to plot the whole of the available figures graphically in order to demonstrate that five hides constitute the norm and that deviations are small or exceptional. Trouble had even been taken by the abbot to group three holdings, containing respectively two hides, two hides and one hide, so as to compose a fee of five hides.[2] And when ordered by the Conqueror to provide a fief for a knight, the abbot carved an estate of precisely five hides from villein tenements belonging to the abbey.[3] Again Round's 'proof to the contrary' proves his own inability to grasp the nature of the problem.

As nearly every page of Domesday Book demonstrates, the intruders had been fitted into a pre-determined framework of tenements, and in southern England, the land of hidation, this framework had been in large part determined by a system of five-hide units of remote antiquity. It follows, therefore, that a Norman military fief, or rather the more important among them, inevitably tended to represent a thegn's estate. If this is true of southern England, there is no reason to doubt that it is generally true also of northern England where direct evidence is wanting. So far as concerns southern England, the evidence from Berkshire appears to be conclusive. We know from Domesday Book that in that county five hides had to furnish one knight (*miles*) for the fyrd.[4] And when we turn to the pre-Conquest assessments of the estates of Abingdon Abbey as recorded in Domesday Book, hundred by hundred,[5] we see that with comparatively few exceptions they are in multiples of five hides. Even the exceptions may be no more than apparent. Thus in Roborough hundred Chiveley is rated at 27 hides, Welford at

pp. 183, 187-8 *n*. These figures were still accepted in 1230, and the reference in the commissions of 13 June of that year to the ordinance (now lost) of John's reign (*Close Rolls, 1227-1231*, pp. 398-402) shows that there had been no change in half a century. This rating, however, had ceased to be realistic and in 1242 it was raised by a half, the knight's fee now being rated at £15 and the half fee at £10 (*Select Charters*, p. 363). It must be emphasised that these figures are minima and in a sense conventional. They were intended as a guide to those responsible for the array of arms. There is nothing to suggest that they were applied to the equally conventional, but independent, assessment for scutage.

[1] *Feudal England*, p. 295.

[2] *Chron. Mon. de Abingdon*, ii.4-5. Some apparent anomalies appear capable of a simple solution. Thus two knight's fees, each composed of ten hides, would seem to be cases of beneficial infeudation; four knight's fees, totalling nineteen hides, and three knight's fees, totalling fourteen hides, also indicate original five-hide units. The date of the list is indicated by the names of the better-known tenants, Herbert fitz Herbert (chamberlain), Hugh Buckland (died *c*. 1115), Gilbert Marshal, Walter Giffard, Walter de la Rivière.

[3] *Ibid.*, p. 7.

[4] D.B., i.56 b 1: Si rex mittebat alicubi exercitum, de v. hidis tantum unus miles ibat.

[5] D.B., i.58 b-59 b. The particulars may be more easily read in the abstract printed in *E.H.R.*, xliv.623; but this has no independent value.

50 hides, Beedon at 10 hides and Benham at two hides. It may well be that at one time Chiveley and Benham together made up 30 hides, giving a total of 90 hides for this hundred. We note also that in Hornmere hundred the 50 hides of Cumnor and the 60 hides of Barton make up 110 hides, so that the abbey's estates in the two hundreds together will provide 200 hides. Again, we may note that in Marcham hundred, though there are two estates at Linford, one rated at seven and the other at three hides, together they give us the ten hides we should expect. We cannot explain away all the exceptions, for behind these assessments there lies much history. Land has been acquired by the abbey and doubtless land has been lost. But we cannot doubt that long ago, perhaps in the tenth century, the estates of the abbey had been somewhat arbitrarily assessed in units of five hides for fiscal and military purposes. We have seen already that, on the estates of Abingdon Abbey, thegns had holdings of five hides or held lands closely approximating to five hides or multiples of five hides, and it was the holdings of those thegns who had followed Harold's banner or had been concerned in a subsequent revolt that escheated and were available for the Conqueror's followers.[1] The inference must obviously be that in Berkshire the obligation to furnish a knight for every five hides had been met by —if we may use a later word—'enfeoffing' thegns with estates of that amount of land or multiples of that amount or perhaps estates that approximated in value to other estates of that amount. Nor is there reason to suppose that there was any special custom in Berkshire: sufficient evidence exists to show that the same process was at work in other parts of southern England.[2]

But here we should perhaps introduce qualifications. The persistence of the five-hide unit has been rightly regarded as the most obvious thread linking pre-Conquest and post-Conquest tenures and obligations. Wherever after the Conquest we find a military tenant with a holding of five hides, we assume an unbroken chain of descent. The assumption may not be infallible for, as we have seen, a five-hide fief might be created after 1066, but in the great majority of cases an alternative explanation is not obvious.[3] Although this is by no means the only indication of continuity, it is important because it is a thread easily recognisable. Those historians who are reluctant to abandon Round's teaching and continue to believe that there was a cataclysmic change soon after 1066, marked by the introduction of knight service, a novelty supposedly unknown in pre-Conquest

---

[1] *Chron. Mon. de Abingdon*, i.484-5, 490-1, 493; ii.3. Doubtless writs had been addressed to the Berkshire county court, as they had to the county courts of Norfolk and Suffolk, requiring the forfeiture of the lands of tenants of religious houses who had been slain in opposing the Conqueror (*Regesta*, no. 40).

[2] Round, *Feudal England*, pp. 293-5; Hollings in *E.H.R.*, lxiii.453-87.

[3] Curiously enough, this was Round's own explanation: 'The circumstance of a fee, in many cases consisting of five-hides, is merely, I think, due to the existence of five-hide estates, survivals from the previous régime' (*op. cit.*, p. 293).

England, can point, as he did, to the many examples of military fiefs existing within a short interval from the Conquest that bear no obvious relation to the five-hide unit. But we cannot assume that the English system of tenure and obligations had been rigid and that on the eve of the Conquest the country was neatly and universally divided into five-hide units or that holdings, greater or less, departing from this scheme were not then to be found.[1] On the contrary, all that we know of the Old English state suggests that, since the remote period when the five-hide unit and the related hundred had been evolved, there had been continuous change and attrition. Burdens had been lightened in some instances and increased in others. The creation successively of burghal districts, of shires and franchises, the Danish conquests, the introduction of mercenaries, could not leave the older structure unimpaired. Beneficial hidation and pejorative hidation—less service for the same hidage, the same service for a reduced hidage—concessions for piety, for favour or for poverty, harder terms for the prosperous or the eager bargainer: there were scores of reasons why the burdens laid upon land should shift and change while conventional reckonings in hidage or hundreds should remain.

When, however, it was a question of replacing an English thegn by a French baron, a freeman by a vavassor, there could have been no nice computation of assessments or values. What, after all, did a hide mean to a Norman? Here was a township, a manor, that had escheated to the king and upon it there were burdens, by no likelihood known with any precision to the would-be acquirer. If he obtained the grant, the new possessor took his fief as a gift or, it may be, as a purchase and as it was, devastated or in full working order: not till afterwards did he slowly learn its boundaries, its value, its potentialities and its burdens. That in this gradual and piecemeal process the number of knights demanded by the king was nicely related to the number of five-hide units or any other units of pre-Conquest service must be the wildest improbability. How the number of knights due from a tenant-in-chief was ultimately settled we can but speculate. As we have made plain, we have not found the speculations of others very profitable and, in particular, the speculations of J. H. Round, which have inexplicably won general favour. We have therefore endeavoured to substitute an inference from the available evidence which seems to us much more probable, which suggests, not an immutable scheme imposed in the first few years of the Conquest, but a gradually evolving series of conventions which did not achieve schematic form until the reign of Henry II.

Let us agree, for the admission is inevitable, that, when the Conqueror granted fiefs to his followers, he can have done so only on

[1] Cf. D.B., i.83 a 1: Bricsi tenuit miles regis Edwardi et geldebat pro xii. hidis.

terms with which the Normans were familiar, though not, as Domesday Book itself bears witness, on those terms alone. Norman precedents were followed at some distance. The situation was an entirely novel one and, whatever ideas of tenure and services the Normans had, these were necessarily applied in circumstances beyond their experience. And then again, the fiefs the Conqueror granted cannot have been made as a rounded whole. The land of England did not become all at once available for distribution. King William cannot have said in 1070, as Round would have had us believe and as the saga may suggest that Harold Fairhair had once said in Norway: 'Here are your fiefs, created out of lands of rebels that have escheated to me as the rightful heir to the English crown. You shall rank as a count and shall do me service with sixty knights.' Nor can he have said to a man not so high in his favour: 'You shall rank as a baron and shall do me service with twenty knights.' True, the span of years between 1066 and 1086 is barely twenty, but in those years much history had been compressed. So far as we can see, escheats, forfeitures, had been individual, not universal, though they might approach universality by 1086. Grants consequently had been made piecemeal. At no time was there *tabula rasa*. Nor can it be a matter of certainty that, as grant was added to grant, so the service demanded of the count or baron was increased. We may doubt, indeed, whether such a picture corresponds at all to reality. Yet if the history of Norman fiefs is any guide to the process by which Frenchmen were settled upon English lands, we must suppose that the idea of knight service was bound up with the idea of a fief. It by no means follows, however, that the service due had, even by 1086, been fixed at a given number of knights or that this quota, whenever and however it was determined, bore any relation to the number of soldiers that King William's followers brought with them or maintained as their troop in the army of occupation which held England down during his reign. When we obtain light on the practice in Normandy—and the most ancient comes from the reign of Henry I —it is evident that the tendency was for the service due to the duke to be much less than the number of knights dependent upon the greater feudatories.[1] Thus the bishop of Bayeux had in his own service 120 knights, but the extent of his service to the duke appears to have been no more than twenty.[2] And we must remember that, although Abbot Turold had a troop of 160, the service due from the church of Peterborough, an exceptionally high quota, was no more than sixty knights.[3] All the men in the abbot's train were, it

---

[1] There is good reason to believe that the return of 1172 (*Red Book of the Exchequer*, ii.624-45; *Historiens de la France*, xxiii.693-8) reflects the arrangements of the eleventh century.

[2] This was the position in 1133 as shown by the inquest of that year (Navel, *L'enquête de 1133*, pp. 14, 43-4) and, by inference, before the death of Bishop Odo in 1097 (*ibid.*, pp. 41-2; Round, *Family Origins*, p. 209).   [3] Above, pp. 69-70.

would seem, such as the compilers of Domesday Book would have called *milites* and the English would have called knights. Not all the men in troops such as this were, however, so fortunate as to be enfeoffed with English lands: there was, in sober fact, no room for all.[1] Some doubtless had no wish to settle away from home; some found no favour; some were discharged; some remained to the end of their days as household knights. But the residue of the rank and file must be represented among the *milites*, too insignificant to be named by their proper name, whose presence is capriciously noticed in Domesday Book. They were fitted, as occasion presented itself, into vacant holdings, sometimes doubtless made vacant by violent disseisins. They were in turn themselves liable to be disseised to make room for others still more favoured.[2] There were fragmentations and aggregations of holdings. But when the upheaval was past, the pattern was very much as it had been: the pieces upon the chequered cloth had changed, but their places and their function remained substantially unaltered.

There were in 1086 knights everywhere in England, many times those who are specifically called knights in Domesday Book, of as many types as there were social grades among freemen; and doubtless some knights were of such humble origin as to be indistinguishable from the unfree peasantry around them.[3] To speak of knighthood in those days as though it depended upon a property qualification is an absurdity. But the conception of knighthood changed; and if we cannot say that the change was rapid, yet we may say that it progressed visibly from generation to generation. The knights in the returns to the enquiry of 1166 are likely to have been men of a much more exclusive status than the knights of Domesday Book; but, even so, it is probable that the one word covered a good many differences of status, even in 1166, and not all the enfeoffed knights of the baronial *cartae* are likely to have been regarded as *barones comitatus*.[4] It follows necessarily that we merely befog ourselves if we seek to relate the *servitia debita* of 1166 to the enfeoffment of knights under the Conqueror, for which we have the evidence of Domesday Book. We cannot fit incommensurables together. The humbler knights of 1086 are not likely to have been succeeded by men who were regarded as knights in 1166. But in so far as knights of a superior status were enfeoffed, since their fiefs had in some way to be related to

---

[1] The constant recruitment of mercenaries for service in England was necessary as the control of the Norman king extended over the country: on this point we have given sufficient references in the preceding chapter. We must rid our minds of any idea that the foreign soldiers in the army of occupation had 'come over with William the Conqueror'. The original force was quite small: a band of adventurers and soldiers of fortune. Its augmentation must have been a relatively slow process.

[2] See the evidence collected by Miss Chew, and especially the case of Evesham Abbey (*Ecclesiastical Tenants in Chief*, pp. 116-9).

[3] Vinogradoff, *English Society*, pp. 74-8.

[4] *Red Book of the Exchequer*, i.186-445. The *cartae* do not seem to have been studied from this aspect: but differences in rank are easily perceptible.

existing holdings, there was a great probability that such a knight would be found in a holding previously held by a thegn and would render the services that had been rendered in the past by English thegns. It is, in any case, a remarkable fact that the tradition of the five-hide unit as a fair basis for the fee of one knight, a superior knight, survived for long in southern and midland England.[1]

At this point we turn to consider the question of sub-infeudation after the Conquest, to which, we venture to assert, a mistaken significance has been accorded as testifying in some way to the introduction of 'military feudalism' in England.[2] Few charters of enfeoffment are, in fact, known for the fifty years after the Conquest. Doubtless they represent no more than a fraction of those actually issued; but it is unlikely that a great many enfeoffments were at this period confirmed by a written deed. If we are forced to the conclusion that few of the Conqueror's grants were committed to writing, we cannot suppose that many of his tenants-in-chief employed written instruments. But though post-Conquest charters are few, they may still tell us something of value. The first we select for notice is a grant by the Norman abbot of Westminster, Gilbert Crispin, to William Baynard. This is not a grant in fee and inheritance: on the contrary it is very strictly limited to the life of the beneficiary. If, as seems certain, the beneficiary, William Baynard, is to be identified with the Bainiard who is recorded in Domesday Book as holding what appears to be the same land, then the date of the grant must be placed in the years 1085-6. Previously the land was held by a thegn named Wulfric, and William Baynard—who, we may note, is a member of a Norman family of some distinction— succeeds to all his predecessor's rights, and since in return for the grant William is to do service as a knight, the inference is that Wulfric had also served as a knight. And then there is a reference to the other knights who hold lands of the abbey, for William is to give the same aids as they do. These knights seem clearly to be quite distinct from the knights who, so Domesday Book tells us, were housed near the abbey and who appear to have been mercenaries quartered upon the abbot. These mercenary knights may well be a new and unwelcome introduction, but the landed knights are, for all that appears to the contrary, the successors to, or, it may be, identical with, the knights who served the abbot under Edward the Confessor. It is only if we place this charter against an imaginary background of cataclysmic change that we can read into it some new invention. There is nothing in it that is 'feudal'. After William Baynard suffered forfeiture, as he seems to have done in 1110, his lands, including the abbey land which he held for life, passed to

---

[1] Vinogradoff, *op. cit.*, pp. 55, 58-9; Hollings in *E.H.R.*, lxiii.454, 464.
[2] Cf. Douglas and Greenaway, *English Historical Documents*, p. 895. Mr Douglas had previously expressed a more acceptable view (*Feudal Documents*, pp. cii-cvi).

Robert fitz Richard, a son of Richard fitz Gilbert, lord of Clare, and so to Robert's descendant, Robert fitz Walter, King John's rebellious baron. But though the land was held in the twelfth and thirteenth centuries in fee and inheritance, this was not the avowed intention in 1086.[1]

This charter does not stand alone, for there are others of the same period which likewise record the grant of a life tenancy in return for knight service. A grant by the bishop of Hereford in 1085 is of interest because, as it is stated in the charter, the grantee's father had held the land on the same terms. Here we have two successive life tenancies, and there is probably an expectation that the land will continue to descend from father to son, but there is as yet no express heritable right.[2] Again, when the abbot of Abingdon, at the behest of the Conqueror, enfeoffed a knight who had been maimed in the king's service, he granted no more than a life tenancy, though in the result the newly created fief was permanently alienated from the abbey's demesne.[3] Even where homage is rendered—and it is a new-fangled ceremony in England—the tenancy is still for life only.[4] Since the surviving documents come from ecclesiastical sources, and monastic houses are more likely to have preserved old customs than laymen, we must hesitate to generalise, but so far as the evidence goes, it suggests that not until the reign of Henry I did it become the rule to grant heritable fiefs[5] and that the change in practice had nothing directly to do with the Conquest. When the change came, it appears to have been essentially a recognition of the fact that land held for life did, by custom, pass from father to son, a custom that is implied in the heriot and that goes far back in the history of Old English society. In the absence of evidence, and indeed in the face of such evidence as we possess, we cannot assume that the nature of tenure changed immediately upon the Conquest.

Let us contrast the post-Conquest charters we have summarised with the famous series of charters whereby Bishop Oswald of Worcester granted leases for three lives in the tenth century. In those charters, or rather as those charters were qualified and expounded in a letter the bishop addressed to King Edgar, Maitland believed he saw nascent feudal tenures.[6] He has been criticised on the ground that neither the leases themselves nor the bishop's letter contained any trace 'of the feudal ideas that the services to be rendered for a tenement should admit of a close definition'.[7] If this is to be the test,

---

[1] Robinson, *Gilbert Crispin*, pp. 38-41; D.B., i.128 a 2. As transcribed, the charter bears the date 1083: but it cannot be earlier than the year of Gilbert's appointment as abbot, which appears to be 1085. For the descent from Richard fitz Gilbert to Robert fitz Walter see Round, *Feudal England*, pp. 472-3.   [2] *E.H.R.*, xliv.371-2.

[3] *Chron. Mon. de Abingdon*, ii.6-7.   [4] Douglas, *Feudal Documents*, pp. 151-2.

[5] We can speak only in the light of surviving private charters: cf. Stenton, *First Century*, pp. 154-6, and Galbraith in *E.H.R.*, xliv.368.

[6] Maitland, *Domesday Book and Beyond*, pp. 304-9. For the charters themselves see Heming, *Chartularium*, pp. 121-240, and Kemble, *Codex Diplomaticus*, nos. 494-683.

[7] Stenton, *First Century*, pp. 123-30 (at p. 125).

then many a charter issued under Norman or Angevin kings may be stigmatised as non-feudal. A more apt criticism would be that the bishop feared that leases of this kind, which presumably were customary, might lead to the permanent alienation of the estates of the church, should the lessees repudiate the terms of their leases. What he was anxious to do was to prevent a leasehold estate from becoming an estate in fee and inheritance, to prevent it from becoming 'feudal'.[1] The fear that a lessee's descendants might establish a title to a leased estate was still present after the Conquest.[2] We need not stop to enquire why such fears passed. All we are concerned to do at the moment is to draw the obvious lesson that, if we were to take Bishop Oswald's leases for three lives as typical of later tenth-century practice and the life tenancies of the later eleventh century as typical of early English 'feudalism', then it would seem that 'feudal' tenures were more precarious than pre-feudal tenures. The evidence is too imperfect to admit of such a conclusion,[3] but it does accord with much other evidence that testifies to continuity and forbids us to believe in abrupt changes in the years following the battle of Hastings.

Continuity does not mean absence of change, and changes were many in the twelfth century. The multiplication of written instruments and the growing precision of legal forms in themselves create a sense of contrast. There is here reflected a movement that was common to Western Europe and was quite independent of any innovations by the Normans. It would seem quite illegitimate to select instruments from the twelfth century and treat them as illustrations of Norman forms or Norman doctrines in the eleventh century. The difficulty that inevitably besets those who stress the influence of Norman ideas upon English practice is the lack of relevant Norman documents of the eleventh century. The persistence of English formulas in twelfth-century charters is sufficient evidence of native influence, but, for the rest, we cannot exclude the influence of continental models. We certainly cannot postulate the influence of the illiterate Normans of the eleventh century. It is highly likely that, if there had been no Conquest, the use of the vernacular would have persisted and that English private charters of the twelfth century would commonly have been written in the native tongue, but they might well have contained very similar provisions to those found in the Latin charters which were actually confected. We do not think that Maitland was at fault when he saw in the Old English polity so much that he called 'feudalism' and that, in any case, resembled the institutions of Norman England. For example, he

---

[1] Cf. Galbraith in *E.H.R.*, xliv.367. [2] *Ibid.*, p. 372.

[3] Maitland drew attention to foreign evidence for leases for a life or lives. Apparently leases for different terms existed side by side (*Domesday Book and Beyond*, pp. 309 *n*, 310). See also Flach, *Les Origines de l'ancienne France*, ii.552 *n*. No instance of a lease for three lives in the Norman period has come to light.

drew attention to the evidence for the 'right of wardship and marriage',[1] and it is abundantly clear that the relief was as well known
in the century before the Conquest as it was in the century afterwards.[2] To the clerks responsible for the compilation of Domesday
Book the tenures that had existed under Edward the Confessor
appeared to be as 'feudal' as those that existed under the Conqueror.
They could write of land that a bishop had held *in feudo* of King
Edward[3] and of other land that had been similarly held *in feudo* in
King Edward's time,[4] just as they could write of post-Conquest
tenants holding of an abbot's fief[5] or of an abbot *in feudo*.[6] A private
charter of the twelfth century is very different in language and form
from a private pre-Conquest charter, but, for all that, it would seem
that such changes in tenure as they reflect might be not very dis-
similar from those that would have evolved independently of
Norman influence.

But close as were the resemblances between English and Norman
tenures—so close that there seems to have been no difficulty in their
assimilation when the Normans settled in England—there was a
difference of some significance. Let us illustrate it by contrasting two
bishops who have already engaged our attention, the bishop of
Bayeux and the bishop of Worcester. Under Henry II both bishops
held fiefs of the king and owed knight service to him, the bishop of
Bayeux the service of twenty knights, the bishop of Worcester the
service of fifty knights. So also it had been in the days of Henry I,
though while the bishop of Bayeux had owed the service of twenty
knights, the quota owed by the bishop of Worcester is uncertain, if
indeed a quota had been determined. It is probable that the service
of the bishop of Bayeux had not changed since the late eleventh
century, but we cannot hope to look beyond that time, for the
earlier history of Normandy is impenetrably obscure.[7] But while we
cannot be certain of the precise position of the bishop of Worcester
in the days of the Conqueror and his sons, we can be reasonably
certain of his position under the Old English kings. Then, in respect
of his franchise of Oswaldslow, he had owed the service of sixty
knights, because the franchise was reckoned at three hundreds. This
force was separately organised and commanded. For the bishop's
extensive lands elsewhere there can be no reasonable doubt that he
had owed the service of one knight for every five hides, but such

---

[1] *Op. cit.*, p. 310.   [2] Above, p. 59.
[3] D.B., i.19 a 2: Alricus episcopus tenuit in feudo de rege Edwardo.
[4] D.B., i.59 a 2: Blacheman tenuit in feudo T.R.E. Note the clear distinction drawn
between a fief and an alod in the immediately preceding entry: Blacheman tenuit de
comite Heraldo in alodio et potuit ire quo voluit.
[5] D.B., i.32 b 2: Willelmus de Wateuile tenet Maldone de feuo abbatis.
[6] D.B., i.33 a: Haimo vicecomes tenet de abbate de Certesy i. hidam et dimidiam in
feudo.
[7] The earliest evidence for Normandy is the inquest of 1133. As Round pointed out,
this carried the history of enfeoffments and knight service in the diocese of Bayeux back
to Odo of Bayeux (*Family Origins*, pp. 208-11).

knights were not separately organised: they took their place beside the knights drawn from other lands in the same hundred and shire. The total number of knights due from the bishop's estates was then a good many more than sixty and they did not constitute a single organised force. In the twelfth century the total had been reduced and the bishop's service was treated as a single whole.[1] This whole may have been no more than notional, a fiscal conception, but its important characteristic is that it bore no relation to the hundred or the hide. No longer is the bishop's liability calculated by looking at the assessment of his estates in hides: this assessment may serve for the purpose of one form of taxation, that of carucage,[2] but it does not serve for the purpose of another form of taxation, that of scutage. Now it may be said that, apart from the advantage the bishop and his tenants gained from the reduction in the amount of service due from the episcopal estates, the practical effect of the change was small. This, indeed, would be our view. Yet still the change is of interest, if not of importance: the liability for military service has been shifted from the administrative unit, the hundred, to a tenurial unit, the fief. Military service has, in this sense, become 'feudal'. It is just this shifting of liability that has created the belief that a territorial form of military service, the 'fyrd', persisted after the introduction of the 'feudal army'. We have exposed this belief for the illusion it is.[3] Had it been a reality, then the change would have been of great historical significance: in sober fact, the change illustrates our thesis of the relative unimportance of any element of 'feudalism' in post-Conquest England.

But it may be objected that we have overlooked the most significant of all the characteristics of 'feudalism', homage, a ceremony apparently unknown to the Old English state. What then was homage? Let us cite the words of one who speaks with authority upon 'feudalism' as it manifested itself on the Continent. 'The rite of homage is a rite whereby a man delivers himself up to his lord. When the vassal places his hands in those of his lord, the act symbolises the subjection of the entire person of the vassal, while the action of the lord in closing his hands upon those of his vassal symbolises his acceptance of this self-subjection.'[4] Is not this rite, we may be asked, this conception of the relationship between lord and

---

[1] Above, pp. 45, 67-8.

[2] Danegeld *eo nomine* was last levied in 1162, but it re-appeared in 1194 under the name of carucage. What the conventional hidage was we do not know in detail for the whole country, though county and estate assessments must have been maintained (Hall, *Formula Book*, ii.28-31) and that for Middlesex has apparently survived (Weinbaum, *London unter Edward I und II*, ii.85-7). There was a reassessment in 1198, which appears to have provided the basis for taxation in the thirteenth century (Mitchell, *Studies in Taxation*, pp. 7-9, 351-5).   [3] Above, pp. 75-7.

[4] Ganshof, *Qu'est-ce que la féodalité?* p. 93: Le rite de l'hommage est un rite de la tradition de soi-même, la remise des mains du vassal dans celles du seigneur symbolisant la remise à celui-ci de toute la personne du vassal et le geste du seigneur fermant ses mains sur celles du vassal symbolisant l'acceptation de cette auto-tradition.

man, a matter of extreme significance? Did not its introduction into England constitute something like a revolution in men's ideas of law and the constitution of society? Our reply must be that continental analogies, even if they were more precisely dated than they seem to be, may hinder rather than help us in understanding the meaning of homage in England when we have a wealth of precisely dated English material from which we can, without great difficulty, deduce its significance.[1]

What seems to be the earliest reference to homage in England occurs in a charter of Abbot Baldwin of Bury St. Edmunds granting a fief to Peter, one of the Conqueror's knights, in return for the service of 'three or four' knights.[2] Though Baldwin had been appointed abbot before the Conquest, he was a French monk from St. Denis and the charter betrays French influence. It does not, however, speak specifically of homage but says that Peter will become the feudal man (*homo feodalis*) of St. Edmund and of the abbot with joined hands (*manibus iunctis*), a reference to the characteristic, if not invariable, ceremony of the vassal's kneeling and placing his hands between those of his lord. Peter's act of homage may have taken place within a very few years of King William's coronation and it appears, as we have said, to be the earliest act of homage recorded to have taken place on English soil. Is this charter, then, the herald of a new order? Let us be chary of giving it this distinction, for symbols live on long after they have lost their primitive meaning, long after they have become an empty show. No man has spoken more eloquently of homage than Thomas Littleton: 'homage', he says, 'is the most honourable service and most humble service of reverence that a franktenant may do to his lord'[3]—and this in the fifteenth century, when nothing had been made plainer than the levity with which men regarded their obligations. But Littleton's attitude is no more than an attitude, copied from those writers who 'seem to lower their voices to a religious whisper when they speak of homage'.[4] And when we proceed from generalities to particular instances, we may well wonder whether homage had at any time very deep significance in England, except perhaps when liege homage was rendered to the king. We must, however, preface our discussion by saying something of the twin ceremony of fealty. If England before the Conquest did not know the rite of homage or, at least, formulas and ceremonies such as were usual in French-speaking lands, yet at least something of the lien symbolised by the rite was well known. When a man took another for his lord, he seems first

---

[1] We do not deny that the conception, much as M. Ganshof states it, was known in England. It appears, indeed, in a fable of Walter Map's; this rite was observed when one sold oneself to the devil (*De Nugis Curialium* (ed. James), p. 166). But it may be observed that the story is set in France.   [2] Douglas, *Feudal Documents*, pp. 151-2.
[3] Littleton, *Tenures*, lib. ii, c. 1. We cite the translation in Coke, *Institutes*, 1, fo. 64.
[4] Pollock and Maitland, *History of English Law*, i.297.

to have come to an understanding with him regarding the obligations he was to assume and then to have sworn to be hold and true, to love what his lord loved and to hate all he hated, not to displease him by word or deed and, finally, to fulfil the terms of their agreement.[1] The form of oath that has come down to us stresses the freedom of choice of the oath-taker. It assumes that he was one of those who was 'free to go with his land to whatsoever lord he would'.[2]

A story told by the Abingdon chronicler illustrates the manner of commendation in the days of Edward the Confessor and the circumstances in which the oath of fealty would be taken. A wealthy freeman named Turkil came to an arrangement with the church of Abingdon and Abbot Ordric with regard to himself and his land so that the lordship of the township he owned passed under the perpetual right of the abbey church. The chronicler does not use the word *commendatio*, though this would be appropriate to the transaction, but he does use the word homage: 'de se cum terra sua . . . ecclesie Abbendonensi et abbati Ordrico homagium fecit.'[3] We must suppose that Turkil took an oath of fealty to Abbot Ordric when he commended himself and his land and that this, by a writer in the middle of the twelfth century, could properly be regarded as an act of homage. The bond between Turkil and the abbey was meant to be a lasting one. In other cases the bond may have been temporary and terminable. But, as we shall see, homage did not differ in this regard. Homage did not necessarily imply a permanent bond; it had to fit many differing circumstances. When, therefore, the Normans came to England, they came to a land where there was a ceremony which had the same practical object as homage, but which differed in its symbolism and seems at one time to have differed in its effect upon the relation between lord and man. For if homage meant 'the subjection of the entire person of the vassal' to his lord, an oath of fealty in pre-Conquest England might still leave a man free to betake himself and his land to whatsoever lord he would. Homage, as introduced into England, involved no oath, but its ceremonial involved the abasement of the vassal. The oath of fealty, on the other hand, was sworn standing upright; and, though the terms of the Old English oath were superseded, among several variant forms of the oath of fealty in use in the thirteenth century there was one which included, like the earlier oath, a promise to render the service due for a tenement at the appointed terms. This form survived, not only to be used by tenants in socage but also by bishops when they declared their fealty at the king's coronation.[4]

When first we hear anything very definite of homage and fealty

---

[1] *Gesetze*, i.396-7.
[2] The usual Domesday Book formula, for which see p. 104, n. 4, above.
[3] *Chron. Mon. de Abingdon*, i.484, 490-1.
[4] Bracton, fo. 80 (Woodbine, ii.232); Littleton, lib. ii, c. 2 (Coke, *Institutes*, i, fo. 67 *b*); 'Little Device' in Legg, *English Coronation Records*, p. 234.

at the beginning of the twelfth century, they seem to be distinct ceremonies. In the agreement between Henry I and Robert count of Flanders in 1101 it is stipulated that the latter will safeguard the king from death, wounding or capture, and that he will aid the king to hold and defend the kingdom of England against all men. Although this is not a formal undertaking to render homage, it is known that Count Robert's successor, Thierry, did homage to Henry I and it is to be presumed that Robert did so before him.[1] While successive counts of Flanders did homage for the money fief they held of the king, the Flemish knights who served the king unde agreement with the count or by individual arrangement seem to have taken an oath of fealty.[2] However, the Constitutions of Clarendon, which appear to state the custom as it stood in the early years of Henry II's reign, require bishops-elect to render both homage and fealty to the king before their consecration.[3] Now the essential words of the bishop-elect's undertaking preserved in the Constitutions are the same essential words as are found in the formulas both of homage and of fealty given by Bracton.[4] The bishop swore that he would bear faith to the king of life and limb and of earthly worship—*de vita sua et de membris et de honore suo terreno*. This oath he took 'saving his order', and this qualification reflects contemporary feeling that it was not altogether right for a churchman to do homage for an ecclesiastical fief. Ultimately this sentiment led to the doctrine that all that was to be demanded of a churchman was an oath of fealty.[5]

If a churchman's position was ambiguous, so also, for different reasons, was a woman's. The author of 'Glanville', who makes no exception in the case of a churchman,[6] declares that in law a woman is incapable of doing homage: 'feminae enim nullum homagium facere possunt de iure'.[7] The grounds for his opinion appear to be these. He is dealing only with that form of homage which later ages were to know as homage ancestral, and the question he is considering is that of the succession of an heir. In the case of a male heir the position is plain sailing. The rendering of homage and the acceptance of a relief were reciprocal acts preliminary to the admission of an

---

[1] For the treaty of 10 March 1101 see *Foedera*, i.7; Vercauteren, *Actes des Comtes de Flandre*, no. 18; *Regesta*, no. 515, where the true date is established. The fact of Thierry's homage and that of his son Philip is recorded in the treaty of 19 March 1163 (Delisle, *Actes de Henri II*, no. 234, p. 379).

[2] This is implied in the treaties mentioned in the preceding note. If they received English fiefs they doubtless did homage (cf. Dept, *Les influences anglaise et française*, pp. 54-5).   [3] *Select Charters*, p. 166.   [4] Bracton, fo. 80 (Woodbine, ii.232).

[5] So Bracton, fo. 78*b*, and as in the coronation ceremony (Legg, *loc. cit.*). But Littleton seems to teach that a bishop should do homage in a passage that gave Coke some perplexity (*op. cit.*, fo. 65*b*). If bishops did not do homage at a coronation it seems certain that, at least since the sixteenth century, they have after consecration performed homage by the ancient ceremonial. For the varying forms see Lea, *The Bishops' Oath of Homage* (1875), pp. 48-52.

[6] Except in the case of land held in frankalmoin (lib. ix, c. 2: Woodbine, p. 126).

[7] *Ibid.*, lib. ix, c. 1 (Woodbine, p. 124).

heir to a fief that came to him by inheritance. Homage and relief were proof of ownership. But a woman was in a different position from a man. If she was unmarried her lord controlled her marriage and could make a profit out of her disposal. On marriage, or if she was already married, her husband rendered homage upon her behalf and was expected to pay the lord relief.[1] The artificiality of this doctrine seems obvious and we may doubt whether it represented more than the opinion of the author. On this point we cannot take him as a safe guide. Before many years had passed after he was writing, a very famous lady, Eleanor of Aquitaine, did homage to the king of France for the *comté* of Poitou,[2] and the rolls of the king's court contain ample evidence that in England homage was rendered and reliefs were paid by women. It may be that the form of homage differed in the case of women and that the form might by some be termed 'fealty'. But whatever the form, and whether it was termed homage or fealty, women assuredly paid relief.[3] Bracton had no doubt that a woman might render homage and he does not hint that the formula in her case was any different from that appropriate to a man; but as he makes clear, there was no single and settled formula and there was plenty of room for differences of opinion.[4] By his time, too, the circumstances in which homage and fealty were to be rendered had become the subject of elaborate distinctions. Some of the distinctions Bracton makes we may note. Every free man, lay or clerical, and every free woman, of age or under age, who held by military tenure or grand serjeanty, rendered homage, but not bishops, abbots, priors or other ecclesiastical persons who held in right of their churches. In practice, however, Bracton admitted, ecclesiastics frequently did so and they also, by custom, gave reliefs to their lords.[5] He teaches, too, that a tenant immediately after rendering homage should take an oath of fealty.[6] This double ceremony, involving the repetition of the same essential words, has a very odd air, and though it would seem from the Constitutions of Clarendon that homage and fealty were at least on occasion combined under Henry II, we may well doubt whether this awkward combination was at all general or persisted very long. Certainly fealty was sworn both to John and Edward I by the barons well before they rendered homage.[7] Later the doctrine gained acceptance that homage and fealty were mutually exclusive and were appropriate to persons of different status.[8]

In the light of the contradictions and inconsistencies, not only in

---

[1] *Ibid.*, lib. ix, cc. 1, 4 (Woodbine, pp. 124, 127).
[2] Rigord (ed. Delaborde), i.146. This was in July 1199: see Richard, *Comtes de Poitou*, ii.353 n.　　[3] *Curia Regis Rolls*, i.298; iii.330; iv.180, 358; xii.24, 214.
[4] Bracton, fo. 78-78b (Woodbine, ii.227-8).
[5] *Ibid.*, fo. 78b-79 (Woodbine, ii.228-9).
[6] *Ibid.*, fo. 80 (Woodbine, ii.232). Littleton, however, cites an instance under Edward III, where husband and wife jointly did homage and fealty (lib. ii, c. 1; Coke, *op. cit.*, fo. 66-66b).　　[7] Below, p. 147.　　[8] Littleton, lib. ii, c. 2 (Coke, *op. cit.*, fo. 68).

the practices but in the law-books of the later Middle Ages, it is difficult to believe that the rendering of homage was subject to any strict rules. Rather it appears to have been a matter of arrangement between grantor and grantee. The homage successive counts of Flanders rendered to Henry I was in respect of a money-fief which was not intended to continue beyond the count's lifetime. This was a strictly personal arrangement. It is true that the arrangement was renewed several times, but the homage rendered on each occasion was not homage ancestral.[1] The same order of ideas is to be seen in the arrangement by which the abbot of Ramsey in the reign of Henry II retained the services of Robert Foliot. Robert had quit-claimed to the abbot a rent of 100 shillings which he had had by the grant of a former abbot and had surrendered the deed. 'And because the aforesaid Robert was of noble birth and a wise man, by the counsel of the brethren and the barons of the church we retained his homage in the service of the church in this fashion. We granted him, in full chapter, with the assent of all the brethren, a thousand eels, which he had in the time of Abbot Reginald [1114-30], and we added another on our own behalf, so that he should have two thousand eels in fee and inheritance, he and his heirs, from the abbot of Ramsey for ever.'[2] Here we have something which can be called homage ancestral, but not in respect of a military fief, and the object of the transaction is to secure the support and counsel of a man of position. But homage might be rendered for something much less than a heritable render of eels or a money fief tenable for life. The author of the 'Leges Henrici' teaches that homage is due from a fermor,[3] and homage might be rendered for very small areas of land, the service for which was a money-rent.[4] Nor should we forget serjeanties and those eccentric or 'jocular' tenures which have always attracted legal historians and are well illustrated in an action of 1201. The point of dispute was whether the service due from a tenant of the bishop of Winchester was that of a knight or was merely the duty of rising in the king's court and making a way for the bishop so that he could speak to the king.[5] This case not only gives an instructive glimpse of the king's court in the twelfth century, but illustrates two points that should always be borne in mind in discussing enfeoffments in the eleventh and twelfth centuries: that grants might be made without any corroborative charter (which is not mentioned and might have settled the point of dispute) and that services might be very loosely defined, if they were defined

---

[1] Cf. Delisle, *Actes de Henri II, ut supra*: Et pro hoc feodo, per istas conventiones predictas, et quia comes Theodericus hominium fecerat regi Henrico, avo istius regis Henrici, comes Philippus fecit hominium isti regi Henrico.

[2] *Cart. Mon. de Rameseia*, i.153; *Chron. Abbatiae Rameseiensis*, p. 276.

[3] 'Leges Henrici', 56.2 (*Gesetze*, i.575).   [4] *Curia Regis Rolls*, iii.47, 81.

[5] *Ibid.*, ii.76. This case has the further interest that, though it is a *placitum servitii* (*ibid.*, p. 74), the method of trial is that of the grand assize. The roll which should record the judgement has not survived.

at all. Precisians, though not unknown, were rare in that age. And then again, since homage might be rendered for very small and diverse grants, it might, as men accumulated landed property,[1] be rendered to many lords in succession and in the process get very much attenuated. Already under Henry I, as the 'Leges Henrici' testify,[2] this was happening, and the doctrine of liege homage had emerged. A man's first duty was to his liege lord,[3] who was assumed to be the lord of the fee on which the tenant lived, 'ille cuius residens et legius est'[4]; and the liege lord was in especial bound to aid his tenant.[5] 'Glanville' has a rule to much the same effect: liege homage, he teaches, was due to the lord of whom the tenant held his principal tenement.[6] But tenures were more complex than this simple scheme suggests, and in Bracton the rule is found whereby rights and duties —especially the rights of the lord—are determined by the priority of feoffment or according to whether some lands and rents are held by knight service and others not.[7]

If we could accept the teaching of 'Glanville', liege homage had still under Henry II something of its ancient significance. A tenant could not act in any hostile way against his liege lord, unless it be in his own defence or unless, at the king's command, he served in the host against his lord.[8] But in the thirteenth century the emphasis was on the profits that accrued to the liege lord, who was entitled to the wardship of minors and the marriage of heiresses to the exclusion of other lords. And just as the doctrines of liege homage and priority of feoffment might attenuate homage almost to meaninglessness in the case of inferior lords or recent feoffments, so there might be a similar attenuation of homage when the parties to a fine rendered homage mutually to each other for the lands that were assured to them. Each is now the other's lord and the other's man.[9] The ceremony is saved from absurdity because the significance of homage attendant upon everyday transactions in land no longer lies in the personal relations of the parties. Those who render and those who accept homage have no thought of arms, of service in the field: they think of reliefs, marriage and wardship, the profits, not the remotely ancient obligations, of military tenure. This is plain from

---

[1] For examples of the accumulation of dispersed properties see the cases of Robert and Henry of Braybrooke and master Philip Galle (Richardson, *English Jewry*, pp. 100-2).

[2] 'Leges Henrici', 43.6, 55.2 (*Gesetze*, i.569, 575).

[3] A man might not even participate in judgements against his liege lord ('Leges Henrici', 32.2; *Gesetze*, i.564).

[4] 'Leges Henrici', 43.6, 55.2, 82.5 (*Gesetze*, i.569, 575, 599). For the application of this rule see the instructive case in 1202 where two men do fealty, saving their homage to their lord 'qui eos feoffavit et in feodo suo manent' (*Curia Regis Rolls*, ii.124).

[5] 'Leges Henrici', 82.4, 6 (*Gesetze*, i.599).

[6] Glanville, lib. ix, c. 1 (ed. Woodbine, p. 124).   [7] Bracton, fo. 79*b*.

[8] Glanville, *loc. cit.* There is a good illustration of this rule in the protection afforded to William of Briouze by William Marshal, though how the former became lord of the latter has never been explained. It looks very much as though the rule was invoked by William Marshal as an excuse for what the king regarded as a questionable action (Orpen, *Ireland under the Normans*, ii.239-40; Painter, *Reign of King John*, pp. 245-6).

[9] *Curia Regis Rolls*, xii.295, no. 1444.

'Glanville', from the many cases that come before the courts where homage is in question, and it is the theme of the statute *Quia Emptores* in 1290: because of sub-infeudation 'the chief lords of fees have many times lost their escheats, marriages and wardships'—there is no word of any other loss.[1]

If by the thirteenth century homage had retained so little of its primitive meaning, how much did homage mean at the time of the Conquest? Though our law-books may preserve ancient doctrine and ascribe a high solemnity to the ceremony, even they cannot hide the debasement, the insignificance, of homage in actual practice; and the more we study the documents, the less shall we be inclined to take the ceremony seriously in everyday transactions. Nor, so far as written evidence goes, is there any suggestion that greater significance had ever attached to homage since its introduction into England. It was a formality, to be observed by Frenchmen because of its antiquity, and so it was observed by French-speaking Englishmen. But homage did not bind men closer to their lord or introduce a new concept of fidelity. Men followed their lord to the death—or betrayed him—after the Conquest as they had done before. Liege homage to the king stands apart; but with or without the ceremony of homage the duty of a subject towards his king would remain.[2] There is nothing to suggest, however, that the introduction of a new ceremony made the slightest difference in men's attitudes, though it might serve for a debating point when the king proceeded against a bishop, not in his spiritual capacity, but as a baron.[3] Homage persisted because of its association with the profits of lordship, very much as in our day, although personal seals have long gone out of use, an imitation seal is affixed to a deed because in English law an instrument under seal has long had special virtues; but it is only corporate bodies, fictitious persons, to whom real seals are of practical utility.[4] So, whatever its convenience as a sign that property had become vested in a new owner,[5] in the ordinary transactions of life homage was as remote from reality as the seal in modern legal practice.

In their origin, it is true, both the Old English military organisation and the French feudal organisation had been based upon

[1] *Select Charters*, p. 473, from *Statutes of the Realm*, i.106.

[2] This is, we think, clear from Bracton's teaching on lese-majesty, fo. 118-119*b* (ed. Woodbine, ii.334-7).

[3] In the case of William of St. Calais, he claimed privilege as an ecclesiastic and he was told that he was being tried as a baron (below, p. 285). In the case of Thomas Becket the bishops claimed that they sat in the king's court as barons—'non sedemus hic episcopi sed barones'—and evaded passing sentence (*Becket Materials*, iii.52-3).

[4] For the modern law see Halsbury's *Laws of England* (3rd ed.), xi.323-81. The distinction between a deed and an instrument under hand, though convenient, is quite arbitrary.

[5] Glanville, lib. ix, c. 1. A lord is bound to accept the homage of the true heir and, until he has done so, he has no right to service or relief or anything else. It is to establish their title that women will bring an action to compel the defendant to take their homage and a reasonable relief (*Curia Regis Rolls*, i.298).

personal service related, directly or indirectly, to the tenure of land[1]; but both systems were extremely difficult to reconcile with the principle of 'feudal' tenures as we know them in the twelfth century. Although land held under a military tenure *in feodo et hereditate* was conventionally charged with knight service, the land was, in fact, transmissible to minors, partible among heiresses, fragmentable by sàle or donation, alienable by gage or lease, divisible by dower, absolvable from any secular obligation by grants in frankalmoin. The conception of property in land with a flexibility approaching the flexibility of property in chattels had overthrown the primitive rigid integrity of the hide and the fief alike with their related services. The history of tenures is the history of a long series of attempts at accommodation between the lingering conception of an immutable nexus between land and service and the rapidly evolving conception of property as a means of gratifying the needs or whims of the possessor. Accommodation could be reached through the agency of money. With the arrival of the mercenary soldier the transformation of personal obligations into pecuniary obligations charged upon land became possible. Personal service could not long survive except in so far as it could adapt itself to the standard of professional soldiering or as a rudimentary police force such as we find in Henry III's ordinance of 1242 and the Statute of Winchester.[2]

We should not, however, pass over entirely without noting the attempt that had been made some years earlier than this to organise the military resources of the kingdom on what may perhaps be called a 'national' basis. John, it will be remembered, had called upon all men capable of bearing arms to resist a threatened invasion in 1205. It is clear that, whether the array of arms had been regularly enforced or not in the recent past, there was in that year no effective organisation of the potential armed forces of the shire.[3] This state of affairs it was evidently sought to remedy. The array of arms was to be enforced and an organisation was set up which grouped the men capable of bearing arms into constabularies with a chief constable in each shire at the head.[4] Whatever effect this reorganisation may have had, it is plain that it did not survive John's war with his barons, and in 1230 the task had to be undertaken afresh. This is the obvious inference from the commissions of array issued on 13 June of that year which were quite specifically intended to re-impose the scheme of the previous reign.[5] So far as freemen were con-

---

[1] But, as we have seen, already under Ine this had ceased to be the rule (above, p. 49).
[2] *Select Charters*, pp. 362-5, 463-6.   [3] Above, pp. 76-7.
[4] Gervase of Canterbury, *Historical Works*, ii.96-7. The document here preserved cannot arise directly out of the emergency of 1205, but is doubtless connected with John's ordinance to which reference is made in the commissions of 1230. This ordinance has not survived, but it must have been made either later in 1205 or in some subsequent year.
[5] *Close Rolls, 1227-1231*, pp. 398-402. These commissions give details, apparently borrowed from John's ordinance. It is from a mandate to the sheriffs of 30 April 1230, which proved abortive, that we learn that John's ordinance had extended to the unfree (*ibid.*, p. 395).

cerned the classification was that of Henry II's reign. In the highest class were the fully armed knights; then came the lightly armed knights[1]; and lastly those who could not afford body armour and wore a purpoint but whose heads were protected by an iron cap. The unfree, who had been disregarded under Henry II, seem evidently to have been drawn into the scheme by John and so there was thus a fourth class, of infantry, who were required to provide themselves with small arms, bows, axes or pikes.[2] The reintroduction of the array of arms was actuated by the fear that the land would be left defenceless with the withdrawal of the available troops for the French campaign of 1230. The new organisation could have no effect upon that fiasco, but it did seem to provide the means for augmenting the forces required to meet the inroads of the Welsh in the following year.[3] Accordingly, on 26 July, the sheriffs of ten western and midland counties were ordered to despatch to the king's army all the men who had been sworn at the array to be clad in armour—and the three classes are named, those with hauberks, aubergels and purpoints—but only a maximum of two hundred men armed with axes were summoned from any county; there was also to be sent, at the king's expense, every available carpenter.[4] The mounted men were not, after all, required and were dismissed almost immediately, though the axemen were retained.[5] The experiment could not have been encouraging. Its bearing upon the obligations arising from military tenures does not seem to have been thought out, and knight service, though in a modified form, continued to be demanded from tenants-in-chief.[6] The experiment is notable, however, as testifying to the right claimed by the Crown to demand the service of all able-bodied men in time of war and as furnishing a precedent for the demands made by Edward I upon the counties for infantry and artisans. But for our present purpose the experiment is particularly noteworthy as testifying to the progress that had been made in dissociating military service from tenure. It seems clear that every mounted man was expected to serve for forty days at his own expense in a rank according to his station in life: only the infantry were to have their expenses found and then by the group to which they belonged. The artisans stand in a class

---

[1] For simplicity we call these two categories knights, but most of those affected had probably never been, and never would be, knighted. As in the Assize of Arms, and doubtless under John, so a distinction is drawn between those holding land by a military tenure and those who are worth fifteen (or ten) marks a year. Apparently by John's reign the man with an income of ten marks had been equated with the half fee and the half fee with the lightly armed knight, *cum planis armis*, who is beginning to lose the title of knight.

[2] For the liability imposed upon the unfree to bear arms under John and in 1230 see p. 113, n. 5, above. Their liability is made even more plain in 1242, when there is a specific reference to villeins (*Select Charters*, p. 363).

[3] For the sequence of events see Ramsay, *The Dawn of the Constitution*, pp. 54-9.

[4] *Close Rolls, 1227-1231*, pp. 595-6.

[5] *Ibid.*, p. 597.

[6] Above, p. 84-5.

apart: theirs is forced labour, but the king recognises his obligation to pay for it.

To pursue further the history of the English army in the Middle Ages would lead us far from our immediate subject. We can take our stand in the year 1231 and look backward. If any lesson is plain, it is that 'feudal' tenures had at no time since the Conquest directly provided an army. For such a purpose they were an encumbrance rather than an aid. They had to be circumvented rather than utilised, to be transmuted into a means of engaging efficient soldiers. The ideas behind the array of 1230 and the summons of 1231 were doubtless mistaken and inadequate and betray the futility of the ministers who advised an incompetent king: the measures fell so far short of anything that could produce an efficient armed force. They mark, however, a culminating-point, a realisation that to continue the old makeshift methods led nowhere. Wealthy kings, like Henry II and Richard I, could dispense with the personal service of mesne tenants and lead mercenary armies to victory. With mercenaries King John could withstand his barons, even though he could not overcome them. But, by comparison, Henry III was impoverished, too impoverished, even if he had the desire, to wage successful war with professional soldiers, and no more than his predecessors could he conjure up a 'feudal' army. The truth is that, by the time 'feudal' tenures were introduced into England, they were already an anachronism. The onerous incidents which they involved had once had a rational purpose in the region where they were first conceived; but by the twelfth century, and indeed earlier, they had ceased to secure their original aim, to provide an army and an administration. The professional soldier, the professional lawyer, the professional civil servant, had made their appearance and were becoming ever more professional and more necessary: without them, the organised state, such as England was, would have collapsed. When, however, we abstract what was essential to primitive feudal tenures, we are left with little more than meaningless 'feudal incidents' that endured because they were a source of profit. And whereas the military obligations of feudal tenures were progressively commuted for money payments, wardship and marriage, especially when exploited by the Crown, became progressively a heavy and vexatious burden.[1] But these are the mere relics of 'feudalism', to be placed beside such a relic of seignorial justice as the right to decide the title to land, a right that in the twelfth century could be exercised in the lord's court only with the permission of the king, signified by a royal writ. Yet the lesson of the grand assize and the writ of right is not that some traces of the principles of feudalism persisted, but that the king's justice dominated such faint workings of those principles as

[1] See Thorne's introduction to Constable, *Prerogativa Regis*, pp. v-xlvi; Hurstfield, *The Queen's Wards*, pp. 3-29; Bell, *Court of Wards and Liveries*, pp. 1-15.

survived.[1] Even so, we must hesitate before we denominate as specifically 'feudal' the determination in the lord's court of disputes regarding the right to land held of him. We have no evidence, but presumably such disputes had been settled in much the same fashion before the Conquest.[2] In the same way we must hesitate to describe the criminal jurisdiction of seignorial courts as feudal: there is no doubt that a similar jurisdiction was exercised in the Old English state.[3] The Normans were already familiar with much that they found in England, but we are not thereby warranted in terming those familiar things 'feudal' or in asserting that England was already 'feudal'.

We must stress the essential continuity of English institutions in England. That there were innovations after the Conquest that affected all men, high and low, is undeniable; but such innovations bore the stigma of violence and injustice. Even though the past could not be wholly recalled, after a brief space of time the desire was all for restoring what had been damaged or taken away. 'Lagam Eadwardi regis vobis reddo', said Henry I. He professed to give back King Edward's law in better form, but it was still King Edward's law.[4] These are not the words, this is not the act, of a man who believes that there have been revolutionary, irreversible changes or who thinks that his barons, who have done well out of the Conquest, have broken with an English past and long to continue in a new and 'feudal' age. Is it conceivable that King Henry was mistaken? We suggest, on the contrary, that he had no desire to be a 'feudal' monarch. When his father allotted among his followers the lands that had fallen into his power, King William, so it has been said, established in England the cardinal feudal doctrine that all land is held of the king.[5] But did the Conqueror introduce a new doctrine? Let us agree that after the Conquest all land in England was, in some sense, held directly or indirectly of the king (as, indeed, it was until 1925)[6] and that this is testified by Domesday Book. But if we go on to assert that this represents some principle hitherto unknown in England, we shall find it hard to prove our case. There is nothing to suggest that William conceived himself as asserting a right that had not belonged to the Confessor or that the Old English kings stood in any different relation to their landowning subjects. A later

---

[1] We first hear of the necessity to obtain the king's or the justiciar's writ in Glanville, lib. xii, cc. 2, 25 (ed. Woodbine, pp. 149, 157). This *consuetudo regni* is not then perhaps very old.

[2] So Maitland conjectures that in Oswaldslow in pre-Conquest days 'the suits of these tenants would come into a court where the bishop would preside by himself or his deputy . . . the justice that these tenants will get will be seignorial justice' (*Domesday Book and Beyond*, p. 311). We doubt, indeed, whether in those days any thegn or cniht would have impleaded his lord in the hundred court, franchisal or not.

[3] *Ibid.*, pp. 89-95, 258:90.

[4] *Gesetze*, i.522; *Select Charters*, p. 119.

[5] Corbett in *Cambridge Medieval History*, v.514.

[6] The rule was abrogated by the Administration of Estates Act, 1925, s. 45 (1) (d).

generation will assert that every man's lord is his ultimate heir,[1] and it follows that the king is the ultimate heir of all his subjects. That men thought in such terms in the eleventh century is unlikely; but there had been no perceptible change in their fundamental ideas. When the lands of Earl Godwin and his sons were forfeited in 1051, their thegns were required to swear fealty to King Edward.[2] If a lordless man, an *alodarius*, committed a breach of the peace or some other punishable offence, he paid a penalty to King Edward: when he died, a heriot, *relevatio*, was due from his land to the king. The principal roads, moreover, were the king's highway and any man who obstructed them paid a heavy penalty to King Edward.[3] We hardly need to look beyond the first page of the first volume of Domesday Book to discover that the Confessor was as much the lord of all English soil, as much the ultimate heir of great men and small, as any post-Conquest king. The king indeed stands at the apex of society, yet the image of the feudal pyramid is inapt to represent any political system that ever obtained in England. True, sub-infeudation 'gave several people different kinds of lordship over the same property'; and, if we read the texts aright, sub-infeudation was no novelty in 1066. What sub-infeudation failed to do in England, whether before or after the Conquest, was what the classical theory of feudalism demands, namely to diminish by fragmentation lordship as a whole—the authority of the king and whatever other lords there might be. It is a strange paradox that the king was never so strong as after what is called 'feudalism' was introduced into England. But to the king we must devote a separate chapter.

And so we come back at last to the meaning of 'feudal' and 'feudalism'. 'Feudalism', we must always remember, is a modern concept, an abstraction, based doubtless upon historical texts, but owing much to the desire of scholars for symmetry, the desire to perceive, and indeed to impose, a rational and coherent order in institutions and events, themselves often irrational and incoherent. Historians of a past generation felt the necessity to distinguish between feudal tenures and feudal jurisdiction.[4] If we concentrate our attention upon tenures, then there is hardly a country or an epoch where an element of 'feudalism' cannot—given the will—be perceived. But it is clear that 'feudal' in this sense means something very different from the adjective 'feudal' applied to jurisdiction or administration. It was in this latter sense that Montesquieu spoke of

---

[1] Glanville, lib. vii, c. 17 (ed. Woodbine, p. 113): Ultimi heredes aliquorum sunt eorum domini.
[2] A.S. Chronicle, D, *s.a.* 1052; E, *s.a.* 1048 (Thorpe, pp. 314, 316; Plummer, pp. 174-5).
[3] D.B., i.1 a 2.
[4] Let us cite Freeman. 'But the words *feudal* and *feudalism* have, in practice at least, two distinct meanings. The so-called Feudal System, that is, the break up of all national unity in a kingdom, undoubtedly grew out of the feudal tenure of land. But the feudal tenure of land does not in itself imply any weakness on the part of the central power' (*Norman Conquest*, v.367).

lois féodales, and it is to this limited sense that historians would be well advised to restrict their use of the word *feudalism* if they wish to be readily intelligible. The administration of mediaeval France can be termed feudal because sovereignty was divided between the king and his feudatories. If in this sense France was 'feudal', England was not. If we call England 'feudal', then we should find some other adjective to apply to France. An adjective so ambiguous and so misleading is best avoided.

VI

LOSS AND GAIN

BEFORE we leave the eleventh century it may be useful to consider a little further the consequences of the Norman Conquest, even though we may be taken some way from the field of institutional history. Not so very many years ago it was the fashion to depreciate the merits of the Old English kingdom and to exalt the qualities of the Normans and their achievements. Thus Stubbs spoke of the 'isolation' of the English people and asserted that the Conquest 'brought the nation at once and permanently within the circle of European interests'.[1] In the face of the available evidence it is difficult to understand how such misconceptions could have arisen. England had never, for many centuries, lost touch with the Continent and its relations with the Low Countries were close, while the Church in England was intimately associated with Rome,[2] far more closely and far more in spirit than the Church in Normandy. It is only by contrasting England in the twelfth century with England slowly recovering from the Danish conquest and the terrors of which Wulfstan has left such a graphic picture[3] that we can foster any illusion of the benefits of Norman rule. Such a comparison is quite illegitimate. We might, however, well marvel that by the middle of the eleventh century England had gone such a long way towards recovery. If we were to contrast Normandy at the same period with England in the twelfth century we might also wonder how it came about that the Normans conformed as well as they did to ordered society and even contributed to it. The explanation is twofold. In the first place they produced two men of outstanding genius, Henry I and Roger of Salisbury, with great gifts for administration, who by a lucky chance came into power together, and whose work after an interval, when the Normans had shown their incapacity for ordered society except under rulers of exceptional strength and resolution, was resumed by Henry II, who had very little that was Norman in him. In the second place, England, like so much of the Continent in the twelfth century, was subject to the forces that largely transformed

[1] *Constitutional History*, i.269.
[2] For a summary statement of the condition of the English Church in the eleventh century see Stenton, *Anglo-Saxon England*, pp. 457-62. His last paragraph is an effective criticism of earlier views.
[3] *Sermo Lupi ad Anglos* (ed. Whitelock), pp. 27-36: for a translation see Whitelock, *English Historical Documents*, pp. 856-8.

European civilisation: the growing literacy among laymen and clergy alike, ecclesiastical reform, new conceptions of law in Church and State that put administration upon a new basis. Of these matters we shall speak later. But there is no reason to suppose that, if there had been no Conquest, those forces would have stopped short at the English Channel. There is much to suggest a different supposition. Two examples may suffice. Reformed monasticism came to Ireland from Tiron, Savigny and Clairvaux many years before Henry II conquered that island[1]: why should we suppose that it would not have come to England, with the same fervour and in much the same way? Again, in the century after 1066 students from England did not resort to Rouen or Caen, but sought the great masters of the new learning at Laon in the first place,[2] and then at Paris and Bologna: it is hard to believe that the Norman Conquest was responsible for this movement or that, if the Conquest had not happened, English students would have trod other paths.

Imaginary reconstructions of history are toys: but in this case they may serve to give us a sense of proportion and deny to the Normans as a body the virtues of the few who kept the rest in check. The rule of Robert in Normandy and Stephen in England should at least warn us that the Normans were not pioneers of civilisation. They were rather, like their Norse forefathers and contemporaries, angels of death and destruction. The absolute value of the vernacular literature of the Old English kingdom may not be high, but it was pre-eminent in Western Europe. This literature came to an end with the Conquest. It is idle to speculate how English letters and the English language might have developed, but that the course was thwarted and changed there can be no question. Nor is it merely as literature that we may regret the demise of Old English poetry and prose. The humanity and wisdom of Ælfric and Wulfstan cannot be matched for two centuries and more, and the high sense of pastoral mission their writings disclose is to be sought in vain among the foreign ecclesiastics who succeeded them, even the Lombards, Lanfranc and Anselm, whose eminent virtues did not extend to the care of their flock, remote alike from their sympathies and their tongue. It was Wulfstan who taught that no Christian man should be condemned to death for a little thing and that God's handiwork should not be lightly destroyed, and his teaching was embodied in Cnut's laws.[3] It was the Normans who introduced trial by battle

---

[1] *Gwynn Studies*, pp. 35-40.

[2] For Laon as the resort of students from England in the early twelfth century see Hermann, *De Miraculis sancte Marie Laudunensis*, ii, cc. 6, 12-13, 15, in *Patrologia Latina*, clvi, 977-83. For Adelard of Bath at Laon see Bliemetzrieder, *Adelhard von Bath* (1935), pp. 52-3.

[3] Liebermann, *Gesetze*, i.308-10 (II Cnut, 2, 1). For Wulfstan's authorship see Whitelock in *E.H.R.*, lxiii.433-52. Compare also the phrase 'Godes handgeweorc 7 his agenneceap þe he deore gebohte' of the Laws with 'Godes gesceafte 7 his agenneceap þe he deore gebohte' of the *Sermo ad Anglos*, lines 92-3, where the sale of slaves overseas is condemned.

into England and the ferocity, the killings and the mutilations of the forest law. This contrast marks a difference between two contemporary societies that redounds, we may think, not greatly to the credit of the conquerors.

True, civilised men are few in any generation, and the lessons of our own time have taught us how many are the barbarians within our gates and how near barbarism is to the surface. Nor must we conceal from ourselves the dark side of Old English society, as dark perhaps as in any land in Western Europe. Not only was there slavery, but men and women were bought and sold as chattels, and there was a slave trade from Bristol that lasted into the twelfth century.[1] Still across the centuries echoes the complaint of Ælfric's ploughman:

I work hard. I go out at daybreak, driving the oxen to the field, and I yoke them to the plough. Be it never so stark winter, I dare not linger at home for awe of my lord; but having yoked my oxen, and fastened share and coulter, every day must I plough a full acre or more. I have a boy, driving the oxen with a goad-iron, who is hoarse with cold and shouting. Mighty hard work it is, for I am not free.[2]

Elsewhere Ælfric tells us of horrible punishments: of a slave girl who for some very slight fault was manacled hand and foot all night preparatory to a flogging in the morning; of an innocent man accused of theft and sentenced to lose his eyes and his ears; of a careless slave, whose master fettered him by the leg.[3] It is sometimes suggested that, while the Normans depressed the peasantry as a whole, they extinguished slavery[4]; but though slavery disappeared in the course of the twelfth century, it is difficult to give the credit to the Normans.[5] It was another Wulfstan, an Englishman, who did most

---

[1] There is a graphic description of the slave trade, which was aggravated by the Danish wars, in the *Sermo ad Anglos*, lines 84-96, 123-7. Wulfstan did not, however, condemn domestic slavery as such: see *ibid.*, lines 43-8, and especially the addition from MS. C. He thought it shameful that a slave who had obtained his freedom by deserting to the Danes should be given the status of a thegn (lines 104-8). Miss Whitelock has a useful note on slavery in *English Historical Documents*, pp. 60-1. For the persistence of the slave trade into the twelfth century see the 'Articuli X', attributed to William I, c. 9 (Liebermann, *Gesetze*, i.488) and Hermann, *De Miraculis sancte Marie Laudunensis*, ii, c. 21 (*Patrologia Latina*, clvi.986). Penal slavery was still so much of a reality in 1127 that it was threatened to unrepentant clerical concubines (Florence of Worcester, ii.88).
[2] *Ælfric's Colloquy* (ed. Garmonsway), lines 23-35: translation by York Powell in Traill, *Social England*, i.187.
[3] Ælfric, *Lives of the Saints* (ed. Skeat), i.452, 458, 466. We cite Ælfric as the author, but he borrowed the first and third incident from the *Translatio et Miracula sancti Swithuni* by his fellow-monk Landferth. Of this instructive work no critical edition exists and there are variant texts; but a text will be found in *Acta Sanctorum*, July, vol. 1 (see p. 294, no. 5), supplemented in *Analecta Bollandiana*, vol. 4 (see p. 406, no. 51).
[4] Poole, *Obligations of Society*, pp. 12-13.
[5] The reasons for the disappearance of slavery and the cessation of the slave trade in the twelfth century are obscure. Vinogradoff's picture of the emancipation of the slave and the depression of the free is conjectural (*English Society*, pp. 463-70). The belief in the rarity of slavery in Normandy (Stenton, *Anglo-Saxon England*, p. 472) rests upon nothing but the absence of documents. There is no reason to suppose that the Normans had abandoned the practices of their ancestors. The story told by William of Poitiers

to combat chattel slavery[1] and, if he did not entirely succeed, his efforts were at least praiseworthy. During his lifetime Norman churchmen were not lacking in England, but there is nothing to show that a single voice was joined with his. It is true that at an ecclesiastical council at Westminster in 1102, perhaps under the influence of Anselm, traffic in slaves was formally condemned; but there is no reason to suppose that this canon was in the least effective.[2] Nor must we forget that manumission has a long history in England and that the surviving deeds of manumission, both before and after the Conquest, are in English.[3] The Normans were not a gentle, compassionate people. And if Christ and His saints had slept under Ethelred and Cnut, they turned again to their slumbers under Stephen.

Then there were taken, both by night and day, those suspected of having any wealth, men and women, and cast into prison and tortured with unutterable torments to extort their gold and silver. Never were martyrs so tortured as they. They were hung by the feet and choked with foul smoke. They were hung by the thumbs or by the head, with their feet weighted with coats of mail. Cords were knotted about their heads and twisted until they pierced to the brain. They were put in dungeons with adders and snakes and toads, and so they were killed. Some were put in a torture-chamber in the form of a short, narrow and shallow chest, and sharp stones were put therein and pressed upon them so that all their limbs were broken. In many castles there was an instrument formed of fetters, so heavy that it needed two or three men to carry one, and this was fastened to a beam, with the sharp iron round a man's neck and throat, so that he could in no wise sit or lie or sleep but must bear the full weight of the iron. And there were many thousands who died of hunger. I lack the power to tell all the miseries and tortures borne by the wretched folk of England. And this endured, growing ever worse and worse, the nineteen winters that Stephen was king.[4]

It was an Englishman who wrote these words, and we must allow for his hatred of the oppressor, as we must allow for the homilist's licence in the sermons of Wulfstan and Ælfric, which tell of the miseries and shames of the doleful days in which they lived. But whatever qualifications our scepticism may suggest, the true picture must have been dark enough. In other chapters we shall describe the fair side of the tapestry and speak of the achievements of the

---

(ed. Foreville, p. 102) of the possibility that Harold might be sold into slavery ('virum quem torquere, necare, vendere potuerit pro libito') is sufficient of itself to show that chattel slavery existed in northern France in the eleventh century.

[1] *Vita Wulfstani* (ed. Darlington), p. 43.

[2] Eadmer, *Historia Novorum*, pp. 143-4; William of Malmesbury, *Gesta Pontificum*, pp. 120, 121 *n*. The traffic had been ineffectually condemned in 1008 (V Æthelred, 2; *Gesetze*, i.238-9).

[3] Thorpe, *Diplomatarium*, pp. 621-44; Earle, *Land Charters*, pp. 253-64.

[4] A.S. Chronicle, *s.a.* 1137 (Thorpe, p. 382; Plummer, p. 264). The text, with a facsimile and useful notes, will be found in Dickins and Wilson, *Early Middle English Texts*, pp. 3-6, 153-8.

twelfth century in the arts of government. Let us not forget the reverse of the fabric.

If there is much to put on the debit side of the ledger—we ask indulgence for the change of metaphor—what can we put upon the credit side? To the work of Henry I and Roger of Salisbury we have already referred, and we shall have much to say in detail later. But of equal significance, though it was no deliberate contrivance, was the accident that the coming of the Normans, and more especially the victory of Tinchebray which united England and Normandy for a century, meant the ascendancy of French speech, the common language of the Mediterranean world. And here perhaps it would be well to enter a caveat against the practice of describing the French spoken and written in England as Norman French or Anglo-Norman. No English king after Stephen can reasonably be called Norman, and he was Norman on his mother's side. The only common description that will fit the kings from Henry II to Richard II is 'French'. The language they and their courtiers spoke was that of northern France, the *langue d'oil*, and when their clerks wrote in French the result was perfectly intelligible to any literate Frenchman, just as documents written in Paris or Champagne or Touraine were perfectly intelligible to any literate Englishman. Bad French was written in England, as it was everywhere; and as the centuries advanced French became an acquired tongue, restricted to a narrow circle. But good, clear French is almost invariably to be found in official documents which represent the bulk of what was written and spoken in England. The diffusion of French, then, meant familiarity with what was spoken and written in France—and little enough was written in Normandy—and therefore the increasing influence of French culture in England.

It is true that basically society remained English in structure and composition. The English way of life, though checked and diverted, pursued its course. In the eleventh and twelfth centuries disputed claims were decided by the testimony of the country that remounted to the days of the Old English kings. No less a figure in the English kingdom than Richard de Lucy, the justiciar, was irked by the indignity that disputes between Normans should be decided by the English.[1] Towards the end of Henry II's reign, however, the distinction between the two peoples had become blurred. If at the beginning of the reign Richard de Lucy could speak of the traps set by the English for the Normans, at its close Richard of Ely could affirm that among freemen it could scarcely be determined who was English by descent and who Norman.[2] The language of the upper classes became, if anything, increasingly French: it was the language of

---

[1] *Chron. Mon. de Bello,* p. 89. Even though this were the chronicler's invention, the sentiment would be significant.

[2] *Dialogus de Scaccario,* p. 53. Walter Map speaks to much the same effect but attributes the fusion of the two peoples to Henry I (*De Nugis Curialium,* p. 218).

court, camp, counting-house and cloister.[1] So the Jews, a race apart, spoke French, not only because English Jews were an offshoot from the community at Rouen, but because, at the level of society at which they moved, French was the language of all intercourse.[2] So also the Londoners, who were predominantly English in origin, conducted their municipal and commercial business in French,[3] although the masses remained English in speech, as the street-names of the City testify.[4] We have then this seeming paradox that, whereas the political institutions of the country had had in their main aspects a continuous existence from pre-Conquest times and, even when modified, preserved a distinctive insular character, they were directed at all levels by men who spoke an alien tongue. But while English institutions were distinctively insular, since the upper classes of English society were French in speech and French by their many ties with the Continent, they inevitably made their own, and imposed upon the country, many of the ideas that prevailed across the Channel. Since, however, contact with France began at an early date, before the restoration and organisation of the French kingdom, and since the juridical institutions of the two countries evolved in very different directions, the similarities are to be found, in the first instance, chiefly in legal concepts and terminology. But French influences are more particularly to be discerned in what is usually regarded as a peculiarly insular institution, that of parliament. Parliaments, all over north-western Europe, were a development of the thirteenth century. They were organised in England in 1258, the year, it is to be observed, preceding the treaty of Paris, which brought Guyenne within the jurisdiction of the French king's parliament. Though one consequence of the treaty seems undoubtedly to have been the assimilation of the functions and characteristics of the English and French parliaments—for it was impossible that representatives of the English king should make periodical appearances in the French parliament and remain uninfluenced by its procedure—yet the influence of French institutions must have reached back for a century or more.[5] With some intermissions, the relations between the two courts had been very close from the days of Louis VII, and intermarriages of royal and noble houses had created many ties. Yet it is noteworthy that it was invariably the

[1] Gerald the Welshman gives some specimens of monastic French in his *Symbolum Electorum* and *Gemma Ecclesiastica* (*Opera*, i.218, 222-4; ii.346). For specimens of the French spoken at Christ Church, Canterbury, see *Epistolae Cantuarienses*, pp. 77, 307.

[2] Roth, *History of the Jews in England*, pp. 93-5; Richardson, *English Jewry*, pp. 128-9. An anecdote told by Gerald the Welshman is to the point: when a Jewess, a deaf mute from birth, was miraculously cured, she spoke in French (*Opera*, vii.24).

[3] No London document written in French appears to have survived from the twelfth century, but the many French documents of the early thirteenth century are sufficient evidence: see the collection from Brit. Mus. Additiônal MS. 14252 in Weinbaum, *London unter Eduard I und II*, ii.5-91.

[4] Ekwall, *Street-names of the City of London*, pp. 19-23.

[5] These questions we discuss later: but see *Trans. R. Hist. Soc.*, 4th series, xi.163-5, and Richardson and Sayles, *Parliaments and Great Councils in Medieval England*, pp. 8-13.

French king who acted as the host to English kings and English princes: it was the French court that was dominant. It is therefore not surprising that the word parliament should appear in England and that sessions of the king's court, to which the name of parliament is given, should be held, however intermittently, a good many years before 1258. But if it is true that, had there been no Norman Conquest, this development is quite unlikely to have taken place, yet the influence of that event was remote and indirect: for the initial cause we must look rather to the marriage of the young duke of Normandy to Eleanor of Aquitaine, which ultimately determined that Henry III, his son and his grandson, should be suitors in the parliament of Paris. And while we recognise the potency of French influences in England from the eleventh to the fifteenth centuries, yet we must also recognise that in the course of reception they were inevitably modified and transformed. Thus, though in the second half of the thirteenth century the English parliament is patently of the same model as the French parliament, by the sixteenth century, still bearing the same name, the two parliaments differ both in function and conception.

Let us, in conclusion, look again at the complex problem of knighthood, not for the purpose of retracing our steps but to cast forward and endeavour to discern the influence of French ideas, and particularly the French idea of chivalry, upon English institutions. There can be no doubt that in the fourteenth century, when the Hundred Years' War once more brought the gentlemen of France and England into close contact with one another, both were imbued with the same ideas of chivalrous conduct. They went to war in very much the same spirit that they went to a tournament. If they desired victory ardently, they did not desire it at the cost of the lives of knights, men of their own class. The lives of knights were too valuable to be sacrificed. Whatever happened to common soldiers, the object was to take knights prisoner, treat them with elaborate consideration and put them to ransom. They were a class apart. Knighthood had become a cult.[1] The studied courtesies that followed the battle of Poitiers and the capture of Jean le Bon are too well known to be recounted: we mention them as typical of the spirit of chivalry at its apogee. That spirit is expressed more completely in Malory's *Morte d'Arthur*, where the strands of religious emotion and respect for women—a limited respect—are entwined with martial virtues. Chivalry had by then become make-believe: a lost ideal of virtue, to which men might aspire but which was quite remote from real

[1] The literature is immense: see bibliography (up to 1929) in *Cambridge Medieval History*, vi.973-6. For a recent account in English of chivalric ideas see Painter, *French Chivalry*, chapters 2-4. A good brief, but more sympathetic, account by G. Neilson will be found in Hastings, *Encyclopaedia of Religion*, iii.565-7, where the influence of classical authors is stressed. On the classical background see the article by H. Leclercq in Cabrol-Leclercq, *Dictionnaire*, iii.1305-7.

life. It is this romantic ideal which colours most modern conceptions of knighthood and has even influenced the conceptions of historians. There is no question that, whether as a guide to conduct or as an ideal, chivalry of this kind was French in spirit and the associated ideas can be traced back to twelfth-century France. But all that is best in chivalry—and we exclude the erotic element—can be traced very much farther back in England. The English word which expresses the chivalric idea was not, however, knightly but thegnly. The song of the Battle of Maldon is a paean in praise of the thegnly virtues. Of Offa, who is cut to pieces in a hopeless fight, it is said that he had fulfilled his plighted word and lay thegnly (ðegenlice) at his lord's side.[1] A true thegn has not only the martial virtues of Offa, but he is honourable and truthful in his everyday conduct. So when the shiremoot of Hereford send three thegns to question a mother whose son has claimed her land, she gives her answer and bids them 'Do thegnly: declare my answer truly before all the good men in the moot.'[2] A thegn, too, will be ready to die for an ideal. So Ælfric, in relating the passion of the Forty Soldiers, tells 'how thegnly they suffered for Christ'. This is the more noteworthy since the men are not thegns but common soldiers (cempan), who act as thegns would be expected to act.[3] Though to Ælfric the virtue of a thegn lay in his conduct and though the ceorl might act as a thegn, we must not suppose that he taught any levelling doctrine. He accepted the established order, even slavery, though he might condemn its abuses. Thegnliness (if we may be excused the abstract noun) was an aristocratic quality: nobility had its obligations and demanded sacrifices. As we have seen, to Ælfric and his hearers the threefold order of society, priests, warriors and labourers—a commonplace of the later Middle Ages—was already familiar.[4] As then, so in the tenth century, the warrior of this trinity is an aristocrat: he is a knight, but he is a thegn, a thegn in the service of God.[5]

It is the thegnly knight, the aristocratic, landed knight, who alone has a significant place in English institutional history. The peasant and the low-born, who apparently formed a large proportion, if not the majority, of knights in the eleventh century, lost all claim to the name before the thirteenth century was very old. The ranks of the thegns, as of the thirteenth-century knights, were not perhaps absolutely closed to those not of noble birth, but exceptions seem to have been rare. Before the Conquest landed knights were likely to be royal thegns. The knights who were the familiars of the Atheling

---

[1] Battle of Maldon, line 294.
[2] Robertson, Anglo-Saxon Charters, p. 152 (no. 78).
[3] Lives of the Saints, i.238.
[4] Guilhiermoz has traced the conception of the three orders of society back to the ninth century (L'origine de la noblesse, pp. 370-8). We may add a reference to King Alfred's Version of Boethius (ed. Sedgefield), p. 40: the king 'sceal habban gebedmen 7 fyrdmen 7 weorcmen'. No such passage occurs in the original Latin.
[5] Above, p. 57.

Athelstan were, of a surety, no common soldiers. Two are mentioned in his will. Ælmær, who seems to have been his dishthegn, had eight hides in one place of the gift of Athelstan and an estate elsewhere which was confirmed by the will: he was also left a horse, a shield and a sword. The other, Æthelwine, received under the will the sword that he had himself presented to the Atheling.[1] These knights were presumably of the same class as those to whom Bishop Oswald of Worcester granted land: his kinsman Osulf (most probably his brother) and Æthelwold, whose relationship to the bishop is not stated.[2] Knights of this kind are described by the Peterborough Chronicle as 'gode cnihtas' and some are named: in 1088, Eustace of Boulogne, the three sons of Earl Roger, 'and all the best-born men that were in this land or in Normandy'; in 1124, Amauri, the steward of the king of France, Hugh fitz Gervase and Hugh de Montfort.[3] And though Domesday Book does not concern itself with grades of knights, yet the distinction between the higher and lower ranks is indicated even there. There is, for example, a list of the knights of the archbishop of Canterbury, which includes important men, like the count of Eu, Hamon the steward (*dapifer*) and Hugh de Montfort, and men of considerable local consequence, like Osbern fitz Letard, Ralf fitz Turold and Robert of Romney. Some knights in the list were plainly men of little consequence, and there are knights of the archbishop, shown elsewhere, both in Kent and Middlesex, who are given no name and who presumably do not figure in the list.[4] This is a problem in itself: but it does not affect the point we have to make, that among the archbishop's knights there were a number whom the chronicler would certainly have described as 'good' and who were of a much higher rank than many knights, probably the great majority, to whom there is a passing reference in Domesday Book, though within this majority there would be gradations and the Domesday knights would obviously not include the large number of landless knights.

How were these 'good knights' distinguished from others? We may doubt whether the mounted soldiers, at one time called knights but who later fell to the rank of serjeants, ever went through a very elaborate ceremony or incurred any great expense in order to gain the title of knight when it was bestowed upon them. But it would seem that already in the tenth century, if not earlier, there was a ceremonial knighting of the well-born. Thus, if William of Malmesbury is to be relied upon, a panegyrist of King Athelstan related how King Alfred had knighted his grandson by investing him with a

---

[1] Whitelock, *Anglo-Saxon Wills*, pp. 58, 60: for Ælmær see also *ibid.*, p. 170.
[2] Robertson, *Anglo-Saxon Charters*, pp. 96, 114, 345.
[3] A.S. Chronicle, *s.a.* 1087, 1124 (Thorpe, pp. 357, 375; Plummer, pp. 224, 253).
[4] For the list headed 'Terra militum eius' (*sc.* archiepiscopi Cantuariensis) see D.B., i.4 a 2, 4 b 1. For other, unnamed, knights on the archbishop's estates see D.B., i.3 a 2, 3 b 2, 127 a 1.

scarlet cloak, a jewelled belt and a sword in a scabbard of gold.[1]
When contemporary chroniclers mention the knighting of the future
Henry I by his father, of Geoffrey of Anjou by Henry I, of the
future Henry II by the king of Scots or of King Malcolm by Henry
II,[2] they are clearly recording a ceremony to which special significance was attached, a ceremony which may have had a continental
ancestry but had an English ancestry also. How far down the social
scale such ceremonies extended we can only guess—in the early
thirteenth century some very small men were knighted—but if we
guess that they extended to royal thegns we are not likely to be
wrong. The thegns, the king's household knights, of whom we read
in the Berkshire Domesday, were knights of a distinctive kind.[3]
Ælfric doubtless would have called them *burcnihtas*, or they might
be described as the king's *hiredcnihtas*.[4] On succeeding their fathers
they paid a relief which is clearly the relief appropriate to royal
thegns prescribed in Cnut's Laws.[5] They were men with good
horses, valuable swords and accoutrements. We seem to pick up the
trail of their successors when we read in the early pipe rolls of the
young knights to whom Henry II presented their arms and accoutrements, costing twenty marks in some cases and in others five
pounds, figures that do not include horses, of which the knights
would be expected to possess two or three.[6] The king's contribution
on these occasions seems to have been a moderate one. The returns
to the Inquest of Sheriffs give some indications of the cost of knighthood to baronial families. The men of Manasser of Dammartin gave
him an aid of fifteen marks when he knighted his son; the men of
Ralf of Munchensy, at the time a ward of the king's, seem to have
given him about ten marks. Another ward of the king's, Hubert of
Rye, was knighted at the instance of his mother, who obtained contributions of upwards of twenty marks from his tenants.[7] Hubert's
knighting has another and noteworthy aspect, because the mother,
Aveline of Rye, did not trouble to get the royal licence and was
fined £200 for her temerity.[8] The incident suggests something of the
importance that was becoming attached to the ceremony. That the
ceremony was expensive in the higher ranks of society is indicated

---

[1] William of Malmesbury, *Gesta Regum*, i.145. There can be no doubt of the existence
of the source: the only doubt can be whether Malmesbury has reproduced the language
of his authority.

[2] A.S. Chronicle, *s.a.* 1085 (Thorpe, p. 353; Plummer, pp. 216-7); Florence of Worcester, ii.19; *Chroniques des Comtes d'Anjou* (ed. Halphen and Poupardin), pp. 178-80 (a
minutely detailed account of the ceremony); Gervase of Canterbury, *Historical Works*,
i.140-1; Geoffrey of Vigeois in *Historiens de la France*, xii.439.

[3] D.B., i.56 b 1: Tainus vel miles regis dominicus moriens pro releuamento dimittebit
regi omnia arma sua et equum, unum cum sella, alium sine sella. For the parallel phrase
'miles de dominica familia regis', see *Pipe Roll, 9 Henry II*, p. 69. For the parallel in
Cnut's law see Liebermann, *Gesetze*, i.358-9, II Cnut, 71.4.   [4] Above, p. 58.

[5] II Cnut, 71.4. The scale is appropriate to royal thegns, not of the king's household,
but related to (or intimately connected with) him (*Gesetze*, i.358-9; iii.212).

[6] *Pipe Roll, 2 Henry II*, pp. 21, 65; *4 Henry II*, p. 113.

[7] *Bulletin John Rylands Library*, xxiv.168; *Red Book of the Exchequer*, ii.cclxxii-cclxxiii.

[8] *Pipe Roll, 14 Henry II*, p. 29.

not only by the custom of demanding an aid when the lord's eldest son was knighted, but by the apparent restriction of the ceremony to two sons of the family.[1] The elaboration and expense, which the introduction of a religious ceremony (still unusual under Henry II)[2] would increase, must in any case have gradually restricted ceremonial knighting to the wealthy, though other circumstances hastened this restriction and determined that only those who were knighted with ceremony should bear the title of knight. But very early there must have been ambiguity in the use of the word, which had acquired one meaning in a social sense and another in a military sense. Already in the later twelfth century there is talk of baronial and knightly families. A *baro* holds directly of the king; a *miles* is a sub-tenant, a vavassor: both, it is implied, are well-born.[3] And while there were still poor knights in the early thirteenth century, by the fourteenth it was assumed that a knight—or at least one socially entitled to this distinction—must have an estate to support his dignity.[4]

The elimination from the ranks of knighthood, not only of the low-born professional soldier but of the lesser landowner, was a recognition of a social division which goes back, as we have seen, a long way before the Conquest. The division was well marked in the Old English kingdom because the line was drawn at the thegn: it was he who was assumed to have the virtues ultimately associated with knighthood. Not all thegns, it is true, were of equal rank; but the problem of the lesser thegn presents no greater problem than the lesser landed knight, those knights, for example, who held of the honour of Mortain.[5] Very much the same differences are found in Normandy, though there the poorer tenants by knight service are distinguished, by the name of vavassors, as members of a lower social rank.[6] This, we may remark, is an unusual use of the word vavassor, which in its origin contained no implication of social inferiority: for a vavassor is a *vassus vassorum*, a mesne tenant.[7] It was never a term in common use in England, though it occurs in Domesday Book. The vavassors there mentioned are freemen of very little consequence, of much the same status as the Norman vavassors; but we know too little of them to be able to say whether they held by some form of military tenure, nor is it easy to understand why the name occurs in only three counties, Buckinghamshire, Hampshire and Suffolk, and only once in each case, though in Suffolk it occurs in a

---

[1] *Rotuli de Dominabus* (ed. Round), pp. 24, 50, 51, 77.
[2] For the ceremony generally see Bloch, *La société féodale: les classes et le gouvernement des hommes*, pp. 46-53. The ceremony is strictly a blessing of the sword, as to which see John of Salisbury, *Policraticus* (ed. Webb), ii.25, and *Sarum Missal* (ed. J. Wickham Legg), p. 454. The subsequent elaboration does not concern us.
[3] *Rotuli de Dominabus*, pp. xxvi-xxvii.
[4] Cf. Tout, *Chapters*, iii.276, n. 1, 278, n. 1; iv.197.
[5] Vinogradoff, *English Society*, pp. 52-4.
[6] Navel, *Enquête de 1133*, pp. 15, 18-21.
[7] For vavassors generally see Guilhiermoz, *Essai sur l'origine de la noblesse*, pp. 183-8.

heading that covers a substantial group of men.[1] We do but mention these Domesday vavassors as an illustration of the practice of the Normans, established in the twelfth century, of distinguishing the *chivaler* from the soldier of inferior status who was not so fully armed and was not clad in a coat of mail.[2] It seems impossible that any such distinction was made generally in Domesday Book: many of the *milites* mentioned there can hardly have been fully equipped *chivalers*.[3] The inference we draw is that, at the time of the Conquest and for a generation or so afterwards, *chivaler*, like knight, was applied to a mounted soldier, without much discrimination. By the reign of Henry I a distinction was at least beginning to show itself, though while in Normandy the men of lower rank are now being termed vavassors and *chivaler* is a name reserved for the fully armed mounted man, by an anomaly we cannot explain the name 'vavassor' is given in England to men who, though mesne tenants, are land-owners of importance, with courts for their own tenants.[4] There is then this paradox that a baron or bishop or minister, who serves the king on both sides of the Channel, will in Normandy call a man a vavassor who is not wealthy enough to be a knight, while in England he will give the same name to a man who would be of knightly rank at any time in the Middle Ages, a man of very considerable social consequence.[5] We emphasise this ambiguity because it is important to realise how circumspect we must be in applying continental analogies to England.

We have said enough of lesser knights who gradually lose any right to that name in England, just as throughout Western Europe *chivaler* gradually becomes restricted to the noble, and all other ranks, except the clergy, fall to the common level of *roturier*.[6] We need hardly explain that 'noble' came to bear a very different meaning on the Continent from its meaning in England, where it became limited to the highest ranks, to the peerage. English insti-tutions insisted upon being or becoming obstinately insular. So it was with English knighthood, those knights of higher rank who retained that title and gradually, through a complex of forces, were reduced to a small number. Two forces were, to begin with, operat-ing simultaneously. There was the moral or religious force, the mystical sense of duty, a single-minded devotion to an ideal, which was heightened by the introduction of a religious ceremony. This force was already operating in the Old English kingdom, but it seems unlikely that the later conception of chivalry owed anything to this source. No English knight of the later twelfth or the thirteenth

---

[1] D.B., i.53 a 2, 146 b 1; ii.446-7. It is noteworthy that the vavassors in Suffolk appear to be all of English or Danish descent, and to hold directly of the Crown.
[2] See above, p. 95, n. 4.   [3] Vinogradoff, *English Society*, pp. 74-8.
[4] 'Leges Henrici', c. 27: cf 'Leis Willelme', c. 20.2 (*Gesetze*, i.506, 562).
[5] It was Robert, earl of Gloucester, who conducted the inquest of 1133.
[6] Guilhiermoz, *op. cit.*, pp. 346-57.

century thought of himself as a thegn: the older tradition had been cut short at the Conquest and a new one had been born afresh on French soil. The moral elevation of knighthood was a sentiment already current at the court of Henry II, as Walter Map's stories bear witness. 'Glory', says one of his knightly heroes, 'is to be attained by valour: it does not come by chance.'[1] Again, he speaks of 'a man of great renown and outstanding knighthood, happy in his manners and his whole estate'.[2] It is no more than a step to Chaucer's perfect gentle knight. But these are aristocratic conceptions, sentiments not to be afforded by professional soldiers of little scruple, with their living to get by hard blows. Then there was the limiting economic factor. To gain social recognition as a knight, one must give oneself to tournaments, to mimic, as well as to real, warfare; and tournaments became an expensive amusement. Whether the accomplished knight was a particularly effective soldier is highly questionable: he was probably a military mistake. But he was what fashion demanded, and he had to have better horses, better arms, better armour than other fighting men. Nor did he go to war singlehanded, but needed attendants, servants. He was a gentleman, who needed a long and careful training in his youth, and whose leisure in manhood was largely occupied with jousting. And because it had become expensive and exclusive, knighthood became an enviable distinction. In England, however, a peculiar twist was given to it.

Quite early in the thirteenth century many English men of standing, with considerable estates in land, were evading knighthood. The evident sign of this is the introduction of distraint of knighthood in the year 1224.[3] Men of sufficient wealth were to be compelled to become knights or were to pay heavily for exemption. What is the explanation of this apparent paradox? Here we come to another illustration of the incompatibility of feudal ideas with English institutions. It has been argued that the reason for this step was to augment the number of knights available for military service,[4] but the assumption that there was any dearth of men trained in arms on the morrow of prolonged civil war is unconvincing: it overlooks the existence of the large class of landless knights. William Marshal is the outstanding example of this class: the younger son of a baronial family who won renown by his knightly prowess and ended his career as earl of Pembroke and *rector regni*. There were many such without his good fortune. The rules laid down by Richard I for the conduct

---

[1] Galo declares 'querenda est virtute gloria non casu' (*De Nugis Curialium* (ed. James), p. 119).

[2] Rollo is described as 'vir magni nominis et preclare milicie, moribus et omni statu felix' (*ibid.*, p. 135).

[3] This appears to have been first established by Nichols in *Archaeologia*, xxxix (1863), p. 202.

[4] Powicke, *Thirteenth Century*, pp. 546-9; Sanders, *Feudal Military Service*, p. 91. There is no evidence that distraint of knighthood had the effect suggested: cf. Denholm-Young, *Collected Papers*, pp. 57-66.

of tournaments in England is perhaps sufficient evidence. The entrance fees, which accrued to the Crown, were regulated by rank: twenty marks for an earl, ten for a baron, four for a landed knight, two for a landless one.[1] Now, two marks was a substantial fee and, though landless knights might in general be poor, the men who could afford to take part in a tournament were not poverty-stricken, but mostly, one may guess, the sons of well-to-do knightly families, still landless, either because they had not succeeded to their inheritance or because, being younger sons, they were not yet provided for by marriage or enfeoffment. Though not all knights, by any means, would be given their arms by their fathers, one of the commonest of feudal aids, that to make the lord's eldest son a knight—and a second son was often knighted, for whom no aid could rightfully be demanded—is evidence enough in itself of the existence of a good many landless knights of superior status, ready, one must suppose, to take service with the king or anyone else willing to reward them for their service in an honourable employment. They were men of a different class from the worthy wandering knight who did well in King Stephen's war but fell into poverty thereafter and took to highway robbery, for which he was hanged under Henry II.[2] This man, however, would probably not have been recognised as a knight, but would have been counted as no more than a serjeant, in the thirteenth century. Of the landless knight in that century we have an apt illustration in a case that came before the king's court in 1220.[3] Five or six years earlier Gilbert of Hendon had given Henry Buccointe his arms, promised him a fee of four marks a year and had taken his homage. Henry alleged that Gilbert had enfeoffed him by charter, but Gilbert denied this, although he admitted the other facts. For our purpose the important feature of the case is not the point of law but the picture of society it presents. Gilbert, who was a Middlesex landowner of no great importance, could take into his household a young man, who came of a prominent London family, and, as he said, promise him advancement if he deserved it. Henry proved disappointing and Gilbert cast him off. But he was of the same stuff as other young men who sought advancement in baronial households and those of worthy country gentlemen of moderate fortune. There could have been no great shortage of such men to serve in the king's wars or, for that matter, against the king in times of civil war. In the late twelfth and thirteenth centuries ecclesiastical tenants-in-chief found it practicable to provide the king with hired knights if they were unable, as often they seem to have been, to exact personal service from their under-tenants.[4] There

---

[1] *Foedera*, i.65; Ralf de Diceto, *Opera*, ii.lxxx-lxxxi. No account appears in the pipe roll, but the fees were collected by Theobald Walter, the justiciar's brother (Howden, iii.268).   [2] *Rolls of the Justices in Eyre for Gloucestershire* etc., ed. D. M. Stenton, p. 167.
[3] *Curia Regis Rolls*, viii.393.
[4] Chew, *Ecclesiastical Tenants in Chief*, pp. 147-56; Sanders, *Feudal Military Service*, p. 55.

was evidently a market for hirelings and a not inconsiderable supply. It is true that the number of knights required from individual tenants-in-chief was by this time small,[1] and a few hundred hireling knights in all would probably have satisfied the utmost demand arising in this way; but it is noteworthy that early in the fourteenth century, by which time the status of the knight had risen, it does not seem to have been considered a matter of difficulty to raise a private troop of forty mounted men-at-arms and ten knights.[2] It is not impossible that some of the knights who hired themselves out owed military service to the king or some lord for their fiefs,[3] but it is unlikely that many substantial landed knights were professional soldiers. When all deductions have been made, we must suppose that there were always a good many soldiers of fortune seeking employment in the later Middle Ages. Quite obviously we can explain indentures of service only on this basis.

The explanation of distraint of knighthood would seem to lie in the legal reforms of Henry II. These had made the civil responsibilities of landed knights extremely onerous. It might be thought that in the later twelfth century there were knights enough and to spare for all the duties, military and civil, that might be imposed upon them. But the requirements of the law were not easily met: the knights must be of the right kind. If they were to bear the record of the country to the king's court they must be *legales milites qui interfuerunt ad recordum illud faciendum*: they must be landed knights and suitors at the county court. The four knights who elected the twelve knights of the grand assize and those twelve knights themselves must be law-worthy knights: the twelve knights who made the recognition must speak of their own knowledge, they must be local landowners.[4] They are knights then with a double qualification: they must be more than dubbed knights, men trained to arms, they must be substantial landowners. How many such there were in the later twelfth century it is hard to say, but early in the reign of Henry III they were scarce enough to cause anxiety. The evident sign of this is the introduction of distraint of knighthood, not because a man was a good soldier but because he was a substantial landowner. That knighthood was evaded is demonstrated also in another way. The aggregate of the new quotas of service that were established in the thirteenth century, though a great reduction on what had been theoretically due in the twelfth, was still considerably greater than the number of knights who appeared in response to writs of military summons for service in the field. This is shown conclusively by the convention, which was already established by 1245, that for one

---

[1] *Ibid.*, pp. 109-14.

[2] Holmes, *Estates of the Higher Nobility*, pp. 122-3: indenture between William Latimer and the earl of Lancaster, 15 May 1319.   [3] Cf. Sanders, *op. cit.*, p. 94.

[4] Glanville, lib. ii, cc. 10-15; lib. viii, cc. 6-10 (ed. Woodbine, pp. 64-7, 120-6; and see notes at pp. 202-4, 242-4).

knight there might be substituted two serjeants. Even tenants-in-chief, who were liable to personal service, might elect to serve as serjeants and bring with them another serjeant to make up the complement of knights for which they had compounded.[1] Even though a landowner had been dubbed knight and undertook the military duties of his rank, he might yet escape his civil responsibilities. If he were wealthy enough he was often willing to pay handsomely to escape the burden of assizes, juries and recognitions. There is no reason to doubt the truth of the barons' complaint in 1258 that the king had granted acquittance from these duties on a large scale.[2] But the king demanded his price and, as Stubbs said, 'it was easier and cheaper to avoid taking knighthood than to purchase such an immunity'.[3] That distraint of knighthood was a weapon aimed at providing knights for civil business can therefore hardly be doubted, nor that respite of knighthood and charters of acquittance were sought and paid for, not to escape military service, but to escape onerous civil obligations. It did not follow that a man who avoided knighthood wished to avoid, or could avoid, military service, though it is true that the mesne tenants of ecclesiastical tenants-in-chief, and presumably of lay tenants-in-chief, seem not infrequently to have evaded their responsibilities.[4] The Assize of Arms was there to ensure that every freeman was equipped, even though he had not exercised himself in arms as a knight should have done; but to dub a reluctant knight, on the other hand, would not convert him into an efficient soldier.

By the thirteenth century knighthood in England had ceased to be a military problem and had become a civil one. The changes in legal procedure and, in particular, the falling into desuetude of the grand assize[5] meant that by the fourteenth century landed knights were not in practice burdened with the onerous duties charged upon them by Henry II's legislation. But a new burden made its appearance when it became increasingly the practice to require the county court to send two knights to represent the shire in parliament. Though the writs of summons for a long time insisted that these representatives should have been ceremonially knighted, in the course of the fourteenth century it was found impracticable to enforce this requirement. It was necessary to admit serjeants and squires, though stress is still laid upon their qualification as gentlemen capable of becoming knights, not men of the degree of yeomen.[6] The English squirearchy was emerging. By a curious evolution England had gained a county aristocracy, which was proud of its gentility, of its right to bear arms, but arms in the heraldic sense; an

---

[1] Sanders, *op. cit.*, p. 93.
[2] *Select Charters*, p. 378; cf. Denholm-Young, *Collected Papers*, pp. 62-3.
[3] *Constitutional History*, iii.564 n.
[4] Chew, *op. cit.*, pp. 147-56; Sanders, *op. cit.*, p. 55.   [5] *L.Q.R.*, liv.387-8.
[6] The facts are summarised by Stubbs, *Constitutional History*, iii.410-6.

aristocracy which, to do it justice, was responsible for conducting most of the public service of the county. By what would have, at one time, seemed a strange inversion, knights were not infrequently squires. If the Old English speech had prevailed, squires would have been called thegns, and in the different circumstances of different centuries they were acting as thegns had acted in the Old English polity. These pacific country squires and the system they represent are sometimes called feudal. That the adjective should become a word of abuse, to stigmatise the universal characteristics of a propertied ruling class, demonstrates of itself how little meaning the word has on English lips.

VII

THE UNDYING KING

A LTHOUGH Stubbs invented a constitution for mediaeval England, he gave his readers but occasional glimpses of it. It was, so he asserted, a parliamentary constitution, a constitution that had had a long struggle for existence, a struggle that ended with the reign of Edward I. The triumph of the constitution—for Stubbs personified it—had involved a surrender by the king to the barons. Yet, strangely enough, before that surrender Edward had 'reigned as Henry II had done, showing proper respect for constitutional forms, but exercising the reality of despotic power'.[1] If, then, we are to know what this constitution was and what were the powers of the king, we must seek our answers in the twelfth century; and Stubbs, indeed, had endeavoured to provide those answers in the final chapter of the first volume of his *Constitutional History*. Here we are concerned with two sections only of that chapter. One of them glances at the doctrine of sovereignty as it is found in contemporary literature, at the claims of English kings to suzerainty over the British Isles, at the homage rendered by them to the French king and by Richard I to the emperor and by John to the pope, at crown-wearings and, finally, at regency during the king's absence: an odd medley. The substance of the other section is sufficiently indicated by a side-note—'the national council in two aspects: as a feudal court and as a stage towards the representation of estates'.[2] To say that Stubbs throws inadequate light upon mediaeval kingship and its limitations would be an understatement. He was handicapped, on the one hand, by the paucity of the sources upon which he relied and, on the other, by his weakness for interpreting the past in the light of what he imagined to be the future of English political institutions. Much could be said in criticism. It will suffice, however, if we, in our turn, attempt to describe the powers and duties of a king after the Conquest.

The best illustration of contemporary ideas on the nature of kingship is the coronation office. Of this there were two main types current in Western Europe: one that had been given shape in England, though its origin was in France, and the other, the so-called *Ordo Romanus*, that originated in Germany. Both types of coronation office circulated in England, though this does not mean

---

[1] *Select Charters*, pp. 38-9; *Constitutional History*, ii.169, 266.　　[2] *Ibid.*, i.592-614.

that any one of the texts that have survived was used at the coronation of any English king. There were many variant texts, and texts
became fused: no resulting text was of any particular authority and
none therefore is a sure guide to practice. We do not even know
which text was used in Westminster Abbey in the twelfth and
thirteenth centuries.[1] Nevertheless it must be understood that the
main elements of every coronation office did not greatly vary and
that we may safely infer that one coronation ceremony in its general
features and in its liturgical content broadly resembled another. For
our present purpose the value of the different texts is that they show
how the unknown ecclesiastics who compiled them regarded kingship.

Exception must be made of the coronation oath. There can hardly
be room for doubt that in England, at least, the oath was administered in the vernacular and that, as on the Continent, it might
bear only a distant relation to any liturgical oath that has come
down to us. The oath administered by St. Dunstan in 978, as it had
presumably been administered on some previous occasions, was a
vernacular version of the liturgical form as it is contained in the
Anglo-French type of office. This engages the king to preserve peace
for the Church and all Christian people; to forbid all kinds of
rapacity and lawlessness; to enjoin equity and mercy in all judgements.[2] But if we can rely upon Florence of Worcester, the oath
taken by the Conqueror was a blending of the Anglo-French and
German forms. It may be that Florence had no certain source of
knowledge and was relying upon a liturgical text that has not come
down to us; but in any case we may be sure that the formula he
gives was current in his day. This formula binds the king to defend
the churches and their ministers and to rule his subjects justly and
with royal prudence, to establish and maintain just laws and to
suppress rapines and unjust judgements.[3] There is very good reason
to believe that William was anxious to follow English precedents,
and we may therefore infer that the form of oath he took had previously been taken by Edward the Confessor: whether it was the

[1] Schramm in *Zeitschrift der Savigny-Stiftung für Rechtsgeschichte*, liv, lv, Kan. Abt.
xxiii.117-242, xxiv.184-332; Bouman, *Sacring and Crowning*, pp. 9-37; Richardson, 'The
Coronation in Mediaeval England' in *Traditio*, xvi.174-89. The reader should perhaps
be warned that the precise dates Schramm has sought to give to certain texts are open
to question.
[2] Text in *Memorials of St. Dunstan* (ed. Stubbs), p. 355, and Liebermann, *Gesetze der
Angelsachsen*, i.214-7. It is uncertain whether the king referred to is Edward (975) or
Ethelred (978), but the inference is that the same ceremony was observed on both occasions. Whether Edgar had taken a like oath in 959 is a matter of conjecture: the
evidence of the *Vita Oswaldi*, on which reliance has been placed for the administration of
the oath in 973, is worthless (Appendix I: below, pp. 399-403).
[3] Florence of Worcester, i.229; *Traditio*, xvi.161-2, 186. There may be an echo of
the coronation oath in Goscelin's description of the Confessor as 'leges iniquas evellens,
justas sapienti consilio statuens' (*Vita Ædwardi*, p. 13). We refer to the Worcester Chronicle
as Florence's without implying that the question of authorship is settled: we are not,
however, convinced by recent arguments that the reference to him *s.a.* 1118 does not
imply his authorship (cf. *Chronicle of John of Worcester*, (ed. Weaver), p. 9 n).

oath Florence gives or another, it is significant that he does not give the easily accessible *tria precepta* of the Anglo-French type of office.

The evidence for the twelfth century is relatively copious and, while we have in no case the actual words spoken, we learn that the oath has undergone further changes. From the time of Henry I onwards kings swore to protect the Church, to do justice to the people and to suppress evil laws and customs. To this oath a further clause —to protect the rights of the Crown—was added, apparently by Henry II, but there is no reason to suppose that in substance the oath was subject to further change until it was entirely recast for the coronation of Edward II.[1] Apart from this additional fourth clause, all the forms of oath, Anglo-French or German or a conflation of the two, embody much the same concepts, however the language might be varied, and varied it certainly was when a vernacular version was prepared for each successive king at his coronation. These variants have their interest, for it was the spoken oath that was elaborated and supplemented in coronation charters until coronation charters were at last superseded by Magna Carta. We need not, however, follow them in detail.

According to the German rite, which was that followed in England, it was not until he had taken the oath that the prince was presented to the clergy and people for their acceptance of him as king, not until then that he was blessed and anointed, that the realm was symbolically committed to him, to rule faithfully according to his oath, and that finally he was crowned.[2] Now doubtless much of this ritual was a matter of form, but if the coronation ceremony conveyed any lesson to the king at all, it was the lesson of the obligations of kingship. The solemnity of the ceremony was heightened by the unction. This exalted the king above other men and bestowed upon him the divine gifts of glory, knowledge and fortitude, gifts he needed if he were to fulfil the duties of his office. Moreover, the anointing of the head—persisted in, despite the protests of high churchmen, even of the pope—mystically sanctified the king: his person became sacred; he was enabled to perform miracles of healing.[3]

If the king has solemn duties, he is also the object of adulation. Before the epistle of the coronation mass, the *laudes* are sung in his honour:

Christus vincit. Christus regnat. Christus imperat. Exaudi Christe!
Willelmo serenissimo a Deo consecrato, magno et pacifico regi,
    vita et victoria!

        *   *   *   *   *   *

Moribus ornatum, Salomonis fonte repletum,
Poscimus Anglorum nostrum salvet basileum.

[1] *Traditio*, xvi.153-73.   [2] *Ibid.*, pp. 178-80.
[3] *Ibid.*, pp. 117-8, 199-200; Bloch, *Les rois thaumaturges*, pp. 67-86. That Edward the Confessor had the power of healing is asserted in the *Vita Ædwardi*, pp. 61-3, written apparently within a year of his death: for date see Southern in *E.H.R.*, lviii.385-400.

Three times a year at the great festivals of the Church will the king wear his crown in state, and that he may be, as it were, re-consecrated, an elaborate votive mass will be sung; the archbishop will be the celebrant; the *laudes* will be chanted; the great ministers will perform their ceremonial offices; there will be feastings and rejoicings. If Stephen and Richard are dishonoured by captivity, in this fashion their honour will be restored to them. Nor is this basileiolatry confined to the king: it is shared by the queen, *serenissima a Deo coronata regina*.[1] Already before the Conquest there are hints of her exaltation: after the Conquest she is *regalis imperii particeps*.[2] And these are no idle words, as the history of the twelfth century was to show.

Whether there was any recognised principle—however faint the recognition might be—that kings were subject to election is a difficult problem. Stubbs was certain that in Anglo-Saxon times kings had been elected[3] and he was inclined to believe that, at least in the case of John, there had been some form of election after the Conquest.[4] The coronation office of the type used in England did indeed provide, as we have seen, for what may not unfairly be termed the simulacrum of an election; but this office was originally drawn up in Germany to suit conditions very different from those obtaining in England. It is from this source, and not from any native source, that the 'recognition' to be found in the coronation office of the fourteenth century derives.[5] There are, indeed, positive statements that John, because of his defective title, was elected king, but these statements are, for different reasons, highly suspect. There is nothing we can see in any liturgical text which suggests that the king was in any real sense elected. It is true that in a pre-Conquest form of coronation office a rubric speaks of 'rex . . . ab episcopis et a plebe electus'[6] and that in the German form of office there is a ceremonial presentation of the prince to the assembled people, who are asked whether they are willing to be subject unto him and to obey his commands. But nevertheless the king is divinely appointed,[7]

---

[1] For the text of the *laudes* under William the Conqueror see Maskell, *Monumenta Ritualia Ecclesiae Anglicanae*, ii.85-8. For later texts see Kantorowicz, *Laudes Regiae*, pp. 171-2. For the *laudes* in England generally see *ibid.* pp. 172-9; for the religious ceremony of crown-wearing see *Traditio*, xvi, 129-32.

[2] See the introductory rubric to the coronation of a queen in the Second Recension (L. G. W. Legg, *English Coronation Records*, p. 21) and the post-Conquest texts in J. W. Legg, *Three Coronation Orders*, pp. 61-3, 173.

[3] *Constitutional History*, i.150-3. The evidence will not support this conclusion (above, p. 23).   [4] *Ibid.*, pp. 553-4.

[5] The Fourth Recension borrows from the Third Recension, which is itself a modified form of the German office (Legg, *English Coronation Records*, pp. 31, 85; *Traditio*, xvi.178-9).

[6] *English Coronation Records*, p. 15. Like words are found in the canons of 786-7, 'legitime reges a sacerdotibus et senioribus populi eligantur'; but the intention is to exclude those born out of wedlock (below, p. 397).

[7] This doctrine is already current in the tenth century. The martyred Edward is God's thegn and his pre-elected vicar on earth: 'suum militem et vice sui regiminis in terris constitutum et praeelectum' (*Vita Oswaldi*, p. 450). Goscelin describes the Confessor similarly: 'Felicissimus mentionis rex Ædwardus ante natalis sui diem Deo est electus, unde ad regnum non tam ab hominibus quam . . . divinitus est consecratus' (*Vita Ædwardi*, p. 60).

a Deo consecratus as the *laudes* put it. As sovereigns from Henry II claimed, they ruled by the grace of God,[1] and it is the ruling king, and not the barons or the bishops, who determines, or seeks to determine, who his successor shall be.

Thus William I disposes of his kingdom to his second-born son[2]: this may be because, according to the rules of tenure with which he was familiar, a man's inheritance passed to his eldest son, while of the possessions he had acquired, his 'conquest', he might dispose as he would.[3] This was, however, hardly a precedent for the future. And if the rules of tenure determined the descent of the Crown, they created difficulty when there was no direct male heir. There can be little doubt that, despite the oaths Henry I exacted from his barons, there were formidable practical reasons against accepting his daughter, the Empress, as queen. It is far from clear how her husband, Count Geoffrey of Anjou, could have failed to share, if not to dominate, her inheritance, by the same title that Henry II became duke of Aquitaine or his son Geoffrey, by his marriage with Constance, became count of Brittany.[4] If the Empress were to be rejected, the alternative was one of the sons of the late king's sister, Adela, countess of Blois; but there is no suggestion of a formal election of Stephen unless it be that by the citizens of London,[5] though in his so-called second charter he claimed that he had been elected king with the assent of the clergy and the people.[6] This, however, seems to be no more than an echo from the coronation office. Henry II regarded Stephen as no better than a usurper. His own title was purely hereditary; but the fact that his mother was set aside in his favour is itself testimony to the difficulty in the way of female succession.

Richard I certainly nominated his successor. In the first place he recognised as heir apparent Arthur, the son of Geoffrey and Constance,[7] and then, for lack of a son of his own and because Arthur had in 1196 been given by the Bretons into the keeping of Philip Augustus, he recognised as heir apparent his brother John.[8] It has been sought to give John a hereditary title by vouching an alleged Norman rule of succession under which the brother was to be preferred to the nephew,[9] and there might be brought in support of this

---

[1] Henry added *Dei gracia* to his style not later than May 1172 (Delisle, *Actes de Henri II*, Introduction, pp. 16-31; *Memoranda Roll, 1 John*, (Pipe Roll Soc.) Introduction, p. xii *n*). The claim to rule by God's grace was, of course, much older. Cf. *Vita Ædwardi*, p. 13: 'omnem Britanniam . . . cui ex Dei gracia et hereditario jure pius rex presedit'.
[2] The picturesque but untrustworthy account of the Conqueror's deathbed in Ordericus Vitalis, *Historia Ecclesiastica*, iii.242-4, has sometimes led to misunderstanding. Freeman, for example (*Norman Conquest*, iv.705-7), seems not to have grasped the sense of Orderic's words 'Non enim tantum decus *haereditario jure* possedi.'
[3] Glanville, lib. vii, c. 1 (ed. Woodbine, pp. 96-101); Pollock and Maitland, *History of English Law*, ii.308.   [4] Cf. Round, *Geoffrey de Mandeville*, p. 33.
[5] *Gesta Stephani* (ed. Potter), pp. 3-4.   [6] *Select Charters*, p. 143.
[7] October 1190 (*Gesta Ricardi*, ii.135).
[8] Not later than August 1197 (Landon, *Itinerary of Richard I*, pp. 121-2, 207-8).
[9] Powicke, *Loss of Normandy*, pp. 193-4. There is this to be said in favour of this argument, that Louis of France, when making his claim to the English throne, implies that

suggestion the conversation between Hubert Walter and William Marshal related in the *Histoire de Guillaume le Maréchal*.[1] But this conversation, like many of the minstrel's tales, is fiction, invented well after the event. For both Hubert Walter and the Marshal, there can be no doubt, had been pledged to support John as far back as 1197.[2] John himself claimed a hereditary title to the throne and he also claimed the unanimous consent and approbation of both clergy and people.[3] This seems to mean no more than the recognition for which the coronation office provided, though on this occasion the recognition may have had something more than formal significance, for John's hereditary title was manifestly weak while Arthur was alive. It was, however, alleged by Louis of France in 1216 that, when Hubert Walter had crowned John, he had declared that he had done so, not because of any right of succession but because John had been elected king.[4] Presumably this was the basis of the fictitious speech that Matthew Paris puts into Hubert's mouth.[5] But there is no strictly contemporary evidence for any form of election, and it is inherently improbable in face of Roger of Howden's statement that Hubert Walter, William Marshal and the justiciar Geoffrey fitz Peter had obtained an oath of fealty from the English barons before John's coronation.[6] The determining factor in John's accession seems clearly to have been Richard's nomination, to which he had obtained the assent of the leading clergy and barons. There was certainly a choice between the two nearest in blood to the king: if we call the choice an election, we must clearly understand what we mean by the word. More distinctly recognisable as a process of election was the action of the barons who opposed John when they offered the crown to Louis of France and arranged a meeting for his formal election.[7] But even Louis felt obliged to concoct a fictitious title *jure uxoris*,[8] and if he had indeed succeeded in winning the throne, it would have been by force of arms. How strong was the claim of hereditary right over any notion of selection among possible candidates is seen in the turn of events. Any title Henry III could have had was simply that of his father's first-born: there could be no question of election, no question of his ability to rule. There was indeed much to be said against him if a choice were really open, for a minority was a new and hazardous experiment in kingship, especially in a land torn by civil war.

a surviving sister should be preferred to a nephew (*Foedera*, i.140): see n. 8, below.

[1] *Histoire de Guillaume le Maréchal* (ed. Meyer), ll. 11878-908.

[2] Only in this way can we explain their appearance as witnesses to John's charters of 8 September and 16 October 1197 which imply that he is heir to the throne (Landon, *op. cit.*, pp. 121-4, 208).   [3] *Foedera*, i.75.   [4] *Ibid.*, p. 140.

[5] *Chronica Maiora*, ii.454-5.   [6] Howden, *Chronica*, iv.88-9.

[7] For the meeting at Northampton *ad regem eligendum*, to which the king of Scotland and the prince of North Wales were invited by the *magnates Anglie*, see *Acts of the Parliaments of Scotland*, i.112.

[8] His wife's mother was Eleanor, daughter of Henry II, born between Geoffrey and John and married to Alphonse III of Castile.

If, however, it is very dubious whether the English king was subject to election, there is, on the other hand, evidence for a ceremony of election in the case of a queen. A hint of this is perhaps to be found in a pre-Conquest coronation office where a rubric directs that the queen is to be blessed and consecrated in church *coram optimatibus*.[1] After the Conquest Adeliza, daughter of the count of Louvain, whom Henry I married in 1121, is said by a contemporary chronicler to have been elected *domina regni* on the day before she was crowned.[2] This election is clearly not to be confused with a form of recognition at the coronation. Again, the Empress was elected lady of the English in April 1141 as a prelude to a coronation which she failed to secure.[3] There could hardly have been any election of Eleanor of Aquitaine, who was already married to the heir to the throne, and indeed there seems no evidence that Henry II ever formally adopted the title of *dominus Anglie* before his accession.[4] For different reasons there could hardly have been an election, not even formal recognition, of Berengaria, who was married to Richard I at Limassol and crowned there. But words are used of Isabelle of Angoulême which we must consider. She was, says a formal instrument confected within four years of the ceremony, crowned queen with the common consent and by the united wish of the archbishops, bishops, earls, barons, clergy and people of the whole realm.[5] These words may mean no more than that there had been a formal recognition in the course of the ceremony or, as in the case of Adeliza, there may have been some preliminary formality of her election. It is inherently probable that the extraordinary authority exercised by Norman and Angevin queens was recognised by some fitting symbolism at their coronation; but we must confess our ignorance. We may be reasonably certain that some form of the *Ordo Romanus* was employed in their case as in the case of kings,[6] but no form that has come down to us contains any hint of an appropriate ceremony.

Already in the tenth century basileiolatry, ruler-worship, was established in England. The king was God's thegn, His vicar upon earth.[7] Greater adulation could not well be bestowed on any king than was bestowed upon Edgar. There can be little doubt that already in his reign there were ceremonial crown-wearings on the Frankish model at the great festivals, when *laudes* were sung in the king's honour[8]; and if it was not claimed for Edgar that he could work miracles, this claim was made for Edward the Confessor.[9] And though the study of Roman law in the twelfth century may have introduced new phrases in which to express the measure of authority

---

[1] Legg, *English Coronation Records*, p. 21.   [2] *Chronicle of John of Worcester*, p. 16.
[3] Round, *Geoffrey de Mandeville*, pp. 60-69.
[4] For Henry's titles before his accession see Delisle, *Actes de Henri II*, Introduction, pp. 120-31. That he claimed to be lord of England would seem, however, to be beyond dispute (below, p. 255).   [5] *Rotuli Chartarum*, p. 128.   [6] *Traditio*, xvi.121-3, 176.
[7] See p. 139, n. 7, above.   [8] Below, pp. 407-8.   [9] See p. 138, n. 3, above.

enjoyed by kings, the concept of autocracy was already to be found in liturgical texts. The sentence from the Institutes cited in 'Glanville' and later by Bracton, 'quod principi placuit legis habet vigorem', may have the sound of absolutism,[1] but surely not more so than the question addressed to the congregation at the recognition, whether they will submit to the king elect as their prince and ruler and obey his commands.[2] The extreme consequence of this concept of the kingly office was drawn by Richard of Ely who, in his dedication of the 'Dialogus' to Henry II, would deny to the subject the right to discuss the king's acts. But he alone speaks without qualification.[3] Others will agree with him that the hearts of kings are in the hands of God, by whom alone they may be judged; but to this they add a qualification which converts the doctrine of absolutism into a doctrine of limited monarchy.[4]

Already Henry I in his coronation charter had recognised that the law might not be changed except by the counsel of the king's barons. True, he speaks thus of the past, of the law of King Edward that had been amended by King William; though he speaks also of himself as having been crowned king by the mercy of God and the common counsel of the barons of the whole realm.[5] We have, however, to wait until the early years of Henry II for an exposition of the nature of kingship in England. The interpolator of the 'Leges Edwardi Confessoris' is the first to enunciate the doctrine that by his coronation oath the king is bound to safeguard the rights of the Crown. To this doctrine we shall return. Here we wish to notice his teaching regarding the relation of the king to the barons. The king must not be guided by caprice but must do all things by the judgement of the nobles, and by the like counsel he must judge rightly and do justice.[6] The author of 'Glanville' speaks in similar terms. English

---

[1] Glanville, Prologue (ed. Woodbine, p. 24); Bracton, fo. 107 (ed. Woodbine, ii.305).

[2] The Third Recension reads 'si tali principi ac rectori se subicere et iussionibus eius obtemperare velint' (*English Coronation Records*, p. 31). Though another variant of the *Ordo Romanus* appears to have been used at Westminster (*Traditio*, xvi, pp. 178-9, 185-7). these words approximate so nearly to those of similar texts that something very like them must have been said at the coronation of English kings: cf. Schramm in *Zeitschrift der Savigny-Stiftung für Rechtsgeschichte*, lv, Kan. Abt. xxiv.312, 317; Hittorp, *De Divinis Officiis*, col. 149.

[3] *Dialogus de Scaccario*, p. 1: 'eorum [*sc.* regum] tamen facta ab inferioribus discutienda vel condempnanda non sunt'. He continues: 'Quorum enim corda et motus cordium in manu Dei sunt.'

[4] Bracton, fo. 107 (Woodbine, ii.305): 'cum cor regis in manu Dei esse debeat': but this imposes moral obligations upon the king. Bracton has already said that 'nemo . . . de factis suis presumat disputare' (fo. 6: Woodbine, ii.33). We discuss Bracton's teaching below.

[5] *Select Charters*, pp. 117-9: the important phrase is 'lagam Eadwardi regis vobis reddo cum illis emendationibus quibus pater meus eam emendavit consilio baronum suorum'. For the doctrine that an edict by the king (in this case Henry I), made without the consent of the barons, was binding only during his lifetime, see *Chron. Mon. de Bello*, p. 66.

[6] Debet etiam rex omnia rite facere in regno et per iudicium procerum regni. Debet enim ius et iustitia magis regnare in regno quam voluntas prava. . . . Debet iudicium rectum in regno facere et iustitiam per consilium procerum regni sui tenere (Leges Edwardi Confessoris', 11, 1.A6, A8, in Liebermann, *Gesetze der Angelsachsen*, i.635-6). For the date see *Traditio*, xvi, pp. 166-7.

laws, he says, are those which, by the counsel of the nobles and with the authority of the prince, are promulgated to settle doubtful points that have been debated in council.[1] With Bracton we get the fullest exposition of kingship. He follows tradition, but he elaborates the doctrine. And here, since contemporary usage has given rise to much misunderstanding, a preliminary explanation may be useful.

In form Bracton's discussion of kingship is based upon the *tria precepta*, for though in practice they had passed into desuetude, they were still regarded as authoritative by ecclesiastics and lawyers. Thus, when in 1185 Henry II asked a council of bishops, abbots, earls and barons to advise him whether he should depart upon a crusade, the decision turned upon the coronation oath. The only text before the council was that to be found in the form of coronation office to be met with most commonly in England, a form that would be accessible to the bishops in their pontificals. This was the so-called Third Recension, a German text modified by elements drawn from an ancient English text, including the coronation oath.[2] So authoritative was this form of oath regarded that Ralf de Diceto gives it as the oath taken by Richard I at his coronation, although he was present himself and heard quite different words uttered.[3] The actual oath, which might vary from one coronation to another, did not pass into circulation and was not generally accessible, and it is not surprising therefore that Bracton relied upon the same text as the clergy had done in 1185 and as the dean of St. Paul's did when writing his *Imagines Historiarum* some years later. It is the text that does duty as the coronation oath in many mediaeval collections.[4]

Bracton, then, has before him the coronation oath in the ancient English liturgical form, and he has also before him the interpolated 'Leges Edwardi Confessoris' (which gives a different form of oath), and he has 'Glanville'. Echoing the 'Leges', he declares that the king is God's vicar and that he may have no equal, let alone a superior; but he is bound to do justice (for if he acts unjustly he serves the Devil and not God) and in the making of law he must act with the advice of his great men.[5] To the king's obligation to act by the advice of the nobles Bracton returns time and again.[6] But writing later, when Henry III was advancing further and further in his career of folly and misgovernment, Bracton has to face the problem of the king who acts unjustly and will not amend what he has done amiss. He first puts forward the doctrine, as Richard of Ely had

---

[1] Leges namque Anglicanas . . . eas scilicet quas super dubiis in consilio definiendis, procerum quidem consilio et principis accidente auctoritate constat esse promulgatas: Glanville, Prologue (ed. Woodbine, p. 24).

[2] Ralf de Diceto, *Historical Works*, ii.33; *Traditio*, xvi, 174-80.

[3] Diceto, *op. cit.*, ii.68-9.   [4] *B.I.H.R.*, xiii.140-1.

[5] Bracton, fo. 107-107*b* (ed. Woodbine, ii.305): he paraphrases Glanville, Prologue (ed. Woodbine, p. 24), 'quod consilio magnatum suorum, rege auctoritatem prestante et habita super hoc deliberatione et tractatu, recte fuerit definitum.'

[6] Fo. 5*b*, 34, 107*b*, 413*b* (ed. Woodbine, ii.32, 110, 305; iv.285).

done, that no man may sit in judgement on the king's acts, and then he gives the reply to this doctrine, a reply that seems to be his own. Truly God is the king's superior, and not only God but the law, by which he is made king; nor these alone, for there is his court of earls and barons whose duty it is to bridle the king if he acts contrary to the law.[1] That Bracton contemplated the constraint of armed force is unlikely, but rather compulsion of the kind that was exercised at the parliament of Oxford in 1258. For elsewhere he had written that, if the king will not amend his wrongful acts, 'satis sufficit ei ad penam quod Deum expectet ultorem'—let him await God's vengeance.[2] There is no solution within the realm of law for the problem of the unjust king who will not yield to argument, and Bracton has no solution. The law must presume, as Bracton did, that the king will do no wrong. What is important to observe is that Bracton assumes, as his predecessors had done, that the king will act by the advice of his barons, that he will not (though Stubbs asserted the contrary) 'exercise the reality of despotic power'. The most devoted of royalists accepted this doctrine. No one was more fervent in his adulation of Edward I than the author of 'Fleta'; but he accepts and adopts the most extreme of Bracton's words.[3]

Nor was this no more than doctrine, a theory of government: it was current practice, as multitudinous records show. The solemn crown-wearings were not merely for the king's glory but also for practical business. We need but give one instance under Henry II. 'The king', says Roger of Howden, 'in this year (1170) held his court in the solemn season of Easter at Windsor, when there were present William king of Scotland and David his brother and nearly all the nobles and great men of England, both bishops and earls and barons. And when Easter was passed, he proceeded to London and there held a great council to discuss the coronation of Henry, his eldest son, and the statutes of his realm; and there he dismissed nearly all the sheriffs of England and their bailiffs because they had dealt evilly with the men of his kingdom.'[4] But let us turn to the thirteenth century. If ever there was an arbitrary monarch, in Stubbs's eyes, it was John; but he, like his father, was constantly consulting the barons on important questions of administration or on some change in the law.[5] Magna Carta is there to testify that John did not, in the barons' view, adequately consult them when

---

[1] Fo. 34 (ed. Woodbine, ii.110). This is the 'Additio de cartis', but there can hardly be any reasonable doubt that it is Bracton's own: see *Trans. R. Hist.*, 4th Ser., xxviii.22 and *Traditio*, vi.87-91.   [2] Fo. 6 (ed. Woodbine, ii.33).

[3] *Fleta*, lib. i, c. 17 (ed. Richardson and Sayles, pp. 35-8).   [4] *Gesta Henrici*, i.4-5.

[5] Quite apart from acts done *communi consilio*, we have a number of examples where this phrase is made specific, e.g.: 'communi consilio baronum nostrorum' (assize of bread, Easter 1204: *Rot. Litt. Pat.*, p. 41); the same phrase occurs in April 1205 when the king's galleys are distributed among various ports (*ibid.*, p. 52b); on the same occasion, it would seem, it was decided that every nine knights should provide a tenth knight for the king's service 'cum assensu archiepiscoporum, episcoporum, comitum, baronum et omnium fidelium nostrorum' (*ibid.*, p. 55).

taxes were imposed[1]; but there is nothing to suggest that they had any complaint of lack of consultation on other matters. The difficulty, of course, was to get the barons together for consultation, except on special occasions such as the great festivals. Henry III's childish vanity and facile piety multiplied crown-wearings to the point at which it was impossible to expect a crowded assembly at court on these occasions.[2] The scheme of a baronial council propounded at the parliament of Oxford might seem to offer a solution; but it was found impossible in practice to keep together a group of fifteen prominent barons and bishops, and the most that could be secured was that they should be represented in the day-to-day work of the council—a ministerial council—by two or three of their number.[3] As in the days when crown-wearings were restricted to the great festivals, three times a year was the extent to which barons could reasonably be expected to attend the king's court in considerable numbers; and three parliaments a year at which there would be a substantial attendance of barons was the scheme envisaged by the Provisions of Oxford.[4] After the collapse of the Oxford scheme, parliaments and great councils provided, until the close of the Middle Ages, the opportunities for consultation that were suited to a limited monarchy, a monarchy limited, not as in Stubbs's imaginary constitution by a parliament of estates, but by the lords of the council. Of these matters, however, we have much to say later.

So far we have discussed the position of the king in mediaeval England with barely a suggestion that it was affected by any of the notions commonly associated with feudalism. It is possible that the obligation upon the feudatory to give his lord counsel did in some measure affect the constitution of parliament. This question is debatable, but is not susceptible of a positive answer. For in parliament there were certainly other elements than feudal, and it is not only the feudal lien that has impelled kings to call magnates to their councils. English kings were doing so a hundred years before the Conquest.[5] Bracton, indeed, uses language that suggests that the feudal lien was far from his thoughts when he considered the relation between the king and his nobles. 'The king's court', he says, 'is one of earls and barons. The former are called *comites* because they are, as it were, the fellows of the king; and he who has a fellow has a master. And therefore, if the king should be unbridled, that is lawless, it is their duty to put a bridle upon him.'[6] Whatever we may

---

[1] c. 12: this embodies c. 32 of the Articles of the Barons.

[2] Henry multiplied them so that in one year there might be as many as sixteen (Kantorowicz, *Laudes Regiae*, pp. 175-6). He appears to have gone on holding crown-wearings until the end of his reign. In 1269 he proposed to wear his crown on the occasion of the translation of Edward the Confessor to his new shrine in Westminster Abbey: the rivalries between the citizens of London and Winchester for the privilege of serving as butlers seem to have led either to the abandonment or modification of the ceremony (*Annales Monastici*, ii.108, iv.458).   [3] *Ibid.* (Burton), i.477.

[4] *Ibid.*, p. 452; *Select Charters*, p. 383.   [5] Appendix I: below, p. 406.

[6] Bracton, fo. 34 (ed. Woodbine, ii.110).

think of the argument, we cannot mistake it for feudal doctrine. And yet homage, liege homage, was of sufficient importance after Bracton's death to cause it to be introduced into the coronation ceremony. How can we account for this apparent contradiction?

If we attach importance to the incidents of feudal tenure—escheats, marriages, wardship—then we may claim importance for feudal ideas in mediaeval England. But if we pursue this line of reasoning we shall find ourselves in difficulty. For these sources of revenue were never so exploited as under the Tudors,[1] and the Tudors are not in the least like conventional feudal monarchs. For the continued influence of feudal ideas we must look, if at all, to the persistence of homage and fealty, though fealty, with its much longer history in England, can hardly be described as feudal. Homage and fealty rendered to the king retained much, at least, of their primitive significance, even though their significance in the case of mesne lords was diminishing to the point of extinction. The Norman and Angevin kings, who became kings only on coronation, took the homage of their barons as soon as possible after the ceremony. Let us illustrate the practice from what we are told of King John.

We have already noticed the emergence in the twelfth century of the title *domina Anglorum*, bestowed upon English queens before their coronation. The title *dominus Anglorum* emerges later in the century and is first known to have been borne by Richard I in the interval between his father's death and his own coronation.[2] In the case of John, his peace as lord of England was proclaimed, and his representatives, Hubert Walter, William Marshal and the justiciar Geoffrey fitz Peter, assembled the earls and the more prominent barons at Northampton and, after giving the assurance that John would respect their rights, took an oath of fealty from them.[3] John was subsequently crowned and on the day following his coronation received 'homages and fealties'.[4] This would seem to mean that he received the homage of the barons and the fealty of the bishops. In any case fealty and homage must be two distinct ceremonies: the former, in the case of a layman, may be sworn to the representatives of the sovereign, but homage seemingly must be rendered to the sovereign in person. That this is the distinction between the two ceremonies is borne out by the rendering of fealty and homage to Edward I on two separate occasions. Within a week of Henry III's death, fealty was sworn to the new king in his absence, for Edward's accession was recognised before his coronation,[5] but homage was seemingly not rendered to him until his coronation. But now the ceremony of homage, as rendered to the king, had changed its significance: it had become part of the coronation ceremony. After the

---

[1] Robert Constable, *Prerogativa Regis* (ed. Thorne), pp. v-xlvi; Hurstfield, *The Queen's Wards*, pp. 3-29; Bell, *Court of Wards and Liveries*, pp. 1-15.
[2] Round, *Ancient Charters*, pp. 91-2.   [3] Howden, *Chronica*, iv.88.
[4] Wendover, *Flores Historiarum* (ed. Coxe), iii.140.   [5] *Foedera*, 1.ii.497.

king had been crowned and had resumed his seat, the prelates and nobles rendered fealty and homage. This they did collectively, taking the appropriate oaths, which, having done, the nobles, standing erect, stretched forth their hands as if to sustain the king's crown. This piece of symbolism was introduced from France and does not appear before 1274: it has been retained ever since.[1] Whether ceremonial of this kind should be called feudal or not, it is certainly unrelated to the primitive ceremony of homage and it derives in no sense from the Norman Conquest. We should note, too, that in the course of the fourteenth century the name given to the nobles who take part in this ceremonial changes from *magnates* to *pares regni*, the peers who stand in a special relation to the king, a relation far more intimate than that between the king and any other of his subjects. This relation could not be more dramatically symbolised than by the rendering of homage at the coronation. Yet the solemn obligations of the peers towards their king, thus signified, did not prevent the deposition of Edward II and Richard II. In each case the act of deposition was accompanied by a formal renunciation of homage and fealty.[2]

Doubtless we may recognise in this renunciation a reminiscence of the feudal *diffidatio*; but this does not mean that feudal custom was still alive in the England of the fourteenth century. Whatever may have been the state of the law in France, *diffidatio*, the renunciation of allegiance, had never been recognised in England as a means of releasing a subject from his duty to the king or regularising a state of war between a lord and his vassals. William of Malmesbury relates that, when Stephen proceeded against Earl Ranulf of Chester and his brother, the king's action was condemned because he had not previously 'defied' them, as was the ancient custom.[3] If Stephen refused to recognise this custom, it would have been strange if his successors had done so. Barons closely in touch with France would not, of course, be ignorant of it, and the dissident barons defied King John in 1215 as a warning that they were prepared to resort to battle to enforce their demands.[4] Equally notable are the letters of defiance given before the battle of Lewes in 1264; but *diffidatio* has changed its meaning. The dissident barons express their unchangeable devotion to the king: it is the king who defies them. The barons declare: 'nos enim vestri fideles semper inveniemur'. The king replies: 'vos tanquam nostrorum inimicos diffidimus.' So also

---

[1] *Traditio*, xvi, pp. 144-5, 194-5. No details of the ceremony appear to have been preserved except in the rubrics to the fourth form of the Fourth Recension of the coronation office (Legg, *English Coronation Records*, p. 99): there is no reason to doubt that these record earlier practice. For the modern ceremony see *ibid.*, pp. 377-8.

[2] For the renunciation in the case of Edward II see *Rotuli Parliamentorum Angliae hactenus inediti*, p. 101, and in the case of Richard II see *Rotuli Parliamentorum*, iii.424. Whether in either case the words recorded were actually spoken is another matter, which does not affect the underlying legal theory.

[3] William of Malmesbury, *Historia Novella* (ed. Potter), p. 47.   [4] Below, p. 458.

do the king of the Romans and Edward, the king's firstborn, defy Simon de Montfort and his associates as public enemies; but they go on to offer battle in the king's court to establish their own innocence of the charges made against them and to prove the guilt of Simon and his friends as false traitors.[1] The men who wrote these letters, whatever terms they used, were not thinking in terms of any feudal law. They were men of the generation of Bracton, who knew of the crime of lese-majesty. Bracton's thought and language are strongly influenced by Roman law. Almost any act that could be construed as an act against the king was lese-majesty. Bracton has a list of acts that constituted the offence, at the head of which stand compassing the king's death, sedition and spreading disaffection in the army.[2] In such a system of law there is no room for *diffidatio*. And, of course, John treated the barons who went to war with him as rebels liable to forfeiture, as did Henry III likewise when he recovered his freedom after the battle of Evesham. The renunciation of homage and fealty in 1327 and 1399 was not an exercise of feudal custom nor in any sense an act sanctioned by the law: it was an attempt, whether justified or not, to cover an extra-legal act with a veneer of legality.

We turn now to the fourth clause of the coronation oath which obliged the king to safeguard the rights of the Crown. That such a duty rested upon the king is a very ancient conception. Long before the Conquest Edgar was praised for doing this by force of arms—*jura regni bellica potestate regaliter protegens*.[3] But it was not only against external foes that the king had to protect the rights of the Crown: he had to protect them against a more insidious enemy, his own imprudence. While this was the king's duty, until the twelfth century there seems to have been no idea of binding him by a solemn oath to fulfil it. The earliest document in which such an oath is mentioned appears to be, as we have said, the interpolated 'Leges Edwardi Confessoris'. The interpolator, let us recall, gives us some fictitious history. He tells us that, when the Danish kings ruled England, right was entombed, laws and customs were put to sleep, caprice and force and violence, and not justice, were the rule. These kings alienated and squandered many of the rights, dignities, lands and islands belonging to the Crown, but the good King Edward restored them, so far as he could, although he had not the power to do so completely.[4] Fictions like this are not told idly: they are a transparent disguise for current history. The interpolator knows that in the Danish kings his contemporaries will see King Stephen and in

---

[1] 'Matthew of Westminster', *Flores Historiarum* (ed. Luard), ii.492-4.
[2] Bracton, fo. 118-118b (ed. Woodbine, ii.334-5). For the underlying romanesque source, Tancred's *Ordo Judiciarius*, see *Traditio*, vi.71.
[3] *Vita Oswaldi*, p. 425. As we suggest below (p. 408) these words seem to be based upon a chant in honour of the king.
[4] 'Leges Edwardi Confessoris', 13, 1 A, in Liebermann, *Gesetze*, i.640 n.

good King Edward the reigning King Henry. He may be unjust to
Stephen, but not more unjust than the monk of Peterborough who
wrote those damning pages on the nineteen years of misrule when
Christ and His saints slept.[1] Unjust or not, it was in such a light that
Henry II and his supporters viewed Stephen's reign, and in this
light we can understand how a new clause came to be added to the
coronation oath.

According to the interpolator this clause pledged the king to
conserve and defend in their entirety and without diminution all the
lands and honours, all the dignities, rights and privileges that belonged to the Crown and, with all his power, to restore to their
original state any rights that had been dispersed or squandered or
lost.[2] Though this oath comes in fictional guise, it is confirmed in
substance and to some extent verbally by later documents of undoubted authenticity. Moreover, we find Henry II in the early years
of his reign doing those things this clause would oblige him to do:
he is recovering the possessions of the Crown that had been lost, not
only by Stephen's alienations but in other ways. He does not do this
arbitrarily and, though he may inflict hardship, the processes of the
law are respected. If we look for the origin of this clause of the
coronation oath, we must look not only to ancient history but to
current ecclesiastical law. The duty had been imposed upon bishops
and abbots to safeguard the possessions of their churches and to
recover any property that had been alienated, and at their consecration they had been required to give a solemn undertaking to do
so. Under Bishop Nigel the church of Ely had suffered greatly from
alienations or usurpations and he had been enjoined by the pope to
recover what had been lost. Now Nigel was not only a bishop but a
strong supporter of Henry, after whose accession he became what
we can describe only as minister of finance. We need hardly look
farther than Nigel for the argument that this salutary rule binding
on prelates should be equally binding on kings.[3] The rule was indeed
salutary to protect Henry III from the consequences of the rash
grants he had made,[4] and the only clause in the coronation oath
which Edward I is known to have invoked was this clause, and he
did so continually.[5] It was a clause devised for the protection of the
king, but it cannot be said to have been disadvantageous to his
subjects in an age when a king was expected to live of his own. But
we would stress its origin, not in feudal custom but in ancient tradition and in ecclesiastical law.

---

[1] Anglo-Saxon Chronicle (Peterborough), *s.a.* 1135-54 (ed. Thorpe, i.381-5; ed.
Plummer, i.263-8).
[2] 'Leges Edwardi Confessoris', 11, 1 A 2, in Liebermann, *Gesetze*, i.635.
[3] *Traditio*, xvi, pp. 151-60. For earlier, if somewhat obscure, references to this rule of
ecclesiastical law see *Cart. Mon. de Rameseia*, i.237-9; *Chron. Abbatiae Rameseiensis*, pp. 219-
20 (*Regesta*, nos. 607, 650).
[4] Powicke, 'The Oath of Bromholm', in *E.H.R.*, lvi.529-39.
[5] *Speculum*, xxiv.49-50.

Until 1272 the king did not begin to reign until he was crowned, and his peace died with him. Where then did authority lie between two reigns? We have already noticed the doctrine that springs up in the twelfth century whereby the heir to the throne can before his coronation claim the lordship of England. The lord of England may have his peace, but it is not clear how it could have been enforced unless it were supplemented by the application of another doctrine, namely that the authority of the justiciar does not cease despite the demise of the Crown. Let us review the history of the interregna at this period and go back to the day when William Rufus was alive and dead. This was on 2 August 1100. By the fifth of the month Henry I had been crowned, before many people had the chance to learn of his brother's death. Henry himself died on 1 December 1135 and Stephen's coronation seems to have taken place within three weeks, on 22 December. Though he had acted so swiftly—to contemporaries it seemed that his seizure of the throne had happened in the twinkling of an eye[1]—he had difficulty in establishing his authority. His coronation can hardly have conferred the sanctity that an undoubted heir could have claimed. His greatest advantage seems to have lain in the support of the justiciar, Roger of Salisbury, who carried the administration with him and whose tenure of office seems to have been uninterrupted by the change of ruler. The next interregnum, the interval between Stephen's death and Henry II's coronation, lasted for two months, but in this interval the peace of the country appears to have been undisturbed. Whether the treaty of Winchester had made the path easy is a matter we shall need to consider in due course; but the preservation of peace seems to have been mainly due to the authority exercised in Church and State by Archbishop Theobald and Richard de Lucy, who appears to have been justiciar under the late king and was continued in office by the new king.[2] Again in 1189, Ranulf Glanville, and in 1199, Geoffrey fitz Peter, the justiciar under the late king, continued in office under the new.[3] The corollary, the significance of which needs to be emphasised, is that in 1199 process was not interrupted in the Bench: the peace of King Richard passed insensibly into the peace of the lord of England or the duke of Normandy, as it is indifferently expressed, and then into the peace of King John.[4] The law knew no void: the king's court remained open.

---

[1] Henry of Huntingdon, *Historia Anglorum* (ed. Arnold), p. 256: 'tam repente omnis Anglia . . . quasi in ictu oculi subjecta est'. The date, 22 December, for Stephen's coronation is that given by William of Malmesbury, *Historia Novella* (ed. Potter), p. 15, and the *Chronicon de Bello*, p. 64. The Peterborough Chronicle gives Midwinter Day (Thorpe, i.382; Plummer, i.263).   [2] Below, p. 166.

[3] The evidence for Glanville's continuance in office will be found in Landon, *Itinerary of Richard I*, pp. 5-7.

[4] This was worked out by Palgrave, *Rotuli Curiae Regis*, i.lxxxiv-xci. Despite every precaution there was inevitably some delay between the first news of Richard's death and the proclamation of the duke's peace; but the law would not tolerate this as an excuse for lawlessness (*Curia Regis Rolls*, i.255, 384).

When we review these facts it does not seem fanciful to detect a theory—or perhaps it would be better to say an assumption—that in some way royal authority resided in the justiciar and that, though the kingdom was for the time being without a king, there was a continuous exercise of authority. An interregnum in the sense of a breach of all authority was thus avoided. We need to glance at the complicated position in 1216 when the courts and the exchequer were closed, although from the *tempus guerrae* a lesson can hardly be drawn. We may note that Hubert de Burgh continued in the office of justiciar. On the other hand it is noteworthy that, although Henry III was assumed to reign from his first, but irregular, coronation at Gloucester, the precaution was taken to remedy any defect by a more regular coronation at Westminster three and a half years later. We cannot hide from ourselves the reality of a divided, warracked land, where the king's writ did not run and no man knew for how long an infant prince would be clad in makeshift trappings of regality. Nevertheless, when we take a longer view, it is, we think, evident that men have been, and still are, feeling their way towards some conception of sovereignty which would avoid the dangers of a lapse of authority. Ultimately this will be achieved when the conception of an undying king is evolved, when men can say *le roi est mort, vive le roi*. In 1216 this conception was still far from men's minds, nor was it yet reached by 1272. Although the new king's peace was proclaimed on the day following his father's death, his reign was not deemed to begin until the fourth day, when fealty was sworn to him in Westminster Abbey beside the still unclosed tomb.[1] A great step in advance had, however, been achieved in dissociating kingship from coronation, and a further step was taken in 1307 when Edward II's reign was assumed to begin on the day following his father's death.

Death was not the only event that left the kingdom without a king, and it is instructive to review the arrangements made for a regency in the event of the king's absence or incapacity. The same assumptions are evidently in men's minds, though modified by another assumption that kingship can be divided, in the first place with the queen, who was *regalis imperii particeps*, and in the second place with an associate king. Such information as we have of the reigns of the first two Norman kings, when the problem of regency first had to be faced, does not suggest that any fixed principle was observed. Under Henry I there appears to be a definite rule that the regency is confided either to the queen or to the justiciar. Exceptionally, after Queen Maud's death on 1 May 1118, the king's son William, although uncrowned, acted nominally as regent, but

---

[1] Henry died on 16 November 1272. Edward's peace was proclaimed on 17 November, fealty sworn to him on 20 November and his peace again proclaimed (*Foedera*, 1.ii.497). His reign was regarded as beginning on the latter day.

there is no other appointment during the twelfth century of an un-anointed prince. There seems to have been a rule under Stephen similar to that under Henry I: Roger of Salisbury is found acting in 1137 when the king is absent in Normandy and Queen Matilda during the king's captivity.[1] It will be recalled that Stephen failed in his attempt to secure the coronation of his eldest son as associate king.[2] Henry II, to his misfortune, achieved this, and during his reign there acted as regent at different times the queen, the young king and the justiciar.[3] The reign of Richard I is remarkable, not only for the continuous administration of England by successive justiciars during the greater part of it, but for the authority exercised by his mother Queen Eleanor. After her revolt in 1173 she had been imprisoned and deprived of all power by Henry II, and she was still under restraint at the end of his reign. Almost the first act of Richard after his father's death was to ensure that in his absence she should assume, in conjunction with the justiciar, the direction of the admin-istration. She was put in the same position in 1193 when the then justiciar, Walter of Coutances, had shown himself incapable of con-trolling Count John who had assumed, without any warrant from the captive king, the office and title of *rector regni*. Eleanor's authority was, so far as we can tell, singular and, indeed, anomalous. During her lifetime her sons' wives were of inferior status, partly doubtless because Berengaria was estranged from Richard and never set foot in England and Isabelle of Angoulême was little more than a child at the time of Eleanor's death, and partly because of Eleanor's dominating character and her personal influence over her sons. She retained after the death of Henry II not only her dower lands, to which she was entitled in law, but also the right to queen's gold, the payment made to the queen regnant upon the issue of royal charters. On the occasion of the solemn crown-wearing at Winchester which marked Richard's rehabilitation after his captivity, she, like a queen regnant, sat facing him in the chancel of the cathedral to hear the *laudes* sung not only in the king's honour but in hers.[4] More than any other queen she exemplifies the truth that in the twelfth century English queens were *regalis imperii participes*.

In the several devices for maintaining the continuity of adminis-tration, there may not be perceptible any consistent doctrine. They are rather expedients, perhaps not in the first instance deliberately contrived, on the one hand, to maintain the principle that the right to govern lies with anointed princes and, on the other, to prevent the fabric of government from being weakened by inexpert hands. The fabric of government grows more complicated year by year and

---

[1] Introduction to *Memoranda Roll, 1 John*, pp. lxvii, lxxxiii. For Henry I's son William see *Regesta Regum Anglo-Normannorum*, ii, p. xvii, nos. 1189, 1191-2, 1201-2.
[2] The best account of the negotiations is by Saltman, *Theobald Archbishop of Canterbury*, 36-8. [3] *Memoranda Roll, 1 John*, pp. lxviii-lxxii; *E.H.R.*, lxxiv.195.
[4] *Ibid.*, pp. 200-3, 209-11; *Traditio*, xvi.129.

this development at once enhances and diminishes the king's authority. His authority is enhanced in that his ministers exercise greater and greater control over the lives of his subjects: it is diminished in the sense that he can act effectively only through his ministers. This truth is strikingly illustrated when, during Henry II's absences, Queen Eleanor or the young king acts as regent. They are anointed princes with all the insignia of royalty, but the administrative machine continues to function uninterruptedly. They do no more than give their royal warrant to the acts of the justiciar. If both they and the king are absent, there is no hiatus in the administration: the justiciar acts as before, but now in his own name.[1] From overseas the king exercises a remote control, and the justiciar, though he issues innumerable writs, may not issue royal charters. But so long as the justiciar enjoys the king's confidence he exercises little short of supreme authority. Nor, as we have seen, does his authority lapse on the demise of the Crown.

Though the position may be thus stated in general terms, we must not ignore the qualities and failings of the principal actors. If for any reason a justiciar failed to act up to his responsibilities or if he lost the king's confidence, plainly the king or someone who could play the part of the king must intervene. Nor could there be a more suitable choice than one who already shared the sovereignty. Such a situation did not often arise and our illustrations must be taken from the reign of Richard I, illustrations we have already used. Richard was fortunate in having Eleanor of Aquitaine for mother. At the beginning of his reign or, to speak more properly, before his coronation he seems to have had no confidence in Ranulf Glanville, who was perhaps failing as he advanced in years and who was shortly afterwards to be replaced.[2] But he could not very well be replaced before Richard was himself king. Eleanor, however, was an anointed queen and, in the strength of her character, she could dominate the kingdom as no one else could. Without the removal of the justiciar, she brought that element of stability which secured tranquillity and unbroken continuity in the administration. There is no reason to suppose that she had any special gifts as an administrator, but she did not need them. By reason of her unction she was a divinely appointed ruler upon whom, moreover, God had bestowed exceptional ability. Again in 1193, it was she who, in the same way, could resolve the crisis brought about by Count John's designs against the captive king. Eleanor's interventions were brief but effective. They bring out the significance of kingship, of the mystic

---

[1] *Memoranda Roll, 1 John*, pp. lxxxiii-lxxxiv. From the attestations to the writs of Henry I's son, William (p. 153, n. 1, above), it seems evident that he, too, was no more than a figurehead.

[2] The stories of the chroniclers conflict, but they point in this direction: see William of Newburgh and Richard of Devizes in *Chronicles of Reigns of Stephen* etc. (ed. Howlett), i.302, iii.385-6; *Gesta Ricardi*, ii.87.

gifts conferred by unction, even in a state such as England, deliberately organised so that the administration should continue uninterruptedly in the king's absence.

The structure of the administration was modified in 1234, when the office of justiciar was abolished, but it was not weakened.[1] It was so strong that, just as it survived the intense strains put upon it in 1193 by Count John's rebellion, so in 1264 and 1265 it was not weakened by the warfare between Simon de Montfort and the royalists. It was disrupted only during the dynastic war under Stephen and in the *tempus guerrae* of 1215-7. Once peace was restored, every effort was made to re-establish the administration and to set it to work with its old complexity and efficiency. The king by himself could do little: he certainly could not hope for prosperity or the reality of power without the aid of a trained civil service and judicature. Since no mediaeval English king was ever, like Louis XIV, *homme de bureau*, his power, whatever his strength of purpose, was limited in practice by his inability to control in person a complicated administrative and judicial system. He was of necessity, as Bracton said, under the law. If he was thus controlled, as it were, from below, he was controlled from above by the greater barons, the group that became known as peers or lords of the council. We do not mention parliament, as Stubbs would have done, in this connexion, because whether in parliament or in great council, whether on stage or off stage, political power, in so far as it was distinct from the power of the king, was exercised in the fifteenth, as it had been in the twelfth century, by the great lords.[2] This system, like every political system, depended for its smooth working upon the wisdom, co-operation and forbearance of those in whose hands power lay. That these qualities were not always forthcoming needs no better illustration than the tragedies of Edward II, Richard II and Henry VI. Yet after each dethronement the political system continues in the expectation that with new men in high places it would work efficiently. The system made immense, perhaps excessive, demands upon the king. Few men were capable of sustaining the burden, and there is no more melancholy reading than the lives of the kings of England. The most charitable must admit that nearly all proved themselves inadequate, nor were the failures merely those who, like Henry III, were weaklings from the start. It was possible for a king to live too long. The extravagances of Edward I or the follies of Edward III in their declining years are as pitiful as the fate of those fallen monarchs who, with the sanctity of royalty still upon them, were too dangerous to be let live.

[1] We deal with the reorganisation of the courts in a later chapter.
[2] We discuss this matter in our second volume: provisionally we may refer to our *Parliaments and Great Councils in Medieval England*, pp. 12-23.

VIII

THE STRUCTURE OF GOVERNMENT
IN THE TWELFTH CENTURY

HOWEVER inadequate and misleading Stubbs's views might be
on the early history of mediaeval England, when he reached
the twelfth century one would expect a surer appreciation
of its characteristic institutions and of their importance for the
future. For in the twelfth century Stubbs was on his own ground.
Before the first volume of the *Constitutional History* was published, he
had already edited the *Chronicles and Memorials of Richard I*, 'Benedict
of Peterborough', Roger of Howden's *Chronica* and the first volume
of the *Memoriale* of Walter of Coventry. Other texts of the same
period were to come. Yet, so it seems to us, Stubbs failed to grasp
the significance for the constitutional historian of the work of Henry I
and Henry II, of the ministers who served these great kings and of
the ministers, trained in the same school, who served Richard I and
John. And though we can hardly blame him when we remember
that, in his haste to complete the formidable task he had set himself,
he was impelled to rely on the printed books available a century
ago, yet it is hard to understand how later historians have failed to
discern, in the light of present-day knowledge, the significant
characteristics of the 'Age of the Justiciars',[1] the age when the
future of the English constitution, the elements of English administration and the unique features of the English judicature and the
English common law were largely determined.

Let us, in the first place, ask why Stubbs came so sadly short of
what he set out to do. Of the structure of government in the twelfth
century he, handicapped as he was by his dependence on printed
evidence, could make very little. In the 1870's the record sources in
print were very limited. There were a few pipe rolls, and these he
did not scrutinise with the minute care necessary to extract their
secrets. There were the excerpts printed by Madox in the *History of
the Exchequer*. There were the plea rolls edited by Palgrave, the 'Dialogus de Scaccario' and 'Glanville'. These sources we still value; but
in the 1870's their perusal needed to be supplemented by a detailed

---

[1] As witness, for example, Poole, *From Domesday Book to Magna Carta* (1955), chapter
xii, 'Justice and Finance'. No document to illustrate the office of justiciar appears in
English Historical Documents, 1042-1189 (1953), edited by Douglas and Greenaway. In
the second volume of the *Regesta Regum Anglo-Normannorum* only half a dozen writs of
Roger of Salisbury are calendared (nos. 1471-2, 1488, 1614, 1814, 1989).

examination of the unprinted pipe rolls and the unprinted charters, a task far more laborious and far more searching than that which enabled Eyton to compile his still useful *Itinerary of Henry II*. Stubbs's interests did not lie in that direction: his knowledge of the public records was small and his ideas about them were confused.[1] Even so, some records which supply necessary clues were then lying unknown among the unsorted Miscellanea of the Exchequer in the Public Record Office. To do what was necessary for an understanding of the processes of administration would have diverted Stubbs's activities and would have frustrated the whole scheme upon which he was engaged. He would not have been likely ever to have emerged from the twelfth century. The gaps in the evidence available at the time might, in any case, have deprived his account of permanent value; but there is no indication that he even guessed what questions should be put in order to elicit the essential facts of twelfth-century administration.

The problem with which Henry I was confronted when he had made good his hold upon Normandy was to provide for the ordered government of his duchy and his kingdom when he was perforce absent. He must divide his time between his two dominions, but all the while he must retain a firm hold on each. The device he adopted was to create the office of justiciar, a minister who was to act as his vicegerent, was to issue writs and was to preside over a central, sedentary court, known both in Normandy and England as the exchequer. We must not credit Henry I with too great originality or too great foresight. Doubtless he used, even though he improved, instruments ready to his hand. There seems, however, to be no contemporary document to show that any great minister had borne the title of chief justiciar before it was conferred on Roger of Salisbury; nor has anyone yet found a reference to the exchequer in either England or Normandy before the year 1109, when, it would seem, the office of chief justiciar was created. But even if we could prove that some earlier minister had borne that title or that the exchequer had existed *eo nomine* on either side of the Channel at the beginning of the twelfth century, we should not have proved that the system which is in operation after 1109 was in operation before that date. For the essence of that system is that it was duplicated in England and Normandy and that it was permanent and no temporary device. The apparatus of the system, as a whole, is found in England under Roger of Salisbury and not before[2]; and, though the evidence is not so detailed or so clear, this is true also of Normandy at the same period and not earlier. We thus state our conclusions at the outset in order that the argument may be present in the reader's mind, and we proceed to adduce the evidence upon which we rely.

[1] *Constitutional History*, i.641.
[2] This seems to be implied by the words of William of Malmesbury: itaque totius regni moderamen illius delegavit justitiae, sive ipse [rex Henricus] adesset Angliae sive moraretur Normanniae (*Gesta Regum*, pp. 483-4).

It is fitting, however, that in the first place we should say something of the origin and career of Roger le Poer, commonly known as
Roger of Salisbury, the remarkable man whom Henry I placed at
the head of the administration in England. Modern historians have,
for the most part, been content to repeat the fables told of him by
William of Newburgh, who was writing two generations or so after
Roger's death.[1] The chronicler's story is, as his *ut dicitur* shows, mere
gossip. He tells how, in the latter years of the eleventh century,
Henry, the youngest son of the Conqueror, came by chance across
an obscure priest in the neighbourhood of Caen and was so struck
by the rapidity with which he celebrated mass that the prince said
to him 'Follow me'. And so he followed the prince as closely as Peter
had aforetime followed the King of Heaven when He spoke the
same words. Need it be emphasised that this is a mere *conte*, devised
to scandalise and amuse? We can give no more credit to this idle
tale than to the statement in the formal certificate of election that
Roger, like every other bishop elect, was *natalibus et moribus nobilis*.[2]
That he was *fere illiteratus*, as William of Newburgh says, may well
be true; but only in the sense that, like many mediaeval and modern
bishops, he was no great scholar. But that he was indifferent to
learning is another matter, and the precise opposite is evidently
true. For he sent his nephews, Alexander and Nigel, to the most
celebrated school of the day, that of Laon, then under the direction
of Master Anselm, where, we are told, they abode a long time.[3] So
it seems that, before he had achieved any great position, Roger had
already determined that his nephews should have the best education
there was to be had.[4] William of Malmesbury, who was Roger's
contemporary and in a position to know, says nothing of such fables
as Newburgh repeats. He is warm in his praises of Roger's devotion
to his duties as diocesan,[5] while Newburgh implies the contrary.
What, Malmesbury says, attracted Count Henry to Roger was his
prudence in conducting the prince's household and restricting unnecessary expenditure.[6] There is no doubt which story we ought to
believe.

Roger's official career—and that is our interest here—may be
summarised thus. At the beginning of Henry I's reign he was one of

---

[1] Newburgh, *Historia Rerum Anglicanum* (ed. Howlett), i.36. That Roger had been
'Abrincensis aecclesie presbiter' was stated when his election to the see of Salisbury was
notified to Archbishop Anselm (Harley Roll A.3), and Avranches cannot by any topographical fancy be described as 'in quodam suburbano Cadomensi'.

[2] For the formula of this certificate at the period see Wharton, *Anglia Sacra*, i.82,
apparently copied from Harley Roll A.3, where it is repeated in the case of a number of
bishops.

[3] Hermann, *De miraculis S. Mariae Laudunensis*, lib. ii, c. xiii, in Migne, *Patrologia Latina*,
clvi.983.

[4] The date of the narrative appears to be 1113 (*History*, xlvi.103). Alexander and Nigel
are then no longer at Laon: they must therefore have been sent there in the early years
of the century. That they were good scholars appears from William of Malmesbury,
Historia Novella (ed. Potter), p. 38.

[5] *Gesta Regum*, p. 484.   [6] *Historia Novella* (ed. Potter), p. 37.

the king's chaplains. He was appointed chancellor soon after Easter 1101 and vacated this office on, or shortly after, his nomination to the see of Salisbury in September 1102.[1] The king, however, retained his services by appointing him as a *justitiarius totius Anglie*[2]—an office we describe later—and in 1109, it would seem, advanced him to the position of chief justiciar. We are led to the conclusion that his appointment was in 1109 by a letter written by the king not long before Anselm's death on 21 March in that year. Henry was then in Normandy and he wished to give the ailing archbishop an assurance that those left in authority in England would act by his advice. The king does not, however, speak of his *capitalis justitiarius* or of the bishop of Salisbury but of his *justitiarii*, who were presumably the *justitiarii totius Anglie*.[3] It seems probable that in July 1108, when Henry left England, he had appointed what we might call a council of regency, though Queen Maud may have been nominally regent.[4] Such an arrangement is not known on the occasion of any later absence of Henry's. The king returned to England at the beginning of June 1109, and very soon after the bishop of Salisbury is certainly chief justiciar and the court of the exchequer, over which he presides, is in being. With practical simultaneity a chief justiciar appears in Normandy.[5]

As chief justiciar, for he was such, though the qualifying adjective is rarely used, Roger of Salisbury occupied an unprecedented position, although there may have been ministers before his time, such as Ranulf Flambard, who wielded for a season equal authority. Orderic, writing a generation later, says of Ranulf 'summus regiarum procurator opum et justitiarius factus est',[6] while a lady who had once formed part of his domestic circle described him as *totius Anglie iudex, secundus post regem*.[7] But, before the appointment of Roger le Poer, there had never been a minister permanently in office who, as the king's *alter ego*, organised and directed a carefully articulated machine of government. Henry of Huntingdon hails Roger as *summus in regno* and *secundus a rege*,[8] descriptions applied unanimously,

---

[1] It seems clear that he had ceased to be chancellor by January 1103: see Introduction by Johnson and Cronne to *Regesta Regum Anglo-Normannorum*, ii, p. ix.

[2] He is so entitled by Henry of Huntingdon (*Historia Anglorum*, p. 245) and in a charter *post* 1124 (*Cartularium Mon. de Rameseia*, i.143) when he was chief justiciar. That he was so employed is implied also by William of Malmesbury's statement that he undertook secular duties with Anselm's consent (*Gesta Regum*, p. 484).

[3] *Anselmi Opera Omnia* (ed. F. S. Schmitt), v.410-11, ep. 461: Decetero de iis quae in Anglia sunt et quae ibi tractentur, volo ut voluntati tuae pareant et consilio tuo disponantur. Quod etiam ego iustitiariis nostris feci agnitum. This letter and the continuation of the correspondence (epp. 462, 470) show that Henry had not delegated matters of importance to the justices.

[4] The editors of the *Regesta*, vol. ii, appear to assume this (nos. 906, 909).

[5] According to C. H. Haskins, not later than 1109 (*Norman Institutions*, p. 93).

[6] *Historia Ecclesiastica* (ed. Le Prevost), iv.107.

[7] *The Life of Christina of Markyate* (ed. Talbot), p. 40. Christina's aunt was Ranulf's mistress. She herself refused Ranulf's advances. The words quoted do not come directly from Christina but from her biographer.

[8] *Historia Anglorum*, pp. 245, 300.

if in varying terms, by other contemporaries,[1] but what was more important was that—to use the words of the Battle Abbey chronicler —*per Angliam iura regia administrabat*.[2] It is when Roger is in office that we first read of the privilege granted to favoured subjects that they were not to be impleaded except before the king or his chief justiciar,[3] that is before the king himself or in the court at the exchequer. It is as president of the king's court at the exchequer that the justiciar exercised the vast powers entrusted to him: it is in this capacity that the greatness of the office is apparent.

The justiciar's powers were seemingly not of gradual growth but were conferred upon him as soon as Roger assumed office. A letter from the bishop of Norwich, which belongs to the first half of the reign of Henry I,[4] illuminates the justiciar's position better perhaps than any other single document that has survived.

To his friend Roger, the pastor of Salisbury, Herbert, his sheep of Norwich, greeting.

Although, during the entire time of your justiciarship, solicitude for my infirmities has been necessary, yet more especially in this hour, when I am fast-bound with sickness and more grievous adversity afflicts me, do I implore your fatherly goodness that him, whom formerly you set upon his feet, you will not, in the press of business, disregard, now that he is cast down. I appeal to you as to a father, I appeal to you as a pastor, with such appeals as a wounded heart is wont to utter. Let the voice of my anxiety pierce, I beseech you, your tender fatherly breast. The sheepfold is broken and I am exposed to the teeth of savage beasts, and unless, in your mercy, you aid me with your protection, I am given over to my enemies who rush to rend me in pieces. What answer shall be returned to the representations of your sheep is for your compassion to decide: I leave it entirely to your discretion to counsel me in my anxieties.

From my lands fifty pounds are demanded for pleas (although my tenants of those lands have offended neither in their response nor in deed), and another sixty pounds for knights, which I find it the more difficult to pay since my resources in recent years have seriously diminished. What is worst of all, my neighbours are seeking to bring under contribution Thorpe, which our lord the king granted for the fabric of the [cathedral] church, as free as ever the manor was when in his hands and as his other manors are. The charter to this effect you have frequently inspected, as well as repeated writs. On this I must take my stand; this must be the burden of my complaint; and this I implore you, from the very bottom of my heart, that our church shall not lose her franchise which hitherto, by the king's grace and on your advice, she has retained in its integrity. Command, I pray you, that Thorpe may be quit, as is customary, or

---

[1] William of Malmesbury, *Gesta Regum*, pp. 483-4; *Gesta Stephani* (ed. Potter), p. 48; Simeon of Durham, *Historia Regum*, ii.302.   [2] *Chronicon Mon. de Bello*, p. 60.

[3] *Foedera*, i.12: nisi coram me vel capitali iustitia meo. This charter, in favour of Holy Trinity, Aldgate, appears to have been expanded, but the existence of an original may be accepted (*Regesta*, no. 1316; *E.H.R.*, lxxv.275, no. 317).

[4] Herbert de Losinga, *Epistolae* (ed. Anstruther), no. 26. Another translation will be found in Goulburn and Symonds, *Life, Letters and Sermons of Bishop Herbert de Losinga*, i.229-33.

grant a respite until our lord the king comes [to England] or, if nothing else may be done, allow a long enough term for me to communicate with our lord the king and request his indulgence. In conceding and doing these things, I am sure that, by the grace of God, you will not find our lady the queen difficult, for, out of her kindness, she has been a very mother to me and she takes advantage of your advice in everything.

If you give the order, I live; and with never-ceasing tears I beseech our Saviour that, in His mercy, you will give the order.

A certain brother of ours is requesting your mercy for his brother in prison: hear his prayer, I beg you, with the same compassion that you desire God to grant your prayers.

Let us first note that the word we have translated as 'justiciarship' is *procuratio*. Bishop Herbert had some claim to be a stylist, and *procurator* is the elegant synonym for *justitiarius*. In the Latin of the twelfth and thirteenth centuries *procurator* may mean a regent or viceroy. The title is given to more than one regent of France; it is applied to the seneschals of Normandy and of Aquitaine and to the justiciars of Ireland[1]; and it was almost certainly used by Roger himself.[2] When Bishop Herbert was writing, Roger had been in office for less than ten years,[3] and the particulars the letter gives show that the system, revealed in detail by the pipe roll of 1130, was already well established. The bishop of Norwich is worried about the demands made upon him for pleas (*placita*), scutage (*pro militibus*) and geld. Of pleas and scutage we need say nothing[4]: but something may usefully be said of geld. The king had granted his manor of Thorpe St. Andrew to the see of Norwich following upon the removal of the cathedral church from Thetford. The manor was to be held by the bishop and the monks as beneficially (*melius*) as the king's father had held it.[5] Did this mean that the bishop was relieved of geld? The barons of the exchequer would not admit such a claim unless it was supported not only by the charter but by a writ expressly granting specific relief. This procedure continued, as Richard of Ely tells us, well into the reign of Henry II.[6] On each occasion, then, that Bishop Herbert had claimed exemption before the justiciar at the exchequer he had had to produce (as he reminds Roger) both his charter and a writ.[7] But freedom from geld implied,

---

[1] Olivier-Martin, *Les régences et la majorité des rois*, pp. 92, 123; Haskins, *Norman Institutions*, p. 168; Gervase of Canterbury, *Historical Works*, i.515; Delisle, *Actes de Henri II*, Introduction, p. 416; Gerald the Welshman, *Opera*, v.334, 347, 359.

[2] The two Reading charters in which he purports to use this style are suspect, but there can be no reason for doubting that they are based upon authentic originals (Johnson in *Tait Essays*, pp. 141-2; *Regesta*, nos. 1471-2).

[3] The extreme date of the letter is May 1118, for the queen died on 1 May. Since the king was absent, the date may be September 1114-July 1115 or April 1116-April 1118. The period August 1111-July 1113 would seem too early.

[4] Round has commented on this passage in the letter in *Feudal England*, p. 270.

[5] *Monasticon*, iv.16, no. 5; *Regesta*, no. 548.

[6] *Dialogus de Scaccario*, pp. 49-52, 105-6; *E.H.R.*, xliii.321-33.

[7] For one of these writs see *Calendar of Charter Rolls*, iv.439; *Regesta*, no. 786: cf. *ibid.*, no. 946.

at least so the bishop suggests, freedom from local exactions (*consuetudines*), and the bishop apparently fears that, unless he resists all attempts at imposing upon the manor liability for any kind of secular burden, he will find that his right to freedom from geld is challenged. Therefore, although there may be no immediate demand for geld, he seeks either from the justiciar or from the king a comprehensive acknowledgement that the land is held by the form of tenure that came to be known as frankalmoin, or free, pure and perpetual alms.

Having said so much, we may put such technicalities of the law aside and turn to the constitutional technicalities of which the letter makes much. First, although Bishop Roger is the effective ruler of the kingdom, any writ he may issue will be expressed in the queen's name, for she is formally recognised as the representative of the absent king. She will act by the justiciar's advice, but she must be at least formally consulted before her seal is put to any instrument.[1] There is a second and more important point: can the justiciar take it upon himself to advise the queen to issue a charter that will confer wide immunities upon the bishop's manor? Such immunities can doubtless be granted by the king, but can they be granted by the queen or the justiciar, who are both but the king's delegates? Bishop Herbert doubts whether they have this power, so he asks for a writ which will enable him to resist any demand either until the king returns to England or until there has been time to approach him in Normandy. There seems to be no evidence that the bishop obtained either writ or charter such as he desired, though the manor continued to be relieved of the payment of geld.[2]

The bishop's worries we may pass over: what is important to us is the clear evidence his letter affords for the existence from the second decade of the twelfth century of the constitutional system that is so plainly to be seen under Henry II and his sons, the system that differentiated England from other monarchies of Western Europe and that determined so many of the characteristics of English mediaeval administration. Nor, when we read this letter, do we wonder that the abbot of Mont Saint-Michel should have addressed the justiciar as 'the reverend lord and father, Roger, by the grace of God bishop of Salisbury, vigorous administrator of the realm of England',[3] or that the bishop of Norwich should have thought it prudent on occasion to approach him through the queen.[4] From Roger there was no appeal except to the king overseas, even though the queen was nominally in charge of the kingdom. Not only might

---

[1] For a writ in the queen's name with Roger as witness see *Regesta*, no. 1190, where it is dated 1116-8.

[2] *Pipe Roll, 31 Henry I*, p. 95.

[3] Reuerendo domino et patri Rogero Saresberiensi episcopo gracia Dei strenuo regni Anglie prouisori (B.M., Egerton MS. 3031, fo. 47).

[4] Herbert de Losinga, *Epistolae*, no. 25.

the queen be the regent,[1] but the heir to the throne might also act as regent, and writs in the name of William, Henry I's son, have survived.[2] We do not know enough of Queen Maud's movements, nor, for the matter of that, of William's movements, to be able to guess on what occasions and for how long either was nominally in charge of the kingdom. In all probability the occasions were not very frequent or of very great duration, for when the king was overseas and there was no royal regent, Bishop Roger issued writs in his own name, and such writs are much more commonly to be found[3] than writs in the name of a royal figurehead. The difference is, however, no more than a matter of form. In whosesoever name a writ is expressed to be made, the same administrative authority lies behind it. The justiciar is of less dignity than the queen or the heir to the throne, but his hand never ceases to control the machine of government. A specimen of Roger's writs[4] will be more instructive than lengthy descriptions.

Roger, bishop of Salisbury, to the archbishop [of Canterbury] and the sheriff and all the barons of Kent, French and English, greeting. I grant that the abbot of Saint Augustine shall have warren in his land of Stodmarsh and of Littlebourne and in all lands appurtenant to them, in woodland and in plain, and no one under a penalty of £10 shall hunt in that warren without his licence. At Westminster. By the king's writ.

The authoritative tone of this writ is impressive, and it is consonant with the obsequiousness of Bishop Herbert's letter to Roger.

When the king was in England, Roger still undertook most of the burden of administration, but now his writs were couched in the king's name, while Roger himself was conventionally merely the witness. Let us look at one such writ: it runs as follows:[5]

Henry, king of the English, to all his barons and lieges of Sussex and of Middlesex, greeting. Know ye that Herbert, abbot of Westminster, has deraigned the land of Parham and of Mapelford against Herbert fitz Herbert before my barons at the exchequer by their judgement that Herbert shall no longer be able to claim anything therein and that the abbot shall have the land in his demesne, if he will, and shall do therewith as he desires. And I command that the abbot shall hold the land as he deraigned it, beneficially and peacefully and without challenge. Witness the bishop of Salisbury. At Woodstock.

Here we see the justiciar notifying to two county courts a judgement of the court at the exchequer. The county court of Sussex is interested because the lands that had been in dispute lie in that county

---

[1] For her writs see *Regesta*, nos. 971, 1000-1, 1190. No. 971 appears to be warranted *per breve regis* and not to be a grant by the queen: its terms are inconsistent with the king's grant (no. 494) and the writ must be regarded with suspicion in its present form.
[2] *Regesta*, nos. 1189, 1191-2, 1201-2, 1223.
[3] Five are noted in the Ramsey Abbey cartulary (*Cartularium Mon. de Rameseia*, i.105-6, 143).   [4] Cotton MS., Julius D.11, fo. 89b: see *Regesta*, no. 1814 n.
[5] *Curia Regis Rolls*, vi.176-7; *Regesta*, no. 1879. Cf. *Dialogus de Scaccario*, pp. 16, 33.

and it is likely that litigation had commenced in that court.[1] The interest of the Middlesex county court would seem to be more remote. It can lie only in the fact that Westminster Abbey is in the county; but it may be that the abbot wishes to bring to the notice of his neighbours and tenants that he has succeeded in his suit in the king's court. In the year 1130, for that is about the date of the writ,[2] the exchequer is not a generation old and a warning to possible disseisors that justice may be had there may be prudent.

Over the court at the exchequer the justiciar, as we have said, presides. This is what we find under Henry II and his sons, and it is what we should infer of the reign of Henry I; but we have direct evidence of the fact in a writ that is addressed to the bishop of Salisbury, the chancellor and the barons of the exchequer, notifying them that the monks of the recently founded abbey of Rievaulx are quit of geld.[3] The purpose of the writ is, of course, to secure that the sheriff shall not be called upon to account at the exchequer for the amount remitted. The bishop is addressed as justiciar, and therefore president of the court, and the chancellor is included in the address because he has the second place there. So closely is the justiciar identified with the exchequer that it is probable that the rather un-expected phrase *justitia mea scaccarii*, which we find in a charter of Henry I's, is meant to apply to Roger: 'my justice of the exchequer' is to do the same justice in respect of money due to be paid by the king's ministers to the monks of Cluny as he would do in respect of the sums due to the king at the exchequer[4].

Writs and references, such as those of which we have given examples, are not, as we have said, to be found before the time of Roger of Salisbury, and it is inconceivable that, if the system they illustrate had been in existence earlier, some trace would not have been found in the numerous documents from previous reigns that have been preserved in just the same way as the documents of the reign of Henry I. Since, however, no political contrivance is ever wholly new, it is possible that there had been barons or ministers who did from time to time exercise functions resembling in part those that Roger exercised fully and continuously for a generation. But to put, as Stubbs does, William fitz Osbern, Geoffrey of Coutances and Ranulf Flambard at the head of a table of justiciars, which continues with Roger of Salisbury and ends with Peter des Roches, is to include the incongruous in one category.[5] And it is going much too far to say, as Stubbs does, that 'there are several other justices,

---

[1] Mapelford is apparently within Parham.
[2] If Herbert fitz Herbert is, as he seems to be, the son of Herbert the Chamberlain, the approximate date is established by the reference to father and son in the pipe roll of 1130: the father seems to have died in 1128 (below, p. 218).
[3] *Cartularium Rievallense*, p. 142; *Regesta*, no. 1741.
[4] *Recueil des chartes de l'abbaye de Cluny*, v, no. 4016; *Regesta*, no. 1691. This is not a product of the king's chancery but was drafted at Cluny: see Chaplais in *E.H.R.*, lxxv. 270, n. 2.   [5] *Constitutional History*, i.688.

mentioned both in records and by the historians, whose position seems to be scarcely inferior to Roger's'.[1] But the measure of his failure to apprehend the nature of Roger's office is indicated by other words of his[2]:

Roger of Salisbury certainly bore the title of justiciar; whether he acted as the king's lieutenant during his absence is uncertain, and even yet it must be questioned whether the name possessed a precise official significance.

Stubbs finds an excuse for his uncertainty in the letter of Henry I's to Anselm which we have already used to date Roger's assumption of the office of justiciar. In it the king informs the archbishop that he has instructed the *justitiarii* to act by his advice.[3] This letter was written to an aged, ailing and unreasonable man. Anselm had time before his death to reply to the king, and his reply shows that the English affairs of which the king wrote and which 'were to be so dealt with as to comply with your wish and to be decided by your advice' were no more than the problems attending the consecration of the newly elected archbishop of York, problems much nearer to his heart than any secular affairs.[4] The correspondence is irrelevant to the question of Roger's authority as justiciar.

Roger of Salisbury is an outstanding, a mighty, figure in English history. Of his Norman contemporaries who held like office across the Channel we know little.[5] It may well be that the duchy was backward and lagged behind, not only in developing the institutions which had reached a remarkable standard of efficiency in England, but in recording what had been imperfectly achieved. There is evidence of ministers from England sent on mission to Normandy, even late in Henry I's reign, to strengthen or reform the Norman financial administration,[6] and it may well be that the duchy was slow in recovering from the disastrous rule of Duke Robert, from civil strife and invasion. Yet poor and fragmentary as the evidence from Normandy is, it is consistent with the inference that there existed a system parallel to that existing in England, and this inference is immensely strengthened by the undeniable existence of the system in Normandy under Henry II. Whether the English and Norman exchequers were constituted by a single royal act, or whether one slightly anticipated the other, we do not know and are not likely to know. That they were both functioning a few years after Tinchebray is all that matters. Although identical in their

---

[1] *Ibid.*, p. 420. Why Orderic (*Historia Ecclesiastica*, v.68) should call Richard Basset *capitalis justitiarius* during Roger of Salisbury's justiciarship is very difficult to understand. For Richard see below, p. 174.   [2] *Constitutional History*, i.378.

[3] *Anselmi Opera Omnia* (ed. Schmitt), v.410-11, ep. no. 461.

[4] *Ibid.*, pp. 411-12, ep. no. 462. It is clear that Anselm took the wide terms in which the king expressed his desire for the archbishop's advice and counsel as being merely complimentary.

[5] Haskins, *Norman Institutions*, pp. 87-99.   [6] *Ibid.*, pp. 113-4; below, p. 223.

general function, it was inevitable that there should be differences between English and Norman practices, because the exchequers were imposed upon pre-existing institutions. The surviving records of the Norman exchequer under English kings impress, however, by their similarities to English records, though one difference we may remark. In Normandy it was more usual to call the justiciar the seneschal, and later in the twelfth century this latter title was the invariable one; but the difference in title implies no difference in function.[1]

At the time of Henry I's death the office of justiciar and his court, the exchequer, were only at the beginning of their history. The system had no deep roots. It had been devised to meet a specific problem, and soon that problem ceased. Stephen would not seem to have had need for a justiciar, a vicegerent, after 1145 when he had definitely lost Normandy, and it may be that none had been appointed to replace Roger of Salisbury after he was deprived of office in 1139. No chronicler mentions a successor to Roger nor have any writs of a successor, if such there were, survived; but there are grounds for believing that towards the end of Stephen's reign Richard de Lucy filled the office. There are writs of Stephen's addressed to him in a judicial capacity[2] which accord with this belief, and his dignity seems to be signalised in the treaty of Winchester, where his attestation follows immediately after the earls' and before that of the other barons.[3] Moreover, after Stephen's death, authority seems to have rested with Archbishop Theobald and Richard who, with other magnates, remained in London awaiting Duke Henry's arrival in England for his coronation.[4] If, too, we can accept Richard as Stephen's justiciar, we can understand how it came to pass that Henry, at his accession, appointed him to the office jointly with the earl of Leicester, an appointment that seems otherwise inexplicable. But though the office may have been maintained after Roger of Salisbury's dismissal or revived after an interval, no later justiciar appointed by Stephen could have exercised more than a fraction of Roger's authority. And if the exchequer survived, as it seemingly did, in name,[5] it is impossible that it could have continued to function as it had under Henry I. But of the decay of the judicature and the financial system we have more to say in subsequent chapters.

Henry II acceded then to a kingdom where the central administration was functioning imperfectly and over only part of the country, and some years were to be spent in the task of reconstruc-

---

[1] *Ibid.*, pp. 164-5, 174, 180, 183-4, 323-6.
[2] For examples see Madox, *Formulare*, no. lxviii, and *History of the Exchequer*, i.33, *n.* 1; Voss, *Heinrich von Blois*, pp. 155-6. The addresses to some of the writs may be ambiguous, but the writ of 1152-3, addressed to 'Richard de Lucy and Terric son of Deorman, justiciar of London, and the sheriffs and ministers of London and Middlesex', shows conclusively that Richard is not addressed as local justiciar.   [3] *Foedera*, i.18.
[4] *Chronicon Mon. de Bello*, p. 71.   [5] Below, p. 226.

tion.[1] The most remarkable feature of the new administration was the appointment of two lay justiciars and the association with them of a nephew of Roger of Salisbury's, Bishop Nigel of Ely, who had served with his uncle as Henry I's treasurer and as a baron of the exchequer. It says much for these men that there is no hint of rivalry and that their association was fruitful in effective government. Richard of Ely speaks in terms of admiration both of his father Bishop Nigel, and of the earl of Leicester, the senior of the justiciars[2]; and, when they died, Henry II maintained in office the other justiciar, Richard de Lucy, until his retirement from the world in 1178.[3] After an interval, Richard de Lucy was replaced in 1180 by another layman, Ranulf Glanville,[4] whose name is imperishably associated with the writ system developed during Henry II's reign. Thereafter bishops and laymen were chosen indifferently for the office until it was abolished in 1234. This is a notable fact, for these laymen must have been sufficiently literate to perform their duties, and indeed the earl of Leicester seemed to Richard of Ely remarkable for his learning.[5] Of the literacy of laymen in the twelfth century we shall have more to say[6]; but here we may remark that it made possible the creation of a body of justices who could sit on the bench at the exchequer or perambulate the country as justices in eyre or of assize. The future of English administration, especially the administration of justice, depended upon the existence of widespread literacy among the baronial class. The twelfth century was as remarkable for a literate laity—an outstanding fact that has been almost universally doubted or denied—as it was for the organisation of an efficient administrative machine, which has been almost equally misunderstood.

The administration directed by the justiciar in England was self-contained, as was also the administration directed by the seneschal-justiciar in Normandy. Every province of the so-called Angevin empire was administered separately, even though outside Normandy some of the English king's French provinces might on occasion be jointly administered by one seneschal.[7] What unity this misnamed 'empire' had was given to it by the king; but he did not introduce common institutions or a common code of law. England and Normandy had, it is true, a closer resemblance than any other two provinces; but this was because many barons held lands on both sides of the Channel, because Norman customs had made some headway in England and such administrative innovations as the king had introduced followed broadly the same pattern in the two countries,

---

[1] Below, pp. 194-7. [2] *Dialogus de Scaccario*, pp. 50, 57-8.
[3] *E.H.R.*, xliii.330.
[4] Apparently in April: see Howden, *Chronica*, ii.215, and cf. Eyton, *Itinerary of Henry II*, p. 231. The references to Glanville's writs, which appear for the first time in the pipe roll of 1180, show that he was justiciar for a substantial part of the year.
[5] *Dialogus*, p. 57: litteris eruditus.
[6] Below, pp. 269-83. [7] For some examples see *E.H.R.*, lxxiv.211-3.

while his ministers, largely of Norman stock, might be called upon to undertake duties in either country. If the efficiency of the administration in England and Normandy is remarkable, so also is the particularism of all the provinces subject to the English king.[1] This particularism, this small-scale administration, was in the twelfth century a source of strength. Of the administration of Anjou, of Poitou, of Gascony, with their more primitive, more feudal, systems we can say little, for little is known[2]; but in England and Normandy the administration, directed by the justiciar, functioned without loss of efficiency or diminution of powers while the king was absent on Crusade or a prisoner in Germany. Even the intrigues, the usurpation of authority, by Count John did no more than shake the fabric. The pipe rolls are there to bear witness how little harm was done to the structure of administration in England, even when John was in open revolt. If the ravages of time have deprived us of most of the plea rolls of Richard I's reign, yet we have enough evidence to show that, whatever minor interruptions there may have been, the king's court remained open. The writ system, of ever-growing intricacy, which had become the main basis of judicial administration, was made possible because the justiciar had power to issue writs on his own authority and to give judgements with the assistance of the royal justices who sat on the bench with him. It was not necessary to seek out a distant king in order to commence an action or to enforce one's right. Justice was available on easy terms for the asking in one's native land and indeed almost at one's very door, if litigants were content that the action should be tried by itinerant justices.[3] In the king's absence all the departments of government functioned without intermission, among them the chancery, if we are to give the name of chancery to the lineal ancestor of the cursitors' office, where writs were regularly issued in the justiciar's name, and not confine it to the clerks of the chapel who followed the king and were responsible for charters and exceptional writs.[4] But we do not need to dispute about names: our concern is with functions.

Plainly the system was what is called in France an impersonal monarchy, and if to have achieved this in the seventeenth century was an important event in French history, it is remarkable and noteworthy to find an impersonal monarchy in England and Normandy

---

[1] This fact lies behind the advice alleged by John of Marmoutier to have been given to Henry II by his father: Henrico heredi suo interdixit ne Normannie vel Anglie consuetudines in consulatus sui terram vel e converso varie vicissitudinis alternatione permuteraret (*Chroniques des Comtes d'Anjou* (ed. Halphen et Poupardin), p. 224).

[2] We say this without depreciating the work that has been done, in especial, on Anjou: see Halphen, *Le comté d'Anjou au xie siècle*; Chartrou, *L'Anjou de 1109 à 1151*; Boussard, *Le Comté d'Anjou sous Henri Plantagenet et ses fils*. The well documented work by Richard, *Les Comtes de Poitou*, is similarly disappointing on the details of administration. It seems likely that documents relating to provincial ad n nistration were never many and would, apart from inevitable losses, have revealed how little organisation there was. The silence of Léopold Delisle on administrative arrangements outside England and Normandy in his Introduction to the *Actes de Henri II relatifs à l'histoire de France* is itself eloquent.

[3] Below, p. 212.   [4] *Memoranda Roll, 1 John*, Introduction, pp. lxxv-lxxxvii.

established in the twelfth century. An impersonal monarchy does not mean that the monarch has lost his personality, but that the functions of the kingly office are performed without his personal intervention, save in exceptional circumstances or in spheres he reserves to himself. And although he delegates much, he is always personally accessible to his subjects and, for good or bad reasons, may intervene to right a supposed wrong or to confer a favour, usually at a price, or even, it is to be feared, to delay or deny justice. The king retains a firm hand upon policy, whoever is the real or nominal ruler to whom his powers are delegated. As we have seen, the queen or the heir to the throne might, in the king's absence, nominally act as regent, though effective power remained in the hands of the justiciar, and for long periods under Henry I, Henry II and Richard I no royal personage was even nominally regent and consequently writs were issued in the name of the justiciar and sealed with his personal seal. Writs issued by the justiciar when the king was present in the country were issued, as we have already noticed, in the king's name and sealed with one of the royal seals, kept in the exchequer for the purpose. Of the existence of the exchequer seal under Henry II and his successors there is conclusive evidence,[1] and there is no good reason for doubting its existence under Henry I. But whosesoever were the image and superscription on the seal and in whosesoever name the writ was couched, the same ministers continued to conduct the business of government. The king, if he were not present in the kingdom and if it were necessary, made his wishes known by his writ 'of oversea', and when he did so, the regent, whether queen, prince or justiciar, cited the king's writ as the authority for any instrument that was issued in consequence.[2] And because the justiciar was throughout the principal minister and acted in complete understanding with the king, the continuity of administration was unbroken.

An important qualification must, however, be made. The justiciar did not control the disbursement of the royal treasure. All but customary and necessary expenditure is incurred under the king's direct authority, and payments are made either by precepts directed to the treasurer and chamberlains or to the sheriffs or from funds that are under the control of the king's chamber, the *camera curiae*. Of the details of this system more will be said in a subsequent chapter, but here we would endeavour to dispel a cardinal error. England was but part of the dominions of Henry I and of the Angevin kings, and from every one of those dominions revenue flowed into the king's chamber. Doubtless England was the king's most important province and doubtless there was a nascent English nation and the faint beginnings of national sentiment. But if we try to look through the king's eyes or through the eyes of the ministers

---

[1] *Ibid.*, pp. lxvi, lxxiii, lxxxv.
[2] *Ibid.*, p. lxxviii: for an example see *ibid.*, p. lxxi.

in attendance upon him, we shall not see affairs in national terms. Especially is this true of finance. Impressed by the stately series of pipe rolls and their inexhaustible details, scholars have sought to wring from them secrets they do not conceal. When the nature of those rolls is understood, it will be appreciated how misguided are the attempts that have been made to construct from them estimates of the king's revenues and how misleading it is to say with Stubbs that they 'contain the summaries and authoritative details of the national account'.[1] The pipe rolls should, above all, teach us caution in approaching the financial history of the twelfth century. The more we study them, the less likely are we to suppose that we can ever tell from our existing sources the story of royal finance, except in the broadest outline. And the reason should be plain. The pipe rolls record the findings of the barons of the exchequer upon specific questions. Certain important items of revenue are not exposed to their scrutiny, at any rate at their regular sessions. The barons, moreover, are not concerned with the total amount of money that finds its way into the treasury, but with the detailed account for which each accountant is responsible; and they approach these questions judicially and not as financiers. The treasurer has a wider view; but once, upon the king's precept, he has delivered up part of the accumulation in his charge he has no concern with its disposal. There is no single minister who is concerned with the king's total revenue and total expenditure. There is no hint that the king himself ever faces in advance the problem of balancing his budget. To think such thoughts is not to think as a man of the twelfth century. Certainly the justiciar and the barons of the exchequer did not think in that fashion. Even the conception of a 'national account' was impossible.

There is another, allied, error constantly repeated, that the chancery enrolments have their origin under John and that the credit for their invention is due to his chancellor, Hubert Walter—though Hubert had formerly been justiciar under Richard I and in complete control of the administration in England. We say that this is an allied error because it springs from misconceptions of the same kind concerning the nature of mediaeval finance and the relations of the justiciar to the king. It is, of course, true that the principal series of chancery rolls, as they now exist, begin in John's reign, but this is a mere accident. There is abundant evidence that chancery enrolments were already in existence under Richard I and that the system which required these enrolments was nearly complete in all its parts in the latter years of Henry II.[2] Enrolments, to begin with, were devised for financial control and served a strictly practical purpose. The earliest of which we have direct evidence are the pipe

---

[1] *Constitutional History*, i.641.
[2] *Memoranda Roll, 1 John*, Introduction, pp. xxi, xxxii-xxxv, liv.

rolls, though there is no reason to suppose that these rolls did not have predecessors. The pipe rolls, however, as we have already explained, are rolls of the exchequer and record the outcome of the barons' deliberations and decisions. They are the product of a complicated system. The English pipe rolls and the corresponding Norman pipe rolls represent only a stage in the process of supplying the king with money. Beyond, there were other stages and other controls until the money was spent and dissipated. But behind the pipe rolls there lay a mass of subsidiary rolls, which tend to be overlooked because they have almost all disappeared, and their nature and purpose can be known only from a few fragmentary survivals and the traces they have left on the pipe rolls themselves.[1] Here we may single out two series of rolls whose origin is illuminating for the history both of the exchequer and the chancery. There was need to notify the English and Norman exchequers of the moneys promised to the king by his subjects and of the debts remitted and grants made by the king to his subjects. In this way arose the series of fine rolls and close rolls: an alternative title for the former is 'rolls of offerings' (rotuli de oblatis) and for the latter 'rolls of grants of lands and money', titles that are sufficiently explanatory.[2] It is these chancery rolls whose origin can be traced back to the reign of Henry II. In course of time the close rolls changed their character, but that does not alter the fact that their primitive purpose was financial.

The king's chancery—the chancery attendant upon the king—was not a great maker of records in the twelfth century. The chancery clerks seem to have kept no record of instruments under the great seal which were primarily of private interest, and when the charter and patent rolls were devised under John, their original purpose appears to us to have been to keep a check upon the fees due for the use of the great seal.[3] In the twelfth century record-making centred, not round the king, but round the justiciar and the exchequer. Nor were these records merely financial. If the plea rolls had their origin in the need to keep a record of the fines and amercements inflicted by the justices, they were before the end of Henry II's reign, as we shall see, used to record the progress of actions through the court at the exchequer and before itinerant justices.[4] The needs of litigation led, too, to the enrolment in the exchequer, for the purpose of record, of charters and letters patent upon which litigants

---

[1] For the early brevia and rotuli of itinerant justices and others, see below, pp. 185-7. The receipt rolls afford a good illustration of fragmentary survivals: only a portion of the roll for the Michaelmas term 1185 and a little of one of 7 Richard I survive for the twelfth century. All of the memoranda rolls, which are known from the 'Dialogus de Scaccario' to have been kept, have disappeared.

[2] Memoranda Roll, 1 John, Introduction, pp. xxi-xxxv.

[3] Ibid., pp. xxxv-xlvi. The financial origin of the charter and patent rolls has been disputed (Painter, Reign of King John, pp. 100-2; Galbraith, Studies in the Public Records, p. 69): but no evidence has been adduced for an alternative origin nor has any alternative explanation been offered for the omission of important documents, notably Magna Carta. Arguments not based on the records leave us unmoved.   [4] Below, p. 214.

relied and also to the invention of feet of fines, the files of which served a purpose similar to the rolls 'of ancient charters'.[1] The peripatetic court held before the king himself is a complete contrast. Though of immemorial antiquity, until the thirteenth century it has left no records of its own[2]: it seems certainly to have kept none in the twelfth century. The significance of the office of justiciar could not be better displayed. If important cases were occasionally heard before the king on his perpetual journeyings, for the most part litigants sought the sedentary court at Westminster with its bench of professional judges. If we may judge by 'Glanville', lawyers in the closing decades of the twelfth century gave hardly a thought to the court *coram rege*: their attention was confined to the court at the exchequer and the courts of the itinerant justices. It was at Westminster that the common law of England was born and grew up. But of these things we must speak at greater length.[3] We have said enough to give an outline of the administrative system as it stood at the close of the twelfth century. It postulated a king, more often absent from his kingdom than present in it, and a justiciar who administered the country with almost regal authority. The loss of Normandy truncated the system, but its usefulness was such that what had been devised to reconcile the exercise of royal authority with efficient local administration in two countries separated by the sea, was continued in England under a king who no longer divided his time between his two principal dominions. There had been devised, under the pressure of circumstances, a system of administration for which there had been no parallel in the West since the collapse of Roman provincial administration. There are many details we shall need to describe in order to complete the picture; but here we may pause and ask whether, if the outline sketched above is a faithful representation of the structure of government, the picture presented by Stubbs in the *Constitutional History*[4] is to be commended to students? It is not only that he was sometimes wrong in detail and more often in inference, not only that he was necessarily ignorant of much that is essential to an understanding of the period, but that the relation of events is misconceived. It is no reply to say that Stubbs recognised the exceptional position of Roger of Salisbury or that he seems to have guessed that the exchequer emerged in both England and Normandy under Henry I, that he was right on this detail or on that.[5] Many of his details, the majority (it may be) are right, but the pattern is false, the architecture is wrong; and to say that is to say all.

---

[1] *Memoranda Roll, 1 John*, Introduction, pp. liv-lix.
[2] The earliest rolls of pleas *coram rege* come from the reign of John, as do the earliest feet of fines levied *coram rege*. This is because the court *coram rege* is served by the same corps of judges as the bench and follows the same procedure. Strictly speaking there are not two separate courts: see below, pp. 384-6.   [3] Below, pp. 210-15.
[4] Vol. 1, chapters 9-13.   [5] *Ibid.*, pp. 377-8, 474-5.

IX

THE ORGANISATION OF THE JUDICATURE

THE office of chief justiciar was created to solve the problem of administering the kingdom during the king's absence in Normandy. As the king's representative and the king's principal minister, he became head of the judicature; but clearly the judicature would have come into existence had the office of justiciar never been created, and it behoves us to trace, if we can, the origin of the administration of royal justice as it is displayed in the records of the twelfth century.

Justice in pre-Conquest England was essentially local justice. If on occasion great causes came before the witan,[1] such occurrences were altogether exceptional. Everyday justice was for the courts of the shire and the hundred. Though it is not impossible that there were times when the Old English kings sent representatives to the shires to settle disputes, there seems to be no evidence that they did so and, so far as we know, the practice of the Conqueror in sending out commissioners to try difficult disputes between highly placed men or to conduct a nation-wide enquiry marked a new departure. Though some men might be employed on such missions on several occasions, as was Bishop Geoffrey of Coutances,[2] there were no royal justices in regular employment. But before the end of the eleventh century it became evident that to protect the king's interests it was desirable to appoint a local justice who would in some sort control the sheriff and act as his coadjutor.[3] Such justices were maintained in office for sixty years or more and had varying fortunes, disappearing for all practical purposes within a dozen years or so of Henry II's accession. Though there is much to learn of their history, it is not so obscure as has sometimes been supposed, and it is necessary to give its main outlines here if we are to understand the organisation of justice in the twelfth century. There is a succinct statement of a justice's duties in Henry I's charter to London, 'ad custodiendum placita corone mee et eadem

---

[1] As, for example, in 1051 and 1052, when Earl Godwin and his sons were outlawed and inlawed, and in 1055, when Earl Ælfgar was outlawed.

[2] Stenton, *Anglo-Saxon England*, pp. 624, 640-2.

[3] Davis, *England under the Normans and Angevins*, p. 520; Round, *Geoffrey de Mandeville*, pp. 106-13, 305, 373; Morris, *The Mediaeval English Sheriff*, pp. 56-8; Cronne in the *University of Birmingham Historical Journal*, vi.18-38. The Leis Willelme', 2.1, suggests that the oppressive sheriff might be subject to the *justice le rei* (*Gesetze der Angelsachsen*, i.492), but this may come from late in Henry I's reign and mean a justice in eyre.

placitanda'.[1] Much more is said in the law-books of the twelfth century but, since these are largely concerned with criminal actions, their
references to local justices give a somewhat one-sided view of their
duties. Homicide and theft were only too common, and it was with
those guilty of these crimes that the justice, sitting as a rule in the
hundred or county court, was mainly occupied,[2] but he presided over
pleas of land as well as criminal actions. A letter written by Roger,
earl of Hereford, to Henry II in 1155 affords a good illustration.
There was a disputed claim to an estate in Gloucestershire which,
the earl said, might be settled in two ways: the abbot of Gloucester
might decide it in his own court or the plea might be heard before the
justice of the shire, when the truth of the matter could be enquired
into by the county court.[3] Our purpose is not, however, to tell the
story of the local justices in any detail. They have a claim to a
greater place in the history of English law than has been given them;
but, when all is said, they appear to have been, as a rule, men of
humble status, who played a useful but undistinguished part in
local courts.[4] The office assumed considerable importance, however,
under Stephen, when it was sought by such men as Geoffrey de
Mandeville, William de Roumare, earl of Lincoln, and successive
bishops of Lincoln.[5] The explanation must be that the weakness of
the central administration of justice gave the local office a significance it had not hitherto possessed and made its control desirable,
for good or ill, in the eyes of local magnates. Once firm government
was restored, the office lost its transient importance and, with the
resumption of judicial eyres, it became superfluous and was allowed
to disappear.

In any case the king needed more effective protection of his
interests than was afforded by local justices, and early in the twelfth
century there appeared a body of justices who were distinguished as
justitiarii totius Anglie: they were so called because their functions
were not confined to any one county. Henry of Huntingdon gives
the title to five men: Geoffrey Ridel, Robert Bloet, bishop of
Lincoln, Ralf Basset and his son Richard, and Roger, bishop of
Salisbury.[6] This is not an exhaustive list. Aubrey de Vere is given
the same title by his son William, whose statement there is no reason
to question.[7] Again, an early charter of Henry I's names Alfred of

---

[1] *Gesetze der Angelsachsen*, i.525; *Select Charters*, p. 129.
[2] 'Leges Henrici', 29.1b, 34.7; 'Leges Edwardi Confessoris', 18.2, 20.1a, 2, 4, 6, 22.5,
23, 23.4, 36, 36.3 (*Gesetze*, i.563, 566, 644-6, 648-9, 666-7).
[3] *Historia et Cartularium Monasterii Gloucestrie*, ii.98.
[4] Despite known exceptions this generalisation appears to be true: but see Cronne, *op.
cit.*, pp. 31, 33. The details are too extensive to be discussed here. It will, however, be
remembered that in later times coroners, who were rarely of equal status with the sheriff,
nevertheless afforded a means of control.
[5] Round, *Geoffrey de Mandeville*, pp. 106-11; *Lincoln Registrum Antiquissimum*, i.60, 63-4.
[6] Henry of Huntingdon, *Historia Anglorum*, pp. 245, 290, 318: the last two references
are in 'De Contemptu Mundi'.
[7] 'Liber de Miraculis S. Osithae' in Leland, *Itinerary* (ed. Toulmin Smith), v.172. For
the author see *Complete Peerage*, x, App., pp. 114-5, 118-9.

Lincoln, together with Roger of Salisbury, as his *justitiarius*: these two justices are apparently going on eyre in the south-western counties in or about the year 1106[1]: here then is a seventh name we can add to the list. There has been a good deal of confusion between the office of *justitiarius totius Anglie* and that of *capitalis justitiarius*, but it is plain that, while there might be several *justitiarii* at a time (and they seem commonly to have acted in pairs),[2] there could be only one chief justiciar and, indeed, all those named above were active while Roger of Salisbury was chief justiciar. Moreover, it seems beyond doubt that there was a parallel and strictly contemporaneous organisation in Normandy, where a number of *justitiarii* are found with a single chief justiciar, John, bishop of Lisieux.[3] It should be added that there were others who appear to have been *justitiarii totius Anglie*, although they are not so styled in any contemporary document that has come to light: in particular, Geoffrey de Clinton, William d'Aubigny the Breton, Walter Espec and Eustace fitz John, of whom more will be said shortly.

Altogether there seem to have been about a dozen *justitiarii totius Anglie* in office at some time during the reign of Henry I, with perhaps a maximum of half a dozen at any one time. They were all prominent *curiales*, identifiable, doubtless, with the *justitie maiores* of the 'Leges Henrici'.[4] Presumably they were employed continuously in the service of the Crown so long as they were *justitiarii*, but there is no reason to suppose that they held office for life. Alfred of Lincoln, for example, who was in office early in the reign, does not seem to have been employed on judicial work for some years before 1130.[5] And while most *justitiarii* were employed on occasion as justices itinerant, this may not be true of all. There is no indication that up to 1129 Aubrey de Vere had been so employed, though he was practised enough in the law to be given later the pejorative description of *causidicus*.[6] We must not, of course, regard any of the *justitiarii* as professional lawyers. William de Vere lays stress upon his father's position as one of the inner circle of the king's counsellors. He says of him, *secretorum ulteriorum non extremus*, which may be translated, 'he was not excluded from the closest secrets'[7]: and there is plenty to show that *justitiarii* were expected to take part in administration. In 1130 Aubrey de Vere and Richard Basset, who were put jointly in charge, as *custodes*, of eleven counties,[8] could not have performed

---

[1] *Cal. Charter Rolls*, ii.132; *Regesta Regum Anglo-Normannorum*, ii, no. 754.

[2] Another early example is that of Geoffrey Ridel and Alfred of Lincoln at the council at Nottingham in October 1109 (*Regesta*, no. 918): later examples are given below.

[3] Haskins, *Norman Administration*, pp. 93-8.

[4] 'Leges Henrici', 59.3, 61.3 (*Gesetze*, i.578, 581).

[5] He is mentioned twice, once because he is pardoned danegeld, and again because of his fine to have the manor of Pulham for life (*Pipe Roll, 31 Henry I*, pp. 15, 16).

[6] William of Malmesbury, *Historia Novella* (ed. Potter), p. 33. Malmesbury also says of him (p. 30): homo causarum varietatibus exercitatus.

[7] *Liber de Miraculis S. Osithae, ut supra.*

[8] *Pipe Roll, 31 Henry I*, pp. 43, 52, 81, 90, 100.

their duties and at the same time have found leisure for other activities. Since, moreover, it was deemed necessary to divert Richard to judicial work elsewhere, the burden upon Aubrey must have been the greater.[1] Geoffrey de Clinton's great activity as justice itinerant did not begin presumably earlier than 1126 when he ceased to be treasurer,[2] for that office would not leave much time for judicial work in distant counties, though we may assume that, like later treasurers, he took part in the judicial work of the exchequer. Every *justitiarius* might doubtless sit on occasion at the exchequer, and there is no reason to suppose that the composition of the court differed sensibly from what it was to be under Henry II. We know that in 1119 there were present the chief justiciar, Robert Bloet, the chancellor and Ralf Basset.[3] Here we have, beside the chancellor, who does not need such a designation, three men who are elsewhere designated *justitiarii*. In a court over which the queen nominally presided, held apparently at the Michaelmas session of the exchequer in 1111, there had been present the chief justiciar, Robert Bloet, Ralf Basset and Geoffrey Ridel.[4] We shall shortly describe the activities of the *justitiarii* when they were on eyre throughout the country, but we may perhaps at this point usefully summarise the evidence we have so far presented. All the essentials of an organised judicature are already present under Henry I. He has instituted an all-powerful minister, the chief justiciar, and he has provided himself with a small body of *justitiarii* who, if not trained lawyers, are experienced administrators. Justice is still, for the most part, a matter for the local courts, but the king's government is in a position to supervise and control the local administration of justice, supervision and control that, so it would seem, it badly needed.

The pipe roll of 31 Henry I, that is, the pipe roll which presents the account as it stood at Michaelmas 1130, affords the bulk of our information regarding the activities of justices itinerant under that king, though, in the absence of earlier rolls, it is not easy to determine the exact significance of many of the facts recorded. So far as appears from the roll, the most heavily employed justice had been Geoffrey de Clinton, who is recorded as having visited no less than eighteen counties, but none of them apparently in the current financial year and only a few very recently.[5] Eyres may leave their

---

[1] He is held solely liable for the escape of a prisoner, and for this and for 'the forfeiture of the counties' of Essex and Hertfordshire he is required to pay £550 and four chargers. He has to find a further 100 marks to be released from the custody of these counties. Richard Basset, presumably because he is employed elsewhere in the king's service, does not share this liability (*ibid.*, p. 53).   [2] Below, pp. 219-20.

[3] *Chronicon Mon. de Abingdon*, ii.160. The statement that complaint was made 'apud regiam iustitiam' implies a decision of the justiciar's court.

[4] *Ibid.*, p. 116: see below, p. 189.

[5] *Pipe Roll, 31 Henry I*, pp. 8-10 (Nottingham, Derby), 17 (Wilts.), 26-31 (York, Northumberland), 50 (Surrey), 55-6, 59 (Essex), 65 (Kent), 69 (Sussex), 73-4 (Stafford), 83 (Northants.), 92-3, 99 (Norfolk), 101 (Bucks.), 103 (Bedford), 106 (Warwick), 112

mark on the pipe rolls for many years. Let us offer proof of this. Scattered over this roll are items which show that Ralf Basset had visited ten counties,[1] and this is certainly not the full tale, for no mention is made of his visit to Leicestershire in 1124.[2] Ralf is believed to have survived until 1129, but he appears to have retired from active judicial work some time before, perhaps in 1127.[3] Consequently it seems quite likely that the pipe roll contains items arising from eyres a decade or so earlier nor, despite the large number of these entries, does the evidence warrant the conjecture that, in the greater part of the country, eyres occurred very frequently, although, when undertaken, they appear to have been exhaustive and rigorous. The eyres which we can be reasonably certain were in progress in 1129 and the proceeds of which were brought to account in 1130 are those of Richard Basset in Sussex[4] and, in company with William d'Aubigny, in Lincolnshire,[5] and that of Walter Espec and Eustace fitz John in the northern counties.[6] These eyres and an earlier eyre by Geoffrey de Clinton and an unnamed companion in Yorkshire and Northumberland—perhaps in 1128 or the early months of 1129[7]—fill large spaces on the pipe roll, in contrast to the brief and scattered entries relating to earlier eyres.

Let us now, with the particulars arising from the three eyres of 1129, endeavour to present a picture of a general eyre under Henry I. We must remember that the primary concern of the barons of the exchequer, when they come to the Michaelmas session, is with the profits of justice, and we shall not therefore expect to find on the pipe roll many details beyond such as serve for the bare identification of a financial item, although we do, in fact, get rather more than this. Nor can we expect to learn of any work the justices did that resulted in no fine or amercement, no offering to the king. But whatever may be lacking, the details we are given represent very fairly, we believe, the bulk of the work the justices accomplished.

Beginning with the Lincoln eyre,[8] we first note that Anschetil the 'collector' is called upon to account for 100 marks of silver and four marks of gold in respect of the pleas of William d'Aubigny; but what is covered by these sums we are not told. Then the burgesses of Lincoln account for 200 marks of silver and four marks of gold so

(Lincoln), 123-4 (Berks.). In Huntingdonshire he had held pleas of the forest (p. 47). The pleas recorded under Nottingham and Derby, York and Northumberland, Essex and Norfolk appear to be more recent than the others.

[1] *Ibid.*, pp. 9 (Nottingham, Derby), 18, 19 (Wilts.), 31 (York), 49 (Huntingdon), 92 (Norfolk), 96 (Suffolk), 110, 114 (Lincoln), 123-4 (Berks.), 145 (London).

[2] Anglo-Saxon Chronicle (Peterborough), *s.a.* 1124 (Plummer, p. 254).

[3] The editors of *Regesta*, vol. ii, assume his presence at Rouen in 1129 (no. 1576). There is no trace in the Pipe Roll of recent activity, and Round in *Dict. Nat. Biog.* assigns 1127 as the possible year of his death. He had probably retired and been succeeded by his son Richard as *justitiarius*.   [4] *Pipe Roll, 31 Henry I*, pp. 69-71.

[5] *Ibid.*, pp. 114-21.   [6] *Ibid.*, pp. 26-7, 33-5, 130-2, 138, 142-3.

[7] *Ibid.*, pp. 26-31.   [8] *Ibid.*, pp. 114-21.

that they may hold the city from the king in chief, and forty marks
of silver and one mark of gold in respect of the pleas of William
d'Aubigny. Roger of Kyme next accounts for 100 marks of silver for
a plea of land against Walter Godwinson. Then two men each
account for sixty marks for a plea of false judgement. Ralf fitz Nigel
and two of his men account for fifty, twenty and sixty marks respectively 'de placitis W. de Albino Britonis', but for what reason we are
not told. Thereafter the sheriff begins to account for amercements
inflicted upon the wapentakes: these entries are scattered but,
collecting them, we have murder fines in Aswardhurn, Aveland,
Corringham and Manley, amercements for breaches of the peace in
Aslacoe and Langoe, and for concealment of treasure trove in
Kirton. Various men account for various sums for breaches of the
peace and for wreck (which they have appropriated instead of
turning to the king's profit). And now Richard Basset has appeared
as William d'Aubigny's colleague[1]: apparently they sometimes sit
together and sometimes separately. There is one item, 'de placitis
Ricardi Basset de minutis hominibus', which we may note and leave
for the moment, since it will be best to discuss it together with
similar entries elsewhere. We come next to items of greater interest.
Roger of La Lacelle has offered 100 shillings in order that a plea of
land may be adjourned until Robert Marmion is knighted. Goislin,
the bishop's steward, has made a causey in the king's highway and
is amerced twenty marks of silver and one of gold.[2] Four *judices* of
the Isle (of Axholm) are amerced eight marks: but we defer the
explanation of this item. Ralf Godricson offers a horse worth sixty
shillings as an alternative to bringing an action to recover his land.
Lambert fitz Peter gives a palfrey (as relief) so that he may have
his father's land,[3] and Ralf fitz Drew does likewise, offering three
falcons and four gerfalcons.[4] Baldwin of Driby offers 140 marks so
that he may have the wardship of Ralf fitz Simon of Driby, with all
his land, until he is ready to be knighted. Wigot of Hackthorn is
amerced one mark because he has failed in a judicial battle.[5] Beside
these informative entries we must set a great number which assign
no reason for the debt, as where the sheriff accounts for fifteen marks
in respect of Leadenham and Fulbeck[6] or £61 6s. 8d. for the pleas
of William d'Aubigny at Boston[7] and we are told nothing more.

The entries regarding Richard Basset's eyre in Sussex are fewer
and less informative,[8] but it is plain that the proceedings followed
the same lines as those in Lincolnshire. We commence with murder
fines inflicted upon eight hundreds and the borough of Lewes. Beyond
this the entries are scanty and for the most part uninstructive. There
are amercements in respect of sureties (*plegii*) who have failed in

[1] *Ibid.*, p. 116.   [2] *Ibid.*, p. 117.   [3] *Ibid.*, p. 118.
[4] *Ibid.*, p. 121.   [5] *Ibid.*, p. 119.   [6] *Ibid.*, p. 119.
[7] *Ibid.*, p. 120.   [8] *Ibid.*, pp. 69-71.

some unspecified way. Ralf of Dean has offered 100 marks for an action between him and Hugh of Varaville, but its nature is not disclosed. The abbot of Fécamp owes sixty marks for half the toll on ships at Winchelsea.[1] We know from another source that this is the outcome of a dispute with the count of Eu.[2] The abbot also owes twenty marks for Salada, his man, who has been amerced by Richard Basset. There follows an entry which is to be compared with one in the account for the Lincolnshire eyre: 102 marks are due 'de minutis hominibus pro defectu hundredorum'. William Malfeth owes a mark of gold for the land that he took with his wife, and the like sum to have right in respect of the land he claims in Sussex. Richard of Héricourt owes twenty marks so that the exchange between him and Robert of Sauqueville may be allowed. And with this the account ends.

While the accounts for the eyres in Lincolnshire and Sussex are easily distinguishable on the pipe roll, those of the eyre of Walter Espec and Eustace fitz John in the northern counties are difficult to disentangle, the more so since these justices, who are very important local personages, have administrative duties also in the same area. It seems likely, too, that their eyre had opened in time for some items to have been put in charge before Easter 1129 and therefore to have appeared in the previous pipe roll.[3] We note that, in addition to other pleas, Walter Espec has been trying pleas of the forest, *placita cervi*. Pleas of the crown are discernible in his delivery to the treasury of a gold ring that has been claimed as treasure trove and in a penalty of twenty shillings imposed for homicide.[4] Again, for neglecting the wall of Blyth castle the barons of Blyth have to pay £20 as a penalty, which Eustace fitz John applies to the necessary repairs.[5] These are all the delicts specifically mentioned in Yorkshire and their fewness contrasts with the considerable number of items relating to land[6]: pro placito terre uxoris sue . . . pro terra patris sue . . . ut haberet escambium terre sue . . . ut teneat in pace terram de Sulinga . . . pro concessione ii. carrucatarum terre et ii. bovatarum et i. domus in Everwic . . . ut rex faciat ei habere saisitionem de terra sua de Willelmo de Albamara . . . ut habeat terram Petri, avunculi sui, in custodia donec redeat de Ierusalem . . . pro recto de terra sua. Some of these items may conceivably arise out of pleas of the crown, but the majority seem certainly to arise from civil actions. Finally we may note an entry under a special heading, 'Placita W. Espec et Eustacii filii Iohannis', which runs 'Iudices et iuratores Eboraciscire debent c. libras ut non amplius sint iudices nec iura-

[1] *Ibid.*, p. 71.
[2] Chevreux and Vernier, *Archives de Normandie*, no. xxxiii; *Regesta*, no. 1690.
[3] *Pipe Roll, 31 Henry I*, p. 27: de placitis W. Espec et Eustacii filii Iohannis. Cf. p. 35 for a similar entry under Northumberland. [4] *Ibid.*, p. 32.
[5] *Ibid.*, p. 33. The castle is better known as Tickhill castle (cf. V.C.H., *Yorkshire*, ii.166).
[6] *Pipe Roll, 31 Henry I*, pp. 32-3.

tores.'[1] From this entry we can infer, despite the silence of the roll, that the eyre has been a general eyre of the normal type; but it will be convenient to defer an explanation.

These miscellaneous and laconic entries may seem to the casual reader a very dull string of uninformative jottings. They are indeed jottings (for a reason we shall explain), but when we have induced a little more order among them, it will be seen that they form a pattern, the pattern of the chapters of the eyre, such as have been preserved for the years 1194 and 1198.[2] In the first place come the pleas of the crown: hence the presentment of murder (in the technical sense), homicide, breaches of the king's peace, treasure trove, wreck. The justices enquire about wardships, marriages, purprestures, any of the king's rights, such as his rights to tolls, that appear to have been infringed. They may enquire about the state of the king's castles and why those who have a duty to repair them have failed to do so. What is especially notable, however, is the large number of cases concerning land which come before the justices. Some of them doubtless arise from their enquiries into the king's right to wardship and to marriage, but a good many appear, as we have said, to be civil actions. Nor does the witness of the pipe roll of 1130 stand alone. Scanty as may be the information we can glean from other sources, it shows the system, as we see it at work in the pipe roll, working in the same way in the early years of the reign. Take first of all pleas of the crown. About the year 1110, William d'Aubigny, who is on eyre in Norfolk, is directed to determine a claim of the abbot of Ramsey to wreck.[3] In 1115-6 Ralf Basset is at Huntingdon and tries an indictment against one Bricstan who has concealed treasure trove.[4] In 1124 he is at Huncot in Leicestershire and sentences fifty thieves, all, with the exception of six, to death and those six to mutilation.[5] And already the justices are trying what will one day be called common pleas. Not later than 1107 Walter Buistard deraigned half a hide of land against the abbot of Ramsey before unnamed royal justices.[6] Not later than 1123 Robert Bloet and Ralf Basset are visiting Lincolnshire and, unless there is a settlement, are to decide a dispute between the monks of Belvoir and a landowner over some appropriate tithes.[7] Isolated, these notices would tell us very little: set against the more abundant details of the pipe roll, they fall into the pattern there disclosed.

If the general pattern of the eyres of Henry I is of the pattern of the eyres of Richard I, of which we have some detailed knowledge, what can we say of the procedure which brings the justices to the

---

[1] Ibid., p. 34.   [2] Howden, Chronica, iii.263-4, iv.61-2.

[3] Chronicon Abbatiae Rameseiensis, p. 228, no. 223.

[4] Ordericus Vitalis, Historia Ecclesiastica, v.123-7; below, p. 186.

[5] Anglo-Saxon Chronicle, Peterborough, s.a. 1124, ut supra.

[6] Cartularium Mon. de Rameseia, i.141, no. 65; Chronicon Abbatiae Rameseiensis, pp. 252-3, no. 274.   [7] Historical MSS. Commission, MSS. of Duke of Rutland, iv.149.

county court, ensures that pleas of the crown and civil pleas are brought before them, enables judgement to be given, and finally brings the king his profit? For the motive that sets this elaborate machinery in motion is largely to safeguard the king's revenue, though let us not refuse to allow the king a higher motive also, for he is, in a very real sense, the fountain of justice. 'A good man he was and there was great awe of him. No man durst misdo against another in his time. He made peace for man and beast. Whoso bare his burthen of gold and silver, no man durst say to him aught but good.'[1] The monk of Peterborough, paying his tribute to the dead king, looks across the sea of troubles of Stephen's reign and sees Henry's England in a light that never was, as indeed we have already given ample proof. But that Henry desired peace and justice to reign throughout his kingdom we may not question. Yet while it behoves us to remember this truth, we must continue to look at the administration of justice from the lower level of everyday life.

Of the commission under which the justices set out upon their eyre and the writs that announced their coming and ensured that the county court should be assembled we can but guess. Nothing has survived of all that must assuredly have been written, though the procedure cannot have greatly differed from that in the thirteenth century.[2] Of civil pleas some, we may suppose, originated in plaints, some in writs, the forerunners of those which were to be standardised under Henry II: again nothing has survived that can be connected with any of Henry I's eyres. But of the way in which pleas of the crown were presented and the way in which they were tried we can, we believe, piece a good many fragments of information together to make a connected story. In the first place let us say something of the men who play the part of juries of presentment and trial. We have already drawn attention to penalties inflicted in the eyres of 1129 on *minuti homines* and the payment made by *judices* and *juratores* of Yorkshire to escape further service. We relate the latter item to two similar items arising out of an earlier eyre in Yorkshire that had been taken by Geoffrey de Clinton: in 1130 thirty-one marks are still due 'de ix. iudicatoribus comitatus' and 336 marks 5s. 6d. 'de minutis iudicibus et iuratoribus comitatus'.[3] And these items we relate in turn, not only to some already cited that arose out of the eyres in Lincolnshire and Sussex, but also to similar items arising out of other eyres of Geoffrey de Clinton: a debt of £17 3s. 4d. 'de iuratoribus comitatus' of Kent,[4] an uncertain sum 'de iuratoribus comitatus' of Sussex,[5] forty shillings 'de iudicibus burgi de Buckingeham'[6] and a like sum 'de iuratoribus et minutis hominibus

---

[1] Anglo-Saxon Chronicle, Peterborough, *s.a.* 1135: Thorpe's translation, p. 229.
[2] As set out by Bracton, fos. 108*b*-112, 115*b*-6 (ed. Woodbine, ii.308-18, 327-9). The text between fos. 112 and 115 relating to another subject is misplaced.
[3] *Pipe Roll, 31 Henry I*, pp. 27-8.   [4] *Ibid.*, p. 65.
[5] *Ibid.*, p. 69.   [6] *Ibid.*, p. 101.

comitatus' of Bedford.[1] To these we can add two items that have been for some time outstanding in Suffolk: a debt of two marks from one of the *minuti homines* who had been amerced by Ralf Basset, which is pardoned by the barons of the exchequer[2]; and a balance of £25 15s. 'de iudicibus comitatus et hundretorum' which the late sheriff, Robert fitz Walter, had failed to collect.[3]

Who are these *judices* or *judicatores*, these *juratores* and *minuti homines*? We have little doubt that the *judices* or *judicatores* are the Old English lawmen, those who pronounce judgement in the county court and hundred court, and that the 'little men' or the 'little judges' are the lawmen of the hundreds, as contrasted with those of the shire. These meanings will fit the context in all the entries where the words occur. But in the light of the known procedure in general eyres under Henry II, we cannot suppose that they have the function of pronouncing judgement or finding a verdict before the itinerant justices. This function we must assign to the *juratores* who can hardly be sworn for any other purpose than to serve on juries of trial. The lawmen, who have already come to a decision in the local courts, must have a different function in the eyre, namely to present their findings to the justices. They are the forerunners of the juries of presentment. These lawmen and jurors, of shire and hundred, who appear on the pipe roll have all failed in some way and have been amerced by the justices. In Yorkshire they have been so roughly handled by Geoffrey de Clinton that they offer the justices, who after a short interval are next sent to the county, £100 to be exempted from further service. And, of course, we can be sure in the light of this entry that the shire and the hundreds were represented before Walter Espec and Eustace fitz John, just as they were before Geoffrey de Clinton, although no other entry on the pipe roll testifies to their presence. Why are these lawmen and jurors so heavily mulcted? A writer earlier in Henry I's reign had a low opinion of *judices*: they hastened to judge matters of which they were ignorant; they were more influenced by the persons concerned than by the facts of the case; men were often elected or made lawmen who were prejudiced against the parties.[4] If such they were, they would cut a poor figure before the justices in eyre; and the justices were ready to punish any slip, any mistake, any deficiency. Nor would the jurors be any better men than the lawmen. Hence the heavy amercements, the desire to escape service. The atmosphere is that of the general eyres of later reigns.

We have expressed our belief that these *judices* are to be equated with the Old English lawmen and we must offer proof. Lawmen are known from references to them in Domesday Book[5] and from one

---

[1] *Ibid.*, p. 103.   [2] *Ibid.*, p. 96.   [3] *Ibid.*, p. 97.
[4] 'Quadripartitus', Ded. 35 (*Gesetze der Angelsachsen*, i.531).
[5] D.B., i.189 a 1, 336 a 1, 336 b 2.

pre-Conquest and one post-Conquest reference in the laws.[1] The word seems obviously to have covered more than one type of judgement-finder, oligarchical at Lincoln and Stamford, elected on the Welsh borders and elsewhere.[2] Sir Henry Ellis suggested, with good reason, that the twelve *judices civitatis* at Chester[3] were what are called *lagemanni* at Lincoln and Stamford.[4] There were *judices* also at York.[5] The *judices burgi* of Buckingham, mentioned in the pipe roll of 1130,[6] cannot be of a different class from the *judices* of other towns forty years or so earlier. This reference supplies the necessary link between the *judices* under Henry I and the *lagemanni* of Domesday Book. The author of the 'Leges Henrici', writing not later than 1118, has a good deal to say of *judices* in the county and hundred courts. A *judex*, described indifferently as *regis judex* and *legum judex*, ought to be a freeholder. A significant difference is drawn between a *baro comitatus* and lesser freeholders; but the latter had to be persons of substance, for freemen, if *viles et inopes*, were ineligible to serve as *judices*.[7] It is anticipated, therefore, that there might be too few duly qualified men in a hundred to constitute a court and that they might need to be afforced from other hundreds.[8] If there were no barons (*senatores*, *proceres*) present in court, the lesser *judices* might refuse to proceed. If there were a difference of opinion, that of the *meliores*, supported by the (county) justice, was to prevail.[9] These *barones comitatus* seem evidently to be the ancestors of Bracton's *buzones comitatus* 'on whose nod the views of the others depend'.[10] The chain of evidence appears to be complete. Leaving aside the towns where a different custom appears to have prevailed, in the country the *judices* consisted of the wealthier suitors of the hundred or county court. In the hundred there could have been little selection, for the number of eligible suitors could rarely have been large. In the county the *barones* would have found it difficult to evade service, for their participation in judgements was essential. As for the lesser men there was inevitably some method of selection, by election or nomination; but as *judices* they carried little weight, though their presence was necessary to make up the complement of the court. Evidently there was some minimum below which the number of *judices* should not fall, but the author of the 'Leges Henrici' is imprecise, doubtless because there was no general rule. That the *judices*, once appointed, continued indefinitely in office is the suggestion underlying all the texts, and it seems evident that their duties

---

[1] *Gesetze*, i.376, 669.   [2] 'Leges Henrici', 31.8 (*Gesetze*, i.564).
[3] D.B., i.262 b 2.   [4] Ellis, *General Introduction to Domesday Book*, i.205.
[5] D.B., i.298.
[6] See above, p. 181.
[7] 'Leges Henrici', 29; 29.1 a (*Gesetze*, i.563).
[8] *Ibid.*, 7.5 (*Gesetze*, i.553).   [9] *Ibid.*, 29.4; 31.2 (*Gesetze*,i. 563-4).
[10] Bracton, fo. 115*b* (ed. Woodbine, ii.327). Cf. *Curia Regis Rolls*, VI.231 (Hilary 1212): milites de comitatu qui consueti sunt interesse falsis judiciis et sunt buzones judiciorum. See also *Pleas before the king or his justices* (ed. D. M. Stenton), ii.48, no. 242 (1201): Willelmus Buzun, unus iiii. militum . . .

GME N

did not begin and end with the periodical sessions of the courts. The most telling piece of evidence is the statement that, when a man accused of felony is subjected to the ordeal of water, the *judices* must be present: they stand with the priest and the executioners who cast the accused into the water.[1]

If we are right in identifying the *judices* with the Old English lawmen, we have here evidence of an ancient procedure that survived the Conquest. Indeed, it is difficult to suppose that there was any breach of continuity if the county and hundred courts were to be maintained in being, as undoubtedly they were. The procedure, however, was devised for self-sufficient local courts, and it was inevitably modified to meet the requirements of royal justice administered by itinerant justices. The part the *judices* were now called upon to play was, as we have already indicated, the part played later by juries of presentment. All serious crime had come before the hundred court or the county court, which was the court of the royally appointed local justice: the *judices* (who, we may recall, are *regis judices*) are the repository of all knowledge of the cases that had been before the courts. They would seem the obvious representatives of shire and hundred to testify in the eyre, nor can we explain in any other way the entries in the pipe roll which concern them. It may be, and we think it certain, that the local justice was also present before the justices itinerant, since he could best check the presentments of the *judices* and, since he was charged with keeping the pleas of the crown, he may have had a written record. But beside the *judices* there are *juratores*, whose presence would be difficult to explain if they did not constitute trial juries. They must be drawn from the same body of men as the *judices*, but they are sworn *ad hoc* to try any issue upon which the justices require a verdict. In Ralf Basset's eyre of 1124 they must have had much work and grim work to do.

Where so much is obscure there is a danger that we may read too much into the evidence, relatively copious though it is. It may be thought that we are inferring a more sophisticated and complex system than is easily credible in the early twelfth century: but no one who has read the 'Leges Henrici' with attention can doubt that the local administration of justice was a complicated business, and we should hesitate to believe that the imposition of controls from above made administration less complicated. Doubtless it is wise, as Maitland recommended, not to believe 'that criminal procedure necessarily involves the use of two juries; as yet the jury which presents the crime is, at least as a general rule, the only jury that there is'.[2] He is speaking of the first quarter of the thirteenth century: we doubt, on the evidence, whether his caution applies to the England of Henry I. After 1130 there seems to be no further mention

---

[1] *Gesetze*, .417.   [2] *Select Pleas of the Crown*, pp. xxiv-xxv.

of *judices* or *judicatores* in royal records, though the name of *judicator* lingered on as a description of some suitors, at least, of hundred courts.[1] There seems no doubt that in the higher courts the place of *judices* was taken by *juratores*. This may be little more than a matter of nomenclature: so far as the evidence of the pipe rolls goes, *juratores* who came before the justices of Henry II performed the same functions and were subject to the same penalties as the *judices* who came before Henry I's justices.[2] It may be that an oath was now administered while at an earlier time *judices* acted without that formality. But in considering the evolution of procedure it is the function, not the formality, to which we should direct our attention.

We think that in yet other ways the eyres of Henry I resembled those of Henry II. To begin with, it is self-evident that the compact series of items on the pipe roll of 1130 relating to the eyres of Richard Basset and Walter d'Aubigny and Walter Espec and Eustace fitz John were derived from records which the justices transmitted to the exchequer. These records were, we believe, called *brevia*. We meet this word in similar circumstances under Henry II when reference is made to *brevia* containing details which were not entered on pipe rolls. These *brevia* were not intended to be permanent records but were necessary in order that the items might be included in the particulars of the amounts the sheriff was required to collect.[3] *Brevia* were used for this purpose until 1175,[4] but in the following year they gave way to *rotuli*,[5] fuller and more permanent records containing a more detailed account of the business transacted by the justices.[6] But the earliest surviving eyre rolls include lists of amercements which must closely resemble the earlier *brevia*.[7] It is, in fact, out of the primitive *brevia* that the justices' rolls evolve.

If, however, the itinerant justices had, in the nature of things, to

[1] Maitland, *Select Pleas in Manorial Courts*, p. lxv, n. 3; Pollock and Maitland, *History of English Law*, i.548, n. 2. [2] Below, p. 204.

[3] Cf. *Pipe Roll, 14 Henry II*, p. 44: vicecomes reddit compotum . . . de essartis Essexe et . . . de wasto foreste et . . . de admerciamentis pro forisfacto foreste, que omnia in summam reducta sunt consideratione baronum secundum breue Alani de Neville quod est in thesauro, quia particule eorum uno rotulo comprehendi non poterant. In the same pipe roll (p. 213) we read of the *brevia* of Richard, archdeacon of Poitiers, and Guy, dean of Waltham, who were justices in eyre in Kent: these *brevia* contained the detailed assessments to an aid. For the use of *breve* in a similar sense see *Dialogus de Scaccario*, p. 62, 'breve de firmis'.

[4] *Pipe Roll, 21 Henry II*, p. 44: nomina et debita subscripta sunt in breui iusticiarum quod liberauerunt in thesauro. *Ibid.*, p. 179: particule sunt in breui quod est in thesauro et de quibus idem vicecomes habet rescriptum.

[5] The uniform formula under the heading *De his qui totum reddiderunt* is 'de minutis misericordiis villarum et hominum quorum nomina annotantur in rotulo quem [iustitie] liberauerunt in thesauro' (*Pipe Roll, 22 Henry II*, pp. 8, 25, 30 *et passim*).

[6] These fuller rolls are described in the 'Dialogus de Scaccario', pp. 70, 77. The financial items were extracted from the rolls at a session of the exchequer. We do not understand Mr Meeking's comment in *Jenkinson Studies*, p. 226. The plea rolls of the Bench presumably originated about the same time. In 1200 rolls of the king's court 'tempore R. de Luci' appear to have survived and to be available for inspection (*Curia Regis Rolls*, i.208, 245).

[7] *Three Rolls of the King's Court*, pp. 136-41: the list is on the otherwise blank dorse of membrane 4 of the roll of an eyre in 1195. The amercements of Hertfordshire, Essex and Middlesex in 1198 are entered very similarly (*Rotuli Curiae Regis*, i.165-70, 178-84, 218-9).

keep a record, it would seem equally evident that they could not have accomplished their task efficiently and speedily unless they had before them something in the nature of a coroner's roll, recording the pleas of the crown that had arisen between the last eyre and the present. We have already suggested that the local justice kept such a roll, and we shall give further reasons for supposing this to have been the case. But the local justice's activities appear to have been supplemented, at least in certain localities, by specially appointed officers also charged with the duty of keeping the pleas of the crown. These officers, if we can generalise from the two instances known to us in the reign of Henry I, were called king's serjeants but had no more specific title. In the account, preserved by Orderic Vitalis, of the trial of Bricstan before Ralf Basset, we read of Robert Malarteis, the king's *minister*, who had no other duty than to spy upon all and sundry, monks or clerks, knights or peasants. It was he who charged Bricstan with concealing treasure trove and appropriating it to his own use, thereby stealing the king's property.[1] Bracton, in describing the offence as a species of treason, uses very similar words,[2] and the procedure he describes is evidently that followed in Bricstan's case: for the accused was attached to await the coming of the justices and, being found guilty, was committed to prison to be heavily ransomed at the king's pleasure. We could indeed hardly find a case more apt to illustrate Bracton's teaching: and it is well to have this further evidence that, even in the technicalities of process, there was but a limited advance between the reign of Henry I and that of Henry III. To return to Robert Malarteis: he was still in office in 1130, for we find him in Huntingdonshire, under the name of Malarteis, in the pipe roll of that year. Clearly he occupied an official position since he was excused the payment of danegeld.[3] Not only did he own land in Huntingdonshire, but also in the neighbouring county of Bedfordshire, where also he was excused danegeld.[4] He was evidently a man of some position. We can put by his side Benjamin, the king's serjeant, in Norfolk, who appears in the same roll. Some while before he had offered the king a substantial sum for keeping the pleas of the crown and had undertaken to make a profit of 500 marks for the king as a result of his activities.[5] In 1130 he was still paying off his debt by instalments and the sheriff accounts for a hundred shillings in respect of pleas of 'Benjamin's money' in the hundred of Clavering,

[1] Ordericus Vitalis, *Historia Ecclesiastica*, v.124-6.

[2] Bracton, fo. 119b-120 (ed. Woodbine, ii.338): quae quidem est quasi crimen furti, scilicet occultatio thesauri inventi fraudulosa.

[3] *Pipe Roll, 31 Henry I*, p. 49. 'Marlarteis' seems to be the same word as the adjective 'malartos' and to mean trickster.   [4] *Ibid.*, p. 104.

[5] *Ibid.*, p. 91. The sum of £4 5s. od. due from him in 1130 is the balance from the previous year. For Benjamin's designation as king's serjeant see the charter, first published by Blomefield in facsimile (*History of Norfolk*, iv.504) and printed by West, *St. Benet of Holme*, p. 174, and again by Loyd in *Christopher Hatton's Book of Seals*, p. 276. The identification of Benjamin of this charter with Benjamin of the pipe roll was made by Hunnisett in 'The Origins of the Office of Coroner' in *Trans. R. Hist. Soc.*, 5th Ser., viii.101.

whence it is clear that a separate account was kept of the profits of justice that had to be credited to him.[1] Benjamin was also engaged in collecting the king's tolls (*lestagium*) in Norfolk and Suffolk, which he farmed for £4 a year.[2] Evidently he, like Robert Malarteis, was a man of position, a well-known figure in East Anglia, so much so that his brother, surely an elder brother, was known as *Ioseph frater Beniamin*.[3]

The appointment of such men as Robert Malarteis and Benjamin to keep the pleas of the crown must obviously have diminished the responsibilities of the local justice, although we can but speculate on the relations between him and king's serjeants of this type. Appointments of the kind were, however, presumably exceptional and were made because it was thought that, by farming the pleas of the crown, a profit might be made both by the king and the fermor. The arrangement was very like the farming of the revenues of a county by the sheriff as an alternative to his holding the county as *custos* and accounting in detail for receipts and expenditure. These two methods of dealing with Crown revenues existed side by side throughout the Middle Ages. It would appear that the majority of king's serjeants did not farm their offices and were subordinate to the local justice, with whom it was in any case necessary for them to cooperate. We do not, it is true, learn very much of the king's serjeants of the twelfth century until the resumption of general eyres under Henry II caused many particulars of their activities and their failures to be recorded on the pipe rolls; but we seem justified in our assumption that in the meantime there had been little change in the position. It is evident that in the early years of Henry II the king's serjeants have much to do with keeping the pleas of the crown. No other interpretation can be put upon entries which concern them.[4] Although we call these officers of hundreds and wapentakes king's serjeants, by contemporaries they are called by a variety of names: king's serjeants, sheriff's serjeants, hundredmen, hundred-bailiffs, hundred-beadles, hundred-reeves.[5] Their duties were many and various, but when they are called king's serjeants it can hardly be for any other reason than that they are keepers of the pleas of the crown. This responsibility inevitably fell upon them. From early in the twelfth century it was the rule that, when anything of value was

---

[1] *Pipe Roll, 31 Henry I*, p. 93.

[2] *Ibid.*, p. 91: *lestagium* may mean port-dues or market-tolls, but here must seemingly mean the former.

[3] *Ibid.*, p. 98; West, *St. Benet of Holme*, p. 80 (no. 141).

[4] Below, pp. 208-9.

[5] Apparently reeve, latinised as *prefectus* or *prepositus*, was the earliest name ('Leges Henrici', 92.8; 'Leges Edwardi Confessoris', 24.2, 3; 32: *Gesetze*, i.608, 649-50, 654). Both *hundredman* and *serviens regis* appear in *Pipe Roll, 15 Henry II*, pp. 102, 149; *bedellus hundredi* and *serviens hundredi* in the eyre rolls of 1194 and 1195 (*Three Rolls of the King's Court*, pp. 100, 143); *ballivus vicecomitis* also appears in 1194 (*Rotuli Curiae Regis*, i.51) and *serviens vicecomitis* in eyre rolls of 1194 and 1198 (*Three Rolls of the King's Court*, pp. 82, 84; *Rotuli Curiae Regis*, i.115).

found, it was the duty of the finder to declare it to the hundred-reeve.[1] This was a matter of police: of preventing crime and protecting the innocent finder of lost objects or of strayed animals. Quite obviously treasure trove or wreck would in this way come to the notice of the hundred-reeve, and he would fail in his duty if he did not claim it on behalf of the king. But the hundred-serjeant (to use the more familiar terminology of the pipe rolls) was the universal policeman and the sheriff's factotum.[2] If there was no one else to perform a necessary duty, it seems to have fallen to him. All aspects of sudden death and crimes of violence came his way, if only because the finders of the body or the witnesses of the deed were anxious to exculpate themselves and escape possible suspicion. Whether his duties were performed as a subordinate of the sheriff or as the king's representative was a matter of indifference and a distinction which probably did not occur to anyone. It is certain that, if the hundred-serjeant failed in his duty towards the king, he was personally responsible and the sheriff was not implicated.[3]

In describing the judicature under Henry I, we have perforce described, for the most part, the functions of the itinerant justices, the local justices and the king's serjeants. It has been especially necessary to do so because historians have passed them over, if not in silence, with hardly more than a whisper, though, unless we understand their place in the administration of justice, we can form little idea of the general administration of the kingdom in the early decades of the twelfth century. To complete the picture we should say no less of the court at the exchequer; but the paucity of the evidence confines us to generalities. A few writs survive which leave us in no doubt that the court of the justiciar under Henry I was very much what it was to be under Henry II.[4] Its functions in regard to matters of justice and finance—if, indeed, these were conceived as distinct issues—were seemingly identical at both periods, and the evidence that *justitiarii totius Anglie* sat at the exchequer to adjudicate upon financial issues is sufficient to establish that some of them would be present when the court adjudicated in civil actions. Indeed, it is inconceivable that they should have adjudicated upon all manner of pleas in the country and not in the central court. But no contemporary description of an action before the barons of the exchequer is known to us.

We have no more information regarding the conduct of actions in the court *coram rege*. There can be no doubt, from the references in surviving writs, that pleas of land were heard with some frequency

---

[1] 'Leges Edwardi Confessoris', 24.2, 3 (*Gesetze*, i.649-50).
[2] Cam, *The Hundred and the Hundred Rolls*, pp. 153-87. The account here given relates to the thirteenth century: the evidence is applicable to the twelfth century only in a general sense and not in detail.
[3] Hence the hundred-serjeant and not the sheriff was amerced (below, p. 208).
[4] Above, p. 176; *Memoranda Roll, 1 John*, Introduction, p. xiii.

before the king and his barons[1] in the same way as they were heard before the justiciar and the barons of the exchequer, and the presumption must be that, although the king's court might be more numerously attended, its personnel had much in common with the justiciar's court. There can be no reason for supposing that the justiciar and the *justitiarii* were absent from the court of Henry I or that he had less assistance from his ministers and judges than was given to his grandson. The real doubt is whether the king's presence is implied in the formula *in curia mea coram me et baronibus meis*. In cases in which he was personally interested he is likely to have presided, but otherwise all that may be implied is that, when the king was in England, the justiciar's court ceased to exist as a separate tribunal.[2] A numerously attended court at which Roger of Salisbury sat with other *justitiarii* in the treasury at Winchester is described in the queen's writ as *curia domini mei et mea*[3]; but the reason is that, if the king is abroad and the queen remains behind in England, she is nominally the regent, while the effective power remains with the justiciar. Although there is ample evidence that Norman and Angevin kings took an active part in the administration of justice, this document is sufficient warning that the king may not preside in the court *coram rege*. Just as the presence of the justiciar at the bench at Westminster may sometimes be a fiction in the closing years of the twelfth century,[4] so the presence of the king may sometimes be a fiction in the court *coram rege* in the early decades of the century.[5] We are already in an age of sophistication. The writs for which Roger of Salisbury is responsible may be ostensibly those of the regents, Queen Maud or William the king's son; many more will be expressed as coming from the king himself, though, since Roger attests them, we know that they are his.[6] In like manner, we conceive, the justiciar's court may become the court held before the king. The available evidence does not enable us to distinguish such an occasion from one on which the king is personally present; but just as a writ is no less authoritative although the king may have no

---

[1] We give four instances in order of date. *E.H.R.*, xxvi.487-9 (*Regesta*, no. 684), 'coram me et baronibus meis' (1105); *Monasticon*, iii.348 (*Regesta*, no. 875), 'ante me et barones meos' (1108); *ibid.*, vii.1043 (*Regesta*, no. 1054), 'ante me et barones meos' (1114); *Chronicon Mon. de Abingdon*, ii.165 (*Regesta*, no. 1478), 'coram me et baronibus meis' (1127), but it is to be noted that the chronicler calls the barons of the writ 'justices' (p. 164). In a fifth case the writ says that the case was heard 'coram me' without mention of barons or justices (William of Malmesbury, *Gesta Regum*, ii.521 *n*).

[2] For a Norman case where the king is present with John bishop of Lisieux, justices and barons, see Haskins, *Norman Institutions*, p. 96.

[3] *Chronicon Mon. de Abingdon*, ii.116 (*Regesta*, no. 1000); above, p. 176.

[4] This doubt is really raised by the early charter rolls, but on the whole the evidence of the justiciar's own writs harmonises with the evidence of the feet of fines (*Memoranda Roll, 1 John*, Introduction, p. lxxxviii), though there were undoubtedly occasions when the justiciar's presence is a fiction (*Pleas before the King or his Justices*, ed. D. M. Stenton, i.87-9).

[5] This is true of the reign of John (D. M. Stenton, 'King John and the Courts of Justice', in *Proceedings of the British Academy*, xliv.125 *n*).

[6] Above, pp. 162-3; *Memoranda Roll, 1 John*, Introduction, pp. lxv-lxviii. See also *Regesta*, ii, *passim*.

personal knowledge of it, so a judgement of his court is no less authoritative, although he does not preside over its deliberations.[1] It is this aspect of English administration under Henry I, his grandson and his great-grandsons that we have summed up in the phrase 'impersonal monarchy'. The king's presence is not necessary to ensure that the royal administration shall continue without intermission: his presence is not necessary in order that royal justice shall be dispensed *coram me et baronibus meis*.

[1] Cf. *Dialogus de Scaccario*, p. 14: Habet enim hoc commune cum ipsa domini regis curia in qua ipse in propria persona iura decernit quod nec recordationi nec sententie in eo late licet alicui contradicere. This is said of the exchequer, but it must be remembered that a little later it is said (p. 15): Non enim in ratiociniis sed in multiplicibus iudiciis excellens scaccarii scientia consistit. We do not think that *judicia* here necessarily or principally imply financial questions.

X

THE DECAY OF THE JUDICATURE
AND ITS REVIVAL

WITH the death of Henry I or, perhaps we should say, when the light shed by the pipe roll of 1130 fails us, we pass into a period of darkness that lifts but slowly until, in 1166, the records become sufficiently full to enable us to reconstruct, with some assurance, the structure of the judicature as it was remodelled under Henry II. There is, however, no reason to suppose that in the early years of Stephen's reign there was any departure from the practices of Henry I. The arrest and dismissal of Roger of Salisbury and his nephews cannot have failed to shake the fabric of government, though there were still some of Henry's *curiales* who adhered to Stephen.[1] A writ, which we assign to 1140, illustrates at once the growing lawlessness of that period and the endeavour of the king to maintain order. Before it was issued Bishop Nigel, in defiance of the king, had taken refuge in the Isle of Ely, the king had besieged and taken his fastness, and Nigel had fled to the Empress.[2] The first phase of the civil war had begun, and the tenants of the abbey of Ely had taken advantage of the confusion to refuse to pay their ferms to the monks. The monks had applied to the king for relief and the king had addressed his writ to the offenders, giving them the alternative of paying what was due or surrendering their fee. If they did neither, Aubrey de Vere would constrain them to make their choice.[3] Aubrey is clearly acting as he would have acted while he was *justitiarius totius Anglie* to Henry I, though whether judicially or administratively is not clear. The writ is, in any case, evidence of the continuity of administration. From nearly the end of the reign there comes an account of an action that was decided at a session for Norfolk and Suffolk over which William Martel presided.[4] Since the point at issue was the claim of the abbot of St. Edmund's to try an appeal of treason in his court, we may be sure that the presiding

---

[1] Aubrey de Vere was the most distinguished. William Martel, who became prominent later in the reign, had been a steward under Henry I.

[2] *Gesta Stephani*, ed. Potter, pp. 65-7; *Anglia Sacra*, i.620.

[3] Stephanus, rex Anglorum, Hugoni de Eschalariis et Stephano, nepoti suo, salutem. Precipio vobis quod cito reddatis monachis de Ely firmam suam ita bene et plene sicut faciebatis priusquam caperem insulam de Ely vel reddatis eis feudum suum quod tenetis. Et nisi feceritis Albericus de Ver constringat vos donec faciatis. Teste Roberto de Oili. Apud Oxeneford. (B.M., Cotton MSS., Titus A.1, fo. 34*b*).

[4] The full text was first published by Miss Cam in *E.H.R.*, xxxix.569-71.

justice was trying pleas of the crown. William Martel is also mentioned in terms which suggest that on another occasion he was
trying civil actions in Berkshire.[1] This is a meagre basis upon which
to generalise, though it is true that, in the absence of the pipe roll of
1130, we should not have a great deal more upon which to base any
conclusion regarding general eyres under Henry I. The argument
for continuity, based upon the analogy of local administration and,
as we shall see, of the court *coram rege*, may seem persuasive, but
against this is to be set the ominous fact that, while in the early years
of Henry II local administration and sessions of the court *coram rege*
proceeded as before, there is little evidence that such eyres as can
be traced were of the same character as general eyres under Henry I.
It would be strange that such eyres should fall into desuetude if they
had been frequently or systematically held in Stephen's reign, and
the conclusion would seem inevitable that, just as the supervision
over the finances of the country hitherto exercised by the exchequer
fell into disuse,[2] so the eyres of the *justitiarii totius Anglie*, which had
centred upon the exchequer, also fell into disuse.[3] Indeed, as the
pipe roll of 1130 testifies, the one implies the other. That the court
at Westminster disappeared is a very different matter, and there
seems no reason to believe that it ceased to function, however
restricted its activities may have been.

That a court *coram rege* continued to be held under Stephen hardly
needs proof, though sufficient positive evidence has survived to
witness to the fact. The few cases of which we have details come
from ecclesiastical sources and doubtless furnish a very imperfect
view of the court. Some of them we shall find it convenient to
examine in another connexion. Here we need say little more than
that there came before the court actions to determine whether a
church and land were held by military service or in frankalmoin
and whether Battle Abbey was free from the jurisdiction of the bishop
of the diocese,[4] a dispute as to the ownership of land granted to
Byland Abbey,[5] an appeal of murder in particularly atrocious circumstances[6] and a charge against Jews of ritual murder.[7] From the
modern standpoint the most notable case is probably an action
brought by the archbishop of Canterbury against the abbot of
Battle, which raised the issue whether it had been within the power

---

[1] *Chronicon Mon. de Abingdon*, ii.182.

[2] When Richard of Ely says that during the reign of Stephen *scaccarii sciencia* was *pene
prorsus abolita* (*Dialogus de Scaccario*, p. 50), he may imply more than the cessation of
financial control, for elsewhere he says that at its highest level the science lies *in multiplicibus iudiciis* (p. 15).

[3] The complaints of the decay of justice during Stephen's reign are very general in
character. The Battle chronicler says 'Quaeritur hinc justitia regalis, inde ecclesiastica,
sed habundante iniquitate ad tempus non invenitur' (*Chronicon Mon. de Bello*, p. 113).
For a similar statement see *Letters of John of Salisbury*, i.231. But the monks of Battle could
hardly complain that they failed to get justice in the court *coram rege* (below, pp. 287-8).

[4] Below, pp. 287-8.   [5] *Monasticon*, v.351-2.

[6] Below, p. 288.   [7] Thomas of Monmouth, *St. William of Norwich*, pp. 92-110.

of Henry I, without consulting his barons, to alter the customary law relating to wreck.[1] These cases suggest that it was only the exceptional action that was heard by the king in person. The right to be heard before the king himself was evidently valued and might be sought by a favoured monastery. The abbot of Abingdon in this way obtained for himself and his men the privilege of pleading before the king in any plea of the crown in which they were concerned. The favour was increased by according the further privilege that any such action should be tried only when the king visited Oxford. Since the writ conveying these privileges is addressed to the justices and sheriffs of Oxfordshire and Berkshire, the intention is presumably to remove any plea of the crown affecting the abbey or its tenants from the jurisdiction of the county court.[2] While we cannot press the argument from silence, especially where the evidence is that of a single writ, it seems significant that there is no mention of the justiciar and no suggestion that pleas of the crown might be tried by itinerant justices. If, as seems probable, there was no justiciar during the middle years of Stephen's reign[3] and if, as we have suggested, there were no regular eyres such as had been organised under Henry I, the burden upon the court *coram rege* must have been heavier, even though it was concerned only with exceptional cases or with privileged litigants. Of humdrum cases we learn little, but it is likely that they were heard by the king's justices in the king's absence, presumably sitting at Westminster. Of one such case, a disputed title to land, we are told that it came several times before the king's justices, who at last remitted the issue to be determined by the oath of the men of the town. The chronicler who tells the story, and was chagrined because his house failed to make good its claim, alleges that the jury were corrupted; but he adds that, by the custom of the country, their testimony, confirmed by oath, was admitted and the tenant remained in possession.[4] Here we seem clearly to have, about the year 1150, an action closely resembling the later grand assize, following to all appearance a well-established procedure. This case is likely to be more typical of the king's court under Stephen than the more spectacular cases that attracted the attention of chroniclers. It suggests that the court held regular sessions, in much the same way as it had done under Henry I, though how it was staffed there seems to be no direct evidence. We can but suppose that, as under Henry I and as under Stephen's successors, the justices who tried actions in the country would be found also in the central court. Nor should we suppose that there

[1] *Chronicon Mon. de Bello*, pp. 65-7. The year is 1139, and Archbishop Theobald must have brought the action soon after his consecration.
[2] *Chronicon Mon. de Abingdon*, ii.181-2.   [3] Above, p. 166.
[4] Walsingham, *Gesta Abbatum*, i.118: quaestioque ipsa coram regis justiciariis saepius ventilatur, tandem judicio curiae regis decretum est quatenus juramenta hominum villae de Luitun quaestio illa terminaretur. This account of the trial was apparently written under Henry II.

were two central courts, one held before the king and one before the justices. As we shall see,[1] when under Henry II the king is in England his court is staffed by the justices who staff the justiciar's court and the one court is subsumed into the other, the lower into the higher, without change in personnel. But, as we have said, it is far from certain, perhaps improbable, that there was a justiciar throughout Stephen's reign, and therefore we cannot postulate the existence of a justiciar's court, although the court of the justices is likely to have been sedentary and to have remained at Westminster. More definite statements we cannot make. We can go but a little way beyond the statement that the sessions of the king's central court were not suspended between 1135 and 1155, and that such evidence as we have points to continuity, unbroken except during the king's captivity.

But though we may accept the continuity of the central court and recognise that *curiales* were despatched into the country more frequently than the direct evidence testifies, the cessation of general eyres inevitably weakened the general administration of justice. In so far as this was maintained, at best sadly interrupted by sporadic warfare, it appears to have been secured by the county justices. It would seem from the addresses of Stephen's writs that local justices were generally maintained in office throughout his reign[2] and we have a little information regarding their activities.[3] There was at first no fresh departure under Henry II,[4] and the way in which reliance was placed upon local justices for the administration of justice during the early years of his reign is well illustrated by the writs preserved in the chronicle of Abingdon Abbey. One, addressed to the king's justices in whose bailiwicks the abbot holds lands, is notable because it gives the abbot licence to appear before them by attorney.[5] Another writ shows that, in default of the sheriff, the

---

[1] Below, p. 213.

[2] Here is a list taken from the writs printed in the *Cal. Charter Rolls*. Bucks. (iv.103), Cambs. (iii.101), Cornwall (v.11), Devon (ii.132; v.11), Dorset (ii.132), Essex (iv.356; v.17, 159, 267), Hants. (iii.338; iv.443), Herts. (v.266-7), Hunts. (iii.243), Kent (v.57), Lincs. (iv.103, 139-40, 162), London (v.17, 267), Norfolk and Suffolk (v.362), Northumberland (iii.290), Notts. (iii.293-4), Surrey (iii.353; v.34, 283), Wilts. (iv.443), Yorks. (ii.438; v.331).

[3] Witness the following writ (B.M., Cotton MS., Titus A.1, fo. 34*b*-35*a*, 48):
Stephanus rex Radulfo de Halstede et Rogero et Willelmo fratribus suis et W. filio Baldewini, salutem. Precipio vobis quod permittatis esse in pace terram monachorum de Ely de Steuechewurde nec amplius vos intromittatis ullo modo nec inde quicquam capiatis. Et nisi feceritis iusticia mea Cantebrigescire faciat fieri ne super hoc inde clamorem audiam pro penuria iusticie. Teste Willelmo Martel.
The place named is Stetchworth.
For Berkshire and Oxfordshire see the writs in *Chronicon Mon. de Abingdon*, ii.178-85. Here the sheriff appears to have been more powerful than the justice.

[4] The following list is compiled from the writs printed in the *Cal. Charter Rolls*: it is not, of course, exhaustive. Bedford (ii.295; iv.183), Berks. (iv.290), Bucks. (ii.34, 295), Cornwall (iii.271), Cumberland (iii.82), Derby (iii.268; iv.141), Devon (iii.271, 331), Dorset (ii.132), Essex (ii.431; v.57, 159), Gloucs. (v.160), Hants. (ii.105; iii.337, 382, 472), Hereford (iv.83), Herts. (iii.19), Hunts. (iv.107-8), Kent (v.57, 59), Lincs. (iii.71, 268, 312; iv.106-7, 110, 145), Norfolk (iii.67; v.160), Northumberland (ii.171-2; iii.393), Notts. (iii.268; iv.141), Oxford (iv.109), Shropshire (iii.292), Staffs. (ii.347), Suffolk (v.58, 59), Surrey (iv.183), Sussex (iv.440), Yorks. (i.61; iii.396; v.472), Westmorland (iii.82).   [5] *Chronicon Mon. de Abingdon*, ii.222.

local justice is expected to remedy a disseisin,[1] and a third that the local justice will compel the knights and freeholders of the abbey to perform their service.[2] Doubtless disseisors or tenants are unlikely to comply without proceedings in the county court, but the important implication of the writs is that, in the usual course, the issue will be determined there and that the local justice will preside. Another aspect of the local justice's activity is, we think, shown obscurely in the early pipe rolls of Henry II's reign. It is noteworthy that, without any evidence for the visitation of itinerant justices, the rolls disclose that murders were regularly notified to the treasurer and murder fines regularly collected by the sheriffs.[3] What is the administrative process that brings this result? Now the attorneys by whom the abbot of Abingdon was allowed to be represented before local justices were attorneys 'ad assisas vestras et ad placita'. There are a good many references to *placita* in the pipe rolls which it seems reasonable to connect with local justices, especially when the *placita* are described as of such-and-such a hundred,[4] for we must remember that local justices sat in the hundred court as well as in the county court.[5] That the *placita* tried in the hundred court were pleas of the crown seems an obvious inference, and this is rendered more certain by an entry that reads 'placita de Galehohundredo pro murdro'.[6] The entry is not so informative as we might wish, but at least it tells us that there was something more than the bare enquiry which at the time ordinarily seems to have led to the murder fine.[7] Now in some way there came to the treasurer a record both of such enquiries and of proceedings in the hundred court[8] which resulted in profit to the king. In what way was this? We might expect the legal treatises, which tell us most about the criminal jurisdiction of local justices,[9] to give some clue to a solution of the problem and we believe they do. The clue may be obscure but let us endeavour to find and follow it. The Laws of Edward the Confessor retail a tradition that if, after a month, a manslayer could not be found, the murder fine was collected and sent under the seal of a baron of the county to the king's treasury, whence it could be reclaimed if the murderer were found within a year.[10] As told, this tale reads like

---

[1] *Ibid.*, p. 223.   [2] *Ibid.*, p. 225.

[3] The earliest reference comes from 1156, though entered in *Pipe Roll, 4 Henry II*, p. 115: Gregory, sheriff of London and Middlesex, owes 50s. 10d. 'de placitis et murdris et donis de tempore suo'. For the following year see *Pipe Roll, 3 Henry II*, pp. 73, 78, 84, 87, 91, 95, 102-3.   [4] *Pipe Roll, 4 Henry II*, pp. 117-8.

[5] 'Leges Henrici', 29.1 b; 'Leges Edwardi Confessoris', 23.4 (*Gesetze*, i.563, 640).

[6] *Pipe Roll, 4 Henry II*, p. 130.

[7] For a parallel see *Pipe Roll, 12 Henry II*, p. 46: quia defecit de apellatione sua de morte sororis sue in murdro. This is a case before justices itinerant in Yorkshire where there was no question of a murder fine.

[8] There seems to be no indication of such proceedings in the county court. The pleas of the bishop of Lincoln in Holland may perhaps arise from the court of the trithing (*Pipe Roll, 2 Henry II*, p. 26). The bishop may be the local justice, as he was under Stephen.

[9] 'Leges Henrici', 29.1 b; 31.2; 34.7; 59.10; 61.8; 'Leges Edwardi Confessoris', 18.2; 20.1a, 2, 4, 6; 23; 36.3 (*Gesetze*, 1.563-4, 566, 579, 581, 644-6, 648, 667).

[10] *Ibid.*, 15.4, 5 (*Gesetze*, i.641).

fiction; but that there was machinery for notifying the treasurer is obvious. Since it was clearly the duty of the hundred-reeve to apprehend the slayer, if he could, and bring him before the justice— in which case the liability of the hundred was discharged[1]—and since the justice had to be notified of fugitives,[2] it seems necessary to infer that the hundred reeve would notify the justice of his failure to apprehend the malefactor and of the consequent liability of the hundred. The justice would presumably thereafter notify the treasurer. The system was doubtless imperfect but, up to a point, it worked. On the other hand, it is doubtful whether, in the early years of Henry II's reign, there was any effective machinery for bringing to the notice of the treasury other pleas of the crown, treasure trove, for example, or wreck. On such matters the pipe rolls are almost completely silent.[3]

On the local justice some few words only remain to be added. Although there were occasional, desultory visitations of *curiales* in the eleven years following Henry's accession, and a general eyre in his twelfth year, there was, as we shall show, no systematic visitation of the country until 1168, from which year such visitations became a prominent feature of the administration of justice for more than a hundred years. Until this system was established, reliance seemingly continued to be placed primarily upon local justices. The pipe rolls show plainly, however, that visitations of itinerant justices were vastly more profitable to the king, and the gradual cessation of references to local justices from about this date suggests that they were regarded as superfluous and generally superseded. It is possible that, for reasons we do not understand, local justices were occasionally appointed here and there until the reign of Richard I,[4] but as an effective branch of the judiciary they disappeared by the late 1160's.

The supersession of the local justice led inevitably to changes in local administration, but before we describe what took place, it will be convenient to resume the story of the itinerant justices. Such knowledge as we have of the visits of itinerant justices in the early years of Henry II we derive almost entirely from the pipe rolls, and in these years the entries are baffling in their brevity. It is plain, however, that late in 1155 or early in 1156 Henry of Essex, the constable, was on eyre throughout southern England[5]: in Kent he was accompanied by Thomas Becket, the chancellor.[6] The justiciar, Robert earl of Leicester, visited Buckinghamshire and Bedfordshire,

---

[1] 'Leges Henrici', 92.8, 9 (*Gesetze*, i.608).
[2] 'Leges Edwardi Confessoris', 20.1a, 2, 4, 6 (*Gesetze*, i.645-6).
[3] For a reference to wreck see *Pipe Roll, 5 Henry II*, p. 42.
[4] For writs of September and October 1189, addressed to the justice and sheriff of Kent and of Essex, see P.R.O. Ancient Deeds A (E. 40) 14404 and *Cal. Charter Rolls*, v.161. In December 1189 the burgesses of Colchester are granted the privilege of appointing a justice (*ibid.*, i.410).
[5] *Pipe Roll, 2 Henry II*, pp. 31-2, 47, 54-5, 57-8, 60-1.
[6] *Ibid.*, p. 65. They also visited Essex where they took an 'assize' (*ibid.*, p. 17).

where Henry of Essex was sheriff[1]; he also visited Lincolnshire in company with the chancellor.[2] The purpose of these eyres is far from clear, but apparently there was nothing in the nature of a general eyre, though some murders seem to have been presented before Henry of Essex.[3] Apart from a few indications that specific actions were occasionally tried by what would be later called justices of assize—and, indeed, these actions are sometimes called assizes— there is little other indication of judicial activity in the country.[4] From scattered entries on the pipe rolls we learn that William fitz John was trying pleas of land in Devon, Gloucestershire, Hereford-shire, Somerset and Yorkshire between the years 1158 and 1160. A few actions of a different kind also came before him, but there is nothing to show that he was trying pleas of the crown.[5] As a quasi-professional judge, the first to be appointed by Henry II, William fitz John is an interesting figure; but he was as much an adminis-trator as a lawyer and in his later years he was chiefly employed on duties connected with the royal household.[6]

We are still some way from an organised judiciary, and it is not until 1166 that there is any sign that general eyres are about to be resumed. This development was associated with a series of measures for the repression of crime and the reform of the land law, which were initiated, apparently, at a council held at Clarendon in the winter of 1165-6 and which received definitive form at a council at Northampton in 1176. These measures it will be necessary to ex-amine in some detail, but one point deserves notice here. During the first eleven years of Henry II's reign there was no attempt, so far as the records show, to restore the administration of justice to the level it had reached under Henry I. The standards to which it had been reduced under Stephen and the methods then perforce adopted, were accepted and continued with little change. The king and his advisers had many other preoccupations. And then, so it would seem, it was determined not only to improve the future administra-tion of justice, but to punish felonies and remedy unlawful acts that had been passed over since the beginning of the reign. The most serious of unlawful acts which did not amount to felony was violent disseisin, for to this men who thought they had an unsatisfied claim to property were always prone in the unsettled times of the twelfth century. Since the original text of the Assize of Novel Disseisin is lost,

---

[1] *Ibid.*, pp. 22-3.   [2] *Ibid.*, p. 26.
[3] *Ibid.*,p. 47.   [4] *Ibid.*, pp. 11, 17; *Pipe Roll, 3 Henry II*, p. 94.
[5] His earlier activities are established by equating entries on *Pipe Roll, 5 Henry II*, pp. 27, 31, 42 with entries on *Pipe Roll, 6 Henry II*, p. 28, *9 Henry II*, p. 58, and *6 Henry II*, p. 51. Other references are on *Pipe Roll, 6 Henry II*, pp. 31, 59; *7 Henry II*, pp. 36, 49.
[6] He was a Norman and until 1157 was actively engaged in the administration of the duchy (Delisle, *Actes de Henri II*, Introduction, pp. 479-80; Round, *Cal. Documents France*, pp. 269, 533). He was given charge of the king's sons, Henry and Geoffrey (*Pipe Roll, 11 Henry II*, p. 73; *12 Henry II*, pp. 71, 96, 100-1; *13 Henry II*, p. 169) and accompanied the king's sister Emma on her way to marry the Welsh prince, David ap Owen (*Pipe Roll, 20 Henry II*, p. 16).

we must approach it from the amending legislation of 1176. This places a new limitation upon the period within which a disseisin must have happened if relief was to be given, namely the date when peace was made between the king and his son Henry, that is 30 September 1174.[1] This limitation was presumably necessary because of the terms of peace which, in effect, excused disseisins during the civil war, though requiring them to be amended.[2] There is here, however, no implication that the original period of limitation was so short as a year and a few months, and it seems probable that, just as the investigation of crimes was to be carried back to the coronation —*postquam dominus rex fuit rex*[3]—so disseisins from the beginning of the reign had fallen within the assize. This would certainly have been the logical course. Not, of course, that crimes had remained generally unpunished or disseisins unredressed: the new procedure was devised to provide more effective remedies and to catch up, so to speak, cases that had escaped the not very effective net of justice during the first eleven years of the reign.

It may be well, before we proceed farther, to make it plain that the 'Assize of Clarendon' has not the importance that historians, led by Stubbs, have attributed to it, and perhaps the preliminary point should be established that the text which passes for the assize does not represent the instructions actually issued to the counties, early in 1166 or late in 1165, for the apprehension and punishment of suspected malefactors. The provisions of the text are not only inconsistent with the references made to the assize ten years later in the Assize of Northampton,[4] but more especially, as we shall see, with the evidence the pipe rolls furnish of the procedure followed in those counties where the instructions were enforced. The *textus receptus* seems to come from a later period, well after the proceedings under the original instructions had been concluded,[5] and it may be a private attempt at bringing those instructions up to date: it is in no sense authoritative in form or content. So far as we can reconstruct the actual procedure, it seems to have been as follows. An enquiry was ordered in every county court and every hundred court to ascertain who were accused or defamed of crimes committed since the coronation: the crimes specified were robbery, murder, theft, coining, arson.[6] Both the perpetrators of these crimes and their

---

[1] *Select Charters*, p. 180, c. 5.   [2] *Foedera*, i.30.

[3] 'Assize of Clarendon', chapters 1, 2. This document (*Select Charters*, pp. 170-3) is apocryphal, but it appears to reflect administrative practice: see Appendix IV on the Assizes of Henry II (below, pp. 438-49).

[4] Chapters 1, 2, 3, 14, 22 of the 'Assize of Clarendon' should be compared with chapter 1 of the Assize of Northampton, which we can accept as authentic.

[5] Since there were no accessible justices in eyre until 1168, chapter 4 clearly cannot belong to the original text, neither can chapter 5. Chapters 17, 18, 19, all refer to procedure which would have been incomprehensible in 1166.

[6] Assize of Northampton, chapter 1. There is no reason to suppose that coining and arson were not included from the first. The compiler of the 'Assize of Clarendon' has merely omitted them.

accessories (*receptores*) were to be formally accused before the local justices and the sheriffs.[1] Twelve of the more substantial and trustworthy men of the hundred and four men of the township were then to state on oath whether they believed the alleged criminals to be guilty. Those thus inculpated were to be arrested and might be dealt with in one of two ways. If a man's lord or the lord's steward or the lord's men or even the men of his tithing[2] were prepared to act as his sureties, he might make his law and so establish his innocence. Alternatively he was given an opportunity to swear that he was innocent and to submit to the ordeal of water. Those who failed to make their law or who failed at the ordeal were mutilated and their chattels confiscated.[3] All this was accomplished locally without the intervention of itinerant justices; for, despite the provisions of the *textus receptus*, the evidence of the pipe rolls makes it impossible to form any other view than that, wherever action was taken by the sheriff and local justice in 1166, it was concluded before the itinerant justices visited the county,[4] and their visitations were far from covering every county.

These local proceedings should have been undertaken in the early months of 1166. The eyre came later. And then no more than two justices or at the most three were employed. The two justices of whom we can be sure were Richard de Lucy and Geoffrey de Mandeville, earl of Essex. Starting apparently in East Anglia in the spring of 1166, they traversed the home counties and went as far north as Northumberland.[5] Alan de Neville seems to have visited Staffordshire with much the same commission,[6] but he was chiefly employed in trying pleas of the forest in Devonshire and Worcestershire and seemingly elsewhere,[7] a preliminary to a forest eyre which covered the whole country and which has left abundant marks on the pipe

---

[1] 'Assize of Clarendon', chapter 1: Et hoc inquirant justitiae coram se et vicecomites coram se. Since there were no itinerant justices early in 1166, the justices must be local. But no clear meaning can be extracted from this sentence.

[2] 'Assize of Clarendon', chapter 3, mentions only the lord, his steward and his men, but the particulars in the Pipe Roll of 1166 show clearly that the permissible sureties were not limited in this way. In Lincolnshire, for example, the men, *homines*, of various vil'ages were the sureties (*Pipe Roll, 12 Henry II*, p. 7), in Yorkshire a township, *villata* (*ibid.*, p. 48), in many counties a tithing, *tedinga* (*ibid.*, pp. 14-15, 31, 70, 87, 92, 108, 129).

[3] This is clear from the Assize of Northampton, chapter 1. Significantly the 'Assize of Clarendon' omits all mention of a penalty, though the original assize certainly stated that 'si perierit, alterum pedem amittat'. The forfeiture of chattels followed automatically upon conviction. This is inferred by the Assize of Northampton and established by the particulars in the pipe roll: see below, p. 201. See also chapter 5 of the 'Assize of Clarendon'.

[4] This is abundantly evident from the pipe roll entries for Lincolnshire, Yorkshire and Nottinghamshire (*Pipe Roll, 12 Henry II*, pp. 5, 7, 43, 46, 56, 57). We infer that all the items proceeding from the assize were put in charge by Easter 1166. No payments are recorded in respect of items arising from the eyre and these must have been put in charge later.

[5] It is only in East Anglia that any payments are shown (*Pipe Roll, 12 Henry II*, pp. 21-30), presumably in response to the Easter summons. A second batch of entries presumably represents items that came too late to be included (pp. 30-1). This is the case also with the entries for Lincolnshire (pp. 7-10), Bucks. and Beds. (pp. 14-15), Yorkshire (pp. 46-9), Notts. and Derby (pp. 57-8), Leicestershire (p. 70), Northumberland (p. 76), Hunts (p. 87), Sussex (p. 92), Surrey (p. 108), Kent (p. 115), Essex and Herts. (pp. 128-9). [6] *Ibid.*, p. 62. [7] *Ibid.*, pp. 39, 82, 95, 104.

roll of 1167. Earl Geoffrey's death at Carlisle within a month of
Michaelmas 1166[1] must, in any case, have put an end to the eyre
as projected: it was not, in fact, continued and much of the country
was left unvisited until eyres were resumed in 1167-8 on a different
plan. While, however, it was part of the duties of Earl Geoffrey and
Richard de Lucy to enquire whether the instructions to the sheriff
regarding malefactors had been obeyed, it would seem clear that
they themselves did not enforce the assize. Not only have we the
evidence of the pipe rolls, which we shall shortly examine, but we
have the evidence of an instructive writ which was despatched early
in 1166. We have already noticed that the royal justices went as far
north as Northumberland. To do so they had to pass through the
palatinate of Durham, where normally the king's writ did not run.
But the assize applied to the palatinate as to other parts of the
kingdom, and it was decided that, without prejudice to the bishop's
immunities in general, Durham should on this occasion be included
in the justices' eyre. The terms in which this decision was announced
to the local justices, sheriffs and ministers of Yorkshire and Northumberland should be remarked.[2] By the advice of the king's barons
and with the leave of the bishop of Durham, one of the king's
justices—this must mean either Earl Geoffrey or Richard de Lucy—
is to visit the territory of St. Cuthbert in order that he may see that
justice is done according to the king's assize concerning thieves,
murderers and robbers. The king's justice, let us stress, is not himself
to do justice but to see that justice is done. We should note further
that the writ is attested not only by Earl Geoffrey and Richard de
Lucy, who were directly concerned, but also by Richard of Ilchester
and Geoffrey Ridel, who were the most active and regular of the
royal justices at Westminster at this period.[3] We can hardly be
wrong in inferring that this group of four, made up of two barons
and two royal clerks, was responsible for the administration of
justice and the enforcement of the new legislation in England.

But let us return to the conduct of the eyre of 1166. To oversee the
activities of the sheriffs and local justices in implementing the provisions of the assize was but part and, it would seem, a relatively
minor part of the task allotted to Earl Geoffrey and Richard de
Lucy. They had wider duties. So far as the assize was concerned they

---

[1] He died on 21 October. According to the Walden Abbey Chronicle, lib. i, c. 18
(early thirteenth century), he was then with Richard de Lucy in command of an army
against the Welsh. We can dismiss this improbable story and assume that he was taken
ill while on eyre. Carlisle, i.e. Cumberland, had been previously visited by Richard de
Lucy in 1162-3 (*Pipe Roll, 9 Henry II*, p. 10).

[2] Sciatis quod consilio baronum meorum et episcopi Dunelmensis licencia mitto hac
vice in terram sancti Cuthberti iusticiam meam que videat ut fiat iusticia secundum
assisam meam de latronibus et murdratoribus et roboratoribus (*Historiae Dunelmensis
Scriptores Tres* (Surtees Soc.), p. 1). The date of this writ must be before the king's departure for France in March 1166 and may possibly have been issued late in December
1165. The king's movements are uncertain (cf. Eyton, *Itinerary of Henry II*, pp. 86-91),
and the writ itself is one of the few pieces of evidence that he was at Woodstock at this
time.   [3] Below, p. 212.

evidently accepted the position as they found it and contented themselves with dealing with any consequential business, and what that business was depended upon the view the sheriffs had taken of their responsibilities and the spirit in which they had discharged them. Nothing would seem to be clearer, however, than that the proceedings under the Assize of Clarendon had failed generally in their immediate purpose. The articles of the so-called Inquest of Sheriffs suggest not only that the king had been defrauded of some of the profits of justice that should have accrued to the revenue, but that innocent men had been unjustly condemned and that for gifts or favour guilty men had been spared.[1] Even without this hint, the pipe rolls would point to much the same conclusion. Thus, the sheriffs of London and Middlesex account for the chattels of only three malefactors; but we cannot deduce that so few were apprehended or that the capital was almost crimeless, for in the same account the sheriffs claim allowance for the expense of putting thirty-four men to the ordeal and mutilating fourteen. Nevertheless it is odd that only three of those who failed the ordeal had anything of value. And we must remember that the special enquiries of the year did not supersede the ordinary course of justice. The sheriffs had meanwhile been maintaining nineteen approvers and had arranged five judicial duels, and they had hanged fourteen convicted felons.[2] If, however, we can in this way explain why the profits that came to the king in London and Middlesex were so meagre, there are no compensating entries to explain why the sheriff of Wiltshire also accounts for the chattels of only three malefactors.[3] Again, in Hampshire not more than four men were sworn to be guilty and one of them had fled.[4] In Worcestershire only a nameless vagabond was apprehended, whose belongings were worth sixteen shillings.[5] In Shropshire, we are specifically told, there was no attempt to enforce the 'assize'.[6] Here and there a more or less determined effort seems to have been made to arrest and punish malefactors,[7] but even where preliminary proceedings were instituted, they seem often to have served as a timely warning to men of ill repute. In Lincolnshire most of those accused appear to have fled after giving sureties: in one manor there were no less than ten fugitives and the total number of fugitives from the county seems to be considerably greater than the number of those whose chattels were seized. The plain lesson conveyed by the pipe rolls would appear to be that the government could not ensure that its decrees would be promptly and readily obeyed over many parts, by no means all of them the less law-abiding parts, of the country.[8]

[1] Inquest of Sheriffs, c. vi: *Select Charters*, pp. 176-7.
[2] *Pipe Roll, 12 Henry II*, pp. 131-2.   [3] *Ibid.*, p. 74.
[4] *Ibid.*, p. 104.   [5] *Ibid.*, p. 82.   [6] *Ibid.*, p. 60.
[7] It is possible that in some counties action was delayed. On the Scottish border chattels of malefactors are accounted for in 1169 (*Pipe Roll, 15 Henry II*, p. 132).
[8] Stubbs drew a very different conclusion in his preface to *Pipe Roll, 12 Henry II*, pp. x-xi.

Doubtless this lesson was learnt by Richard de Lucy and guided him in framing a better system of criminal justice. But, as we have indicated, any review of these local proceedings against malefactors was but incidental to the purpose for which he and Earl Geoffrey were visiting the counties. The chief interest of their proceedings lies in the fact that they were conducting a general eyre, for the first time perhaps since the reign of Henry I, certainly since the coronation of Henry II, and, we might add, almost certainly since the early years of Stephen. It is for this reason, and not for a mistaken connexion with the Assize of Clarendon, that their eyre is memorable. The counties of Lincolnshire and Yorkshire afford the best evidence of the nature of the eyre. In Lincolnshire[1] there had evidently been an effort to carry out the instructions to apprehend malefactors and a great many sureties had been given, but there had been a wholesale flight of the accused. As each wapentake comes before the justices the sureties are amerced, sometimes individuals, sometimes whole townships, sometimes the men of the lord of the accused. This is the aftermath of the earlier local proceedings. But the justices are not themselves seeking to enforce the instructions the sheriff and local justice should have carried out: they are punishing the defaults of the sureties, just as they would punish other defaults. Again, the local proceedings have revealed some murders of which no account had yet been rendered to the treasurer, and these the wapentakes now present, one or two or three, as many as six in Aveland wapentake. There are also amercements for a breach of the peace, *pro falso clamore*, for withdrawing from a judicial duel, for absence from a *jurata feodorum militis*. Other entries arise from the Assize of Novel Disseisin and other pleas of land. The entries relating to Yorkshire are still more informative.[2] No murder fines are recorded, for the good reason that the custom of exacting such fines did not obtain in the county. There are entries which refer to homicides, but they seem to arise from presentments that would in any case be made before the justices: a township has failed to prosecute a homicide, and some of the pleas of the crown that have been concealed concern violent deaths. What is noteworthy is the number of entries which can be related to articles appearing in later texts of the chapters of the eyre. Thus, besides amercements *pro placito corone concelato*, we find others *pro ceto quodam*, for the king has a claim to whales and other graspeys. A man has married the widow of the moneyer of York and must pay fifteen marks. An heir has offered five marks for his relief. There have been purprestures in a marsh at Pallethorp,[3] and at Malsonby the king's highway has been ploughed up.[4] At York one man owes fifty marks for the king's mint: elsewhere a man

---

[1] *Ibid.*, pp. 5-10.   [2] *Ibid.*, pp. 46-9.
[3] *Ibid.*, p. 49. 'Torpe', in the parish of Bolton Percy in Ainsty Wapentake.
[4] Wrongly spelled 'Malsatebi': the corrected spelling 'Malsanbi' will be found in *Pipe Roll, 13 Henry II*, p. 91.

is amerced for a leaden penny. There are entries which may arise from disseisins: two men are amerced *quia duxit bladem super assisam*; land has been ploughed despite a prohibition; a mill has been erected *super assisam regis*. Lastly, let us mention the men of Harthill wapentake who are amerced *pro quodam homine qui fugit pro alia asisa et rediit et non monstrauerunt justiciis*. We do not need great ingenuity to group such entries under appropriate articles in the chapters of the eyre of 1194 and 1198[1]: *de placitis corone, de omnibus assisis, de dominabus, de valettis, de purpresturis, de viis domini regis extreciatis, de falsonariis, de fugitivis retatis reversis post ultimam assisam*. Then there are many entries which could come under the general article *de defaltis*. There have been appeals of felony and claims that have failed. A man has wrongly alleged that another man had been out-lawed. A man has denied that he was summoned and has then admitted it; another has failed to come before the justices; another has failed to prosecute his plaint; another has refused to give a pledge to the king's serjeants (*ministris*). Malger the clerk has presided over a court (can it be of the wapentake?) where an approver (it would seem) has been required to fight two judicial duels in one day: not only is Malger amerced, but twenty-one men who were present in court at the time and nine others who failed to present the wrongdoing. This body of evidence is conclusive: we need not seek for further testimony to the nature of the eyre of 1166.

The eyre of 1166 was brought to a close by the death of Geoffrey de Mandeville. General eyres were resumed early in 1168 or perhaps late in 1167 upon a more ambitious plan and continued into 1170. The main burden fell upon four justices, Richard of Ilchester, archdeacon of Poitiers, Guy (Rufus), dean of Waltham Holy Cross, Reginald de Warenne, and William Basset.[2] Richard de Lucy, sole justiciar since 5 April 1168, also took part and again visited York-shire[3] and Staffordshire.[4] Some assistance was given by Henry fitz Gerold, chamberlain of the treasury,[5] Ogier the steward,[6] Gervase of Cornhill,[7] John Cumin,[8] the two Alans de Neville[9] (whose normal employment was to take pleas of the forest) and two local men, Robert de Stuteville and Hugh de Moreville, in Cumberland and Northumberland.[10] This was certainly the most thorough and ex-haustive eyre that had yet been carried out: a number of counties were visited more than once, and the entries on the pipe rolls for

---

[1] We take the headings from the chapters of both years in Howden, *Chronica*, iii.263-4, iv.61-2.

[2] *Pipe Roll, 14 Henry II; 15 Henry II; 16 Henry II, passim.*

[3] *Pipe Roll, 14 Henry II,* p. 85. Perhaps Cumberland also (p. 109).

[4] *Pipe Roll, 16 Henry II,* p. 131.

[5] *Pipe Roll, 14 Henry II,* p. 414.

[6] *Pipe Roll, 15 Henry II,* p. 147; *16 Henry II,* p. 10.

[7] *Pipe Roll, 16 Henry II,* p. 102.

[8] *Ibid.,* pp. 64, 102, 117.

[9] *Pipe Roll, 15 Henry II,* p. 66; *16 Henry II,* pp. 42, 63, 72, 89, 116, 147.

[10] *Pipe Roll, 16 Henry II,* pp. 33, 52.

three years testify to the diligence with which the justices performed
their duties. Doubtless we must see in this the driving force of
Richard de Lucy (for the king was overseas), and it can hardly be
a coincidence that the eyre of 1166 had been carried through, so far
as it went, in the absence both of the king and of the senior justiciar,
Robert earl of Leicester.[1] We see, too, that there has been instituted
a small body of men, which we can call a regular judiciary, resembling the *justitiarii totius Anglie* of Henry I. Of the business of the eyre
not a great deal need be said. It is quite obvious from the large
number of amercements *pro disseisina facta super assisam* and the like
that the action of novel disseisin had rapidly become popular,[2] but
though the most numerous, these are by no means the only pleas of
land to come before the justices, as the many entries of debts *pro
recto terre*[3] or *pro fine duelli* show.[4] It is hardly necessary to remark
that the chapters of the eyre were such as they are known to have
been in the last decade of the century.[5] Another point worth remarking is the eagerness of the hundred juries to compound in
advance for any defaults of which they might otherwise be found
guilty by the justices: as the eyre progresses it becomes common
form for the county to compound in place of individual hundreds.[6]
These entries recall the *judices*, *judicatores* and *juratores* who were
amerced by Henry I's justices. But the close correspondence between
the general eyre under Henry I and Henry II, the constitution in
both reigns of a regular judiciary of much the same character, are
facts that hardly need further stressing. And though more must be
said of the judiciary, to pursue further the history of the general
eyre is unnecessary: much that could be said would be repetitive,
for there seem to have been few developments of equal importance
in the later decades of the twelfth century or in the thirteenth century, although articles of enquiry continued to be added and special
emergencies may be reflected on occasion in the chapters of the eyre,
the eyre rolls and pipe rolls. To take an instance in the twelfth
century: in 1194 and 1195 the rebellion of Count John and the

---

[1] Cf. Eyton, *Itinerary of Henry II*, pp. 92, 99.

[2] *Pipe Roll, 14 Henry II*, pp. 27, 31, 43, 69, 85-6 (fifteen entries) *et passim*. The assize
covered nuisance: e.g. 'pro quodam fossato iniuste facto' (p. 43), 'pro sepe quam fecit
fieri super pasturam' (p. 44), and similar entries at pp. 214, 219: see also p. 107, 'pro
divisa fracta super assisam'. Villeins cannot bring an action: see *Pipe Roll, 15 Henry II*,
p. 149, 'quia petierunt assisam sicut liberi et fuerunt rustici'.

[3] *Pipe Roll, 14 Henry II*, pp. 135, 195; *15 Henry II*, pp. 53, 65, 116, 139; *16 Henry II*,
p. 12.   [4] *Pipe Roll, 14 Henry II*, p. 135; *15 Henry II*, p. 116; *16 Henry II*, pp. 44-5.

[5] One of the most striking items is the amercement of Avelina of Rye in the sum of
£200 'quia fecit fieri filium suum militem qui erat in custodia regis' (*Pipe Roll, 14 Henry II*,
p. 29). Among the many entries referring to pleas of the crown we may note treasure
trove (*ibid.*, p. 67), wreck (*ibid.*, pp. 136-7), chattels of a usurer (*Pipe Roll, 16 Henry II*,
p. 72), graspeys (*ibid.*, p. 147). The king is asserting all his rights.

[6] *Pipe Roll, 14 Henry II*, p. 26, 'ut possent audiri sine occasione'; p. 28, 'ut pacifice
audirentur'; p. 31, 'ut audirentur sine occasione'. The thirty hundreds of Northampton-
shire make a joint payment on this account (pp. 54-5). The wapentakes of Lincolnshire
make individual payments for similar reasons or 'de promissione sua' (pp. 67-75). The
following year counties are compounding 'pro defectibus et misericordiis' (*Pipe Roll,
15 Henry II*, pp. 28, 65, 71, 80, 85, 90, 91, 132, 139).

ransom of Richard I figure largely.[1] But in its essential character the general eyre shows no change to the end of its history.[2]

There are, however, two closely connected subjects which we cannot leave unnoticed: first, the evolution of the jury, and secondly, the evolution of the system of keeping the pleas of the crown from which the coroner emerges in the thirteenth century.

The opinions of historians on the evolution of the jury in England have been greatly influenced by Heinrich Brunner, who taught that the jury originated among the Franks and was introduced into England by way of Normandy.[3] Of recent years there have not wanted doubters who have been perplexed by the lack of all evidence for a Norman jury before 1066. Indeed, there appears to be no known record of a Norman jury before 1133, and on this occasion the inquest was held before an English earl[4] who, it may be noted, had previously been employed on important administrative duties in England.[5] On the other hand, there is respectable evidence for a body of men who look very much like an English jury and who date from the reign of Ethelred the Unready.[6] Whether, however, the English jury is of English origin or whether it came in with the Conquest is not a question that need greatly concern us here. What is of consequence is the employment of a body of men who perform such duties as jurors perform when they come into the full light of history. Function is of more importance than forms. But even in the matter of forms there seems a *prima facie* case against those who cling to a belief in a Norman origin for the jury. The word 'jury' implies an oath, which the German equivalent *Schwurgericht* brings forcibly to our notice, and Brunner was especially concerned with the formalities under which the jurymen undertook their duties. Now, in matters of law it is very dubious whether the Normans were great

---

[1] Howden, *Chronica*, iii.263-4; *Three Rolls of the King's Court*, pp. 84-5, 87-8, 91-2, 94 *et passim* (the references to *auxilia* and scutage also are to the taxes for the king's ransom); *Pipe Rolls, 6-7 Richard I, passim*.

[2] The introduction of the bill in eyre in the thirteenth century is perhaps the most noteworthy innovation. Of this we speak later.

[3] *Die Entstehung der Schwurgerichte* (1871). Brunner had no real evidence for the eleventh century: the English evidence he did not seriously examine. It is remarkable that, if the sworn inquest was communicated to Normandy from France, there appears to be no evidence for its employment in the latter country until the middle of the twelfth century, and a recent investigator has suggested that this was under the influence of Anglo-Norman practice: see Yvonne Bongert, *Recherches sur les cours laïques du xᵉ au xiiiᵉ siècle*, especially pp. 262-5. Nor is there any evidence for the survival of Carolingian institutions in Normandy: such scanty facts as are known point strongly in the opposite direction (M. de Bouard in *B.I.H.R.*, xxviii.1-14).

[4] The inquest into the estates of the church of Bayeux, as to which see above, pp. 46, 53. The assembly of bishops and barons at which the Norman *Consuetudines et Justicie* were drawn up in 1091 (Haskins, *Norman Institutions*, pp. 277-84), though sometimes called an inquest, had nothing of the jury about it. Haskins' own argument in favour of the priority of the sworn inquest in Normandy turns, curiously enough, on the use of the word *assisa* 'in the sense of royal legislation' in the second half of the twelfth century (*ibid.*, pp. 196-238). Whether he was right or wrong in his interpretation of the word, his argument seems quite irrelevant to the issue.

[5] The earl of Gloucester: see below, p. 225.

[6] In particular Hurnard in *E.H.R.*, lvi.374-410. Van Caenegem has re-examined the evidence and lists the extensive literature on the subject (*Royal Writs in England*, pp. 57-77).

swearers. They preferred to decide questions of right by judicial battle and not by the English methods of ordeal or compurgation, which demanded many oaths.[1] A Norman, again, was bound to his lord by the rite of homage, which required no oath, while the Englishman was bound by an oath of fealty.[2] And then, again, there have survived a good many Old English formulas for oaths to be taken on various occasions,[3] but no parallel ancient Norman formulas. We must beware of the fallacies that may underly the argument from silence; but when we speculate upon the basis of very little evidence or, as in the present case, on the basis of no directly relevant evidence at all, it is well to bear in mind what we can learn of national habits. And we should, we think, be more ready to assume the existence of a jury, the sworn inquest, among those with whom swearing was a habit rather than among those who, it would seem, made little use of oaths as a means of judicial proof.

It is agreed that in 1166 juries of some sort were in existence in England. The Assize of Clarendon has been accepted as evidence for what has been called the 'accusing' jury or jury of presentment[4]: indeed, it has been said to mark the establishment of the 'grand jury'.[5] If we are right in our conception of the events of 1166, this cannot be the case. What was novel in the procedure was the attempt to bring to justice those against whom there was no conclusive evidence. The several steps in the procedure appear to have been (*a*) delation, (*b*) the declaration of the jury of their belief in the guilt (or innocence) of the accused and (*c*) compurgation or ordeal. The jury were not concerned with the red-handed manslayer, the back-bearing or hand-having thief, but with the man against whom the evidence was at best circumstantial. They did not accuse; they did not present. Their function was not one we can readily place in any of the categories known to the law when ordeals had become a thing of the past and compurgation was in disfavour. But if the occasion was novel, there is no reason to suppose that the method of investigation was novel. For this is not the only kind of jury known in 1166. We have already mentioned the man who was amerced because he was absent from a *jurata feodorum militis*.[6] To understand what the purpose of this jury was, we must recall that in 1166 there was an enquiry into the number of knight's fees which had been created by the king's tenants-in-chief, and many of the returns made by these barons have survived.[7] It appears that not

---

[1] This is clear from one of the two authentic pieces of legislation by the Conqueror, entitled by Liebermann 'Lad' (*Gesetze*, i.483-4). That the Normans did on occasion resort to compurgation is, however, indicated by the reference in para. 1.1 to the oath to be taken by a Frenchman with his oathhelpers according to Norman law; but this was an alternative forced upon him when an Englishman declined battle.
[2] Above, pp. 105-12.   [3] Liebermann, *Gesetze*, i.396-9.
[4] Pollock and Maitland, *History of English Law*, i.152.
[5] Plucknett, *Concise History of the Common Law*, p. 112.   [6] Above, p. 202.
[7] *Red Book of the Exchequer*, pp. 186-445; Round, *Feudal England*, pp. 236-46.

only were these returns made, but that enquiries into the facts were made, on occasion, by juries.[1] Juries were also employed to 'recognise' the facts in actions of novel disseisin, which were put on a new footing, but did not originate, in this year.[2] Nor can we limit trial by jury to any particular forms of action. It is evident that in the early years of Henry II procedure by way of jury was extremely flexible and readily adaptable.[3] Any idea that it was a novelty in any of its aspects is untenable.[4] The major argument, though by no means the only argument, for its antiquity seems to us to be the close resemblance—we had almost said the identity—between the general eyres of Henry II and those of Henry I. It is hard to believe that there was any substantial difference between the presentment and trial of criminals over the thirty or forty years that intervene. We have already assigned the part of an accusing or presenting jury to the lawmen, the representatives of shire and hundred, and the part of a trial jury to the *juratores*. Whether the lawmen were sworn on this occasion or not, we do not know: that they were admitted to office without an oath is incredible. But the point would seem to us irrelevant. The only possible alternative to our hypothesis is that under Henry I juries, sworn *ad hoc*, already represented the hundreds before the itinerant justices. That the function of presenting criminals was then performed in one way or the other, either by the *judices* or by specially sworn *juratores*, cannot reasonably be doubted.

When we pass to the eleventh century we find the administrative machinery of shire and hundred employed for the Domesday Inquest and other enquiries. The tale has often been told and we need not retell it.[5] To only one trial under the Conqueror do we wish to call attention, that in which Gundulf, bishop of Rochester, claimed, as the property of his church, land in Cambridgeshire which the sheriff had treated as royal demesne. The minutely detailed narrative that has come down to us is not strictly contemporary, but it comes from a highly respectable source[6] and it receives some confirmation

---

[1] Cf. Round, *op. cit.*, p. 245.   [2] Van Caenegem, *op. cit.*, pp. 57-77.

[3] As a further example there may be instanced its employment to ascertain a man's means. Samuel, priest of Pilton, had been amerced 100 marks but had pleaded poverty and in consequence 'admensuratus est de misericordia c. marcarum in quam positus fuit per Willelmum filium Iohannis pro xl. marcis per sacramentum vicinorum suorum' (*Pipe Roll, 11 Henry II*, p. 64; *14 Henry II*, p. 141).

[4] The evidence for the continued employment of juries under Henry I and Stephen, if scanty, is ample. For Henry I see, beside the 'Winton Inquest' (D.B., iv.531), *Regesta*, nos. 1283, 1341, 1423, 1833. For Stephen see the documents printed by Madox, *History of the Exchequer*, i.108, *n*. h and *Formulare*, no. lxviii, and also the proceedings concerning the church of Luton (below, p. 286) which Maitland recognised as a predecessor of the assize *utrum* (*History of English Law*, i.145).

[5] For a recent presentation of what may be called the classical view see Stenton, *Anglo-Saxon England*, pp. 644-8. A much modified view is presented by Galbraith, *The Making of Domesday Book*, pp. 28-44, who ascribes to the landowners a greater part in furnishing information and so reduces the rôle ascribed to the jurors. We ourselves would go further in the same direction: but the division of duties is not a matter we need pursue.

[6] *Textus Roffensis* (ed. Hearne), pp. 149-52: compiled in the first half of the twelfth century. A defective text had previously been printed by Wharton, *Anglia Sacra*, i.339, of which a translation is given by Stenton, *William the Conqueror*, pp. 434-5.

from Domesday Book.[1] Briefly, the story we are given is that the
dispute was referred to the county court and that Odo of Bayeux
presided. The suitors as a body declared that the land was the king's,
but this they did out of fear of the sheriff, and Odo, who was not
satisfied, ordered a jury of twelve to be elected and sworn. This jury
confirmed the previous judgement, but later some of the jurors admitted that they had perjured themselves. They were then summoned to London, together with a second jury of twelve,[2] to appear
before a court attended by many barons from all over England.
Here they were adjudged 'both by the French and the English' to
be guilty of perjury. If we are to accept this narrative—and there
seems no reason to question its substantial accuracy—within twenty
years of the Conquest there were employed not only a jury of trial
but a process of attaint. That this advanced procedure was a recent
introduction by the Norman king and was without roots in the Old
English past defies all probability: where is a Norman parallel to
be found? The originality of the Norman and Angevin kings lies
rather in the despatch throughout the country of royal commissioners
and royal judges who made use of English institutions for the purpose
of local enquiries and the local administration of justice. The system-
atisation of this practice, first by Henry I and then by Henry II, and
its integration with the court of the exchequer laid the foundations
of the judicature in England.

We turn next to the evolution of the office of coroner. The English
king was sworn to do justice to the people committed to his governance, and he relied upon the profits he drew from the rights of
the Crown to maintain his dignity. It was well that profit and
justice should go together, for a most important source of profit lay
in the penalties inflicted on wrongdoers. To secure those penalties
the king needed, all over the country, men who were vigilant in
keeping a record of serious crime and of infractions of the king's
rights. We have seen how this duty had fallen upon the king's serjeants, who acted in co-operation with the local justice. We have
also seen that the evidence of the early pipe rolls of Henry II, slight
though it may be, points to the continuation of this system so long
as local justices remained in office. With their disappearance, the
serjeants of hundreds and wapentakes appear to be themselves
keeping the pleas of the crown. No other interpretation seems
possible of entries in the pipe rolls of 1168 and 1169 which show them
amerced for failing to claim pleas of the crown tried in franchisal
courts,[3] or for conniving at the concealment of violent deaths,[4] or for

---

[1] D.B., ii.381.
[2] This appears to be a jury of attaint. They repudiated the verdict of the trial jury,
but could not clear themselves by ordeal of complicity in the original judgement of the
county court. Consequently the whole county was amerced £300.
[3] *Pipe Roll, 14 Henry II*, p. 30; *15 Henry II*, pp. 149-50.
[4] *Pipe Roll, 14 Henry II*, pp. 87, 151 (two instances).

failing to inform the sheriff that a plea of Englishry had been prof-fered,[1] or for failing to arrest men accused of concealing treasure trove.[2] The serjeants seem also to have replaced the local justices in receiving the abjuration of confessed felons,[3] to have arrested sus-pects, inspected bodies before burial, received evidence of Englishry and so forth.[4] Nor can we attach great importance to the direction in the chapters of the eyre of 1194 that four *custodes placitorum corone* were to be elected before the justices[5]: no similar article occurs in later chapters of the eyre, though there is evidence to show that elections of this kind did take place in some eyres at least.[6] The scheme of 1194, however, lapsed, and there is wide variation in the number of *custodes* or coroners appointed.[7] In any case it is impossible to believe that the direction given in 1194 marked the creation of the office of coroner and the end of the hundred-serjeant's duty to keep the pleas of the crown. Hundred-serjeants performed that duty long afterwards and their supersession by specially appointed *cus-todes placitorum corone* was a gradual process.[8] These *custodes*, who later came to be known as coroners,[9] had their forerunners, as we have seen, in the king's serjeants who farmed the pleas of the crown under Henry I; but they were the inheritors of the powers and duties of the local justices and the hundred-serjeants.

There is diversity in the contrivances to which the king resorts in securing his rights; but there is an essential continuity, even, we believe, in points of detail. One point we would stress, for it goes to the very root of the administration of justice in England, the use of the written record. Long before there were any coroners there was, if we may be excused the paradox, a coroner's roll. An entry in the pipe roll of 1169 shows that in the general eyre of 1168-70 a record of pleas of the crown was expected to be kept in writing and to be produced before the justices.[10] Nor can it be supposed that a written

---

[1] *Ibid.*, p. 164.   [2] *Ibid.*, p. 67.
[3] *Three Rolls of the King's Court*, pp. 100-1.
[4] Hunnisett, 'The origins of the office of coroner', *Trans. R. Hist. Soc.*, 5th Ser., viii.92-6. For other references see *Three Rolls of the King's Court*, p. 143; *Rotuli Curiae Regis*, i.215. For the arrest of suspects see 'Leges Henrici', 92.8 (*Gesetze*, i.608); *Pipe Roll, 14 Henry II*, p. 67; *Three Rolls of the King's Court*, p. 51.
[5] Howden, *Chronica*, iii.264. These four *custodes* figure twice in surviving records, in 1194 and 1198 (*Rotuli Curiae Regis*, 1.50-1; *Curia Regis Rolls*, i.39).
[6] Hunnisett, *The Medieval Coroner*, p. 151.
[7] There appear to be three *custodes* in Somerset and in Dorset in 1201 (*Pleas before the King or his Justices*, ii, nos. 733, 743), two in Leicestershire in 1207 (*Curia Regis Rolls*, v.18), six in Yorkshire in 1210 (*ibid.*, vi.115), two in Somerset in 1214 (*ibid.*, vii.98). For Hamp-shire, Kent and Sussex see Hunnisett, *op. cit.*, pp. 134-5.
[8] Hunnisett, 'The origins of the office of coroner', *ut supra*, p. 93.
[9] *Custodes placitorum corone* continued to be the official term, even when Bracton was writing (fo. 149b, 153b; Woodbine, ii.423, 434). Cf. *Curia Regis Rolls*, i.166, iii.156; v.18; vi.265; vii.110. But *coronarius* and *coronator* gradually superseded the more formal title (cf. *ibid.*, ii.180; iii.164, 221; vi.10, 115, 264, 292, 341, 350), and Bracton uses *coronator* except when citing writs.
[10] *Pipe Roll, 15 Henry III*, p. 148: Galfridus de Scalariis . . . pro scripto de placitis corone regis quod non habuit. Geoffrey was a member of the well-known Cambridgeshire family of 'Scales'. Although he is not here qualified as a hundred-serjeant, there can be little doubt of his office. The use of a written record is confirmed by an entry in *Pipe Roll*,

record of this kind was an innovation in the early years of Henry II. Such records would seem necessary for the proper functioning of the eyre system and therefore to date from the reign of Henry I.

We have already said a little of the court *coram rege* and of the court of the justiciar at the exchequer, and our purpose now is to show how the central courts became integrated with the courts of the itinerant justices and how there was evolved a corps of judges ready, as need might require, to sit *coram rege* or in the common bench or to travel the country on eyre. But first let us endeavour to dispel the error that still persists which would treat the common bench and the exchequer as different tribunals, the one with judicial, the other with financial, functions.[1] We have already reproduced a writ of Henry I's which recites how the abbot of Westminster had deraigned certain land against Herbert fitz Herbert before the barons at the exchequer.[2] Let us now leap forty years onwards to find that men are willing under Henry II to pay substantial sums in order that a civil action may be adjourned or removed to the exchequer or before the justices at the exchequer.[3] We must not imagine that any difference is implied when 'justice' is the word employed and not 'baron'. There is abundant evidence to show that in the twelfth century the two words were interchangeable when reference was made to those of the king's ministers who adjudicated upon issues coming before the court at the exchequer.[4] These issues, in so far as they raise points of law rather than of finance, are mainly pleas of land, but criminal matters are also referred to the exchequer,[5] for, as William fitz Stephen said, it was there that pleas of the crown were adjudicated upon.[6] And it was to the impartiality, as between rich and poor, of the justice administered in the exchequer before Ranulf Glanville that Walter Map gave his testimony.[7] In the course of the twelfth century the barons or justices tended to specialise, some upon judicial and some upon financial work; but even in the reign of John there was no complete separation. Entries that are essentially judicial will be made upon the memoranda roll, which is primarily intended for fiscal business,[8] while fiscal business will appear upon a plea roll.[9] And though, by then, the distinction between a judge who sits on the bench to adjudicate in civil actions and a baron who sits at the exchequer to

25 *Henry II*, p. 77: quia fecit iniuste imbreviari Reginaldum de Elveden' de morte cuiusdam hominis. Again, the office of the culprit is not stated.

[1] The contrary seems, in fact, to be asserted by Richard of Ely when he says 'Non enim in ratiociniis sed in multiplicibus iudiciis excellens scaccarii scientia consistit' (*Dialogus de Scaccario*, p. 15).   [2] Above, p. 163.

[3] *Pipe Roll, 14 Henry II*, p. 197; *15 Henry II*, p. 66; *17 Henry II*, p. 73.

[4] *Memoranda Roll, 1 John*, Introduction, p. xiii.

[5] *Three Rolls of the King's Court*, pp. 96, 103.

[6] *Becket Materials*, iii.51: 'scaccarium . . . est regis tabula nummis albicoloribus ubi etiam placita corone regis tractantur.'

[7] *De Nugis Curialium*, v, c. 7 (ed. James, p. 253).

[8] *Memoranda Roll, 1 John*, Introduction, p. xciii.

[9] *Pleas before the King or his Justices*, i.108.

adjudicate upon fiscal matters is becoming marked, the barons of the exchequer will take the place of the justices of the bench and the proceedings before them will be entered on the plea rolls without any break or apparent change of venue.[1] Even in the early years of Henry III common pleas were on occasion tried by the barons.[2]

The personnel of the king's court, whether it is held before the king himself or before the justiciar, is disclosed chiefly by the fines of land which have survived from the twelfth century. Until 1195 there are chance survivals in original or transcript: from that year they have survived as the feet (or third copies) of fines, which were systematically filed in the treasury. Until 1195, therefore, our information is fragmentary. In the pipe roll of 1175, however, as it happens, there is a long series of entries of pleas and agreements before William fitz Ralf, Bertram of Verdun and William Basset *in curia regis*.[3] This court, it would seem, must be the court at the exchequer, for the king was absent from England until May of this year.[4] Since these three justices were often engaged on eyres, we have here satisfactory proof of the employment of royal judges, now in one capacity and now in another. Why these three men sat as a tribunal in this year we do not know: perhaps it was an experiment, for there does not seem to be evidence of a like kind on other rolls. Fines of land, indeed, suggest that the court at the exchequer was, as a rule, much more numerously attended by others besides the regularly employed royal judges,[5] but the long lists of those present may be illusory and may be a mere convention of the chirographers. However, we are here concerned with the judges regularly employed. We can as yet hardly call them judges by profession; they do not seem to be trained lawyers. William fitz Ralf, for example, was shortly afterwards appointed seneschal of Normandy, where he had a long and distinguished career, and before he sat on the bench he had served as sheriff.[6] William Basset, whose father and grandfather had been *justitiarii totius Anglie* under Henry I, might perhaps for that reason have a greater claim to be regarded as a judge by profession,[7] but he served for long periods as sheriff, as did also Bertram of Verdun.[8] These men were, in fact, of the same kind as the *justitiarii totius Anglie* of Henry I, who might, as occasion required, act as sheriff, go on eyre or sit at the exchequer. These three are not,

[1] *Rotuli Curiae Regis*, ii.155; *Curia Regis Rolls*, i.115-7; *Pleas before the King or his Justices* i.294-6. For later evidence of the same kind see D. M. Stenton 'King John and the Courts of Justice' in *Proceedings of the British Academy*, xliv.116.

[2] *Curia Regis Rolls*, viii.316; x.142, 156.

[3] *Pipe Roll, 21 Henry III*, pp. 47, 55, 69, 78, 98, 124-5, 132, 143, 163, 181-2.

[4] Eyton, *Itinerary of Henry II*, pp. 183-90.

[5] The numbers of justices not uncommonly run to eight or more named, together with others unnamed, and are invariably more than three. There are many examples in the fines printed by the Pipe Roll Society and in the fines of earlier date not yet assembled in print.

[6] Delisle, *Actes de Henri II*, Introduction, pp. 481-3.

[7] See notice in Foss, *Judges*, *s.v.*, and references in Eyton, *op. cit.*, p. 312.

[8] Delisle, *op. cit.*, pp. 359-60; Foss, *ut supra*; Etony, *op. cit.*, p. 342.

in fact, the most eminent of the judges who sit at the exchequer. Apart from the justiciars themselves, those who sit most regularly from the 1160's onwards appear to be Richard of Ilchester and Geoffrey Ridel, both archdeacons, who in 1173 will be elected to the sees of Winchester and Ely but will continue to sit on the bench.[1] They are men with a different background, men with some knowledge of canon law and perhaps of civil law, though we know nothing of their academic training. For all that, they are not primarily lawyers, but king's clerks, civil servants, administrators. They are of a type which will become prominent in the thirteenth century and will produce such distinguished judges as William of Raleigh and Henry of Bratton, whom we know more familiarly under the perverted form of 'Bracton'.

From the bench we turn to the itinerant justices regarding whom our information is relatively plentiful, for brief particulars of the eyres are provided by the pipe rolls, particulars that are supplemented by the surviving fines. We cannot enter into many details, but certain entries on the pipe rolls of 1177 and 1178 invite comment.[2] They disclose that two of the six groups of justices who had been on eyre in 1176 sat at the exchequer to complete their business. These two groups consist of Hugh de Gonzeville, William Basset and William fitz Ralf, and Bertram of Verdun, William fitz Stephen and Turstin fitz Simon. These entries are valuable for two reasons. They show that, already under Henry II, the practice, which is well attested under John,[3] had been adopted of bringing to a conclusion at Westminster the business of an eyre that had been unfinished in the country. They also show that, when the regularly employed judges were sent on eyre, they were given as companions men of the same type with less judicial experience, for Hugh de Gonzeville, William fitz Stephen and Turstin fitz Simon had all served either as sheriff or in other official capacities.[4] The four other groups of three who went on eyre in 1176 are of similar composition.[5] Even when the law had become a profession and the judges can reasonably be called professional, a like practice was followed of appointing as itinerant justices inexperienced and, it is to be feared, unlearned men as associates of the judges of the benches.[6] We emphasise these points, for they bring home a truth it is important to establish, that the judicial system of the thirteenth century was, in its essentials, already in being under Henry II.

---

[1] For printed examples see Round, *Ancient Charters*, no. 41; *Curia Regis Rolls*, x.334; West, *St. Benet of Holme*, nos. 10, 193; Madox, *History of the Exchequer*, i.213 n.; Dugdale, *Origines Juridiciales*, pp. 50, 92; *E.H.R.*, xii.300-1; Douglas, *Feudal Documents from Bury St. Edmund's*, pp. 183-4; Salter, *Thame Cartulary*, p. 131, no. 186; D. M. Stenton, *Pleas before the King or his Justices*, i.365-6. There is much other evidence.
[2] *Pipe Roll, 23 Henry II*, pp. 31-2, 45, 112-3; *24 Henry II*, pp. 4-5.
[3] D. M. Stenton, *op. cit.*, p. 146.
[4] See Foss and Eyton, *ut supra*, and the notice of Hugh de Gonzeville in Delisle, *op. cit.*, pp. 389-90.   [5] 'Benedict of Peterborough', 107-8.   [6] *Traditio*, vi.80.

It was, as we have said, at Westminster that the common law was born and grew up, and there the professional lawyer had his origin. The court *coram rege* differed from the court at Westminster in that it was peripatetic, was absent from England for prolonged periods, especially in the closing decades of the twelfth century, had no regular judges of its own[1] and, so far as we can tell, kept no records of its own until the reign of John. When in England this court, though numerously attended on formal occasions, had as its nucleus much the same members as the justiciar's court. Thus, when Henry II was sitting at St. Edmund's in 1157 to try an action between the bishop of Chichester and the abbot of Battle, there were present a number of those whom we have already seen acting as justices—the chancellor, the two justiciars, Henry of Essex, Reginald de Warenne —and we may note in addition Warin fitz Gerold, the chamberlain.[2] In 1163 an action at Westminster between the bishop of Lincoln and the abbot of St. Alban's was tried by the king, who sat with a large body of bishops, abbots and earls, but also much the same body of ministers as in 1157: the two justiciars, Geoffrey Ridel, who is now keeping the great seal, Henry fitz Gerold, who has succeeded his brother Warin as chamberlain, and Richard of Ilchester, who is rapidly rising in the official hierarchy and who has a seat at the exchequer.[3] As the reign proceeds we find the justiciar and the regular judges present in the court *coram rege*, as well as many others, bishops and barons, who may add dignity to the proceedings but can have added little to the wisdom of the court.[4] If we can safely draw a conclusion from the few accounts that have come down to us of trials held before the king or the fines levied before him, he was present only when there was some issue in which he was personally interested. And while the inference must be that for the time being the differentiation between the court *coram rege* and the justiciar's court disappeared, it seems likely that these occasions were rare and that, even when the king was in England, the justiciar's court continued to function, just as the justiciar continued to issue writs. Doubtless as the king progressed through the country, suitors came to his court asking for justice,[5] and for the existence of a peripatetic court *coram rege* distinct from the King's Bench there is much evidence

[1] The king would not act judicially without the assistance of justices, even in an appeal of treason (*Rotuli Curiae Regis*, ii.30). Cf. *Curia Regis Rolls*, i.394, which shows Henry II sitting judicially at Marlborough with Ranulf Glanville and William Ruffus.

[2] *Chronicon Mon. de Bello*, pp. 84-104.   [3] Walsingham, *Gesta Abbatum*, i.157.

[4] At Westminster in 1175 there were present the archbishop of Canterbury, six bishops, an earl, the justiciar and seven others (B.M., Egerton MS. 3031, fo. 23b-24). At Clarendon in 1187 there were present the king's son John, the justiciar, Hubert Walter, three archdeacons and four others (*Cartularium Mon. de Rameseia*, i.121-3).

[5] It may not be superfluous to repeat here that the arrangement in 1178 recorded by Roger of Howden ('Benedict of Peterborough', i.207) was exceptional and does not mark the origin of either the King's Bench or the Common Bench (Sayles, *Select Cases in the Court of King's Bench*, i.xii-xiv, xx-xxii). Curiously enough this was one of the passages expunged by Howden when he revised his chronicle: evidently he attached little importance to it.

in later centuries.[1] But of this less formal side of twelfth-century justice we know nothing and, with other minor jurisdictions, this minor court *coram rege* lies apart from the general structure of judicial administration.

From July 1188, when Henry II left England for the last time, to 1199, when John ascended the throne, the bench at Westminster was left almost undisturbed by the king's presence. The king's ministers and judges, if they could not introduce great changes, could consolidate and extend the innovations in the judicial system that had been brought into being from 1166 onwards. It is from this period that we get the earliest surviving plea rolls: they differ little in character from those surviving from the next decade, and we hazard the guess that they differed little from those of the last ten years of Henry's reign which are lost to us. To this same period belong the law-book we know as 'Glanville', the first of the rolls of the grand assize,[2] the first files of feet of fines[3] and, we may add, the first surviving file of original writs returned to the bench.[4] This is adequate evidence of an advanced and well organised judicial system which the greater store of records surviving from the reign of John serves to confirm. For these records but continue those of the two earlier reigns which are mostly lost to us: we must not think of the early years of the thirteenth century as a period of innovation because hazard has preserved more historical material.[5] Now doubtless between 1176, when plea rolls *eo nomine* had begun to be kept, and 1215, when the ordered administration of justice came to an end for the space of the *tempus guerrae*, doubtless in these forty years there had been changes, improvements in the details of procedure, clarifications of the law. But the general picture the relative abundance of records permits us to draw of English judicature in the early years of John is, we believe, substantially that of English judicature under Richard I and in the closing years of the reign of Henry II.[6] At the centre is the court at Westminster. It is staffed by judges of whom a high degree of competence is demanded and to whom the description of professional can, by this time, hardly be denied, though they are not professional in the sense that judges of the later Middle Ages were, men who had begun their career as apprentices and had attained the degree of serjeant before their elevation to the bench. Though technically competent, the judiciary could hardly

---

[1] Sayles, *op. cit.*, iii, p. lxxxv, ns. 5-7.

[2] *Curia Regis Rolls*, i.1-14: see *Memoranda Roll, 1 John*, Introduction, pp. lii-liv, for a description.

[3] A few survivors are printed in *Feet of Fines, Henry II* and *Richard I* (Pipe Roll Soc.): see endorsements at pp. 21, 26, 79.

[4] D. M. Stenton, *Pleas before the King or his Justices*, i, app. ii. Most of the writs are, however, of a date after Richard I's death.

[5] *Memoranda Roll, 1 John*, Introduction, pp. xxi, xxxv.

[6] For the judicature under John see *Pleas before the King or his Justices*, ed. D. M. Stenton, i.51-149, and 'King John and the Courts of Justice' in *Proceedings of the British Academy*, xliv.103-27.

be said to be deeply learned. Some of them may have had a passing acquaintance with Roman law, for an elementary knowledge of it was widespread; but no great gap separated the professional judges from the prelates, barons and ministers who, from time to time, were called upon to reinforce them. This corps of judges, regular and adventitious, with the justiciar as their head and director, staffed, as occasion required, the bench, the court *coram rege* and the eyres. The essential unity of this body explains the ease with which an action might be transferred from one tribunal to another[1] and the case with which tribunals could coalesce and divide. In principle the bench is sedentary at Westminster and the court *coram rege* is ambulatory; but, in the early years of John, the bench may be found for a time at Northampton and, when the king is resident for some weeks at Westminster, the bench loses its separate identity. If there is a general eyre, demanding the full strength of the judiciary, the sessions of the bench may be suspended for a term or two. If the business of an eyre is unfinished in the country, the judges may, as we have seen, bring it to a conclusion at Westminster. Though the justiciar is the president of the bench, he may sit in the court *coram rege* and the bench may function without him. Nor is the separation between bench and exchequer yet complete, and the one will be found performing functions which normally belong to the other, and, despite changes in the personnel and venue of the court, process continues uninterrupted. There is a maze of jurisdictions and a confusion of records which have baffled historians, but, if we have the patience to trace the threads, the pattern becomes plain, the convenience of seeming anomalies apparent. The whole machinery of justice revolves round the justiciar, as does the machinery of finance: as it was under Henry I, so it is under Henry II and his sons. Differentiation in personnel and function proceeds slowly and is never entirely stabilised until, in 1234, the office of justiciar is abolished and the king's bench, common bench and exchequer are at last separated and their modern history begins.[2]

---

[1] An excellent example from the years 1200-1 has been given by G. B. Adams, *Council and Courts in Anglo-Norman England*, pp. 243-4.
[2] We deal with this development in a later chapter.

XI

FINANCIAL ADMINISTRATION:
THE TREASURY

IN the reign of Henry I, so Stubbs believed, 'a supreme court of
justice, called the Curia Regis, presided over by the king or justiciar... managed the assessment and collection of the revenue, and
for this purpose had a separate and very elaborate organisation. ....
The Exchequer of the Norman kings was the court in which the whole
financial business of the country was transacted.'[1] Stubbs's conceptions of mediaeval financial administration, like those of his followers
and successors, were dominated by the researches, undertaken in the
early eighteenth century, by the learned and laborious Thomas
Madox and, in particular, by Richard of Ely's *Dialogus de Scaccario*,
which Madox was the first to publish. Of the writers since Stubbs's
day, the most significant contributions have been made by that way-
ward scholar, J. H. Round; but unfortunately, he could rarely apply
himself to the prolonged and connected investigation of any subject,
and in his occasional excursions into mediaeval finance he was, with
an equal show of authority, as likely to come to a wrong conclusion as
to a right one. And whilst T. F. Tout contributed much to the later
history of financial administration, in the twelfth century he was on
unfamiliar ground and as yet fresh to his task: and what he had to
say that was new was of little value and was sometimes, indeed, positively misleading. Neither Round nor Tout called for any serious re-
consideration of current conceptions concerning administration in the
twelfth century, and Stubbs's teaching, except perhaps for a reserva-
tion here and there, is still accepted. What have we to put in its place?

The essential difficulty in the way of constructing an easily intelligible account of financial administration under the Norman and
Angevin kings lies in this, that its basis must be sought in scattered
and largely unrelated documents and that what might seem to be
the main source, the splendid series of twelfth-century pipe rolls,
regards the subject from the standpoint of an auditor and an auditor
of but a portion of the king's resources. The pipe rolls are not concerned with the whole of the revenue and they record the expenditure of but a fraction of the king's resources. It is only occasionally
and incidentally that the pipe rolls reveal anything of larger and
wider matters. We should like to know what were the king's re-

[1] *Constitutional History*, i.407.

sources in cash and credit, how much he spent and upon what, how much he saved. But to these questions the pipe rolls supply no answer. Nor do they tell us very much, though they tell us a little, of the financial system before the earliest surviving pipe roll, that of 1130. Yet it is important to know whether, with the coming of the Normans, there were fresh departures or whether the conquerors were, for the most part, content with the resources and the system that had been developed under English kings. Not the least of Round's services was his demonstration that some, at least, of the features of Norman finance were of pre-Conquest origin.[1] But if the sources of revenue available to English kings were maintained practically unchanged, though they might be augmented by the Normans, is it not highly probable that the system under which they were collected and disbursed continued practically unchanged also? We may put the question in another way: did the Norman kings employ ministers of the same kind and with the same functions as their English predecessors? If we cannot answer this question fully and directly, we can at least point to evidence that reveals an apparently unbroken line of treasurers from William I to Stephen, a line that, there is some reason for believing, began under the Confessor. The details are perhaps tedious, but they are essential to our understanding of the history of financial administration.

It will be convenient to begin with a writ of the last year of the eleventh century which Henry I addressed to Eudes *dapifer* and Herbert the chamberlain. This is, in substance, a writ of *liberate*, though the formula is not that which became customary in the twelfth century. The writ orders that, whenever the king wears his crown in one of the three abbeys of Westminster, Winchester and Gloucester, full livery (*plenaria liberatio*) shall be given to the monks and an ounce of gold to the chanters, and the address tells us who were the two ministers at the time in charge of the king's treasury.[2]

First, let us ask, who was Herbert the chamberlain? Herbert, a married clerk, was a man of substance, with a good deal of property in Winchester and elsewhere in Hampshire.[3] Two quite independent chroniclers describe him, not only as chamberlain, but as the king's treasurer (and there is no doubt of their reliability on this point),[4] while two writs addressed to Roger of Salisbury and Herbert the

---

[1] *Commune of London*, pp. 66-75.

[2] Henricus rex Anglorum Eudoni dapifero et Herberto camerario, salutem. Precipio quod conventus Westmonasterii et Wintonie et Gloucestrie in omnibus festivitatibus quibus in eisdem ecclesiis coronatus fuero plenariam de me habeant liberacionem et earum cantores unciam auri habeant, sicut Mauricius episcopus Lundoniensis testatus est tempore predecessorum meorum eos habuisse. Teste Willelmo electo Wintoniensi apud Westmonasterium (Robinson, *Gilbert Crispin*, p. 141, no. 18; *Regesta*, no. 490).

[3] For his property see D.B., i.42*b*, 45*b*, 48*b*, and 'Winton Domesday' (iv.532-8). That he was a clerk appears from his description in a charter of 1101 (*Monasticon*, iv.17*a*: see also p. 16*a*). For his family see below, pp. 426-8.

[4] Continuator of Hugh the Chanter (*Historians of the Church of York*, ii.223) and John of Hexham (Simeon of Durham, ii.317) from a common source, which was independent of *Chronicon Mon. de Abingdon*, ii.43, 134-5.

Chamberlain, one notifying them that Abingdon Abbey had been exempted from contributing to an aid granted to the king by the barons,[1] and the other that the bishop of Norwich was quit of scots and gelds,[2] must presumably be an instruction to them in their capacities of justiciar and treasurer respectively. These writs appear to come from the year 1110. Again, Herbert was one of a commission of five who, early in the reign of Henry I, were responsible for the survey known as the Winton Domesday,[3] and he was also a member of the king's court 'at Winchester in the treasury' over which Roger, bishop of Salisbury, presided, probably at Michaelmas 1111.[4] Herbert was dead before Michaelmas 1130,[5] and had died within the last few years, perhaps in 1128.[6] If he is to be identified with Herbert the chamberlain of Domesday Book and with Herbert the king's chamberlain of Winchester who witnessed a grant to Westminster Abbey under William Rufus,[7] he must have lived to a ripe age, and it might perhaps be suggested that we have to do with two Herberts, father and son. When, however, we come to examine the evidence for the other officers of the treasury under Henry I, it will appear that Herbert had ceased to have any responsibility there for some years before his death. This may have been the consequence of his advanced age and is consistent with the assumption that he is to be identified with the chamberlain of 1086.[8] And it looks as though Herbert were a chamberlain of the treasury under William Rufus and treasurer under Henry I. A chamberlain, we infer, might be assigned for duty in the treasury, but he was not a chamberlain of the treasury before he took up that duty or after he relinquished that duty. It follows, of course, that there is nothing inconsistent in a chamberlain's serving as treasurer or in his being a chamberlain of the treasury at one time and treasurer at another. To those who are acquainted with the later history of the lower exchequer this may seem a strange doctrine, but, as we shall show, some of the characteristic institutions of the later twelfth century were unknown about the year 1100.

---

[1] *Ibid.*, p. 113: *Regesta*, no. 959. Hugh of Buckland, who is included in the address, was presumably addressed as sheriff.

[2] *Regesta*, no. 946. Ralf of Belfou must similarly be addressed as sheriff.

[3] *Winton Domesday* (D.B., iv.531). That he is named here next after the bishop of Winchester and before Ralf Basset and Geoffrey Ridel indicates that he is an ecclesiastic. The date of the commission has to be inferred, but it was certainly not later than 1115 (see Round in *V.C.H. Hants*, i.528) and must for the reasons explained later be earlier than the election of William of Warelwast as bishop of Exeter in 1107. If the writ in favour of Hawise Mauduit (below, p. 429; *Regesta*, no. 729) is not later than 11 05, then the survey cannot be later, for Robert Mauduit was at the time of the survey in possession of the property in Winchester to which Hawise made good her claim (below, pp. 429-30).

[4] *Chronicon Mon. de Abingdon*, ii.116; *Regesta*, no. 1000.

[5] *Pipe Roll, 31 Henry I*, pp. 37, 125.

[6] Certainly before Michaelmas 1129, since the odd sum of 353 marks due from Herbert's son for his father's debt (p. 37) must represent a balance from the pipe roll of 1129, after the payment of one or two instalments.

[7] Robinson, *Gilbert Crispin*, p. 146, no. 27.

[8] Round came to this conclusion on other grounds (*E.H.R.*, xxvi.725).

While Herbert was serving as chamberlain of the treasury his colleague as treasurer appears to have been one Henry. A treasurer, Henry, is named both in Domesday Book and in the Winton Domesday.[1] When the latter survey was made he was already dead, but we learn from it that he had held property in Winchester before the Conquest. Although his Hampshire lands had been acquired since the time of the Confessor, it is possible that he had served King Edward. One point, in any case, is clear, that the office of treasurer did not pass to Herbert through any tenurial connexion with Henry. Whether Henry was a clerk does not appear: he was certainly married and left a widow.[2]

But we must say something of Herbert's associate and superior of 1100. Eudes *dapifer* was, of course, a very much more considerable figure than Herbert. Legend made him the chief steward under William Rufus, but there is no knowing what grain of historical truth lies in this story.[3] The writs addressed to Roger of Salisbury and Herbert, in favour of the monks of Abingdon and the bishop of Norwich, afford an obvious parallel to the writ addressed to Eudes and Herbert. In each case, it looks as though Herbert is addressed as treasurer. Eudes, however, was certainly not justiciar, though we must suppose that as steward he was performing much the same function in relation to the treasury as Roger of Salisbury was to perform a few years later. He may have presided over a court, in the nature of a board of audit, that preceded the court of the exchequer. Clearly he had authority over disbursements from the treasury, but he was not the treasurer.

If Herbert was treasurer at the beginning of Henry I's reign and if he relinquished office some time before his death, who succeeded him? The answer would seem to be 'Geoffrey de Clinton'. Geoffrey was one of those *curiales* who, according to Orderic, had been raised from the dust by Henry I.[4] There is no reason to doubt that Geoffrey de Clinton is the same man as Geoffrey the chamberlain who witnesses a writ of 1103-6[5] and who appears as tenant of a house in the Winton Domesday.[6] Later, presumably after he had acquired his estate at Glympton, he is rarely given in charters any other qualification than 'de Clinton'. But in a few charters, one of them his own, he is called Geoffrey de Clinton, 'treasurer' or 'treasurer and chamberlain'.[7] The text of these charters may be suspect but, however unsatisfactory they are in the form in which they have come down to us, there is no reason why the monks of Kenilworth should have interpolated the title 'treasurer', and on the evidence of these

---

[1] D.B., i.40; *Winton Domesday* (D.B., iv.539).   [2] *Winton Domesday, loc. cit.*
[3] Colchester Chronicle in *Monasticon*, iv.607: on this fabrication see Freeman, *William Rufus*, ii.464.   [4] Ordericus Vitalis, *Historia Ecclesiastica*, iv.164.
[5] *Cal. Charter Rolls*, ii.102; *Regesta*, no. 630. Other writs, similarly witnessed, appear to be later.   [6] *Winton Domesday* (D.B., iv.540b).
[7] Madox, *History of the Exchequer*, i.58(a); *Monasticon*, vi.221, 223.

charters it would seem that Geoffrey held that office about the year 1125.[1] Of his successor, there can be no question, for Nigel the treasurer is a witness to a charter that may be dated 1127, where he appears in company with the king, Bishop Roger, and Geoffrey the chancellor.[2] Whatever doubt there may hitherto have been about the identity of Nigel the treasurer who witnesses other charters of the same period, there can be no doubt here, and we have therefore adequate corroboration of the statements by Richard of Ely and Alexander Swereford that Bishop Nigel had held that office.[3] But by 1137, at latest, another king's treasurer appears, by name Athelhelm (Adelelmus),[4] and this makes it highly probable that Nigel relinquished his relatively lowly office on becoming bishop of Ely in 1133.[5] Since Athelhelm the treasurer appears as witness to a mandate of Bishop Roger's, issued in his pastoral capacity,[6] and to a charter where he is associated with Roger's nephew, Bishop Alexander,[7] the inference is that he was connected with the family of le Poer and is presumably to be identified with the unnamed nephew on whose behalf Bishop Roger besought the treasurership at the beginning of Stephen's reign.[8] He may, without difficulty, be identified also with Athelhelm the archdeacon, who witnesses a charter of Bishop Alexander's[9] and who later became dean of Lincoln.[10] The infrequency of the name and Athelhelm's connexions leave practically no doubt on this point.

Here there is a break in our information regarding the office of treasurer and, before we pass to consider the further evidence relating to the chamberlains of the treasury, it may be convenient to summarise the conclusions to be drawn from the evidence so far adduced. The list of treasurers we can construct is, then, as follows:

KINGS	TREASURERS
William I	Henry the Treasurer
William II	[Probably the same]
Henry I	Herbert the Chamberlain
	Geoffrey de Clinton
	Nigel
Stephen	Athelhelm

[1] Farrer, *Itinerary of Henry I*, p. 111; *Regesta*, no. 1428.
[2] Brit. Mus. MS. Egerton 3031, p. 38, a charter of Robert earl of Leicester in favour of Reading Abbey. It was issued before the death of William of Tancarville in 1129 and is dated at Eling, Hants., where the king was awaiting his passage to Normandy in August 1127: cf. Round, *Feudal England*, p. 269 *n*. For other references to Nigel the treasurer see C. H. Haskins, *Norman Institutions*, p. 108, n. 105, and Round, *Cal. Docts. France*, no. 1388. The *Historia Eliensis* (p. 283) also states that Nigel was treasurer before his election in 1133. The subsequent statement (p. 284) that after his consecration Nigel 'thesaurorum regis et reipublicae custos extiterat' is manifestly an exaggeration, but the implication is that he ceased to be treasurer.
[3] *Dialogus de Scaccario*, p. 50; *Red Book of the Exchequer*, i.4.
[4] *Thame Cartulary*, p. 1.
[5] Since chancellors vacated their office on their elevation to the episcopate, it is almost inconceivable that, at this period, a bishop would act as treasurer.

If, as suggested, Nigel relinquished the office in 1133, it is probable that Athelhelm then began to serve under Henry I. But in every case, the dates of entering and leaving office are uncertain.

Under Henry II and his successors, the treasurer has two invariable companions, the chamberlains 'of the treasury' or, as they were known later, 'of the exchequer'. Every writ that requires the payment of money out of the treasury is addressed to these three ministers. The treasurer is a clerk, while the two chamberlains are laymen whose office comes to be regarded as running with the tenure of lands that Henry II granted to William Mauduit and Warin fitz Gerold: in other words these two chamberlainships are serjeanties. The history of the chamberlains of the treasury has been made to look simpler than it is by the hypothesis that this was always so, as far back as the days of the Conqueror, and that the problem was to trace the descent of the lands which the two chamberlains were holding under Henry II. The hypothesis is, as we shall show, baseless, and there must be a different approach.[1] If we turn to the Winton Domesday we shall find as landowners in Winchester four men who, we have good reason to suppose, were at some time chamberlains of the treasury; they are Herbert the chamberlain, who seems certainly to have been treasurer at the date of the survey; Geoffrey the chamberlain, who seems certainly to be identifiable with Geoffrey de Clinton[2]; Robert Mauduit who, though not described in the survey as chamberlain, is known to have been one[3]; William of Pont de l'Arche, who is later entitled chamberlain, but seems not to have been such at this date.[4] All four of these men are named in the pipe roll of 1130. Of Herbert there is no need to say more than has already been said. Robert Mauduit had apparently died in 1129 and William of Pont de l'Arche had, as the roll shows, purchased his office and his daughter.[5] Since Robert's brother William succeeded to the (unspecialised) chamberlainship which their father, William Mauduit, had held, it is quite clear that William of Pont de l'Arche did not purchase that chamberlainship. The inference is that the office that was sold was the chamberlainship of the treasury, which William Mauduit II was himself to acquire in 1153 after the death of William of Pont de l'Arche.[6]

The grounds for supposing that Geoffrey de Clinton was chamberlain of the treasury have already been indicated. It is suggested that he held that office early in the century, succeeded Herbert the

[6] Egerton MS. 3031, p. 51b; Harleian MS. 1708, p. 190b: 'Teste A. thesaurario apud Wintoniam'.   [7] *Thame Cartulary*, p. 1.
[8] William of Malmesbury, *Historia Novella* (ed. Potter), p. 39: in initio regni eius nepotibus suis uni cancellariam, alteri thesaurariam . . . impetravit.
[9] *Lincoln Registrum Antiquissimum*, ii, no. 219.
[10] *Ibid.*, iii, nos. 797, 939; iv, no. 1295.

[1] See Appendix III: below, pp. 422-37.   [2] *Winton Domesday* (D.B., iv.540).
[3] *Ibid.*, pp. 533, 534.   [4] *Ibid.*, pp. 531, 534, 535, 537.
[5] *Pipe Roll, 31 Henry I*, p. 37.   [6] See Appendix III: below, p. 430.

chamberlain as treasurer and then relinquished the latter office in favour of Nigel, while retaining his original office. Geoffrey is, however, shown in the roll of 1130 as having purchased an office.[1] The fact that he owed 310 marks in 1130 for this does not necessarily imply that the purchase was recent: the odd amount suggests that he had already paid off part of the debt and that the purchase had been arranged in some previous year. What then was the office he had purchased? The Latin description is *ministerium thesauri Wintonie* and it has been assumed that this means the office of chamberlain of the treasury, though the Latin for that is undoubtedly *cameraria thesauri* or *cameraria de thesauro*.[2] Geoffrey surely had no need to purchase the chamberlainship of the treasury in 1130 or a few years before, but he might have thought it advantageous, on relinquishing the treasurership, to purchase the custody of the treasury at Winchester. That there was such an office is to be deduced, not only from the words of the pipe roll, but from the testimony of the *Gesta Stephani* and the Colchester chronicle. The *Gesta* implies that Roger of Salisbury and William of Pont de l'Arche were in control of the treasury in 1135.[3] Roger, of course, was justiciar, while William is described as the 'guardian and disburser of King Henry's treasuries'.[4] The Colchester chronicle, although it transfers William's rôle to the year 1100, describes him, apparently accurately, as holding the *claves thesauri Wintonie*.[5] Presumably William had succeeded to the office on the death of Geoffrey de Clinton in 1132.[6] The inference is that William, having acquired the office of chamberlain of the treasury on the death of Robert Mauduit, proceeded on Geoffrey's death to acquire the custody of the treasury. This must mean that of the two chamberlains of the treasury, one in particular had direct charge of the treasure and held the keys. We do not, in fact, know that William of Pont de l'Arche had a companion chamberlain in 1135. Geoffrey de Clinton had a son of the same name, who is entitled chamberlain,[7] but that does not necessarily imply that he became chamberlain of the treasury under Henry I or at any time. Certainly he did not serve Henry II in that capacity. The conclusion then is that under Henry I there was a treasurer, who might be a clerk or a layman, and two chamberlains of the treasury, one of whom was in direct charge of the treasury. There is nothing whatever to suggest that the office of chamberlain of the treasury was heritable or held by serjeanty. Nor is there any reason to suppose that the system found under Henry I originated with him: the

---

[1] *Pipe Roll, 31 Henry I*, p. 105.   [2] See Appendix III: below, pp. 423, 427.

[3] *Gesta Stephani* (ed. Potter), p. 5.

[4] 'Willelmus quidam, fidissimus thesaurorum regis Henrici custos et resignator.' Mr Potter translates *resignator* as 'steward', but the sense required is 'one who issues or pays out'.   [5] *Monasticon*, iv.607.

[6] For Geoffrey's death see Farrer, *Itinerary of Henry I*, p. 143, n. 11.

[7] *Cartulary of Oseney Abbey* (Oxford Hist. Soc.), i.3, 5, 6, 425; Salter, *Early Oxford Charters*, p. 69; Round, *Cal. Docts. France*, p. 299.

terms of the writ that Henry I addressed to Eudes *dapifer* and Herbert the chamberlain are sufficient to refute any such supposition. The probabilities are that the system, like the treasurership, had evolved before the Conquest and that Hugh the chamberlain (*cubicularius*), who figures in two well-known stories of the Confessor, was the chamberlain who was in direct charge of the treasury.[1] Though we should not use quite the same words, we do not dissent from Stubbs's conclusion: 'Edward the Confessor . . . as we must infer from Domesday, had a centralised system of finance, a treasury with its staff of keepers and assessors.'[2] Whether or not the pre-Conquest officers were termed *thesaurarius* and *camerarius* in Latin is a question of the same kind as whether or not the Old English sheriff could be latinised as *vicecomes*. If there were substantial identity of function before and after 1066, differences of nomenclature are, for our present purpose, of minimal significance.[3]

It is, of course, obvious that in the year 1106, the treasury of the king of England was self-contained, as it had been in the eleventh century. When the king of England became duke of Normandy, was there any change in the position? Was there a common Anglo-Norman financial administration? It is clear from the pipe roll of 1130 that certain officers of the English treasury have, in the recent past, been on duty in Normandy. Two of these officers were Robert Mauduit and Geoffrey de Clinton. Their visit cannot have been later than 1129 and may have been several years earlier while Geoffrey was still treasurer. They had been responsible for the safeguarding, and presumably for the receipt, of money in Normandy, and evidently they had been found in deficit, for which Geoffrey was still held to be accountable at Michaelmas 1130.[4] Another pair who had been on duty in Normandy and had received money in the treasury there were Nigel (the treasurer) and Osbert of Pont de l'Arche.[5] What office Osbert had then held does not appear. Taken together the entries suggest that the English treasurer, accompanied by an officer serving in the capacity of chamberlain, had crossed over to Normandy for the purpose of assisting the financial administration there. We can, however, exclude the possibility that a common staff served the treasuries of the two countries, since the existence of a line of Norman treasurers has been proved.[6] Moreover, we may see a parallel to these visits in the visits paid by a later English treasurer, Nigel's son, Richard of Ely, who was sent to Normandy by Henry II.[7] The facts point to a very flexible system which would enable the king to employ on either side of the Channel

---

[1] *Lives of Edward the Confessor*, pp. 53, 79-81; *Chronicon Abbatiae Rameseiensis*, pp. 170-1.
[2] *Constitutional History*, i.406; cf. p. 408 *n.*
[3] For the evidence see Larson, *The King's Household in England before the Norman Conquest*, pp. 124-33, and R. L. Poole, *The Exchequer in the Twelfth Century*, pp. 21-5.
[4] *Pipe Roll, 31 Henry I*, p. 37.   [5] *Ibid.*, pp. 54, 63.
[6] Haskins, *Norman Institutions*, pp. 107-10.
[7] *Pipe Roll, 21 Henry II*, pp. 187-8; Delisle-Berger, *Actes de Henri II*, i.194, 516.

men experienced in financial administration: but this is a different matter from a common staff and a common administration.

We may see here the beginning of the process by which the treasury would become detached from the household, and the exchequer would be transformed from a court into a department of state. There can be no doubt that originally the treasurer was a member of the household, whether of the king of England or of the duke of Normandy; and the *Constitutio Domus Regis*, which represents the situation as it stood in the early years of Stephen's reign, shows the treasurer as still belonging to the royal household.[1] But just as king and duke were conjoined in the person of Henry I, so the household of king and duke became fused. English treasurers and Norman treasurers, like other officers of the royal and ducal households, became equally members of Henry I's household. The inevitable duplication made the position of individual officers anomalous, and some offices which hitherto had demanded, in principle, continuous personal service upon the king or duke tended to become localised. The various chamberlainships afford an illustration of this evolution. The Tancarville chamberlainship was originally Norman, but William of Tancarville, who died in 1129, is said to have been 'chamberlain of England and Normandy'. However, the well-known story of a later William of Tancarville, who insisted on serving Henry II in person, suggests that in Normandy he enjoyed precedence over other chamberlains.[2] The origin of the Mauduit chamberlainship is obscure, but the William Mauduit, who was the resident chamberlain of the *Constitutio Domus Regis*, held lands in both Normandy and England which were associated with his hereditary office.[3] The Mauduits, however, acquired another chamberlainship, that of the English treasury, which localised what came to be regarded as their principal office, though this did not preclude them from serving Henry II in the chamber.[4] There were many chamberlains in the twelfth century, and with the growing importance and complexity of chamber business, there was a natural tendency to specialisation and this leads in the end to the evolution of the office of chamberlain of the exchequer which had no connexion with the chamber.[5]

The divorce of the treasurer from the household was rather more rapid. From the beginning his office had been specialised. Moreover, a treasury must tend to be fixed or, at least, to have fixed headquarters, however many subordinate treasuries there might be: a large bulk of treasure, of regalia, of records, is not made easily ambulatory, even though, as we shall see, astonishing quantities of

---

[1] *Dialogus de Scaccario*, p. 133.
[2] *Complete Peerage*, X, appendix F, pp. 47-54; *E.H.R.*, lxix.600.
[3] Below, pp. 429-30.   [4] *E.H.R.*, lxix.600-4; below, pp. 423, 429-36.
[5] This is not apparently formally recognised until the reign of John (*Memoranda Roll, 1 John*, Introduction, pp. xii, lxxii, lxxiv).

coin were constantly being transported across many miles of indifferent roads in order to satisfy the exigencies of administration.[1]
But if the treasury becomes fixed, so does the treasurer also tend to
become fixed; his duties are sedentary; his activities cannot be dispersed. It was doubtless the formidable administrative and physical
difficulties which precluded the creation of a single office of treasurer
to serve both England and Normandy. The need for a single central
organ of finance was met by the chamber.[2]

Both a Norman treasury and an English treasury were therefore
retained by Henry I and he also devised, for reasons we have already
explained, a Norman exchequer and an English exchequer. And
while there were certain points of contact between the two systems
—a debt due in one country might be discharged in the other[3]—the
two systems were distinct. We must, however, emphasise that, at this
period, the treasury was no part of the exchequer. The function of
the exchequer in relation to finance was to audit the accounts of
certain Crown debtors, who were due to make payments into the
treasury. The treasury itself was subject to quite a different kind of
control.

The pipe roll of 1130 alludes to an audit conducted by the earl
of Gloucester and Brian fitz Count.[4] It was Round who established,
contrary to earlier views, that this audit was entirely distinct from
the accounting that took place before the barons of the exchequer
and that its purpose was to verify the amount remaining in the
treasury after balancing issues against receipts.[5] Such periodical
audits were obviously necessary in order to control the officers in
charge; but since these audits were quite apart from, although they
might be complementary to, the control exercised over Crown
debtors, no notice would be taken of them in the pipe rolls, except,
as in this instance, where the reference was quite incidental. The
occasion arose in connexion with the accounts of Geoffrey Escolland,
who was responsible for the revenues accruing from the vacant
bishopric of Durham. Ranulf Flambard had died on 5 September
1128, and William of Pont de l'Arche had been sent by the king to
take possession of the bishopric. It was he, doubtless, who selected
Geoffrey, a local man and one of the bishop's barons,[6] to be keeper
and arranged that he should farm the revenues for a fixed sum. This
arrangement was to date apparently from Michaelmas 1128, while
he was to account also for any receipts for the preceding period,
which was loosely called the *tempus episcopi*. Geoffrey's first account
was not rendered until the Michaelmas term 1130, but he must have
made at least one proffer (that is, a payment on account) in the

---

[1] Below, pp. 235-7.   [2] Below, pp. 229-39.
[3] *Pipe Roll, 31 Henry I*, pp. 7, 13, 27, 39, 54, 63, 122, 145.
[4] *Ibid.*, pp. 129-31, upon which the particulars following are based.
[5] *Commune of London*, pp. 76-8. There are some errors in detail here.
[6] Simeon of Durham, *Historia*, i.141, 158.

interim, for he was present at the treasury on the occasion of the audit by the earl of Gloucester and Brian fitz Count. There appears to have been difficulty in making up a round sum of money (presumably £100) to put into a forel for storing in the treasury and Geoffrey had provided £4 4s. for the purpose. Note was, as we should suppose, taken of this contribution but, because it was not a normal payment into the treasury, no tally was issued against it. Credit for the sum was, however, given to Geoffrey when his account was heard in 1130, and it is from the entries concerning the transaction that we can fix the date of the audit of the treasury as falling within the twelve months ended Michaelmas 1129.[1] Nor is this the only incidental transaction that took place on the occasion of the audit. We learn that, when William of Pont de l'Arche had taken possession of the bishopric, a sum of £30 had come into his hands, and for this sum he had accounted to the earl and Brian and not to the barons of the exchequer. From the point of view of the latter, the matter was regularised by debiting Geoffrey with the £30 and then crediting him with the amount because William had accounted for it elsewhere. These details are illuminating, because they indicate that the treasury was subject to more than one authority, which might come into conflict and whose actions it might take some ingenuity to reconcile. There is a warning here, if it were necessary, to be careful not to identify the treasury with the exchequer at this date.

Scanty as our knowledge is of the treasury under Henry I, it is much less for the reign of Stephen. We must, however, assume that, until the arrest of the bishops at Midsummer 1139,[2] administration in England proceeded as formerly. Then it was inevitable that there should be a period of confusion and, so far as the treasury is concerned, it is significant that William of Pont de l'Arche went over to the Empress, with whom he is found early in 1140.[3] Nevertheless, for a time, the exchequer was kept in being, at least in principle. Importance has been attached to a charter of Stephen's, given in 1141, that refers to accounting at the exchequer. But this phrase is used by both contending parties in the same year, by the Empress as well as the king. The Empress addresses a writ of *computate* to the barons of the exchequer in favour of the canons of Osney,[4] while the king in his grant to Geoffrey de Mandeville of the counties of Essex

----

[1] Not 1130, as Round stated. The audit was probably in the Easter term when we should expect Geoffrey to make his proffer.

[2] William of Malmesbury, *Historia Novella* (ed. Potter), pp. 26-7.

[3] He witnesses a charter of the Empress after the death of Bishop Roger in December 1139 and apparently before her election as *domina Anglorum* in April 1140 (B.M., Cotton MS. Vesp. E.v. fo. 78). For William's subsequent relations with the Empress, see B.M., Additional Charter 20420 (*Facsimiles*, no. 19); *Monasticon*, v.409; *Hatton's Book of Seals*, no. 514; *Gesta Stephani* (ed. Potter) p. 100. He was dead by 1148: see *Winton Domesday* (D.B., iv.555, 558).

[4] Salter, *Early Oxford Charters*, no. 68, which is complementary to no. 96: the date of both appears to be July 1141.

and Hertford provides that any *terrae datae* shall be computed as a reduction in the farm.[1] These two instruments can hardly have both been effective and they may both have been dead letters. There is nothing to show that either was ever used. If this could be shown, we should have precisely the evidence we now lack, namely that, in 1141 or thereabouts, accounting took place at the exchequer at the regular terms, as it had under Henry I and as it was again to do under Henry II.

As we shall see, Duke Henry maintained his own financial organisation, his own treasury in England, although the duke's treasurer did not find a place in the treasury when it was reorganised by Bishop Nigel at the beginning of Henry's reign.[2] Instead we find acting as treasurer in 1156 an otherwise unknown William who had presumably held the office from the coronation.[3] Soon after, however, and perhaps before the end of 1156, he was succeeded by Richard of Ely, the bishop's son.[4] The two chamberlains of the treasury in the new reign were William Mauduit and Warin fitz Gerold. Warin had already served as chamberlain to Duke Henry, perhaps as chamberlain of the treasury, and his appointment as such is confirmed in a charter that may be dated with great probability at Michaelmas 1155. William Mauduit seems to have relied upon the charter granted before Henry's accession and not to have sought a confirmation from the king.[5] Although, therefore, the duke's treasurer was not continued in office, the inference is that, in theory, the duke's treasury had become the king's treasury and that, like all the other acts of Stephen's reign, his control of the finances of the country was regarded by King Henry as a usurpation and a nullity. The revenues the *de facto* king, and others, had illicitly collected could not be recovered, but the legality of the proceedings could not be admitted. So far as there was continuity in administration, this was traced through the duke's acts, although on becoming king he had little scruple in repudiating his former favours and grantees were well advised who deemed it expedient to obtain royal confirmation of ducal grants.[6]

At least in the early years of Henry's reign the staff of the treasury continues, in principle, to form part of the household, as it had under Henry I and Stephen.[7] Only as his reign progresses does the treasury become identified with the exchequer. A number of writs have survived to show that the source of payment, which formerly had been called the treasury, was by the 1160's being called the ex-

---

[1] Round, *Geoffrey d' Mandeville*, p. 142. The date ascribed is Christmas 1141.
[2] Below, p. 263.
[3] *Pipe Roll, 2 Henry II*, p. 47: at p. 16 the treasurer is mentioned but is not named.
[4] *E.H.R.*, xliii.163-6. If the 'Ricardus thesaurarius' of the instrument printed by Delisle-Berger, *Actes de Henri II*, i.194, is Richard of Ely, this is evidence that he was in office in 1158 and was accompanying the king to France.
[5] See Appendix III: below, p. 430.
[6] Below, pp. 261-2.   [7] Above, p. 224.

chequer,[1] and when in the late 1170's Richard of Ely was writing his 'Dialogus de Scaccario', the treasury, or one aspect of it, had become known as the lower exchequer or the receipt.[2] At the same time, the exchequer is still thought of as an occasion rather than a place.[3] Certain officers of the lower exchequer, as well as some of those of the upper exchequer, are paid their liveries 'dum scaccarium est', that is, Richard explains, from the day when the barons are assembled to the day when they disperse.[4] There is no reason to suppose that the assimilation of treasury and exchequer was the result of a single deliberate act. All we know suggests a gradual, almost insensible, change associated with the transfer of the centre of government from Winchester to London. It is easy to understand how a direction that payment was to be made on the occasion of a session of the exchequer would, as the place of session became fixed at Westminster, come to be construed as a direction that payment was to be made not only at a certain time but at a certain place: habitation and occasion would be confused. But this confusion would not be shared by the treasurer and chamberlains, and the process by which they became absorbed into the exchequer and the exchequer became a department of state with a continuous existence remains obscure. There is, however, nothing in the early history of the treasury and its assimilation to the exchequer which conflicts with the inference to be drawn from the records of legal transactions *ad scaccarium*, that the exchequer was the justiciar's court which adjudicated equally on legal and financial issues and from which the common bench eventually separated out as a distinct tribunal.[5] But though the exchequer adjudicated on financial issues, it is untrue to say (to use Stubbs's words) that the exchequer 'was the court in which the whole financial business of the country was transacted'.[6] The real centre of financial control and the principal 'spending department' was the king's household. Below that we perceive, however indistinctly, a network of agencies, receiving, storing, paying, recording and accounting, throughout England and Normandy and the other dominions of the king. The exchequer is only one wheel, however important it may be, in a complicated machine.

---

[1] Round, *Cal. Documents France*, pp. xliii-xlv; *Memoranda Roll, 1 John*, Introduction, pp. xii-xiii.

[2] *Dialogus de Scaccario*, pp. 8-13. The treasury is described, however, as the *domus* of the treasurer and chamberlains, which would have been equally apt under Henry I.

[3] Hence the phrase 'consumato scaccario' in *Pipe Roll, 29 Henry II*, p. 139.

[4] *Dialogus*, p. 13.   [5] Above, pp. 213-5.   [6] *Constitutional History*, i.407.

XII

FINANCIAL ADMINISTRATION: THE CHAMBER

O F the king's chamber, the *camera curie*, of the twelfth century Stubbs knew nothing. It had been passed over, with a few hesitant remarks, by Thomas Madox,[1] and what was obscure to him was ignored by later writers, until investigation into the details of finance under Henry II was facilitated by the publication of the pipe rolls. There are no twelfth-century accounts of the chamber to set beside the wardrobe accounts of the later thirteenth century, when, so Stubbs said, 'the whole accounts of army, navy, and judicial establishments appeared in the computus of the wardrobe along with the expenses of the royal table, jewel chests and nursery'.[2] But there was adequate evidence in print to show that such expenses were being borne by the royal household under John, and it was a fair inference that the system was then no innovation. Bewilderment may be caused by changes in internal organisation and in nomenclature, so that activities attributed to the chamber at one period are attributed to the wardrobe at another[3]; but to recognise the great and far-reaching activities of the wardrobe in the thirteenth century and to fail to look for a counterpart in the twelfth is a failure in historical imagination. A wide gap was left in Stubbs's account of the structure of government under Norman kings, a gap most oddly filled by attributing, in vague terms, to the exchequer a universal competence in financial affairs that it had at no time possessed.

There are two points that it will be well to emphasise from the outset. The first point is that the king had but one chamber and that it was inseparable from the household that accompanied him upon his journeys. There were not, as appears to be sometimes believed, two chambers, an English chamber related to the English treasury and a Norman chamber related to the Norman treasury or exchequer.[4] The second point is that in the twelfth century the chamber

---

[1] *History of the Exchequer*, i.264-5.

[2] *Constitutional History*, ii.582. There is an element of exaggeration in this description.

[3] Tout, *Chapters*, ii.158-69, 186-205. There has also been confusion between the chamber and the chamberlains of the exchequer, arising from a mistaken extension of the abbreviation *cam'* (*Trans. R. Hist. Soc.*, 4th Ser., xv.70-6).

[4] Packard, *Miscellaneous Records of the Norman Exchequer*, p. 66: 'The relationship between *Camera* and Exchequer remains as elusive as ever, but this transcript from the *Camera* records . . . brings us nearer the Norman *Camera* than does any other extant published document.' *Ibid.*, p. 90: 'The history of the *Camera*, Norman or English, remains to be done.'

was, as it was later, the great spending department, particularly for military purposes, and that, contrary to what T. F. Tout seems to have supposed,[1] the chief sources of supply were the accumulations in the king's treasuries.

It is unfortunate that we must, in the main, derive our knowledge of the chamber in the twelfth century from incidental references in the pipe rolls. Light from other records does not become available until the reign of John. The chamber is already well established in 1130: this is plain from the pipe roll of that year. How long had it had a distinct and individual existence? J. H. Round seems to have had no difficulty in assuming that it was already in existence in the year 1100. The writ of that year addressed to Eudes *dapifer* and Herbert the chamberlain[2] served, he thought, a double purpose. Eudes is addressed as steward, as the officer whose function it was to supply 'liveries', and Herbert as chamberlain, the officer whose business it was to find the ounce of gold to be bestowed on the chanters of the *laudes* and whom Round identifies with the later treasurer of the chamber.[3] If liveries and alms were supplied only by officers of the household, the argument would doubtless be valid. But it is quite clear from the pipe roll of 1130 that the liveries paid to the barons of the exchequer were normally a direct charge on the treasury. Even the chancellor, who might seem entitled to receive his livery from the household, received his livery with the other barons, and when he was absent from a session of the exchequer, he might deduct the value of the liveries due to him from the monies in his hands for which he was required to account.[4] It is plain, too, from the *Constitutio Domus Regis* that the liveries of members of the king's household might be issued either from the treasury or from the chamber and that, in either case, the master-marshal kept the tallies.[5] Again, the liveries to which William of Pont de l'Arche is entitled, when he is journeying from Normandy to take possession of the bishopric of Durham, are paid from the revenues of the see and are allowed to the custodian of the bishopric.[6] To cite a final example from the reign of Henry I: the sheriff of Norfolk is authorised to pay St. Paul's Hospital at Norwich threepence a day in respect of the livery that Odlent used to have.[7] Liveries then were not necessarily in kind but might be paid in money, and they might be paid from the treasury or from monies that would otherwise be paid into the treasury.

The writ of 1100 need not, therefore, be taken to imply that the household had then a financial department separate from the

---

[1] *Chapters*, i.231.   [2] Above, p. 217, n. 2.
[3] *The King's Serjeants and Officers of State*, p. 324.
[4] *Pipe Roll, 31 Henry I*, p. 140. Cf. *Dialogus de Scaccario*, p. 39, for other liveries payable *ad scaccarium*.   [5] 'Constitutio Domus Regis' in *Dialogus*, p. 134.
[6] *Pipe Roll, 31 Henry I*, pp. 129, 131.
[7] *Cal. Charter Rolls*, iii.71; *Regesta*, ii, no. 1608.

treasury, and it is not at all evident why such a separation should be necessary. But when Henry I became duke of Normandy as well as king of England and divided his time between his two dominions, the need for a separate financial department for his household would seem obvious. The household now draws funds from two main sources, the English treasury and the Norman treasury, and an additional means of controlling receipts and payments would inevitably be required. This is not to suggest that there was not a king's chamber physically distinct from the treasury in 1100: the existence of chamberlains implies a chamber, just as a treasurer implies a treasury, and a duke's chamber can be traced in Normandy before the battle of Tinchebray.[1] All that is argued is that the financial organisation of the chamber, as we see it later in the twelfth century, can hardly antedate the union of Normandy and England under Henry I.

We get few details of the chamber from the pipe roll of 1130. William Mauduit is recorded as having received money in the chamber, but this is in the past.[2] In 1130 the two chamberlains who act as receivers there appear to be William of Pont de l'Arche and his brother Osbert, for this seems to be the most probable interpretation of the *ministerium camere curie* for which William had agreed to pay twelve marks and one ounce of gold on his own behalf and two marks of gold on behalf of his brother.[3] The continuous history of the chamber can, however, be traced only from 1154. In the pipe roll of 1155 several payments into the chamber are recorded,[4] and in subsequent pipe rolls we see something of its organisation. Warin fitz Gerold, who is now chamberlain of the treasury, acts also in the chamber, where he may have acted before Henry came to the throne. His companion and apparently his subordinate is Geoffrey Monk. These men act not only as receivers: they defray the household expenses of the king and queen and pay the wages of huntsmen and soldiers.[5] The smaller details of chamber administration we can, however, pass by. Let us establish that the king had only one chamber.

As we have said, there are a good many references to the chamber in the early pipe rolls of Henry II and they continue, though intermittently, throughout his reign. The absence of such entries from some pipe rolls of Henry II has been regarded as an insoluble puzzle[6]; but the explanation appears to be quite simple. When the

---

[1] Haskins, *Norman Institutions*, pp. 40, 41.   [2] *Pipe Roll, 31 Henry I*, p. 134.
[3] *Ibid.*, p. 37.   [4] *Red Book of the Exchequer*, pp. 650, 654, 655.
[5] Another chamberlain, Stephen, also occasionally acts as receiver (*Pipe Roll, 2 Henry II*, p. 27; *3 Henry II*, p. 87), and there are other subordinates who do so, Ralf fitz Stephen and Stephen of Tours (*Pipe Roll, 4 Henry II*, pp. 125, 129, 155, 168), but the duty falls in the main upon Warin fitz Gerold and Geoffrey Monk. For their expenditure (met by the sheriffs) see *Pipe Roll, 2 Henry II*, p. 65; *3 Henry II*, pp. 89, 107; *4 Henry II*, pp. 113, 136, 155, 160, 171. That Geoffrey was subordinate to Warin is suggested by the entry 'Et Gaufrido Monaco pro Warino filio Geroldi x.l' (*Pipe Roll, 2 Henry II*, p. 66). On the general question of the staff of the chamber at this period see *E.H.R.*, lxix.600-4.
[6] Tout, *Chapters*, i.103.

king crossed overseas his chamber went with him, and unless debtors in England followed the king to the Continent and made payments in his chamber there, no entries recording such payments would occur on the English pipe rolls. The silence, for example, of the rolls from 6 to 9 Henry II corresponds to the king's absence abroad from August 1158 to January 1163.[1] Similarly the Norman exchequer roll of 1180 appears to contain no reference to the chamber —the king having crossed to the Continent in the latter half of the fiscal year and having spent some time beyond Normandy—while in the English pipe rolls of the same year there is evidence that receipts which normally would have been paid into the treasury were diverted directly into the chamber.[2] Again, the pipe rolls of Richard I cease to record payments in the chamber when he is on his crusade.[3] When he is in France a number of such payments are, it is true, recorded, the explanation being that the debtors have discharged their debts in the king's chamber abroad and have obtained a written receipt which they have duly presented to the exchequer.[4]

The receipts from English sources, so far as the exchequer rolls show them, are, however, trivial in comparison with the receipts from Norman sources. Direct comparison is limited to two years for which rolls are available from both countries, but there is no reason to question their general significance. In the English pipe roll of 1195 there appear to be three entries relating to payments into the chamber and in that of 1198 four entries: in the Norman exchequer roll of 1195 there are nearly a score,[5] in that of 1198 nearly fifty entries.[6] In part the difference may be due to methods of accounting, since in Normandy certain payments from and into the chamber became subject to audit by the [upper] exchequer and entailed entries the like of which we shall look for in vain in the English pipe rolls.[7] Payments from the treasury into the chamber are not mentioned in the English pipe rolls, at any rate in those of the twelfth century[8]: the largest sums mentioned in the Norman exchequer rolls

---

[1] Two entries in *Pipe Roll, 5 Henry II*, pp. 42, 63, may relate to an earlier year or perhaps to payments in France: the latter item is warranted *per breue regis*.

[2] *Pipe Roll, 26 Henry II*, pp. 38, 112.

[3] There is a gap between *Pipe Roll, 2 Richard I*, pp. 89, 116, 136 and *Pipe Roll, 6 Richard I*, pp. 13, 75, 194. An entry on the former roll (p. 155) illustrates the difficulty of attributing a payment into the chamber to the current year. It reads: Et in camera domini regis patris £83:12:8d. per breue ipsius regis quod clausum venit ad scaccarium. But for the fact that the warranting writ was one of Henry II's, we could not have known that it was presented at least fifteen months after its issue.

[4] *Pipe Roll, 6 Richard I*, pp. 13, 194; *7 Richard I*, pp. 25, 178, 190; *8 Richard I*, pp. 87, 119, 279, 280; *9 Richard I*, pp. 76, 92, 154, 178; *1 John*, p. 98. In certain cases it is stated that payment was made to the king himself and some are warranted *per breue regis de ultra mare*.

[5] *Magni Rotuli Scaccarii Normanniae*, i.132, 135, 138, 155, 221, 235-8, 260. Most of these payments are to Brice the chamberlain.

[6] *Ibid.*, ii.301, 306, 307, 311, 327, 328, 330, 334 *et passim*.

[7] The earliest example appears to be in 1201 (*Chancellor's Roll, 3 John*, p. 220).

[8] Payments from the treasury for castle-building, shipping, pay of knights and serjeants, the mint, may be found occasionally in the latter part of the twelfth century, but none of these concerned the chamber except indirectly: see *Pipe Roll, 30 Henry II*, p. 150, and

as paid into the chamber—amounts of £3500,[1] £2400,[2] with others of £1000[3], £700 and £500[4]—come directly or indirectly from the treasury at Caen. Naval prizes and tallages, it may be remarked in passing, also provide large sums: £2200,[5] £1743,[6] £1600,[7] £1540,[8] £880.[9] The Norman exchequer rolls give some indication too of the scale of chamber expenditure: thus, one set of accountants received £9375 in one year and £8883 in the next for castle building.[10] These are all Angevin *livres* and would look much smaller if expressed in sterling, for then we must divide by four,[11] but the amounts both of receipts and payments are still large.

Before leaving the question of the financing of the chamber in the twelfth century, it is desirable to mention one other source of revenue, that of loans. The credit transactions of the Angevin kings are too complicated a subject to be discussed in detail here. The pipe rolls, in recording the repayments to creditors made by sheriffs on the king's instructions, afford but glimpses of what has happened. One instance will suffice to establish that loans were paid into the chamber, which was thus temporarily accommodated until funds should accrue in the treasury. In 1163 William de Chesnay went out of office as sheriff of Norfolk and Suffolk and is shown as indebted to the Crown in the substantial sums of £319 9s. 8d. blanch and £150 numero.[12] Two years later it is noted that Isaac the Jew has attorned for the debt, as shown by the roll of the chamber and by the roll of the archdeacon of Poitiers.[13] 'To attorn' here means to acknowledge responsibility for the amount. It is not, however, until 1168 that William produces the king's writ, authorising him to make payments amounting to £476 to Isaac, which supplies the missing element to make the story complete.[14] The Jewish moneylender had made a loan to the king: this fact and subsequent transactions connected with it had been recorded in a roll kept in the chamber and also, it appears, in another roll kept by Richard of Ilchester, whom the king had appointed to discharge a number of supervisory duties in the exchequer. Repayment (either of the whole, or a large part, of the loan) was made neither from the chamber nor

entries under Dover in later rolls to *Pipe Roll, 34 Henry II*, p. 209; *Pipe Roll, 2 Richard I*, pp. 1, 4, 8; *3 Richard I*, p. 148.

[1] *Magni Rotuli Scaccarii Normanniae*, ii.485.   [2] *Ibid.*, i.136.   [3] *Ibid.*, ii.485.
[4] *Ibid.*, i.236.   [5] *Ibid.*, ii.311.   [6] *Ibid.*, ii.400.   [7] *Ibid.*, ii.447.
[8] *Ibid.*, ii.328.   [9] *Ibid.*, ii.400.   [10] *Ibid.*, ii.309.

[11] This equation was established in 1184 and held good until the loss of Normandy: for examples see *ibid.*, i.110, 120, 136, 156, 235; ii.300, 301, 443, 501. Previously the rate seems to have fluctuated, but the Angevin *livre* was valued slightly higher: *ibid.*, i.50, 57, 66, 92. The rate in the English pipe roll of 1189 (*Pipe Roll, 1 Richard I*, p. 229) cannot be cited as an exception, since it is a case of an exaction imposed upon a Jew. On the whole question see the paper by Léopold Delisle in *Bibliothèque de l'École des Chartes*, x.187-96.

[12] *Pipe Roll, 9 Henry II*, pp. 28-9. We should perhaps explain the terms *blanch* and *numero*. In the former case the coin was assayed and a deduction made for any deficiency in the value of equivalent standard coin of full weight; in the latter case payment was accepted by tale in current coin.

[13] *Pipe Roll, 11 Henry II*, p. 4.   [14] *Pipe Roll, 14 Henry II*, p. 17.

from the treasury, but by a precept on a sheriff, doubtless to meet
the creditor's convenience. This fact is as significant as the other fact
which emerges that loans to the king (of which we are thus indirectly
informed by the pipe rolls) were paid into the chamber. Nor were
these loans derived only from Jewish money-lenders. In 1164, in
similar language to that used of Isaac in 1165, the large sum of
£606 8s. 2d. is said to be 'attornata Willelmo Cade': there had been,
that is to say, a similar transaction with the Flemish money-lender
William Cade, who had in this instance been repaid, in whole or in
part, from the treasury.[1] But, as with Jewish money-lenders, the
usual reason for any note of Cade's transactions is because a payment has been made on a precept addressed to a sheriff.[2] Such notes
are sufficiently numerous to show that Henry II was largely financed
by loans in the earlier part of his reign, though they do not provide
data for estimating the extent of his borrowings.[3]

For light upon some aspects of twelfth-century finance we must
rely upon information from the early thirteenth century, before any
great changes in administration had taken place. Doubtless such
information has to be used with caution, and the argument that
what we learn of a later period may enable us to interpret the fragmentary records of an earlier period has its dangers. There are
dangers either way, for it seems to be supposed that there was a
marked development in the activities of the chamber under John,[4]
although any impression that this was so appears to derive from
the relative abundance of records for his reign. We must, however,
guard against the fallacy that, because we know more of the early
years of thirteenth century than of the closing years of the twelfth,
there was therefore more to be known. If we leave aside the exceptional financial contrivances made necessary by the *tempus
guerrae* from 1215 to 1217, no obvious reason suggests itself why
John's ministers or John himself should, in the absence of proof, be
credited with notable departures from the practice of the past.
There are no grounds for believing that Richard's wars and preparations for war had been less costly than John's or that Richard's
chamber was called upon to make smaller disbursements than
John's. It is possible, indeed, that John's resources were smaller than
Richard's, for John ceased to have the revenues of Normandy to
draw upon, although he had another source, Ireland, as well as
some counties of England, of which Richard did not avail himself.
It seems safe then to regard the information that comes from John's
reign as illuminating Richard's reign as well. The fresh sources of

[1] *Pipe Roll, 10 Henry II*, p. 34.
[2] Hilary Jenkinson in *E.H.R.*, xxviii.215, 219: see also *E.H.R.*, lxix.605-7.
[3] Richardson, *The English Jewry under Angevin Kings*, pp. 50-66.
[4] Jolliffe, 'The Chamber and the Castle Treasuries under King John' in *Powicke
Studies*, pp. 120-2. Mr Jolliffe's view is adopted by Poole, *From Domesday Book to Magna
Carta*, p. 422.

information we obtain, not only in the chancery enrolments but in
the earliest surviving records of the chamber, enable us to fill in
much detail and confirm the inferences we should draw from the
scantier sources for the earlier reigns. We may note in particular a
number of references in the early years of John's reign to large sums
brought to Normandy from the English treasury and paid either into
the chamber or used for chamber purposes,[1] and also many references to the payment of tallage in Normandy directly into the
chamber.[2] Substantial sums too reached the chamber in Normandy
from the revenues of the English forests, sent direct by Hugh de
Neville,[3] who appears to have paid nearly 4,000 marks into the
chamber within six and a half years between 1201 and 1208.[4] The
chamber roll of 1212-3 discloses that the wardrobe has developed
into the department in charge of the money and muniments of the
chamber,[5] its relation being parallel to that of the treasury to the
exchequer. The sums of money handled are very substantial and
may amount to thousands and tens of thousands of marks[6]: on one
occasion four carts with nineteen horses make a long journey of
many days with the treasure,[7] and on other occasions five and six
carts are employed, the coin being specially packed in barrels for
transport.[8] There is necessarily much reckoning of money, and the
cloth purchased for the purpose in October has apparently to be
replaced by May, so hard-used was it.[9]

The transport of treasure leads naturally to the question of its
deposit and to the control of the local treasuries thus created. Even
a casual examination of the records must suggest that considerable
sums were normally kept in the principal royal castles in the twelfth
and thirteenth centuries. In March 1204, for example, treasure from
Ireland was required to be delivered to Thomas of Rochford, constable of Bristol.[10] Later in the year his successor, Robert of Ropsley,
received 350 marks from the treasury at Winchester,[11] and he, in
turn, is found shortly afterwards delivering coin to Nottingham.[12]
In 1205 4100 marks were deposited in Northampton,[13] and in 1208-9
there was sufficient money there to enable a payment of more than
10,000 marks to be made to Engelard de Cigogné.[14] In July 1207,
11,000 marks were sent under the conduct of Robert de Vieuxpont
from the treasury at Winchester to Nottingham.[15] This money, it is

---

[1] *Rotuli Normanniae*, pp. 31, 36, 65, 69, 72, 75.
[2] *Ibid.*, pp. 47, 53, 60, 101-3, 107.
[3] *Rot. Litt. Pat.*, pp. 18b, 22, 27, 29b, 35b.
[4] *Memoranda Roll, 10 John*, p. 64. When accounting at the exchequer he produced a
writ for 3350 marks and claimed to have paid into the chamber a further 500 marks.
[5] Cole, *Documents illustrative of English History*, pp. 236, 238, 239, 243, 256, 265.
[6] *Ibid.*, pp. 236, 241, 242.   [7] *Ibid.*, pp. 246-9.   [8] *Ibid.*, p. 260.
[9] *Ibid.*, pp. 243, 265. The cloth used in the exchequer had apparently to last a year
(*Dialogus de Scaccario*, p. 6).   [10] *Rot. Litt. Pat.*, p. 38.
[11] *Rot. Litt. Claus.*, i.6b. From the note of warranty 'per Petrum de Stokes', it would
seem probable that the money passed technically to the chamber.
[12] *Rot. Litt. Pat.*, p. 48.   [13] *Rot. Litt. Claus.*, i.20.
[14] *Pipe Roll, 12 John*, p. 214.   [15] *Rot. Litt. Claus.*, i.88a, 88b.

to be remarked, passed formally out of the custody of the treasurer and chamberlains into that of the chamber before being despatched to Nottingham. In the same year a thousand marks were paid out of the treasury at Rochester to Reginald of Cornhill: this treasury was, there can be no doubt, under the control of the exchequer, for the transit of the treasure was supervised by serjeants of the treasurer and chamberlains.[1] In April and May 1208, two convoys, each with 1500 marks, were received at Gloucester castle, the money being apparently for the use of Gerard of Athée.[2] A year or so later the men of Bristol and Redcliffe paid 1250 marks to Engelard de Cigogné in four sums to be deposited in the king's treasury at Bristol.[3] The *Misae* Rolls of 11 and 14 John show that these local treasuries were supplied not only from the central treasury but also from monies in the control of the king's chamber. In August 1209 nearly 1000 marks —the proceeds of a fine from the archdeacon of Durham—were delivered to Brian Delisle to keep at Knaresborough, and shortly afterwards 100 marks appear to have been paid out of this money for chamber purposes.[4] On 30 January 1210 fifty marks which had been paid over by Thomas of Samford were returned to him to be placed in the treasury at Devizes.[5] On 2 February 300 marks, which had been received from Brian Delisle 'in respect of the churches and prebends of the archbishopric of York' were handed over to Robert of Braybrooke to place in the treasury at Northampton.[6] On 26 February Engelard de Cigogné received 100 marks out of the chamber to keep at Bristol.[7] In July 1212 no less than 48,000 marks were removed from the treasury at Bristol into the custody of Philip Marc at Nottingham where, by command of the king, a tower was being built; and in September a further 1000 marks were deposited there, 900 from Marlborough and the balance from the chamber itself.[8] Before the autumn of 1213 the enormous sum of at least 120,000 marks had been accumulated at Nottingham, only to be returned for the most part to Bristol.[9] These are but specimen items from the rolls, taken at random to impress upon the reader, even by their dull iteration, the great and constant traffic in treasure from castle to castle, for ends and purposes it would be vain to guess. Isolated entries certainly tell us nothing, and it may be well to observe that, although the incident took place almost on the eve of the outbreak of civil war, there was nothing at all unusual or specially significant in sending, early in 1215, £1000 from the Tower of London to Oxford[10] or in the movement of treasure in June and July of that year.[11] All such operations must be viewed in the light of past practice:

---

[1] *Ibid.*, i.90; *Rot. de Oblatis*, p. 393; P.R.O., Ancient Deeds, L.110.
[2] *Rot. Litt. Claus.*, i.113b, 114b.   [3] *Pipe Roll, 12 John*, pp. 143-4.
[4] *Rot. de Liberate*, pp. 127, 129.   [5] *Ibid.*, p. 147.   [6] *Ibid.*, p. 148.
[7] *Ibid.*, p. 152.   [8] Cole, *Documents*, pp. 235, 236, 241.
[9] *Rot. Litt. Claus.*, i.153.   [10] *Rot. Litt. Claus.*, i.192b; Pipe Roll, no. 61, m. 2d.
[11] J. C. Holt, *The Northerners*, p. 125.

they cannot be isolated and cited in support of some random hypothesis.[1] Nor did the practice of depositing treasure in castles cease
with John's reign. The whole of the fifteenth levied in 1225, amounting to nearly 90,000 marks, was required to be deposited in the
castles of Devizes and Winchester.[2] Monies collected for the aids of
1232 and 1235 were deposited in Hereford castle.[3] That this was the
usual place in which to lodge, at any rate, revenue collected locally
is shown by the existence of a serjeanty with the service of conveying
treasure from Hereford castle to London. The earliest reference to
this serjeanty appears in the returns to an exchequer enquiry of
1250[4]: when it was created is uncertain, but there is no reason to
doubt its existence in the twelfth century.[5]

For the twelfth century there is adequate evidence for a system of
castle treasuries in Normandy.[6] The English evidence for the reign
of Henry II—there is little for that of Richard I—gains meaning
from the evidence from the early thirteenth century. Apart from
notices of journeys to and from London and Winchester and the
southern ports, we are rarely given more information in the pipe rolls
than that treasure was carried 'per diuersa loca Anglie pluribus
vicibus'. Such entries leave us in no doubt that the money received
in the central treasury was distributed in quantity over the country:
and when we learn, as we occasionally do, that the destinations included such places as Gloucester,[7] Colchester,[8] Salisbury, Oxford
and Guildford,[9] we may be pretty sure that many of the journeys
were made with the purpose of filling the treasuries in the king's
castles. In the case of Salisbury there is, in fact, in the pipe roll of
1182, a reference to the construction of a treasury in the castle and
the provision of treasure-chests,[10] and the rolls of later years record
issues from the Salisbury treasury.[11]

There are indications in the early thirteenth century, it will have
been observed, that some castle treasuries were under the control
of the chamber and some under the control of the treasurer and

---

[1] It is inferred by Mr Holt (*loc. cit.*) that these operations indicate that 'John was
mustering his ultimate financial resources', which suggests remarkable prescience on the
king's part. Even less warranted is the deduction that, because money had been sent
from Corfe and Bristol to Portsmouth or because money was deposited with the Templars
and paid out by them, the king was short of money at the end of 1214 (*Pipe Roll, 16 John,*
pp. xxv, 44, 55, 84). Castle treasuries were there for the purpose of meeting emergencies,
such as the war in Poitou, while deposits with the Templars were for the purpose of
enabling them to act as international bankers, in this instance to make payments in
Flanders (cf. Richardson, *English Jewry under Angevin Kings*, p. 58 and references cited).
[2] Mitchell, *Studies in Taxation under John and Henry III*, p. 167.
[3] *Book of Fees*, p. 406.   [4] *Ibid.*, pp. 1186-7, 1246-7, 1274.
[5] There was a similar serjeanty at Cirencester that went back to Henry II's reign.
'Terra Roberti de Pirrie deffendit se conducendo thesaurum domini regis infra comitatum
ad custum suum et extra comitatum ad custum domini regis' (*Curia Regis Rolls*, xii.303).
[6] Haskins, *Norman Institutions*, pp. 107, 115, 117.
[7] *Pipe Roll, 17 Henry II*, p. 40.   [8] *Pipe Roll, 19 Henry II*, p. 183.
[9] *Pipe Roll, 28 Henry II*, p. 85; *33 Henry II*, pp. 194-5.
[10] *Pipe Roll, 28 Henry II*, p. 84: cf. Introduction, p. xxiv.
[11] *Pipe Roll, 29 Henry II*, p. 126; *30 Henry II*, p. 92. See also Mr R. A. Brown's paper
in *Jenkinson Studies*, pp. 35-49.

chamberlains of the exchequer. But we lack precise information and know little of the division between treasury and chamber. This was a matter of great concern to the ministers saddled with the responsibility for the treasure and led to precautions, of which some traces are left on the chancery rolls, and to the preparation of records that have long since lost their purpose and disappeared. But though the immediate authority over them and the limits of their responsibility might mean much to the local custodians of the king's treasure, to the king himself these were minor points of administrative convenience. In the twelfth century financial administration is evidently still very fluid. The king appears normally to have plenty of ready money at his command, and the ultimate result is the same whether payments are made from the chamber or out of the treasury or by a sheriff out of monies that would otherwise have been paid into the treasury. In effect these three sources form a common purse. This indeed seems to be very much the language of the twelfth century. The pesour (or weigher) of the exchequer is paid twelve pence a day from the king's 'purse',[1] and from the same source fivepence a day is paid to David the lardiner[2] and twopence a day to John, the controller (contratalliator) of the king's wines.[3] Later the word bursa was restricted in its meaning and was applied to the king's privy purse,[4] but originally it had no such limitation. The lardiner was paid his daily fivepence by the sheriff of Yorkshire from the farm of the county,[5] the controller of wines his daily twopence by the burgesses from the farm of Southampton,[6] while the pesour was paid from the treasury.[7] It is to be remarked also that there was as yet no rigid differentiation between the staff of the treasury and the staff of the chamber. William of Pont de l'Arche serves in both under Henry I and so does Warin fitz Gerold under Henry II. Moreover, the rolls of the chamber are accessible to the exchequer. Treasury and chamber are complementary: at this period, at least, there can be no idea of rivalry.

To pursue the subject further would be to overload this chapter with details, already, it may be thought, accumulated to the point of weariness. But it has been necessary to present them in this fashion in order to disperse the errors and anachronisms which have distorted the current teaching on mediaeval finance. That the control of finance centred in the royal household and was the imme-

---

[1] Coker, Survey of Dorsetshire (1732), p. 15; Cal. Inquisitions, Miscellaneous, i.456 (no. 1626).

[2] Ibid., i.163 (no. 501). Henry II's grant appears to have taken effect from Michaelmas 1164: see Pipe Roll, 11 Henry II, p. 46.

[3] Cal. Inquisitions, Miscellaneous, i.19 (no. 61).

[4] Borrelli de Serres, Recherches sur divers services publics, i.88. The word is used in this restricted sense in Rot. Litt. Claus., i.217, and Rot. Litt. Pat., pp. 183, 189b.

[5] Pipe Roll, 11 Henry II, p. 46, and later rolls.

[6] Pipe Roll, 2 Henry II, p. 53, and later rolls. The reference to the king's wines is usually omitted and contratalliator becomes abbreviated to talliator. In Pipe Roll, 14 Henry III, p. 201, we find talliator vinorum regis.   [7] Dialogus de Scaccario, p. 10.

diate concern of the king, whose resources flowed in from all parts
of his dominions, are truths which cannot be overemphasised. The
exchequers of England and Normandy played but a subordinate rôle
in such matters. To speak, as Stubbs did, of the English exchequer
as 'the court in which the whole financial business of the country was
transacted' is, in the light of facts as easily ascertainable in his time
as in ours, an inexcusable blunder. What is remarkable is that his
fallacies have for so many years remained unexposed and that even
now the chamber is regarded, not as the centre and controlling organ
of the financial system, but as ancillary to the English exchequer.
The picture presented by the most recent summary of twelfth-
century history is as misleading, in its own way, as the picture of the
financial system presented by Stubbs. 'When the exchequer broke
away from the household to become a separate department, the
chamber', so we are told, 'continued to be a place where the king
kept a current account into which moneys were directly paid without
passing through the hands of the exchequer officials'.[1] Those who
have had the patience to follow us so far will not need to be re-
minded, we trust, that the exchequers of England and Normandy
were never and could not form, if they were to fulfil their function,
part of the household and could not therefore break away from it.
Of the dominant rôle of the chamber in financial administration
there can be no question.

[1] Poole, *From Domesday Book to Magna Carta*, pp. 9-10.

XIII

THE HOUSEHOLD AND THE EXCHEQUER

W E are conscious that the subject of the two preceding chapters is likely to appear difficult and complicated to the reader, partly perhaps because the view it presents of mediaeval finance is in some ways novel and partly perhaps because the exposition, based upon the accumulation of detail, makes for hard reading. Let us therefore attempt to draw a simplified picture, which may aid in relating to one another in a coherent pattern not only the facts we have given but the many facts of a similar kind that can be found in contemporary documents.

At the centre is the king. He is the great spender. He has no separate funds for his private pleasures and his public duties; for his clothes, his jewels, his weapons; for his sport and his wars; for his alms and his buildings, domestic, military, ecclesiastical. He draws no distinction between his privy purse and public revenues. This does not mean that there are no specialised services and specialised servants, but there is as yet nothing in any way corresponding to a civil list or to departmental estimates, nor is there any control on royal spending, except lack of money, though the greater of our kings cannot be reproached as spendthrifts. Indeed, they managed to amass large treasures: and this, as we have seen, is true even of King John, until his finances were plunged into the maelström of civil war. But not only were our kings lords of England, they were also—with the exception of Stephen for the greater part of his reign —lords of extensive dominions oversea, from all of which they drew revenues and all of which occasioned spending. To some extent local revenue was used for local needs, but the surplus—and surpluses were considerable—came undifferentiated into the king's pocket, if the metaphor be allowed us. Henry I had no separate English pocket or Norman pocket, nor had Henry II separate Angevin, Poitevin or Aquitanian pockets. To compare great things with small, these kings were rather like modern financiers, with interests in half a dozen countries and some scores of companies, who draw, if they can, income from each.

In the twelfth century, as in earlier centuries, kings were great travellers, and especially English kings. Their household travelled with them and, while it was much encumbered with baggage, it could not carry with it money sufficient for the king's needs. So there was deposited in many castles a larger or smaller store upon which the king could draw. We know little of these stores except in England and Normandy, but quite certainly they must have existed in Anjou and Poitou and Aquitaine. And though the king's main source of wealth was England, he was very frequently overseas, and Henry II, for example, spent considerably less than half his time this side of the Channel, while Richard I was a stranger to the country. All the lands over which the king ruled and from which he drew his wealth had a separate, ancient administration, which, except in Ireland, had been maintained. Henry II combined in himself the ancestral traditions of Anjou, Normandy and England: his wife brought with her the ancestral traditions of Poitou and Aquitaine. To Ireland he brought the traditions of Anglo-Norman administration and John implanted them firmly, so that Irish institutions, lagging behind somewhat, became almost a replica of those of England, with a treasurer on the English model to supply his contribution to the king's resources[1], a king who so rarely saw this dominion of his that we can count upon our fingers the number of visits paid by English sovereigns between Henry II and Victoria. Every one of the king's dominions was so organised that, if he should take up his residence as duke of Normandy or count of Anjou, duke of Aquitaine or count of Poitou, king of England or lord of Ireland, the administration would be complete within itself and he would displace for the time the minister who ruled in his name, the justiciar in England or Ireland, the seneschal-justiciar in Normandy, the seneschal in the other French provinces. But until John was expelled from Normandy and Anjou, the king paid but intermittent visits to any of the lands he ruled: an interval of two or three years was nothing exceptional. And so all the provinces were self-contained and went their own way.

There had been a time when the English king abode permanently within his kingdom as the duke of Normandy abode in his duchy and the count of Anjou in his *comté*. Then there was no need for elaborate controls. The prince's household sufficed for all the purposes of central government, and, in particular, the clerks of the king's chapel, the chamberlains and the treasurer. In the Old English state it had been possible to maintain this primitive organisation, for as the heptarchy slowly made way for a unified kingdom under the hegemony of Wessex, though the volume of business might be increased, the king's household sufficed for all there was to do. But it was impossible to unify in this way England and Normandy and, while there could not very well be two royal households, the services of the treasurer were not so intimate that it was impossible to detach him, to leave him localised, while the king with the rest of the household departed on their way oversea. This is the

---

[1] Richardson and Sayles, *Administration of Ireland*, pp. 21-6.

first significant division of administrative functions. The king has but one chapel, but one chamber, for these are personal to himself; but he has now two treasurers, for their task as providers of money can be exercised from without the household. Custom determined that the treasurer should still be considered a member of the household, but he is, as it were, an honorary member. If he travels, as he sometimes does, with the king, it is not in pursuance of the duties of his office.[1] But now that the treasurer is no longer a full member of the household, no longer resides in the king's presence, but has in his keeping much of the king's property, he needs supervision. We must remember that as yet the treasurer's office is not very dignified. If he is a clerk, his services may at some time be rewarded, like the chancellor's, with a bishopric, but this will be the signal for his retirement. The day is yet distant when bishops will be prepared to serve as chancellors or treasurers,[2] and still more distant the time when men will speak of Lord Chancellors or Lord Treasurers. At first, it would seem, the treasurer was supervised by one of the king's stewards, who was a prominent baron; but when the office of justiciar was created, the treasurer became subordinate to him.[3] Quite independently, however, of the justiciar, the state of the treasury might be surveyed by a baronial committee.[4] Nothing could indicate more clearly the new status of the treasurer and the treasury: the first government department had been created.

Parallel with this development, a writing establishment evolved distinct from the king's chapel. The justiciar necessarily found that he had need of a staff of clerks for the administration he conducted in the king's absence and continued to conduct during the king's intermittent visits. In England this writing establishment was in origin a branch, a detachment, of the staff of the chapel, the chancery proper, though it acquired a separate identity and name, the *scriptorium*. The clerks of the *scriptorium* were employed in the business of the exchequer, the justiciar's court that had two regular sessions a year in the Easter and Michaelmas terms but occasioned much work throughout the year, for the whole judicial and financial administration of the country centred upon the justiciar.[5] The nature of the exchequer and, indeed, of the justiciar's administration as a whole has been obscured, rather than illuminated, by one of the most remarkable books of the twelfth century, the 'Dialogus de Scaccario', written as an office manual by Henry II's treasurer,

---

[1] For his position in the household see 'Constitutio Domus Regis' in *Dialogus de Scaccario*, p. 133. He is sometimes, if rarely, a witness to the king's charters. For Nigel's presence with the king at Eling in August 1127 see above p. 220, and at Rouen in May 1131 see *Regesta*, no. 1691. In September of this year he is attending a great council at Northampton (below, p. 249). For Richard of Ely's attestation of Henry II's charters see Delisle-Berger, *Actes de Henri II*, iii.203.

[2] This does not happen until the reign of Richard I when Longchamp combines the offices of chancellor and justiciar and Richard of Ely retains the office of treasurer after his elevation to the episcopate as bishop of London.

[3] Above, p. 222.   [4] Above, pp. 225-6.   [5] Below, pp. 246-7.

Richard of Ely. To assert that this book has made for obscurity must sound paradoxical and we must explain our meaning. We have already stated that one of the functions of the exchequer was to audit the accounts of Crown debtors, and the 'Dialogus' is concerned with this function. Richard of Ely seems to have projected a second book that would have taken a wider view, but, so far as we know, this second book was never written.[1] This is the more regrettable since historians have been misled, as Stubbs was misled, into supposing that the very limited operations described in the 'Dialogus' covered the whole field of royal finance.[2] It is as though, armed with a treatise upon the audit of company accounts, we thought that we were given a view of the whole field of industry or as though, with the departmental instructions of the Comptroller and Auditor General in our hand, we believed we could obtain an insight into the complex of modern public administration. The value of the 'Dialogus', however, lies principally in the assistance it gives to the understanding of the pipe rolls, the only continuous series of records for the second half of the twelfth century. Incidentally we are told much else of value for our understanding of the history of Henry II's reign, but also we are told some fictions,[3] and we must always be on our guard against accepting, without verification, the treasurer's apparent statements of fact: he sometimes describes as practice his own ideals. We shall shortly see the significance of this warning.

Of the processes described in the 'Dialogus' we have said little, because they are subordinate to the main business of administration, and we may venture the caution that they can be made to figure too largely in the history of administration. This is not to deny that the book is a very remarkable one to have been written in the twelfth century, a book that testifies to the maturity of the contrivances of government in the England of Henry II, just as what we may describe as the companion volume, the treatise known as 'Glanville', testifies to the maturity of the judicial administration. But we must retain a sense of proportion. The 'Dialogus' covers a very small part of the field and, with it and 'Glanville' before us, we feel all the more the lack of parallel contemporary treatises on the financial administration of the chamber and on the practice of the chancery, two matters of greater importance than the technicalities of audit, matters that fell, if not within the immediate cognisance of the king, within the competence of those of his servants who immediately attended upon him.

We turn therefore to examine briefly the distinction between the duties that fell upon the ministers who followed the king in his perambulations and the duties that fell upon the justiciar and the

---

[1] The 'Dialogus' does not purport to contain 'totam scaccarii descriptionem . . . alterius egens inquisitionis'. The Master adds: 'His igitur ad presens supersedeo in alterius diei disputationem eadem reseruans' (pp. 126-7).

[2] *Constitutional History*, i.407, cited above, p. 228.

[3] Below, p. 247, n. 3.

ministers who remained in England. We may state the problem succinctly by asking what were the respective duties of the royal household and the exchequer. Clearly both are working to the same end and their relations must be intimate, but for long periods they are many miles and many days apart.

We have described the chamber in its financial aspect, the aspect in which it came into close contact with the exchequer. Intimately associated with the chamber is the king's chapel, and it is through the clerks of the chapel that the king controls his finances. The clerks of the chapel provide the staff for the chancery, the writing office attached to the king's person, for the preparation and sealing of instruments under the great seal which the chancellor controls. There is, as we have said, another writing office, attached to the justiciar, for the preparation and sealing of instruments (either under the justiciar's seal or under the exchequer seal) required for the more routine purposes of administration and justice in England: but this office, which is the ancestor of the cursitors' office, must be clearly distinguished from the chancery proper.[1] Of the clerks of the chapel at work, we get a number of contemporary glimpses.[2] Gerald the Welshman relates how, after King John had agreed to the terms of letters to be sent to Geoffrey fitz Peter and Hubert Walter regarding the election of a bishop of St. David's, the clerks of the chapel, who were partisans of the archbishop of Canterbury, and the keeper of the seal, who was the archbishop's agent, changed the form by adding a clause that restricted the choice of the chapter.[3] A similar allegation was made in 1189 by a monk of Christ Church, Canterbury. He relates how, after he had interviewed Henry II, it was left to the dean of York (Hubert Walter) to dictate the form of words of an appropriate letter. This letter the monk had sealed. While the letter was thus being prepared for issue, Archbishop Baldwin, then in attendance at court, was informed: he came at once and asked to inspect the letter which had not yet left the chancery (*cancellaria*). He did not go there himself but sent Hubert Walter and Peter of Blois, who broke the seal and showed the letter to the archbishop. He disapproved of its terms and insisted that it should be altered. Thereupon he entered the chamber (*thalamus*) and there added three clauses to the letter. Coming out, he had the revised letter engrossed and sealed in duplicate. He retained one of the duplicates for himself and the other he handed to the monk. These two stories establish (if that were necessary) the identity of the chancery staff with the clerks of the chapel[4] and indicate that the chamber and the chancery were in adjacent apartments. With an ambulatory household—the scene in the one case is Quilleboeuf, in the other Le Mans

---

[1] *Memoranda Roll, 1 John*, Introduction, pp. lxxv-lxxxvi.
[2] Their growing professionalism is indicated by their study of Roman Law, which Peter of Blois deprecated (*Epistolae*, nos. 14, 150).
[3] Gerald the Welshman, *Opera*, iii.302.   [4] *Epistolae Cantuarienses*, pp. 282-3.

—the arrangement of the several departments could not follow a fixed plan, but wherever the household went, the clerks of the chapel and the clerks of the chamber would find themselves in close proximity. It is only in this way that we can explain the numerous entries on the chancery rolls of John which record transactions affecting the chamber. The chancery was issuing, in the interests of Crown creditors and debtors, writs of *liberate*, *allocate* and *computate* to the exchequer, many of the writs being connected directly or indirectly with chamber business. We cannot, however, draw a line to separate the activities of the chamber from the chancery. In a sense, the chancery is the agent of the chamber and acts upon instructions, but all notifications to the exchequer pass through the chancery and do not go direct from the chamber.[1] The chancery, too, is itself a financial department in that it records (and doubtless arranges in large part) the fines made with the king, which constitute a substantial part of the revenue and are in due course notified to the exchequer. Though we obtain details only in the reign of John, it seems clear from incidental references on the pipe rolls that the system was already operating, with full apparatus of writs and rolls, in the latter years of Henry II and, presumably in a more rudimentary form, from the beginning of his reign.[2] It follows, then, that, as we have already endeavoured to make clear, the central organ of finance under the Angevins, as under earlier kings, was not the exchequer but the chamber.

We emphasise the distinction between the household and the exchequer. The doctrine that the staff of the exchequer is 'the staff of the king's household put to financial tasks and slightly influenced by their duties',[3] that the court of the exchequer was constituted 'on the model of the Carolingian household',[4] misconceives what was involved in the institution of the justiciarship. We cite modern authorities, but they do no more than echo some words of Stubbs:

The officers of the Exchequer are the great officers of the household; the justiciar who is the president, the chancellor, the constable, two chamberlains, the marshal, and the treasurer, with such other great and experienced counsellors as the king directs to attend for the public service, and who share with the others the title of Barons of the Exchequer.[5]

Stubbs, in turn, is doing no more than to repeat, and to gloss, the teaching of Richard of Ely in the 'Dialogus de Scaccario'. But even for the twelfth century this conception is manifestly open to the preliminary objection that, since the household followed the king abroad for long periods, the principal officers of the court could not

[1] See the references to chancery rolls in the preceding chapter, pp. 235-6.
[2] *Memoranda Roll, 1 John*, Introduction, pp. xxxii-xxxiii, xxxv.
[3] *Dialogus de Scaccario* (Oxford edition), p. 13.
[4] *Dialogus de Scaccario* (ed. Johnson), p. xxiii.
[5] *Constitutional History*, i.409.

conceivably have been present at the regular sessions of two sedentary exchequers, one in England and one in Normandy, unless indeed
there had been a system of deputies, for which there is, in fact, no
evidence. Nor do we need to probe very deep to disprove the hypothesis that, if the principal officers of the king's household are not
to be found sitting at the exchequer in person, they are represented
by deputies. Admittedly two of the principal officers, the butler and
the steward, are absent. The chamberlains who are present at the
exchequer are in no sense deputies of the master chamberlain.[1] The
justiciar, the king's *alter ego*, cannot be said to be a member of the
king's household: indeed, his functions are quite incompatible with
personal service on the king and, though he is the most important
of all the king's ministers, no place is found for him—and surely for
the most obvious of reasons—in the 'Constitutio Domus Regis'. The
presence of the chancellor, the constable and the marshal, in person
or by representative, is to be explained not on this hypothesis but
by practical, functional, reasons.

Of the chancellor's connexion with the exchequer we must speak
with caution. Even when Richard of Ely was writing the 'Dialogus',
it was little more than a memory. Already in the early years of
Stephen, when the 'Constitutio Domus Regis' was drawn up, the
scriptorium and the king's chapel, though both under the chancellor,
were separately organised.[2] Later in the century, perhaps from the
beginning of Henry II's reign, there are two distinct organisations,
the clerks of the chapel, who follow the king, and the clerks of the
scriptorium who remain in England when the king is abroad.[3] The
leading clerk in the *scriptorium* in 1156 (perhaps earlier) seems to
have been Richard of Ilchester,[4] whose career is bound up with the
exchequer and who has no obvious connexion with the chancery.
Later in the reign we find 'clerici domini regis de scriptorio' acting
as clerks to justices in eyre.[5] The *scriptorium* constitutes, in fact,
though we should not guess it from the 'Constitutio Domus Regis',
the writing office of the justiciar, and the clerks are employed in
executing the many functions that fall upon the justiciar, one of
which is the supervision of itinerant justices. But meanwhile prominent officers of the exchequer and treasury have attached to themselves their own personal clerks, who, however, come to be engaged
on public duties. Thus, by the side of two clerks of the *scriptorium*
who accompany the justices in eyre, we find a clerk of Walter of
Coutances,[6] and in 1189 the clerks of the treasurer and chamber-

---

[1] See Appendix III: below, p. 428.
[2] *Dialogus de Scaccario* (ed. Johnson), p. 129.
[3] *Memoranda Roll, 1 John*, Introduction, pp. lxxv-lxxxvii.
[4] The earliest reference to him as *scriptor curie* appears to be in *Pipe Roll, 2 Henry II*,
p. 30. We doubt whether he was ever *magister scriptorii*: see *Memoranda Roll, 1 John*, Introduction, p. lxxxv.   [5] *Cartularium Rievallense*, p. 66. The date is 1178.
[6] *Ibid.* For Walter's connexion with the exchequer see Richardson, 'William of Ely',
in *Trans. R. Hist. Soc.*, Fourth Series, xv.71.

lains are employed on preparing the writs of summons, a task that had earlier fallen upon the clerks of the *scriptorium*.[1]

The 'Dialogus' implies that the exchequer seal was controlled by the chancellor. Only in his presence was the solemn procedure to be observed for putting that seal into use.[2] If it is not to be said outright that Richard of Ely is giving currency to fictions, his words at least require a liberal interpretation if they are to be reconciled with facts. Who would guess, without the evidence, that, when Richard says that the exchequer seal was only to be used for exchequer business,[3] this phrase would cover a writ summoning the monks of Christ Church, Canterbury, to appear before the justiciar and other justices? Yet so it was, and the writ was described by the recipients as 'littere domini regis de scaccario'.[4] The all-embracing functions of the justiciar inevitably resulted in the development of a staff of clerks independent of the chancellor and the king's chapel. In exercising his functions the justiciar made alternative use of writs in two forms, authenticated by different seals. Normally, as we have already explained, when the king was absent, the justiciar's writs were made out in his own name and sealed with his personal seal, while, when the king was present in the kingdom, the justiciar's writs were made out in the king's name and sealed with the exchequer seal.[5] These alternative forms were merely technical: the same clerical staff and the same administrative processes were employed.[6] But the chancellor could not be held responsible for the justiciar's personal writs or for the justiciar's personal seal, and any responsibility he might be supposed to have for writs in the king's name, sealed with the exchequer seal, was obviously the thinnest of fictions. The desire of the chancellor to dissociate himself from the business of the exchequer is plain from Richard's own words,[7] which make it clear also that the barons of the exchequer were loth to break with a tradition that had become meaningless.

The position of the constable and marshal was quite different from the position of the chancellor. The several alternative ways in which the king could pay his servants meant that there must be links between his chamber, the treasury and the exchequer.[8] Since the expenditure was largely for warfare and to some extent for sport, the constable and marshal were principally concerned. The object of their association with the exchequer was to secure that, from whatever source stipends were paid, there was neither overpayment nor

[1] *Memoranda Roll, 1 John*, Introduction, p. lxxxv.

[2] *Dialogus de Scaccario*, pp. 19, 62.

[3] Hoc enim facte summonitiones et alia, pertinentia dumtaxat ad scaccarium, regis mandata signantur (p. 62).   [4] *Epistolae Cantuarienses*, no. 391: cf. nos. 377 and 378.

[5] *Memoranda Roll, 1 John*, Introduction, pp. lxvi-lxxv; above, p. 163.

[6] *Ibid.*, pp. lxix-lxxi, lxxv-lxxxiv.

[7] 'Et, sicut viris magnis visum est, de omni scriptura rotuli cancellarius eque tenetur ut thesaurarius' (*Dialogus*, p. 19).

[8] There are some illuminating examples of the dangers of double payment in the chamber roll of 1212-3 (Cole, *Documents*, pp. 232, 255).

GME R

underpayment, and it is sufficiently plain from the 'Dialogus' that the functions of the representatives of the constable and marshal lay in ensuring proper financial control.[1] This seems to explain their presence quite adequately without resorting to the hypothesis that the court of the exchequer was modelled, consciously or unconsciously, upon Carolingian precedents.

This model is admittedly an inexact one, since it has to be supposed that the justiciar (an officer unknown to the Carolingians) can be equated with the steward. The functions of the twelfth-century justiciar have, however, not a great deal in common with those of the ancient steward, who is, in fact, still found in the household in his historical capacity.[2] It is true that in Normandy the seneschal and justiciar were identical,[3] but no one has suggested that in Normandy the court of the exchequer was modelled upon the Carolingian household. Yet the one exchequer cannot be explained in terms that will not apply to the other. We possess a good many lists of the barons (or justices) constituting the court of the exchequer both in England and Normandy in the twelfth century,[4] and other lists can be compiled of those who appear from the pipe rolls to have enjoyed the 'libertas sedendi ad scaccarium'. Not only do the lists bear little relation to the king's or duke's household but they have no striking similarity to the court as described in the 'Dialogus'.[5] Doubtless the personnel varied according to the importance of the occasion, the other occupations of the members and the nature of the business. A court, composed as Richard of Ely describes it, was presumably intended to deal with financial business. Is this court a traditional adaptation of the king's household or are the particular arrangements he describes quite a recent innovation? Richard of Ilchester and Master Thomas Brown, who cannot by any stretch of language be described as officers of the household, have a place at the exchequer; but clearly they do not owe their seats there to the force of precedent or tradition: they are there solely because the king has so ordered.[6] It may be objected, therefore, that we should disregard these newcomers and any other changes that may have been introduced under Henry II and go back to the early

[1] Dialogus, pp. 19, 20. The marshal seems to have acquired certain additional duties, which may not have been his primitively.

[2] It is significant, as we explain in a later chapter, that when, from 1234 onwards, the King's Bench is separated formally and finally from the Common Bench, the stewards of the household are judges of the former court and do not sit as judges of the latter court which is the descendant of the justiciar's court at the exchequer.

[3] Above, p. 176.

[4] Besides those given below, others will be found in final concords levied in the king's court at the exchequer, references to a number of which will be found in Memoranda Roll, 1 John, Introduction, p. xiv, n. 1.

[5] Perhaps the one obvious exception is the earliest notice of the exchequer in Normandy, where we find sitting as a judicial tribunal a seneschal, two constables, a chamberlain, a marshal, the treasurer and two other clerks; but the same document shows that the court had been differently constituted on a previous occasion (Haskins, Norman Institutions, pp. 88-9). The date is about 1130.

[6] As Richard of Ely himself states (Dialogus de Scaccario, pp. 17-18).

years of the century when presumably the court will more nearly reflect primitive conditions. What, however, do we find then? When we look at two lists that have come down to us from the reign of Henry I, the composition of the court does not seem to bear the impress of the household. In 1119, the four members named are the justiciar, the bishop of Lincoln (Robert Bloet), the chancellor and Ralf Basset,[1] all four *justitiarii totius Anglie*.[2] In the court held in the treasury at Winchester eight years or so earlier, of these four three are present, while the chancellor is presumably abroad with the king: among the rest of the fifteen members we can distinguish the treasurer (Herbert the chamberlain), but none other of the officers whom Richard of Ely would have at a session of the exchequer.[3] Apart from the treasurer, no leading members of the household are present, though there seem to be some inferior members of the steward's department, a sewer and a larderer.[4] Yet upon both occasions the business of the court is financial, such as Richard had in mind. It is probable that only on the occasion of a great council, such as that at Northampton on 8 September 1131, would there assemble all the ministers who, if Richard of Ely's ideal were realised, would constitute the court of the exchequer. Here we find the justiciar, the chancellor, the keeper of the seal (the head of the *scriptorium*), Nigel, nephew of the bishop of Salisbury (the treasurer, though he is not so designated), Geoffrey de Clinton and William de Pont de l'Arche (the chamberlains, also without designation). A constable is certainly there also in the person of Miles of Gloucester,[5] though if John the marshal were present at the council, as is likely, this humble officer[6] is not noticed as a witness to any surviving charter that may be attributed to this date and place.[7] We may reasonably conclude that all the allegedly constituent members were present, but we may with equal reason conclude that it was not the occasion of a session of the court of the exchequer.

If we cannot find any corroboration for Richard of Ely's description of a session at the exchequer in the records of Henry I, he is no better corroborated by the records of Henry II and Richard I. Let us take as examples some documents of a date a few years after the 'Dialogus de Scaccario' had been revised, when, if at any time, we should expect his teaching to be exemplified. When we look at a list of barons of the exchequer in 1193, while we shall find the justiciar,

---

[1] *Chronicon Mon. de Abingdon*, ii.160; *E.H.R.*, xliii.329.
[2] Above, p. 176.   [3] *Dialogus*, pp. 15-18.
[4] *Chronicon Mon. de Abingdon*, ii.116; *Regesta*, no. 1000. The sewer is William de Curci and the larderer William de Enesi; see Farrer, *Itinerary of Henry I*, p. 69, no. 323.
[5] Round, *The King's Serjeants*, p. 79.
[6] *Complete Peerage*, x, App. G, 'The rise of the Marshal'; *Dialogus de Scaccario*, pp. xxx-xxxiii, li.
[7] The fullest list of witnesses is in the dated charter relating to the church of Malmesbury in favour of the bishop of Salisbury, who is therefore not a witness (*Sarum Charters*, pp. 6-7, no. 6). For other charters, see Farrer, *Itinerary of Henry I*, pp. 139-41, and *Regesta*, nos. 1712-6.

John the marshal and William Mauduit the chamberlain, of the rest two are regularly employed justices, Roger fitz Renfrey and Osbert fitz Hervey, and two are administrators with a variety of employments, Henry of Cornhill and Otho fitz William.[1] A longer list comes from 1191 with twenty names, three of them subordinate clerks, whom we can ignore. Among the seventeen there is the chancellor, but only because he is also the justiciar, William Longchamp. The treasurer too is there, Richard of Ely himself, now bishop of London, as well as John Marshal and William Mauduit. This appears to be the extent of the correspondence between the list and the list of barons of the exchequer we should expect on the testimony of the 'Dialogus'. Of the rest, seven appear as justices in a fine of the same date. We may add that the justiciar and the treasurer also appear as justices in the fine.[2] There is therefore a large common element in the personnel of the court of the exchequer in its financial aspect and in its judicial aspect or, to put it another way, between the barons of the exchequer and the justices of the bench. This is no new phenomenon, but seems to be true also of the reign of Henry I. It is this element that Richard of Ely ignores, while at the same time he exaggerates the part played by officers of the household. If we were asked what motive the treasurer could have had in misrepresenting the facts in a dialogue devised for the instruction of the junior staff of the exchequer to whom the truth would soon become known, we could give no answer better than a guess. But we should assert that the evidence of contemporary records is to be preferred to his and that, when his statements are tested in this way, it is by no means unusual to find them wanting.[3]

Let us end by emphasising that the exchequer is no emanation of the royal household. True, at the beginning of the twelfth century the treasurer is still a member of the household, but at the end of the century the treasury is a constituent of the exchequer; yet the process of its absorption has been lengthy and gradual. To begin with, the exchequer is quite distinct from the treasury: it is, as we have shown, the justiciar's court, a sedentary court, not a court of the ambulatory household. In this lies the explanation of the large judicial element, the element that Richard of Ely and later commentators have ignored.

[1] *Law Quarterly Review*, xlviii.422. The document is misdated 1191.
[2] *Ibid.*, pp. 421-3.
[3] E.g. on blanch ferm, on the sheriff's ferm, on assay, on the escort for treasure in transit, on entries of remission on the pipe rolls: see Round, *Commune of London*, pp. 64-73, *Dialogus de Scaccario* (Oxford edition), pp. 28-31, *Trans. R. Hist. Soc.*, 4th Ser., xv.68-79, *E.H.R.*, xliii.330-1.

XIV

DUKE AND KING

THE history of the concluding, as of the earlier, years of Stephen's reign will not be satisfactorily told until his writs and charters, and not only his but those of the Empress and Duke Henry, have been collected and methodised. But while the situation in England in 1153 and 1154 is, on many points of detail, still obscure, it does not require undue research in order to be satisfied that Henry had little interest in resolving the administrative confusion that overhung the country, even after the peace of Winchester in November 1153. The view still current that, once peace was concluded, the way was paved for the smooth and almost painless accession of Henry II to the throne is illusory. It seems to be assumed that Stephen's disappearance within the year was ineluctable, almost part of a plan. If, indeed, there was a plan, it miscarried, for the contest between Stephen and Henry did not end at Winchester. But, to make the position intelligible, we must first clear away a misapprehension of Stubbs's which has coloured the views of more recent historians.[1] He believed, on the strength of a passage incorporated by Ralf de Diceto in his *Imagines Historiarum*,[2] that, as part of the settlement between Stephen and Henry, there had been drawn up an elaborate 'scheme of reform', and he regarded it as 'extremely unfortunate that the exact means by which it was to be carried into execution are not recorded'.[3] But this 'scheme of reform' seems to be no more than the imaginings of an anonymous writer, who has transposed to the year before Henry's accession the work he actually performed after he became king. Appropriately enough, the writer pointed the moral with borrowings from the prophecies of Merlin.[4] We can be reasonably sure of no more than that there was an agreement that any who had been violently disseised on either side should be restored to their possessions and that adulterine castles should be destroyed, though, when it came to implementing the agreement, the king and duke, not unnaturally, differed on which

---

[1] Norgate, *England under the Angevin Kings*, i.400-3; Ramsay, *Foundations of England*, ii.451-3; Adams, *History of England, 1066-1216*, pp. 251-3; Davis, *England under the Normans and Angevins*, pp. 179-80. Mr A. L. Poole appears silently to reject Stubbs's teaching (*From Domesday Book to Magna Carta*, pp. 165-6).

[2] Ralf de Diceto, *Opera*, i.296.　　　　　　　[3] *Constitutional History*, i.360-1.

[4] Stubbs's note to Diceto shows that he himself later regarded the passage with suspicion. The source from which Diceto drew was available to Matthew Paris, who incorporated more of the text (*Chronica Maiora*, ii.191-2).

castles should be left standing and which dismantled.[1] Of co-operation between king and duke in restoring order—beyond what has been temerariously inferred from the treaty of Winchester itself—there appears to be no more evidence than this dissension over adulterine castles; and this evidence points the same way as all our other evidence does, not to mutual trust and common enterprise between erstwhile rivals, but to enduring dislike, mutual suspicion and active opposition, scarcely veiled for a few months. It may be a fair interpretation of the terms of the treaty of Winchester that the parties agreed to Henry's acting as 'Stephen's collaborator',[2] but this, in fact, he never was. The practical consequences of the treaty are depicted sufficiently accurately for us, not by the obviously ill-informed chroniclers,[3] but by the duke's own *acta*.

Let us ask, however, what were the antecedents of the peace of Winchester, for a knowledge of these is essential to an understanding of the treaty itself. In the late summer of 1153 the war was at its height. Henry had besieged Bedford, where the burgesses were inflexibly opposed to him, and, failing to take the castle, he had left the town and its two churches in ashes.[4] The date we cannot fix with precision. It has been suggested that from Bedford the duke moved on to Wallingford, where, in face of the reluctance of many on both sides to continue the fighting, he entered into a truce with the king.[5] Such an order of events seems highly improbable, but, in any case, it is clear that the failure at Bedford took place before 31 August when Henry was 'at the siege of Stamford'.[6] Thence he seems to have proceeded to Nottingham, presumably early in September, but was forced to retire from the siege because the defenders of the castle fired the town.[7] Meanwhile, so we are told by the chroniclers, Archbishop Theobald and Bishop Henry of Winchester had begun their

---

[1] John of Hexham in Simeon of Durham, *Opera*, ii.331; Henry of Huntingdon, *Historia*, pp. 289-90; Robert de Torigni in *Chronicles of Stephen etc.*, p. 177; Gervase of Canterbury, *Historical Works*, i.156-8. The number of adulterine castles given by both Robert of Torigni and Ralf de Diceto as 1115 is, of course, quite impossible.

[2] Poole, *op. cit.*, p. 166.

[3] It is impossible to reconcile the discrepant statements of Henry of Huntingdon, the *Gesta Stephani*, John of Hexham, Robert of Torigni and Gervase of Canterbury, either between themselves or with documentary sources.

[4] *Curia Regis Rolls*, xii.513; *Gesta Stephani* (ed. Potter), p. 155; Newnham Priory Cartulary (Harleian MS. 3656), fo. 27. The burgesses were still opposed to Henry after his accession, and they were fined 20 marks, 'quia fuerunt in castello contra regem' (*Pipe Roll, 4 Henry II*, p. 139). On one or other of these occasions Henry was struck by a stone cast from the castle (*Curia Regis Rolls*, iv.270).

[5] Potter in Introduction to *Gesta Stephani*, pp. xxiv-xxviii. This suggestion is in direct conflict with the text, p. 155, where it is stated that Henry went straight from Bedford to Stamford. It seems more probable that, though the *Gesta Stephani* does not mention the abortive siege of Nottingham, the writer is correct in placing the truce immediately before the negotiations for peace. If this were not so, it would seem that Henry broke the truce.

[6] *Lincoln Registrum Antiquissimum*, i.96-7 (no. 150); Delisle-Berger, *Actes de Henri II*, no. 60*.

[7] Henry of Huntingdon, p. 288; Robert of Torigni, p. 174; William of Newburgh in *Chronicles of Stephen etc.*, i.89. Is it possible that the repulse from Nottingham took place before the siege of Stamford?

efforts to bring the contending parties to terms.[1] They, or at least
the archbishop, succeeded in arranging a meeting between Stephen's
heir, William earl of Warenne, and Duke Henry, at which there were
present Theobald himself and the leading royalist barons. This
meeting, for which we have the evidence of an eyewitness, presumably took place in October.[2] Here agreement was reached, at
least in broad outline, for a *dies pacis et concordie* was arranged, which
must doubtless be 6 November at Winchester. The fact that the
principal negotiator on the king's side was his son William—who was
not only earl of Warenne in right of his wife, but had succeeded to
the *comté* of Boulogne on the death of his brother Eustace (mid-
August[3])—explains why 'the terms secured by the young count of
Boulogne occupied a very large place in the treaty between Stephen
and Henry'.[4] It is worthy of remark that William can have been
barely of age, if so old, at the time, although he had been married
for six years or so.[5] His precocity can have been scarcely inferior to
that of the young duke. It would be astonishing if Stephen had
trusted him to negotiate with Henry, and it may well be that the
king had not, in fact, assented to these preliminary negotiations.[6]
However that may be, Stephen must have approved their outcome
and seems evidently to have assumed this position, that if his right
to the crown were recognised during his lifetime, his heir could make
what terms he chose. These terms were doubtless the result of hard
bargaining. We may be sure that it was only because he was in no
position to drive a better bargain that Henry agreed to terms which
made William (again to use Round's words) 'too powerful for
Henry's safety as a king'.[7] Henry was even believed to have added
to the undertakings in the formal treaty a promise that William
should have the deciding voice in the affairs of the kingdom—*princi-
patus super negotia regni*.[8] It may be so. Henry was not the man to
stint promises when in difficulties, and Henry's difficulties were
pressing. Whatever his prospects, his present resources were small,[9]

[1] Henry of Huntingdon, p. 289; John of Hexham, p. 331. Theobald, however, had
been with Henry at 'the ford of Stockbridge' on 9 April, as had also been the bishop of
Winchester and other bishops (*Sarum Charters*, p. 22). Later Theobald was with Henry at
the siege of Crowmarsh (*Lincoln Registrum Antiquissimum*, i.97-8, no. 151), that is, in the
operations based upon Wallingford.

[2] William de Vere, 'Liber de Miraculis sanctae Osithae', in Leland, *Itinerary* (ed.
Toulmin-Smith), v.171.

[3] Robert de Torigni, p.176.

[4] Round, *Peerage and Family History*, p. 169.

[5] Clay, *Early Yorkshire Charters*, viii.14-15.

[6] Stephen could hardly have been ignorant of the archbishop's association with the
duke, and he must have regarded Theobald's attitude as ambiguous, if not positively
hostile.

[7] Round, *op. cit.*, p. 170.

[8] John of Hexham in Simeon of Durham, *Opera*, ii.331. This narrative is quite unreliable: in particular, the part ascribed to Bishop Henry of Winchester is unhistorical.

[9] The slenderness of the forces Henry brought with him to England is a matter of
comment by Henry of Huntingdon, *Historia Anglorum*, p. 285. The author of the *Gesta
Stephani*, pp. 152-3, puts the matter differently, to the effect that Henry brought a body of
foreign mercenaries with him, most of whom had to be sent back.

he was fighting with borrowed money,[1] he had suffered more than one military reverse,[2] and his presence in France was soon to be urgently needed.[3] Though his campaign—in sober fact confused and scattered skirmishes, sieges, burnings and ravagings—has been hailed by modern historians as a 'triumphal progress', Henry himself knew better. At the end of August, lying before Stamford, he was contemplating failure. He had been followed thither by the canons of St. Paul's, Bedford, whose church and houses he had destroyed, and he readily promised compensation; but he had nothing tangible to give. The canons were not satisfied with the promise of the haw-gafol of Bedford,[4] which was not the duke's to bestow, or of land that belonged to another,[5] and he was forced to offer them compensation in country under his own control (*in pace mea*), if he could not redeem his promise. But Henry added that if, by God's will, he should make good his just claim to England, he would augment the endowments of the church. This is hardly the language of a triumphant conqueror with the prize within his grasp, and the charter the canons received[6] could not have brought them much comfort. They may have guessed—it did not demand great powers of divination—that Henry was prepared to promise anything to buy off importunate demands. We can, however, acquit him of any intention of abiding by these or any other engagements[7] that might prove inconvenient, if he could possibly avoid doing so. Certainly he did not honour his obligations.

Let us have no illusions about Henry's attitude and intentions at this period. Let not the glamour of the great king he proved to be cast a golden light over the young and unscrupulous duke of Normandy, struggling passionately, and perhaps desperately, for his lawful inheritance. From beginning to end Henry was fighting for his own hand. He gave up nothing and he asserted his claim to as much as he could. He had no hesitation in disposing of the rights of the Crown. For example, at some time early in 1153 he confirmed to the canons of St. Augustine's, Bristol, all lands and revenues pertaining to the Crown of England which he or any other had granted or should in future grant to them.[8] About the same time he granted the stewardship of England and Normandy to the son and heir of

---

[1] As shown by his indebtedness to William Cade, William Trentegeruns and other money-lenders (Richardson, *English Jewry*, pp. 50-5).
[2] His failure at Nottingham marks the end of the 'triumphal progress' with which Mr Poole credits him (*op. cit.*, p. 164).
[3] See especially Robert de Torigni, pp. 179-81.
[4] Sciatis me dedisse . . . hagaflam Bedefordie, i.e. the house-dues of Bedford.
[5] Selam (i.e. a field called La Sele) . . . si eam de Petro de Goldintona deliberare potero.
[6] B.M., Harleian MS. 3656, fo. 27.
[7] The pipe rolls do not show any reduction of the ferm of the county in respect of endowments given to Bedford Priory or its successor, Newnham Priory, nor does there seem to be any indication of royal grants in the cartulary, Harleian MS. 3656. See also the charters in *Monasticon*, vi.374.
[8] *Ibid.*, vi.366; *Actes de Henri II*, no. 49*.

the earl of Leicester.[1] In another charter, apparently of June or July 1153, Henry speaks of 'my forest of Cannock'.[2] And although by the terms of the peace Henry had assented to Stephen's exercising sovereignty (*regalis iustitia*) throughout the whole kingdom, both in the duke's portion and the king's portion,[3] there is no indication that Henry's attitude was modified in any way. It is difficult to give a precise date to most of his charters of this period, but one that can be confidently ascribed to January 1154 is significant. This charter, in favour of the monks of Meaux, follows *literatim* (except in the formal clauses adapted to Henry's titles, parentage and witnesses) the charter given to the monks by Stephen, apparently at a few days' interval. The king confirms to the monks their endowments quit and free from danegeld, murder-fines, and all other gelds and secular services and demands: the duke does the same. The king refers to the monks' benefactors as 'my barons': the duke also refers to them as 'my barons'. The duke makes no allusion to the king: the charter would not read differently if he were exercising absolute sovereignty.[4] A charter a little later in date grants to the monks of Bermondsey 100 shillings charged on Edredeshithe (the future Queenhithe) in London and forty shillings on the farm of Southwark 'que pertinent ad coronam regis'.[5] It is said by Gervase of Canterbury that Stephen ordered Henry to be proclaimed lord of England.[6] This is doubtless a misapprehension by a chronicler writing long after the event. We have, however, the authority of Earl Reginald of Cornwall, Henry's representative in England, that the duke claimed the title of *dominus terre* much earlier than the treaty of Winchester.[7] Here is a complete explanation of the duke's grants: he was exercising a sovereignty to which he claimed to be entitled without waiting for the ceremony of coronation. His treaty with the king led to no modification of his claim. It thus becomes impossible to reconcile his charters issued after the conclusion of peace with the interpretation placed by Stubbs and his followers on the treaty of Winchester.

The duke returned to Normandy before Easter (4 April 1154)[8] and his charters continued to be expressed in the same strain as hitherto. He directs that, out of the farm of Winchester, the monks of Tiron are to receive payment of a sum of fifteen marks granted by Henry I, together with an augmentation of five marks granted by the Empress.[9] Now while it might be objected that it is just possible that

---

[1] *Ibid.*, no. 47*. Later the duke repeated the grant to the earl himself. This was after he had assumed the title of duke of Aquitaine; but the charter, which is imperfect, cannot be precisely dated (Harcourt, *His Grace the Steward*, pp. 58-9).

[2] *Actes de Henri II*, no. 63*. [3] *Foedera*, i.18.

[4] Farrer, *Early Yorkshire Charters*, iii, nos. 1385, 1386.

[5] *Cal. Charter Rolls*, iv.185. In dating the duke's charters we have been guided by the suggestions and conclusions of Z. N. and C. N. L. Brooke in *E.H.R.*, lxi.86-8.

[6] *Opera Historica* (ed. Stubbs), i.156: dominumque totius Anglie predicari eum precepit.

[7] *Sarum Charters*, pp. 23-4, no. 26: si dominus meus Henricus terre dominus preceperit. This is dated 21 June 1152, but 1153 seems to be intended.

[8] *E.H.R.*, lxi.87. [9] *Actes de Henri II*, no. 72*.

this charter was given after the death of Stephen and before Henry had crossed to England for his coronation,[1] no such objection can be made in the case of the writ which we next adduce and which it is well to cite in full,[2] for its whole tenor and, in particular, the final sentence seem incompatible with the attitude of one who was the indisputable lord of England and was shortly to be crowned king.

Henry, duke of the Normans and of the men of Aquitaine and count of the Angevins, to Reginald the abbot and to the whole convent of Reading, greeting and affection. I command and order you, as you value my regard and have confidence in me, that you hold stable and unshaken the arrangement that was made by me and before me concerning the church of Berkeley; and Earl Reginald, who is my lieutenant in England for this and other affairs of mine, will assign to your church in perpetual alms the fifteen librates of land which I have undertaken to give you and which are to be taken from my demesne. Therefore at a term which he will appoint to you, setting aside all hindrances, you are to come to him and receive that land; and whatever he shall do for you I will hold firm and stable. And I should have assigned the land to you long ago, had I not been impeded by many and heavy affairs. These are the witnesses: Reginald earl of Cornwall and Robert of Dénestanville. At Eu.

Especially to be noted is the statement that Henry would long since have dealt with the matter, if he had not been impeded, for this implies that he would have taken action, involving the alienation of part of the demesne of the Crown, when he was at best a claimant to the throne. From his standpoint, the treaty of Winchester had made no difference to his status: before and after he was lord of England. The writ implies also that Duke Henry's pretensions were not everywhere respected or his commands readily obeyed, and perhaps some further words of explanation may be desirable. The abbot of Reading to whom the writ was addressed, Reginald by name, had recently been elected in place of Abbot William who seems to have been an adherent of Henry's.[3] Reginald had been keeper of King Stephen's seal before he entered religion and, doubtless with the king's backing, had risen rapidly to be prior and then abbot. Henry soon came to object to Reginald's presence at the head

---

[1] It will be noted that Henry does not style himself *dominus Anglorum*, and no writ in which he does so has yet come to light.

[2] B.M. Egerton MS. 3031, fo. 26.

Henricus dux Normannorum et Aquitanorum et comes Andegauorum Reginaldo abbati Radingie et toti conuentui, salutem et dilectionem. Mando vobis et precipio quatinus, sicut amorem meum diligetis et sicut in me confidere vultis, compositionem que per me et coram me facta fuit super ecclesia de Berkeleia ratam et inconcussam teneatis. Comes enim Reginaldus qui in hoc et in aliis negociis meis locum meum tenet in Anglia xv. libratas terre, quas vobis dare pepigi, vobis assignabit ecclesie vestre in perpetuam elemosinam obtinendas de dominio videlicet meo. Vos autem in termino quem ipse vobis constituerit ad eum veniatis et terram illam omni occasione remota recipiatis. Ego vero ratum et firmum habebo quod ipse vobis faciet. Et iam diu terram illam vobis assignassem si negociis magnis et multis impeditus non fuissem. Testibus Reginaldo comite Cornubie et Roberto de Dunstanuilla. Apud Augem.

[3] Abbot William witnesses the duke's charter (*Actes de Henri II*, no. 73*), which we date June or July 1153.

of a royal abbey and within four years of his accession to the throne he secured the abbot's deposition.[1] The writ certainly suggests that, while Stephen was king, Abbot Reginald was reluctant to fall in with Duke Henry's wishes and this would not lessen the disfavour with which he regarded those closely connected with Stephen.[2]

If the date of this writ is what it seems to be, that is between Henry's departure from England late in March or early in April 1154 and Stephen's death on 25 October, then, upon this evidence alone, we should conclude that the duke maintained an administration independent of the king's. But we have other evidence of this. In particular, he had a treasury with officers to administer it. We can name the treasurer and a chamberlain of the treasury he appointed. If there was a second chamberlain of the treasury at this period, positive evidence has not been found, though there are indications that the second post may have been in existence. The treasurer was Henry, son of Robert fitz Harding, who was already acting in that capacity before Duke Henry assumed the title of duke of Aquitaine in the spring of 1153 and who continued to act thereafter.[3] The chamberlain (or one of the chamberlains) of the duke's treasury was William Mauduit, who may well have been acting earlier than the date of the charter granting him the chamberlainship of 'my treasury', which seems to have been issued at Whitsuntide 1153.[4] Plainly Henry the treasurer was not the king's treasurer nor was William Mauduit the chamberlain of the king's treasury. Duke Henry had his own financial organisation, centred perhaps at Bristol, while King Stephen obviously controlled the ancient royal financial organisation, still centred presumably at Winchester. When, therefore, we find Earl Patrick of Salisbury accounting in the Michaelmas term 1155 for a small balance due for the ferm of Wiltshire in 1153,[5] we should not take this as evidence that he had accounted at King Stephen's exchequer. Earl Patrick was Duke Henry's man,[6] and if he had paid his ferm anywhere he had paid it into the duke's treasury. What is of interest is that the accounts kept by the duke's treasurer were plainly at the disposal of the barons of

[1] For Reginald's early career see the Walden Chronicle lib. i, cap. 14. His deposition is noted in the *Flores Historiarum*, ii.75.

[2] Henry did provide Reginald with compensation of a sort, for he gave, or secured for, him the priory of Walden; but this was at the time a new and miserably poor foundation.

[3] Historical MSS. Commission, *Fourth Report*, App., p. 364; *Berkeley Charters*, no. 2; *Cal. Charter Rolls*, iii.377-8 (where Henry's style has been interpolated, as will be seen by Stephen's confirmation which follows).

[4] Warin fitz Gerold may have been acting with him. But there is no positive evidence that Warin, though a chamberlain, was chamberlain of the treasury before Henry's accession to the throne. For the whole question see Appendix III: below, p. 436.

[5] *Pipe Roll, 2 Henry II*, p. 56. Cf. G. J. Turner, 'The Sheriff's Farm' in *Trans. R. Hist. Soc.*, New Ser. (1898), xii.127, where, however, he suggests that this is evidence for the existence of pipe rolls in the later years of Stephen. We are in no doubt that rolls of accounts were kept on Stephen's behalf, but not in the ordered tradition of Henry I's exchequer.

[6] He was with Henry throughout 1153, though he had previously acted as sheriff of Wilts. under Stephen (*Complete Peerage*, xi.376).

King Henry's exchequer when they became responsible once again for the whole country. How they set to work we shall see later.

The confusion into which the country's finances had been plunged is strikingly illustrated by the first pipe roll of Henry II's reign, and the facts disclosed should, of themselves, dispose of any idea that there had been an ordered scheme of reform, with Stephen and Henry working in collaboration in pursuance of the terms of the treaty of peace.

Normally a pipe roll should relate to the accounts and revenues of the preceding twelve months, and since this roll was made up as at Michaelmas 1155, it would, if it were a normal roll, show the receipts for the last twenty-six days of Stephen's reign, for the fifty-four days during which Henry was lord, but not king, of England, and for the nine months and a few days between Henry's coronation and Michaelmas.[1] It has, indeed, been asserted that the pipe roll covers these three periods,[2] but in fact it is far from doing so. If we compare this roll with the roll for the following year, we shall find that no account at all was rendered for five counties, Bedford, Buckingham, Hampshire, Rutland and Warwick.[3] For Cambridge and Shropshire, there was an account for three months only[4]; for Huntingdon, London and Suffolk for half the year[5]; for Gloucestershire, Herefordshire, Kent and Sussex for three-quarters of the year.[6] It is doubtful whether all the sheriffs of the remaining counties accounted for the full twelve months. Even so, there is evidence from the accounts that revenues which should have accrued to the Crown had been diverted. Thus, for the first quarter of the year the borough of Northampton had paid its farm to Earl Simon and he had obtained a further £11 15s. that should have gone to the farm of the county.[7] We may guess that some of the deficiencies elsewhere had been similarly diverted.[8] What is evident is that, with few exceptions, no account of these deficiencies was ever rendered at the exchequer. Richard du Hommet is charged with the farm of Rutland on the pipe roll of 1158,[9] and account is rendered in 1161 for the half-year's farm of London from Michaelmas 1154 to Easter 1155,[10] but regarding the other missing payments, the later pipe rolls are silent.

If we were to plot upon a map the counties for which a full year's

---

[1] Precisely, in fact, as *Pipe Roll, 1 Richard I*, is made up.

[2] Poole, *From Domesday Book to Magna Carta*, p. 156.

[3] It should perhaps be remarked that there is no reason to suppose that anything has been lost by mutilation. That the roll, when abstracted, was complete is implied by the entry in *Red Book of the Exchequer*, ii.658, at the end of the extracts: Et terminatur hic annus regis Henrici primus, quoniam de aliis comitatibus, qui hic non annotantur, hoc anno non audiebantur compoti.   [4] *Ibid.*, pp. 653, 655.

[5] *Ibid.*, pp. 652, 653, 658.   [6] *Ibid.*, pp. 648, 650, 654.   [7] *Ibid.*, p. 655.

[8] The earl of Chester is alleged to have diverted money due to the king (*Gesta Stephani*, p. 128).

[9] *Pipe Roll, 4 Henry II*, p. 136: the 'firma quarti anni' is, of course, the farm of the fourth year previous to the account.   [10] *Pipe Roll, 7 Henry II*, p. 17.

account was rendered and those for which either an account for some fraction of the year or no account at all was rendered, we should get no recognisable pattern, no clear geographical division. We could not draw a line and deduce that on one side of it there had been continuity of administration and on the other side discontinuity. It is clear that Henry's adherents had had control of some counties since Michaelmas 1154, Geoffrey Abbot in Leicestershire, Earl Patrick in Wiltshire, William Cumin in Worcestershire, all of whom accounted for a full year.[1] But for Gloucestershire, for example, which presumably Henry had for long controlled, the sheriff, Osbert of Westbury, accounts only from Christmas; and similarly Maurice, the sheriff of Hereford, accounts *post coronationem regis*, that is, strictly, from 20 December.[2] On the other side, however, Richard de Lucy and William Martel, the late king's most faithful adherents, account in full for Essex and Surrey,[3] which they had doubtless been administering under Stephen, and so perhaps may (though the case is doubtful) Henry of Oxford who had been Stephen's sheriff of Oxfordshire.[4] It is impossible to explain, except quite conjecturally, the circumstances in each county that determined the period for which it was possible to obtain payments for the benefit of the treasury or the reasons why, for varying periods, recovery was abandoned. We must conclude that Henry began to appoint sheriffs upon his coronation and that he gradually established his authority during the next nine months. At Michaelmas 1155 a number of changes and new appointments were made. Of the sheriffs who were continued in office, Richard of Raddon (Dorset), Richard de Lucy (Essex), Jordan of Blosseville (Lincolnshire), Robert of Stafford (Stafford), William Martel (Surrey) and Earl Patrick (Wiltshire) accounted from Michaelmas 1154; Ralf Picot (Kent) and Bertram of Bulmer (Yorkshire) accounted from Christmas; Pain the sheriff accounted from Easter 1155 for Huntingdon and from Midsummer for Cambridge; William fitz Alan accounted for Shropshire also from Midsummer; while Richard de Reviers accounted for Devon from an uncertain date. Of some of those who were not continued in office, it is difficult to believe that they were strictly speaking sheriffs at all. They were rather men put in temporary charge of counties to meet an emergency, men such as the bishop of Chichester, who accounted for Sussex from Christmas 1154 to Michaelmas 1155, or Earl Hugh Bigod who accounted for Norfolk and Suffolk, apparently for half a year.[5] It was long ago

---

[1] *Red Book of the Exchequer*, ii.649. In 1156 Earl Patrick accounted for a balance due in respect of the 'firma de Wiltescira tercii anni', that is for the year ended Michaelmas 1154 (*Pipe Roll, 2 Henry II*, p. 56).

[2] *Ibid.*, pp. 650, 655, 656. [3] *Ibid.*, pp. 650, 654.

[4] *Ibid.*, p. 657. For his tenure of office under Stephen, see *Chronicon Mon. de Abingdon*, ii.184.

[5] All these particulars are from the *Red Book of the Exchequer*, pp. 648-58, and *Pipe Roll, 2 Henry II*.

remarked, we may add, that the early pipe rolls of Henry II are compiled with what, in later years, would have been regarded as extreme carelessness; that gradually, year by year, they show greater care and accuracy; that they exhibit the staff of the exchequer as, to begin with, in a state of inexperience, confusion and disorganisation; that they suggest that the energies of the king's ministers were directed to the discovery of his rights and the recovery of his revenue rather than to the niceties of accounting.[1] But whatever interpretation we may put upon the dry facts contained in the pipe rolls, recorded without bias or ulterior purpose, it cannot be consistent with orderly administration in the last years of Stephen's reign or with an orderly transfer of power to Henry II.

Stephen's early death came opportunely for Henry. Had the conditions that followed the abortive peace of Winchester continued for some years—the usurpation by Henry of royal power, the rival administrations, the simmering hostility, the infinite possibilities of open conflict—all hope of compromise would have vanished. The authors of the treaty themselves foresaw this consequence. As its language testifies, no man supposed that faith would be kept without the giving of hostages or the coercion of the Church. The treaty provided for the likely contingency—there is not even a facile *quod absit*—that the duke would recede from his engagements: then, it is agreed, his earls and barons were to withdraw from his service until he should mend his ways. By the same rule (*simili lege*), the king's earls and barons were to withdraw from his service if he should recede from his engagements.[2] The treaty is eloquent of its own fragility. But however lightly Henry regarded his obligations and however dubious the validity of the treaty might be ten months after its ratification, there was no reason why the king's barons should prefer the count of Boulogne to the duke of Normandy, if it came to a choice between them. The rule of primogeniture did not yet apply to succession to the throne, the count's claims were no stronger than the duke's, and there can be no reasonable doubt that the duke had come to an understanding not only with Robert earl of Leicester, who had forthwith deserted to his side,[3] but with such leading figures in the royal administration as Richard de Lucy (who appears to have been justiciar) and William Martel.[4] And though Henry had little scruple in breaking his engagements, the acquiescence in his claims by men such as these was of the utmost importance

---

[1] G. J. Turner, *op. cit.*, pp. 128-30. We have ventured to modify some of Mr Turner's phrases.

[2] The text of the treaty in *Foedera*, i.18, can be checked on some points by the earlier (imperfect) copy in Historical MSS. Commission, *Twelfth Report*, Appendix, part ix, pp. 119-21.

[3] For the prospective grant of the stewardship see above, p. 255, n. 1. For the earl's presence with the duke in Normandy in October 1154, see *Actes de Henri II*, no. 80*.

[4] These two must have been among the king's barons who met Henry at Colchester; they both subscribed to the treaty of Winchester; and the shires they administered under Stephen were transferred without a hitch to the new administration.

to him. It was therefore as much to his interest to keep faith with them as it was to theirs to secure their position under the new king. As for Stephen's heir, we may make Round's judgement our own: 'it might well seem better to the young count of Boulogne . . . to have these estates [his inheritance, his wife's lands and his father's grants] secured to him by Henry of Anjou than to claim a contested crown'.[1] It is true that the duke met with some resistance after his accession, but it was sporadic, at isolated centres,[2] and there is no reason to suppose that the count was a party to it. In any case his early death, in 1159, removed any threat to the new king from that quarter. Even so, Henry had had time to go back upon his solemn undertakings towards the count.

Henry's treatment of the count was not an isolated incident. Count William was forced to surrender 'Pevensey and Norwich and whatever he held of the Crown and all his own castles both in Normandy and in England'[3]; but so also were many other men required to surrender such parts of the ancient demesne of the Crown as had fallen into their hands. Robert of Torigni groups the king of Scots with the count of Boulogne as a victim (if that is the right word) of Henry's insistence upon the surrender of the royal demesne.[4] It is easy to add other names,[5] including, it may perhaps be emphasised, William of Ypres, who, however, was not subjected, as has been supposed, to a savage vengeance for serving King Stephen in the way that other Flemings had served and were to serve other kings of England.[6] As for the surrender of castles, this demand was quite general throughout England and Normandy[7] and was one that English kings frequently made. The count of Boulogne was not therefore treated in any exceptional way: he remained loyal to Henry, in whose service he died,[8] and his enjoyment of his ancestral estates and of the estates of his wife was not disturbed. We have already explained the legal basis for the resumption of estates that had formed part of the demesne of the Crown. At his coronation Henry had sworn an oath to protect the rights of the Crown, an oath which, either expressly or by implication, extended to the recovery of rights that had been alienated. Henry's interpretation of this undertaking covered not only the extravagant alienations of King Stephen, but

[1] Round, *Peerage and Family History*, p. 169.
[2] The main facts are stated by Stubbs, *Constitutional History*, i.487-91; see also Ramsay, *Angevin Empire*, pp. 5-6. For the resistance at Bedford see above, p. 252, n. 4.
[3] Robert of Torigni, p. 193.   [4] *Ibid.*, p. 192.   [5] *Traditio*, xvi.153-5.
[6] This legend derives from William fitz Stephen who asserts that, within three months of the coronation, that is in March 1155, William was forced to depart from England 'cum lacrymis', on the advice of Becket, the clergy and the barons (*Becket Materials*, iii.19). We have but to look up the pipe roll of 1 Henry II to find the refutation of this story, for at Michaelmas 1155 William of Ypres was clearly in possession of the lands Stephen had granted him in Kent (*Red Book of the Exchequer*, ii.648-9). For the process by which those lands were retrieved see *Traditio*, xvi.153-5. For Flemings in the service of English kings up to the reign of John, see above, p. 73.
[7] Robert of Torigni particularly mentions Hugh Bigod (p. 193).
[8] Robert of Torigni, p. 206.

his own alienations before he came to the throne. He treated William Mauduit, whom he had bought with lavish grants and promises, in the same way as he treated Count William.[1] Nor did he do this arbitrarily: solemn inquests were held into the extent of the royal demesne and the process of resumption was leisurely and did not exclude the possibility of regrant.[2]

The resumption of alienated estates was doubtless an inevitable act of statecraft necessary for the stability of the throne, an act to which Henry may well have been urged by his minister of finance, Bishop Nigel, who had personal reasons to be aware that canon law imposed upon prelates the obligation to recover ecclesiastical estates that had been dispersed by their predecessors.[3] Should not the principles of ecclesiastical law apply also to secular affairs? But the king's actions raised embarrassing questions, if not of morals, of law, and one question in particular, for the treaty of Winchester had solemnly assured to Count William precisely those things that Henry required him to surrender. It was a nice question: did the coronation oath relieve Henry of the oath which bound him to the treaty? Only the pope could settle the issue, and to the pope the count appealed: his death forestalled the judgement.[4] If we were now to try the issue, we might find that Henry was justified, though perhaps only on the ground of expedience; but we should find it hard to acquit him of bad faith, for other actions of his followed the same pattern without the legal justification of his resumption of alienated royal demesne. Let us mention one that is adequately documented. Although he had undertaken in the most solemn terms to restore to the bishop of Salisbury the castle of Devizes of which he had despoiled him on the plea of necessity, yet when that plea was no longer valid, he would not let the castle pass out of his hands but offered the bishop compensation instead. It is significant that from the outset the bishop had no faith in the duke's word and had invoked the aid of the pope to enforce the agreement. Nevertheless, with Archbishop Theobald's assistance, Henry got his own way.[5]

Henry's resolve on becoming king to free himself from the imprudent undertakings of the duke of Normandy would have been more to be admired, had his actions appeared to be free from vindictiveness. We have seen that he dismissed Reginald, abbot of Reading, who had been keeper of King Stephen's seal: he dismissed equally Gervase, abbot of Westminster, who was Stephen's son.[6]

---

[1] Below, p. 433.   [2] *Traditio*, xvi.155.
[3] *Ibid.*, xvi.151-9.   [4] John of Salisbury, *Letters*, i.82.
[5] The story of the castle is told in the *Sarum Charters*. Henry was already in possession during his visit in 1149 (no. 17). His undertaking to restore it was given in April 1153 (no. 25). Papal approval of ecclesiastical censures if Henry should break his undertaking was given by Anastasius IV on 1 January 1154 (Holtzmann, *Papsturkunden in England*, ii.254-5). For the bishop's quitclaim and Theobald's confirmation see *Sarum Charters*, no. 26. See also *Pipe Roll, 4 Henry II*, p. 161, and Saltman, *Theobald Archbishop of Canterbury*, pp. 40, 465-6.
[6] The dismissal of these abbots, as well as the deprivation of the earl of Warenne of

Yet he was prudent in his abasings and rejections. If it is true that he had promised the chief place in the administration to the youthful count of Boulogne, he did well to give the office of justiciar to the experienced Earl Robert of Leicester and Richard de Lucy. If he allowed Aubrey de Vere to buy back the dignity of master chamberlain, he did not recognise the grant of the chancellorship his mother and he had made to Aubrey's brother William. Aubrey's vacillations were sufficient justification for disregarding a grant that had been part of the price promised for his loyalty.[1] Henry might then with reason regard his hands as freed and, since William de Vere and Thomas Becket were both members of Theobald's household,[2] there was no reason why he should not be guided by the archbishop's advice in his choice of a candidate for the chancellorship. And while we cannot be certain of Henry's reason for dismissing Henry fitz Harding, who had served him as treasurer before his accession, it is probable that the king gave Bishop Nigel a free hand in organising the financial administration of the country.[3]

We need not, however, follow further the measures taken by Henry to restore the administration of the country, measures which showed, on the whole, little discrimination either in favour of those who had supported him in his struggle for the throne or against those who had supported Stephen. What we seek to do is to disperse any notion that, before coming to the throne, Henry had taken steps to give England unified government, to aid Stephen in the task of administration, except in so far as the cessation of open hostilities, which was not likely to be more than brief, contributed to that end. To credit Henry with a consciously pursued constructive task from November 1153 onwards is to fall into the historian's worst fallacy, that of reading history backwards and perverting it in the process. There is no reason to suppose that Stephen was then in visibly failing health or that his early death could be foreseen. In October 1154 he was adjourning until the following Hilary term an action coming before him in person which raised the fundamental issue of the jurisdiction of the king's court over criminous clerks, and there was no expectation that he would not be present to try the issue.[4] So far

his castles, can be assigned to the period April 1157-August 1158, when the king was in England. For Gervase, see Appendix II: below, p. 418. For Reginald, see above, pp. 256-7. Reginald must have been youthful, since he lived on until 1203; but his subsequent career as prior and abbot of Walden shows that he was capable and, if we can trust the chronicle of that house, he was pious and learned. His appointment as abbot of Reading was doubtless due to Stephen's influence; but it was no more irregular than that of his predecessor, Robert de Sigillo, who had been keeper of Henry I's seal.

[1] See Appendix III: below, p. 428. For the charters see Round, Geoffrey de Mandeville, pp. 180-3; Vincent, Discoverie of Brooke's Errors (1622), pp. 397-400.

[2] The fact that William de Vere was present at Colchester as a member of Theobald's household (Leland, Itinerary, v.171) is conclusive proof that he was not Henry's chancellor. He was at the time Theobald's chaplain (Letters of John of Salisbury, i.217: cf. Saltman, Theobald Archbishop of Canterbury, pp. 321-2 (no. 100), for a charter of 1152 witnessed by William de Vere). The William who witnesses Henry's charters as duke of Normandy is William fitz Gilbert (cf. E.H.R., lxi.88-9).

[3] As Richard of Ely implies (Dialogus de Scaccario, p. 50).   [4] Below, p. 288.

GME S

as we can tell, he could then reasonably look forward to many years of life. His end within a fortnight or three weeks came suddenly and unexpectedly.

If we are to reconstruct history, let us ask what Henry would have done through long years of waiting for the reversion of the throne. We have surely a good inkling in those acts of his which we have reviewed. He would have continued to fight for his own hand without thought for the well-being of the people of England. To act otherwise would have been to strengthen his rival's hold upon the throne. When, against all expectation, he was called upon to succeed him in October 1154, the disorder alike in the financial and judicial administration of the country was such that it was years before the level attained under Henry I could be restored. To this disorder the Empress and, more particularly, her son had been principal contributors to the very end of Stephen's reign. To say this is not to impute blame: it is to state a fact.

XV

STATECRAFT AND LEARNING

EDWARD I, said Stubbs, 'had all the powers of Henry II without his vices and he had too that sympathy with the people he ruled, the want of which alone would have robbed the character of Henry II of the title of greatness'.[1] Comparison between Edward I and Henry II came frequently to Stubbs's mind and, though his idealisation of Edward made it impossible for him to hold the balance fair, he recognised the greatness of Henry's achievement in England. Stubbs knew far more about Henry than he did about Edward. He knew more of Henry's background than he did of Edward's. His two lectures on 'Learning and Literature at the Court of Henry II', though now antiquated in form and scholarship, stand above the general level of the *Seventeen Lectures* and show how widely he had read in the historical sources of the twelfth century.[2] Of the handicaps under which he laboured in approaching the history of administration we have already spoken, but he was further handicapped in his approach to Henry II by his insularity and by his attribution of perpetual validity to the moral standards of his own age. One wonders sometimes whether his idealisation of Edward I would have survived the discovery that his hero had at least one son born out of wedlock.[3] Certainly he made no allowance, in Henry's case, for the sexual laxity which, however reprehensible in principle, was accepted, almost as a matter of course, among all classes of mediaeval society, high and low, laity and clergy.[4] Henry was not, in this respect, exceptionally depraved, and the most scandalous charge against him, that he seduced Alice of France, his son's betrothed, is certainly a fiction, even though the fiction may be contemporary.[5] As for Henry's other failings, they rest largely upon the testimony of the enemies which, it was inevitable, his policies in Church and State raised up against him; and the favourable testimony of his friends largely discounts the adverse criticism of those who were out of

[1] *Constitutional History*, ii.104.
[2] *Seventeen Lectures*, pp. 132-78.
[3] John Botetourt: the authority for his paternity is the chronicle of Hailes Abbey, a house closely connected with the royal family (Cleopatra D. III, fo. 51). His royal birth explains the distinction accorded him under Edward I and Edward II, for which the editors of the *Complete Peerage*, ii.233, were unable to account. He was born before his father came to the throne.
[4] As Stubbs largely recognised (*Constitutional History*, iii.384-5).
[5] *E.H.R.*, lxi.311-3.

sympathy with him. But a man, able, energetic, forceful above the common, must needs hurt those who oppose him.

Before sitting down to write his *Constitutional History*, Stubbs had already declared that 'if we could distinguish between the man and the king, between personal selfishness and official or political states-manship, between the ruin of his personal aims and the real success of his administrative conceptions, we might conclude by saying that altogether he was great and wise and successful'.[1] Stubbs himself was never able to view a king as a ruler in disregard of the man's private virtues and vices, real or imagined; but this disability falsi-fied the character he gave to other kings more than it falsified the character of Henry II, whose qualities no reservations on moral grounds could diminish or disguise. Nor was Stubbs's rigid applica-tion of his own standards of personal conduct so great a fetter on his judgement as his insularity which persistently falsified his apprecia-tion of characters and events. He saw the Norman and 'Plantagenet' kings of England as Englishmen, not as Frenchmen called upon to rule far-flung dominions. 'Henry II', he said "had laboured to the utmost to obtain foreign territory for his sons, but had allowed only one of them to marry at home, and had sent all his daughters abroad.'[2] Henry II spent in England considerably less than half the thirty-five years covered by his reign: a fact that makes it difficult to suppose that England was the centre of his interests, his 'home'. Edward I gave England somewhat more of his time, if not of his thought, but that he had great sympathy with the people of England is an assumption for which Stubbs never offered proof, though we need not doubt that Edward wished to rule well, after his fashion, all the subjects committed to his charge. But what of Henry? Surely he was a conscientious ruler: 'I know, indeed I know, nor can heart think or voice declare, how much I have laboured for my people', are the words that Peter of Blois puts into his mouth.[3] Of the admin-istration of Henry's own *comté* of Anjou and of the duchy of Aquitaine which he acquired in the right of Queen Eleanor, we have much less information than we have of the administration of England and Normandy, though it is certain that the system which, in its major outlines, was common to England and Normandy was not extended to Henry's other dominions. There was never an Angevin 'empire', and Henry was an adaptor and an improver rather than an inno-vator. In England and Normandy, there can be no question, he re-

---

[1] 'Benedict of Peterborough', ii, p. xiii.   [2] *Constitutional History*, ii.436.
[3] Peter of Blois, 'Dialogus inter Regem Henricum II et Abbatem Bonaevallensem' in *Opera*, iii.302: Novi ego, novi, nec possum aut corde cogitare aut voce proferre quantum laboraverim pro populo meo. Cf. *Epistolae*, no. 66 (*ibid.*, i.195): Ad pacem populi pertinet quicquid cogitat, quicquid loquitur, quicquid agit; ut quiescat populus suus labores anxios et enormes incessanter assumit. . . . Ad pacem quoque populi spectat immensitas illa pecuniarum quam donat, quam recipit, quam congregat, quam dispergit. Ralf de Diceto has words to the same effect: de communi salute magis et magis sollicitus . . . (*Opera*, i.434-5).

called and resumed the work of Henry I and of Roger of Salisbury: there was no completely fresh departure. The task of assimilating Anjou, not to speak of Poitou and Aquitaine, to a novel and alien system would have been, indeed, formidable, and there is no reason to suppose that it was ever contemplated.[1] But within whatever limitations Henry pursued his work, when we regard England and Normandy as they were governed in 1150 and in 1200 and consider the development of administration and law in that half-century, we cannot resist the conclusion that he was a great ruler. It is true that he commanded the services of many able administrators and that much of what we admire in Henry's reign was their work, but the results were achieved because he generally chose his ministers well.

Henry's greatest mistake was in choosing and trusting the flashy, shallow and egotistic Thomas Becket, though this was, initially at least, the mistake of a young and inexperienced man who relied upon the judgement of an old and experienced one, Archbishop Theobald.[2] It is probable that he would, in any event, have incurred the enmity of high-churchmen, but Becket's martyrdom gave them a stick to beat him with and must have alienated popular sympathies. Nor was it only in this that he alienated popular sympathies. Henry had a manner of life that did not commend itself to a young and chivalrous generation. In Peter of Blois' description of Henry's court and Bertran de Born's description we perceive the contrast between the old and the new ideas. 'As often as he can get breathing space amid his business cares, he occupies himself with private reading or takes pains in working out some knotty question among his clerks. . . . With the king of England it is school every day, constant conversation of the best scholars and discussion of problems.' So the scholarly Peter.[3] To Bertran, on the other hand, the atmosphere of Henry's court was deadly weariness and boorishness: 'there was no banter, no laughter, no giving of presents'.[4] In the eyes of Gerald of Wales also, who reflects the fashionable view of the circles in which he moved, the amiable, open-handed paladin was the ideal type of noble[5]: it was the type beginning to be cultivated throughout French society.[6] It was the type to which Henry's sons endeavoured

---

[1] Above, pp. 167-8.

[2] Theobald himself was completely disillusioned, as his letter to Becket shows (John of Salisbury, *Letters*, i.224-5).   [3] Peter of Blois, *Epistolae*, no. 66 (i.194-5).

[4] Bertran de Born, *Poésies complètes* (ed. A. Thomas), p. 126:

Ont om no gab ni no ria:
Cortz sens dos . . .
E agram mort sens falhia
L'enois e la vilania . . .

(A slightly different text is given by A. Stimming, *Bertran von Born*, p. 125). Peter of Blois on the contrary extols Henry's generosity: nullus magnificentior in donis (*loc. cit.*).

[5] As in his description of the young king in *Topographia Hibernica*, dist. iii. capp. 49, 51 (*Opera*, v.194-5, 198), repeated in *De Principis Instructione*. Comparing him with his father, Gerald says 'de magno major, de luce lucidior'.

[6] E. Faral, *La vie quotidienne au temps de Saint Louis*, ch. 3, gives a good, if brief, view of aristocratic society in the late twelfth and early thirteenth centuries.

to conform, and it may well be that in this we should see the source of their enmity with their father. He was a difficult man to live with; a serious, studious, frugal man, at a time when frivolity, lavishness, extravagance were the means of conquering the hearts and commanding the good-will of youth. Nor can we suppose that the excellence of Henry's administration was appreciated at its true worth, except by the *curiales*, for it was costly and bore hardly on many. There were few contemporaries with the perspicacity to set the king's achievements above his errors and oddities, his failures and defects. The achievements remain.

The controversy with Becket overhangs Henry's reign and tends to obscure our vision. The literature that surrounds it is so great and forms so substantial a part of contemporary historical sources that our sense of proportion is distorted. In due course we shall comment upon it at greater length. Here we mention it but in passing lest it should seem that we have overlooked an important aspect of Henry's life, perhaps his one great failure. But we find it impossible to believe that the tragic outcome of the controversy deflected Henry more than momentarily from his course or materially affected the relations between Church and State. The tragedy was but an incident in the history of administration, an incident confined to the province of Canterbury.[1] The archbishop of York was not involved in the king's quarrel with the archbishop of Canterbury, nor were the archbishops of other ecclesiastical provinces within the king's dominions. His approach to the provinces on one side of the Channel did not differ from his approach to the provinces on the other side of the Channel. If then there were changes in Henry's attitude or relations with the Church in England, we should expect to trace their counterpart on the Continent. This we do not find. Here again, an insular view is a partial view: we cannot judge Henry or his policies if we confine our enquiries to English affairs.

Henry then pursued his great, wise and successful administration, harassed but not, in the end, seriously disturbed or deflected by his conflicts with the Church or with foes within and without. Nor were his successes evanescent. His work did not dissolve when he died, a broken man. It lived on, but circumstances determined that in England it should have its greatest measure of permanence. Henry's work stood as a whole, despite the long absence of Richard I on crusade and in captivity, and it stood in England, despite John's downfall and the loss of Normandy. It stood, no doubt, because, as we have explained, there had been achieved the conception of an impersonal monarchy, a royal administration that would function without the royal touch. But an impersonal monarchy would have been impossible, had there not been agents able to keep it in motion

---

[1] As Stubbs said, 'its interest is rather moral or personal than constitutional' ('Benedict of Peterborough', ii, p. xxxix).

It appears in the twelfth century, and not before the twelfth cen-
sury, because until then learning had not been secularised. The
recularisation of learning—or perhaps literacy would be the better
word—made possible Henry's achievement and gave it permanence.

Henry himself was a scholar—'with the king of England, it is
school every day'—and doubtless he was exceptional in his tastes
and his competence, but he was no isolated phenomenon of a literate
layman. It was to the extension of learning among men of knightly
tank, gentlemen of modest fortune, that Marc Bloch attributed the
rise of the new monarchies of the twelfth century, the monarchies of
Henry II and Philip Augustus. 'The use, the appreciation, the possibility of the written instrument permitted these states to assemble
those administrative archives without which they could have had
no truly continuous existence.'[1] While doubtless every historian
would, on reflection, accept the view that continuous and efficient
administration depended upon the extended use of written instruments, the belief that the secularisation of learning was a dominant
factor in this evolution is certainly not widely shared, although,
quite obviously, it was because the secular rulers, the laity, used and
desired the written word that the written word transformed the arts
of government. Though this truth may be obvious, it is yet assumed,
with rare exceptions,[2] that in the twelfth century laymen were employed on duties appropriate to the illiterate, and on this assumption
the administrative devices of the exchequer are explained. This explanation, even when it is applied to the exchequer, leaves, as we
shall show, too much unexplained; and when we look beyond the
twelfth century and discover evidence that laymen were becoming
increasingly literate and yet the characteristic devices of the exchequer remained, the explanation becomes less and less convincing.
We shall never understand the institutions of the twelfth century if
we study them in isolation and do not relate them to the society they
served. Even Stubbs, extensive as his knowledge was, never brought
into relation, one to the other, the learning and the administrative
achievement to be found, side by side, at the court of Henry II.

We may perhaps best approach the problem in this way. No one
would suggest that a layman in public employment in the fifteenth
century, in the age of Littleton and Fortescue, of Humphrey duke of
Gloucester, of Caxton and Pynson, was to be presumed illiterate.
No one would make that presumption of the fourteenth century, the
age of Chaucer and Gower, of the lay chancellors of Edward III and
Richard II, the age when all the judges on the bench were laymen
who had served as apprentices and serjeants-at-law. No one would

---

[1] *Société féodale: les classes et le gouvernement des hommes*, p. 216; cf. *ibid.*, *les liens de dépendance*, p. 422.
[2] A dissenting note was struck by J. Westfall Thompson, *The Literacy of the Laity in the Middle Ages* (1939). The wide scope of the work did not, however, permit much detailed investigation.

make that presumption of the thirteenth century, the age of Simon de Montfort, of Arnald fitz Thedmar, the London chronicler, and of those literate knights, the discovery of whom seems to have surprised T. F. Tout.[1] Was there then some social change, some extension of education, about the year 1200, that will account for a hypothetical passage from universal illiteracy to, at least, partial literacy? On the contrary, there are suggestions that, as contrasted with the twelfth century, the thirteenth showed a decline in learning.[2] But if we ask whether there was a social change, an extension of education, about the year 1100, we can give an affirmative answer with some confidence.

Let our first witness be Gilbert of Nogent. He was born in 1053 and he recalled that in his childhood there was such a lack of Latin masters (*grammatici*) that in villages practically none and in towns hardly any were to be found and such as existed had so little learning that they could not compare even with the wandering clerklings (*clericuli*) of the twelfth century.[3] The implied contrast between his youth and age—he was writing soon after 1114—is significant. Nor does Gilbert stand alone. A contemporary of his, writing at much the same time, seeking to refute an allegation by Theobald of Étampes, asserts that in France, Germany, Normandy and England there were, if not more, almost as many skilled schoolmasters as there were collectors of taxes and officials, not only in cities and towns, but even in villages.[4] However much we may discount these statements, we can hardly assume that they are the direct opposite of the truth and that there was a dearth of teachers, at least in northern France, in the early twelfth century. Nor does there seem to be any reason to suppose that England then lagged behind,[5] even though in the realm of higher learning no schools were to be found to compare with certain of the schools to be found on the other side of the Channel. Even so, we must not imagine that political boundaries or the narrow seas were an obstacle to those who sought a better education than was easily to be found in England. In the early years of the century the schools of Laon, when master Anselm was teaching there, were not only distinguished but fashionable. Among Anselm's pupils there were five from England who became

---

[1] *Chapters in the Administrative History of Mediaeval England*, i.205, 288, n. 2; cf. *ibid.*, iii.202.

[2] Thompson, *op. cit.*, pp. 145, 181; J. de Ghellinck, *L'essor de la littérature latine au xii⁶ siècle*, i.12-16, ii.312-21. There is some risk of confusion here. That there was a decline in learning in the higher sense seems certain. On the other hand, though in the thirteenth century the standard was lower, there was a wider familiarity with Latin, as the rise of the universities and the increasing activities of the government and the courts show. The wide use first of French and then of English for literature and for communications in writing marks an increasing literacy among all ranks of society except the lowest.

[3] *Vita*, lib. i, cap. iv (ed. Bougin, pp. 12-13).

[4] From the anonymous *Rescriptum pro Monachis*, written apparently in England, in answer to Theobald of Etampes' *Improperium in Monachos*: the text is printed by T. H. Holland in Oxford Hist. Soc., *Collectanea*, 2nd Series (1890), p. 158. and by Leach, *Educational Charters*, pp. 102-6.   [5] *Ibid.*, pp. 54-102.

bishops, William of Corbeil, Algar, a future bishop of Coutances, Robert of Chichester, a future bishop of Exeter, Alexander and Nigel, nephews of Roger of Salisbury. To Laon, too, Ranulf, Henry I's chancellor, had sent his sons, not as pupils of master Anselm but to be instructed by William of Corbeil.[1] Nor must we assume that, because five of master Anselm's pupils, whose names we happen to know, became bishops, that all those attending the schools at Laon were destined for an ecclesiastical career. Perhaps all were in some sort clerks, but the distinction between a clerk in minor orders and a literate layman was hardly more than formal and there was nothing to prevent a clerk from adopting a secular career.[2]

If we lack adequate knowledge of such men in the first half of the twelfth century, the *Otia Imperialia* of Gervase of Tilbury gives us more than a glimpse of scholars of much the same sort in the second half of the century. Gervase, who was born about 1152, went, while still a lad, to Italy and studied at Bologna, where he became a master and taught canon law. His companion in the schools was his kinsman, Philip, the son of Earl Patrick of Salisbury. Though Gervase himself was doubtless in minor orders, there is nothing to suggest that Philip was in any sense an ecclesiastic, and Gervase's own career shows how little difference there might be between a clerk and a layman. With his friend Philip he followed for a time the court of Henry II, and he was thereafter attached successively to Henry, the young king, to William, archbishop of Reims, and to King William II of Sicily. The early nineties found him married to a wealthy wife at Arles and his connexion, through her, with the archbishop of Arles led eventually to his appointment by the Emperor Otto IV to the honorific post of marshal of the kingdom of Arles, a military office, which, however, he was able to serve, as he says, with his ready tongue. He seems to have followed the imperial court, through triumph and disaster, until Otto's death, and then, in old age and disappointment, to have found refuge at last in a house of religion in England.[3] But the lesson we would draw from Gervase's career is not a moral one, of the vanity of earthly things, but that it differed so little from that of any well-born layman with a taste for learning. Earls' sons might find themselves in the schools as well as ecclesiastics, and whether, as clerk or layman, they served Church or State was very much a matter of fortune: they might be equipped for either.

We have chosen Gervase and his friend Philip as examples, because of others who followed a secular career in the twelfth century we

[1] Hermann, *De miraculis S. Mariae Laudunensis* lib. ii, capp. 6, 12, 13, 15, in Migne, *Patrologia Latina*, clvi.961 sqq. For date and authorship see *History*, xlvi.103, n. 8.

[2] An early instance is that of Aubrey, the youngest son of Hugh of Grandmesnil, who 'in pueritia litteris studiit, sed in adolescentia, relicto clericatu, ad militiam se contulit' (Ordericus Vitalis, *Historia Ecclesiastica*, iv.456). Since Hugh died at an advanced age in 1094, Aubrey must have changed his profession in the eleventh century.

[3] Richardson, 'Gervase of Tilbury', in *History*, xlvi.104-14.

get sparse details, hardly more than hints of the kind of education they received; but what we learn points to the universality of education among the highborn and well-to-do.[1] It should be remarked that the man chiefly responsible for the education of Henry fitz Empress had previously taught Henry's aunts.[2] Under this same tutor, Master Matthew, there sat by Henry's side Roger, the future bishop of Worcester.[3] In the education of the young Henry, Stubbs saw something exceptional and, to explain it, he emphasised the tradition of culture at the Angevin court which, he thought, was not commonly met with elsewhere[4]: this, however, may put us on a false scent, for it is by no means certain that the counts of Anjou were so exceptional as he supposed.

At the threshold of the twelfth century we are confronted with a lay correspondent of the bishop of Norwich, Herbert of Losinga. Herbert praises the exquisite style of this layman and we are given what purports to be a letter from him. This letter is written with the fashionable empty elegance of the day and its inclusion in Herbert's own correspondence suggests that it may have been improved for the purpose of publication. Of the real existence of this layman there can, however, be no doubt, though the particulars we are given are insufficient to enable us to identify him. We know that he was resident in England, that his name was John, that he was a man of means and had travelled to Rome; but apart from a few personal touches we know nothing more.[5] Whether he had attended the schools in France or in Italy, whether he had had a master of his own, as seems not to have been unusual: between these alternatives we cannot choose. That these alternatives were open to laymen of rank in the year 1100 is a matter of the greatest significance for us; for we must emphasise that the prospect of an ecclesiastical career was not the only motive which inspired a desire for learning. Learning might be desired for its own sake or as a fitting accomplishment for born leaders of men.[6] Henry I provided a *tutor et paedogogus* for his family in the person of Otwel, a son of Earl Hugh of Chester, a Norman baron who, perhaps, would hardly be suspected of any leaning towards letters. If Otwel were in orders, Orderic, who tells

---

[1] J. W. Thompson comes to much the same conclusion (*op. cit.*, p. 180).

[2] For what is known of Master Matthew see *E.H.R.*, lxxiv.193-7. Is it possible that Matthew was the master of Saintes who, according to an anonymous chronicler, was entrusted with Henry's education by Count Geoffrey (*Historiens de la France*, xii.120: cf. p. 415)? There appears to be no authority for giving this master the name of Peter (Thompson, *op. cit.*, pp. 190-1). We doubt whether either Adelard of Bath or William of Conches can be said to have been in any real sense Henry's master: see, however, Haskins, *Studies in History of Mediaeval Science*, pp. 28-9; Bliemetzrieder, *Adelhard von Bath*, pp. 133-41, 340-52; Thompson, *op. cit.*, pp. 175, 191.

[3] Fitz Stephen in *Becket Materials*, iii.104.   [4] *Seventeen Lectures*, pp. 136-7.

[5] Herbert de Losinga, *Epistolae* (ed. Anstruther), nos. 45, 58. The latter is John's purported composition. Translations will be found in Goulburn and Symonds, *Life, Letters and Sermons of Bishop Herbert de Losinga*, pp. 10-16.

[6] This point of view is expressed in the letter, composed by Peter of Blois for Archbishop Rotrou of Rouen, addressed to Henry II, urging that the younger Henry should have a literary education (Peter of Blois, *Epistolae*, no. 67).

us that he perished in the White Ship, does not say so.[1] Among Henry's family who were instructed by him we should probably include the king's favourite illegitimate son Robert, whom he created earl of Gloucester. It was Robert, himself a well-educated man[2]— not, it must be remarked, Count Geoffrey of Anjou—who was responsible for arranging the education of Henry II, and this education, as we have said, the young prince shared with Robert's own son, Roger. It is by accident that we learn these facts, but we must not regard them as in any way unusual. Rather we should assume that there were not a few noble households where future statesmen and future prelates, and indeed future ladies of high rank, studied side by side under a domestic tutor. Not only did Earl Robert have a reputation for learning but so had two contemporary earls, the brothers Waleran, count of Meulan and earl of Worcester, and Robert, earl of Leicester, who seem also to have been pupils of Otwel's.[3] A little below this exalted rank, another prominent contemporary, Brian fitz Count, was a man of some education, who wrote a pamphlet in support of the claims of the Empress, now lost,[4] but whose vigorous letter, denouncing those who had gone back on their oath to her, survives to tell us something of the quality of his Latin.[5] Incidental references to educated laymen will be found elsewhere, as when the bishop of Exeter submits to Pope Alexander III the case of a *literatus et nobilis vir* who had engaged himself to marry and then, thinking better of it, had decided to retire to a monastery.[6] A little later we learn the name of the master engaged for the grandsons of the earl of Oxford,[7] while Gerald of Wales has a story of a *miles literatus* whose favourite amusement was capping Latin verses.[8] Without rashly generalising from what may perhaps be called a handful of cases, it may fairly be said that they create a presumption that a man of noble birth will in his youth have had the opportunity of learning something of Latin letters.

We may think this presumption justified when we consider the succession to the office of justiciar.[9] Beginning with Roger, bishop of Salisbury, we have Richard de Lucy, Robert, earl of Leicester, Ranulf Glanville, William Longchamp, Walter of Coutances, Hubert

---

[1] Ordericus Vitalis, *Historia Ecclesiastica*, iv.418.

[2] William of Malmesbury, *Historia Regum*, ii.355-6. Cf. *Historia Novella* (ed. Potter), p. 23: vir ille qui plena satietate literarum scientiam combiberat; Geoffrey of Monmouth, *Historia Regum Britanniae* (ed. Griscom), pp. 86, 219; Walter Map, *De Nugis Curialium* (ed. James), p. 213: vir magne prudencie multarumque literarum.

[3] Their father died in 1118 and the brothers were taken into the king's household and educated with his own children (Ordericus Vitalis, *Historia Ecclesiastica*, iv.438). For their learning see William of Malmesbury, *Gesta Regum*, ii.482, 519; Geoffrey of Monmouth, *ut supra*, pp. 86, 220; *Dialogus de Scaccario*, p. 57.

[4] Gilbert Foliot, *Epistolae*, no. 79 (ed. Giles, i.94).   [5] *E.H.R.*, xxv.297-8.

[6] X, 4.1.16; Jaffé-Loewenfeld, no. 13905.

[7] *Monasticon*, vi.309. The date cannot be later than 1187.

[8] Gerald the Welshman, 'De Principis Instructione', dist. iii, cap. 28 (*Opera*, viii.310). The knight lived in the twelfth century.

[9] Stubbs had another explanation of the succession of clerical and lay justiciars, but it is at variance with the facts (*Constitutional History*, i.379-80).

Walter, Geoffrey fitz Peter, Peter des Roches, Hubert de Burgh, Stephen Segrave—five ecclesiastics, six laymen. Of the literacy of Robert, earl of Leicester, there is unquestionable evidence; and who can doubt the literacy of Ranulf Glanville, of whom even Gerald the Welshman speaks in terms of admiration?[1] But on general grounds it is impossible to believe that an administrative office, which was served indifferently by ecclesiastics and laymen, could be filled successfully by an illiterate. Certainly from the time of Ranulf Glanville onwards, the justiciar, in his capacity as president of the Bench, had necessarily to be master of an elaborate procedure, based largely upon writs and recorded in rolls and chirographs expressed in technical language. But if it is conceded that justiciars must needs know enough Latin to read a writ or a roll or a fine, the same ability must be accorded to the lay justices who sat on the bench with them. It is significant that, when a glossator of the treatise that bears Glanville's name had occasion to mention the diverse opinions of the judges of Henry II, he named two justiciars, both laymen, Richard de Lucy and Glanville, and three justices, of whom two were laymen, Osbert fitz Hervey and Hugh Bardolf, and the third an ecclesiastic, Hubert Walter.[2] The opinions of all five are treated with respect and, though the points of difference did not depend upon book-learning, it would have been odd if a competent and instructed lawyer, for such the glossator must have been, would have troubled to record the opinion of an unlearned judge. And if we persist in assuming that Henry's justices might be illiterate, we have to make the most improbable assumption that John's justices might be illiterate also, for at least one of the laymen who sat upon the Bench under Henry II continued to sit there in the thirteenth century.[3] We may presume then that a layman who exercised an office demanding the use of written instruments was literate, just as we presume that a clerk who might be called upon to exercise an office in the Church was literate. In either case, we may have to allow for exceptions, though the generalisation holds good. And though the arguments are perhaps at their strongest with the judges of the Bench, there is reason for believing that the argument will extend to other laymen. The two auditors of the treasury in 1129 were the earl of Gloucester and Brian fitz Count,[4] for whose literacy we have independent evidence, and we shall argue that the evidence points to the conclusion that those who accounted at the exchequer

---

[1] Gerald the Welshman, *ut supra*, p. 258: At ille, sapiens ut erat simul et eloquens, solita gravitate eloquentiam ornante . . . respondit.

[2] *E.H.R.*, lxv.87-8. We think it far more probable that these names appeared in glosses than that they were, as Professor Southern suggests, part of the original text: see *Juridical Review*, lxvii.168-9.

[3] Osbert fitz Hervey (Hunter, *Fines*, p. lxi). Michael Belet and Hugh Bardolf were also employed under John (*ibid.*, pp. lxi-lxii); but they were not regular members of the Bench. Master Thomas of Hurstbourne also survived until John's reign; but he was an ecclesiastic and canon of St. Paul's.   [4] Above, p. 225.

or, at least, the principal accountants there were sufficiently literate.

If we presume that laymen employed in administration were literate, then we must accept the corollary that they were drawn from classes which normally provided education for their sons. While there is ample evidence for the widespread existence of schools in twelfth-century England,[1] we know little of the pupils. If Fitz Stephen's description of London tells us something of the curriculum, we can only speculate upon the careers the schoolboys subsequently followed.[2] That the sole career before them was the Church or that they all became clerks or ecclesiastics is, as we have seen, unlikely. But if we are to advance beyond speculation we must look for direct evidence of reading and writing by laymen. There is, in fact, a not inconsiderable number of documents which purport to be replies by laymen to enquiries addressed to them in Latin, notably the *cartae* of 1166 and the returns to the Inquest of Sheriffs of 1170. Doubtless the greater men who replied were in a position to delegate to clerks the task of preparing their answers; but what of the lesser men? It is unlikely that the latest-discovered return to the Inquest of Sheriffs was written by a clerk, for it is in French and inelegant French at that.[3] Another return to the same enquiry is the earliest known written plaint, couched in uncouth Latin: if it is not the work of the complainant, but of a clerk, the clerk was notably unskilled.[4] Such examples raise the presumption that the more informal documents, those that have no marks of clerkly skill, were written by laymen. The same presumption is raised by some of the *cartae* of 1166, the returns to a demand for particulars of knight service due from tenants-in-chief. This naïve reply of William of Colkirk, who owed service for no more than half a knight's fee, can hardly have been written by a trained clerk:

Ego Willelmus de Colecherche debeo domino meo Henrico Regi servitium dimidii militis in Norfolcia de antiquo tenemento a Conquestu Anglie. Nolo enim ut servitium meum celetur quin fecerim quod facere debeo. Et homagium feci vobis, O domine, et meo domino Henrico filio vestro, et vestris vicecomitibus servitium feci.[5]

And what are we to make of the return for the fee of Bertram of Bulmer who, at the date of the enquiry, was dead? The letter, for such it is, purports to be written by one of his tenants, David the lardiner.[6] It begins:

---

[1] Leach, *Educational Charters*, pp. 66-138.
[2] *Becket Materials*, iii.4-5; Leach, *op. cit.*, pp. 82-4.
[3] *Bulletin of the John Rylands Library*, xxiv.168-72, xxvii.179-81.
[4] *Red Book of the Exchequer*, ii, p. cclxix, no. 8: cf. Richardson and Sayles, *Select Cases of Procedure without Writ*, p. lxiv.
[5] *Red Book of the Exchequer*, p. 400: 'I, William of Colkirk, owe to my lord King Henry the service of half a knight in Norfolk for an ancient tenement held since the Conquest of England, for I do not wish to conceal my service but to do what I ought to do. And I have done homage to you, my lord, and to my lord Henry your son and I have done service to your sheriffs.' [6] *Ibid.*, pp. 428-9.

Venerabili domino suo et illustri Regi Anglorum Henrico, David, lardarius suus, salutem et fidele servitium. Domine, literis istis vobis notifico quot milites Bertram de Bolemer de vestro feodo habuit.[1]

There follow details of the knights' fees, including a sentence regarding David's own holding:

Et ego David lardarius quintam partem militis tempore avi vestri et modo similiter.[2]

Why should the task of making the return have been delegated to David, if David was unable to write? It is true that he had a number of duties to discharge on behalf of the king, but this was not one of them.

The *cartae* of 1166 read in many instances as though they were the work of the putative authors. We need not cite more of them, for they are all in print and easily accessible. Let us, however, put beside them the farewell addressed to Henry II in 1158 by his chamberlain Warin fitz Gerold.[3] It begins:

In novissimis agens et viam universe carnis ingrediens, domine mi karissime, vos alloquor, neque vos ulterius visurus nec a vobis videndus. Exaudite, obsecro, extrema verba, que non iam tam a corpore veniunt, quod sentio defectissimum, quam ab anxiis affectibus anime . . .

This moving letter, which is too long to give in full, ends on the same tone:

Domine karissime, anima mea vos salutat. Salutat vos, inquam, anima mea extrema salutatione. Valete perpetua prosperitate.

Warin's dying fingers are not likely to have held the pen; but are we to suppose that he did not know what was being written on his behalf? The letter sounds too individual, too personal, to be other than what it purports to be, and it was addressed to a recipient who could read it without difficulty and was not easily deceived. Nor would any purpose have been served by fabricating the letter, which asks the king to confirm the death-bed gift that Warin had made to the monks of St. Edmund's. The monks preserved Warin's letter, which they presumably conveyed to the king, but their title to the lands he had given rested upon more formal documents, Warin's

---

[1] 'To his revered lord Henry, the illustrious king of the English, his lardiner David sends greeting and loyal service. My lord, by this letter I notify you how many knights Bertram of Bulmer held of your fee.'

[2] 'And I, David the lardiner, held a fifth part of a knight's fee in the time of your grandfather and now likewise.'

[3] Douglas, *Feudal Documents from the Abbey of Bury St. Edmund's*, pp. 164-5 (no. 180). The extracts may be translated thus: 'As I lie at the point of death, going the way of all flesh, to you, my dearest lord, I speak, though never more shall I see you or be seen by you. Hear favourably, I beseech, these last words, which come not so much from my fast-failing body as from the anxious desires of my soul. . . . Dearest lord, my soul greets you. My soul, I say again, greets you in a final greeting. Farewell in everlasting prosperity.'

own charter, the confirmation of his overlord, Earl Geoffrey de Mandeville, and the confirmation of the king.[1]

As a final example we choose an unpublished letter of the same period from an under-tenant, Otwel Delisle, addressed to the king's justices, presumably those on eyre in Kent.[2] It was written because land in Beckenham was in dispute between the canons of Holy Trinity, Aldgate, and John of Orpington, and the canons had vouched Otwel to warranty. Otwel was too old and infirm to appear in person before the justices, but he sent his son, who presumably took the letter with him.

Justiciis domini regis Othewelus de Insula salutem. Sciatis quod prior et canonici sancte Trinitatis Lund[onie] tenent quandam terram in Becham de me in feodo et hereditate per seruicium dimidii militis sicut tenuerunt de patre meo et de fratre meo Willelmo et sicut carte nostre testantur. Et ideo volo ut sciatis quod nec Alexander de Orpent[une] neque filius eius Iohannes nec Osbertus Uitdeniers per me ingressi sunt terram illam set contra me et sine consensu meo et iniuste et contra omnem racionem; et propter hoc mitto Othewelum filium meum ut huius rei testimonium perhibeat. Et ego ipse ad hunc diem venissem nisi senectus mea et grauitas infirmitatis me impediret. Cum vero necesse fuerit pro loco et tempore ego veniam et stabo cum priore et canonicis et faciam quod facere debuero sicut dominus eiusdem terre quam de me tenent sicut supra prediximus. Valete.[3]

This has the look of personal composition, with none of the set phrases which are the mark of the trained letter-writer. We might, if we wished to set it aside as evidence, imagine the employment of a clerk to whom Otwel dictated the letter and who caught, and translated to a marvel, the unstudied message the younger Otwel was to take to the judges. And to account for the other examples given above we might imagine the same process to be happening all over England. The simpler explanation of a sufficiently literate laity seems preferable.

We do not seek to draw wide inferences from the presumption we have endeavoured to establish, that laymen engaged in public administration involving the use of written documents were sufficiently literate for the task. We do not attribute great learning to them or suggest that, in a century when writing materials were scarce and

---

[1] Ibid., p. 98 (no. 88), 165-6 (nos. 190-1). [2] P.R.O. Ancient Deeds, A.5937.
[3] 'To the justices of our lord the king Otwel Delisle sends greeting. You should know that the prior and canons of Holy Trinity, London, hold certain land in Beckenham from me in fee and inheritance, by the service of half a knight, as they held it from my father and from my brother William and as our deeds testify. And therefore I desire you to know that neither Alexander of Orpington nor his son John nor Osbert Huitdeniers has entered upon that land through me but against me and without my consent and unlawfully and against all reason. And therefore I send my son Otwel that he may bear witness to these things. And I should myself have come to-day had not my age and serious illness prevented me. If, however, it should be necessary, I will come at an appointed place and time and stand with the prior and canons and do what I ought to do as the lord of that land which they hold of me as I have said above. Farewell.'

books were rare and dear, they spent their leisure in reading or that
they could have read books with ease, had they been available. Nor
do we conceive that more than a small fraction of the laity had
enough Latin to read official documents or formal instruments. In
a population that cannot have greatly exceeded, even if it attained,
two millions, some hundreds of literate laymen would suffice to do
all the business that professed clerks did not perform. Ability to read
and write in the vernacular, whether French or English, is another
question, upon which adequate light is not likely to be shed until
non-literary documents have been studied with more interest and
care than have hitherto been accorded them. It would seem, however, that while, in the second half of the twelfth century, a command
of Latin implied a command of French, there were those who could
write in the vernacular but who were ignorant of Latin. For the
requirements of public administration such a limited qualification
was inadequate. At the same time, the Latin vocabulary, even of
royal clerks, might be very limited and might need to be eked out,
on occasion, with French.[1] There is good reason to believe that
proceedings in courts of law, including the exchequer, were conducted in that language,[2] that Latin was a stumbling-block and was
rarely spoken, except when a document was read. It follows that a
limited knowledge of Latin, a knowledge to be easily and rapidly
acquired by any intelligent youth, was all that was necessary. And
it is only on the assumption that such knowledge was widespread
that we can explain the curricula of mediaeval universities and the
schools that preceded them in the twelfth century. Since instruction
was in Latin, it is evident that an elementary knowledge of the
language was demanded from the outset, and this from boys barely
in their teens. To call knowledge of that standard 'literacy' would
perhaps have been an abuse of language in the Middle Ages, when
literati were men with some pretension to learning.[3] For our present
purpose, literacy means a good deal less than learning, though yet
a certain skill in reading and writing Latin. Perhaps we might apply
to the more educated laymen the words that Gilbert Foliot addressed
to Brian fitz Count: 'quum literas non didiceris, in campum tamen

---

[1] Here are a few examples. *Rot. Curiae Regis*, i.40: 'dedit ei unum palefridum bai';
Pipe Roll, 1 John, p. 290: 'Homines de Dunewiz reddunt compotum de . . . x. chascurs
et v. girfalcs'; *Pipe Roll, 7 John*, p. 277: 'W. de Braosa reddit compotum de . . . v. chascuris
et xxiiij. seuz' (a type of greyhound); *Rot. de Liberate*, p. 79: 'facias ei habere hif et nervos
et cornu ad balistas faciendas'; *ibid.*, p. 235: 'ad expensas canum gupillerez quos custodit'
(i.e. foxhounds).

[2] The preceding examples show that French was the spoken language of the courts.
We can reinforce this evidence by what is told us by William of Drogheda of ecclesiastical
courts. In one place he says that, just as Greek may be used, 'sic et advocatio Anglicis vel
Gallicis acsi Latinis [verbis]', and again 'et fiat expositio appellationis Gallice et Anglice'
(*Summa Aurea* (ed. Wahrmund), pp. 91-4, 252-3). These passages are, however, concerned
with laymen.

[3] So Walter Map, speaking of a youth who had great facility as a scribe (and could
therefore read), says that he was not literate: 'puerum . . . inter nos et a nobis educatum
. . . cum non esset literatus quod doleo, quamlibet literarum seriem transcribere sciret'
(*De Nugis Curialium*, p. 138).

literarum non mediocriter impegisti'.[1] To the less educated, such words would be extravagant flattery; for it sufficed if they could read a writ, make a return to it, and keep accounts.

Let us now turn to the question of the qualifications of the sheriffs and other laymen who came to account at the exchequer. These laymen, it is assumed, were illiterate: their inability to read and write made necessary the devices of the tally and the chequered cloth that served as an abacus.[2] These assumptions do not rest upon explicit statements by contemporary writers, but are inferences, it would appear, from the 'Dialogus de Scaccario'. If the inferences were valid, we should be driven to conclude that, since tallies and abacus were still in use in the exchequer, laymen continued to be illiterate until the sixteenth century and perhaps, since tallies (if not abacus) continued to be employed for many hundreds of years, that laymen had not ceased to be illiterate in the nineteenth century. Clearly the argument leads nowhere, and a conclusion must be based upon other premises.

As a preliminary, a few words may be said both on tallies and the chequered cloth. The advantage of the tally does not lie in its simplicity, in the convenience it affords for scoring a total by means of notches. The technique of the exchequer tally was, in fact, elaborate,[3] and, let it be emphasised, a tally to be of any use at all had to be inscribed[4]: it was not devised for illiterates. Its advantage was the almost complete protection it provided against fraud: stock and foil, when brought together, must correspond, and could correspond only if cut from the same stick. The device of proving identity by fitting together two edges cut by a knife was not confined to tallies: it was employed equally with writings on parchment, indentures in their many forms.[5] The wooden tally was, however, cheaper than parchment and was equally effective in its own sphere. Nor will Richard of Ely's questionable assertion, that the phrase *ad scaccarium* had replaced the phrase *ad taleas* to describe the court we know as the exchequer,[6] bear the inference that, within the twelfth century, the abacus had superseded some more primitive methods of accounting that involved merely the use of tallies. No such method is recorded, and it is difficult to conceive any method of the kind. The method of accounting employed in the eleventh century is unknown, but there is no ground for excluding either some form of abacus or some simple arithmetical calculations on parchment. The

---

[1] Gilbert Foliot, *Epistolae*, no. 79 (ed. Giles, i.94): 'although you have not had a literary education, you have striven valiantly in the field of letters.'
[2] *Dialogus de Scaccario*, Introduction, pp. xxviii, xxxv-xxxvi.
[3] As Sir Hilary Jenkinson showed in various articles: see especially *Archaeologia*, lxxiv.289-351.
[4] For specimens see the plates appended to the article mentioned in the previous note and in the *Introduction to the Study of the Pipe Rolls* (Pipe Roll Soc.), pp. 64-8.
[5] As Hubert Hall pointed out many years ago (*ibid.*, p. 64).
[6] *Dialogus de Scaccario*, p. 7.

certainty that many other features of exchequer practice in the twelfth century have a pre-Conquest origin[1] raises a presumption in favour of the abacus.[2] As for the phrase *ad taleas*, it is, in any case, well attested that the justices were already known early in Henry I's reign as *barones de scaccario*. The court, however, was not termed the *curia de scaccario* but the *curia regis*, though there might be an indication that it was sitting *in thesauro* or *ad scaccarium*.[3] No known document supports Richard of Ely's statement, and of anything that happened before the time of Roger of Salisbury he was not likely to have had certain knowledge. It would be rash therefore to assume as a historical fact that at some remote period there was a court that was said to be 'at the tallies'. The *scaccarium*, the chequered cloth itself, may well have been an introduction under Henry I, before whose time no reference to the exchequer has been traced, though, whether introduced then or earlier, it does not seem to have been a concession to illiteracy, but the corollary of treating an audit as a judicial process. If the court and the parties were to follow the proceedings, there must be a continuous ocular demonstration of each step in arriving at a final balance. This demonstration it was possible to give by placing counters upon the chequered cloth, with its columns a foot or so wide. Whether the accountant was literate or illiterate is beside the point.

Not all accountants at the exchequer were laymen, and of those who were laymen some, of a certainty, were not illiterate. Take, for example, the evidence of the first pipe roll of Henry II. Among those whose accounts are included there are three whom no one could suspect of illiteracy: Hilary, bishop of Chichester, William Cumin, who had served as chancellor to the king of Scotland, and one of the justiciars, Richard de Lucy.[4] In 1161 two clerks, Alexander and Richard, account for Stafford and Wiltshire, and the bishop of Chichester again accounts for Sussex.[5] At other times clerks, chaplains and archdeacons act as sheriffs.[6] In Henry's reign, too, Ranulf Glanville, a future justiciar, will frequently account as

---

[1] For the pre-Conquest ancestry of exchequer practices see Round, *Commune of London*, pp. 69-74.

[2] Knowledge of the abacus had certainly reached England before the end of the eleventh century and seems to have been applied to royal accounts (Haskins, 'The Abacus and the King's Curia', in *E.H.R.*, xxvii.101-6). But there is a good deal of evidence for arithmetical calculations or memoranda upon parchment (*brevia*) in the exchequer in the twelfth century, e.g. *Pipe Roll, 14 Henry II*, p. 213. The *breve de firmis* (*Dialogus*, p. 62) presumably had its counterpart in the eleventh century, as did also the roll for danegeld (*Red Book of the Exchequer*, ii.659).   [3] Above, p. 163.

[4] *Red Book of the Exchequer*, ii.650, 654, 656.

[5] *Pipe Roll, 7 Henry II*, pp. 8, 13, 41.

[6] Henry the archdeacon in Sussex in 1162; David the archdeacon in Bedfordshire in 1170; Wimar the chaplain in Norfolk in 1170 and 1175; Alexander the clerk in Staffordshire in 1170; Nicholas the dean or the clerk from 1164 in Essex (for his identity see *Pipe Roll, 14 Henry II*, p. 36, and *Pipe Roll, 15 Henry II*, p. 121). For dates see P.R.O. *List of Sheriffs*. Though a man is not so qualified in the Pipe Rolls, we may learn from another source that he is a clerk, as Walter of Grimsby in Lincolnshire in 1170 and 1174, for whom see *Becket Materials*, vii.147.

sheriff,[1] while under Richard I another bishop, Hugh of Nonant, will be sheriff of three counties.[2] And then, among the sheriffs of London, William fitz Isabel, will account for several years: he was a prominent money-lender, and money-lenders in a large way are not likely to be illiterate or unskilled in book-keeping.[3] But let us take what may seem a more impressive example. Of the eighteen justices who were sent on eyre in 1176 twelve had served or were to serve as sheriffs.[4] Are we then to infer that, of the eighteen, two-thirds were illiterate? But if we take the more probable view that all the eighteen justices were literate, are we not forced to believe that the *justitiarii totius Anglie*, who were similarly employed under Henry I and two of whom were bishops, were literate also? And a number of these *justitiarii* certainly served as sheriffs[5]. Moreover, if we are right in deducing that the local justices who kept the pleas of the crown, and at least some of the king's serjeants who were concerned in the same business, of necessity kept written records[6], even in the early decades of the twelfth century, we must count the laymen in the king's service who had some elementary knowledge of Latin letters, if not by the hundred, by the score. There does not seem to be any alternative to this conclusion that does not involve improbable assumptions and lead to absurd fantasies. The pipe roll of 1130 cannot be explained away.

It may be that not every sheriff who, we suggest, must be presumed to have been literate accounted at the exchequer in person. The more dignified sheriffs frequently did not do so[7]; but is it to be supposed that they were represented by illiterates? When a sheriff (and presumably a sheriff's deputy) appeared before the barons, he would be accompanied by his clerk[8]; but this was not, we conceive, because the sheriff was presumed to be illiterate, but because he had many other things to do besides keeping accounts. The clerk could doubtless prompt the sheriff on details, but he could not take the sheriff's place. A sheriff's clerk might become a sheriff himself[9] and, though just as able as he was before to deal

---

[1] For Westmorland and Yorkshire between 1175 and 1189 (*Pipe Roll, 23 Henry II*, p. 123; *Pipe Roll, 1 Richard I*, p. 74).

[2] Sheriff of Staffordshire and Warwickshire and Leicestershire.

[3] Sheriff in 1156, 1162, 1178-87, 1193. For his money-lending see Richardson, *English Jewry under Angevin Kings*, pp. 44-59.

[4] For the eighteen see 'Benedict of Peterborough', i.107-8. There are brief biographies of all of them in Foss, *Judges of England*. Two of the commissions were entirely composed of men who had served as sheriffs, those on the second and fifth circuits as listed in the chronicle.

[5] Geoffrey de Clinton in Warwickshire as well as Richard Basset and Aubrey de Vere. It is more than likely, however, that there was difficulty in getting suitable men for the post: hence the concentration of shires in the hands of Hugh of Buckland. For all these men see *Regesta Regum Anglo-Normannorum*, vol. ii.   [6] Above, pp. 184, 186.

[7] This is true generally of magnates, who were represented by stewards, themselves of much the same class as sheriffs' clerks (*Memoranda Roll, 1 John*, Introduction, pp. xciv-xcv).

[8] This is implied by a passage in the *Dialogus de Scaccario*, p. 84: et resideat solus cum suis ad interrogata responsurus. The sheriff's staff (*sui*) must have included at least one clerk and probably more.

[9] *Memoranda Roll, 1 John*, Introduction, p. xcv. Under-sheriffs might be in a similar

with accounts, would have a clerk with him when he appeared as a principal before the barons. Doubtless a sheriff who had seen service as a sheriff's clerk would prove a good accountant, but that does not mean that a sheriff without that experience would be a bad one. If we are to proceed from the known to the unknown, to estimate the qualities of the men of whom we have no knowledge from the qualities of those with whom we have some acquaintance, then the presumption cannot be that sheriffs were illiterate or that the procedure at the exchequer was devised for illiterates. And we must not overstress the part played by tallies in accounting. The primary purpose of the exchequer tally was to serve as a receipt for sums paid into the treasury. Many payments might be made by a sheriff on the authority of a writ, and such writs he had to hand to the chancellor's clerk, who then read them aloud.[1] When lands were newly granted out and an allowance was claimed in respect of them, a writ had again to be produced and scrutinised.[2] An illiterate sheriff, even with a clerk at his elbow, would be very much at a disadvantage if any question arose as to the propriety of a payment or an allowance of this kind.

We have not exhausted the evidence for the wide extension of literacy in the twelfth century. We have not considered the merchants and the financiers who could not have pursued their calling on any large scale without the use of written instruments. Merchants and financiers only occasionally make their appearance in public records: William Cade, who advances money to the king as well as to many of his subjects[3]; Geoffrey of Val Richer, the trusted financial agent of Richard I and John,[4] who checks the great sum of money brought from the English exchequer to Rouen[5]; the burgesses of Bristol, who perform a like service at Gloucester[6]—we cannot suppose these men to be illiterate. But we have said enough for our purpose. The advanced administrative system of the twelfth century was viable because literacy was widespread enough throughout society to make possible an ever increasing use of written documents. The ability of a growing number of laymen to read and write was matched

position to sheriffs' clerks: a good example is Robert Braybrooke, a Christian money-lender, who became a sheriff: for an outline of his career see Richardson, *English Jewry under Angevin Kings*, pp. 100, 270-1.

[1] *Dialogus*, p. 87.   [2] *Ibid.*, p. 86.

[3] For William Cade see Jenkinson's articles in *E.H.R.*, xxviii.209-27, and in *Poole Essays*, pp. 190-210. For other Christian money-lenders who made loans to Henry II and appear upon the pipe rolls see Richardson, *op. cit.*, pp. 51-5.

[4] Geoffrey of Val Richer or 'le Cangeor' was a prominent citizen of Rouen (Delisle, *Actes de Henri II*, Introduction, p. 348; B.M. Additional MS. no. 28024, fo. 22) and he is frequently met with in the Norman pipe rolls (*Rot. Magni Scaccarii Normanniae*, i.136, 235 sqq.; ii.300 sqq, 348 sqq, 415-6, 548, 562 *et passim*). These references and others show the trust reposed in him: cf. *Rot. Normanniae*, p. 49; *Rot. Litt. Pat.*, pp. 14-15*b*; Packard, *Miscellaneous Records of the Norman Exchequer*, pp. 18, 26, 73. There seems nothing to indicate that he was a professional money-lender, as Sir Maurice Powicke appears to suggest (*Loss of Normandy*, (1961), pp. 223, *n.* 239). A *cambiator* seems invariably to have been placed in charge of a mint and Geoffrey may have been master of the mint at Rouen.   [5] *Rot. de Oblatis*, p. 72.   [6] *Rot. Litt. Claus.*, i.113*b*, 114*b*.

by the availability of a growing number of clerks who, little more than nominally in the service of the Church, undertook the burden of the humbler tasks of royal and private administration. But the importance of the literate laymen is that they had not the divided interests that were liable to divert even the humblest clerks from the service of the State. We cannot doubt that it was a source of strength to Henry II and to all his successors that, to an ever increasing extent, public and local administration was in the hands of laymen who could read for themselves all the documents of their office and could, if need be, conduct their own correspondence. The clerk, who might have been the master, became the servant of the State.

Henry II is the symbol of a new age and he was fortunate in his hour. His achievement would not have been possible had there not been men ready to enter his service and to undertake the tasks of a new conception of government, a growing conception, not of one grand pattern, but advancing from expedient to expedient, making possible new and undreamt-of advances. For the far-seeing statecraft which Stubbs attributed to Henry II, in common with his Norman predecessors, we can find no evidence, a statecraft, pursued with earnestness and policy, consciously aimed at balancing the powers of the State, which, for Stubbs, were 'the people of the towns and villages', the 'commons', on the one hand, and the 'feudatories', the 'barons', on the other.[1] All this—'the league between the king and the nation at large which alone could keep the great nobles in their proper subordination'[2]—all this is surely illusion. Is such statecraft to be perceived in Normandy, in Anjou, in Aquitaine, or is it only in England that the eye of faith discerns it? No, this Angevin, in his practical way, lived from day to day, accepting the world as he found it, but wishing it to be at peace and well governed by the standards of the twelfth century. If he transcended those standards as they stood in his boyhood, it was not only because he was a man of exceptional energy and ability, who knew how to progress step by step and who rarely made a false step. He was fortunate in finding servants equipped to do his bidding in a society that was increasingly using for its own purpose the arts which were necessary for the exaltation of the State. To this end, also, the revived study of Roman law tended; and in that Roman law captured the imagination of men in his lifetime he was fortunate too.[3] But withal he accepted the laws and customs of his dominions as he found them, on either side of the Channel,[4] even though he transcended them and supplemented them. This acceptance of old and new, though it brought with it

[1] *Constitutional History*, i.571. [2] *Ibid.*, ii.368.
[3] So Daniel of Morley in the prologue to his *Philosophia*: in partibus illis discipline liberales silentium haberent et pro Ticio et Seio penitus Aristoteles et Plato obliuioni darentur. For the text see *Archiv für die Geschichte der Naturwissenschaften* viii.6-40, ix.50-1: the prologue had previously been published by the Oxford Historical Society, *Collectanea*, ii.171-9. [4] Above, p. 167.

passing difficulties and maladjustments, made for the ultimate stability of the institutions he did so much to remodel, if not to create. Consider two outstanding monuments of his reign, the law-book we know as 'Glanville' and the 'Dialogus de Scaccario'. These are not monuments of systems newly and wholly devised by Henry and his ministers. Complete and rounded as 'Glanville' may seem, we know that the system it expounds was built up writ by writ, action by action, by adapting, fashioning, normalising the processes of the past, rarely by devising something entirely new, though in the result there was composed a system the counterpart of which had never before been conceived in England.[1] And however much the control imposed by the exchequer improved upon the past, it is evident from the witness of the pipe rolls themselves that in substance the financial system of Henry II is the system of Henry I.

If, when we have weighed the evidence, Henry II appears to be a lesser figure, both in his failings and his attainments, than Stubbs would have him, if it seems a mockery to say of him, as of those with whom he is compared, that 'he stands with Alfred, Canute, William the Conqueror, and Edward I, one of the conscious creators of English greatness',[2] we have but reduced him to human, to historical, proportions. We see him as a child of his age, a child of his native Anjou, resting at last in the land of his fathers, among the nuns serving God in the Angevin abbey of Fontevrault.[3]

---

[1] This was shown by M. M. Bigelow in 1879 in his *Placita Anglo-Normannica*: see especially his Introduction, pp. xxiii-xxviii. Later investigations have clarified and confirmed his conclusions: see Van Caenegem, *Royal Writs in England*, part ii.
[2] 'Benedict of Peterborough', ii, p. xxxiii.   [3] *Ibid.*, ii.71.

XVI

CHURCH AND STATE IN THE TWELFTH CENTURY

THE Becket controversy brought to a head a difference between Church and State that was the inevitable outcome of a changing conception of the tribunal which should decide ecclesiastical questions. Broadly speaking, the king and his advisers were conservative, while the Roman Curia and those who sympathised with the Roman point of view sought to oust the customary jurisdiction of the king's court. Those who took this view desired a clear separation of the things belonging to God from the things belonging to Caesar. The Conqueror had already gone some way to meet the views of Rome. In a famous decree he had enjoined that ecclesiastical causes should not henceforward be tried in the hundred court and that laymen offending against canon law should be tried in the bishop's court.[1] The king is legislating for the local courts: he has no word to say of a higher court, the court held before the king himself. There is perhaps an implication that the king will abide by his own rule, but this rule is, at best, a general principle which might be interpreted in more ways than one when it came to particular instances. The jurisdiction of the king's court was, in fact, challenged sixteen years or so later by William of St. Calais, bishop of Durham, who claimed to be tried under canon law when charged with complicity in a plot by Odo of Bayeux or, as the bishop chose to put it, with perjury and breach of faith. Lanfranc's comment, real or invented, is well known, but it may be useful to recall it. 'We are trying you', he said, 'not in your capacity as bishop but in regard to your fief; and in this way we judged the bishop of Bayeux in regard to his fief before the present king's father, and that king did not summon him to that plea as bishop but as brother and earl.'[2] Here a distinction is recognised between ecclesiastical offences and secular offences; but the limits of the jurisdiction of the king's court received no clear definition and, as time went on, it emerged that there was a large area of disputable

---

[1] Liebermann, *Gesetze der Angelsachsen*, i.485. The suggested date is April 1072.
[2] There is an account of the trial in the anonymous tract *De Iniusta Vexacione Willelmi episcopi* in Simeon of Durham, *Opera*, i.120-95. The date of composition has been put as late as the second quarter of the twelfth century (Offler in *E.H.R.*, lxvi.321-41), but in any case the tract reflects the views current within half a century or so of the Conquest. Lanfranc's speech is at p. 184. If not authentic, it seems to be traditional: compare the words attributed to him by William of Malmesbury, *Gesta Regum*, ii.361.

ground over which either *sacerdotium* or *regnum* might claim jurisdiction.

For long, however, there was no serious clash. William of St.
Calais received scant sympathy from his fellow prelates, and his
claim to be tried elsewhere than in the king's court was viewed as
no more than an attempt to evade an accusation which could not be
denied. As yet there was no general assertion that a clerk should be
tried and sentenced only in an ecclesiastical court, even for a secular
offence. Laymen, however, were, in fact, willing to meet the clergy
more than half way in their claim for respect for spiritual things.
Let us give an example. It was for this reason that the possession of
churches by laymen was deprecated, and in the course of the
twelfth century the proprietary church gradually disappeared from
England, quietly and without any collision between the two powers.
The landowner's proprietary right was not entirely lost but was
transmuted into his right of patronage, though there were many
cases where a church had been transferred by lay owners to an
ecclesiastical lord who, from the point of view of the parish and its
priest, might be no better a proprietor than a layman would have
been.[1] The result of this peaceful concession to the Church's claim
to be mistress in her own house may be regarded as typical of the
compromises reached in other fields where the same claim led to
controversy. Something was gained by one side and something lost
by the other: rarely were issues pressed to the limit. Although claims
might be asserted in high-sounding terms, controversies were as a
rule pursued by opinionated and self-seeking men of limited aims
and vision, who in the end were willing to accept a grudging settlement too often repugnant to morals or common sense.[2]

Acute controversy did not, however, arise until Becket fell foul
of Henry II. To get matters in perspective let us go back to the days
of King Stephen. A commonplace dispute over the right to a parish
church will serve as well as any to illustrate the general position at
the time. In 1138 Earl Robert of Gloucester had given the church
of Luton to Gilbert de Clare, earl of Pembroke, who desired it for
his kinsman, a royal chaplain named Gilbert of Chimay. The king
and the earl presented this Gilbert to Bishop Alexander of Lincoln
for induction; but William the Chamberlain, a tenant of the earl of

---

[1] P. Thomas, *Le droit de propriété des laïques sur les églises et le patronage au moyen âge*,
pp. 105-48, traces the process by which the canonists transformed the conception of
dominium into *ius patronatus*. For the proprietary church in England see Boehmer, 'Das
Eigenkirchentum in England', in *Texte und Forschungen: Festgabe für Felix Liebermann*, pp.
301-53, and Douglas, *Domesday Monachorum of Christchurch, Canterbury*, pp. 5-14. Examples
of appropriations to religious houses in the twelfth century will be found in Hartridge,
History of Vicarages in the Middle Ages, pp. 25-9, 209-17.

[2] For the compromises on the determination of legitimacy and the right of presentation
to churches see Mary Cheney in *E.H.R.*, xlvi.188-95. In matters of dower the absurd
position was reached that, if it was in money or chattels, the ecclesiastical courts had
jurisdiction, if in land the secular courts (*Curia Regis Rolls*, xiv.113, no. 574; *Bracton's
Note Book*, no. 442). The one obvious victory for the Church was in the matter of criminous
clerks who were given benefit of clergy.

Gloucester's, was in possession of the church and its lands, which he claimed as his lay fee. The bishop, for his part, was not prepared to remove William except by due process of law, and he therefore appointed a time and place for the trial of the issue between Gilbert and William. The latter refused to appear and sent a message to the effect that, since he did not hold in frankalmoin but in inheritance by military service, he did not admit the bishop's jurisdiction. The bishop summoned him a second and a third time. At this stage Gilbert produced a mandate from the legate, Alberic of Ostia, who happened to be in England, ordering the bishop to enquire whether the land William held belonged to the church of Luton, while William himself procured a writ from the king ordering a recognition by the men of Luton to ascertain who had right to the church and whether the land belonged to the church. The bishop gave an order to like effect. The recognitors found that the church and all the land had been held in frankalmoin until William had converted the ecclesiastical franchise into a military tenure. This finding was certified by the corporal oaths of three of the recognitors chosen for the purpose, and the church was thereupon seized into the bishop's hands. Gilbert then asked to be inducted, but the bishop adjourned the matter to a council held at Oxford early in 1139 in the presence of the king. There the proceedings were recited and, by judgement of Archbishop Theobald and Bishop Alexander, Gilbert was given seisin of the church and the land.[1] The picture we have here is one of close collaboration between Church and State, ending in remarkably speedy justice. There is no hint of a clash of jurisdictions.

Let us take, as a further illustration, a case some years later which arose out of the assertion by the bishop of Chichester of his right to exercise jurisdiction as diocesan over the abbot of Battle. The abbot, for his part, claimed to be exempt by virtue of a charter of the Conqueror's and was formally suspended by the bishop. Thereupon the abbot complained to the king, and the bishop was summoned to answer the abbot before a court over which the king presided in person and which included the bishops of Winchester and Ely and the abbot of Westminster as well as lay barons, sitting in a chapel in the Tower of London. The bishop of Chichester seems to have withdrawn from the court at an early stage and the action proceeded in his absence. The abbot exhibited the charters granted by the Conqueror and his successors, which were read by the bishop of Winchester, and the king, having taken counsel, decided that the church of Battle should not be in any way subject to the bishop of

---

[1] The story is told in the life of Abbot Robert of Gorham (1151-68), one of the *Vitae Viginti Trium Abbatum* passing under the name of Matthew Paris, who seems to have changed little in the text. The original was apparently written before the end of Henry II's reign from documents and personal knowledge. It is accessible, but poorly edited, in Walsingham's *Gesta Abbatum* (Rolls Series), i.110-82. The legal proceedings under Stephen are at pp. 113-5.

Chichester. It is necessary to remark, however, that this was no ordinary dispute over the limits of ecclesiastical jurisdiction, for Battle had the status of a royal chapel and belonged, as it was said, to the king's demesne and crown. And though the abbot had gained his cause in the king's court, he still remained under the sentence of suspension, imposed by the bishop on the ground of his contumacy. Since the bishop was not in court, there was no immediate remedy, but the king proposed to summon him and arrange for the sentence to be lifted. This, however, did not happen, and since the abbot was still contumacious after the lapse of a year, the bishop in a diocesan synod excommunicated him *secundum canonum statuta*. Shortly before, Stephen had died and Henry was not yet king. At Richard de Lucy's instance, however, Archbishop Theobald sent a messenger to the bishop, requiring him to relax the sentence of excommunication pending a reconciliation between him and the abbot.[1]

A third illustration adumbrates the coming clash over the treatment of criminous clerks. In June 1154 Archbishop William of York died suddenly after celebrating mass. The king was in York at the time, and one of the archbishop's clerks came to him and appealed Osbert, an archdeacon of York, of murder, alleging that the sacramental wine had been poisoned. The archdeacon was summoned to appear before an afforced court,[2] apparently the Michaelmas court in London at which Roger of Pont l'Évêque was elected to fill the vacant see.[3] Here Archbishop Theobald and his fellow bishops claimed jurisdiction. The king, however, refused to hand the accused over to an ecclesiastical tribunal on two grounds: the heinousness of the crime and because the appeal of murder had been made to him. The hearing was, however, adjourned until the octave of Epiphany,[4] but before the action could be tried King Stephen was dead.[5]

And now, having seen something of the relations between King Stephen and the Church, we may perhaps ask what meaning is to be given to the words in his so-called second charter, by which he granted and confirmed to ecclesiastics and all clerks that they and their possessions should be subject to the justice and jurisdiction of the bishops and that control over ecclesiastical offices should be in the same hands.[6] It has been suggested, by one from whom we

---

[1] *Chronicon Mon. de Bello*, pp. 68-72, 95, 99.

[2] In John of Salisbury's Latin, 'in quodam conuentu celebri', translated 'solemn council'; but Gilbert Foliot clearly uses *conuentus* as a synonym for *curia* (*Epistolae*, ii.13).

[3] William of Newburgh, *Chronicon*, i.94-5.

[4] That is, the feast of St. Hilary (13 January). This suggests that the traditional law terms were already observed.

[5] *Letters of John of Salisbury* (ed. Millor, Butler and Brooke), i.26.

[6] Ecclesiasticarum personarum et omnium clericorum et rerum eorum justitiam et potestatem et distributionem honorum ecclesiasticorum in manu episcoporum esse perhibeo et confirmo (*Select Charters*, pp. 143-4). The word *honorum* appears in the surviving original charters and seems to be intended, but it was early rendered *bonorum* and the sense completely altered (William of Malmesbury, *Historia Novella* (ed. Potter), p. 19; Richard of Hexham, *Historia* (ed. Howlett), p. 148).

would not lightly differ, that these words mean that the king 'admitted whatever claims of immunity could be fairly made in the name of canon law'.[1] Yet, if these words meant that clerks should be immune from the jurisdiction of secular tribunals, we must surely go further and argue, for example, that the king admitted the right of ecclesiastical courts to determine such issues as disputed claims to advowsons and disputed claims to exemption from diocesan jurisdiction. If, however, Stephen did promise a wide immunity for the clergy, he was grievously forsworn. William of Malmesbury, indeed, declares that the king failed to honour his undertakings in almost every respect and, with the charter immediately before him, he gives what we may presume to be the worst examples. Churches were robbed of their treasures and lands; churches belonging to ecclesiastics were alienated; bishops were imprisoned; abbeys were granted to unfit persons.[2] So runs the catalogue; but of the violation of the immunities of the clergy, of usurpation by the king's courts of causes which belonged properly to courts Christian, there is not a word. There has, we submit, been a misunderstanding, arising not with the contemporary chronicler, but from taking out of its context one sentence in a long and obscurely drafted paragraph of Stephen's charter, the burden of which is that Stephen undertakes that the Church shall be put back into the same position as it was when the first King William was alive and dead. Taken as a whole, the paragraph may suggest that William Rufus and Henry I had despoiled the Church of some of its rights and possessions, but it can hardly mean that Stephen is making fresh concessions, that he is doing more than meeting grievances.[3] And if we understand William of Malmesbury's reproaches aright, they are that Stephen despoiled the Church as his predecessors had done, listening to the counsel of his courtiers who told him that he need never lack money while monasteries were full of treasure. We may doubt whether these reproaches were entirely deserved, but we cannot doubt their meaning.

Nor can it be argued that, because the Constitutions of Clarendon purported to set out the customs, liberties and prerogatives of the king's ancestors and specifically of Henry I,[4] therefore there must have been some concessions made by Stephen which Henry II was endeavouring to withdraw.[5] If this had been so, much surely would have been made of it in the subsequent controversy and we should surely have noticed some traces of these concessions in our sources

---

[1] Pollock and Maitland, *History of English Law*, i.452.   [2] *Historia Novella*, p. 20.

[3] Boehmer, believing that the charter displays wide concessions to the high church party, sees in it not a little we cannot find (*Kirche und Staat in England . . . im XI. und XII. Jahrhundert*, p. 322).

[4] *Select Charters*, p. 163, where the punctuation appears to be wrong. We read: facta est ista recordatio vel recognitio . . . consuetudinum et libertatum et dignitatum antecessorum suorum, videlicet regis Henrici avi sui et aliorum (*sc.* regum), quae observari et teneri debent in regno.   [5] Cf. Pollock and Maitland, *op. cit.*, i.449.

for the history of Stephen's reign. But nothing of this sort do we, in fact, find. In truth, the reference back to the days of the king's grandfather is a commonplace in Henry II's grants: he studiously avoids recognition of the acts of the usurper who preceded him. On the evidence, admittedly fragmentary, we do not think it can be maintained that Stephen's attitude towards any claims that may have been made by high-churchmen was noticeably different from the attitude of his predecessors or, we may add, his successors, except perhaps in the appointment of bishops.[1] Indeed, it seems to have been Henry II who made the greatest and most grievous concession, which he sought later to withdraw.

The three actions under Stephen, of which we have given an account, all had consequences in the early years of Henry II's reign. After Gilbert of Chimay had managed to establish his title, the monks of St. Alban's had managed by rather devious means to obtain possession of Luton church and to have their title confirmed by Stephen. On Henry's accession, however, they lost the church after it had been found by a local inquest to belong to the royal demesne, and only by bribing Richard of Ilchester were the monks able to get it restored to them.[2] This sequel is of interest in the present connexion as illustrating the right of the secular courts to decide who held *dominium* in a church, for more was at issue than the *jus praesentandi*.

The sequels to the other cases are more pertinent to our present discussion. The dispute between the abbot of Battle and the bishop of Chichester continued, with the abbot still resisting the authority of the bishop, despite a mandate from the pope,[3] until, at the instance of Richard de Lucy, the abbot's brother, the king sent a writ to the bishop ordering him to leave the abbot, a royal chaplain, in peace until he himself returned to England. Henry, therefore, as Stephen had done before him, claimed the right to decide the issue, and the case came before him at Whitsuntide 1157 when he wore his crown at St. Edmund's, an occasion on which there would be a large attendance at court. The court moved on to Colchester where the hearing took place. The bishop protested that no layman, not even a king, had the right to confer ecclesiastical dignities or liberties and argued consequently that the Conqueror's charter (which Henry had confirmed) was invalid. To this the king replied in anger that the bishop was calling in question the authority conferred upon him by God at his coronation and asked for the support of the assembled archbishops and bishops. Deserted by his colleagues, the bishop nevertheless persisted in his claim, while denying any inten-

---

[1] Boehmer, *op. cit.*, pp. 371-94. Stephen's inability to control the appointment of bishops is more evident than his failure to control the appointment of abbots, and it is difficult to set aside William of Malmesbury's testimony.

[2] Walsingham, *Gesta Abbatum*, i.116-8, 123-6.

[3] *Chronicon Mon. de Bello*, p. 78; Jaffé-Loewenfeld, no. 10002: 1 March 1155.

tion of disputing the rights of the Crown. In the hostile atmosphere of the court, however, he was driven to repudiating the papal mandate, which he asserted had been obtained without his know-ledge, and finally, at the king's order, resigned all claim to juris-diction over the abbey, the king insisting that he should declare that he did so of his own free will.[1] Instructive as this case is, it must be remembered that it turned upon a narrow issue, whether a royal chapel was subject to the jurisdiction of the diocesan, whether it was, in modern language, a peculiar. Once it was admitted that Battle Abbey was part of the royal demesne and a royal chapel, the bishop had no hope of succeeding in the king's court. That the bishop, who had a great reputation as a lawyer and was much con-sulted by Archbishop Theobald,[2] should fail in pressing the superi-ority of papal authority against local custom, is significant. If we are to believe the *ex parte* story of the Abbey chronicler, none of the assembled bishops ventured to support him, and prominent in ad-vancing the argument in favour of the royal privilege was the chancellor, Thomas Becket.

We turn to the third case. At Henry's accession, the archdeacon of York still lay under the accusation of administering a poisoned chalice to his archbishop. The circumstances in which the case came before Henry II's court are not disclosed by the available sources of information. All we know is what Archbishop Theobald told Adrian IV: 'from the king's hands we just and only just suc-ceeded in recalling the case to the judgement of the Church, with much difficulty and by strong pressure, to the indignation of the king and all his nobles'.[3] We need not at the moment follow the fortunes of the archdeacon, except to remark that he failed in his compurga-tion but escaped the consequences by appealing to the pope.[4] What is noteworthy is that Stephen's decision to try the case himself appears not to have departed widely from the legal position that had been accepted by canonists, namely, that a clerk accused of an atrocious crime should be judged by a secular court, although the canonists would insist that, as a preliminary, the clerk should first be tried and degraded by ecclesiastical authority.[5] Since the arch-deacon's crime appeared to be undeniable,[6] this preliminary step might well look like a formality to a secular tribunal. Henry's yield-

---

[1] *Chronicon Mon. de Bello*, pp. 84-103.

[2] *Letters of John of Salisbury*, Introduction, p. xxvi; Knowles, *Episcopal Colleagues of Archbishop Thomas Becket*, pp. 24-6.

[3] *Letters of John of Salisbury*, i.26.   [4] *Ibid.*, p. 27: see below, p. 304.

[5] Génestal, *Le Privilegium Fori en France*, ii.8-13, 102-3.

[6] His failure to purge himself is significant, as is also the fact that he resigned, or was removed from, his archdeaconry (below, p. 304). Gilbert Foliot, however, believed in his innocence and wrote to Adrian IV on his behalf (*Epistolae*, i.152). His trial was a *cause célèbre*, and many years later William of Newburgh wrote a defence of Osbert (*Chronicon*, i.80-1). Accusations of poisoning in the case of sudden death were, however, common-place. Robert de Sigillo, bishop of London, was alleged to have been murdered with poisoned grapes (John of Hexham in Simeon of Durham, *Historia Regum*, ii.324). Adrian IV is likewise said to have been poisoned (Walsingham, *Gesta Abbatum*, i.136).

ing to Theobald's insistence seems to have had for its motive a desire to please the churchman to whom he owed most rather than any recognition that the custom was unlawful which brought to trial in the king's court clerks accused of atrocious crimes.

There are two other cases in the early years of Henry's reign of which some mention should be made. At the same Whitsuntide court in which the case of Battle Abbey was decided, a parallel action was heard between Archbishop Theobald and the abbot of St. Augustine's, Canterbury.[1] What was in dispute was the profession to be made by the abbot to the archbishop. There seems, however, to have been only a preliminary hearing on this occasion, and the case was adjourned to a meeting of the court at Northampton in July. Here two mandates from the pope, which obviously the arch-bishop had procured,[2] were read; but though they directed the abbot to make his profession, this direction was dependent upon proof that the abbot's predecessors had made their profession to former archbishops. This fact the abbot denied. Whereupon the archbishop produced a number of aged monks who swore that they were present when Abbot Hugh, the present abbot's predecessor, had made his profession to the previous archbishop, William of Corbeil. By the unanimous judgement of the court, therefore, the abbot was required to make his profession and the judgement was embodied in an instrument to which seven bishops set their seals.[3]

The fifth case is also one of the jurisdiction of the diocesan.[4] The monks of St. Alban's were determined to be exempt from the juris-diction of the bishop of Lincoln and, when Alexander III succeeded Adrian IV, the abbot at once sent an agent to the Curia to obtain confirmation of the abbey's privileges before the bishop could him-self persuade the pope to annul them. By means of heavy bribes the abbot obtained what he wanted. The bishop, for his part, went to the king, who was then in France, and, with his authority, prepared to make a visitation of the abbey. The abbot resisted. Thereupon the bishop obtained a writ from the king, addressed to the earl of Leicester as justiciar (and witnessed, it may be remarked, by Becket as chancellor), directing him to cite the bishop and abbot to appear before him and, with three bishops[5] and the abbot of Westminster as assessors, to hear the parties and to report what the relations of the bishop of Lincoln and the abbey had been in the time of Henry I. At the hearing the parties were represented by trained advocates,

---

[1] *Chronicon Mon. de Bello*, p. 88.
[2] Theobald had been in correspondence with Eugenius III as well as Adrian IV (*Letters of John of Salisbury*, i, nos. 8, 11, 12), but little has survived. It is clear, if proof were necessary, that he had requested the mandates: see Adrian's letter of 23 January 1156 (Elmham, *Historia Mon. S. Augustini Cantuariensis*, pp. 411-3) which refers to one of the mandates (Jaffé-Loewenfeld, no. 10237; Gervase of Canterbury, *Opera*, i.163-4). The other mandate, dated 13 January 1156, is Jaffé-Loewenfeld no. 10124=Gervase, *op. cit.*, p. 163.   [3] Gervase, *op. cit.*, pp. 164-5.
[4] Walsingham, *Gesta Abbatum*, i.137-57.
[5] Hilary of Chichester, Richard of Coventry, William of Norwich (*ibid.*, p. 139).

both apparently doctors of law.[1] After an adjournment the case was reserved for trial before the king himself, who had unexpectedly returned to England. In the meantime the bishop had procured a mandate from the pope, remitting the cause to two of the bishops who had already heard the action before the justiciar.[2] These judges delegate were not to determine the cause but were to report fully to the pope who would give judgement. However, at the trial, which was held in March 1163, the abbot made the preliminary point that, while he was prepared to argue his case before either tribunal, the action should be concluded before one or the other, so that, if he succeeded in the king's court, he should not be compelled to appear before an ecclesiastical court. Turning to the two archbishops, Thomas of Canterbury and Roger of York—for by this time Becket had succeeded Theobald—the king remarked that the abbot's point was a reasonable one, for it would not be to the king's honour if an action decided in his court were subject to a second judgement in the pope's consistory. He then withdrew from the court, accompanied by the earl of Leicester, Richard du Hommet[3] and Richard of Il-chester, Geoffrey Ridel joining them later.[4] Here apart, the abbey's privileges were examined by the king and his advisers, after which he returned to court and adjourned the case until the morrow, when the bishop was to be heard. On the second day the bishop, having admitted that his claim did not rest upon documents but on prescription, was advised by the king to confer with the dean and chapter of Lincoln and decide whether to continue to fight the action or to reach a compromise with the abbot. When the bishop agreed to seek a compromise, the king advised the abbot to compensate the bishop by a gift of land in return for a renunciation of his claims. On this basis the action was settled, the terms being embodied in instruments executed by the parties and confirmed by the king and the archbishop.[5]

We have set out these cases in some detail because in no better way can the everyday relations between Church and State in the mid-twelfth century be depicted, the political climate evoked, the background rendered visible before which the quarrel provoked by Becket was played out. Generalities leave too much unexplained. We must endeavour to see the situation from the standpoint of those who sat in the king's court, often in the king's presence, to experience their reactions when conventions, hitherto accepted, were wantonly challenged to the derogation, it must have seemed, of the king's

---

[1] Master John of Tilbury for St. Albans, 'quidam legis peritissimus' for the bishop (*ibid.*, p. 142).
[2] Chichester and Norwich (*ibid.*, p. 144). They were, of course, the nominees of the impetrant, the bishop of Lincoln.
[3] Constable, later justiciar of Normandy (Delisle, *Actes de Henri II*, Introduction, pp. 429-31; Haskins, *Norman Institutions*, pp. 162, 166, 325).
[4] Both archdeacons and both destined to be royal judges and bishops.
[5] Walsingham, *op. cit.*, p. 156.

rights and dignity. We must look at affairs as they appeared at Westminster, rather than as they appeared at Canterbury. We must regard Becket not as a martyr, but perhaps as the fatuous fool that Gilbert Foliot in his anger called him.[1] But before we proceed, it may be well to add something on two other matters which are intimately connected: the relations between English bishops and the king and the relations between the king and the pope.

An English bishop might often be faced with the problem of conflicting loyalties. Though we speak of English bishops, they were bishops of the Universal Church. Normally in the twelfth, as in earlier centuries—Stephen's reign apart—they were nominated by the king, but they were canonically elected and consecrated. If, however, the king could make bishops, he could not unmake them. If they offended him or were immovable in their opposition to him, the ultimate sanction he could impose was to drive them into exile. Though we may not accept as verbally accurate the words which the Battle Abbey chronicler puts into Henry II's mouth long before his quarrel with Becket—'It is very true that a bishop cannot be deposed, but he could be expelled'—these words at least expressed the actual situation, and we may believe the chronicler that they would meet with the general assent, if not the approval, of both ecclesiastics and laymen.[2] When driven to their logical extremes, the pretensions of *sacerdotium* and *regnum* were irreconcilable. But prudent men did not seek to carry to extremes the principles for which they stood. As the wisest of English prelates, Gilbert Foliot, said to Becket, if the king should wield the temporal sword as Becket had wielded the spiritual sword, there was no prospect of peace, no hope of compromise: in this lay the archbishop's fatuity.[3] As a later English canonist, Gervase of Tilbury, saw clearly, insistence upon the abstract claims of Church or State could lead only to disaster. God, he told the Emperor Otto IV, was the author of both *sacerdotium* and *regnum* and the protector of both. Neither was greater than the other, nor should one ask which was the superior but which of the two powers was most faithful in discharging its duty.[4] This is not the point of view of the ecclesiastical controversialists, whose prejudices inform most of the sources upon which modern historians have relied. But if we regard Becket or, for that matter, Anselm through the eyes of their adherents and advocates, we shall not see the whole man. Saints and martyrs do not necessarily make good archbishops. Is it not written, 'the children of this world are in their generation wiser than the children of light'?

---

[1] Verum qui semper fatuus, tua in te hodie apparebit fatuitas (Herbert of Bosham in *Becket Materials*, iii.305). William fitz Stephen reports the speech differently: 'semper fuit stultus et semper erit' (*ibid.*, p. 57).   [2] *Chronicon Mon. de Bello*, p. 91.
[3] Si rex suum exserit gladium ut tu nunc tuum exseruisti, quae poterit esse decetero inter vos reformandae spes pacis?' (Herbert of Bosham in *Becket Materials*, iii.305).
[4] *Otia Imperialia*, Preface, in *M.G.H., Scriptores*, xxvii.363-5.

Not only Becket but, before him, Anselm and Theobald, and, after him, Langton and Winchelsea went into exile, and not only these archbishops but bishops who have little claim to sanctity or high principles, William of St. Calais, Bishop Nigel of Ely—the catalogue is too long to recite of children of this world as well as of children of light. The kings who drove them into exile were not only those who are conventionally 'bad' but some who are conventionally 'good'. To suggest that all the exiles were in the right and all the kings in the wrong would be to suggest the incredible, that, indeed, those who supported the king at the time—and even John had almost universal support against Innocent III and Stephen Langton[1]—were, one and all, utterly misguided and unreasonable. Sorely tried, King Stephen had been high-handed in his treatment of bishops, but he did not act without precedent. Suspecting Roger of Salisbury and Alexander of Lincoln of treachery, he had not hesitated to order them to surrender their castles and, when they defied him, to arrest them.[2] His mistake had lain in treating them with indignity, but otherwise it is difficult to see that he overstepped any bounds that his predecessors had observed. Bishops, he held, might attend ecclesiastical councils abroad only with his consent, and Archbishop Theobald's first exile was the result of disobeying the king's prohibition.[3] Stephen's forbearance in the face of Theobald's ambiguous conduct—if not open disloyalty—in the closing years of his reign is remarkable.[4] We cannot suppose that the archbishop's conduct was a matter of indifference to the king: perhaps he was biding his time or feared that reprisals would still further endanger his hold on the throne when so many, including his own son, were protecting their own future by coming to terms with the pretender. Nor must we suppose that the pretender, the young duke of Normandy, had a less exalted idea of his rights and dignity than had Stephen, or that, young as he was, he had any illusions as to the motives for the support Theobald gave him. And if Henry, on his side, when he came to the throne, made concessions to the archbishop and, for example, surrendered criminous clerks to him, the archbishop also had to make concessions. Theobald's action in conniving at Henry's seizure from the bishop of Salisbury of the castle of Devizes[5] was, in after years, repudiated by Becket, and during his lifetime Theobald had to support the reproaches of Adrian IV for conspiring with the king in suppressing appeals to the Curia.[6]

There has been much discussion of appeals from England to Rome in the twelfth century and of the attitude of Henry II before and

---

[1] Below, p. 341-2.
[2] William of Malmesbury, *Historia Novella*, pp. 27, 31; *Gesta Stephani*, pp. 51-2.
[3] Saltman, *Theobald archbishop of Canterbury*, pp. 25-30.   [4] Above, pp. 252-3.
[5] Becket to Alexander III, 1170 (*Becket Materials*, vii.241). Theobald is not named, and this sentence, like the rest of the letter, is characteristically disingenuous. For the transaction see above, p. 262.   [6] Elmham, *Historia*, p. 412.

after the concordat of Avranches in 1172.[1] But the problem should be approached in rather different fashion if we are to understand the relations between Church and State, and we propose to show that any idea that Henry, at any time, had consistently restricted access to the Curia is manifestly out of the question. To begin with, it may be well to refute the statement of a contemporary, Henry archdeacon of Huntingdon, that the evil practice of appealing to Rome began during the legation of Henry of Blois, bishop of Winchester.[2] The legation, which was granted to Henry, possibly in March 1139, by Innocent II, was not published until the end of August.[3] More than three years before this, however, there had been a disputed election to the bishopric of London, following upon the death of Gilbert the Universal in August 1134. The see was still void on the accession of Stephen, and the new king proceeded to take steps to fill it at the council he summoned to meet at Westminster at Easter 1136. There it was found impossible to secure the unanimous assent of the canons of St. Paul's to any candidate, but a party of them, without the king's approval, elected Abbot Anselm of St. Edmund's. The dean, and the canons more intimately allied with him, appealed to the pope against the election, not perhaps at the king's instance, but certainly with his approval. Despite the king, Anselm's party sent representatives to Rome to obtain papal confirmation, but in the confusion resulting from the schism they were forced to return home without accomplishing anything. Meanwhile the dean's representatives had been favourably received by Innocent II who, as a preliminary to hearing the appeal, wrote to the suffragans of Canterbury (that see being void) and to Archbishop Thurstan of York, asking them to report on the life and conversation of the bishop elect. Their replies were read in the consistory which considered the appeal. Presumably Thurstan's letter, of which we are given the substance, is typical: he commented drily that it would be better to remove Anselm from his abbacy rather than to promote him to the church of London. In the result, Anselm's election was quashed on the ground that it had not received the assent of the dean who, in law, should have had the first voice in the election.[4]

When the dean's appeal had been decided, it was the turn of one of his proctors, Richard de Belmeis, to present his own appeal. Richard claimed to be the rightful archdeacon of Middlesex: and, to understand how his appeal came to the pope, we must remember that both the sees of Canterbury and London were void—the election

---

[1] The principal contributions are by Z. N. Brooke in *Cambridge Historical Journal*, ii.213-28, and again in *The English Church and the Papacy*, pp. 208-26, and Mary Cheney, 'The Compromise of Avranches', in *E.H.R.*, lvi.177-97.

[2] Henry of Huntingdon, *Historia Anglorum*, p. 282.

[3] William of Malmesbury, *Historia Novella*, p. 29.

[4] Ralf de Diceto, *Abbreviationes Chronicorum, s.a.* 1156-8, in *Opera*, i.248-51. This account appears to be contemporary. Cf. *Memorials of St. Edmund's Abbey*, iii.5.

to London having just been invalidated—and that the pope was the universal ordinary. We are given the speech of Richard's advocate in the consistory, but we need not recite the grounds for his appeal. All we need note is that the pope appointed the bishops of Hereford and Lincoln as judges delegate to determine the cause and that they decided in Richard's favour well before Henry of Blois was appointed legate.[1] Now, not only do these two cases dispose of any suggestion that appeals were unknown in England before 1139, but the details we are given indicate that the procedure was well understood, the path well worn, at the time of Stephen's accession. There is nothing in the least to suggest that the dean of St. Paul's or the would-be archdeacon of Middlesex was embarking on an uncharted sea. There is other evidence to show that appeals to Rome were not unknown under Henry I and that they continued unabated, though in what volume we can hardly guess, under Stephen.[2] But no evidence is so striking as these appeals from St. Paul's in Stephen's earliest years, evidence that seems hitherto to have been generally overlooked.[3]

It is true that Henry II did on occasion prohibit appeals to the Curia. The first instance was in 1159, on the occasion of a disputed election to the papacy, when he did not wish the position to be prejudiced by appeals to either of the rivals, Alexander III or Victor IV, until he had decided, after mature deliberation, which of them to recognise. But the very terms of the writ addressed to Archbishop Theobald, the bishops, abbots and all clergy subject to him, which is almost apologetic in tone, show that in the ordinary way the king did not interfere with appeals. The king urges ecclesiastical judges so to conduct the administration of justice that none will have just cause for complaint or suffer injury which would give ground for appealing to the apostolic see. At the same time, but for the same limited period, the king forbade the clergy to leave England for the purpose either of meddling in the dispute or of prosecuting appeals.[4] Doubtless Henry addressed similar writs to the clergy of the other ecclesiastical provinces within his dominions and for the same reason, and presumably he was obeyed because disobedience, if brought to light, might have unpleasant consequences. But he had no effective means at his command to prevent access to the Curia. He was in no better position than Stephen when the bishops proposed to send some of their number to Rome to complain of the treatment of Roger of Salisbury. 'If one of you', Aubrey de Vere told them, 'should presume to do so and leave England against the king's wish and the royal prerogative, he might have some difficulty in getting

---

[1] Diceto, *op. cit.*, pp. 251-2. [2] *E.H.R.*, lvi.178-80.
[3] The appeal by the dean against Anselm is noticed, however, by Boehmer (*op. cit.*, pp. 372-3).
[4] Saltman, *op. cit.*, p. 543. The writ is witnessed by the bishops of Bayeux and Evreux, which is evidence enough of the concurrence of the episcopate.

back', adding, rather lamely, that the king was himself appealing to Rome against the bishops.[1]

Bishops and abbots, as a matter of course, employed agents at the Curia. It seems now to be accepted that Archbishop Theobald employed John of Salisbury in this capacity in the time of Eugenius III,[2] with scant success, it must be admitted, in the archbishop's dispute with the monks of St. Augustine's, who also had their agents, and perhaps better ones, at the Curia.[3] The monks of St. Alban's and Battle, the bishops of Lincoln and Chichester, had their agents there. Which bishop or great religious house had not? A minute fraction of papal mandates obtained by English litigants has come down to us, but we cannot doubt that there was once a multitude of them,[4] a multitude to which no English king could take any conceivable objection. The pope was the universal ordinary and the universal court of appeal. Nor was there one system of ecclesiastical law, one mode of procedure, upon the Continent and another on this side of the Channel. Nor would the king wish it otherwise: he was himself too often a suppliant at the Curia to desire to be at cross purposes with the pope. Stephen had solicited the support of Eugenius III for his scheme to associate his son in the kingship.[5] On the accession of Adrian IV, Henry II, himself recently crowned, sent proctors to the pope, a distinguished company, the abbot of St. Alban's and three Norman bishops, Le Mans, Lisieux and Évreux.[6]

It was an impressive delegation, political rather than jurisprudential, though the members, certainly the abbot, found their stay at the Curia convenient for the transaction of private business that impinged upon ecclesiastical law. For this they necessarily employed local agents, but they did not then make the acquaintance of Italian lawyers for the first time. The Italian lawyer had made his appearance in England by the middle of the century.[7] Vacarius had been brought to England by Archbishop Theobald.[8] The abbot of St. Alban's sent his learned Italian clerk, Master Ambrose, to act at the Curia on his behalf.[9] The abbot of Battle desired to retain an Italian lawyer as advocate before the legate's court.[10] We stress these facts in order to emphasise the universality of canon law, the impossibility of conceiving a system in which England at this period was insulated from the *jus commune* of the Western Church and the appellate jurisdiction of Rome. The Italian canonist was everywhere,

---

[1] William of Malmesbury, *Historia Novella*, p. 33.
[2] *Letters of John of Salisbury*, i, Introduction, pp. xvii-xxiv; Saltman, *op. cit.*, pp. 169-74.
[3] *Letters of John of Salisbury*, i.14-15.
[4] Cf. *ibid.*: monachus sancti Augustini contra me multitudinem obtinuerit litterarum. If this phrase is to be taken literally the letters cannot all have been from Adrian IV. For instruments by Eugenius III in favour of St. Augustine's see Elmham, *Historia*, pp. 392-406.   [5] Saltman, *op. cit.*, pp. 36-39.
[6] Walsingham, *Gesta Abbatum*, i.125-9.
[7] Cf. Pollock and Maitland, *History of English Law*, i.214.
[8] See the introduction by F. de Zulueta to Vacarius, *Liber Pauperum*, pp. xiii-xvii.
[9] Walsingham, *Gesta*, i.136-7.   [10] *Chron. Mon. de Bello*, p. 173.

and an Italian canonist who did not accept as axiomatic the necessity for papal authority to decide vexed questions of ecclesiastical law would be a monster. Trained English lawyers were, it is true, gradually coming to the fore in their own country; but they were trained in the fashion of Italy, where they seem for the most part to have learnt their law.[1] If they were not Italian, they were Italianate.

We can give here but a glimpse of the intricate web which bound together Western Christendom, a web from which no man could escape, even if he so desired, be he prince or pauper. This is the *sacerdotium*. But did men desire to escape from the web? Yes, there were those who sought a perfect life outside the fold of the Church, the sect we call Catharist, Albigeois, and by other names; but princes were zealous in driving out such heretics, beating and branding them in England, burning them in France.[2] Kings were nothing if not orthodox. If a pope was the vicar of Christ, so also was a king: and God had created the *regnum* as well as the *sacerdotium*. Under Christ the pope was the superior over all men's souls. Under God the emperor was the lord over all men's bodies, and kingship, the *jus regis*, was divinely instituted.[3] What then was to be rendered unto Caesar? It was here that the conflict between Church and State, pope and king, began and ended. They fought over a narrow field, to which there were no defined boundaries either in England or in any country, not a continuous combat but desultorily as occasion arose; consequently we can understand what were the objects of contest only by giving examples.

Let our examples be taken from the early years of Henry II's reign. As we have seen, soon after Henry's accession Robert of Gorham, abbot of St. Alban's, was employed by him upon a mission to Adrian IV, and the abbot obviously found it convenient to further at the same time the interests of his house. So far was the king from disapproval that he wrote to the pope, asking that the abbot's business might be regarded as favourably as his own. We know of two matters in which the abbot succeeded: one was a privilege exempting St. Alban's from diocesan jurisdiction; the other was a letter of censure addressed to the abbot of St. Benedict-sur-Loire because he had failed in his duty of hospitality when Abbot Robert was on his way to the Curia. On the abbot's return to England he attended a royal council at which he exhibited certain papal mandates he had

---

[1] The abbot of St. Alban's retained Master John of Tilbury (Walsingham, *Gesta*, i.142): his name suggests kinship with Gervase of Tilbury, who learnt his law at Bologna, where he subsequently taught (*History*, xlvi.105-6). There was a growing school of civilians and canonists in England and Normandy, but their teaching was dominated by Bologna (Kuttner and Rathbone, 'Anglo-Norman Canonists of the Twelfth Century' in *Traditio*, vii.270-339).

[2] For England the references are collected by Maitland, *Roman Canon Law in the Church of England*, pp. 161-75. For France see William of Newburgh, *Chronicon Anglicanum*, pp. 121-4, and *Annals of Anchin, s.a.* 1183, in *Historiens de la France*, xviii.536. By 1210 the penalty of burning had been introduced into England.

[3] Gervase of Tilbury in *M.G.H., Scriptores*, xvii.365.

obtained: one of these required the general celebration throughout England of the feast of St. Alban; another the attendance of the clergy and laity of Hertfordshire at an annual procession at the abbey. When these mandates were read, the representatives of the bishop of Lincoln at once entered an appeal against them to the pope. Shortly afterwards St. Alban's obtained additional privileges, including the right of the abbot to wear a mitre. On the accession of Alexander III, the abbot obtained further privileges, which were to lead to an action brought by the bishop of Lincoln before the king himself. Before this action could be heard, however, the bishop procured a papal mandate, citing the abbot in the same cause before judges delegate and reserving judgement for the pope himself. This mandate excited the king's anger, at first against the abbot, who, he thought, had procured it; but the abbot was able to reassure him that it was the work of the bishop, who wished to ensure a trial before prejudiced judges. At the actual trial all the abbey's privileges were produced for the king's inspection. The only one to which he took exception had been granted by Celestine II: this contained a clause providing for an annual payment of an ounce of gold to the pope in recognition of the dependence of the abbey upon the Holy See. 'This article, my lord abbot', said the king, 'is in derogation of our dignity: you have no right to make my church tributary to Rome without my assent.' The abbot protested that it was not he who had procured the privilege but a predecessor. 'Whoever did it', retorted the king, 'acted illegally.' The king then asked to see the other privileges, especially those to which the bishop of Lincoln took exception. In handing the king the privilege conferring the mitre, the abbot excused himself, with questionable honesty, asserting that Adrian IV had sent it without his prior knowledge. The king, however, showed no displeasure, saying that, so far as he was concerned, every abbot might wear a mitre.[1]

We have set down these things in the unstudied order in which the chronicler records them, hoping in this way to give a fair impression of the constant traffic with the Curia in matters great and small and of its impact upon authority, ecclesiastical and secular, in England. We may supplement these examples from St. Alban's with parallels from Battle, where also there was a long-standing dispute between the abbot and the bishop of Chichester over the authority of the diocesan. In an action before the king himself in 1157, the king made his position quite clear. He objected to the bishop's plea that the king could not confer ecclesiastical liberties and dignities and also to his impugning royal charters that purported to do so. The king also demanded to know whether the bishop had procured a papal mandate derogatory to the royal authority: this the bishop impudently denied, making the brazen suggestion

[1] Walsingham, *Gesta*, i.126-53.

that the abbot had done so.[1] From these examples certain truths quite clearly emerge. The king did not control access to the Curia but, on the contrary, learnt of any papal privilege or mandate after the event; on the other hand, the impetrant was expected to conform to the law of the realm. The temptation to ignore the limitations imposed by law was doubtless strong in a litigious age, when privileges and mandates might be obtained in almost any terms for an adequate payment. But when papal instruments that offended the king's dignity were challenged in the king's court, especially before the king himself, the boldest litigants were driven to prevarication and renunciation. Such occasions were, however, rare, and possible conflicts between ecclesiastical and secular jurisdiction in no way inhibited litigants from recourse to the Curia. Some might think it prudent to consult the king beforehand[2]; but whatever steps litigants might take for their own protection, privileges and mandates were sought quite openly and were as openly exhibited, nor could they, indeed, have served any conceivable purpose had not this been the position. Pope Adrian's complaint that Archbishop Theobald had conspired with the king to suppress appeals and that no one dared in their presence to appeal to the apostolic see is manifestly based upon a malicious tale.[3] It springs from the undeniable fact that disputes regarding diocesan jurisdiction over monasteries had been determined in the king's court and in the archbishop's presence. Theobald was not, in the event, deterred either by the pope's protest or by his threat of reprisals should the archbishop persist, for, as we have seen, the action which gave rise to them, that between Theobald and the monks of St. Augustine's, was decided to his satisfaction in the king's court.[4] There had not, of course, been any attempt either by the archbishop or the king to suppress appeals in general or to render them abortive. A letter from Theobald to the pope, reminding him that it was open to anyone to appeal if he wished,[5] should be sufficient to dispel any such idea, and the early letters of John of Salisbury are replete with references to appeals to the Curia from ecclesiastical courts all over the province of Canterbury, appeals concerning what may seem to us quite trifling disputes.[6] Whether such appeals were pursued or not was of no moment to anyone except the litigants.[7] But it is easy to understand the resentment felt at Rome when a disappointed litigant complained, as the monks of St. Augustine's evidently complained, that an appeal of

---

[1] *Chron. Mon. de Bello*, pp. 91-2, 96, 101-2.

[2] Apart from the case of Richard of Anstey the evidence is difficult to interpret: cf. Saltman, *Theobald Archbishop of Canterbury*, p. 155.

[3] Elmham, *Historia*, p. 412.　　　　　　　　　　　　　　　　　　　[4] Above, p. 292.

[5] *Letters of John of Salisbury*, i.20: noueritis liberum esse omnibus appellare.

[6] Cf. *ibid.*, Introduction, p. xxxii.

[7] If we understand aright Gilbert Foliot's letter to Alexander III (*Becket Materials*, v.205), the king made it plain that he claimed no more than that by ancient custom he was entitled to control appeals touching secular matters: *ob civilem causam*.

some importance was being frustrated because it was drawn into the king's court.

It may, however, fairly be said that, except perhaps in the matter of criminous clerks, there was no serious point of dispute between *sacerdotium* and *regnum* in the early years of Henry II's reign. The subjection of abbeys to diocesan jurisdiction, which engaged the attention of the king's court with some frequency, was hardly a matter of contention between Church and State. The pope was as ready to accord exemption to favoured monasteries as was the king. The bishops were the parties most deeply concerned, and their quarrel was not with the king but with the privileged, or would-be privileged, monks. The pope might be piqued that his jurisdiction was ousted on occasion, but, however vehement his protests, they were so much sound and fury. Nor was the king active in drawing such suits into his court: whether the issue was tried by judges delegate or in the king's court was a matter primarily for the ecclesiastical litigants. Nor were the two tribunals necessarily very different in composition. Certainly, when actions came before the king in person, he was likely to be well attended by bishops and abbots as well as barons. Nor was this the position only in the highest court. The action between the bishop of Lincoln and the abbot of St. Alban's was, in its initial stages, tried in a court, presided over by the justiciar, that included three bishops and an abbot. When the bishop of Lincoln sought to remove the cause to an ecclesiastical court, the judges delegate appointed on his nomination were two of those who had sat in the king's court, the bishop of Chichester and the bishop of Norwich. These, the abbot alleged, were chosen because they were themselves embroiled in similar disputes, the one with the abbot of Battle, the other with the abbot of St. Edmund's.[1] With the bishop of Lincoln the choice of an ecclesiastical tribunal was not a matter of principle but an expedient to gain his own ends. Clerical litigants, indeed, resorted to ecclesiastical or secular tribunals as they estimated their chances of success. Their first thought was to win their actions, not to uphold any lofty ideal. When the abbot of Battle sought to recover a church of which he had been deprived, he proceeded, as the chronicler says, 'nunc in curia regali, nunc in ecclesiastica'.[2] This it was possible for him to do because he could proceed against an intrusive incumbent before judges delegate and in the king's court against the layman who claimed the advowson.[3] When the abbot proceeded against an incumbent in the king's court, the chronicler excuses him on the ground that this was not to the detriment of the right and dignity of the Church because the only question to be determined was upon whose presentation the incumbent was instituted.[4] We may get such echoes of high principles, but they are

---

[1] Walsingham, *Gesta*, i.138-9, 144.
[2] *Chronicon. Mon. de Bello*, p. 113.
[3] *Ibid.*, pp. 116-8.
[4] *Ibid.*, p. 125.

distant echoes. The abbot was not so much concerned with the pretensions of the Universal Church as with the material interests of the church of Battle. In everyday life litigants seized the weapon most serviceable in their hands.

If we seek an apt phrase in which to express the general relations between Church and State at this period we shall have difficulty in finding it. A mutual tolerance may mask a grudging acceptance by churchmen of a situation incompatible with the principles they professed. No clerk would dispute the king's claim to jurisdiction in temporal matters, no layman that of the Church to jurisdiction in spiritual matters; but as to which jurisdiction belonged such matters as we have seen coming before the king's court there might be two opinions. Successful litigants would be content that the king's court should have cognisance of matters that certainly impinged upon the spiritual. Unsuccessful litigants, like Bishop Hilary of Chichester, who had a great reputation as a canonist[1] and boasted of his acquaintances at the Curia,[2] might be inclined to question, as he did, the foundations of royal authority. Yet to all seeming, despite such differences of opinion, churchmen could accommodate themselves to a situation which, however anomalous, rarely irked them. Into this calm atmosphere the acute controversy provoked by Becket came as a sudden thunderstorm on a summer day. The king was quite unprepared for the claims the new archbishop advanced. As chancellor he had attested royal writs, in the king's court he had advanced arguments, which asserted the royal prerogative to the full.[3] Now he was prepared to question every claim to jurisdiction where the Church was involved. The story has been told from many angles and we need not seek to repeat it. There is general agreement that the controversy had been provoked by the treatment of criminous clerks and continued to revolve round it, despite the extraneous questions introduced by each side. Let this be the basis of our approach.

It would seem unquestionable that the clause in the Constitutions of Clarendon governing the treatment of criminous clerks was a simplification of the facts. The Constitutions, in none too plain language, laid it down that a clerk, accused of felony, should be tried in an ecclesiastical court and, if found guilty, should be degraded and handed over to royal justice for punishment.[4] It was claimed, and with reason, that this accorded with canon law.[5] Whether it

---

[1] For Bishop Hilary see Knowles, *Episcopal Colleagues of Archbishop Thomas Becket*, pp. 24-7.

[2] Ego autem in illa curia omnibus notus sum (*Chronicon Mon. de Bello*, p. 102).

[3] Above, pp. 291-2.

[4] Maitland, *Roman Canon Law in the Church of England*, pp. 133-9.

[5] The argument on behalf of the king is set out by Herbert of Bosham (*Becket Materials*, iii.266-7). Maitland's comment on this passage will be found in *Roman Canon Law in the Church of England*, pp. 140-5. It is significant that Henry was prepared to stand or fall by the decision of the Gallican Church or the masters of the school of Paris in regard to the

accorded with the custom hitherto prevailing in England is more questionable. The case of Archdeacon Osbert, at which we have already glanced, was notorious. Had the rule in the Constitutions been applied, he would, after failing to purge himself, have been handed over to the king's court. As it was, he had appealed to the pope and, though retaining the style of Osbert the archdeacon, was now living as a knight unmolested in England.[1] In face of this precedent it seems impossible to contend that the more recent cases of criminous clerks which figured in the Becket controversy fell outside an arrangement to which Henry had given a reluctant sanction when he had yielded to Archbishop Theobald's insistence and waived Stephen's claim to deal with the archdeacon in the king's court. From the details which Becket's biographers give of the trial of criminous clerks in the years before the Constitutions brought a long rankling grievance to the point of crisis, it is clear that many others were treated as the archdeacon had been. In a case of murder there appears always to have been in the first instance an appeal of felony, followed by a claim of privilege for the accused, his transfer to the bishop's jurisdiction, and his trial in an ecclesiastical court.[2] Nor must we assess the quality of ecclesiastical justice by the case of Philip de Broi, the case which in especial roused the king's ire. It was in the days of Archbishop Theobald that Philip, a canon of St. Paul's, Bedford, was appealed of the murder of a knight but purged himself in the bishop's court. Popular indignation was aroused because he was generally believed to be guilty. He was therefore again brought before the sheriff, apparently to the end that he should stand a second trial in a secular court. He claimed that he had already been acquitted and then, presuming upon his high birth, was imprudent enough to revile the sheriff. But the sheriff, Simon fitz Peter, was not to be trifled with: as a *curialis* he had the ear of the king, to whom he went with his complaint. Meanwhile Philip had put himself under the tuition of the court of Canterbury. Though these events are briefly related in our sources, they must have been spread over some years, and the archbishop now was Becket. Not unreasonably, as it would seem, Becket refused to re-try the charge of murder, but he did try Philip on the charge of insulting the king's minister, a charge Philip did not deny. The accounts given of the penalty differ, but he seems to have been scourged, suspended for a year or more and exiled, a sentence which looks far in excess of the gravity of the offence.[3] Neither this sentence nor the indignation

whole of the Constitutions and that Becket evaded this test (*Becket Materials*, vii.164; Ralf de Diceto, *Opera*, i.336-7).

[1] C. T. Clay in *Yorkshire Archaeological Journal*, xxxvi.277-9.

[2] *Becket Materials*, iii.45-6, 264-6.

[3] The story is variously told by Edward Grim, William fitz Stephen, Herbert of Bosham and an anonymous author (*ibid.*, ii.374-6, iii.4-5, 265-6, iv.24-5). The account by William of Canterbury is worthless (*ibid.*, i.12-13). Simon fitz Peter is described as an itinerant justice: he was, in fact, sheriff of Bedford, 1156-9. For Philip de Broi see

aroused by the case is easy to understand unless we presume that Philip was in fact responsible for the knight's death and that his compurgators had perjured themselves. In the other cases reported there seems to be no hint of a miscarriage of justice, although the penalties evidently appeared to laymen to be inadequate. We hear of one case where a priest, who had been appealed of murder, failed in his purgation, was degraded and confined in a monastery to undergo perpetual penance, and we are told that other criminous clerks were treated similarly.[1] Lay opinion, however, demanded death or mutilation.

It is important to bear in mind that, though the differences between Church and State may have been exacerbated by Becket, at least in the matter of criminous clerks they were not of his creation, and it may be well to cite another piece of evidence. It is contained in a story told by William fitz Stephen, which has often been used as an illustration of the corruption of inferior ecclesiastical courts, but it has a much wider implication. The facts are briefly these. Early in his reign Henry appears to have issued an edict,[2] prohibiting the extortion of money by judges: the text has not come down to us, but the intention seems to have been to make it apply to both ecclesiastical and secular courts.[3] In consequence, a burgess of Scarborough complained to the king, who was then at York, that a rural dean had extorted money from his wife by bringing against her a charge of adultery which was false and unsupported by witnesses. The king ordered the dean to be brought before him in the presence of Richard de Lucy and other barons, Archbishop Theobald, the bishops of Durham and Lincoln, and John of Canterbury, then treasurer of York. The dean alleged that, when he tried the case, there had been witnesses to the woman's guilt, a deacon and a layman; but since he failed to produce them, the king demanded judgement upon him. The barons and clergy retired to consult. John of Canterbury was the first to give his opinion: the money extorted should be returned to the burgess and the dean should be remitted to the archbishop of York, his diocesan, for sentence. At this Richard de Lucy turned to him and asked: 'What will you adjudge to our lord the king, against whose edict this man has offended?' (meaning, of course, that he should be amerced). 'Nothing', replied John, 'because he is a clerk.' Thereupon Richard refused to be a

---

V.C.H. Bedford, i.378. He was still in possession of his canonry in 1166, or later, when the endowments of St. Paul's, Bedford, were formally transferred to an Augustinian foundation (Harl. MS. 3656, fo. 16). He, or a namesake, was employed to pay the wages of knights at 'Canterbothan' at some time before Michaelmas 1161 (*Pipe Roll, 7 Henry II*, pp. 22, 54). Philip's would seem to be a very early instance of a tuitorial appeal, for which see Churchill, *Canterbury Administration*, i.427-8, 460-5.

[1] *Becket Materials*, iii.264-5. Later this severity seems to have been relaxed, but reimposed in the thirteenth century, though the practice in England is uncertain (Cheney in *E.H.R.*, li.218-9, 233-4).

[2] It is described as 'lex prohibitionis' or 'constitutio'.

[3] Haskins suggested that the edict was confined to inferior ecclesiastical courts (*Norman Institutions*, 329-32). But if the legislation is related to that summarised by Robert de Torigni (ed. Howlett), p. 327, it applied to secular courts as well as to ecclesiastical.

party to the judgement and, leaving the clergy behind, returned with
the other barons to the king. When the clergy themselves returned
and expressed their agreement with John, the king rejected their
judgement as perverse (*falsa*) and appointed another day for consideration of the matter. Before that day could arrive, he was, however, called away from England and nothing further was done.[1] This
is an illuminating case. It gives us a view of the court held before
the king himself, corresponding exactly to the picture presented by
other accounts when the king is determining such issues as the exemption of monasteries from diocesan jurisdiction. It also presents
us with a new issue, because here the clerk was not accused of
felony, but of what we should call a statutory offence. Doubtless he
was guilty of an ecclesiastical offence, for which he would be punished. Should he be punished also for the civil offence? The answer
of the clergy seems evidently already to be, *non bis in idipsum*: a man
should not be punished twice for the same offence.

In the face of so much evidence for the early part of Henry's reign
it is impossible to take any other view than that, for nine years or
more before the Constitutions of Clarendon were framed, the
practice had grown up of remitting criminous clerks for trial and
punishment by an ecclesiastical court. While, therefore, an older
custom, a custom spread throughout Frankish lands,[2] may have been
to punish criminous clerks in the king's court, at least in the case of
grave felonies, leaving to ecclesiastical courts merely the formal
process of degradation before execution of sentence, this custom had
lapsed. Consequently, it is difficult to avoid the conclusion that, faced
with the deplorable consequences of Henry's concession to Theobald,
the king's advisers had found a way out by dressing up as a custom
a new rule that could be plausibly defended as canonical. The custom,
they said in effect, was for accused clerks to be brought before the
king's court and, if found guilty in an ecclesiastical court, punished
as laymen.[3] If in this way the draftsmen of the Constitutions sought
to check an abuse, they would not be unmindful that the procedure
yet left a loophole. Should the accused be at liberty to appeal to
the Curia, he might be as fortunate as Archdeacon Osbert. This
loophole, we suggest, the draftsmen sought to close by another
clause which made such appeals subject to the king's assent. This
clause demands scrutiny, for we doubt whether it has always been
correctly interpreted. It envisages appeals of one restricted type only,
in suits commenced in an archdeacon's court. From the archdeacon
there was an appeal to the court of the bishop and thence to the
court of the archbishop. If the archbishop failed to render justice,
the case was to come to the king and by his direction was to be
determined in the archbishop's court. This left open the possibility

[1] *Becket Materials*, iii.43-5.
[2] Génestal, *Le Privilegium Fori*, ii.xxiii-xxvii, 110, 115-8.   [3] Above, p. 291.

of an appeal from the archbishop to the Curia, but only with the king's approval.[1] There is this limited restriction on appeals to the pope, but certainly no general restriction. How very limited the restriction was can be appreciated by considering the nature of an archdeacon's jurisdiction. Cases of great difficulty or magnitude did not ordinarily come before him: no disputes regarding a monastery's claim to exemption, episcopal or abbatial elections or such high issues, but ecclesiastical crimes, matrimonial causes, testamentary matters and a few other causes of little importance.[2] Except in regard to their criminal jurisdiction the king had little interest in archdeacon's courts, as, indeed, another clause in the Constitution suggests, a clause designed to regulate their procedure so that a layman, accused of an ecclesiastical crime, should be assured of a fair trial.[3]

We cannot suppose that appeals to the Curia which affected the rights and dignity of the Crown were intended to be governed in any way by the Constitutions. Of such appeals we have already had some examples before us. When the abbot of St. Alban's and the bishop of Lincoln were engaged in a continuous series of disputes, the bishop endeavoured to circumvent the abbot by obtaining a papal mandate for a preliminary hearing before judges delegate, leaving the determination of the cause to the pope. When in a royal council the abbot exhibited papal privileges obnoxious to the bishop, his representatives at once gave notice of an appeal to the pope. Appeals to the pope against Becket were likewise freely threatened at the council of Northampton in 1164,[4] very much as appeals had been made or threatened at the council at London in 1151.[5] But appeals of this sort were quite remote from appeals of the kind restricted by the Constitutions. A very different clause would have been drafted had it been proposed to restrict such appeals otherwise than in the very effective way already employed: an impetrant who was so rash as to seek to infringe the king's prerogative would incur the king's displeasure and might, if he persisted, be driven into exile.

In the course of his quarrel with Becket the king did take wider action in regard to appeals to Rome, in the first instance late in 1164 and again apparently late in 1169. The most reliable source of information regarding the first incident is a writ, or rather the substance of a writ, said years later to have been addressed to all the sheriffs of England.[6] It seems, in fact, to have had a very restricted

---

[1] Constitutions of Clarendon, cap. viii (*Select Charters*, p. 165).

[2] As we shall see, at this period actions regarding advowsons might come before archdeacons, but this was prohibited by cap. i of the Constitutions.   [3] Cap. vi.

[4] *Becket Materials*, iii.65-6 (fitz Stephen), 308-9 (Bosham). For these appeals and the consequent appeals in subsequent years see Knowles, *Episcopal Colleagues of Archbishop Thomas Becket*, pp. 95-101.

[5] Henry of Huntingdon, *Historia Anglorum*, p. 282. It is at this point that the chronicler alleges that such appeals were unknown before the legation of Henry of Blois, bishop of Winchester.

[6] *Becket Materials*, v.152, where it is dated about Christmas 1164. The reference to St. Thomas in the rubric shows that the transcript is much later.

circulation. Its first clause instructs the sheriff to whom it is addressed, presumably the sheriff of Kent, to arrest any clerk or layman in his bailiwick who may have appealed to the Curia and to keep him in custody until the king's pleasure be known. The other clauses instruct the sheriff to seize all rents and possessions of Becket's clerks and to take security from their relatives pending further instructions. There is nothing in the writ to suggest more than local precautions against acts hostile to the king, and it is certainly not evidence of any general prohibition of appeals. It is true that John of Salisbury[1] and Becket[2] write as though there had been such a general prohibition, but they both seem to be wilfully misinterpreting the Constitutions. Becket is indulging in a mere debating quip: 'the king', he says, 'first of all enjoined that there should be no appeal to the apostolic see, but now he has been brought to the point that he must have recourse to the see of Peter and invoke the pope's name'. Our knowledge of the second occasion is derived from a highly suspicious document, which is certainly fictitious in the variant forms in which it has been preserved and is, in parts, incomprehensible. It has the marks of a clumsy piece of Canterbury hagiography, though there are doubtless some elements of truth underlying it. The basic facts appear to be these. Becket having, with papal authority, threatened to lay England under an interdict, the king gave instructions that no mandate to this effect should be introduced into England. The bishops were required to promise not to countenance any such mandate, and laymen were required to swear neither to receive nor to obey one. Upon these bare facts 'the king's new constitutions', as they are called, embroider. There are to be no appeals to the archbishop or the pope and no judicial proceedings are to be initiated upon a papal mandate or any mandate from the archbishop (as legate).[3] These are perhaps the logical consequences of the king's action in countering the threatened interdict; but if there were any positive directions to this effect, it is evident that they were given in a particular emergency and would be dropped as soon as the emergency ended. In fact, the interdict was never imposed.

In these ways Becket and the king between them managed to bring the whole question of appeals into the dispute, but, ironically enough, with the result that the system we have seen at work in the

---

[1] *Ibid.*, p. 382.   [2] *Ibid.*, vi.55.

[3] The text given by William of Canterbury, *s.a.* 1165 (*ibid.*, i.53-5), and that existing as an independent document (*ibid.*, vii.147-9) are nearly identical. That given by Roger of Howden, *s.a.* 1165 (*Chronicon*, i.231-3), has a good many variants, while Gervase of Canterbury gives a text obviously improved to make it fit the year 1169 (*Opera*, i.214-5). It is clear that Edward Grim and William fitz Stephen know nothing of the *Novae Constitutiones*, nor do the anonymous lives show any knowledge of the document (*Becket Materials*, ii.405-6, iii.102, iv.65-6, 118-9). Ralf de Diceto, though well documented, is equally ignorant (*Opera*, i.317-37). Herbert of Bosham ignores the whole incident. Grim says that the king prohibited appeals by word of mouth, and the first anonymous life alleges that it was at Clarendon that he did this. The letter attributed to Becket and supposed to refer to the document (*Becket Materials*, vii.146) is too silly to be credited even to him.

early years of the reign received papal approval and was, if anything, modified and rather strengthened to the king's advantage.
The right conceded to the king of taking security from any appellant
that nothing would be sought to the prejudice of the king or the
kingdom was wide enough to bar any appeal to which objection
might be taken.[1] Despite the clear terms in which this right was
recognised at Avranches, it has been supposed that, whereas earlier
in Henry's reign appeals to Rome had been restricted, after his
formal submission in September 1172 appeals from England were
unhindered, and Stubbs lent his authority to this view.[2] But Stubbs
also acknowledged that throughout the Middle Ages effective means
were open to the king, by restraints on the person, to prevent appeals
to Rome, if ever it should be worth while to use them.[3] Into the later
history of the relations between English kings and the papacy we
must not enter here, but we may perhaps usefully add a few words
on the situation in the twelfth century. It cannot be supposed for one
moment that, whatever was conceded on one side or the other at
Avranches, it was intended that, in the matter of appeals, there
should be one rule in England and another in Henry's continental
dominions. The Church in England was not *sui generis*, as Stubbs
liked to think. We must then regard this question, not as a facet of
the king's quarrel with Becket, but in the ambience of Western
Christendom. In this wider context, having regard to the ascertained
facts of papal relations with England on the one hand and with
France and Europe generally on the other, it seems impossible to
maintain that the course of history was affected, except in the
matter of criminous clerks, by any innovation or change of mind on
Henry's part. Certainly nothing he did or failed to do had any
material bearing upon the appellate jurisdiction of the Curia or upon
its wide extension in the later years of the twelfth century.

But if the volume of appeals was unaffected by the Becket quarrel,
there were other questions which figured in the concordat of Avranches.[4] Of what significance were these? We need not consider
transitory matters of penance or restitution nor Henry's undertaking
to recognise as pope only Alexander III and his successors, which
outweighed, at the moment, anything else the king could give. We
are concerned especially with his undertaking to abandon all customs inimical to the churches of his realm that appeared to have
been introduced in his time. No custom is specified. The Constitutions are not mentioned, and in any case they purported to cover
only points in dispute. The limited range of the Constitutions does
not seem to be generally appreciated; but a final clause states specifically that there were many other customs and prerogatives (*digni-*

[1] *Ibid.*, vii.517, 520.
[2] *Ecclesiastical Courts Commission Report*, Historical Appendix (1), p. 30a.
[3] *Ibid.*   [4] *Becket Materials*, vii.517-8, 519, 521-2; *E.H.R.*, lii.466-7.

tates) of importance, as well of the Church as of the king and his barons, which were saved to each side.[1] In this wide field the king, for his part, thought that few or no customs had been introduced,[2] and he seems unquestionably to have been right, for few are mentioned in the final settlement with the legate, Hugh Pierleoni, in 1178 and only one of these had been covered by the Constitutions. It was now agreed that clerks should not be subject to proceedings in secular courts except in regard to forest offences and lay fees. The other heads of agreement covered only one major question, that of vacant bishoprics and abbeys, which the king undertook not to retain in his hands for more than a year save in exceptional circumstances. The agreement that slayers of clerks should suffer forfeiture, as well as the punishment customarily awarded to laymen, and that clerks should not be compelled to fight judicial duels refers to quite obscure grievances, possibly isolated incidents, of which we know nothing with certainty.[3] The former clause may have some reference to the doctrine that the punishment of offences against clerks was reserved for the Church, and it may have in view the notorious fact that Becket's murderers had escaped all secular penalties, though seemingly penance had been imposed upon them by the pope.[4] The latter clause may contain a hint that in some cases putative clerks appealed of felony had had to justify themselves by combat and had had no other form of trial. But whatever may lie behind these clauses, they relate to minor matters on which the king could make a concession without any sacrifice of principle. What is plain is that the area of dispute, if disputes there still were, had become very narrow. On every main issue the king had maintained his ground, nor can it be said that he and his successors ever honoured punctiliously the agreement with the legate. On only one matter, however, need we dwell, the treatment of criminous clerks.

Let it be said at the outset that to apply the agreement of 1178 exactly as it was worded was impracticable. Any attempt at putting it into execution would be arrested at the outset by the necessity to determine whether or not the suspect was a clerk. Many a clerk wore the garb and lived the life of a layman, and many a layman, as experience was to show, would claim benefit of clergy. The practical difficulties of the situation led to the procedure, unchallenged so far as we know in England, whereby the accused was put on his trial in the king's court,[5] pleaded his clergy, was claimed by the bishop's

---

[1] *Select Charters*, p. 167.
[2] *Becket Materials*, vii.519: quas quidem aut paucas aut nullas aestimo.
[3] Ralf de Diceto, *Opera*, i.410.
[4] Cf. Pollock and Maitland, *History of English Law*, i.456-7. For the fate of Becket's murderers see the note by Walberg to Guernes de Pont-Sainte-Maxence, *La Vie de Saint Thomas le Martyr*, pp. 295-8.
[5] Maitland objects that in the king's court there was no trial but an inquest *ex officio* (Pollock and Maitland, *op. cit.*, i.442); but Bracton himself speaks of secular judges having cognisance of crimes by clerks (fo. 401*b*, 407) and of passing judgement on clerks (fo. 411), though he seems to speak in a contrary sense at fo. 123*b* (Woodbine, iv.250,

representative and handed over to the Church. Whether this was precisely the procedure followed in the last decades of the twelfth century we can but speculate; it is not until the thirteenth century that we are able to speak with any certainty. The king's courts are then exercising an increasing control over the conduct of the proceedings in order to supplement the weakness of canonical procedure. In effect the guilt of a criminous clerk is determined by a secular court. If Bracton's teaching were to be relied upon—and it seems to depart far from actual practice[1]—the punishment of a convicted clerk was left to the Church and was limited to degradation: there was no further penalty.[2] Though, therefore, there was a trial in the king's court, there was no violation of the spirit of the agreement. The principle for which Becket had stood—*Non judicabit Deus bis in idipsum*—was thus respected.

The compromise achieved was confined to England: it did not become part of the procedural law of the continental dominions of the English king. However, though in other directions the effect of the Becket controversy was negligible, in regard to the trial of criminous clerks it seems to have left its mark, first upon canon law and then upon secular law on the Continent. It may be no more than a coincidence, but, about the year 1177, Alexander III, in replying to a whole series of questions addressed to him by the archbishop of Salerno, touched upon the question of the criminous clerk. 'Even if clerks', said the pope, 'have been convicted before a secular judge, they are not for this reason necessarily to be condemned by their bishop: a sentence delivered by one who is not qualified to judge is not binding.' And if a clerk is degraded, the pope added, he should not be handed over to a secular judge: he should not be afflicted twice. Originally this reply was related solely to a question put by the archbishop and, whatever may have passed through the pope's mind, the reply had no connexion with the distant quarrel that had distracted the English clergy some years earlier. But the decretal, perhaps because of its wide range, passed rapidly into the early collections of decretals, to find a place in the *Compilatio Prima* and finally in the Gregorian collection.[3] In this way one brief excerpt, beginning with the words *At si clerici*, by which it is cited, became

265-6, 278; ii.348-9). After Bracton's day clerks frequently, if not usually, stood their trial and awaited the jury's verdict before claiming benefit of clergy (Gabel, *Benefit of Clergy in England*, pp. 30-51). This may have happened earlier, though the evidence is not decisive: cf. A. L. Poole in *Tait Essays*, pp. 239-46. How a clerk appealed of felony avoided trial by battle is not clear.

[1] Despite the assurances given to the prelates in 1245 (Cole, *Documents*, p. 356), complaints of irregular practices by secular tribunals continued and in 1257 had become stronger and more specific (Matthew Paris, *Chronica Maiora*, vi.356). It is now said that clerks accused of felony may be kept in prison for five or six years before trial by justices in eyre and on conviction may be hanged before the ordinary can claim them.

[2] Cum autem clericus sic de crimine convictus degradetur non sequitur alia pena ... (Bracton, fo. 123b). Elsewhere Bracton does not imply any such limitation.

[3] Génestal, *Le Privilegium Fori*, ii.20-26. For the text of Alexander III's letter see Jaffé-Loewenfeld, no. 14091.

known to every canonist as the law of the Church. Influenced presumably by this decretal, when under Richard I a settlement was
reached in Normandy over the conflicting claims of the secular and
ecclesiastical courts to jurisdiction, it was agreed that clerks accused
of capital crimes, while they might be arrested by the lay power,
should be handed over to the Church for trial and punishment.
Hitherto, it had been the practice to hang them on conviction,
doubtless after degradation[1]: in the view of the school of thought, of
which Becket and Alexander III are in this matter representative,
these clerks had been punished twice.

This Norman parallel is, we suggest, most instructive. It shows
that, when Stephen expressed his determination to try Archdeacon
Osbert in his own court, he was not making any new or extraordinary
claim. It explains the reluctance of Henry II and his barons to
relinquish the archdeacon of York to an ecclesiastical tribunal and
their reluctance again, in 1178, to concede to the legate the abroga-
tion of the right of the king's court to try and punish criminous
clerks.[2] As we have said, the king and his advisers were conservative;
they were upholding ancient customs. It is for this reason that, while
Becket could create a tempest, he could achieve so little. Even if, in
a sense, he gained a victory in retrieving criminous clerks from
secular tribunals, it was seemingly only because the king had already
conceded the right of trial to Archbishop Theobald. Having already
abandoned the king's customary right, Henry was on the weakest
ground in endeavouring to regain it under another guise.

Becket's murder added a new saint to the calendar, inaugurated
a new cult, made the repression of crime more difficult, allowed a
multitude of peccant clergy to escape with their lives, but it left the
relations between Church and State otherwise undisturbed. If we
would sense the atmosphere a few years after the murder and after
the concordat of Avranches, which wiped out old scores, let us look
in at a trial that took place at Westminster in 1176. In the previous
year there had been sent to England as legate Cardinal Hugh
Pierleoni. He arrived towards the end of October and summoned a
legatine council to meet in Westminster Abbey at mid-Lent.[3] The
tumultuous proceedings at this abortive council, which were sufficiently scandalous, need not detain us. All we need note is that, at
the same time as he received a summons to attend the council, the
abbot of Battle was cited to appear before the legate to answer
Godfrey de Lucy in a suit concerning the church of Wye. Godfrey,
the son of the justiciar, Richard de Lucy, had been presented to

---

[1] Génestal, op. cit., ii.95-124. The agreement with the seneschal, William fitz Ralf,
appears to have been in 1191. The king's approval was given at La Roche d'Orival: no
date is given, but Richard was there in 1198 (Landon, Itinerary of Richard I, pp. 126, 132).
[2] Henry II to Alexander III: 'licet plurimum resisterent et reclamerent regni nostri
maiores et magis discreti' (Ralf de Diceto, Opera, i.410).
[3] 'Benedict of Peterborough', i.112-4; Ralf de Diceto, Opera, i.402-6.

the church by the king and instituted by the archbishop-elect of Canterbury while the abbacy was vacant. The monks of Battle contested the validity of these proceedings on several grounds. Godfrey, for his part, contended that the monks were keeping him out of a moiety of the church and demanded full possession. But we may pass over the technicalities of the suit. Godfrey, who was absent at the schools, had for advocate Master Ives of Cornwall. The abbot sought among those present at the council an equally skilled advocate. He approached Master Gerard la Pucelle, Bishop Bartholomew of Exeter, Master John of Salisbury, all of whom excused themselves on various pretexts, but actually because they feared the ire of Richard de Lucy. Failing these, the abbot retained an Italian lawyer in the train of the legate, who undertook the defence for a fee of a mark; but during the night the Italian sent word that he must withdraw lest he should incur the anger of the king and the nobles. The morrow dawned and the abbot was still without an advocate. After Master Ives had opened his case, the abbot turned again to those who had declined to act for him, but again they refused for fear of the king, the archbishop and the justiciar. At last Master Waleran, archdeacon of Bayeux, taking Master Gerard apart, proposed that they should come to the abbot's assistance, and, after a short conference with him, they returned to court, where Master Gerard spoke for the defence. There followed the inevitable compromise, which gave Godfrey for his lifetime possession of the church, while the monks were glad to secure the abbey's title to the church thereafter.[1] It is not, however, the result of the action that need concern us, but the atmosphere of the trial. There could scarcely be a more independent ecclesiastical tribunal than a court held under the authority of a legate, certainly no more independent court could be found in England, but overhanging all those present is the fear of offending the king and the justiciar. Gerard, Bartholomew, John, had all been, to greater or less extent, concerned in the Becket controversy. They all knew that Richard de Lucy had, in Becket's eyes, been the head and front of the offending[2]; that, after the king, he had been the man to fear. Whatever triumph Becket may have achieved by his death, Richard was still the man to fear. Nothing had changed.

The lesson to be drawn from the Becket controversy is that, in the very narrow field open to dispute, the king was in an almost impregnable position so long as he could rely upon ancient custom in the face of assaults based upon novel doctrines advanced by canonists. Just as Henry, handicapped though he might be by the emotional

---

[1] *Chronicon Mon. de Bello*, pp. 170-9.
[2] *Becket Materials*, v.174: odiosus ille Ricardus de Luci. See also *ibid.*, pp. 383, 388, 390, 395; vi.559, 572, 590, 594, 602. It was in vain that Gilbert Foliot remonstrated with Becket over his treatment of this 'vir magnus et sapiens moderator regni Ricardus de Luci' (*ibid.*, v.524).

reaction to Becket's murder, remained at the end of the battle in possession of the field, so, as we shall show, John, after his quarrel with Innocent III had been resolved, remained in possession of the ancient right for which he had contended.[1] Let us emphasise that, despite the extravagant language, the customary hyperbole, which came readily to the tongue or pen of any papalist engaged in controversy, no issue of faith or morals was involved in these disputes, but plain questions of jurisdiction. In principle the Curia conceded nothing of its claims: in practice, with the one exception of the treatment of criminous clerks, the Crown retained everything for which it had fought. Let us give an illustration.

We put side by side a judgement in the king's court in 1219 and a text from the Gregorian Decretals. The first reads:

Et ideo prohibitum est ei ne teneat aliquod placitum in quo fiat mentio de advocatione.[2]

The second reads:

Causa vero iuris patronatus ita coniuncta est et connexa spiritualibus causis quod non nisi ecclesiastico iudicio valeat definiri.[3]

Perhaps to complete our citations we should add the first clause of the Constitutions of Clarendon:

De advocatione et presentatione ecclesiarum, si controversia emerserit inter laicos vel inter laicos et clericos vel inter clericos, in curia domini regis tractetur et terminetur.

An advowson is precisely the right of patronage, the privilege of presenting a clerk for institution to a benefice. Both king and pope, then, claim exclusive cognisance of suits concerning advowsons: and there is a piquancy in the papal claim to jurisdiction and its rejection, if we remember that the decretal is drawn from a letter addressed by Alexander III to Henry II, a letter of uncertain date but of certain connexion with the Becket controversy.[4] The Curia withdraws none of its pretensions. The king goes on his own way, determining disputed claims to advowsons and issuing writs of prohibition to those who would draw such suits into ecclesiastical courts, writs that it would be imprudent to disregard. In some cases there might be a way of escape, the prescriptions of canon law observed, and a church yet recovered. A plaintiff might bring an action for intrusion before an ecclesiastical court, and this, we take it, was the course Godfrey de Lucy adopted in his action against

---

[1] Below, pp. 357-8.   [2] *Curia Regis Rolls*, viii.75.
[3] X, 2.1.3; Jaffé-Loewenfeld, no. 13727.
[4] Presumably before 1172. Soon after, in a letter to Abbot Simon of St. Alban's, Alexander III tacitly recognises the *Angliae consuetudo* whereby the *jus patronatus* is determined in the king's court (Gilbert Foliot, *Epistolae* (ed. Giles), ii.104-5: Jaffé-Loewenfeld, no. 12636). This letter passed into the collections of decretals and appeared in X.3.38.19 without any reference to English custom.

the abbot of Battle in the legate's court. But this path was beset with difficulty and a litigant would be exceptionally fortunate if, in later days, he took this course and was not confronted by a prohibition.[1]

The triumph of the king may seem all the more remarkable if we ask whether the jurisdiction he claimed did, in fact, rest upon ancient and undisputed custom. There seems no doubt that, in the days of Stephen and in the early years of Henry's reign, disputes regarding advowsons had come before all manner of ecclesiastical courts from archdeacons' upwards and that there had been frequent appeals from those courts to the pope.[2] It may well be that a concurrent jurisdiction had been exercised by the king's court,[3] as, indeed, the case of the church of Luton suggests. This case, it will be recalled, was determined co-operatively, if we may so express it, and a final decision made in the king's presence.[4] Nor is this a solitary instance of co-operation. Early in Henry's reign we find a dispute as to the *jus patronatus* of a church in Derby determined by a mixed inquest of clergy and laity over which the sheriff and the archdeacon presided. This is all the more noteworthy because the inquest was taken in response to the king's writ.[5] And we have, at much the same point of time, writs from the king requiring the bishop of Norwich to enforce the judgement of the bishop's court which established the right of the abbot of St. Benet of Holme to the church of Repps. If the bishop fails in this, the archbishop of Canterbury, so he is told, will give effect to the judgement.[6] Here we have another aspect of co-operation between Church and State. We can take the story back to the days of Henry I. It will be recalled that Robert Bloet was at once bishop of Lincoln and *justitiarius totius Anglie*. There came before him, apparently about the year 1115, a dispute regarding the church of Shillington in Bedfordshire, to which both Ramsey Abbey and a layman, Autin of Huntingdon, laid claim. The action was determined *canonice*—that is by the bishop in his capacity as diocesan—and ended in a compromise under which the monks bought out for a money payment any claim Autin or his son Bartholomew might have. Upon Autin's death, however, some years later Bartholomew renewed his claim to the church and brought a writ, which we may perhaps call a writ of novel disseisin,[7] addressed to

---

[1] It was an action of intrusion before an ecclesiastical court, followed by a writ of prohibition, that led to the judgement by the justices of the Bench cited above (*Curia Regis Rolls*, viii.74-5). Of course, if the parties came to an agreement with the acquiescence of the bishop, there was no longer a *lis* and no place for a writ of prohibition, which in any case issued only at the instance of one of the parties. The difficulty suggested by Professor Darlington (*E.H.R.*, lxvii.564-5) does not therefore arise.

[2] *Letters of John of Salisbury*, i, 5-6, 91, 115-6, 123-6, 131-3, 163.

[3] Cf. *ibid.*, pp. 91, 123, 163, where there are indications of writs of prohibition or an assize.   [4] Above, p. 287.

[5] *E.H.R.*, xxxii.47-8; *Cartulary of Darley Abbey*, p. 71.

[6] West, *St. Benet of Holme*, i.18, nos. 25 and 26.

[7] Baldewinus . . . quaesivit per breve regis ut resaisiretur . . . in breve regis continebatur ut per rectum resaisiretur. We are given no further indication of the terms of the writ, but compare the specimens printed by van Caenegem, *Royal Writs in England*, pp. 445-53,

the abbot of Ramsey. The abbot then offered him right judgement either in his own (secular) court or in the bishop's court, where the dispute had previously been determined. At this stage the bishop intervened and ordered Bartholomew, as his parishioner, to appear, together with the abbot of Ramsey, before his own court. In other words, the bishop proposed once more to determine the issue canonically. In the bishop's court the earlier agreement was recited, Bartholomew withdrew his claim and seisin was formally given to the abbot by a rod which Bartholomew and his brother handed to him. It is to be noted that the sheriff was present at the proceedings, at least in the concluding stages.[1] Quite obviously the circumstances were especially favourable to co-operation in this case because the bishop united in his person both secular and ecclesiastical authority. Nevertheless the likeness to later cases, where these particularly favourable circumstances did not exist, indicates that, over half a century or so, there had been no exclusive jurisdiction over advowsons and that there had been a large measure of co-operation between ecclesiastical and secular authorities.

How it came about that by 1164 the king could claim exclusive jurisdiction over advowsons, a claim in which the majority of bishops were prepared to acquiesce,[2] is a puzzle we cannot pretend to solve. Any hope of formal agreement was, however, defeated by Becket and, in principle, the Church would not admit the right of the king's court to determine conflicting claims to advowsons, while it became customary to maintain the king's prerogative by addressing writs of prohibition to ecclesiastical judges. But it took some time to evolve a set procedure, and it is of some interest to observe Church and State once more co-operating in the period between the concordat of Avranches and the final settlement with Cardinal Hugh Pierleoni when, if the king's claim to jurisdiction was not tacitly admitted, it was not contested. The year is 1175. The monks of Reading and the canons of St. Augustine's, Bristol, have been disputing their respective claims in the church of Berkeley and its dependencies and there has been an appeal to Rome. The bishop of Hereford and the abbot of St. Alban's have been appointed judges delegate to hear the cause, but before they can come to a decision, the king has intervened, not, however, to issue a prohibition but to join with them in effecting a settlement. The king sits in his court with the judges delegate, who nevertheless claim to be acting with apostolic authority, and, as is usual when the king hears an action in person, there is present a large and distinguished company of

nos. 65, 68, 69, 72, 75, 79, 80: compare also p. 420, no. 17, which is classified as a writ of right.

[1] *Cartularium Mon. de Rameseia*, i.138-9.

[2] They assented to all the articles of the Constitutions of Clarendon, according to William fitz Stephen (*Becket Materials*, iii.66). The effect of what Herbert of Bosham says is much the same (*ibid.*, pp. 288, 308).

ecclesiastics and laymen. Besides the judges delegate there are the archbishop of Canterbury and five bishops, Earl William de Mandeville, the justiciar Richard de Lucy, and seven barons. The majority of those present are employed regularly or with some frequency as royal judges, including three of the bishops, Richard of Ilchester, Geoffrey Ridel and John of Oxford.[1] If we did not know the special circumstances which brought them together, we should say that this was a normal sitting of the court *coram rege*. The striking fact is that —the presence of judges delegate apart—we have here a reversion to the type of court we have seen determining ecclesiastical disputes in the days of Stephen and the early years of Henry's reign, a court with which Richard de Lucy was familiar.

The point we would stress, however, is the ineffectiveness in England of the decretal of Alexander III, claiming exclusive jurisdiction for ecclesiastical courts in disputes regarding the *jus patronatus*: it might be binding upon the Universal Church, but it fell on deaf ears in the country to which it had been addressed. Nor is this by any means a solitary example. Scattered up and down the 'Corpus Juris Canonici' there are not a few texts that failed to secure practical recognition in this country. There was a decretal of Innocent III's which forbade the anointing of the king's head at his coronation, a precept that ran contrary to English custom and was completely ignored in a ceremony which could not be performed without the participation of bishops and in especial of the archbishop of Canterbury.[2] We need not multiply parallel instances.[3] They served Stubbs as a justification for his view that the Church in England had the right to accept or reject papal legislation. The true view is that they testify to the limitations within which the papacy could command respect for its injunctions, limitations resting upon the rights and dignity of the Crown.[4] In such matters it was not a question of the acceptance by the pope of a reasonable local custom,[5] but of tolerating a custom that to the papalist was the reverse of reasonable.

It has been necessary for us to speak much of *sacerdotium* and *regnum*, but we must remember that to few of those concerned with the relations of Church and State were these more than remote abstractions, useful, it might be, to lawyers or philosophers, but with little bearing upon the problems of daily life and with as little influence on conduct. Let our last words, therefore, be of clergy and laity, of those who had to live together and work together, however much they might be pulled apart from time to time by political notions which it is now the fashion to call ideological. To those upon whom the burden of administration mainly lay the Becket

---

[1] Egerton MS. 3031, fo. 23*b*-24, 47*b*-48. For a parallel case two years later see Morey, *Bartholomew of Exeter*, pp. 140-2.   [2] X. i.15.1 §5; *Traditio*, xvi.117.
[3] A number will be found in Maitland, *Roman Canon Law in the Church of England*, p. 84, n. 4, citing Stillingfleet, *Ecclesiastical Cases*, p. 356.
[4] Above, pp. 7-12.   [5] Cf. Maitland, *op. cit.*, pp. 41-2.

controversy was an unseemly and unnecessary quarrel which, once ended, no one wished to revive. The hagiology that surrounds Becket must not mislead us: it is no more a guide to responsible opinion than any other hagiology surrounding a pinchbeck saint. Nor is the popularity of the cult of St. Thomas of Canterbury, which arose from the dramatic, easily visualised, circumstances of his murder, any testimony to the popularity of his ideas or his politics, though his martyrdom made possible the most improbable reconciliations. His inflexible opponent, Richard de Lucy, without abating his principles in the least, dedicated an abbey to him and retired from the world to die there.[1] Barons and prelates resumed their intimate association in public affairs and any rifts there may have been were quickly smoothed away.

How close that association could be is illustrated by the case of the church of Luton, of which we have spoken at some length and which, as we have said, was settled co-operatively between the bishops and the king's justices. This is, of course, no isolated incident, for the presence of bishops in the courts held before the king is attested by many documents. Since these come from monastic sources, the presence of the bishops, it might be thought, was to be explained by the nature of the business, which obviously touched ecclesiastical interests. But, as the Constitutions of Clarendon show, the king insisted upon their presence in his court so that they might take part in its judgements generally, except in criminal causes where the sentence might be death or mutilation. They were to be present as tenants-in-chief, not as representatives of a separate order.[2] And it is a commonplace of history that bishops, abbots and many of the lower clergy did take a prominent part in the administration of secular justice, even though they might not escape the reproach that they were participators in judgements of blood.[3] The pattern is unaltered throughout the twelfth century. Hubert Walter is the first archbishop of Canterbury to be also justiciar, and he has for his colleagues on the bench the bishops of London, Rochester, Salisbury and Winchester and the archdeacons of Ely and Hereford.[4] If bishops and archdeacons are somewhat less prominent in the king's service under John, his first chancellor will be the archbishop of Canterbury, a bishop of Winchester will be justiciar, and no one will be more active in civil administration than the archdeacon of Taunton.[5] Bishops were called upon to take part in civil administration throughout the Middle Ages, and in the fifteenth century they are still prominent in council and parliament. But in the adminis-

---

[1] *Monasticon*, vi.456-7; Ralf de Diceto, *Opera*, i.425-6; 'Benedict of Peterborough', i.238. He seems to have retired from office at Michaelmas 1178 (*E.H.R.*, xliii,330).
[2] Cap. xi (*Select Charters*, p. 166).   [3] *E.H.R.*, xliii.171 *n.*
[4] *Feet of Fines, Henry II and Richard I, passim.*
[5] The chancellor is, of course, Hubert Walter and the justiciar Peter des Roches. The archdeacon is William of Wrotham, of whom there is some account in the *D.N.B.*

tration of the law the Crown calls upon the clergy less and less as the centuries advance. Gradually bishops cease to sit upon the bench, abbots cease to go on eyre, cathedral dignitaries are no longer to be found among the judges.[1]

The twelfth century is the last century of the old order and it carries with it the elements of change. One element is the literacy of the laity, already evident but increasing steadily until there is hardly a profession that could not be as well served by laymen as by clerks. The civil service, it is true, will continue to be staffed overwhelmingly by clerks, but this is because their remuneration is largely provided by ecclesiastical benefices. But the ordinary clerk in a government office in the later Middle Ages could, from the nature of his employment, be an ecclesiastic in little more than name: he eschewed marriage not by vocation but from fear of poverty.[2] It is in the field of law that the cleavage between clerk and layman is most marked. This cleavage had begun, though it was as yet imperceptible, at the end of the twelfth century. The exclusion of ecclesiastics from secular tribunals was the inevitable consequence of the growing technicality of the laws appropriate to Church and State. The chronicler of Battle Abbey ends his account of Gerard la Pucelle's speech before the legate's court with the words: 'and so Master Gerard made his peroration in this fashion in the hearing of all and proved his case by citations from the laws and decrees too long to insert here'.[3] By the 'laws' is meant, of course, Roman civil law and by the 'decrees' Gratian's 'Decretum'. This was in 1176. In the case prepared for the monks of Christ Church twelve years later in their action against Archbishop Baldwin over his proposal to found a collegiate church at Hackington, there are, if our reckoning is correct, ninety-three citations of the 'Decretum', forty-four of the 'Digest', thirty-nine of the 'Code', five of the 'Institutes' and one of the 'Authenticum'.[4] This precise citation of authority for every clause in the argument is characteristic of all pleading before ecclesiastical tribunals, of every textbook of canon law.

But before the end of Henry II's reign there appeared the first textbook of the common law of England embodying a very different system. This book is assuredly the work of a man strongly influenced by the romanesque treatises on procedure of his time, *ordines judiciarii* as they are called. There are, however, no books of authority, no *lex scripta*, he can cite: at best he has before him a *registrum brevium*, and it may be that he has had to construct such a register of writs himself. He is well acquainted with the practice of the courts with which

---

[1] Bishops do not seem to have sat as regular judges of the Bench (or King's Bench) after the reign of John. Occasionally abbots and bishops are on commissions of justices in eyre under Henry III, though the actual judicial work seems to have been done by others (cf. *Traditio*, vi.80-1). Clerks continued to sit on the Bench under Edward I and Edward II, but there seem to have been no cathedral dignitaries among them except Hengham. [2] Tout, *Chapters in Mediaeval Administrative History*, iii.209-10, v.94-5. [3] *Chronicon Mon. de Bello*, p. 178. [4] *Epistolae Cantuarienses*, pp. 520-30.

he is concerned, the king's court at the exchequer and before the itinerant justices.[1] He is probably himself a judge, though not Ranulf Glanville, under whose name the book has passed throughout the centuries.[2] He is writing, it would seem, for his fellow judges and for officers of the courts rather than for students. The book is not one for practitioners, for there is as yet no body of men we can call a profession learned in the common law. Herein lies a great contrast with the other system, which had been served by academically trained lawyers in profusion for many years. This new system will grow steadily more and more complex, more and more technical. In due course it will demand an organised profession, its own schools of law; but in the age of Glanville all this lies in the remote future. For a time there will be on the Bench men, such as the author of 'Glanville' himself, with a knowledge of both systems, who drew to no inconsiderable extent upon Roman law, civil and ecclesiastical. To this dual learning there are two monuments in the thirteenth century, the 'Regiam Majestatem' and Bracton's treatise. But however we may rate the Roman learning of the authors, we cannot mistake their work for that of civilians or canonists: what they take from civil or canon law they do their best to transmute.[3] The divergence between the two systems is already marked by the middle of the century when these two books were written; before long a great gulf will be fixed. When churchmen disappear from the Bench and the common lawyers become exclusively laymen, the law of the Church and the law of Justinian will be so much foreign law in the English courts. Only in the court of chancery will ecclesiastics still linger, but the law they administer will bear little resemblance to canon or civil law.[4] Elsewhere in the courts the divorce between *sacerdotium* and *regnum* will be complete.

[1] An adequate edition has yet to appear, though Woodbine's edition of the *beta* text is serviceable. An edition of the *alpha*, or original, text is promised.

[2] Both Hubert Walter and Geoffrey fitz Peter have been suggested as the author. The former seems to have the right background and qualifications, but it would be strange if his authorship had passed unnoticed by contemporaries. The latter seems not to have had the requisite academic training.

[3] For the Roman elements in the 'Regiam Majestatem' see *Juridical Review*, lxvii.155-87; for Bracton's adaptation of Roman law see *Traditio*, vi.83-4.

[4] Holdsworth, *History of English Law*, iv.275-83. Ecclesiastics did sit in the court of the constable and marshal, but as experts in civil law.

XVII

THE KING OF ILL REPUTE

W HEREVER his constitutional theories led him, Stubbs was impelled to make his characters conform to the parts allotted to them. He found a 'hero' in Edward I because he conceived that king to be the architect of the constitution. He found a villain in John. John was 'unfit to reign'[1]: his tyranny overthrew 'that balance of the powers of the State which his predecessors had striven with so much earnestness and so much policy to adjust'.[2] For the full measure of Stubbs's condemnation of John we must look outside the covers of the *Constitutional History*,[3] but it will be well to have before us his denunciation of the evil king as it stands there. It helps to explain why he could not appreciate that John might have an arguable case in the great issues of his reign, why he does not scrutinise the evidence against John or realise how much of it is tainted. The verdict is settled before the case has been argued, if, indeed, it is ever argued. Here then is John's character, as Stubbs paints it in the *Constitutional History*:[4]

He was the very worst of all our kings: a man whom no oaths could bind, no pressure of conscience, no consideration of policy, restrain from evil; a faithless son, a treacherous brother, an ungrateful master; to his people a hated tyrant. Polluted with every crime that could disgrace a man, false to every obligation that should bind a king, he had lost half his inheritance by sloth, and ruined and desolated the rest. Not devoid of natural ability, craft or energy, with his full share of the personal valour and accomplishments of his house, he yet failed in every design he undertook, and had to bear humiliations which, although not without parallel, never fell on one who deserved them more thoroughly or received less sympathy under them. In the whole view there is no redeeming trait; John seems as incapable of receiving a good impression as of carrying into effect a wise resolution.

Until recently the judgement passed upon John by modern historians was almost unanimous. Though expressed in different words and explained in different ways, the sum and substance had been the same. All agreed with Stubbs: John was irredeemably bad. It was

---

[1] *Constitutional History*, i.534.
[2] *Ibid.*, i.571.
[3] Walter of Coventry, *Memoriale*, ii.xi-lxxx.
[4] *Constitutional History*, ii.17.

also a contemporary judgement, a judgement put into picturesque words by the Minstrel of Reims:[1]

Et fu sacrez à roi et fu li pires rois qui onques fust, meis li rois Herodes, qui fist les enfanz decoleir; car cil rois Jehans, dont je vous di, fu mauvais chevaliers et avers et treitres, si comme vous dirai.

Recently the balance has begun to swing in the opposite direction, perhaps too far.[2] And before a conclusion is reached, it may be well to consider the evidence and confront some, at least, of the witnesses. Equally desirable is it to regard John in his own time and place, in the company of his father and mother, his brothers, his friends and enemies.

Let us explain, however, what we mean when we say that it is desirable to regard John in his own time and place. Consider this sentence of Stubbs's.

John [he says] was employed, after the conclusion of the peace in May [1200], chiefly in divorcing his wife, Hawisia of Gloucester, and marrying Isabella of Angoulême, acts which caused in England the alienation of the whole of the Gloucester influence from the king, and in France the active and malicious hostility of the house of Lusignan, to whose head Isabella had been betrothed.[3]

In this summary statement there are sufficient mistakes and misapprehensions to require pages to refute in detail; but what we are concerned to emphasise is that Isabelle (not Hawisia) of Gloucester was never John's wife in the eyes of the Church and that it was only because the putative marriage was a nullity that a divorce was possible. If by modern standards John's conduct would be reprehensible, in the year 1200 his conduct was in strict conformity with the law governing Christian marriage, for Isabelle was related to John within the forbidden degrees and no dispensation had been obtained to validate their union. They had, indeed, been separated, not long after the marriage ceremony, by the archbishop of Canterbury, and there is no evidence that since this separation they had lived together. The proceedings leading to a formal divorce were protracted, but it is certain that months, at least, before May 1200 final judgement had been pronounced and John was then free to make another match, calculated and passionless, with the daughter of the count of Angoulême, who appears not yet to have attained twelve years of age.[4] Let us emphasise that John's marriage was calculated and passionless, for the story of his mad infatuation with a

---

[1] *Récits d'un ménéstral de Reims*, p. 129 (para. 244): 'And he was anointed king and was the worst that ever was, even than King Herod who had the children beheaded. For this King John of whom I speak, was a bad knight and avaricious and a traitor, as I am about to relate to you.'

[2] For recent views see Painter, *The Reign of King John*, pp. 18-19, 152-3, 226-30, 237-8; Poole, *From Domesday Book to Magna Carta*, pp. 425-9; Warren, *King John*, pp. 256-9.

[3] *Constitutional History*, i.555.   [4] *E.H.R.*, lxi.289-95; lxv.361-2.

beautiful princess,[1] already the prize of another, is a piece of foolish romance, the wanton invention of modern writers, a story that offends chronological congruity and ignores the elementary require-ments of canon law.[2] And since his union with Isabelle of Angoulême has been held to be proof of John's folly from the very commence-ment of his reign, let us endeavour to disperse the clouds of error in which historians have befogged themselves. Let us begin with the purchase of the *comté* of La Marche by Henry II in 1177.[3] Thereafter there were three claimants to the *comté*: the count of Poitou (for his son Richard succeeded to Henry's claim), the count of Angoulême and the lord of Lusignan. Of these Count Wulgrim of Angoulême died in 1181, leaving an infant daughter named Matilda who became a ward of Richard's, as Wulgrim's feudal superior; and she con-tinued in his custody when he became king of England.[4] At the time of Richard's death the count of Angoulême was Audemar (a younger brother of Wulgrim's), whose only child was Isabelle. It is quite clear therefore that, in the event of Audemar's death, both Matilda and Isabelle would have a claim to both Angoulême and La Marche and that Matilda might be thought to have the better claim. It is clear, too, that whoever married either of these claimants would himself become a claimant and therefore that both the lord of Lusignan and the king of England, as count of Poitou, were greatly interested in the marriage of the two girls. There was a further com-plication. While the lord of Lusignan, Hugh le Brun, had been loyal to Richard and continued for some time to be loyal to John,[5] the counts of Angoulême had been throughout at enmity with Richard and, as soon as he was dead, Audemar and his half-brother Aimar, viscount of Limoges, had sought the protection of Philip Augustus, who had undertaken to do right in the matter of the disputed claim to La Marche.[6] This meant that the claims, not only of Audemar and Hugh, but the claims also of Richard's successor, whoever that might be, and of Richard's ward, Matilda, would be determined in the French king's court. Further, in order to frustrate any claim Matilda might have, either to La Marche or to Angoulême, Audemar betrothed his daughter to Hugh.[7] This may not have prejudiced Matilda's claims in law, but her prospect of enforcing them was made difficult.

When John obtained recognition as Richard's heir, he was thus faced with a tangled and formidable situation. It was to his interest

---

[1] That John may later have become enamoured of Isabelle is another matter. The best testimony to this is that of the minstrel of Béthune, though what he relates is clearly malicious gossip that cannot be trusted in detail (*Histoire des Ducs de Normandie*, pp. 104-5).
[2] *E.H.R.*, lxv.370-1.   [3] *Gesta Henrici*, i.197.
[4] 'Chronica Gaufredi Prioris Vosiensis', c. 72, in Labbe, *Nova Bibliotheca*, ii.328.
[5] Painter in *Speculum*, xxx.378.
[6] Teulet, *Layettes du Trésor des Chartes*, i.201, nos. 492-4.
[7] *E.H.R.*, lxi.296. Audemar's motive is not stated by any chronicler but it must be inferred.

to pacify Poitou, to avoid any action that would alienate Hugh le Brun, but, while doing this, to conciliate Audemar, if conciliation was possible. Unfortunately the difficulties with which he was confronted had been made worse by the slaying of the viscount of Limoges by Richard's son, Philip, in revenge for Richard's slaying at the castle of Chalus.[1] A blood feud had thus been added to the dispute over La Marche, a dispute that had been removed to the court of John's feudal superior. Richard or Henry II would have ignored that jurisdiction altogether, but John, for the time at least, was hardly in a position to do so, although, as events were to show, he was not prepared to plead in the French king's court. The problem with which he was confronted might seem insoluble, but he held one good card in his hand—the possession of Matilda with her claims to Angoulême and La Marche—and he played his hand with admirable skill. He betrothed himself to Isabelle, thus conciliating her father by securing her succession to Angoulême and, by the same stroke, composing the feud with the young viscount of Limoges.[2] At the same time he relinquished his claim to La Marche in favour of Hugh le Brun[3] and gave Matilda in marriage to him.[4] These easily ascertainable facts are in striking contrast to the idle tale of John's violation of Hugh's marriage to Isabelle, a tale told by chroniclers who have no word to say of these dealings of John's with Hugh or of Hugh's marriage with Matilda.[5] Hugh obviously was not prejudiced by John's marriage to Isabelle, but on the contrary was placed in a much more favourable position. He had been put under an obligation to John and not, as has been imagined, set at enmity.

Careless as Stubbs may have been and gross as may have been his misinterpretation of the evidence, his mistakes were as nothing compared with the mistakes of later writers who have embroidered upon the absurdities of the chroniclers. And, since their errors are not yet abandoned, it may not be superfluous to emphasise that if, as is supposed, John had abducted Hugh's wife, his own marriage to Isabelle would have been irregular. Clearly it was not so, for we have the most positive contemporary evidence that it was strictly canonical.[6] The explanation is that, although Isabelle had been

---

[1] Below, p. 329.
[2] The presence of the bishop of Limoges at the marriage is sufficient testimony (*Rot. Normanniae*, p. 36; *E.H.R.*, lxi.305).
[3] On 28 January 1200 (*Rot. Chartarum*, p. 58b; *Foedera*, i.79).
[4] The date has to be inferred. On Count Audemar's death on 16 June 1202, Hugh endeavoured to assert his claim to Angoulême (*Chroniques de Saint Martial de Limoges*, p. 67, n. 3), but his title derived solely from his marriage with Matilda. Since Hugh was at enmity with John and Count Audemar before 8 March 1201 (*Rot. Chartarum*, p. 102) and the marriage could have taken place only with their agreement, it is probable that Hugh had married Matilda in 1200, very much at the same time as, if not before, John's marriage to Isabelle.
[5] The chroniclers are Rigord and Guillaume le Breton (*Oeuvres*, ed. Delaborde, i.153, 207; ii.153); Ralf de Diceto, *Opera*, ii.176; Ralf of Coggeshall, *Chronicon*, pp. 28-9; *Histoire des Ducs de Normandie*, p. 91; *Histoire de Guillaume le Maréchal*, ll. 11996-12000.
[6] *Rotuli Normanniae*, p. 36.

contracted in marriage to Hugh, the contract was voidable by reason of the child's tender years.[1] Nor could there be any question of breach of faith, since Hugh received ample compensation for acquiescing in the avoidance of the contract. The whole prosaic transaction would have passed without contemporary misrepresentation, had not a quarrel flared up upon another issue between John and the house of Lusignan, a quarrel that finally involved him in the loss of Normandy.[2] That larger question we do not propose to discuss. We are concerned for the moment only with the initial problems with which John was confronted after his accession. We leave them with the conclusion that John's second marriage—or perhaps we should say second marriage ceremony—in no way offended against contemporary law or contemporary morals and that, for the time being at least, it extricated him from much political embarrassment. His reign did not begin with an act of impetuous folly but with an act of calculated statesmanship.

Next, to get John into focus, let us try to sketch in a few pages the company he was forced to keep: Henry II, Eleanor of Aquitaine, Philip Augustus, Richard I, Innocent III. For we must judge John not only by the standards of contemporary law and contemporary morals but also by contemporary manners.

Perhaps we should view Henry at his worst. There is a well-known portrait of him drawn by Gerald the Welshman[3]:

He was from beginning to end the oppressor of the nobility. He judged that to be right or wrong, lawful or unlawful, as it served his purpose. He sold justice, yet acted as accuser. He was untrustworthy and deceitful, not only in his words but in his pledges, and lightly broke his oath. He was an open adulterer; he gave neither thanks nor devotion to God; he was the hammer of the Church and a child born to calamity.

Gerald was then a bitterly disappointed old man, vindictive and salacious. He did not hesitate to repeat, or invent, the most reckless calumnies about his enemies. Eleanor of Aquitaine he accused of adultery with Count Geoffrey, her husband's father,[4] and he put into St. Bernard's mouth a puerile prophecy of Henry's fate, 'De diabolo venit et ad diabolum ibit.'[5] Gerald's personal wrongs and his devotion to the extremest pretensions of the Church robbed him of the

---

[1] E.H.R., lxi.306. For the assertion that Isabelle was fourteen years of age Mr A. L. Poole cites no evidence (From Domesday Book to Magna Carta, p. 380): had she been so old, it is difficult to understand how she was released from Hugh.

[2] While Kate Norgate completely misconceived the circumstances of John's marriage, she saw that the quarrel of the Lusignans with John had another basis, though she thought that the marriage had made them angry (John Lackland, pp. 78-84). Sir Maurice Powicke could not see any ground for connecting the two matters (Loss of Normandy, pp. 215-9). The connexion assumed by recent writers seems to be due to G. B. Adams who wrote 'John had given the [Lusignans] now a legal right of appeal to his suzerain and a moral justification of rebellion' (Political History of England, 1066-1216, p. 397; cf. Poole, From Domesday Book to Magna Carta, p. 380).

[3] Gerald the Welshman, 'De Principis Instructione', ii, c. 3 (Opera, viii.160).

[4] Ibid., p. 300.   [5] Ibid., p. 309.

desire and power to understand Henry's task and purpose; but his judgement of the king might be very like the judgement of Henry's sons, of John who was at one time Gerald's friend.[1] We have good reason to believe that Henry's sons had little sympathy for their father, that his frugality and seriousness of purpose were not to their liking and were beyond their appreciation. His way of life was not their way of life. They were not likely to see the good in him: they could hardly fail to see, and to exaggerate, the bad.

Eleanor of Aquitaine it is easy to judge harshly.[2] It may be that she was cursed by fate in being born a woman. Of indomitable energy and courage, her long life seems to have been passed in the service of her children. Her devotion to them, and perhaps her dislike of her husband, led to the greatest mistake of her life—her part in the conspiracy of her sons against Henry II. If she had ever cared for Henry, her passion soon exhausted itself; but the probability is that she cared as little for her second husband as for her first, Louis VII of France. With her, marriages were politics. Whether she shared at all in the view of life which found expression in the *amour courtois* there is no means of telling: her participation in 'courts of love' is mere fiction. When we have separated fact from legend, there is little to make us suppose that Eleanor was frivolous, and in her later years she gave herself to piety within the cloister of Fontevrault, in so far as she could withdraw from the pressing business of state-craft. That she was devoted to John the history of her last years seems to leave in no doubt. That she was capable of teaching him prudence or restraint is very much in doubt.

The best that can be said of Philip Augustus is that—in the words of Gerald the Welshman—he reclaimed the rights of the French Crown from those who had usurped them.[3] He was the founder of the mediaeval French monarchy and as such has a high place in history. But what would have been written of him had he died before Richard I, after the disaster of Fréteval in 1194, when he fled in utter rout before the English king? Again, if Richard had not been prematurely slain, it is quite unlikely that Philip would have conquered Normandy, quite unlikely that he would have gained any such victory as that at Bouvines: and Bouvines determined the destiny of the Capetian dynasty and of France itself. Philip, however, was blessed by fortune and, if not of outstanding ability, he had a fixed purpose and knew how to turn an opportunity to advantage.

---

[1] *Ibid.*, i.86: quem familiarem habebat.

[2] Of Eleanor there is no good biography, for no biographer has had the patience to collect her *acta* and to ascertain the indubitable facts of her life, the personnel of her household, and so forth. For an introduction to the subject see *E.H.R.*, lxxiv.193-213. It can be said of the most recent biography, that by Miss Amy Kelly, *Eleanor of Aquitaine and the Four Kings*, that it is better than its predecessors.

[3] Gerald the Welshman, 'De Principis Instructione', iii, c. 1 (*Opera*, viii.228): iura corone contra tot et tantos detentores tam viriliter etiam in tenera etate revocavit. Gerald's choice of words implies that Philip was fulfilling the duty imposed upon a king: see above, p. 150.

Opportunity certainly came to him through the dissensions between Henry II and his sons and between those sons themselves. Philip's conduct can be made to appear in an odious light, and it is difficult to regard as pleasant the support he gave to the sons in their rebellion against their father. If the situation had been as simple as that (and sometimes English historians write as though it were), then the case against Philip might be black indeed. But the situation was complicated by the web of feudal relationships that Henry II could not desist from weaving or attempting to weave. The feudal relationship between the French king, the English king in his capacity as duke of Aquitaine, and the latter's vassals was intricate. The French king seems never to have been loth to accept the homage of one of those vassals, with the object of obtaining jurisdiction in any dispute between the vassal and the duke. When, therefore, Henry II invested his sons with French fiefs, the relationship in which he placed them to the French Crown provided every opportunity for mischief, if the sons' ambitions should overcome their filial duty. The situation was of Henry's own making and he might have unmade it, but he would not.[1] Philip Augustus was not the man to refuse to take advantage of it, merely because the English king's vassals were also his sons. In this Philip was not exceptionally cynical or base. Louis VII had not shrunk from supporting Henry's sons against their father; but he had at least the excuse that two of them were his sons-in-law, and he affected to be concerned about the welfare of his daughters who were in Henry's keeping.[2] Philip's support of John against Richard is a much blacker business and reveals his lack of scruple, but on other occasions he was not without a colourable excuse for his conduct. If Philip was unscrupulous in his political actions, he was unscrupulous also in his personal relations. It is significant that Gerald, who is fertile in inventing stories to extol the Capetians, is silent on Philip's morals. Louis VII and Louis VIII were, if we could believe the Welshman, paragons of virtue[3]; but all the world knew of Philip, of his queen Isambour of Denmark and of Agnes of Méranie who had usurped her place,[4] and it would have been idle to circulate a discrepant fiction.

Richard, the athlete, the born warrior, does not cut so sorry a figure as his sickly opponent, Philip Augustus. The truth of the soubriquet Bertran de Born applies to him, 'Oc e No',[5] is borne out

[1] Though we cannot accept as his *ipsissima verba* the speech put by Peter of Blois into Henry's mouth, it must represent what were believed to be his sentiments: 'Filios meos exheredare non valeo nec volo nec debeo: quamvis enim decreta et leges repellant eos ab hereditate paterna qui contra patres suos arma moverunt, nolo tamen filios meos ab hereditate repellere, etsi exheredare eos possem, cor meum hanc duritiam non posset sustinere' (*Opera*, iii.300). [2] Below, pp. 343-4.
[3] Gerald the Welshman, 'Gemma Ecclesiastica', ii, c. 11; 'De Principis Instructione', i.20 (*Opera*, ii.216-7; viii.131-3).
[4] Gerald carefully avoids these topics.
[5] It may be convenient to give page references to the texts of Antoine Thomas (*Poésies*, pp. 55, 72, 76-8, 82, 89, 121) and Albert Stimming (*Gedichte*, pp. 63, 93, 98, 101, 104, 124)
GME Y

by Gerald's description, 'in purpose and word of fixed constancy'.[1] In the light of some well-known incidents in his career we may think this reputation for integrity rather easily earned; but there can be no questioning contemporary opinion. Richard stood out in contrast to the Poitevin barons among whom he passed his early career, to Philip Augustus, perhaps to his own father, certainly to his brother John. In some odd way Richard must have justified to himself, and reconciled with his code of honour, his armed rebellion against his father. Contemporary writers do not help us to solve the riddle: it is hard to believe the explanation that Richard took up arms against Henry in 1189 because his father wished to make provision for John at his expense. Henry's intended provision for John was implemented by Richard, and it seems clear that it amounted to £4000 a year from English lands, the county of Mortain in Normandy, as well as the lordship of Ireland.[2] A handsome provision, no doubt, but something quite different from Richard's disherison. Moreover, John was found in the same camp as Richard in 1189, a fact that seems quite inconsistent with any idea of animosity between the brothers and quite consonant with the affection and generosity that Richard later displayed towards John. Gerald of Wales was prepared to assert the worst of Henry II and to sing Richard's praises, but he hints, not obscurely, that Richard was his father's murderer.[3] The enigma of Richard's conduct remains. The root of the matter may very well be that father and son had very different views on life.

Richard was one of those noble knights, typical of his time, with whom all things were for sale and who expended his gains without counting the cost. When money was short, then fresh expedients had to be devised. The best-known perhaps is his trick in requiring the re-sealing of charters on the pretext that his first seal had been lost.[4] He is credited with vast dreams of empire, but he had no conception of the relation of financial means to political ends and it is evident that he had no practical interest in administration. No administrator would have displayed his princely generosity, even in compliance with his dead father's wishes, by making over to his brother the revenues and administration of six English counties, a brother in whom he had so little trust, despite his affection for him, that he bound him by oath not to set foot in England during his own absence.[5] Though we cannot place upon Richard the entire blame

[1] Gerald the Welshman, 'Topographia Hibernica', iii, c. 1: 'tam animi quam verbi firma constantia', repeated in 'De Principis Instructione', iii, c. 8 (*Opera*, v.196; viii.248).

[2] Details in Norgate, *John Lackland*, pp. 26-8. The story of Henry's intended disherison of Richard in favour of John rests only on the word of Gerald in an obviously malicious passage of *De Principis Instructione*, iii, c. 2 (*Opera*, viii.231-2).

[3] His father's corpse bleeds at his approach. The same story is told in the 'Vita Galfridi' and 'De Principis Instructione' (*Opera*, iv.372; viii.305) and by Howden ('Benedict of Peterborough', ii.71).   [4] Landon, *Itinerary of Richard I*, pp. 175-80.

[5] Of the manner in which John was released from his oath we have two different stories. Gerald, professedly repeating John's own words, says that the chancellor, that

for the anarchy induced by the uncertainty of his fate in 1192 and in 1193, events showed that in politics, as in administration, his acumen was deficient. His best service to England was to leave the government of the country to Hubert Walter and Geoffrey fitz Peter during the last five years of his life. But even though his deficiencies were counterbalanced by the qualities of his latest ministers, his reign had become irksome before his death,[1] though as John's reign wore to its close Richard's seemed a golden age.[2]

And if we are to see Richard whole, we must consider his end. He died not in any heroic contest, but in a mean Poitevin quarrel over buried treasure. Some wonderful gold-work of classical times had had been found on the lands of a vassal of Aimar, viscount of Limoges, and to this both Aimar and Richard laid claim. Richard would hear of no compromise and went to take by force the treasure which he seems to have believed was in safe-keeping at Chalus. He laid siege to the castle and, imprudently venturing out insufficiently protected, was struck by a bolt from a crossbow and died from the inexpertly treated wound.[3] Since he had been slain in a quarrel with Aimar, it was incumbent upon Richard's son Philip (born, of course, out of wedlock) to avenge his father, and Philip slew the viscount.[4] The feud was composed, as we have said, by John's marriage to Isabelle of Angoulême, Aimar's niece. Richard's end was typical of the man. The heir to the vast Angevin dominions bequeathed to his own son neither rank, land nor money, no better legacy than a squalid blood-feud.

Finally, let us say a little of Innocent III, pope from 1198 to 1216, John's whilom antagonist, but, at the end, his firm supporter and friend. Innocent's lasting achievement is represented by the legal texts that stand under his name embodied in the Gregorian Decretals; among papal law-makers he is second only to Alexander III. But his other achievements crumbled into dust, though the aims and methods of his politics might seem eminently successful. He died on the crest of the wave, but a wave that brought the papacy to the sinful city of Avignon, from which it emerged with only a shadow of its former greatness. Innocent's politics, the pursuit of temporal power, were not his invention but an inheritance he gladly accepted. The obligations of his inheritance he fulfilled with the utmost piety, without intermission and without scruple. There had been many

is Longchamp (as justiciar), absolved him ('De rebus a se gestis', c. 23 (*Opera*, i.86); Howden says that Richard was persuaded by Queen Eleanor to give him leave to return to England (*Gesta*, ii.106).

[1] Perhaps the best evidence for this is John's 'Constitution' of 7 June 1199 which condemns the evil customs introduced by Richard in making excessive charges for the great seal (*Foedera*, i.75-6; *Memoranda Roll*, 1 *John*, pp. xxxv-xxxvi).

[2] So Matthew of Rievaulx: Anglia sub rege Ricardo tuta fuisti, tota potens, misera nunc conditione subacta (Faral, *Les arts poétiques*, p. 26; *Revue Bénédictine*, lii.33).

[3] Details in Norgate, *Richard the Lion Heart*, pp. 324-9.

[4] Howden, *Chronica*, iv.97. Philip then went to England under John's protection (*Pipe Roll, 3 John*, p. 283).

indications that the course the papacy had set would inevitably bring it in conflict at innumerable points with the secular rulers of Western Europe, both in matters where the lay power was exercised for ill and where it was exercised for good—if peace and justice be good. Successive popes pitted might against might, to discover in the end, in the bitter school of experience, that their material resources could be controlled by secular rulers and that ecclesiastical weapons wear out with usage. Christ's Vicar was slow to learn that His kingdom is not of this world. Innocent thought the contrary.

We have said enough, for our immediate purpose, of John's friends and enemies. Angevins, Capetians, popes: all were engaged in a struggle for empire, sometimes inevitably at the others' expense, and they were not nice in their methods. 'On ne construit pas un empire avec des premières communiantes', remarked Marshal Lyautey, who was not without experience. By the standards of candidates for confirmation these kings and popes were doubtless bad, and bad too was Eleanor of Aquitaine; and it was in association with all this badness that John grew to manhood and in turn became a bad man. Yet there is room for the conjecture that perhaps John was not so very bad when he was young. Perhaps he was not without qualities that deserved his father's anxious care and his brother's sorely tried affection, that merited Gerald's anticipations for his future when he was on the threshold of kingship: 'May God long preserve, for the calm peace of the people and the liberty of the Church, the fourth of King Henry's sons, who yet survives.'[1] How soon did his fall from grace become evident? 'When he had the temerity to quarrel with Innocent III' would seem to be the answer implied by the monastic chroniclers who, writing after that event, were able to discover much that was reprehensible in John's otherwise unrecorded past. Let us examine some of their stories.

A favourite authority with modern historians is the 'Great Life' of Hugh of Avalon, bishop of Lincoln.[2] Gerald the Welshman had already written a life of the saint, but this, it was apparently thought, lacked something of colour and incident. So, about the year 1212, a successful fiction-writer, to whom we owe the *Vision of the Monk of Eynsham*, was commissioned to write a bigger and better hagiography. Gerald had known Hugh, but Adam, for that was the favoured author's name, had, although a religious, been the bishop's companion for some years. A sincere and personal narrative would have put posterity in Adam's debt: but he went far beyond his own knowledge and produced, what was doubtless more welcome, a

---

[1] 'De Principis Instructione', iii.28. This passage from an earlier version of the book was, curiously enough, preserved by Gerald, who added a note in the later version to say that the promise had proved false (*Opera*, viii.308).

[2] *Magna Vita Sancti Hugonis Episcopi Lincolniensis* (ed. Dimock). The editor's idea of the 'very conclusive evidence of [Adam's] strictest truth and honesty' (p. xli) is not ours. The text has been re-edited in 1961 by D. L. Douie and H. Farmer.

romance. It is altogether in keeping with his writings that, after rising to be abbot of Eynsham, he was deposed in 1228 for perjury and malversation.[1] Evidently this is a dubious witness, for whose statements it is desirable to have corroboration. He is, however, the sole authority for John's alleged irreverence at mass, his refusal to communicate after he had attained years of discretion, his ill-omened dropping of the lance when invested with the duchy of Normandy.[2] If there were any truth in these stories we should expect to find corroboration either in the many references to John by Gerald the Welshman or in the 'Histoire de Guillaume le Maréchal'. The latter gives credit to the Marshal for John's accession to the duchy, but there is not a word about an unusual incident at the investiture, no hint of an ill omen, although a prophecy of disaster is put into the mouth of Hubert Walter.[3] Again, Gerald knows nothing of any of these stories. He never charges John with irreverence; but he does mention one occasion when he found the king at mass, and then he notes that John stayed to the end and did not discuss business until it was over.[4] There is, moreover, as we shall see,[5] adequate evidence to show that John's attitude towards the sacrament was that normal to men of rank at the time. He was neither more nor less reverent than the common run of his fellows. Gerald, again, was in London at the time of John's coronation and, though he does not expressly say whether he was present at the ceremony, he could hardly have been ignorant of any refusal on the king's part to communicate and he was not the man to let such an incident pass in silence.[6] What he does relate is a legend of a countess of Anjou, a mythical ancestress of John's, who did not communicate,[7] and this suggests the origin of Adam's tale. But as we make our way through the stories of John's depravity, we find ourselves in a sea of legend.

There was a pleasing Canterbury story, arising out of a disputed claim by the monks of St. Augustine's to the church of Faversham. The monks manfully shut themselves in the church and parsonage and denied access to the king's ministers and the archbishop's officials. When this came to the king's ears, in fury he ordered the church and other buildings to be set on fire with the monks and their supporters inside.[8] No one, however, would carry out this evil order, but all joined in dissuading the king from perpetrating such an awful crime. So in the end, abating his anger, he merely ordered the sheriff to expel the monks. Then there was the Dunmow story, which attributed the origin of the Barons' War to John's illicit passion for Maud, the beautiful daughter of Robert fitz Walter. Because her

[1] Annales Monastici (Dunstable), iii.109.   [2] Magna Vita, pp. 291-4.
[3] Histoire de Guillaume le Maréchal, ll. 11904-6.
[4] 'De Iure et Statu Menevensis Ecclesiae', v (Opera, iii.301-2).
[5] Below, pp. 347-8.   [6] 'De rebus a se gestis', c. 12 (Opera, i.111).
[7] 'De Principis Instructione', iii, c. 27 (Opera, viii.301).
[8] William Thorne, Chronica, in Twysden, Decem Scriptores, col. 1846.

father would not give her to the king, Robert's castle in London (Castle Baynard) was destroyed and the castles and lands of other barons seized into the king's hand. Robert, with two other barons, fled to the king of France, leaving Maud at Dunmow. There an emissary of John's sought her out and, because she would not yield to the king, he poisoned her food, so that she died and was buried in the choir of Dunmow Priory. The king of France then invaded John's possessions, in defence of which he crossed to the Continent. An armistice having been arranged, the two armies faced each other across an arm of the sea. When they were in that position, an English knight challenged the French to send a champion to joust for his lady love. Without disclosing his identity, Robert fitz Walter accepted the challenge and easily overcame the English champion. John's admiration was such that, when he learnt who the victor was, he restored him to his barony. Peace was then made between the two kings by Robert's mediation, John recalled all the exiles, restored them to his favour and gave them licence to rebuild their castles. They were for ever faithful to him thereafter.[1]

St. Alban's, too, had its stories about John. Roger of Wendover narrates how, when the news of John's excommunication, which it was endeavoured to suppress, began to be whispered abroad, Geoffrey, archdeacon of Norwich, sitting one day at the exchequer on the king's business, began secretly to discuss the matter with his colleagues, giving it as his opinion that it was not safe for beneficed clergymen to remain in the service of an excommunicate king. Saying this, he himself retired, without leave, to his home. Shortly afterwards these things came to the king's knowledge. Greatly incensed he sent a knight, named William Talbot, with an armed force, to arrest the archdeacon and cast him, bound in fetters, into prison. There, after a few days, by the king's order he was sheathed in a cope of lead and starved to death.[2] Matthew Paris has a more wonderful tale of a secret embassy despatched by John to the admiral Murmelius, the great king of Africa, Morocco and Spain, a tale he heard with his own ears from Robert of London, one of the mission, who subsequently was granted the custody of the abbey. This Robert claimed that he had given in confidence to the Moorish king a candid description of John. 'His wife,' Robert had said 'was detested by the king and she hated him. She was unchaste, an evildoer and an adultress. She had often been found out and the king had ordered her paramours to be strangled with a halter on her bed. He, however, had made many of his barons and even his kinsmen jealous and had corrupted their nubile daughters and sisters. As for the king's profession of Christianity it was (so Robert had heard) uncertain and hesitant.'[3]

---

[1] *Monasticon*, vi.147.   [2] Wendover, *Flores*, iii.229.
[3] *Chronica Maiora*, ii.559-64.

Pleasant monastic gossip, of which these specimens may suffice, however revealing the tales may be of the intellectual level and moral tone of the convents in which they once were told, would not be worth notice here, had they not been treated as evidence of another sort by modern historians. It is therefore not superfluous to indicate why these tales must be rejected. The Canterbury story of the king's intentions is obviously improbable in itself and could not be within the knowledge of the writer. The Dunmow story, based though it is upon actual incidents, is of the stuff of *chansons de geste* and may be drawn from one now lost. If Matthew Paris believed, and did not invent, Robert of London's story, he was simpler than he appears to be: we know sufficient of Queen Isabelle's frequent maternities and of John's relations with her to be certain that what is said of her is false[1]; and the rest therefore deserves no credit.

These stories can be briefly dismissed; but Wendover's story requires a more extended examination, for though it is plainly fabulous, historians have been reluctant to abandon it.[2] They will admit that, since the archdeacon lived to be rewarded with the see of Ely in 1225, Wendover was mistaken in his man, but since there was another Geoffrey of Norwich connected with the exchequer, they have sought to keep the chronicler in credit by supposing that it was this Geoffrey who suffered in his leaden cope. The fact that the incident must have taken place in 1209, as Wendover knew, if it took place at all, and that the other Geoffrey lived on until at least June 1212, seems not to be regarded as an insuperable difficulty, because another version of the story alleges that Geoffrey's offence was complicity in the plotting of Robert fitz Walter and Eustace de Vesci. But all these variants are merely stages in the growth of a legend. What is apparently the original version is found (under a wrong year) in a St. Edmund's chronicle, a simple statement that a noble clerk, Geoffrey of Norwich, because it was alleged that he had read the pope's rescript before the barons of the exchequer, was summoned by the king to give an explanation, [but he fled and] was taken at Nottingham and loaded so heavily with irons that he died.[3] There is nothing here but the story of a fugitive arrested and dying in prison before trial; there is no suggestion that the king had a hand in the death or that it was by intent that the clerk met his end: just a grim incident in a mediaeval prison, and no more. But, circulating through Western Europe in the thirteenth century, there was a tale of a leaden cope as an instrument of torment.[4] Its use was attributed to the Emperor Frederick II, and this tale was known to

[1] *E.H.R.*, lxi.310-1.
[2] Poole dismisses it (*From Domesday to Magna Carta*, p. 427 *n*), as does also Warren, *King John*, pp. 12-13. It is defended by Painter, *Reign of King John*, pp. 270-3.
[3] Liebermann, *Ungedruckte Anglo-Normannische Geschichtsquellen*, p. 139; *Memorials of St. Edmund's Abbey*, ii.25.
[4] F. Olivier-Martin, 'Les chapes de plomb', *Mélanges Mandonnet*, ii.283-7.

Dante.[1] It has woven itself into—perhaps the legend originated from—a French translation of the Institutes of Justinian.[2] So, as is the way with romances, the tale of the fugitive clerk and the tale of the leaden cope became fused; and, as the romance passed from mouth to mouth, the scene changed from Nottingham to Dunstable and Bristol, details were varied, fresh characters were introduced. We have no reason to suppose that Wendover did more than abbreviate in Latin the story that reached his ears in the vernacular, but his credulity is no excuse for ours. As evidence against King John the story is ludicrously inadequate, whatever basis it may have and whoever may have been Geoffrey of Norwich.

There were in circulation, however, two stories of John's cruelty which appear to be well-founded: the doing to death of Arthur and of Maud of Briouze and her son. These misdeeds were remembered when mere scandals were forgotten. Of the manner of death of these three victims of John's there is no certain knowledge. What seems certain is that John had Arthur put to death as a dangerous pretender to the throne.[3] Less certain, but highly probable, is it that Maud of Briouze was imprisoned lest she should relate what she knew of Arthur's death[4]: whether, as rumour told, she was starved is another matter, but she did not emerge from prison alive.[5] It may well be that not only fear but spite and vengeance were motives in these tragedies. It is not easy otherwise to explain why Maud's eldest son should share his mother's fate, although it is true that a daughter was spared, and there is an ugly parallel in the execution of the son of Peter of Wakefield with his father. Peter of Wakefield has passed into history as the foreteller of the king's death, who was hanged when his prophecy was belied.[6] The chroniclers know little of Peter.[7] He appears in this one episode and is gone. Nor have historians been curious about him, though he is a figure worth more than passing attention. He is described as a hermit, but this seems to mean merely that he was a man of piety, frugality and strict life. He was, in truth, the head of a heterodox sect, which seems to have

---

[1] Inferno, xxiii.61 sqq:
> Egli avean cappe con cappucci bassi . . .
> Di fuor dorate son si ch'egli abbaglia,
>   ma dentro tutte piombo, e gravi tanto,
>   che Federico le mettea di paglia.

[2] *Les Institutes de Justinien en français* (ed. Olivier-Martin), p. 29.

[3] Ch. Petit-Dutaillis, *Le déshéritement de Jean sans Terre*, pp. 18-29. It is, however, remarkable that the minstrel of Béthune (not noticed by Petit-Dutaillis), who is very frank about John, does not hint at a violent death, and presumably the story of the murder is later. All he says is 'il mist Artu son neveu en prison en la tour u il moru' (*Histoire des Ducs de Normandie*, p. 95).   [4] Powicke, *Loss of Normandy*, (1961), p. 320.

[5] The minstrel of Béthune gives a very precise and horrible story: it is as likely to be as near the truth as any other (*Histoire des Ducs de Normandie*, pp. 114-5). Miss Norgate collected the accounts of other chroniclers in *John Lackland*, p. 288.

[6] Stubbs notices him in *Constitutional History*, i.561, 563.

[7] Again the minstrel of Béthune, who calls him Peter of Pontefract, seems the most reliable conveyor of current rumours (*Histoire des Ducs de Normandie*, pp. 122-3, 125-6). Other accounts are in Walter of Coventry, *Memoriale*, ii.208, 211-2; *Chronica Mon. de Melsa*, i.403; Ralf of Coggeshall, *Chronicon*, p. 167; Wendover, *Flores*, iii.240, 255.

originated in the reign of Henry II and to have received an impetus from the mission of Eustace, abbot of the Norman abbey of Saint Germer de Fly, who came to England at the beginning of John's reign. The sect was evangelical and puritanical. In apocalyptic utterances its members called upon all men to repent. They affixed calls to repentance to church doors and altars. They believed that they were in special and direct communication with Christ, and they called their leaders His 'elect'.[1] It is easy to understand how, mystical and exalted, Peter, the 'elect', might warn the king and be understood to be prophesying his death: he may, indeed, have done so. Of his trial we know little for certain, but the king seems to have presided and Peter, it would appear, called upon him to repent 'lest in the terrible day of judgement his household, body and soul, should be adjudged to Hell for ever'.[2] Peter was found guilty of lese-majesty and condemned to death as a traitor. We cannot say that his condemnation was unjust or unlawful[3]; in other reigns men have been condemned to death for imagining the king's death. But what seems contrary to justice is the condemnation of Peter's son as an accessory.[4]

Mediaeval history, however, like modern history, knows many unrighteous deaths perpetrated by secular and ecclesiastical rulers. In this matter John has the company of not a few English kings. Were they all bad men or bad kings? A king, it would seem, may be allowed a few murders for political ends. A distinguished French historian, indeed, terms the death of Arthur a 'political execution'.[5] But though Innocent III was disinclined to condemn John, contemporary opinion did not judge John leniently. There was a feeling that, as between the two, Arthur might have a better right to succeed Richard than John. This is written for all to read in the 'Histoire de Guillaume le Maréchal', where a discussion on the rival claims is put into the mouths of William Marshal and Hubert Walter.[6] In the writings of the sect of Peter of Wakefield, Arthur's death, the imprisonment of his sister, Eleanor, and the deaths of Maud of Briouze and her son 'by hunger and thirst', are singled out as John's most atrocious crimes—the execution of Peter and 'his innocent son'

---

[1] What remains of the writings of the members of the sect after Peter's death is to be found in Vespasian E. III, fo. 171-8. This is our principal source of information.

[2] Cumque electus meus Petrus senior Iohanni . . . verba et sermones misericordie mee coram omnibus retulisset, ne in inferno domus eius cum corpore et anima in die iudicii terribili sine fine efficeretur (Vespasian E. iii, fo. 175b).

[3] That it was felony to imagine or, in the contemporary phrase, to announce (denunciare) the king's death is clear from an appeal in 1214 (Curia Regis Rolls, vii.94-5, 166-73).

[4] Testified by Vespasian E. III, fo. 175b, as well as the Histoire des Ducs de Normandie, pp. 125-6, Walter of Coventry, Memoriale, ii.212 and Wendover, Flores, iii.255.

[5] Petit-Dutaillis, op. cit., p. 28. We do not follow M. Petit-Dutaillis in every detail and particularly in the matter of the date of Arthur's death, nor do we accept his view of the complicity of Geoffrey fitz Peter.

[6] This conversation (ll. 11861-918) is, of course, apocryphal and should not be treated as historical. The circumstances in which John succeeded have been explained above, p. 147.

apart.[1] Be it so. But when we have sifted the mass of tales told to John's discredit, the number of crimes and fleshly sins that we can be reasonably certain he committed are no more than those committed by other kings whose reputation is by no means low and who are judged on their ability to rule. It is by this test that John's reputation should stand or fall.

[1] Vespasian E. III, fo. 175*b*, 177.

XVIII

THE KING AND THE ARCHBISHOP

I F John is Stubbs's exemplary bad king, Stephen Langton is his exemplary archbishop.[1] The two are foils, puppets in his historical melodrama. Stubbs's John is incredible at any time or place; his Langton is incredible as a mediaeval archbishop. The constitutional virtues with which Stubbs endeavours to endow the archbishop would have seemed vices in the eyes of his contemporaries; and yet Stubbs's conception of Langton has passed unchallenged. Of him a recent historian of the reign of King John has written:

He had hoped to establish a reign of law in English secular politics. To that end he had persuaded a group of disaffected barons, who hated the king and lusted for lands, castles, and privileges, to formulate a general program of reform—one that would benefit not only the barons but all the freemen of England.[2]

Stubbs could not have written these words: perhaps rightly, he did not view the Magna Carta barons in this light. But unless Stubbs had perverted history as he did, it is unlikely that Professor Painter would ever have attributed to Stephen Langton a part he did not and could not play. This is a matter of evidence. But in drawing a conclusion from the evidence, we must remember that, just as we should judge John by his ability to rule his kingdom as a mediaeval king should, so, in the context of constitutional history, we should judge Langton by his ability to play the part of an archbishop of Canterbury in the early thirteenth century.

It should be clear that Langton's personal qualities are largely irrelevant to the political struggle under John, if only because the contestants disregarded them. Suffice it to say that, unlike that of his distinguished predecessor on the throne of Augustine, Langton's training had been academic, not administrative or political. He was eminent in the barren learning of contemporary theology.[3] He was an unquestioning papalist. He was an active, indeed a leading, participant in the stupidly cruel persecution of the Jews.[4] One conspicuous action of his was the condemnation to death of the

---

[1] *Constitutional History*, ii.313, 418.
[2] Painter, *The Reign of King John*, p. 347.
[3] Powicke, *Stephen Langton*, pp. 23-74.
[4] Langton's interest in the Jewish problem is suggested by the dedication to him of a disputation between a Christian and a Jew (Hunt in *Powicke Essays*, pp. 143-56).

apostate deacon who had fallen in love with a Jewess[1]; another was a persistent, though abortive, attempt to place disabilities upon Jews in England and to force them to wear the distinctive badge that had been prescribed by the Lateran Council of 1215.[2] If, within his limitations, he was a man of inflexible integrity, plainly he was not a man of independent thought, but narrow, legalistic and uncharitable. Events were to show that no more inept choice could have been made of a successor to Hubert Walter; but, in any case, Langton was a mere pawn that could be removed without loss from the chess-board of papal politics. These things it is necessary to emphasise at the outset so that we may get free from the sentimentalities borrowed from the chroniclers, and in large measure from the unveracious Roger of Wendover, which still find a place in sober histories.

It was initially through no fault of his own that deep enmity sprang up between the king and the archbishop. The essential facts are these.[3] On Hubert Walter's death on 13 July 1205, the method of the election of his successor as archbishop of Canterbury was in dispute. There is no question that Hubert himself had been elected by the Christ Church monks on the nomination of Richard I and that the chapter had evaded co-operation with the bishops of the province. On the occasion of the election of Hubert's successor, the bishops of the province again claimed the right to elect the archbishop jointly with the chapter. The monks resented the interference of the bishops, and both parties appealed to the Curia. Without waiting for the result of this appeal the monks secretly and provisionally elected their sub-prior, Reginald, with the object of avoiding the necessity of electing the king's nominee. Subsequently, at the king's instance, there was a formal election by the chapter when the king's nominee, the bishop of Norwich, was unanimously chosen. Innocent quashed this election as uncanonical, disallowed equally the election of Reginald, and directed a fresh election by representatives of the chapter present at the Curia. It was apparently at Innocent's suggestion that they elected Stephen Langton. The king's proctors refused to ratify this election and Innocent therefore made a direct request to the king. After a period of temporising John refused to accept Langton, and Innocent attempted to coerce the king.

But we must go into a little detail. Innocent's action, in arranging the election of Langton and ignoring the king's interest in the matter, was, at best, of dubious legality, and he seems, as was not unusual

---

[1] For the various versions of the incident see Maitland, *Roman Canon Law in the Church of England*, pp. 158-75. That the deacon was condemned in a council over which Langton presided does not admit of doubt. His condemnation is Bracton's only authority (fo. 123b-124: Woodbine, ii.349) for the doctrine that apostasy was punishable by death in English law.   [2] Richardson, *English Jewry under Angevin Kings*, pp. 182-7.
[3] The facts were established by Knowles in *E.H.R.*, liii.211-20, as against the account by Roger of Wendover, which was in substance adopted by Stubbs and subsequent writers. For some further details see Painter, *op. cit.*, pp. 164-71.

with him, to have decided a judicial issue for a political objective in which he was himself interested. The pope could have been under no illusion regarding John's standpoint in the matter of episcopal appointments. By February 1203 the pope had found cause for complaint at John's actions in regard to English, Irish, Norman and Poitevin sees.[1] We cannot examine all these disputes, and we select two of them, in the first place that over the election of the bishop of Séez, which is particularly well documented and which shows the contestants in their characteristic attitudes.[2] This see had become void on the death of Bishop Lisiard in September 1201, and the canons resolved that his successor should be chosen from among their own number. The king objected and first proposed the dean of Lisieux as his candidate and then, when the canons demurred, asked them to nominate three canons and three strangers from whom he would make his choice. The canons named five candidates, all from the chapter, and at the king's mandate sent representatives to Argentan to make the election. There, however, they refused to consider a royal nominee and elected unanimously one of the five they had named. Following the refusal of the archbishop of Rouen to confirm this election—the archbishop, we must remember, was Walter of Coutances, a former justiciar of England—dissensions arose and the chapter split into two parties, both of which appealed to the pope. The prior's party favoured the candidate first elected, but he died on his way to Rome, and the prior and the canons who accompanied him then elected another of the five, Silvester, the archdeacon of Séez. After much argument, but without consulting John, Innocent approved Silvester, holding that his election was, despite the circumstances, canonical. Silvester was still only bishop elect and in the normal course it would have fallen to the archbishop of Rouen to consecrate him, but in face of the king's opposition to the election of a candidate not of his choice, Archbishop Walter declined to proceed. Not to be thwarted, Innocent ordered the archbishop of Sens to consecrate, but John refused to permit the bishop to take possession of his see. The pope riposted by ordering the archbishop of Rouen to lay Normandy under an interdict unless the king submitted within a month. This was in May 1203.[3] Whether or not Archbishop Walter dared obey the pope's instructions, it seems that already an attempt to impose an interdict had been made by the archbishop of Sens and that John retaliated by harassing

[1] Migne, *Patrologia Latina*, ccxiv.1175-7. The sees in question were Lincoln, Dublin, Coutances, Séez, Limoges, Poitiers.

[2] The episode is described by Elsie Gütschow, *Innocentz III und England* (1904), pp. 116-20 and again by Packard, 'King John and the Norman Church', *Harvard Theological Review*, xv.20-4. The *ex parte* statements by the two parties in the chapter are set out at great length in Innocent's letter of 24 June 1202: *Patrologia Latina*, ccxiv.1038-44 (the text seems to be corrupt in places).

[3] *Ibid.*, ccxv.69-70. See also *Rot. Litt. Pat.*, p. 16: clerks in the bishopric of Séez are not to aid Silvester (12 August 1202).

those of the clergy who were minded to comply, while at the same time he appealed to the pope.[1] But the tide of war was setting strongly against John, and by October 1203 he was in no position to resist further. He therefore gave orders to the seneschal of Normandy to permit Bishop Silvester to take possession of his see and to compensate him for any losses he had sustained. John gave way, so he said, out of reverence for the pope and the church of Rome, but he added that he was nevertheless seeking for justice to be done to him according to the ancient and approved custom of the duchy.[2] He made it plain that he had renounced none of his claims to control episcopal elections.

Meanwhile another conflict, raising the same issues, had been in progress in Ireland, following upon the death in 1201 of the archbishop of Armagh, Thomas O'Connor. We have not the same detailed information regarding this dispute as we have of the Séez election, but the main facts are known. To begin with, the king nominated Master Humfrey of Tickhill, a royal clerk employed in Ireland[3]; but Humfrey did not secure the general suffrage of the electors, who seem to have been the suffragan bishops and the chapter of Armagh, and it was possible for two other candidates to claim that they had been elected: Simon, bishop of Meath, and Ralf, archdeacon of Meath.[4] It was apparently in an endeavour to resolve the conflict that a fourth candidate was elected, Echdonn Mac Gilleuidhir—latinised as Eugenius—a canon of Bangor.[5] Although this election was made without the king's consent, canonically it was evidently difficult to impugn. John, nevertheless, appealed to Cardinal John of Salerno, as legate to Ireland, and, failing to obtain satisfaction, appealed direct to the pope.[6] At the same time negotiations were opened with the archbishop elect to induce him to withdraw in favour of Humfrey. He was offered a pension until he should be elected to another see but, though at first he appeared to be amenable, he decided to seek confirmation at Rome. The king was apprehensive that he would be consecrated by papal authority and forbade his suffragans to recognise him as archbishop.[7] Even after Humfrey had died, John maintained his opposition to Eugenius and endeavoured to secure the recognition of the archdeacon of Meath as archbishop elect.[8] This was in February 1204; but within a twelvemonth Eugenius had evidently obtained possession of his see

---

[1] *Rot. Litt. Pat.*, p. 22b. The implication of the order of 26 October 1203 to the seneschal and baillis of Normandy that the abbot of Blanchelande is to enjoy his rents despite the interdict (*ibid.*, p. 35) must be that other ecclesiastics had been deprived of them.

[2] *Rot. de Liberate*, p. 72 (9 October 1203).

[3] *Rot. Litt. Pat.*, pp. 2b, 4, 29.

[4] *Rot. Chartarum*, p. 133b.

[5] *Patrologia Latina*, ccxiv.1067. He was a regular canon, perhaps of the Arroasian order (Dunning in *Irish Historical Studies*, iv.311-2).

[6] The actual correspondence has not survived, but its purport is known from references in the enrolments of the king's letters: *Rot. Litt. Pat.*, pp. 16b, 29, 29b.

[7] *Ibid.*, pp. 28-9.   [8] *Rot. Chartarum*, p. 133b (10 February 1204).

and was universally recognised in the province.[1] For a long time the king deferred the restoration of the temporalities,[2] even although he recognised Eugenius as archbishop and had in July 1207 commissioned him—there being no archbishop of Canterbury—to execute the episcopal office in the diocese of Exeter, which was then without a bishop.[3]

John's ultimate acquiescence, first in the appointment of Silvester as bishop of Séez and then of Eugenius as archbishop of Armagh, reluctant as it had been, may have given the impression at the Curia that his consent could safely be dispensed with whenever an election was disputed. His objections had not prevailed in either instance, and any right he may have had to give or withhold his assent to the candidate finally adopted had not been recognised. But appointments to Irish bishoprics were very different from appointments to English bishoprics—Norman bishoprics were no longer in question —and, for all that the archbishop of Armagh was primate of Ireland, his political significance was very different from that of the archbishop of Canterbury. Nor could the English king claim an immemorial custom to appoint bishops in Ireland as he could, with much justification, claim in the case of English bishops. But whatever weight we attach, as a matter of law, to the claims of king and pope, there can be no doubt that Innocent's action in proceeding with the consecration of Langton was deliberately provocative and politically maladroit. He lived to regret his unwisdom. John's case, if not unimpugnable, was grounded in law and in politics. The legal position, as he saw it, was put to the pope at the time both by letter and by the mouth of his messengers,[4] and it was again stated in letters which, at his instigation, were issued long afterwards by the English and Irish barons. The baronial statement we may give at some length, for it is a clear and very carefully drafted exposition of the king's case. 'They have heard', the barons say, 'with grief and surprise of the pope's intention to absolve from their fealty the subjects of the king of England because he has resisted the wrongs done to him in the matter of the church of Canterbury. They well know that all that has been done in this connection has been directed despitefully against his dignity and the privilege customarily enjoyed by the English Crown, to his disherison and that of his heirs. It is notorious that in ancient times, before the coming of the Normans, the kings of England, even those now canonised, granted cathedral churches to archbishops and bishops entirely at their pleasure. Since the Conquest elections have been subject to the king's assent and

---

[1] So we must infer from a letter of Innocent III's of 1 July 1205, referring to a sentence of excommunication passed by Eugenius and certain of his suffragans on any who infringed a treaty between Hugh de Lacy and John de Courcy (*Patrologia Latina*, ccxv.681-2).

[2] *Rot. Litt. Pat.*, p. 72b (30 August 1207): cf. *ibid.*, p. 76b.

[3] *Rot. Litt. Claus.*, i.88.

[4] The king's letter has not survived: its purport is indicated in Innocent's reply of 26 May 1207 (*Selected Letters of Innocent III*, pp. 86-90).

hitherto have been carried out strictly in this form. . . . King John has done nothing against the constitutions of the realm.'[1] This is the legal case. Politically the case for refusing to accept Langton was that he was personally unknown to John and that he had lived for a long time in France among the king's enemies.[2] And since, among English bishops, the archbishop of Canterbury stood in a special relation to the king, it is manifest that only a man known to him and approved by him could be regarded as a suitable candidate. No one who considers the arguments dispassionately can deny that John's case was weighty, and it is plain that, except for a number of the higher clergy and some of the monastic communities, he was generally supported in England. The Margam Annalist (not, indeed, a very satisfactory authority) goes so far as to assert that every lay-man and nearly every clerk approved and assented to the king's actions, as well as many religious of every order.[3]

Langton perhaps could not have stood apart from the struggle between the *regnum* and the *sacerdotium*. His principles could not leave him a detached observer, even if his quite justifiable personal ambitions had not made him a partisan. What is remarkable is his lack of foresight, his inability to realise that, even if the pope achieved a complete victory, thereafter must come peace and conciliation and that, in order to achieve either the spiritual or temporal mission of his office, he must live on good terms with the king. Langton was more papalist than the pope. The limitations of his mind, his un-awareness of the responsibilities of an archbishop of Canterbury, are displayed without disguise in his letter addressed to the English people in 1207.[4] He tells the barons that, unless John repents, they are absolved from the fealty they owe to him, for otherwise the service they would render to the king would be treachery to God. Why? Because John stood upon what he conceived to be his legal rights and defied the pope in the matter of Langton's election to the metropolitan see. *Vox Papae, vox Dei!* This vast, laboured, academic epistle could have been known to few, and no more than an echo may have reached the king's ears. But if Langton had deliberately contrived to justify John in refusing to recognise the papal candidate, he could hardly have chosen apter language. But he had not the wit to appreciate this, as subsequent events were to show.

The king was more supple in mind, more calculating and more prudent. After his first burst of resentment against the monks who had been prevailed upon to elect Langton and against the pope who

---

[1] We have only the text of the declaration of the Irish barons, for which see Richardson and Sayles, *Irish Parliament in the Middle Ages*, pp. 285-7. That the declaration of the English barons was in similar terms is clear from the king's letters to William Marshal and the bishop of Norwich of October 1212 (*Rot. Litt. Claus.*, i.132b).

[2] *Selected Letters*, p. 87. Innocent's rejoinder is a quibble, though he cannot dispute that John's knowledge of Langton is merely by repute.

[3] *Annales Monastici*, i.28.

[4] Gervase of Canterbury, *Opera*, ii.lxxxi-lxxxii; *Acta Stephani Langton*, pp. 5-6.

had consecrated him, John, strong in the support of the English clergy and laity, was prepared to negotiate, provided his prerogative right to control elections to the episcopate was safeguarded. For long the pope failed to give assurances that John deemed satisfactory and, when negotiations broke down, endeavoured to coerce the king to accept his own terms. An interdict was laid upon the kingdom on 24 March 1208 and, because it proved ineffective, in October 1209 John was excommunicated. The Interdict lasted formally until July 1214. Before, however, we attempt to assess its effect, it will be well to regard it in perspective. It is easy to speak, as some historians have spoken, of the 'horrors of an interdict', but the difficulty, as every investigator learns, is that facts are hard to come by and that the horrors, if such there were, are elusive. At the threshold of the enquiry we cannot fail to note that an interdict, like excommunication, could be threatened or imposed by men whom we could hardly regard as measured and sober in their actions and who were actuated by animus and self-interest.[1] And even popes might threaten or impose an interdict with a levity and recklessness that would be remarkable if, in fact, an interdict invariably had serious consequences. Let us take an example. In 1173 Henry II's sons rose in rebellion against him, but there remained with him Margaret of France, who was married to the young king, and Alice of France, who was betrothed to Richard. The girls' father, Louis VII, was in league with the rebels and affected to be concerned for his daughters' welfare. He therefore approached the pope, Alexander III, who required Henry to deliver the girls to their husbands (*viri*), telling him that, if he failed to do so within forty days of a formal summons, the province in which the girls were detained would be laid under interdict.[2] There is, of course, no reason to suppose that they were in detention: they were probably quite happy members of Henry's family, with whom Alice was to live for many years.[3] It seems clear that Louis did not know precisely where the girls were, and it is evident that they might at any time be moved elsewhere without his knowledge. But even if their whereabouts could be ascertained, there was no practical means of enforcing an interdict in the province where, for the moment, they happened to be; and a circular letter addressed vaguely to the archbishops, bishops, abbots, prelates and

---

[1] We give particulars later of the interdict imposed by John Cumin, archbishop of Dublin. In the course of the dispute over the election at Séez, the prior placed the cathedral church and bishopric under interdict (*Patrologia Latina*, ccxiv.1040). Early in the 1180's, arising out of a trivial quarrel, the church of Arkesden was placed under an interdict by Archbishop Richard, and in the early 1190's the church of Walden was similarly placed under interdict by the bishop of London (Walden Abbey Chronicle, lib. ii, c. 10; lib. iv, c. 5).

[2] *Patrologia Latina*. cc. 965-6. A short extract passed into the early collections of decretals and thence into the Gregorian collection, X.4.1.11. Henry was to be summoned to deliver the girls by a commission of three, headed by the archbishop of Tarentaise.

[3] Ralf de Diceto notices their crossing over to England in July 1174 (*Opera*, i.382). For Alice of France see *E.H.R.*, lxi.311-3.

clergy of England and of Henry's overseas dominions, which was all that Louis obtained, would not help to achieve that end. Henry was not the man to be perturbed by idle menaces—and it is uncertain whether he heard of these—and the girls remained where they were. The incident is trivial; but it has this interest, that for once we are given precise details of what the interdict, if effective, would involve. The only spiritual ministrations permitted would have been baptism and absolution of the dying. No other sacraments would have been administered; no marriages would have been blessed; no dead would lie in consecrated ground. These were the penalties—the horrors, if you will—to be imposed indiscriminately upon men and women who had no concern in the quarrel between Henry and his sons, no knowledge of the girls, no power to influence their movements.[1] Are we to suppose that Alexander III, the astute lawyer, was ever serious in his threats or unaware of the frivolity of his proceedings—he certainly did not know the facts[2]—or that for so light a matter he would have embroiled himself with the king whose support he ardently desired?[3] As for Henry, he had some experience of interdicts and he had means at his command to prevent their enforcement.[4] Doubtless the pope was willing to make a show of obliging the king of France, and idle threats cost little and hurt nobody. We must not mistake comedy for tragedy.

As churchmen became more combative, the interdict became a more and more favoured weapon: the golden age of the interdict, it has been said, was the pontificate of Innocent III,[5] not indeed because it then proved most effective but because it was most frequently employed. And well before 1208 John had had much experience of it. Soon after his purported marriage with Isabelle of Gloucester in 1189, Archbishop Baldwin had laid his lands under an interdict because Isabelle was related to him within the forbidden degrees and there had been no dispensation. The opportune arrival of the legate, John of Anagni, enabled Count John to get the interdict relaxed, on the ground that Baldwin had hastily imposed it while an appeal to the pope was pending.[6] Again, in 1197 John Cumin, the archbishop of Dublin, had laid an interdict upon his province after he had come into conflict with Hamon of Valognes, the Irish justiciar.

---

[1] This form of interdict was known as 'ambulatory', as opposed to a general interdict. The theory was that it followed the culprit from place to place and, assuming that popular indignation forced him to move rapidly, was not a great hardship on the innocent. In some instances an ambulatory interdict appears to have effected its purpose (Krehbiel, *The Interdict*, pp. 78-81). As a weapon against a powerful king it was not likely to succeed.
[2] If Alexander had known the precise relationship of Richard to Alice, he would hardly have ordered her to be restored to her husband (*vir*), for Richard had not married Alice and never did marry her.   [3] Above, p. 309.   [4] Above, p. 294.
[5] 'Avec Innocent III commence ce que l'on pourrait appeler l'âge d'or de l'interdit': L. Godefroy in Vacant, *Dictionnaire de théologie catholique*, vii.2282. The article *Interdit*, cols. 2280-90, gives a good brief introduction to the subject. The book by Krehbiel, cited above, is a detailed examination of the interdict at our period, excluding the Interdict in England, 1208-14.
[6] Ralf de Diceto, *Opera*, ii.72-3; 'Benedict of Peterborough', ii.78.

John crossed the seas to lay his grievances before Richard I, Count John and the pope,[1] and some kind of reconciliation seems to have been effected, for Richard, John and the archbishop were all in Normandy together in May 1198.[2] But, rather oddly, Innocent III remonstrated with John later in the year for his treatment of the archbishop,[3] although they must have remained upon friendly terms, for the archbishop was present at John's coronation on Ascension Day 1199 and again at a crown-wearing at Easter 1201.[4] Thereafter a fresh quarrel developed; the archbishop went again into exile; and in May 1203 Innocent threatened John with an interdict.[5] Whether or not this threat had any effect, it is plain that, if negotiations for the archbishop's return had not already begun, they were soon in progress, for in July he had letters of protection and was making preparations for his return to Ireland by the following November.[6] For some unknown reason he delayed his departure[7] and, quite inexplicably, he obtained from the pope in December 1204 a further threat of an interdict.[8] However, negotiations were not broken off. The archbishop was in John's company in September 1205,[9] and in the following December the Irish justiciar was notified that, at the pope's request, he had been pardoned and was to be compensated.[10] We give these rather dull details in order to emphasise how lightly the Curia could be moved to send a letter of reproof or issue a formal threat of interdict. We can perhaps acquit Innocent of personal knowledge of them, for it seems evident that such threats were made without any serious consideration of the issues and upon the *ex parte* statement of the impetrant. The explanation of this remarkable way of conducting negotiations seems to be that John Cumin had a liking for the weapon of the interdict. When in 1197 he laid his own province under interdict, he sought to heighten its effect by giving orders that every crucifix and every image in his cathedral should be removed and placed upon the ground, hedged about with thorns. Though this melodramatic action was followed, at least so it was reported, by a miracle, his fellow-bishops refused to be impressed and ignored the interdict.[11] Doubtless the archbishop thought the negotiations for his return from his second exile might be speeded by papal threats of interdict, obtainable readily enough on an *ex parte* application. There is, however, no reason to suppose that they had any such effect or that anyone was in the least moved by them. Indeed, the archbishop may have thought it prudent to suppress them: they are ignored in the official correspondence on the chancery rolls.

[1] Howden, *Chronica*, iv.29-30. [2] Landon, *Itinerary of Richard I*, pp. 126, 128.
[3] *Patrologia Latina*, ccxiv.345-6 (18 September 1198): cf. *ibid.*, col. 1175.
[4] Howden, *Chronica*, iv.89, 160. [5] *Patrologia Latina*, ccxv.61.
[6] *Rot. de Liberate*, p. 105; *Rot. Litt. Pat.*, p. 32. [7] *Ibid.*, p. 38*b*.
[8] *Patrologia Latina*, ccxv.484. [9] *Rot. Chartarum*, p. 158.
[10] *Rot. Litt. Pat.*, p. 38. [11] Howden, *Chronica*, iv.29-30.

We have already seen that Normandy had been threatened with, and perhaps actually laid under, an interdict in the course of John's quarrel with the bishop of Séez.[1] In the middle of June 1202 he had to meet a similar threat, this time of an ambulatory interdict, by reason of his quarrel with the bishop of Limoges.[2] Again, in 1207 the province of York was threatened with an interdict because of John's treatment of the archbishop, his brother Geoffrey, who had obstructed the collection of taxes from the clergy.[3] There may well have been other threats, besides those we have noted, in the course of the many minor conflicts between John and the Church, and there were certainly interdicts threatened or imposed by less exalted dignitaries than the pope. Hardly a year could have passed without an interdict in one corner or another of John's dominions, and the story had been much the same during Richard's reign.[4] When, therefore, an interdict was imposed upon England in 1208, the king was highly experienced in the appropriate tactics to counter it. From the first the king had taken steps to prevent its enforcement: any refusal to celebrate divine service was to be met by sequestration,[5] and an effective procedure was devised for securing this. In every township four local men were appointed to seize the stored barns of the recalcitrant.[6] In a few cases only can such sanctions have been applied, for there was no appreciable revenue from this source,[7] and the implication is that, in general, the clergy made their peace with the king and continued to officiate. If it is true that nearly all the rectors in England redeemed their property,[8] this can mean only that, while they at first observed the Interdict, sooner or later they obeyed the king rather than the pope. And it is clear that the pope was forced to make concessions, to recognise grudgingly what he had no power to prevent. Reviewing the evidence known to him, Stubbs concluded that 'at the worst the observance of the interdict would not reduce the mean religious services beyond the model voluntarily adopted by some protestant communities at the present day'.[9] This result would perhaps have been regarded with indifference by the many who failed to understand or appreciate

---

[1] Above, p. 339.   [2] *Patrologia Latina*, ccxiv.1036.

[3] *Ibid.*, ccxv.1262-3 (18 December 1207). The threat was renewed on 27 May 1208 (*ibid.*, 1403-4), presumably upon the assumption that the Interdict already promulgated on England and Wales would shortly cease.

[4] Krehbiel, *op. cit.*, pp. 32 *n*, 88-90.

[5] Instructions were given in advance on 18 March to sequestrate the lands and chattels of those 'qui divina extunc celebrare noluerunt' (*Rot. Litt. Pat.*, p. 80b). It follows that sequestrations would be relaxed only when the offender agreed to celebrate.

[6] For the four men see C. R. Cheney in *Bulletin of John Rylands Library*, xxxi.302-3, and *Trans. R. Hist. Soc.*, 4th Ser., xxxi.130-1.

[7] This we may infer from the particulars of corn sold in the Salisbury diocese (*Pipe Roll, 13 John*, p. 245). The *dona clericorum* recorded (*ibid.*, pp. 93, 245) stand, of course, on a different footing from profits arising from sequestration. Not all receipts from the clergy appear on the pipe rolls, and our information is very limited.

[8] *Magna Vita sancti Hugonis*, pp. 303-4. This is not a very trustworthy authority.

[9] Walter of Coventry, *Memoriale*, ii.xlv-xlvi *n*. Little more that is positive has been discovered since: cf. Cheney in *Bulletin John Rylands Library*, xxxi.296-300.

normal religious practices, but there was a sufficient number attached to customary observances to cause widespread resentment at any attempt to curtail them. It is possible that in the very early days of the Interdict the clergy were more zealous in attempting to put it into effect than they later ventured to be. So long as the bishops were at their posts, parish clergy were liable to pressure. But the bishops of London, Ely and Worcester, who had been appointed executors of the Interdict, thought it prudent to withdraw soon after it had been pronounced; and after the king had been excommunicated, nearly all the remaining bishops left the country.[1] Meanwhile the king's counter-attack, though it could not be made effective everywhere at once, was not relaxed. The probabilities are therefore that the Interdict was progressively less and less effective. A deed of William of Sainte-Mère-Église has been cited as evidence that Londoners dying during the Interdict were buried in unconsecrated ground. This deed sanctions the use for burials of land adjoining St. Bartholomew's Hospital because ordinary Christian burial was impossible; but since it must be dated between 24 March 1208 and the bishop's flight, it cannot be inferred that the land was ever used for the purpose.[2] Nor can there be any doubt of the attitude of the Londoners, for when in the years 1216 and 1217 the city lay nominally under an interdict, the citizens defied it.[3]

Whatever the attitude of the populace at large, the king's interest and pride were touched and he was determined that, so far as in him lay, religious ceremonies should continue unimpaired. We can confidently deny that the Interdict was respected in the king's household. The household accounts from Ascensiontide 1212 to Ascensiontide 1213 are conclusive.[4] The king fulfilled his religious duties with a regularity beyond praise. His alms were lavish, notably when, as was his practice, he broke a fast-day.[5] He distributed his maundy to thirteen poor men on Holy Thursday and crept to the Cross with his knights on Good Friday.[6] If we are not directly told that he communicated on days of obligation, there is the significant fact that, like his predecessors, he had a bath before each of the great feasts.[7] Elsewhere, too, there are indications that he did communicate[8] and, while the circumstances may have been excep-

---

[1] Precise details of the bishops' movements are irrecoverable: for such information as exists see Cheney, *ut supra*, pp. 310-11.

[2] Krehbiel, *op. cit.*, p. 61; a translation, including the witnesses omitted by Krehbiel, will be found in Webb, *The Records of St. Bartholomew's, Smithfield*, i.109-10.

[3] *Histoire des Ducs de Normandie*, pp. 171-2; Wendover, *Flores Historiarum*, iii.357, 369; E.H.R., xlviii.252-4.   [4] Cole, *Documents*, pp. 231-69.

[5] *Ibid.*, pp. 232-8 *et passim*.   [6] *Ibid.*, p. 258.

[7] *Ibid.*, p. 262: some of his other baths, not precisely dated (*ibid.*, pp. 237, 249), may have been taken before he communicated. For the like practice in the early twelfth century see 'Constitutio Domus Regis' in *Dialogus de Scaccario*, p. 133.

[8] That the king had communicated became known to the Curia and it was believed that others in like state had done so: it is significant that no objection is taken to the administration of the sacrament to those who were not excommunicate (*Selected Letters of Innocent III*, pp. 139-40).

tional, it is not to be overlooked that Stephen Langton himself celebrated mass publicly in the king's presence on 20 July 1213, a year before the Interdict ended.[1]

Any attempt at presenting a general picture of England under the Interdict is hazardous. Those monastic chroniclers who notice it are rarely descriptive and hardly ever contemporary. There is no city chronicler to give us the details of life in London or in any other town: the villages have no chronicler. So far as monasteries are concerned there seems to have been no uniformity of observance as between one house and another, even within the same order: we can select none as typical. We may be sure, however, that nowhere was a zealous obedience given to the pope's command. From the outset the Cistercians, for example, held that their privileges entitled them to disregard the Interdict, and though their claim was disallowed by the pope,[2] it is far from certain that in any Cistercian house there was more than the minimum of compliance. If we may trust what appears to be a contemporary narrative of the monastery of Meaux, the Cistercians there adhered to their ordinary routine except for closing their doors and burying their dead in an unconsecrated cemetery. The chronicler asserts that this was the extent to which the Interdict was observed by other exempt and privileged houses.[3] Even, however, if it may be assumed that all monasteries observed the Interdict as strictly as this,[4] we could not stretch the assumption to parish churches. Especially may we discount stories of corpses lying unburied, flung into byways and ditches.[5] Ralf of Coggeshall, describing the interdict in France in the year 1200, declares that the dead were deprived of Christian burial, the stench of the corpses infected the air, and the horror of the sight filled the minds of the survivors with terror.[6] This is a conventional horror story, a mere embroidery of Ralf's, who does not notice, if he knows, the fact that in many French dioceses, if not all, the interdict was disregarded.[7]

---

[1] Wendover, *Flores Historiarum*, iii.261; Walter of Coventry, *Memoriale*, ii.213; *Annales Monastici* (Winchester), ii.82.

[2] Gervase of Canterbury, ii.cix-cx; *Patrologia Latina*, ccv.1563-4.

[3] *Chronica Mon. de Melsa*, i.351. This is clearly an earlier text than that at p. 343, and appears to reproduce substantially an early thirteenth-century narrative: cf. the editor's remarks at pp. lxxi-lxxiii.

[4] Monastic chronicles rarely mention any departure from customary observances. At St. Albans a cemetery was set apart that was subsequently consecrated (*Gesta Abbatum*, i.269-70; Liebermann, *Ungedruckte anglo-normannische Geschichtsquellen*, p. 172). At Tewkesbury the public celebration of mass seems to have been discontinued, since its resumption is noted (*Annales Monastici*, i.61). Both of these houses were Benedictine. At St. Bartholomew's Hospital in London unconsecrated ground was set apart for the burial of brethren and inmates (Krehbiel, *op. cit.*, p. 61 *n*). Even such details as this may be sought in vain elsewhere, and no generalisation is possible.

[5] So the unveracious Roger of Wendover (iii.222): corpora quoque defunctorum de civitatibus et villis efferebantur et more canum in biviis et fossatis sine orationibus et sacerdotum ministerio sepeliebantur.

[6] Ralf of Coggeshall, *Chronicon Anglicanum*, pp 112-3. An actual case of unburied corpses is attested by the Walden Abbey Chronicle, lib. ii, c. 10. A dispute between the archbishop of Canterbury and the bishop of London resulted in an interdict on the church of Arkesden. The scandal was so great that the justiciar, Ranulf Glanville, intervened.   [7] Cf. Krehbiel, *op. cit.*, pp. 110-25.

The chronicler of Meaux impresses by his sober statement that, when the dead were buried in unconsecrated ground, this was done with decency, in a cemetery appropriated for the purpose, beneath a great wooden cross.[1] And it is noteworthy that Ralf of Coggeshall, who is eloquent over the horrors of the French interdict, has no word to say of the horrors of the English Interdict, of which, while holding office as abbot, he was a witness. At most he will notice the king's exactions or the modifications in the observance of the Interdict permitted by papal authority: he has no word of the burial of his deceased brethren in any unusual fashion, no word of unchristian burials of the laity outside the privileged precincts of his own Cistercian house.[2] There was nothing so unusual, it appears, as to call for notice. We refrain from any argument drawn from his silence, but we may perhaps venture upon a parallel. When, not long afterwards, Innocent III laid an interdict upon London, though in a few religious houses it was observed, everywhere else it was disregarded. It is true that the citizens and parish clergy were encouraged in their defiance by the barons and the canons of St. Paul's, but the menaces of the king during the earlier Interdict could hardly have been less compulsive.[3] There may have been a similar contrast between monasteries and parish clergy in the years from 1208 to 1214, not only in London but in other towns. We have every reason to suppose that the king's authority was steadily and continuously exerted, wherever it might stretch, to check any attempt at a public manifestation of compliance with the pope's command. And while the king's agents were everywhere, the pope was far away, with no agents anxious to enforce his will: for the bishops were in exile and there were no bold prelates, zealous to step into their place and face the king's anger. With no popular support and with no driving force behind it, how the Interdict could be maintained is very hard to see. When the bishops returned, the position was doubtless altered; but, in the absence of evidence, we must hesitate to suppose that, even so, in the last eleven months for which it was prolonged the Interdict was rigorously imposed upon the country at large.

And at this point we may perhaps adduce the unwitting testimony of Stephen Langton. In the face of the hostility with which he was greeted, the archbishop resolved to justify his actions publicly, and he did so at a large gathering at St. Paul's on 25 August 1213. The text of the *apologia* he prepared has been preserved[4]: and though we must assume that his sermon was delivered in French, for it was addressed to the laity, yet its substance must be represented in the academic Latin version. Langton is in no mood to minimise the hardships an interdict entailed but rather to represent them as a

---

[1] *Chronica Mon. de Melsa,* loc. cit.
[2] *Chronicon Anglicanum,* pp. 163-6.
[3] For references see p. 347, n. 3. above.
[4] Printed by Lacombe in *Catholic Historical Review,* xv.408-20.

proper retribution for the oppressions the Church had suffered. Yet there is no hint in his sermon of any 'horrors': that the dead lay unburied or that the living were deprived of the sacraments. The criticism he has to meet is that, though there has been a reconciliation, the voice of the Church is silent and the churches are shut. So he turns upon his critics and asks whether, if their mother were convalescing from fever, they would feed her on coarse beef and fat goose: would they expect her to dance? So, he replies, it must be with Mother Church: she must have a period of quiet and abstinence. It was a manifestation that king and people had not yet been reconciled with the Church or the Church with her despoilers.[1] Whatever we may think of the argument, do not Langton's own words suggest that, however irksome the Interdict might be, its practical effect, even after the bishops' return, was no more than to curtail outward observances, elaborate ritual, bell-ringing?[2]

There is one further, and surely not unrelated, fact that it seems desirable to emphasise. The royal records appear to prove conclusively that the whole routine of church administration continued uninterrupted throughout the Interdict. We need give but one example of the observance of routine. In January 1209 the pope—at whose instigation we know not, but presumably Langton's—sent letters to the chapters of Chichester, Coventry, Durham, Exeter and Lincoln, instructing them to elect bishops to fill the vacant sees. A letter in similar terms was sent to the king.[3] Whether this was delivered or not, he, of course, became aware of what was on foot and, in the case of Coventry, we have a minute account of the subsequent course of events.[4] As a preliminary, the prior was dispossessed, and reinstated only at the price of a fine of 300 marks. The king then sent the abbots of Waltham and Osney, with Robert of Vieuxpont, requiring the monks to elect the archdeacon of Stafford (Henry of London). When the monks objected, the king offered them the choice of the abbot of Bindon and Richard Marsh. The prior asked permission to elect Walter Grey, the chancellor. After much wrangling, and objection on the part of the monks to the participation of the canons of Lichfield in the election, the choice, with the king's approval, rested on Walter Grey. Full as the account of the proceedings is, with each step detailed and with reports of the speeches on each side, there is no word of the Interdict, no suggestion that because of it anyone was under restraint, no standing on principle, except that the monks should not have anyone distasteful thrust upon them and that, if they could prevent it, the canons of Lichfield should

---

[1] Ibid., pp. 417-8.
[2] If Wendover (iii.263) is to be relied upon, Langton did on this occasion ameliorate the Interdict to the extent of permitting the canonical hours to be recited in a low voice in both conventual and parish churches.
[3] Selected Letters of Innocent III, pp. 115-6.
[4] Monasticon, vi.1243.

have no say in the matter. At his beck and call, the king has the earls and barons and the higher clergy, prompt to do his bidding. It may be said that all this was yet in the early months of the Interdict and that the king was not yet excommunicate. But so far as the evidence goes—and it is copious—there is nothing to show that the course of ecclesiastical administration in England was at any time interrupted during the Interdict.[1] And it is noteworthy that, when peace was restored between king and pope and the see of Coventry again required to be filled, the proceedings before the legate followed the same lines as in 1209, with the monks objecting to candidate after candidate, objecting to the participation of the canons of Lichfield, and finally agreeing upon a king's man, William of Cornhill.[2]

The difficulty of establishing the existence of general hardship, much less of 'horrors', during the years 1208 to 1214 seems to lie, as we have suggested, in the fact that hardships were few and rare. This is not to say that any of the contestants could derive satisfaction from the lingering years of uncertainty and antagonism, with a future beyond them that no man could spell out. If the masses were little affected, to the governing classes the position was unquestionably irksome. Though the flight of the bishops did not disrupt the internal relations between Church and State, any provisional substitute for the normal machinery of intercourse was awkward and unsatisfactory. Customary ways and ancient ties are not easily set aside without feelings of frustration and impatience. An essential element in the routine of administration had gone and a painful void was unfilled. To put an end to the interminable dispute must have been in the mind of every responsible man; but having been borne so long, the situation was not so troublesome that it could not be borne a little longer. The difficulty was to arrange terms that would not humiliate one side or the other. That King John was at last stimulated to accept terms of peace by a threat—men thought a papally inspired threat—of invasion from France[3] did not mean that

---

[1] Cf. Cheney in *Bulletin of John Rylands Library*, xxxi.307-10.

[2] *Monasticon*, vi.1243-4.

[3] There is no evidence that the pope formally deposed John, but rather the contrary; nor is there documentary evidence that he instigated Philip Augustus to invade England. Upon these points we must agree with Professor Cheney in *Powicke Essays*, pp. 100-16; but the points are perhaps rather academic. Not only had Langton argued that, if the king remained obdurate, the Interdict itself was sufficient to release subjects from their allegiance—and John's excommunication strengthened the argument—but the pope was threatening formal deposition in 1211 and again in 1213 (*Selected Letters*, pp. 129, 132). It was certainly believed by the barons in 1212 that John was about to be formally deposed (above, p. 341), and the conspiracy of Robert fitz Walter and his associates could be justified only on the hypothesis that they were released from their allegiance. Doubtless Philip needed little prompting, if he shared the popular impression that John, while excommunicate, could no longer lawfully claim the allegiance of his barons, but it seems to have been generally believed that the threatened invasion was first instigated and then forbidden by papal authority. Professor Painter contended that this belief was justified: to the references given by him (*op. cit.*, p. 191) add *Chronica Mon. de Melsa*, i.402, derived apparently from an independent contemporary chronicle. There is no need, however, to suppose that the pope would commit himself in writing.

he made an abject surrender. The singularity of the great Interdict is that, after battle had been waged with unexampled obstinacy, it came to a conclusion which both sides could claim as a victory. Yet for the papacy it was a Pyrrhic victory. The ineffectiveness of an interdict as a means of coercion had been made manifest; and though the weapon was not at once abandoned, after Innocent's death it was used less and less for political ends. And if the lesson of the great Interdict was not enough, there was the ensuing lesson of the melancholy failure a little later to coerce the Londoners and the dissident barons by interdict and excommunication. Some few of the higher clergy, some few parish clergy, suffered in consequence, but more for their adherence to Louis of France than for their ecclesiastical mutiny. As for the laity, no ill consequences followed their defiance of the pope's commissioners and the legate.[1] The sword whose edge was thought to be so sharp had been blunted by overmuch use and was soon put aside to rust in its scabbard.

But we must return to Langton's arrival in England in July 1213, for there is yet something to say that seems significant regarding him and his relations with the king and the barons. Two important documents have survived from the latter part of the year which have been little used by historians but which are of considerable help in dispersing the haze of sentimental affection through which, under the guidance of the St. Alban's chroniclers, this bitter, self-righteous man has been regarded. Of one of these documents, Langton's sermon at St. Paul's, we have already made a little use. The other document is the letter from the cardinal legate, Nicholas of Tusculum, written on 21 October 1213 to Innocent III, when, confronted with the archbishop's intransigence, he sought to learn the pope's real intentions so that he might be guided in his negotiations, on the one hand with the king and on the other with the English episcopate.[2] Innocent's lack of foresight, the rash letters he had written in support of Langton, had made negotiations extremely difficult. The king, for his part, was anxious that the Interdict should be lifted without delay, not only for his own credit and as an overt sign of his reconciliation with the pope, but, on the practical plane, in order to avoid friction with the returned bishops, who had no option but to obey the pope's commands. By the surrender of his kingdom, John had met Innocent more than half way and it was reasonable for him to expect that bygones would be treated as bygones. The king himself had not only been absolved and so was no longer excommunicate, but he had been personally released from the Interdict[3]; if, however, the Interdict continued, while he would be free from any

---

[1] Wendover, iii.354-7, 361-2; E.H.R., xlviii.252-8.
[2] Printed by Mgr A. Mercati in Poole Essays, pp. 274-89.
[3] Selected Letters, pp. 154-5, 172; Poole Essays, p. 278. Apparently the intention had been that John should be absolved, but that the Interdict should remain upon him as upon the rest of the kingdom. Langton seems to have misunderstood his instructions.

ecclesiastical penalty or restriction, his people—or, at least, the devout among them—would suffer. The irrational absurdity of the situation was patent, but Langton had a logic of his own. As for himself, he declared publicly, he would not have the Interdict relaxed until everything of which the Church had been deprived was restored. Those who vituperated him or criticised him for this ought rather to give him their prayers and affection. He was, he explained, acting as he did for the honour of the Church and not (as had evidently been suggested) out of cupidity. He had no patience with the laymen who complained that, since he had returned to England, the doors of the churches had remained shut. 'You laymen', he retorted, 'ought to have sufficient confidence in your prelates to believe that in all these matters they act with discretion and prudence: in any case the pope is lord of Christendom and must be obeyed.'[1] This was, as we have said, on 25 August 1213, a little more than a month after he had absolved John.

It seems less than candid on Langton's part to have put the onus upon the pope; but he had perhaps allowed himself to be misled. He was surprisingly ignorant of the ways of the Curia. Innocent had sent Nicolas of Tusculum to England as a plenipotentiary to conclude a final settlement with John. He landed on 20 September in an atmosphere not at all favourable to amicable negotiations.[2] Evidently the legate was all for hastening the final steps and re-establishing normal relations between the kingdom and the Curia, but Langton stood in the way. He was resolved, as he had already made plain at St. Paul's, that the Interdict should not be lifted until the clergy had been fully compensated for the losses they had suffered; and he flourished in the legate's face the pope's uncompromising letters[3] written to terrify the king, with no thought that one day they would be produced to clog his diplomacy. And though the legate was in a sense a plenipotentiary and the negotiations with the king were in his hands, in this matter he had to win Langton's assent to every step he took. The archbishop, not without reason, mistrusted the king and feared that any concession he might make would prejudice the settlement of the claims of the clergy for compensation. Nor could he fail to have a shrewd suspicion, based, if on nothing else, on the attitude of the legate, that the pope's favour was shifting to the king. The only firm ground he had to stand upon was to be found in the pope's letters in his possession, setting out the original and, in practice, quite impossible terms for settlement, and he would consider nothing else. The legate was embarrassed and per-

---

[1] *Catholic Historical Review*, xv.417-8.

[2] *Poole Essays*, p. 277. Langton's hostility to the legate is manifest (*ibid.*, p. 282).

[3] *Ibid.*, pp. 280-3. The king had heard of other letters, besides those Langton showed to the legate, but these Langton would not disclose. Two of those 'contra ipsum et heredes suos expresse' may be nos. 48 and 49 in *Selected Letters of Innocent III*, pp. 141-2. It is a commentary on papal diplomacy that the legate was not informed of this embarrassing correspondence.

haps puzzled by Langton's attitude. He reported to the pope that many persons of credit had told him that the archbishop and his colleagues sought to defer the relaxation of the Interdict so that England might be still further afflicted and disturbed.[1] He did not himself express this view, but he did not dissent from it. It is evident that he was far from singular in thinking Langton unreasonable and perhaps vindictive. What reply the legate received from the pope we do not know. In the embarrassing position in which Innocent found himself, he affected at first to be inflexible and insisted that the king should pay 100,000 marks cash down before the Interdict was relaxed.[2] But the legate must have received confidential instructions in a very different sense, and he continued in his endeavours to bring the two parties together. The result was that some months later representatives of both the king and Langton met in the pope's presence and agreed on far less stringent terms.[3] There can then be no room for doubt that, if the delay in bringing the Interdict to an end caused hardship to the English people—as, indeed, it was intended to do—the responsibility and intention were Langton's. And before we break off, let us stress this patent truth: the archbishop was no popular hero, allied with the barons in an endeavour to shake off the yoke of a tyrannous king, but, on his own showing, mistrusted and disliked. Yet it is on the occasion of the meeting at St. Paul's, when Langton faced a hostile and suspicious audience, that—so Roger of Wendover would have his readers believe—he confided to the assembled barons his discovery of Henry I's charter.[4] Of the archbishop's real purpose, of his defence of the Interdict, Roger has no word.

There is little to commend in Stubbs's reflections upon John's contest with the pope:

Engaged in a quarrel from which a little circumspection would have saved him, he chose to enter the lists against Innocent III; matching his own low cunning at once against the consummate diplomacy of the Curia and the aspiring statesmanship of the greatest of all the popes.[5]

The Interdict was, indeed, a piece of political blackmail—blackmail attempted once too often—and John had had the good sense to defy the blackmailer. The result was that he gained his original point, that his assent was required to episcopal elections. The elections supervised by the cardinal-legate Nicholas, after he arrived in England in September 1213, were conducted with due respect for the king's wishes.[6] It was as though the disputed Canterbury election

---

[1] *Poole Essays*, p. 286.　　　　　[2] *Selected Letters of Innocent III*, pp. 171-2.
[3] *Ibid.*, pp. 188-90; *Rot. Chartarum*, p. 199.　　　　[4] Wendover, *Flores*, iii.263-6.
[5] *Constitutional History*, i.558
[6] As he was instructed to do by the pope (*Selected Letters of Innocent III*, pp. 166-7). His procedure is vividly illustrated by the surviving account of the Coventry election, to which we refer later.

had never been. Quite obviously John's conduct in this matter had not been a matter of low cunning, nor had the diplomacy of the Curia been consummate. The king had done no wrong. His quarrel with the pope had not been about faith or morals but about a point of law, and the pope had found it prudent to give way. John, for his part, made concessions: he gratified Innocent's desire for power by becoming his vassal; he accepted, or rather professed to accept, Langton; and he compensated, if inadequately, the exiled clergy for their losses.[1] Some of the senior clerks in his service were suspended from their ecclesiastical offices and benefices and were required to seek absolution at Rome, because they had assisted the king since his excommunication or had obtained benefices at his hands or had openly partaken of the sacrament with him.[2] But this seems to have been mere face-saving. The most prominent among these royal clerks was Richard Marsh, and his journey to Rome, while it secured him absolution without difficulty, was as a member of a diplomatic mission from the king to the pope.[3] Another of the clerks was Gilbert de l'Aigle who in 1209 had been intruded by the king into the see of Chichester. But though he lost his bishopric, his election can hardly have been the reason why he had to journey to Rome.[4] Of the three other bishops who had been intruded by John in 1209, Hugh of Wells had already been accepted by Langton as bishop of Lincoln; Henry of London, the elect of Exeter, had been promoted in 1212 to the archbishopric of Dublin; while Walter Grey exchanged in 1214 the see of Lichfield for the see of Worcester. Only Gilbert de l'Aigle was unprovided for. Evidently there is a story behind the seeming caprice with which nominal punishments and real rewards were meted out; but that John was touched in the persons of his servants or that he threw over those who had stood by him is certainly not the inference to be drawn.[5] Perhaps the inference should be that, in the diplomatic comedy, both sides must preserve appearances. And, whatever the appearances, John lost little or nothing. The Interdict had brought in large sums from the property of the exiled clergy, as well as from those who remained and desired to live at peace with the king. Apparently the total exceeded £100,000.[6] If a balance of receipts and expenditure could be struck,

[1] It is not known how much was paid: since the arrangement was that 40,000 marks should first be paid and then half-yearly sums of 6000 marks and since the first half-yearly instalment was authorised, it is probable that the clergy received 46,000 marks, but it seems unlikely that they received more: cf. *Selected Letters of Innocent III*, p. 189 *nn*, and Painter, *Reign of King John*, p. 197.

[2] *Patrologia Latina*, ccxvi.780; *Annales Monastici* (Dunstable,) iii.40.

[3] Painter, *op. cit.*, pp. 197-8.

[4] Nothing more seems to be known of master Gilbert de l'Aigle. There are many later references to a baron of the same name, who died in 1231 (*Patent Rolls, 1225-1232*, p. 458), but none apparently to the former bishop.

[5] Cf. Cheney in *Bulletin John Rylands Library*, xxxi.312.

[6] This is the figure given in the *Red Book of the Exchequer*, pp. 772-3, as the total. The particulars will not add up to this sum, but they are clearly defective: only twelve dioceses are included and some of these incompletely. There seems to be no reason for questioning

it is very doubtful whether the contest would be found to have been financially onerous, and politically John had made substantial gains. His resistance to the pope had for the time secured him popular support, if not popularity, and his reconciliation had earned him the support of the papacy.

When in July 1213 Langton came back from exile he had learned nothing and forgotten nothing. He believed that the issues which had divided the king and the pope were matters of principle that should not be waived. He was incorruptible and inflexible. The lack of tact displayed in his letter of 1207 is again shown in his sermon at St. Paul's and in the dating of his *acta*, not by the dominical year or by the year of his pontificate, but from the relaxation of the general Interdict, a pointed and unnecessary adaptation of an old-fashioned style.[1] Inevitably his troubles began afresh. The politicians at the Curia—cynical Italian sceptics as perhaps they were,[2] to whom religion and law were weapons in the quest for power—were anxious to let bygones be bygones. They had obtained their price and they had conceded John's point: vacant sees should be filled with bishops agreeable to the king. The agent of the Curia in arranging this was, as we have said, the legate, Nicholas cardinal bishop of Tusculum, whom Innocent sent 'as an angel of healing and peace'.[3] That the legate acted wholeheartedly in the king's interest is shown, not only by the names of the men chosen to be bishops but by the details we have of his proceedings at Coventry. The legate offered the monks the choice of four candidates, but repeatedly urged upon them John's creature, the disreputable abbot of Beaulieu. When, after many days, the monks persisted in their objection to this candidate, they were allowed their choice of the others and eventually, after consulting the justiciar Peter des Roches, they chose William of Cornhill, a prominent clerk of the king's.[4] The elections were in the hands of the legate,[5] but Langton was not

the total so far as the information in the exchequer went, and presumably the exchequer clerks would have access to the chamber accounts, through which some of the revenue passed (cf. *Poole Essays*, p. 286).

[1] *Acta Stephani Langton*, pp. xlii, 16-30. One such document undoubtedly came before the king (*ibid.*, pp. 19-21, 158). The phrase, 'in termino Epiphanie proxime post relax-accionem interdicti' occurs in a safe-conduct (*Rot. Litt. Claus.*, p. 126*b*), but this is not a parallel usage.

[2] To defend this view would require much space, though we think the whole of this chapter supports it. To those who would dissent we commend the passage in the letter from the legate to the pope regarding the 2000 marks exacted from the dying Geoffrey fitz Peter; it runs, 'Ad hec noueritis quod, cum iusticiarius regni Anglie, qui ad moni-tionem meam resumpserat signum crucis, quasi ageret in extremis et de vita eius nullatenus speraretur, eum a labore peregrinationis absolui, receptis ab eo duobus milibus marcharum mittendis in subsidium terre sancte. Quod nisi tam caute fecissem et cito, nichil inde penitus habuissem, cum antequam lator presentium iter arriperet expirauit' (*Poole Essays*, pp. 286-7).

[3] *Selected Letters of Innocent III*, p. 150 (to the king, 6 July 1213): quasi angelum salutis et pacis. A similar phrase is used in letters to the bishops and barons (*ibid.*, pp. 152, 154).

[4] *Monasticon*, vi.1243-4.

[5] *Patrologia Latina*, ccxvi.928; *Selected Letters of Innocent III*, pp. 166-7 (to the legate). The chapters were sent letters in similar terms and were left in no doubt that they were

prepared to stand wholly aside. While the monks of Coventry were wrestling with the legate over the candidature of the abbot of Beaulieu, the archbishop sent them a sympathetic letter and afterwards came in person to offer his consolation and support.[1] He may not have gone further but, according to a highly coloured story of Wendover's, he protested against the elections made under the legate's supervision and appealed to the pope on the ground that the new bishops were intruded rather than elected.[2] If he went so far as this, it is not surprising that he was snubbed for his pains. There is, in any case, no doubt that the question of episcopal elections lay very near the archbishop's heart, and on 21 November 1214 he secured from the king the formal concession to all cathedral and conventual churches of freedom of election.[3] Coming, as it does, after Bouvines, this charter has been interpreted as a sign of weakness on the king's part, as a bid for Langton's support and as an attempt to separate the clergy from the barons.[4] But if we compare the terms of the charter with earlier statements of the king's claims, it scarcely appears that he was conceding anything more than words.[5] His assent to the choice of the chapter is still necessary and no election may take place without his licence. The concession of free election was quite illusory, and we have contemporary evidence that John desired papal confirmation of the charter, not to gratify Langton, but for his own protection against any invasion of his prerogative. So greatly did he value the pope's approval of the formula the charter contained that he delayed his assent to the election of the abbot of St. Edmund's until his messengers had returned from the Curia with Innocent's reply. John did not, in fact, give his assent until well after the time when the pope's confirmation must have been in his hands.[6] Whatever Langton may have believed the Church had secured, John's view was clearly that he had now obtained all that he had contended for in his repeated contests with the pope over episcopal elections. We cannot suppose that Innocent was deceived on this occasion: he had every opportunity for interrogating the king's messengers. Nor must the high-flown language of the bull deceive us any more than the language of the charter. Innocent's confirmation shows how completely king and pope understood one another and how grossly Langton misunderstood the situation in

to acquiesce in the legate's orders and advice and, with the king's assent, to choose the 'regi fideles et regno utiles'.

[1] *Monasticon*, vi.1243.   [2] Wendover, *Flores*, iii.278-9.

[3] The text is accessible in *Select Charters*, pp. 283-4. The post-dating of the charter to January 1215 in the copy sent to the pope was doubtless intended to convey the suggestion that there had been no delay in seeking his confirmation: otherwise the text is identical with the original, the place and names of witnesses being unaltered (*Selected Letters of Innocent III*, pp. 198-201).   [4] Stubbs, *Constitutional History*, i.568.

[5] See especially the king's letter to Langton on 12 January 1214, written before his departure to Poitou (*Rot. Litt. Claus.*, i.160). A form of election has been agreed which has put an end to controversy, but this form saves the king's right on all points: salvo in omnibus iure nostro.

[6] 'Electio Hugonis', pp. 124-8, in *Memorials of St. Edmund's Abbey*, vol. ii.

which he found himself. It was such a document as this that John
had been refused when he demanded a papal privilege preserving
his prerogative as a condition of his acceptance of Langton as archbishop.[1] It is possible that, as a contemporary chronicler asserts,
following upon the charter monasteries were given freedom to elect
their abbots, but all the accustomed forms of *congé d'élire* and royal
assent were preserved;[2] and there was certainly no significant change
in the established procedure for filling episcopal vacancies. The concordat was embodied in Magna Carta, where it stands at the head
of the provisions. It is not there at the request of the barons, but
doubtless at the instance of Langton. We must credit him with at
least this much influence on the terms of the Great Charter, though
assuredly neither the king nor Pandulf could have had the least hesitation in agreeing that the grant of freedom of election, in the sense
in which they understood it, should be once more confirmed.

In the constitutional struggle of the closing years of the reign, the
rôle assigned by the pope to Langton and his suffragans was that of
mediators between king and barons, and there is abundant evidence
that they endeavoured consistently to reconcile the contestants. At
John's instance, Innocent reproached the bishops for their in-
activity,[3] but, if this reproach had ever been deserved, it soon ceased
to be. This is plain in the record of the negotiations which preceded
the Great Charter, in several clauses of the Charter itself, and in the
recorded proceedings of the council that met at Oxford to complete
the work left unfinished at Runnymede.[4] If we could trust a very
confused chronicler at Barnwell, the bishops made a last desperate attempt at mediation after the second breach between king and barons
in late August 1215.[5] The position of the bishops, and especially of
Langton, as mediators was quite incompatible with their participation in the formulation of the baronial demands upon the king. The
contrary notion, that Langton was an accomplice of the barons, is
an idea which Stubbs has foisted upon modern historians. As the
footnotes to the *Constitutional History* show, he adopts Roger of
Wendover's chronicle as the basis of his own narrative. That this
chronicle is always cited under the name of Matthew Paris confirms

[1] Apparently an actual privilege—for the meaning of this term see R. L. Poole, *Papal
Chancery*, pp. 100-13—had been prepared and deposited at the abbey of Claremareis,
but John could not obtain even a transcript of it (Gervase of Canterbury, *Historical Works*,
ii.c, cx, cxii). Not unjustifiably he suspected a trap: its terms were presumably known by
Langton and the papal agents to be unacceptable.

[2] *Annales Monastici* (Dunstable), iii.42. No more may be meant by free election than
that the chapter elected one of their own number, who received royal approval. For the
system at work and the close control exercised by the king, see the letters patent of December 1214 and January 1215 relating to Selby, Darley, Battle and Faversham (*Rot. Litt.
Pat.*, pp. 125-7). This does, indeed, contrast with the practice in the twelfth century when
royal nominees were appointed from outside: see Appendix II, below, pp. 413, 421.

[3] *Foedera*, i.127; *Selected Letters of Innocent III*, p. 196.

[4] Richardson, 'The Morrow of the Great Charter' in *Bulletin John Rylands Library*,
xxviii.422-9; and see Appendix V, below, pp. 450-62.

[5] Walter of Coventry, *Memoriale*, ii.223-4.

THE KING AND THE ARCHBISHOP

the conclusion which his treatment of the evidence suggests, that he had never subjected his principal source to critical scrutiny.[1] If some idle tale seems to suit his thesis, Stubbs adopts it. Thus Wendover retails a story, for which he will not vouch. Upon this we have already commented: it centres round an allegation that Langton had brought to light Henry I's coronation charter and had secretly communicated it to the barons who were opposing the king.[2] Now let us give Stubbs's comment:

Probably few knew what the laws of Henry I were; but the archbishop took care that they should soon be informed. Another council was called at St. Paul's on the 25th of August and there Henry's charter was produced. It was seen at once that it furnished both a safe standing-ground and a precedent for a deliberate scheme of reform.[3]

We note, first, Stubbs's apparent confusion of the 'Leges Henrici' with the coronation charter.[4] Furthermore, since this charter was already easily accessible at the time both in Latin and in French,[5] we need not speculate upon the element of credibility behind the story: there is none. But Stubbs cannot stay for the laborious process of verification: he is engaged in building up a spurious reputation for Stephen Langton,

who deserves more than any other person the credit of undoing the mischiefs that arose from that system [i.e. the administrative system of Henry II], maintaining the law by making the national will the basis of the strength of government.[6]

Langton's opposition to John did not take this form at all. His attitude was determined by his strict impartiality, and, if he has a claim upon our admiration, it is by reason of his stand for a few weeks in 1215, not only against the king, but against the pope, in the interests of justice. It is true that, in his enmity for Langton, John endeavoured to cast suspicion upon him, to insinuate that he

---

[1] Constitutional History, i.556-83.

[2] Note Wendover's qualification, 'ut fama refert'. Langton is supposed to refer to his absolution of the king at Winchester and to continue, 'inventa est quoque nunc charta quaedam Henrici primi regis Angliae, per quam, si volueritis, libertates diu amissas poteritis ad statum pristinum revocare' (Flores, iii.263). Paris makes slight changes of no significance (ibid., v.165). The more reliable Histoire des Ducs de Normandie, pp. 145-6, while stating that the barons demanded the observance of Henry I's charter, makes no mention of Langton and places the meeting with the king after John's arrival in England in October 1214.   [3] Constitutional History, i.566.

[4] The 'Leges Henrici' open with the charter. Stubbs, of course, knew this; but he seems to have thought that the title 'Leges Henrici Primi' might be confined to Henry's coronation charter and his charter to London: see his Lectures on Early and Medieval English History, p. 143.

[5] That Henry I's charter was easily accessible in Latin is now conceded (cf. Powicke, Stephen Langton, pp. 113-6): this in itself is sufficient to discredit Wendover's story. But it was accessible also in French, as in Harleian MS. 458, which contains also translations of Stephen's and Henry II's coronation charters. The translation of Henry I's charter was printed by Liebermann, Trans. R. Hist. Soc., New Series, viii.46-8; but his dating of this manuscript is incomprehensible (p. 37). It is significant that, according to the Histoire des Ducs de Normandie, pp. 145-6, the barons linked together Henry I's and Stephen's charters. They would naturally make no reference to that of Henry II since they accused him of introducing evil customs.   [6] Constitutional History, i.677.

was covertly abetting the barons. 'There are some', says the pope, echoing the words of the king's advocate, 'who believe and assert that you afford the barons aid and favour in the issues they have recently raised against the king.' The only ground for suspicion is, however, that such issues were never raised in the time of Henry II or Richard I or, indeed, in John's time until after peace had been made between him and Langton.[1] This flimsy allegation was made by Walter Mauclerc in March 1215.[2] Had there been substance in the allegation, had the baronial representatives, who were before Innocent at the time, admitted its truth, more would have been made of it and more would have been heard of it, for could it have been sustained, no charge would have been more damaging to Langton or more welcome to John. But since no more is heard of it, we may be sure that it is baseless.

To understand the conflict in which pope, king, barons and, quite incidentally, Langton were involved we must bear steadily in mind that, from the point of view of the Curia, what was in dispute was something to be settled by process of law. By John's surrender of the kingdom England had become a fief of the supreme pontiff and the Church of Rome,[3] and the differences between the king, who held of the pope, and the barons, who held of the king, were justiciable before the papal court. Innocent reiterated his desire and intention to do justice between the parties, and both were, in fact, at a preliminary stage, represented before the Curia.[4] Thereafter, however, the barons persisted in pursuing their own methods of settlement out of court and, by putting constraint upon the king, they made themselves, as Innocent said, judges and executioners in their own cause.[5] From the pope's standpoint, the standpoint of a judge with litigants before him, the barons were contumacious and the only methods of coercion open to him were excommunication and interdict. In applying these sanctions he had need of a local agent, and the obvious agent was the archbishop. Langton received a mandate on several occasions to pronounce the barons excommunicate, but on each occasion he failed to do so, not because he was remiss or wilfully disobedient, but because he believed that he was, in law, entitled to disregard the mandate.[6]

The position perhaps needs to be explained. A mandate (or letter of justice) was obtained on the application of a litigant and contained an *ex parte* statement by him which could be rebutted. Usually it was addressed to three commissioners (judges delegate) who had

---

[1] *Bulletin John Rylands Library*, xxix, pp. 188-96.
[2] *Ibid.*, p. 120.
[3] So described by Innocent: feudum summo pontifici et Romane ecclesie (*Selected Letters of Innocent III*, p. 181).
[4] The account of William Mauclerc of proceedings in Rome is clear evidence of this (*Foedera*, i.120). The whole spirit of the papal letters at this period is that Innocent is adjudicating between litigants.   [5] *Selected Letters of Innocent III*, pp. 214, 217.
[6] *Bulletin John Rylands Library*, xxix, pp. 188-96.

been named by the party. Exceptions could be made by the other party against the judges, who might be partial, or against the substance of the mandate on such grounds as that it suggested a falsehood or suppressed the truth.[1] Further, since the journey from England to Rome took about thirty days at the speediest, it is obvious that more than two months and possibly nearly three months must elapse before instructions given in England could be translated into a mandate and returned for execution. The facts that had justified a request for a mandate might be irrelevant to the situation two or three months later.[2] Again, mandates (and papal bulls) did not execute themselves: they came into the hands of the parties who had applied for them and might be withheld for a time or suppressed entirely. These very relevant considerations have not always been regarded by historians, who have been inclined to accept instruments at their face value and have sometimes, it is to be feared, neglected also the time factor.

Now in 1215 the position was extremely complicated because, while the barons had withdrawn from the litigation at Rome, John continued it. At the same time the barons and John were in treaty out of court and, as the barons viewed the matter, had compromised the action. It is in this sense that the Great Charter was called the *concordia* of Runnymede,[3] this word being the technical term for a compromised action. We must remember that the pope (whether we regard him as party or judge) had been represented at Runnymede by Pandulf, who had consented to the charter and who later referred to it as *triplex forma pacis* or threefold treaty[4]: from this point of view it was an agreement between pope, king and barons. Whether the charter was a *concordia* or *forma pacis*, all parties, if they had been honest, would have accepted it as the basis of subsequent negotiations. It was, of course, known to the barons that the king had his agents at the Curia and that he had enlisted the aid of the pope

---

[1] There is a good summary of the law in Tancred's *Ordo Judiciarius*, lib. ii, tit. 5 and 6, dealing with exceptions and recusations (ed. Bergmann (1842), pp. 139-50).

[2] Appendix V: below, pp. 450-62.

[3] *Curia Regis Rolls*, viii.16. See also the endorsement on the Lincoln exemplar of the charter: Concordia inter Regem Johannem et Barones pro concessione libertatum ecclesie et regni Anglie. Facsimiles will be found in *Foedera* and *Statutes of the Realm*.

[4] *E.H.R.*, xliv.92. Professor Painter questioned the identification of this threefold treaty with the Great Charter and suggested that there had been a proposal put by the pope to the barons in March 1215 which could be so described (*Reign of King John*, pp. 345-6). But *forma pacis* is a common phrase for a treaty (for example, that of Le Goulet), and Ralf of Coggeshall (p. 172) applies it to Magna Carta: Mox igitur forma pacis in charta est comprehensa. In any case, since the pope knew nothing on 18 June of any *concordia* and made no reference to specific proposals, we can dismiss any suggestion of the kind: see the summary of the pope's letters of 19 March and 18 June in Appendix V: below, pp. 457, 460. Professor Cheney supports Professor Painter, 'The Eve of Magna Carta' in *Bulletin John Rylands Library*, xxxviii.316-7. Apart from minor difficulties, neither meets the major difficulty that the hypothesis would require us to suppose that Pandulf, who had been a party to the Great Charter, ignored it when calling upon Langton and his suffragans to excommunicate the barons. That Pandulf should ignore the elementary requirements of established legal procedure seems incredible. He, at least, knew all about exceptions and recusations.

against them. Nor could they complain because, some weeks before a settlement was reached, the king had applied for a mandate for the excommunication of all disturbers of the king and kingdom and for spacing their lands under interdict. But they would argue that the selttlement, finally negotiated between 15 and 19 June, automatically superseded any mandate that might be issued. The mandate was, in fact, issued on 7 July, necessarily in ignorance of the happenings at Runnymede, and reached the king about the second week in August.[1] Meanwhile a council had met at Oxford, in the third week of July, to complete the work left unfinished at Runnymede, and, after protracted negotiations, there had been an adjournment to 20 August. It would seem that it was while the council was in session at Oxford that John had sent a request to Rome for a bull annulling the Great Charter: this was issued on 24 August and reached the king about the end of September.[2] All these dates, confusing as they may be, are important, for on them our judgement upon the principal actors must depend.

Until 20 August the barons had no reason to suspect that the king was deceiving them and that the negotiations for a settlement were a means of gaining time. Upon that day the blow fell. John did not come to the meeting, but his representatives appear to have communicated to the assembled bishops and barons the mandate of 7 July and intimated his intention of enforcing it. Further negotiations were obviously out of the question: the barons again defied the king and war was resumed.[3] What of Langton and his fellow bishops? But we must distinguish. The Poitevin bishop of Winchester, Peter des Roches, and the Italian elect of Norwich, Pandulf, were John's men: they had been his advisers at the council at Oxford and without doubt they were privy to his request for the annulment of the Great Charter. In any case, they stood apart: they were the executors of the mandate of 7 July which, on the face of it, required the archbishop to give instructions that the sentence of excommunication, in which the barons were already involved by the decision of the pope, should be published every Sunday and holiday until the barons submitted completely and entirely to the king. Langton objected: precisely what form his exception took is not certain, but evidently he made the point that the mandate had been issued on inadequate information. The obvious ground for his exception was the agreement at Runnymede. Peter des Roches and Pandulf met this objection, not by impugning the Great Charter, which, perhaps incautiously, they praised as being honourable and fair and acceptable to God-fearing men, but by declaring that the barons had violated the terms of the agreement.[4] If that were so, the other

---

[1] *Selected Letters of Innocent III*, pp. 207-9.
[2] *Ibid.*, pp. 212-6; Appendix V: below, pp. 461-2.
[3] *Bulletin John Rylands Library*, xxix.192-3.
[4] *E.H.R.*, xliv.92-3.

parties were not bound and the position was as it had been before the agreement: the mandate was therefore effective. The weakness of this argument seems manifest: the parties were still in negotiation when the king had decided to make use of the mandate, and it was he who declined to attend the council appointed for 20 August. Whatever his precise reasons, Langton refused to obey the injunction of the commissioners that he and his suffragans should act on the mandate, and, in face of his persistent refusal, the commissioners suspended him. He appealed to the pope and left for Rome, where he arrived towards the end of October. The king's proctors were also there, and the hearing was speedy. By 4 November Innocent had given his decision: Langton's suspension was confirmed.[1] John had succeeded in getting rid of the detested archbishop, for whom Rome had now no use. He would not accommodate himself to the political manoeuvres of the Curia: he was no Peter des Roches or Pandulf. Still, a cardinal cannot remain long suspended without scandal, and his suspension was soon lifted, but he was detained in Rome and did not see England again until the spring of 1218, and even then for three years he was in subordination to the legate.[2] Other, more accommodating, more subtle, agents were needed for the pope's business in England.

Stubbs's knowledge of Langton is no more than superficial, but his judgement is yet more superficial. It seems never to have occurred to him that Langton's rejection both by the king and by the pope is evidence of his unsuitability for his office or that, if an indictment were to be framed against a mediaeval archbishop, it would be difficult to present a more damning count than that he had inspired and comforted the king's enemies. The count is baseless, but Stubbs accepted it and thought it creditable. In truth, there is not, nor did Stubbs produce, a vestige of evidence that Langton was one of the architects of the Great Charter, let alone the principal architect, and to cast him for such a rôle is an absurdity.

---

[1] *Foedera*, i.139; *Selected Letters of Innocent III*, p. 220; Wendover (iii.345) gives a concurrent letter dated 3 November, which appears to be a day too early. Cf. *Bulletin John Rylands Library*, xxix.195-7. [2] Powicke, *Stephen Langton*, pp. 132-46.

XIX

THE KING AND THE BARONS

O F recent years, as the records of his reign have been scrutinised, much stress, undue stress, has been laid upon the
evidence they afford that King John was personally interested in the details of administration. While it is well that John's
intimate concern with such details should be realised, it should be
realised also that no mediaeval king could free himself from them.
John may well be contrasted with his brother Richard, who took
little interest in England except as a source of revenue, and certainly
did not favour England as a place of residence. But the contrast
cannot be pressed very far; for John, if he had had the opportunity,
would have spent much of his time in France. His continued residence in England was not by choice, but a reluctant alternative
thrust upon him by his failure to make good his hold upon his
continental dominions. The evidence does not warrant us in treating
John as in any way exceptional in his devotion to his duty as an
administrator and as a judge. We may have more evidence in his
case, for the simple reason that the surviving records of his reign are
more plentiful than the surviving records for any earlier period: but
we must not confuse abundance or paucity of evidence with evidence
of the relative frequency or infrequency of any action performed by
the actors. However, the frequency with which some act during the
reign of Henry II is warranted *per breve regis de ultra mare* shows that,
even when the king was absent and was represented by a royal
regent or an experienced justiciar, he could not free himself from
detail.[1] And though, as we have been at pains to show, Henry II,
like his grandfather before him, delegated a great deal in routine
matters, he was always liable to be sought out by suitors from England: there were always problems that demanded his personal
attention and control.[2] Moreover, though we lack any plea rolls for
his reign and though it may be doubtful whether any rolls ever
existed to record the pleas heard *coram rege*, yet we have in monastic
chronicles and correspondence ample evidence of Henry's personal
intervention in judicial proceedings.[3] Nor, as his writs and charters

---

[1] Delisle, *Actes de Henri II*, Introduction, pp. 173-5; *Memoranda Roll, 1 John*, p. lxxi.
And see the Pipe Rolls, *passim*: seven such writs are noted in the index to *Pipe Roll,
14 Henry II*, p. 258.
[2] *Memoranda Roll, 1 John*, pp. lxx-lxxi, lxxviii-lxxxi.
[3] Above, pp. 213-4. Henry II's personal interest in the dispute between the monks of

show, could Richard I, even if he would, escape the trammels of detail.[1] And if it be questioned whether writs and charters are reliable evidence of personal interest, we can point to the narrative of the monk of Walden Priory who sought Richard out in Poitou and found him at St. Jean d'Angely.

Believing therefore the time and place to be opportune, he approached the king with due reverence, saluting him with head bowed in humility, and announced to him, in simple and few words, the business with which he had been charged. God, in whose hand are the hearts of kings, inclined the king's heart to hearken to the monk's words, and when the king had inspected and understood the original charters of our patrons, which the monk had ready at hand, he granted and confirmed by his royal authority, in a charter sealed with the royal seal, all the possessions that Earl William had left to us and our house.

The interview was prolonged because the messenger had a yet more important and delicate request to make, that the king would agree to the elevation of the house from a priory to an abbey. Richard granted this petition too and sent letters accordingly to the justiciar, William Longchamp, and to the bishop of the diocese. As a final act of generosity, the king refused to accept any gift for his favours.[2] It is through the accident of personal touches, such as this, in contemporary chronicles and letters that we learn of the daily life of kings. Such accidents have made us well acquainted with the almost patriarchal conduct of affairs by Saint Louis but, if we abstract Louis' piety, the picture we have left would fit nearly any king of the twelfth or thirteenth century.

We may accept it then as true that John was diligent, perhaps with an enforced and unhappy diligence, in the affairs of government. But a mediaeval king had another equally essential duty: he must be a skilled military commander. Here John, when put to the test, fell short. He had been trained in the best of contemporary schools of warfare, that of Richard I. He had the same commanders, the same troops, the same resources: but where Richard was invincible, John could do nothing right and collapsed completely and irrevocably. For this many explanations have been offered. We have no complete explanation to propose, but some facts seem significant. Though John was of middle height, he was thickset and inclined to corpulence and, it seems, to indolence and self-indulgence.[3] In

Christ Church and the archbishop of Canterbury is abundantly illustrated by the *Epistolae Cantuarienses*: no. 240, describing the hearing at Clarendon, is particularly instructive.

[1] Most of those which bear a date are summarised by L. Landon in his *Itinerary of Richard I*. He did not, for his purpose, require to notice those writs which bear no indication of date.   [2] Walden Abbey Chronicle, lib. iii, cc. 4, 5.

[3] Gerald the Welshman seems to be the only contemporary witness to John's personal appearance: see the references collected by Ramsay and the evidence compared with the measurements of John's skeleton (*Angevin Empire*, p. 367: cf. Poole, *From Domesday Book to Magna Carta*, p. 486 n). For John's self-indulgence see Gerald the Welshman, 'De rebus a se gestis', c. 23 (*Opera*, i.86): he is borne out by the minstrel of Béthune (*Histoire des Ducs de Normandie*, pp. 104-5).

strong contrast to the tall, long-limbed, athletic Richard,[1] John cannot have been an impressive figure. Few deeds of prowess are
ascribed to him.[2] It may be that the contrast with his knightly
brother lay at the root of John's inadequacy; and men soon had
cause to regret Richard's death, a regret that increased as the years
went by. At first the regret was for the loss of a military commander,
a great warrior, for Richard was little else: not, indeed, regret from
the very first, because Mirebeau in 1202 looked like a crowning
victory. But the fruits of victory, or so it seemed to observers, were
frittered away by John's ineptitude.[3] Mirebeau was a flash in the
pan. Put to the proof of a long campaign, John proved himself to be
no great leader of men. Contemporary warfare called for little
strategy, for little military science. Big battles were of the rarest.
Small bodies of knights and serjeants engaged in cavalry charges
where tactics and personal prowess were the only things that mat-
tered. Or they might shut themselves up in a castle and stand a siege:
here again the object of the besiegers was to effect a breach and
come to grips in hand-to-hand fighting. Whatever skill was lavished
on arms, armour and siege-engines, it was sheer physical strength
and aptitude for single combat that counted most, and John was
at a great disadvantage in taking the place of Richard. If his initial
success had been followed up, John might have overcome his disadvantage, but failure robbed him of any confidence that men
might have in him and led to further failure. That he lost confidence
in himself is likely enough, and this may account in large part for
the stories told of his extremes of indolence and inertia, for indolent
as he may have been by nature, when the spur was there he could,
on occasion, act with a speed and determination that few could
equal. We must accept, even if we cannot explain, these apparent
contradictions. It is, however, less important to explain John's
failures than to realise that military incompetence, crushing defeat,
meant to contemporaries failure to act the part of a king. A defeated
king lost the respect and eventually the loyalty of his barons.

John, of course, did not admit defeat and he was always planning
to retrieve his loss of Normandy. So long as there was a prospect of
this, his barons might mitigate their judgement of him and, luckily
enough, his standing was greatly improved by his quarrel with
Innocent III. The story of the quarrel as presented by monastic
chroniclers is, naturally enough, *ex parte*. The interests of English re-

---

[1] For Richard's personal appearance see Gerald the Welshman, 'Topographia Hibernica' and 'De Principis Instructione' (*Opera*, v.198; viii.248), and *Itinerarium Regis Ricardi*,
p. 144.

[2] He is credited by the minstrel of Béthune with one feat at Mirebeau: et li rois
meismes i entra et, au premier cop que il feri, coupa-il le puing un chevalier, tout armé,
de s'espée (*Histoire des Ducs de Normandie*, p. 95).

[3] So the *Histoire de Guillaume le Maréchal*, ll. 12105-9. This is not first-rate evidence of
contemporary opinion, but it is supported by the minstrel of Béthune who, however, gives
the principal credit for the victory to William des Roches (*Histoire des Ducs de Normandie*,
pp. 93-6).

ligious houses were little affected by the choice of an archbishop of Canterbury or the manner of selecting him; but Black Monks naturally sympathised with their exiled brethren of Christ Church, the wealthy Cistercians groaned under the royal exactions,[1] and, as the quarrel progressed, the regular clergy were put in the unenviable position of having to decide between the contestants and suffering for their enforced antagonism to the king. A sense of outrage vented itself in anger and abuse, of which monastic chroniclers are the vehicles to posterity. Since their writings have been the basis of the narratives of modern historians—and Stubbs was no exception—it is not surprising that John is usually made to appear in an adverse light. But, as we have already said, in his own view, and in contemporary public opinion, his case was unanswerable. Looking back, John could, in September 1214, regard the years of the breach with Rome as years of domestic tranquillity: until peace had been made with the Church, the barons had not troubled him with the vexatious issues that now beset him.[2] It may be that he was making light of past conflicts, that there were animosities he did not recall, that there were undercurrents of which he was unaware. But there had certainly been no general outward manifestation of hostility to the king, and if 1212 had been a year of disaffection and conspiracy against him, it had also been the year of a notable, if hardly spontaneous, manifestation of support for him in his quarrel with the pope.[3] And yet hardly had that quarrel been settled when everything began to go wrong and, well within a year of the relaxation of the Interdict, the barons were in arms against the king.

Warfare between barons and their prince was nothing unusual: England had seen a good deal of it in the twelfth century and France much more. But what made the warfare between John and his barons remarkable is that the contest was over political principles and was not, as such warfare had been in the past, a dynastic quarrel or mere baronial disorder, with private gain or lawlessness at the bottom of it. The points and principles in dispute are known to all because they were embodied in the Great Charter. If John had been an abler man, it is unlikely that any instrument of the kind would ever have existed and it is unlikely that anyone would have been worse off for the lack of it. Apart from the clauses specifically directed against John in 1215, which were removed when the Charter was subsequently reissued, it may seem a cause for wonder that there should be any serious quarrel at all, so reasonable or so insignificant is the matter. If this be so, it is important to know why the barons demanded the Charter, why John attempted to thwart them, and

---

[1] The enmity with which the Cistercians for a time inspired John may be due to the fact that, while at first they ignored the Interdict, they later complied with the pope's mandate. It is significant that the exchequer kept a separate account of the sums extorted from them (*Red Book of the Exchequer*, ii.773).

[2] *Rot. Litt. Pat.*, p. 182.   [3] Above, pp. 341-2.

why they attempted to coerce him. How did the Great Charter come into existence and why was there so much pother about it? These may seem light words and we do not doubt that they would have seemed frivolous to Stubbs. For what did he say of the Great Charter?

The Great Charter is the first great public act of the nation after it has realised its own identity: the consummation of the work for which unconsciously kings, prelates and lawyers have been labouring for a century. . . . It is in one view the summing up of a period of national life, in another the starting point of a new period, not less eventful than that which it closes . . . the whole of the constitutional history of England is little more than a commentary on Magna Carta.[1]

But let us, for the moment, endeavour to forget what, under the guidance of lawyers and politicians, historians have contrived to find in Magna Carta; let us put aside the sentimental regard for it that has grown with the centuries; and let us approach the problem as though the demanding, the granting and the annulling of the Great Charter were as indifferent to us as the causes and consequences of the siege of Troy.

The first question we should perhaps ask is why the barons' struggle with John was political and not a mere contest for power or material gain. To begin with, it may be well to say a little of the barons themselves,[2] for there seems to be some danger lest they should come to be written off as unintelligent, self-seeking, scoundrelly conspirators,[3] so violent has been the reaction against the idealisation of the very ordinary men who wrested the Great Charter from an arbitrary and short-sighted king. Doubtless, since they shared our common infirmities, they should have been better men than they were; but no one, it might be thought, who had read the Articles of the Barons and the Charter itself could have failed to recognise that behind these documents there lay a development in men's minds and in their attitude towards public affairs that was of outstanding historical significance, a development to which no parallel can be found in any earlier century. Even if the intrinsic merit of the articles and the charter be questioned, the fact that they are the first of their kind establishes in itself their importance, for they are evidence that the barons who devised them had become politically conscious. Here we have a law, the foundation of our

---

[1] *Constitutional History*, i.571-2.

[2] Powicke, *Stephen Langton*, pp. 207-13, supplies particulars of the twenty-five barons named in Magna Carta. Professor Painter gives particulars of the baronage at the beginning of the reign and of those in opposition to the king (*Reign of King John*, pp. 19-55, 286-99): despite his occasional pungent comments, not always happily inspired, we gain very little light upon the motives and conduct of the principal actors. Nor on this point are we much the wiser from J. C. Holt, *The Northerners*, pp. 17-34, where details are collected regarding a particular group of barons.

[3] We excerpt two sentences from a recent work: 'It is hard to believe that Fitz Walter and Vesci were anything more than baronial roughnecks. . . . Fitz Walter was altogether disreputable and mischievous, rescued from ignominy by his great fiefs . . .' (Warren, *King John*, p. 230). We cite a similar view of Eustace de Vesci later.

statute-book, imposed not from above, as were Henry II's assizes, but from below, by those who, it is true, would normally constitute an important element in the king's council, but who, on this occasion, take the initiative. Just as the Great Charter is the first of our statutes, so the Articles of the Barons stand at the head of that long line of formal statements of grievances which we can trace through the Petition of the Barons of 1258 to the common petitions of Edward III's reign and which have given us the characteristic forms of English legislation. If we do not, like Stubbs, see in this sequence the hand of Providence; if we recognise that the authoritarian legislation of Edward I stood upon a higher plane than any statutes which preceded it or followed it for two centuries or more[1]; if we perceive that the parliamentary petition was at best a clumsy contrivance that had either to be cast aside or become a mere mask for measures promoted by the government; yet, on however low a plane we place the articles and the charter, whatever blunders and imperfections we see in them and the men who made them, they demand a high place in our consideration as marking a stage in the political development of the country and the evolution of legislative forms. If we dismiss from our minds the monstrous fable that the Great Charter was the work of Stephen Langton—a work so unlike the veritable work that came from his hands—then we must see it as the work of men who, in the school of bitter experience, had learnt something of the art of politics, men who, we must assume, had some tincture of learning, men certainly with wide experience in administration and command. If the Great Charter was admirable when it was conceived to be the masterpiece of an imaginary genius who was confused with an historical archbishop, it cannot be less admirable when we recognise it to be the work of others, whatever be the load of infirmities with which we burden them. And let us have good warrant before we denigrate the baronial leaders.

We need but take one example of this very dubious process. Robert fitz Walter, we have been told, was not a man with a good record behind him; he had become an object of ridicule and contempt both in England and France; it is difficult to credit such as he with a high sense of responsibility and public duty.[2] This is the modern reading of his character: this is the portrait we are asked to accept as veridical. But the difficulty is that the barons who opposed John had, quite evidently, a very different opinion of Robert. They knew

[1] Richardson and Sayles, *The Early Statutes*, pp. 21-3; *Trans. R. Hist. Soc.*, 4th Ser., xxviii.27.
[2] Poole, *From Domesday Book to Magna Carta*, p. 470. This owes much to Ralf of Coggeshall (p. 144) who, however, here borrows a tag from the Vulgate 'in derisum omni populo . . . canticum eorum tota die' (Thren. iii.14). Nothing can be based upon such borrowings: cf. Powicke in *E.H.R.*, xxi.296. Better evidence is supplied by the minstrel of Béthune: 'dont il furent molt blasmé et dont li Englois furent moult abaudé' (*Histoire des Ducs de Normandie*, p. 97). On a later page Mr Poole speaks of 'unscrupulous and reactionary barons', meaning apparently all those actively opposed to the king (p. 476). This is a cliché with which we deal later.

his record and his qualities and they chose him to be the marshal of the army of God and Holy Church.[1] Let us discount this grandiloquent title, obviously devised as a thrust against John, the dedicated crusader, and his backer, Innocent, the vicar of Christ. Are we invited to believe that the barons would deliberately choose as their leader in the serious business of war a man of bad character and a notorious poltroon? No one would even have considered such a possibility, had it not been for Kate Norgate's very proper reaction against the extravagant laudation of the dissident barons and particularly against T. F. Tout's incautious words extolling Robert fitz Walter as 'the first champion of English liberty'. She rightly drew attention to the inadequacy and uncertainties of the sources, which offered no support for this perversion of history.[2] And whatever is obscure, there is no reason to doubt that Robert's hostility to the king, far from originating in political controversy, was quickened by John's quarrel with Geoffrey de Mandeville, Robert's son-in-law, and that the enmity between Geoffrey and the king had been occasioned by John's behaviour towards Geoffrey's wife.[3] Robert, however, had a long-standing grievance of his own against the king. Put in command of the castle of Vaudreuil, jointly with his cousin Saer de Quency, the two had, on the king's instructions, surrendered to Philip Augustus without offering any resistance. They were in consequence the subject of much obloquy, which was not entirely dissipated by John's acknowledgement of his responsibility.[4] The whole incident is as incomprehensible to us as it was to contemporaries —an act of insanity, it has been suggested, on John's part[5]; but there is no ground for doubting the truth of John's written statement or for crediting him, as Miss Norgate did, with 'exaggerated generosity' towards two men who, if they had not acted under orders, would have been guilty of a gross act of treachery. One result of their common misfortune seems to have been to unite Robert and Saer in a fast friendship. Like other barons who felt themselves to have suffered wrong at John's hands, they were leaders in the opposition to him, but it is notable that they were concerned together in the negotiations preceding the intervention of Louis of France[6] and that, when

---

[1] *Foedera*, i.133-4; Ralf of Coggeshall, *Chronicon Anglicanum*, p. 171.

[2] *John Lackland*, pp. 289-93. In fairness to Tout it must, however, be said that, apart from this phrase, his article in the *Dict. Nat. Biog.* is a sober and well-documented account of his subject.

[3] We depend for the facts upon the contemporary writer of the *Histoire des Ducs de Normandie*, pp. 116-21. He leaves us in no doubt that the king's advances to Fitz Walter's daughter were the origin of the quarrel, though his narrative is far from clear and is, of course, hearsay.

[4] *Rot. Litt. Pat.*, p. 31. This does not seem to have become generally known. The minstrel of Béthune, who mentions the incident, makes no reference to John's instructions (*Histoire des Ducs de Normandie*, p. 97).

[5] Powicke, *Loss of Normandy*, p. 162f.

[6] Whether or not Wendover (*Flores*, iii.359) is correct in saying that they went to France together, Fitz Walter, as the baronial commander, was implicated in the negotiations: cf. Painter, *Reign of King John*, p. 367.

his cause was lost, they set off together on crusade.[1] We cannot explain this friendship by labelling Robert and Saer (who had been created earl of Winchester in 1207) as cowards and traitors, outcasts sharing a common misery, nor can we thus explain the esteem in which Robert fitz Walter was, without question, held by his fellows. However much may be puzzling in the stories that have come down to us, one fact at least stands out: Robert was a man of good repute in his day, a nobleman of distinguished birth, renowned in arms, as Matthew Paris puts it.[2] And when he is found with Eustace de Vesci making common cause, at least for a limited purpose, with Stephen Langton and when special provision is made for these two men in the conditions of reconciliation between Innocent III and the king, we must at least assume that Robert had satisfied both Langton and the pope's representative, Pandulf, of his integrity and the genuineness of his grievances.[3] In her scepticism, in her reluctance to find anything worthy in him, Miss Norgate was driven to the supposition that Robert succeeded in deceiving the subtle Pandulf,[4] unlikely enough in itself and beyond belief in view of the ease with which he would have been unmasked in the course of the protracted negotiations with the king that the settlement involved. That Robert was, in fact, reinstated and recompensed for his losses is the best evidence we could have of the merit of his case.[5] Let it be granted that Robert and Eustace had been plotting against the king before they fled: much contemporary opinion must have held that they were justified. The picture of a worthless schemer, with no better claim to distinction than his estates, cunningly disguising his real character and hoodwinking his fellow barons into giving him their confidence, outwitting Pandulf and over-reaching the king, may be amusing, but it has no other merit. The events in which Robert fitz Walter played a prominent part can best be explained on the assumption that he was, like his associates, a credible human being.

If we would get the Great Charter into perspective we must compare it with earlier treaties of peace that put an end to civil war in England; for though the charter was regarded by later ages as a statute, as an act of legislation, it was also a treaty, a *forma pacis*, both when it was first issued in 1215 and when it was again conceded in 1216 in a bid to win for the boy king the loyalty of the barons who had taken up arms against his father. Let us look at the treaty of Winchester of 1153. It purports to settle a dynastic quarrel, awarding

[1] Wendover, *Flores*, iv.44; *Annales Monastici*, ii.292, iii.56. There are other reference to their acting together: e.g. *Patent Rolls, 1216-1225*, pp. 103, 134.
[2] *Chronica Maiora*, iii.334.
[3] *Selected Letters of Innocent III*, pp. 131, 161; see also Innocent's letter to Eustace de Vesci, where he implicitly accepts the view that the 'confederations and conjurations' against John were occasioned by the breach with Rome (*Foedera*, i.126).
[4] *John Lackland*, pp. 292-3.
[5] *Rot. Litt. Pat.*, p. 101 (19 July 1213); *Rot. Litt. Claus.*, i.146.

to one claimant to the throne the succession on the present king's death and securing to the king's heir the estates that were his by inheritance and those with which the king had endowed him from the royal demesne. Some other territorial claims are met. Of good government, however, the only thing that is said is by afterthought in the last clause, where it is provided that the king shall exercise royal justice over the whole land, both in that part which belongs to Duke Henry and that which belongs to the king: but this division of immediate jurisdiction, which nullified the whole clause, is not removed by the treaty.[1] Again, let us look at the treaty of 1174. This is little more than a family settlement to which Henry II and his sons, Henry, Richard and Geoffrey, are parties. It proclaims a general amnesty and provides for the rectification of violent disseisins, but the only clause that asserts a legal principle is that which, while admitting to the king's peace those who followed his sons in rebellion, lays down that they are to stand their trial for murder, treachery or mayhem.[2]

How are we to account for the changed outlook between 1174 and 1215? Though personal wrongs were doubtless an important factor in the revolt against John, they will not afford a sufficient explanation. The explanation that, while the revolt of the barons was wholly selfish, the influence of Langton transferred it to a higher plane, fails, not only because it lacks evidence, but because it is against the evidence. A necessary element was the change in the political climate between the first twenty years of Henry II's reign and the beginning of the thirteenth century. This change had been induced largely by Henry, but there were other important factors. To Henry we must give the credit for the creation of a strong central administration and of a system of law, uniform in its application, which is embodied in the law-book that goes under the name of 'Glanville'. But the influence of Roman law, both as an academic discipline and as an authority to be applied in determining legal issues, is all pervading. Moreover, the debt of canon law to Roman law was direct and immense: it is not too much to say that in this field the authority of Justinian was as great as that of the Decretals. The debt of English law to Roman law was indirect but still great. 'Glanville' owes its form and spirit, though little of its substantive law, to Roman law as it was applied in the latter part of the twelfth century, especially to the romanesque *ordines judiciarii*.[3] But the influence of Roman law was more potent than 'Glanville' may suggest, and its adoption to supply deficiencies in the English common law is exemplified in Bracton's treatise and the Scottish 'Regiam Majestatem'. These later law-books are evidence enough that for sixty or seventy years after 'Glanville' was written, the 'Corpus Juris Civilis' and the

---

[1] *Foedera*, i.18; above, p. 253.   [2] *Ibid.*, p. 30.
[3] Van Caenegem, *Royal Writs in England from the Conquest to Glanville*, pp. 372-86.

current textbooks that depended upon it were still exerting, and perhaps increasing, their influence.[1] Men brought up in this tradition inevitably had a growing conception that a system of law should be precise and universal in its application, a rational system in which there was nothing arbitrary. At the same time Roman law exalted the function of the king as ruler and law-giver. This is a doctrine most emphatically stated in the 'Dialogus de Scaccario', but there is no reason to suppose that this work was known outside a narrow official circle. The much more influential 'Glanville'—embodied, for example, in Roger of Howden's chronicle—while it looks to Justinian's 'Institutes' as an ideal statement of the written law, for which the author endeavours to supply an English counterpart, does not, however, conceive of the king as an autocrat, but as a supreme ruler, who is nevertheless limited by the necessity to consult his council, the great men of the realm.[2] In this he is in the English tradition, represented above all by the recension of the Laws of Edward the Confessor that was produced early in the reign of Henry II. This recension was at one time believed to reflect the views of the dissident barons under John.[3] While we must put the date of the book half a century or more earlier,[4] none the less the similarity in the political outlook stated there and the political ideas attributed to the barons is noteworthy. The emphasis laid upon righteous rule, the condemnation of the exercise of arbitrary power by the king, the necessity of co-operation with the baronage, the maxim that a king forfeits his right to kingship if he does not rule well:[5] all these things are close to the ideas with which we may reasonably credit the barons who chafed under John's misrule. There may be no element of truth in the unlikely story that Stephen Langton absolved John from excommunication on condition that he swore to observe the good laws of his ancestors and especially the laws of King Edward,[6] yet the story gives some indication of where men looked for an exposition of the duties of a king.

We need not suppose that any of the barons who were active in their opposition to John had read a line of 'Glanville' or of the 'Laws of Edward the Confessor', much less of Roman law. It was not necessary to do so in order to appreciate the virtues of the system of law under which they lived or to condemn arbitrary government. They would be as unlikely to know the sources from which their political ideas were derived as modern politicians are unlikely to know the sources of the political ideas they take for granted. There is perhaps one hypothesis we should mention, if only to express our

---

[1] *Traditio*, vi.83-5; *Juridical Review*, lxvii.155-87. [2] Above, pp. 143-4.
[3] Liebermann, *Über die Leges Anglorum . . . Londoniis collectae*, pp. 91-100.
[4] *Traditio*, xvi.166-7. [5] *Gesetze der Angelsachsen*, i.635-7.
[6] Wendover, *Flores*, iii.266. That such a condition should be imposed by the Curia is incredible and it would require independent testimony to establish that Langton imposed this or any other condition of his own motion.

dissent from it, that the barons sought 'to undermine the whole fabric of the judicial system'.[1] Inevitably one result of the creation of an efficient centralised judicial administration was to curtail baronial administration of the law and, it may be added, the jurisdiction of the county court. But the advantages of a permanent central court, with a precise system of procedure and precise rules of law, were so great that there was little antagonism. This is evident from the plea rolls of Richard I, which show that the magnates as well as other ranks of contemporary society, except the lowest, made free use of the new procedure. From the barons' demand that common pleas should be tried in a sedentary court and that justices of assize should make frequent visits to the counties, it is evident that they wanted more royal justice and not less.[2] Royal justice was not, of itself, oppressive nor was it burdensome upon litigants. On the whole the administration of justice was inexpensive because judges and ministers were largely remunerated through the grant by the king of ecclesiastical benefices, wardships and the like and by fees and gifts from the parties, for it was not yet thought reprehensible to smooth the course of the law. It was not centralised administration, as such, that caused dissatisfaction, and there is nothing to suggest that the barons wished to revert to more primitive methods of government. For causes of dissatisfaction we must look rather to the recurrent drain of treasure spent upon foreign war which could not be met from the ordinary revenues of the Crown. This may not have been the only cause, but it was the principal cause of the pressure of the fisc. And we must remember that, if John inherited an efficient instrument of centralised administration, he inherited also the possibilities it afforded for misuse. What the dissident barons demanded of him, and what indeed he affected to offer them, was the reform, not only of the evil and oppressive customs he had himself introduced, but those of Richard I and Henry II.[3] There might be differences of opinion on what was evil and what was oppressive, but that the customs that irked the barons were of long standing and gradual growth admitted of no question. The rights of the Crown were exploited to increase the revenue, and the central and itinerant courts could be used as an effective instrument of exploitation. Eyres *ad omnia placita* were, in particular, unpopular throughout their existence because they enabled the Crown to extort substantial pecuniary penalties in the remotest countryside for technical breaches of the law.[4] This form of extortion had, however, narrow limits, and resort was had increasingly to general taxation. The same central administration that dispensed justice and controlled the ordinary revenues could be used to enforce taxation. Richard I

---

[1] *Magna Carta Essays*, p. 97: see below, p. 388, n. 3.
[2] Below, p. 387.   [3] *Foedera*, i.129: letter of 29 May 1215.
[4] Pollock and Maitland, *History of English Law*, i.201-2.

made use of other devices and, though he had imposed heavy taxes, the greatest grievance against him seems to have been the extortionate fees demanded for sealing royal charters and letters. This is the grievance singled out in what is, in effect, John's coronation charter, the 'constitution' of 7 June 1199. In this the king stigmatises the 'vile and wicked customs which had arisen either from cupidity or from ill counsel or some other unlawful impulse' and which, as he recognised, he was bound by his coronation oath to put down. And whatever exactions he may have perpetuated, there is every reason to suppose that John did moderate the fees for the great seal, reverting to the scale in force under Henry II.[1]

John, however, was unable to keep down expenditure without acting as no mediaeval king in a like position could be expected to act. He was committed to making war in order to maintain, if it were possible, his position in France, and it was a reproach to him that he had not completed the conquest of Ireland.[2] Warfare was becoming increasingly expensive. As we have explained, military fiefs did not provide an army. It is true that the king expected his barons to take part in his wars, but wars were not waged by means of the service due for lands held of the king: they were waged at the king's expense, and the soldier, whether he were a humble archer or an armoured knight, in many cases held not a rod of English land. The mercenary had established himself by the twelfth century and his appearance marks the beginning of a new era.[3] John was but following the trend of the times in keeping large numbers of armed men in his pay, some permanently, some for special occasions.[4] When we add to the expenditure on pay the cost of supplies and transport, it is easy to understand how formidable were the sums required for the wars and the hardly less expensive preparations for war that fill the years of John's reign. And how little was accomplished! It is true that John subdued William the Lion and forced Llewellyn to sue for peace; but we must not exaggerate the importance of what, in modern terms, were police operations. These princes were feudatories, and any transient success that John achieved in checking their ambitions was more than counterbalanced by the hatred he induced. It is unlikely that John had any Welsh or Scottish policy,[5] that he saw beyond what he conceived to be the

[1] *Foedera*, i.75-6; *Memoranda Roll, 1 John*, pp. xxxv-xxxix.

[2] Gerald the Welshman, 'De rebus a se gestis', c. xxiii (*Opera*, i.86): potius autem in Hiberniam iret et pleno conquestui regni illius interim et incastellationi indulgeret.

[3] Above, pp. 73-4.

[4] The Flemish were the most important and have been best studied: see Dept, *Les influences anglaise et française dans le comté de Flandre*, pp. 28-32, 54-66, 108-15, 121, 157-62.

[5] It seems to be agreed that, in regard to Scotland, John had no objective except to retain control over the northern counties which William the Lion sought to bring within his own kingdom. As regards Wales, A. L. Poole makes out a case for a policy (*From Domesday Book to Magna Carta*, pp. 298-300): but that John planned to bring 'the whole country . . . under the despotic rule of the English Crown' is an assumption that goes beyond the evidence. For details of the abortive preparations of 1212 see *Pipe Roll, 14 John*, pp. xv-xvii.

needs of the day; but whether he deemed himself to be politic or whether he acted without reflection on the impulse of the moment, the judgement on his activities is written in four chapters of the Great Charter.[1] He drove the princes of Wales and Scotland to make common cause against him with the English barons. Except for the expedition to Ireland—which, beyond its avowed object of bringing William de Briouze to justice, did for a time bring the land under subjection and lead to a reform in its administration[2]—there was nothing to show for all the treasure that had been poured out. John turned everywhere for money. He succeeded in compelling the clergy to contribute to the thirteenth of 1207: and this single tax yielded £60,000. So heavy a burden could not soon be repeated, and, in any case, the conditions arising from the Interdict both complicated the position and gave the king a different and substantial revenue from this source.[3] His taxation of the Jews reached an unprecedented height in 1210 and was accompanied by unprecedented cruelty. This tax, again, could not be repeated and was, indeed, not fully collected at the end of the reign.[4] Until the outbreak of war with the barons, taxation nevertheless brought in very considerable amounts by the standard of the times, and whether by taxation or by more devious means John amassed a very great treasure in ways that were considered oppressive. He was not, however, let us make plain, singular in this. 'It may be asked', said Gerald of Wales, 'how it came about that King Henry II and his sons, in the midst of so many wars, abounded in such riches. The explanation may be given that, although their regular revenues were smaller than their predecessors', they took care to make good the amount from exceptional sources, relying more upon occasional profits than upon steady income. Truly, wherever by any manner of means something is to be gotten, there, of a surety, every effort will be made to thieve: unrestingly and delicately the robber prowls, on the chance that a weak spot will be found somewhere.'[5]

Though the name of tyrant has been somewhat freely applied to John, by contemporaries as well as later writers, it must not be imagined that he acted in important matters without counsel, whatever value he attached to it. The assent of the barons is carefully mentioned in instruments recording, for example, the surrender of the kingdom to the pope and the concession of the free election of prelates.[6] In like manner assent was given to the assize of bread,

---

[1] Magna Carta, cc. 56-59.
[2] Orpen, *Ireland under the Normans*, ii.235-77; Richardson and Sayles, *Irish Parliament in the Middle Ages*, pp. 12, 14.
[3] Mitchell, *Studies in Taxation under John and Henry III*, pp. 84-93, 106-8. See also above, pp. 355-6.   [4] Richardson, *English Jewry under Angevin Kings*, pp. 167-72.
[5] Gerald the Welshman, *De Principis Instructione*, iii, c. 30 (*Opera*, viii.316).
[6] For the one see *Foedera*, i.115: 'bona nostra spontaneaque voluntate ac communi consilio baronum nostrorum'. For the other see *Select Charters*, p. 283-4, where the formula is: 'liberaliter mera et spontanea voluntate, de communi consensu baronum nostrorum'.

the allocation of the king's galleys among various ports, and the limitation of knight service when it was decided that every nine knights should provide a tenth.[1] But since no rule seems to have been observed for summoning the barons for important business, the composition of the king's court on any particular occasion was, to some extent, a matter of chance. A prudent king would doubtless arrange, as Henry II evidently did, that weighty matters should be reserved for the great feasts, when the king ceremonially wore his crown, the *laudes* were sung and the court was exceptionally well attended. John certainly observed the traditional practice of crown-wearing[2] and his court was doubtless crowded on these occasions, but whether he took advantage of these occasions to seek counsel and, if he sought it, followed it, is another matter. If we regard chapters twelve and fourteen of the Great Charter, we must get the impression that there had not been adequate opportunity to consider the king's demands for extraordinary taxes, but the occasions on which such taxes had been levied were exceptional. The barons, however, objected as well to scutage being taken without their consent, and John's scutages had been frequent and in general extraordinarily heavy as compared with those demanded by his brother and his father[3]: it may have been the frequency or perhaps the amount, rather than the principle, that was objectionable, for it could not be reasonably contested that scutage was not due from those who after summons did not serve the king in arms. But to the scutage of Poitou objection had been taken on the ground that service there was not due from English barons, and this grievance too may be reflected in the barons' protest.[4] The demands of the barons as a whole and John's reluctance to concede or discuss them are in themselves proof that the opportunities for counselling the king, or rather for making counsel effective, had been inadequate, and we need no better evidence.[5] It is noteworthy, however, that it is only in regard to taxation that the barons demanded a formal summons with adequate notice: apparently the mere method of obtaining and giving counsel in other matters was not seriously in question.

The essential difficulty was that John was at odds with his barons, and the reason must lie in his attitude and conduct towards them. Still, we must bear in mind that such different men among his

---

[1] *Rot. Litt. Pat.*, pp. 41, 52b, 55. For some other examples, including extraordinary taxation, see Mitchell, *op. cit.*, p. 369 n.

[2] Kantorowicz, *Laudes Regiae*, p. 174.

[3] For particulars see Ramsay, *Revenues of the Kings of England*, i.261, and cf. *ibid.*, pp. 195, 227.

[4] The barons' case has been treated somewhat lightly (e.g. Painter, *Reign of King John*); but the king's argument, echoed in Innocent's letter of 1 April 1215 (*Selected Letters of Innocent III*, p. 202), that the scutage of Poitou was due because 'regibus Anglie reddere consueverint ab antiquo' is manifestly fallacious, since no king before Henry II had exercised authority there. The barons were prepared to concede liability for service in Normandy and Brittany ('Unknown Charter of Liberties', c. 7: McKechnie, *Magna Carta*, p. 486), and the historical basis for this is obvious.

[5] See Appendix V: below, pp. 455-62.

successors as Henry III, Edward I, Edward II and Richard II were also at variance with their barons, and that in each case there was an obvious conflict over the control of administration, which, in the king's view, meant control of the king. John was not the great exception. Political differences may, however, be exacerbated by personal differences, and seemingly this happened in John's case, although the facts are not easy to ascertain. There was doubtless much exaggeration in the widespread charge against John that he dishonoured his barons' womenfolk. Monastic chroniclers could, indeed, bring wild and baseless accusations against him. Matthew Paris puts the charge into the mouth of Robert of London amid much scandalous nonsense that destroys its credibility.[1] The sober chronicler of Meaux arouses our suspicions by prefacing a general charge against John with the most improbable allegation that he 'frequented' the wife of his brother Geoffrey, that is Constance of Brittany.[2] But if we ask for specific instances of John's indiscretions, we are given at least one, his unsuccessful attempt at corrupting the daughter of Robert fitz Walter, who was married to Geoffrey de Mandeville. That this incident was woven into a *chanson de geste* and eventually found a place in a monastic chronicle and a long-popular romance does not mean that it is imaginary: we can take the word of the matter-of-fact minstrel of Béthune that Robert fitz Walter made constant reference to it.[3] The story seems to account for much of the rancour between the king and these two barons and is surely inherently probable. Again, while the stories of John's cruelty may have lost nothing in the telling, there are sufficiently unquestionable atrocities to explain how these stories arose.[4] It is a commonplace that John was faithless in greater matters: is it to be supposed that he was faithful in lesser matters? Is it not evident that he was suspect by those who knew him best? He himself doubtless suspected the loyalty of those around him, not least of those he had offended. The mutual suspicion between king and barons needs no better proof than the number of hostages he demanded. There was nothing novel in the taking and giving of hostages, but the Great Charter is there to witness that, in the view of the barons, John's demands had been excessive and unjustifiable.[5] Nor will all the modern denigration of

---

[1] *Chronica Maiora*, ii.563: 'filias corrupit nubiles ac sorores'. For Robert of London see above, p. 332.

[2] *Chronica Mon. de Melsa*, i.403: 'uxorem fratris sui Galfridi iam mortui frequentavit, uxores et filias nobilium defloravit, feminae nulli saltem pepercit quin eam libidinis ardore vellet maculare'.

[3] *Histoire des Ducs de Normandie*, pp. 119, 121. The writer too says (p. 105): 'de bieles femes estoit trop couvoiteus'.

[4] 'Crues estoit sor toz homes', says the minstrel of Béthune (*Histoire des Ducs de Normandie*, p. 105); and see above, pp. 334-5.

[5] For some particulars see McKechnie, *Magna Carta*, pp. 441-3. John's practice is well illustrated by his proceedings in Ireland, for which see Orpen, *Ireland under the Normans*, ii.264-6. How interwoven the giving of hostages was with feudal relations, as they were understood in France, is well illustrated by the story told by the minstrel of Béthune of William des Roches, when he learnt that John had imprisoned Arthur. It had been agreed

Robert fitz Walter and Eustace de Vesci explain away the indubitable fact that, though they were accused of the blackest of contemporary crimes, treachery to their lord, they obtained the protection of the Church and were not only welcomed back from exile by the baronage in general but adopted as their representatives and leaders. Not only does this fact make nonsense of the denigration to which they have been subjected, but it shows that, in contemporary opinion, they were justified and the fault lay, not with them, but the king. John's evil reputation was that of his own time and was well based. The other side of his character, which historians have recently discovered with rather naïve surprise, his contemporaries took for granted. He fulfilled, without any particular distinction, the duties expected of a king. Like Innocent III, he was a determined persecutor of heretics.[1] We have but to read his household accounts to see that he was not devoid of the virtues of good-fellowship, charity, piety, affection.[2] The loyalty his French captains gave him we may perhaps dismiss as interested, but in times of adversity they stood by him and they continued to stand by his son. He certainly stood by those clerks who remained loyal to him during the Interdict.[3] And as late as 1212 the barons of England and Ireland testified that John had been faithful to them and that they had no knowledge of any offences committed by him against the constitutions of the realm or against his liegemen.[4] Doubtless we cannot take at its face value a declaration instigated by the king and expressed in terms he wished and perhaps dictated; but the struggle with the papacy had in some measure reconciled the barons to the king and had doubtless inclined him, however reluctantly, to circumspection in handling them. It is not without significance that William Marshal, no eager doer of John's bidding, was active in securing the adherence of the Irish barons to this declaration.[5] But John did not command the devotion that was given so emphatically to his brother Henry, a devotion we find very hard to understand, so worthless does the young king seem to us.[6] It is clear that John had little charm, that

that the treatment of Arthur would be governed by William's advice: 'et ses consaus estoit que il boine seurté presist de lui [Arthur] ke il dès ore mais loiaument le sierviroit, et Artus l'en donroit assés des fils as haus homes de sa tierre en hostages, et sor chou l'en lassast aler' (*Histoire des Ducs de Normandie*, pp. 95-6). The passage may be translated: 'and his counsel was that John should take good security from Arthur that henceforth he would serve him loyally, and Arthur would give him as hostages a sufficient number of the sons of the magnates of his land, and on this condition John would set Arthur free'.

[1] See his letter of 30 November 1214 to the seneschal of Gascony, ordering the extirpation of the Albigensian heretics in the province. John wrote concurrently to the cardinal legate Peter of Benevento, asking for his co-operation (*Rot. Litt. Pat.*, p. 124).
[2] Cole, *Documents*, pp. 231-69; Misae Roll, 14 John. For John's perhaps ostentatious piety during the Interdict see above, pp. 347-8.
[3] Above, p. 355: cf. Cheney in *Bulletin John Rylands Library*, xxxi.312.
[4] Above, pp. 341-2. The Irish barons may not have made their declaration until early in 1213. [5] See John's letter to him in *Rot. Litt. Claus.*, i.132b.
[6] Cf. Norgate, *England under Angevin Kings*, ii.220-2. The best description of the young king is that written by Walter Map, who knew him well, but the enigma of his attraction remains (*De Nugis Curialium*, iv, c. 1 (ed. James), pp. 139-40).

he was no leader of men. Whatever his virtues, his barons had no
affection for him and, says the dispassionate minstrel of Béthune, all
the people hated him.[1] Those who had suffered wrongs at his hands
found no reason to forgive him, and if they had perforce to disguise
their resentment, they nursed their grievances.

Two unrelated events precipitated the crisis: the accommodation
with Innocent III and the destruction at Bouvines of John's hopes
for revenge on Philip Augustus. The first of these events, as the
course of events shows, loosened the bond that had temporarily
united king and barons, while the surrender of the kingdom to the
pope gave John a feudal overlord to whom both the king and his
subjects could appeal.[2] There is no reason to doubt that the assent
of the barons to the surrender of the kingdom to the pope, which
was expressed in the formal instrument, had been a real, and not an
assumed, assent. Before the pope their representatives claimed credit
for it,[3] and let us remember that Robert fitz Walter and Eustace de
Vesci had returned from exile under the pope's aegis. The barons
looked, mistakenly as it proved, to the pope for support against the
king. This is not to say that the surrender was popular. We have
good warrant for saying that the detestation which Matthew Paris
expresses was but echoing one phase at least of contemporary opinion.[4] As for the battle of Bouvines, although John had not himself
been beaten in the field and was apparently anxious to continue the
war, the defeat of the emperor was none the less a personal disaster
that could not be concealed, while the five years' truce between the
kings, which followed, held a message that all could read. A mediaeval king found it hard to survive defeat. *Proh pudor de rege victo! proh
pudor!*[5] And it is not surprising that malcontents at home should
think the moment opportune to press their advantage.[6] John returned to England on 13 October 1214,[7] and he must have been
presented almost immediately with a request for reform. If from
this point our knowledge of the sequence of events is defective, we
yet can construct a network of dates and events which enables us to
put documents in their context and reduces to a minimum the need
and possibility of conjecture, of which we have been given overmuch.

---

[1] *Histoire des Ducs de Normandie*, p. 123: il veoit que tout chil de sa tiere le haoient.
[2] Above, p. 360.   [3] *Foedera*, i.120
[4] Matthew Paris, *Historia Anglorum*, ii.134. Contemporary opinion is represented by
Matthew of Rievaulx (Faral, *Les arts poetiques*, pp. 25-6; *Revue Benedictine*, lii.32):

> Christe Ihesu . . .
> Dissolvas hanc rem, scelus hoc, opus istud, et illud
> Exitiale iugum citius tu contere; certe
> Est insigne mori quam libertate carere.

(Christ Jesus, do Thou destroy this thing, this shame, this work, quickly break this deadly
yoke. Truly it is nobler to die than to lose one's liberty.)
[5] Alleged to have been said by Henry II on his deathbed (Gerald the Welshman,
'De Principis Instructione', iii, c. 26, in *Opera*, viii.297).
[6] The Northerners appear to have been already at variance with the king, but no
particulars are given by the Dunstable annalist who records their reconciliation on
1 November 1213 (*Annales Monastici*, iii.40).   [7] Below, p. 455.

To avoid overburdening the text with detail, we have consigned to an appendix the calendar we have constructed[1]: it should be used to check our account of the sequence of events and the parts played by the principal actors, and it may be useful in checking the suggestions of others.

This, however, we should emphasise. The received account of the prelude to the Great Charter, the story told by modern historians, which is substantially that told by Roger of Wendover, will hardly bear confrontation with the plain message of printed records.[2] We have said that, after his return to England, the king must have been presented almost immediately with a request for reform. We say this because the leaders of the dissident barons, the 'Northerners', are found in his company early in November and again in the fourth week of November, as they are once more at Epiphany, when there is a prolonged meeting of which we have a good deal of knowledge. The baronial leaders throughout are Robert fitz Walter, Geoffrey de Mandeville and William d'Aubigny. If these men were plotting against the king, they were doing a singular amount of it in the king's presence.[3] Doubtless in the background stood the implacable Eustace de Vesci, but the negotiations were in other hands, negotiations that demanded a deal of persistence and patience, not perhaps on one side only, negotiations that must have seemed promising before the meeting at the New Temple in January 1215. This was an exceptionally well-attended gathering of prelates, earls and barons, but from the start it went ill for the king. To John's chagrin, he found that he could look for little support from the bishops and, in his spite, he insinuated to the pope that they were hand in glove with the barons, a baseless charge in which he did not persist. In the presence of the bishops, however, he was gracious, and the only tangible outcome of the meeting was to transmit to the pope for confirmation the charter granting to cathedral and conventual churches freedom of election, an empty enough concession, but placatory and an outward sign of good-will, while at the same time serving the king's own purpose.[4] But almost from the start of the meeting John had decided to submit the differences between himself and the barons to the pope, for preparations were already being made on the second day after Epiphany for the journey to the Curia of the king's representative. Since the meeting lasted thereafter for several days, the king's intention could not have been made known to the barons. When they learned of it, they had no alternative but to put their case to the pope also, though there is nothing to suggest that this was their desire. It is significant that they chose

---

[1] Below, pp. 455-62.
[2] We refer to the general accounts of John's reign and the Great Charter. Recently Professor C. R. Cheney and Professor J. C. Holt have endeavoured independently to construct from the records a firm basis for discussion: see Appendix V, below, pp. 450-62.
[3] Below, pp. 455-9.   [4] Above, pp. 357-8.

as one of their two representatives a clerk of Eustace de Vesci, who had stood aloof from the negotiations. Another sign that the relations between the Northerners and the king were strained almost to breaking-point is the arrangement of a truce between them until Low Sunday (26 April).[1]

The expiration of the truce and the news of the pope's decision came almost simultaneously. The decision did not in any way touch the merits of the dispute between the king and the barons. Innocent accepted without question John's presentation of the case. The king, he held, was under no obligation to make any concession and the barons had no right to demand any. It was for them first to reconcile themselves to the king, by proving their loyalty and obedience, and then to make their requests humbly and without insolence. Above all, they were not to engage in leagues and conspiracies against the king. The pope will go no farther than to urge him to give gracious consideration to any just petitions the barons may put forward.[2] This dismissal of their case and the empty advice that accompanied it, to enter afresh upon friendly negotiations with John, robbed the barons of any trust they may have had in Innocent's impartiality. But their defiance of the king on 5 May brought new and varied offers of negotiation from his side. All were rejected, because all reserved the last word to the pope, whom the barons were determined to exclude. If, to reinforce their arguments, the barons made a show of armed force, nevertheless the two sides never lost touch, and on 27 May preparations were already on foot for the final negotiations at Runnymede, with Langton and his suffragans acting as intermediaries, though two days later John made yet another offer to submit the issues to the pope for his decision.[3] He could have had little expectation that this offer would be accepted. Serious discussions upon quite another footing were begun on 10 June and were seemingly concluded on the fifteenth, although a few more days were required for settling the draft of the final instrument,[4] which like other treaties took the form of a charter.[5] Runnymede then was the culmination of negotiations that had begun seven months and more earlier, that had been suspended by the reference of the dispute to

[1] Below, pp. 456, 458.
[2] *Selected Letters of Innocent III*, pp. 194-7.   [3] Below, pp. 459-60.
[4] Three dates appear to be established beyond question: 10 June, when John, who was lodged at Windsor, went to the 'pratum de Stanes' and stayed for a long time (*Electio Hugonis*, p. 128); 15 June, the date given to the charter; 19 June, the date when the barons renewed their homage (i.e. Friday after Trinity) and the date of the writs which assume that copies of the charter are, or will be, available (*Rot. Litt. Pat.*, p. 180b). Since the date of the charter is generally assumed to be the date of agreement between the parties, it is inferred that the Articles of the Barons were sealed in token of the king's acceptance. The dates 15 and 19 June stand, whatever delays there were in preparing copies of the writ and the charter and despatching them throughout the country: for this see Richardson, 'The Morrow of the Great Charter', *Bulletin John Rylands Library*, xxviii.425-9.
[5] Compare the opening protocol of the treaty of Le Goulet: . . . universis ad quos presens carta pervenerit, salutem. Noveritis quod hec est forma pacis. . . . Text in *Foedera*, i.179, and *Actes de Philippe Auguste*, ii.178-85 (no. 633).

the pope and had been resumed when his decision proved unacceptable to the barons. There is no reason to suppose that, in essentials,
the barons' demands changed from first to last, though their alliance
with the Londoners in May 1215 doubtless led to some minor additions, while others were introduced in the course of negotiation. Nor
is there any reason to doubt that the barons' case rested throughout
upon their contention that Henry II, Richard and John had all
introduced 'customs' to which they had a right to object.[1]

Of the Great Charter itself we need say little. The text is one that
every mediaevalist is expected to master, and it has been the subject
of endless commentary. The vast store of learning to be found in
McKechnie's *Magna Carta* is the harvest of many generations.
Buried in this enormous apparatus, the charter tends to be obscured,
for though each clause may be put into its historical setting, something portentous is created out of a document intended to deal with
an immediate situation, a document that was given a fictitious importance by the passions of the contending parties. It is generally
agreed that the Charter was not intended to create new law but to
express what the barons conceived to be the law, which, being
written down, would save the king's subjects from arbitrary interpretations or arbitrary exactions by the king's ministers. The
charter as a whole became, however, symbolic of the curb that the
barons sought to put upon the king. That the Charter should be
offensive to the king was made inevitable by what Stubbs considered
to be 'clauses of special and transient interest',[2] those requiring the
king to surrender charters and hostages that he had demanded as
sureties and to expel his mercenaries and foreign ministers, and
especially that clause which set up a body of twenty-five barons to
secure the execution of the charter. Their immediate importance,
there can hardly be any doubt, far outweighed all the rest of the
charter. Provisions of this kind may have been unavoidable, but
they were the inept work of fearful men, of men who knew in their
hearts that only under constraint would the king live at peace with
them, though the mere threat of constraint made the king's acceptance a mockery, a mere device to gain time.

But except in the clauses aimed directly at the king and devised
as sanctions in the event of his default, the Great Charter was not
a revolutionary document. The more carefully its provisions are
examined in the light of contemporary records, the more clearly it
appears that their main object was to protect the king's subjects
from oppressions or even mere inconveniences in the administration
of the law. Thus clause 34, which was framed to restrict the use of
the writ *praecipe*, was not, as was once supposed, an attempt to restrict the jurisdiction of the royal courts, but was an attempt,

---

[1] See the king's letter to the pope of 29 May 1215 (*Foedera*, i.129: below, pp. 459-60).
[2] *Constitutional History*, i.578.

which, as it fell out, was misconceived, to simplify the procedure under which a lord claimed an action for his own court. It seems to have given no greater jurisdiction to baronial courts nor to have deprived the king's courts of any jurisdiction, though unintentionally it increased the complexity and cost of litigation.[1] Similarly clause 17, which provided that common pleas (that is actions in which the king was not concerned) should not follow the king's court but should be held at a precisely determined place, seems to have involved no great change. But at this point it may be well if we introduce some explanatory sentences, since the constitution of the courts under John presents a good many complications that need to be elucidated, not only for the understanding of this clause but in order that the later history of the courts may be made intelligible.

When John became permanently resident in England—apart from occasional military expeditions beyond the borders of the kingdom— the Common Bench and the court *coram rege* tended to coalesce, especially when the king's journeyings brought the two courts to the same place. This was no new phenomenon: the two courts had not been conceived as distinct and separate tribunals and they were served by one corps of judges.[2] However, until the Trinity term 1209 two separate tribunals were maintained in principle and largely in practice[3]; but thereafter, for more than three years, there appears to have been but a single ambulatory tribunal that followed the king.[4] It has been suggested that the suppression of the Bench is to be explained by a paucity of judges, due to the reluctance of churchmen to serve under an excommunicate king.[5] But there is little evidence of any such reluctance,[6] and John's reputation cannot be saved by blaming the embarrassments of the Interdict. The restriction of the central courts in this fashion is one of those gratuitous acts of folly of which John, for all his cleverness, was capable in a blind access of resentment. We say this, because there are two facts that cannot be dissociated: the suspension of the Bench and the exclusion of the

---

[1] N. D. Hurnard, 'Magna Carta, Clause 34' in *Powicke Studies*, pp. 157-79.

[2] Above, p. 215.

[3] There is a meagre plea roll of the Bench for the Hilary and Easter terms 1209 (*Curia Regis Rolls*, v.321-8). No plea roll has survived for the Trinity term, but the existence of two courts is shown by the surviving feet of fines, though the Bench seems to have been sitting at Westminster in June only (*Feet of Fines, Lincoln* (Pipe Roll Soc.), nos. 301-2; *Suffolk*, nos. 530-1). For the court *coram rege* between May and July see *Feet of Fines, Lincoln*, nos. 303-4; *Norfolk*, nos. 235-8; see also D. M. Stenton, 'King John and the Courts of Justice', *Procs. Brit. Academy*, xliv, p. 117.

[4] The surviving rolls from Hilary 1210 to Trinity 1212 are printed in *Curia Regis Rolls*, vol. vi. For the evidence of the feet of fines see Hunter, *Fines*, i.lvi-lvii.

[5] D. M. Stenton, *ut supra*, pp. 112, 118. Lady Stenton justifies her suggestion by references only to Jocelyn and Hugh of Wells and Eustace of Faucunberg. Jocelyn does not appear to have acted as judge after he became bishop of Bath and Wells in 1206. Hugh went abroad after the king's excommunication, but though his name is occasionally found as a judge in the preamble to a fine, he does not seem to have been regularly employed after his election to the see of Lincoln or, indeed, before it. What happened to Eustace is in doubt, but a case in 1211 does not suggest that he had left England (*Curia Regis Rolls*, vi.127).

[6] C. R. Cheney in *Bulletin John Rylands Library*, xxxi.312.

justiciar from all judicial work from May 1209 to November 1212.[1]
John's dislike of Geoffrey fitz Peter and his spite against him, his
envy of his power and wealth, were common gossip, and any indication there may be of an outward reconciliation in 1212 does not
discredit the stories the minstrel of Béthune tells of the rift between
the two men.[2] The measure of John's folly is seen in 1210 when the
business of the remaining central court was suspended from the day
he left England for Ireland until his return.[3] The explanation seems
to be that, while he would not permit the justiciar to hold a court, at
the same time he required the senior judge, Simon of Pattishall, to
accompany him overseas.[4] No doubt there was work for Simon to
do in Ireland[5]; but no responsible ruler would have been so reckless
as to disorganise the courts to gratify his pique. By the summer of
1212 John's folly had run its course, and in the Michaelmas term
1212, while there appears still to be only one central court, it is in
permanent session at Westminster. At times the king is certainly
present, but when he leaves Westminster, the justiciar presides.[6]
This arrangement was continued for another term, Hilary 1213.[7]
Then, under the threat of invasion, the king suspended the sittings
of the court[8] and it appears not to have re-assembled until after
Michaelmas when it met at Westminster, to remove in November
to Oxford.[9] The court does not seem to have become sedentary again
until the reconstitution of the Bench during the king's absence overseas. It then sat at Westminster, under the presidency of the new
justiciar, Peter des Roches, during the Hilary[10] and Easter terms 1214

---

[1] Hunter, *Fines*, i.lvi-lviii, lxiii; D. M. Stenton, *ut supra*, p. 117.

[2] *Histoire des Ducs de Normandie*, pp. 115-6. Evidence of a reconciliation is suggested by
Geoffrey fitz Peter's entertainment of the king at Ditton in May 1212 (Cole, *Documents*,
pp. 232-4) and by the grant to him of the forest of Huntingdon in July 1213 (*Rot. Chartarum*, p. 194). We cannot follow Lady Stenton's argument, *ut supra*, p. 118.

[3] *Curia Regis Rolls*, vi.50-1: Omnia placita que terminata fuerunt coram domino rege
in i. mensem post Pascha et die mercurii proximo sequenti ponuntur in respectum per
preceptum eiusdem domini regis usque a die qua transierit Saverniam in reditu suo
versus Angliam in i. mensem in eo statu quo fuerunt ipsis diebus. Here *terminare* means
'set down for hearing'.

[4] *Rot. de Liberate*, p. 188.

[5] There is evidence that the administration of the law in Ireland was reformed during
John's visit. As it was said in 1226, 'ipse duxit secum viros discretos et legis peritos, quorum
communi consilio et ad instantiam Hiberniensium statuit et precepit leges anglicanas
teneri in Hibernia' (*Patent Rolls, 1225-1232*, p. 96). There is, however, no strictly contemporary evidence: see Richardson and Sayles, *Irish Parliament in the Middle Ages*, pp.
12-15, 21-3.

[6] No rolls for this or the following term have survived, but see *Feet of Fines, Norfolk*,
nos. 270-2; *Suffolk*, no. 555.

[7] Hunter, *Fines*, i.84, 149, 253, 255; ii.69, 70; *Feet of Fines, Norfolk*, no. 273; *Suffolk*,
nos. 556-7.

[8] All pleas were adjourned 'pro exercitu Kancie' apparently until the Michaelmas
term (*Curia Regis Rolls*, vii.25, 90, 92, 95, 172, 238). There are no plea rolls for the Easter
and Trinity terms.

[9] D. M. Stenton, *ut supra*, p. 125. A single roll covers the Michaelmas term 1213 and
the Hilary term 1214 (*Curia Regis Rolls*, vii.1-112).

[10] There are fines levied before the king and dated at Westminster as at the octave
and month after Hilary (*Feet of Fines, Lincoln*, nos. 331-3; *Suffolk*, no. 562). Since the king
seems to have been at sea on the latter day (10 February) and on the Hampshire coast
on the former (20 January), his presence at Westminster is a fiction, but the court may

and apparently continued to sit there until active hostilities broke out between the king and the barons in August 1215.[1]

The vagaries and inconsistencies of John's policy towards the courts—if so polite a word as policy is permissible—cannot be explained upon rational grounds. But we must not leave the impression that the litigant was treated with an entire lack of consideration. If the king was recklessly improvident, his servants were not. Wantonly as the fabric of the judicature had been mutilated, within its limitations the convenience of the parties could be met. There was a constant demand for hearings at Westminster, a demand that is reflected in the entries on the fine rolls of sums that litigants were prepared to pay for the privilege of a trial there. The rolls are defective, but there is nothing to suggest that the popularity of trials at Westminster decreased. If we compare the entries for, say, the seventh and the sixteenth years, the suggestion is rather that the demand had increased.[2] When there was only an ambulatory court *coram rege*, litigants had, of course, to wait until its journeying brought it to Westminster,[3] and if all sittings were discontinued for a term or two terms, as in 1210 and 1213, the parties might well feel aggrieved. There is other evidence to suggest that, when litigants did not wish to come to Westminster,[4] some trouble was taken to accommodate them, so that actions to which they were parties should be tried within a reasonable distance of their homes.[5] Favours, of course, had to be paid for, and, regard the situation as indulgently as we may, there was evidently ample ground for the barons' demand that justice should not be sold or delayed or denied, with its implication that John had done all these things. Much has been read into chapter 40 of the Great Charter that is entirely without warrant, and it has been observed with some surprise that, so far as concerns what may be called the legitimate costs of litigation, little difference

well have been following him. A fine also dated at Westminster a month after Hilary is levied before the justiciar and judges (*Feet of Fines, Suffolk*, no. 563). We may conclude provisionally that, after accompanying the king, the judges returned to Westminster.

[1] There is ample evidence for the presence of the Bench at Westminster in the Easter term 1214 (Hunter, *Fines*, i.88, 149, 256; ii.70; *Feet of Fines, Lincoln*, no. 334; *Norfolk*, no. 274; *Suffolk*, no. 564). There are plea rolls for the Trinity and Michaelmas terms 1214 (*Curia Regis Rolls*, vii.113-311). If the fragmentary roll for the Hilary term 1215 (*ibid.*, pp. 312-26) belongs to the Bench, the court apparently removed to Oxford (*ibid.*, p. 235); but the Bench was at Westminster on 2 March (*Feet of Fines, Norfolk*, no. 278). Two fines of even date, the quinzaine of Easter, show the justiciar and justices at Westminster (*Feet of Fines, Lincoln*, no. 337) and the king, justiciar and another group of justices at the New Temple (*Feet of Fines, Norfolk*, no. 279) where John's itinerary shows him to be from 7 to 9 May. There are references elsewhere to the justices of the Bench in April 1215 (*Rot. Litt. Claus.*, i.203*b*) and July 1215 (*Rot. Litt. Pat.*, p. 218).

[2] In the rolls as printed, there appear to be 21 cases for 7 John and 22 cases for 16 John (though the roll for this year is incomplete), as against 13 cases for 1 John (*Rot. de Oblatis*, pp. 1-75, 371-464, 526-50).

[3] Apart from Hardy's *Itinerary*, there are available as an indication of the presence of the court at Westminster the particulars in Hunter, *Fines*, i.lvi-lix, and those given by Lady Stenton, *ut supra*, pp. 118-23.

[4] In an action of novel disseisin a plaintiff offers half a mark to have the recognition *coram domino rege* (*Rot. de Oblatis*, p. 412).

[5] D. M. Stenton, *ut supra*, pp. 118, 121-4.

is perceptible in practice before and after 1215.[1] The simple explanation of the chapter is that it offered a remedy for the arbitrary restrictions and interruptions in the administration of justice for which John had been responsible, restrictions and interruptions which are not found in later reigns. Chapter 40 must be read with chapters 17 and 18.

Chapter 17, as we have said, involved no great change. What the barons demanded was that the reconstituted Bench at Westminster should be maintained, if not there, then at some fixed place. Chapter 18, providing for regular visits of justices of assize, is unnecessarily divided from chapter 17 in the *textus receptus* of Magna Carta: both spring from one clause in the Articles of the Barons. The barons were demanding that what had already been irregularly practised should be converted into a system. In the year 1210, for example, three groups of justices, mainly local men, had visited the counties. Those who sat in the summer months presumably supplied to some extent the lack of a central court during John's absence in Ireland: their appointment, it may be observed, was due not to the king's prevision but to the initiative of the disgraced justiciar, Geoffrey fitz Peter.[2] Chapters 17 and 18, taken together, were calculated to ensure relatively cheap and speedy litigation with the minimum of inconvenience to the suitors of the county court.[3] The barons, it is to be noted, made no proposals regarding actions other than common pleas. It is not that they were uninterested in pleas in which the king was directly concerned, pleas which were almost of necessity tried *coram rege*; but they had no intention of infringing the royal prerogative. Moreover, since the king was the fountain of justice, complainants and litigants had the right of access to him as he had the duty of relieving them; and the demand that common pleas should not follow the king's court but should be tried in a fixed place, did not mean that such pleas would not be tried *coram rege*—the rolls of the king's bench, after it comes into being in 1234, are full of common pleas[4]—but that litigants would not be obliged to resort there.

We need refer to but one other chapter of the Great Charter. The technical discussions to which chapter 2 has given rise, on the obscure problem of which tenants-in-chief were considered major barons and which were not, did not, of course, trouble the men of

[1] McKechnie, *Magna Carta*, pp. 395-8.

[2] Information comes almost solely from the pipe rolls, where little is disclosed beyond the financial results of these eyres. It is clear, however, that the justices appointed by Geoffrey fitz Peter were charged *inter alia* with the duty of correcting the irregularities of an earlier group (*Pipe Roll, 12 John*, pp. xiv-xvi; *13 John*, pp. xxxiv-xxxvi). That these justices were empowered also to try civil pleas and pleas of the crown is indicated by the justiciar's writ of 3 August to the Berkshire justices (*Memoranda Roll, 1 John*, p. lxxv; again printed, D. M. Stenton, *ut supra*, p. 128). The third group of justices included Simon of Pattishall, Richard Marsh and Saer de Quency, lately returned from the Irish expedition.

[3] Chapter 19, it may be remarked, is merely a proviso to chapter 18 and is designed to release the majority of the suitors if, on the day when the county court met, the assizes had not been determined: see the note by McKechnie, *op. cit.*, pp. 282-3.

[4] Sayles, *Select Cases in the Court of King's Bench*, i.xxxviii-xl.

1215, who were not precisians and did not read into its wording more than was specified in clause 1 of the articles, that reliefs should not be arbitrary but should be paid according to a scale which was claimed to be ancient and customary. The true interest of the chapter lies in this that, as J. H. Round showed, 'the feudal extortions remedied by the Charter were not introduced by John, but are found in full existence under Henry II'.[1] The demand that these long-standing abuses should be remedied stands in the forefront of the barons' petitions.

If we were to review the Charter, chapter by chapter, in the light of the records, the same general impression would be left. Apart from the clauses aimed at immediate grievances, which were not a matter of law and which, with a few others (those, for example, concerned with Jewish money-lending),[2] were held over for maturer consideration when the charter was re-issued in 1216, there is nothing to suggest that the barons who demanded the Charter were asking for more than could be justified as reasonable reforms that experience, and not the experience of the rule of John alone, had shown to be necessary. The conception attributed somewhat unfairly to G. B. Adams, that 'the Charter is simply the programme of a pack of feudal reactionaries seeking to undermine the whole fabric of the new judicial system'[3] or, as Professor Painter described them, 'a group of disaffected barons who hated the king and lusted for lands, castles and privileges',[4] springs from multiple misconceptions of law and of fact and, it may be, a relish for paradox that have no place in sober history.

With these words we come back to the question we put earlier. How do we account for the breadth of outlook expressed in the Articles of the Barons and the Great Charter? Plainly certain clauses do reflect personal and local grievances or apprehensions. Broad principles of law are found side by side with clauses about fishing weirs in the Thames and Medway, London franchises, the hostages given by Llewellyn and the king of Scots, the expulsion of foreign

---

[1] *Magna Carta Essays*, pp. 46-77: the citation is from p. 62.

[2] The clauses concerning the Jews do not appear to embody any new principle. The courts had for long protected the widow's dower against Jewish creditors (*Curia Regis Rolls*, i.417; vii.70-1, 339). In the 'Unknown Charter', which apparently belongs to the spring of 1215, clause 11 provides that usury shall not run against the infant heir of a tenant-in-chief (McKechnie, *Magna Carta*, p. 486). It apparently follows that this restriction had not yet been established by the courts.

[3] Powicke in *Magna Carta Essays*, p. 97. This view, in fact, goes back to the 1870's at least, since Stubbs refers to 'the fashion to depreciate the value of Magna Carta as if it had sprung from the private ambition of a few selfish barons and redressed only some feudal abuses'. He contests this view and attributes 'the glory of this monument' to Langton and William Marshal (*Lectures on Early and Mediaeval English History*, pp. 345-6). Adams's own views are stated at length in *The Origins of the English Constitution*, pp. 207-74. His conclusion at p. 261 is of more interest than some of his assumptions and arguments: 'there is evident on the part of the barons an honest intention to state their rights only within the limits of the law, to deprive the king of nothing to which he could justly lay claim, or having done so to withdraw the demand, and to make their statements of the law more clear and full, more accurate and just, wherever they learned of the possibility of improvement'.   [4] Above, p. 337.

mercenaries and foreign ministers. There are the sanctions against the king himself. But when such clauses are eliminated, as they were for the most part in subsequent reissues of the Charter, there is left a considerable number of enactments of more than transitory importance, reforms of substance or restatements of the law. These are not matters of individual grievance, but such as would be propounded if men were to ask themselves on which points the common law required amendment. It was all very well to condemn in general terms the evil customs introduced by the king, his brother and his father: every king had done much the same at his coronation.[1] The barons had been driven to make specific proposals. It needed no *deus ex machina* to formulate them. This was to do no more than the knights and burgesses were to do repeatedly in the parliaments of Edward III, guided partly by their native wisdom and partly by suggestions from outside.[2] The result tended in all cases to be a rather disorderly jumble. As we have said, the importance of the Articles of the Barons and the Charter lies in their priority: they are the first of their kind, and, being the first, they deal, for the most part, with something more than personalities or trivialities. In general the barons accepted the common law as they found it and the administration of the law as they knew it. Their object was to improve both. Naturally there is much in the Charter that can be labelled 'feudal', but this is because the common law was, at that stage, pre-eminently land law.

How soon the king approached the pope with a request that he would quash the Great Charter is a matter of inference. The probabilities are that John came to no decision until the session of the council of Oxford in the latter half of July 1215, which met for agreeing the detailed application of the terms of settlement. He could not fail then to be convinced that the barons were not prepared to be conciliatory and, while conceding nothing, proposed to press their advantage and their demands to the full. Seemingly, however, it was not until 20 August that John disclosed his intention of breaking off relations with the barons: this he did at a meeting on that day, which he failed to attend as had been arranged, but to which he sent representatives.[3] So far as he was concerned the Charter was now patently a nullity, in fact if not in law, but he still desired to justify his conduct. Accordingly Peter des Roches and Pandulf, the pope's representative, soon after denounced the Charter on the ground that the barons had violated the terms of the agreement it embodied.[4] Since this conclusion was clearly disputable and was, in effect, disputed by the archbishop, Stephen Langton, the issue remained open; but any questionings were set aside by the bull *Etsi*

---

[1] Above, p. 375.
[2] Richardson and Sayles, *The Early Statutes*, pp. 21-3, 36; *Trans. R. Hist. Soc.*, 4th Ser., xxviii.33-6. [3] Richardson in *Bulletin John Rylands Library*, xxviii.429-30; xxix.192-3.
[4] Powicke in *E.H.R.*, xliv.87-93; *Bulletin John Rylands Library*, xxix.193-4.

karissimus, which arrived in England about the end of September and which, on quite different grounds from those given by Peter des Roches and Pandulf, formally relieved the king of his obligations.[1] With this bull in his hands John felt a free man again, armed with a new weapon against his enemies.

The tangled story of the last twelve months of John's life has often been told and we need not spare the space to tell it again. What is necessary for our purpose can be said in a few sentences. The effect of the bull was much less than the king could have hoped. The barons had lost all trust in Innocent's impartiality, and papal pronouncements had lost much of their authority. If the king chose to regard the Charter as dead, the barons regarded it as very much alive, and few fell away from the baronial cause.[2] The sixty-first chapter of the Charter had, indeed, provided for this very emergency. It had made provision for a baronial council of twenty-five which would co-operate with the king in implementing the agreement or, if necessity arose, would coerce him to do so. The twenty-five were an alternative to the king's government, temporary, transitory, but still a government, which acted by a sub-committee of four earls. We see them issuing their writs and administering the counties under their control.[3] At first they were not without hope that a reconciliation with the king was possible, but when it became clear that John would not yield on the essential issue of the Charter, they chose Louis of France as their king and lord in his place.[4] Louis lacked the resources, and perhaps the ability, to win the crown, and John, at his death on 19 October 1216, was still king. It was his treasure, amassed in his castles up and down the country, that had enabled him to retain his hold, but there was no means of replenishing it. The exchequer was closed and, though an irregular revenue could be exacted from the country under the king's control, this would not sustain the burden of war conducted largely with the aid of foreign mercenaries.[5] The barons had but to hold out and victory was assured, for a stalemate was all they required. Well within a month of John's death, the legate and Henry III's other advisers capitulated. The Charter was reissued on 12 November. So the threefold treaty that Innocent had denounced a short while before as base and shameful, illegal and unjust, to the utmost diminution and derogation of the king's right and honour, was again conceded to the honour of God, the exaltation of the Church and the amendment of the realm. The way had been cleared, not only by John's death, but by that of Innocent, dead three months before him.

As a practical remedy for everyday grievances experienced in the

----

[1] *Selected Letters of Innocent III*, pp. 212-9; below, pp. 461-2.
[2] *Bulletin John Rylands Library*, xxviii.438-9. Professor Painter's presentation of the facts may give a rather exaggerated notion of the desertions from the baronial cause (*Reign of King John*, pp. 369-72).   [3] *Bulletin John Rylands Library*, xxviii.433-8, 442-3.
[4] *Ibid.*   [5] Richardson, 'William of Ely', in *Trans. R. Hist. Soc.*, 4th Ser., xv.55-8.

prosaic England of 1215 the Great Charter was reasonably satis-factory. To criticise it minutely, clause by clause, as is sometimes done, from the standpoint of some timeless Utopia is unhelpful. In a sense it is a hasty, imperfect draft, which was revised from time to time until it reached its final form in 1225, the form in which it appears upon the statute-book.[1] It belongs to its time and place, and much of it became so antiquated that it was either forgotten or re-interpreted to fit different circumstances. This is the common fate of legal enactments. But the Charter was no ordinary enactment: it became a symbol and assumed mystic properties. It became the symbol of the rule of law, the vindication of the right of the barons to maintain the law and to be consulted on changes in the law. The mystical aura surrounding the Charter was the result of the attitude of the kings from John to Edward I. To John the Charter was a shameful invasion of his rights. To Henry III it was a boon, to be sold for money, or granted, as it was to Ireland, as a reward for good behaviour.[2] In Edward's excited imagination it was a fetter from which he must free himself.[3] It was not until the reign of Edward II that the Charter was unfeignedly accepted,[4] by which time it had become so integrated into the statutory law that it would have been impossible to undo it, though its undoing had been con-ceived by the failing intelligence of the king's father.

The exaggerated importance placed by kings upon the Charter inevitably gave it an exaggerated value in the eyes of the barons, and the struggle for the charters did much to secure for the baronage that position in the English parliament which largely determined the lines of its evolution, with a chamber of peers as a tribunal and a lower house of commons to voice the grievances of the people.[5] But, though these results may spring remotely from John's obduracy, they should not affect our judgement of the contestants of 1215. The barons were not the fathers of the constitution, nor was John its enemy. What the barons did do—and this is their merit—was to point the way to the rule of law. That there were personal wrongs which stimulated the opposition to John's rule and its vagaries, we cannot doubt. But these find little place in the Articles of the Barons. The wrongs suffered by the king of Scots and by Llewellyn have a place, the wrongs suffered by those barons who had been forced to give hostages and bonds to the king have a place; but there is nothing of the wrongs suffered by the family of Briouze, by Eustace

[1] Richardson and Sayles, *The Early Statutes*, pp. 11-15.

[2] The concluding article of the reissue of 1225 puts the matter without disguise: Pro hac autem concessione . . . dederunt nobis quintam decimam partem omnium mobilium suorum (*Select Charters*, p. 350). To Ireland the charter was sent 'in signum fidelitatis vestre tam preclare, tam insignis' so that 'libertatibus regno nostro Anglie a patre nostro et nobis concessis de gracia nostra et dono in regno nostro Hibernie gaudeatis vos et vestri heredes in perpetuum' (*Patent Rolls, 1216-1225*, p. 31).

[3] *Trans. R. Hist. Soc.*, 4th Ser., xxiii.133-6; *Speculum*, xxiv.75 *n*.

[4] *Trans. R. Hist. Soc., ut supra*, pp. 150-1; *Speculum*, xxiv.69-70.

[5] *Trans. R. Hist. Soc.*, 4th Ser., xxviii.25-7.

de Vesci[1] or Robert fitz Walter or any other victims of John's vengeance or lust. Despite all the welter of hatred that surrounded the king, the demands of the barons are singularly impersonal. They object to arbitrary government, to capricious exactions, and for a remedy they seek the limitation of the powers of the Crown and a statement of the obligations of the king in those matters where his authority had been abused. They are not, however, consciously seeking to limit the royal prerogative. They are looking backward to a golden age when kings did not abuse their office. They are seeking to restore, not to reconstruct or to invent. They believe, to use Bracton's words, that the king's power should be tempered by law and that law is above the king.[2] John's view was different. If he made any concession to the barons, this was an act of grace, and in this view he had the support of the pope. It was under duress that he had conceded the Great Charter and it was on this ground that the pope quashed it. These two irreconcilable principles were not harmonised when the Charter was reissued. They remained to defeat all the ingenuity of Bracton to resolve them into a coherent theory of sovereignty. He vacillates between the conception of a king who is answerable only to God and that of a king who, if he rejects the bridle of the law, must be bridled by his court, by the earls and the barons[3]—the king, indeed, of real life, a king such as John and Henry III. Nor was Bracton singular in failing to find a solution. The dilemma is inherent in any form of authoritarian government, indeed, in any form of government that confides power to an executive, in name a servant, in reality a ruler. John doubtless was guilty of many breaches of the moral law; but it would be hard to establish that he had broken the law of the land or, to use the words the barons used in 1212, the constitutions of the realm.[4] When he refused, as he did for many months, to commit himself to any formal acceptance of the demand for reform, he may have been unreasonable, but his refusal was not unlawful. John's error was political, in prevaricating, in persisting in his refusal until he tried the patience of the barons beyond endurance. If the Charter of November 1216 was consistent with the king's right and honour,[5] the same terms con-

---

[1] For the evidence for John's advances to Eustace de Vesci's wife see K. Norgate, *John Lackland*, p. 289. It is late and unsatisfactory and no deduction can be drawn as to when the incident took place; Miss Norgate's comments are vitiated by her prejudice.

[2] Bracton, fo. 34: Rex habet superiorem, Deum scilicet, item legem, per quam factus, est rex; fo. 107b: Temperet igitur potentiam suam per legem, que frenum est potentie (Woodbine, ii.110, 305).

[3] Exercere igitur debet rex potestatem iuris, sicut Dei vicarius et minister in terra (fo. 107b). Rex habet superiorem . . . item curiam suam, videlicet comites et barones, quia comites dicuntur quasi socii regis, et qui socium habet, habet magistrum. Et ideo si rex fuerit sine freno, id est sine lege, debent ei frenum apponere (fo. 34: Woodbine, ii.110).

[4] Richardson and Sayles, *Irish Parliament*, p. 287: nec audierimus eumdem dominum nostrum contra constitutiones regni sui . . . deliquisse.

[5] Cf. Innocent III's letter of 24 August 1215 (*Utinam in persecutione*): statuemus ea . . . per que . . . rex suo sit iure ac honore contentus (*Selected Letters of Innocent III*, p. 219).

ceded in 1214 would not have been derogatory. To stand upon an abstract right, which he conceived he possessed, of refusing concessions, until at last the issue was decided by the threat of civil war, was political ineptitude, just as it was politically inept of Innocent to sustain John in his disavowal of the Charter after the representative of the papacy had assented to this threefold treaty. John, indeed, was not bound in law to concede the demands of the barons and his concession had been made under duress. But this point of law—a point barely more than one of procedure, once it had been recognised that concessions had to be made—the point upon which both John and Innocent took their stand, was, in the circumstances, a frivolity. This was one of those legal issues which it is unwise to press to their logical conclusions, for the reason that behind it lay a political issue in which any code of law was an irrelevance. But law was a cloak and a pretext. No upright man would have resorted to the deceptions to which John resorted in the summer of 1215, and in his dishonesty he was counselled and abetted by Pandulf, Innocent's familiar.

If, however, we are to judge John on this issue, let us retain a sense of proportion. Clearly enough, if it was depravity on John's part that he did not gladly accept the demands of the barons and that he sought the annulment of the Charter, it was depravity on Edward I's part that he came to resent the Charter and that he also sought its annulment. Yet Edward, not only to Stubbs but to almost all historians, is a conventionally 'good' king. Between the conduct of the two kings, if the course of their actions is examined without prejudice, there seems, in fact, little to choose. In each case the Charter was the symbol rather than the gravamen of the quarrel, though John had more ground for objection in the clauses that affected him personally. But the Charter did not decide the great underlying issue. If it afforded a rallying cry to those who opposed the arbitrary acts of kings, neither its original ratification nor its many re-issues and confirmations effected a settlement or sensibly modified the attitude of the contestants. The same quarrel that brought John and his barons to armed conflict was fought out again in a different guise under Henry III at Oxford, Lewes and Evesham, and was renewed in the closing years of Edward I.

If John remains a king of ill repute, he is not the only English king who deserves a bad name and for much the same reasons. But before we weigh his failings as a king, his personal failings, so far as we can be certain of them, must be put aside. By the standards of Victorian England, not only John, but Henry II and Eleanor of Aquitaine, Richard I, Philip Augustus, Innocent III, even Stephen Langton, would have been personally unacceptable. This is doubtless to the credit of the later nineteenth century, but the moral standards of one age will not help us to judge the actors of another. Kings and statesmen must be judged by their greater actions, viewed against the circumstances of their time. John was involved in three great issues. His quarrel with the Roman Church, which scandalised monastic writers, carried no guilt with it, and it earned the approbation of his subjects. In any case, he gained his point. If it seems harsh to condemn him for the loss of Normandy, for his military failures, let us reflect how different the judgement of history would have been on Napoleon I and Napoleon III, had they been victorious in the end. A military monarch is inexorably condemned if he is defeated. But the major count against John is that he was not prudent or considerate enough to live on good terms with his barons and that he provoked them to civil war over an issue not worth an armed conflict. In lacking the wisdom to concede in due time what must inevitably be conceded, he lacked the essential quality of a wise ruler and, indeed, of a righteous ruler, for political wisdom is the righteousness of princes.

APPENDIXES

CORONATIONS AND CROWN-WEARINGS
BEFORE THE CONQUEST

VIDENCE that the anointing of kings was an established practice
in England comes from the last quarter of the eighth century,
not very much later than the evidence for the existence of the
ceremony among the Franks, which commences in 751 with Pepin.
The two significant texts are the canons of 786-7, to which agreement was obtained by the papal legates George and Theophylact
from all the ecclesiastical and secular authorities in England,[1] and
secondly the notice by some northern annalist (preserved in part by
Simeon of Durham and in part in three of the Saxon Chronicles)
relating to the consecration of Eardwulf of Northumbria in 796.[2] In
the first document the language of the twelfth canon does not permit
us to suppose that any new ceremony was contemplated. *Ordinatio
regum* is mentioned as an accepted rite, and the primary purpose of
the canon is to prevent the consecration of any king who was not
the issue of a canonical marriage. This is clear from the words: 'nec
christus Domini esse valet . . . qui ex legitimo non fuerit connubio
generatus.' In prescribing penalties for regicide emphasis is laid
upon the sacred character of the king 'quia christus Domini est', and
the canon concludes with a reminder of the fate that had frequently
overtaken regicides in England. The question of origins is inevitably
difficult, but there is no obvious reason why the introduction of
royal anointings into England should be ascribed to the example of
the Franks.[3] What seems certain is that in 786-7 the English rite was
already of some antiquity. The second document gives an indication
of the nature of the ceremony. Eardwulf is raised [to the throne and
invested] with the insignia of royalty[4] and consecrated in the church
of St. Peter's, York, before the altar of St. Paul. There officiated
Archbishop Eanbald of York, Æthelberht of Hexham, Hybald of
Lindisfarne and Baldwulf of Whithorn. The form of words might lead
us to suppose that there was a double ceremony, a secular investiture
and an ecclesiastical consecration, but in any case there would seem
no doubt that the elements of later coronation ceremonies were

---

[1] Haddan and Stubbs, *Councils and Ecclesiastical Documents*, iii.447-62.
[2] Simeon of Durham, *Historia Regum*, pp. 57-8; Saxon Chronicles, *s.a.* 795 (ed. Thorpe,
i.103; ed. Plummer, i.57).
[3] As asserted by Schramm, *History of the English Coronation*, p. 15. Bouman challenges
this view, *Sacring and Crowning*, p. xi.
[4] *Historia Regum*, p. 58: 'regni infulis est sublimatus'.

present. Whether the insignia of royalty included a crown we are left to conjecture. Unless, however, the references by Simeon of Durham to the crowning of Æthelred of Northumbria (774) and the 'diadema regni Merciorum' borne by Coenwulf (796), as well as his statement that, after conquering Kent, Coenwulf took 'coronam in capite sceptrumque in manu', are all misguided embellishments of a later age,[1] the presumption must be that Eardwulf too was crowned.

It may be worth remarking that royal consecrations are rarely mentioned in the Saxon Chronicles, not because they were rare but presumably because they were commonplace. As Plummer pointed out, there is good evidence for the coronation of Eadred in 946 and of Eadwig in 955, although the Chronicles are silent.[2] It follows that, although the first consecration to be mentioned is that of Ecgfrith in 787, there is no justification for the inference that he was the first English king to be consecrated.[3] If we seek for a reason for the entry, it may well be the unusual nature of the consecration, for Ecgfrith was made king of Mercia while his father Offa was still alive. It may be, too, that the reason why the consecration of Eardwulf is noticed in one group of Chronicles is because that ceremony also had hitherto unknown features.

We must not suppose that, because English kings were anointed, and presumably crowned, in the eighth century, there was as yet any formal coronation office. At most there were available to the officiating bishops formulas for royal consecrations which were the common property of the Western Church.[4] And though we may doubt whether in their origin royal consecrations in England—or ordinations, as the canon of 786-7 calls them—owed anything to Frankish practice, yet from an early date continental texts became known in England and English texts upon the Continent.[5] While we can be certain only of the fact that King Eardwulf sought refuge at the court of Charlemagne when he was expelled in 808,[6] this fact in itself makes it probable that his period of exile under King Æthelred, which lasted for four or five years,[7] had also been spent at the Frankish court and that he had learnt much of the way in which the Franks regarded kingship. That the bonds between Northumbria and the Frankish kingdom were for some decades very close admits of no doubt.[8] It may well be, therefore, that the ceremony observed at Eardwulf's coronation owed something to Frankish practice. The so-called First and Second Recensions of the English Coronation Office and the parallel continental texts show how closely the tradi-

---

[1] *Ibid.*, pp. 45, 58-9. We may add to these instances Raedwulf who in 844 'successit in regnum, qui confestim diademate insignitus' (Wendover, *Flores*, i.283, from otherwise unknown Northern annals).   [2] *Two Saxon Chronicles*, ii.145-6, 149-50.
[3] Schramm, *loc. cit.*; Stenton, *Anglo-Saxon England*, p. 217.
[4] Cf. Bouman, *op. cit.*, pp. 2-8.   [5] *Ibid.*, pp. 9-15, 17-21.
[6] Haddan and Stubbs, *op. cit.*, iii.561, 563, 566-7.
[7] Simeon of Durham, *Historia Regum*, pp. 52, 57-8.
[8] Stenton, *op. cit.*, pp. 93-4.

tions of England and France had been bound together by the tenth century.[1] None of these texts can be dated with any precision, but we can give a precise date to an event of some significance, the marriage and coronation of Judith, the Frankish wife of King Æthelwulf of Wessex, in 856. Since the ceremony took place at Verberie (near Senlis), it was not, of course, a royal coronation in the ordinary sense of the term, but it set a precedent for the crowning of English queens and so influenced the English rite.[2]

The First Recension of the Coronation Office is unlikely to have been employed at any coronation in England,[3] and of it we need say no more. We are, however, much concerned with the Second Recension which has at least some claim to be regarded as a historical document; but this claim depends primarily upon the supposed assertion of the hagiographer who wrote the 'Vita Oswaldi' about the year 1000, that this form of office was followed when Edgar was crowned in 973.[4] Now the 'Vita Oswaldi' has very considerable historical value. It reflects faithfully the ideas and manners of the late tenth century and it embodies much material that otherwise would be lost. But the writer was careless and muddled in the use of his sources.[5] His reliability may be gauged by his statement that the half-brothers Edward (the Martyr) and Ethelred (the Unready) were both sons of the same mother Ælfthryth.[6] Elsewhere he states categorically that Dunstan died after the battle of Maldon,[7] whereas he was dead more than three years earlier. These events happened within perhaps a dozen years of the time when the 'Vita' was being written: we need to be cautious in accepting anything the author tells us of a remoter date.

That Edgar was crowned with ceremony at Bath at Whitsuntide 973 cannot be questioned, although the circumstances in which this happened have for long been a matter of conjecture. In the Saxon Chronicles there are two, possibly independent, statements, one in verse and one in prose, that he was then hallowed king—'gehalgod to cyninge'[8]—and there is the third, diffuse, statement, unrelated to

---

[1] The principal texts are printed by Schramm in *Zeitschrift der Savigny-Stiftung*, liv, Kan. Abt., xxiii.201-42.

[2] *Annales de St. Bertin*, pp. 89-90; M.H.G., *Leges*, i.450-1 (*Patrologia Latina*, cxxxviii.639-42); *Asser's Life of King Alfred* (ed. Stevenson), p. 11; but see *ibid.*, pp. 200-2.

[3] Of the three known manuscripts, with varying texts, one, the so-called Leofric Missal, is undoubtedly of continental origin; two, the Egbert Pontifical and the Lanalet Pontifical are of English origin. Bouman (*op. cit.*, pp. 156-7) has argued that the 'Order of Egbert' was actually used in England. He does not explain why the king was not to be crowned but to have a helmet (*galeum*) placed on his head, although English kings had been crowned since the eighth century. The three texts have been collated by L. G. W. Legg, *English Coronation Records*, pp. 3-9, and by Schramm, *ut supra*, pp. 221 sqq.

[4] *Vita Oswaldi*, pp. 436-8; reprinted by Schramm, *ut supra*, pp. 231-3.

[5] With the suggested attribution of the 'Vita Oswaldi' to Byrhtferth we need not deal. To account for some of the many difficulties in the text it has been suggested that the primitive 'Vita' was expanded in a Mercian monastery (D. J. V. Fisher in *Cambridge Historical Journal*, x.257-9). But to whomsoever the confusions and contradictions are to be attributed, the passage with which we are principally concerned seems to be part of the original and has certainly been regarded as authoritative. [6] *Vita Oswaldi*, p. 429.

[7] *Ibid.*, pp. 456-7. [8] A.S. Chronicle, ed. Thorpe, i.224-5; ed. Plummer, i.118-9.

the Chronicles, in the 'Vita Oswaldi'. This purports to give a detailed account of Edgar's coronation, without, however, mentioning the year or the place, an account that has been accepted not only as a true description of what happened in 973 but also as evidence that the Second Recension was devised for the occasion.[1] Now there is no question but that the story in the 'Vita Oswaldi' is derived in large part from the Second Recension.[2] The author himself makes this quite clear. He follows the text of the office closely, but he stops short at copying out the long prayers. He therefore summarises that part of the office in this fashion:

Explicitis promissionibus stetit archipraesul et oravit pro eo orationes quae in illorum libris scriptae sunt.

That is, he refers to a pontifical for the text of the prayers. The plural *illorum* is explained by his next sentence:

Deinde secundam dixit Oswaldus, Christi minister, satis eleganter post haec, sicut constituit pater cuius imperiis omnes parebant.

Presumably he means that Dunstan, the *archipraesul*, recited the first prayer, *Te invocamus, Domine*, and Oswald an *alia*. He assumes that the two archbishops will have had similar pontificals, such as the example that was available to him at Ramsey Abbey. This, of course, is excellent evidence for the presence there, about the year 1000, of a pontifical containing a copy of the Second Recension, but precisely nothing more. As evidence for the date of that recension the author's statement is worthless: it may have been in existence in 973; it may have been composed later. That issue must be determined on quite different grounds.[3] If, however, there had been in existence in 973 two pontificals containing the same form of office, the obvious inference must be that the office had been composed well before that date. If, as has been supposed, Dunstan had composed the Second Recension for the ceremony of 973, there is no process known to us whereby it could have found its way into other bishops' books by Whitsunday of that year. The process by which liturgical texts were transmitted in the tenth century may be imperfectly understood, but there is no evidence of rapid diffusion or speedy duplication.

The context into which our hagiographer chose to thrust his extracts from the coronation office was drawn from a very different document, a document so incongruous that we may be quite sure he did not invent it, though he mishandled it sadly. Its nature may

---

[1] Schramm, *ut supra*, pp. 178-80, 221; *History of the English Coronation*, p. 20; Bouman, *op. cit.*, p. 157. Dean Armitage Robinson had previously suggested that the office might have been prepared for Edgar's coronation in 959 (*Journal of Theological Studies*, xix.72).

[2] This seems to have been first indicated by Sir James Ramsay, *Foundations of England*, i.319-20, 328.

[3] As Schramm indeed argues, *Zeitschrift der Savigny-Stiftung, ut supra*, pp. 167-77.

best be demonstrated by quoting the final sentences. Since the writer appears to have improved upon his original and his choice of language makes for obscurity, we substitute an English translation:

The queen entertained the abbots and abbesses at a feast. Clad in a robe of fine linen, embroidered with precious stones and pearls, she was raised high above the other matrons, as befitted her royal dignity [because after the death of the great ealdorman, she had been deemed worthy to enter the royal chamber]. When the splendid nuptials of the royal wedding came to an end, the whole company returned to their own place, blessing the king and the queen likewise and wishing them the tranquillity of peace, such as kings of old had merited.[1]

We have placed one clause between crotchets since it interrupts the narrative and is clearly an interpolation, derived perhaps from a gloss to the original document. In the 'Vita' it is certainly superfluous, because some pages previously the marriage of Edgar to Ælfthryth and her former marriage to the ealdorman Æthelwold had been mentioned.[2] But this interpolation gives us the clue to the nature of the document which the author chose for conflation with the coronation office, a description of Edgar's marriage in 964 or 965.[3] How the incompatibility of the two documents conflated in the 'Vita' has hitherto escaped remark we find it difficult to understand.

Nor is this the only incompatibility. The king, so the 'Vita' states, was already crowned when he entered the church.[4] If he were so, it would be quite inconsistent with the rubrics of the coronation office, and to get over the difficulty the author was forced to interpolate the text before him. He therefore represented the king as removing the crown from his head when, as the rubrics prescribed, he prostrated himself before the altar.[5] The author did not, however, read the office with sufficient care. All the versions that have come down to us provide for the coronation of the queen[6] and we cannot suppose

---

[1] *Vita Oswaldi*, p. 438: Regina vero cum abbatibus et abbatissis convivium habuit, quae vestita carbasea veste erat, circumamicta varietate lapillorum et margaritarum, suffulta elatius caeteris matronis, quam compsit regalis dignitas [quoniam post mortem pretiosi ducis thalamum regis promeruit introire]. Peractis egregiis nuptiis regalis thori, reversi sunt omnes in locum suum benedicentes regem pariter et reginam, pacis eis tranquillitatem desiderantes quam antiqui promeruerunt reges.   [2] *Ibid.*, pp. 428-9.

[3] The year given in the Chronicles is 965, but this appears to be at least a year late. Æthelwold had died in 962. See Plummer, *op. cit.*, ii.158-9, and Harmer, *Anglo-Saxon Writs*, p. 551.

[4] *Vita Oswaldi*, p. 436: Coronatum atque electum regem gloria et honore perduxerunt ad ecclesiam. The significance of these words was pointed out by Armitage Robinson, *ut supra*, p. 57.

[5] *Vita Oswaldi*, p. 437: Cumque pervenissent in ecclesia et rex ante altare se prosternendo deponendo prius diademam de capite . . . The corresponding rubric reads: Perveniens ad ecclesiam prosternat se coram altare.

[6] For a list of texts see Bouman, *op. cit.*, pp. 18-19. Ramsay, *op. cit.*, p. 320, argued that Queen Ælfthryth must have been consecrated, but assigned the ceremony to 973. Nicholas, a monk of Worcester, writing to Eadmer about the year 1120, stated that Edgar's first wife, Æthelflæd, 'licet legaliter sibi desponsata et sibi copulata, regni consors et domina Angliae esset, non tamen uncta in reginam esset', but that Ælfthryth 'sacram unctionem cum corona suscepit' (*Memorials of St. Dunstan*, p. 423). Æthelflæd does not seem to have been entitled queen, while Ælfthryth undoubtedly was (Stevenson's note to *Asser's Life of*

that the Ramsey Abbey copy was deficient in this particular. But although, if the author's narrative is taken at its face value, the queen must be assumed to be present, not one word is said of her consecration or coronation or, indeed, of her taking any part in the religious ceremony, although she and the king preside at the subsequent feasts. Is it not clear that, far from possessing any knowledge of the ceremony he professed to describe, the author conflated two unrelated and disparate documents and concocted a story that should have deceived no one, so clumsily did he do his work? He himself had no desire to deceive, but his knowledge was very limited and his critical sense of a low order. He was concerned solely with magnifying the part played by Oswald in the affairs of the kingdom: accuracy or even probability was of little moment. There is no escape from the conclusion that, for the framework in which to place his account of Edgar's consecration, he chose, by an unlucky mistake, the description of a wedding. The wedding ceremony was of so special a kind as to explain his error. But before we give the explanation, it will be well to set down what can be known of the actual circumstances of Edgar's coronation.

None of the Saxon Chronicles that have come down to us says a word of Edgar's consecration on his accession in 959, and it has been generally assumed that the ceremony of 973 was the first and only consecration to which he submitted.[1] But we have seen that the silence of the Chronicles has no significance. Otherwise, indeed, we should be forced to conclude that no king had been consecrated since Athelstan[2] and very few before him. Nor does the 'Vita Oswaldi', however misleading it may be, imply that Edgar was not crowned before 973: it implies the contrary. Before the author describes the king's coronation, to which, we must remember, he gives no date, he speaks of him as already *coronatus* or *sceptris et diadematibus pollens*.[3] Nor is this all. In recording Edgar's death he says: 'peractis plurimis annis postquam consecratus est . . . repente rapitur ex hoc seculo.' No deduction could safely be made from the author's own erratic chronology, but here we can be reasonably sure that he is reproducing the source which gave him the exact date of the king's death, viii. Idus Julii.[4] If Edgar died many years after his consecration, obviously this is not a reference to the ceremony of 973, for he died little more than two years later. And even if the testimony of

---

King Alfred, p. 202). This suggests that the union with Æthelflæd was in some way irregular, though her issue was regarded as legitimate, which may explain a great deal. Nicholas claimed to have derived his information from chronicles, popular ballads and other writings. He is certainly not to be completely trusted, but he may be right in this particular.

[1] Stubbs, following Robertson, *Historical Essays*, pp. 203-15, evidently had his doubts (*ibid.*, p. ci).

[2] A.S. Chronicle, *s.a.* 924-5 (ed. Thorpe, i.198-9; ed. Plummer, i.104-5). The consecration of Eadred is mentioned by Florence, *Chronicon* (i.134), but not in any surviving version of A.S. Chronicle, where no other consecration is mentioned until Ethelred, *s.a.* 979.

[3] *Vita Oswaldi*, pp. 425, 436.   [4] *Ibid.*, p. 443.

the 'Vita Oswaldi' was not enough, standing by itself, the fact of Edgar's early coronation is surely put beyond doubt by the definite statement of Æthelweard that he was crowned at the beginning of his reign. 'Eadwig', he says, 'tenuit namque quadriennio per regnum amandus, denique Eadgar coronatur in regnum.' Æthelweard continues with an obscure Latin rendering of part of the metrical account of Edgar's reign to be found in the Saxon Chronicles A, B and C. This describes the ceremony at Whitsuntide 973 when 'coronatur anax', but the initial statement that Edgar was crowned on his accession stands unaffected.[1] There is, moreover, this difficulty which those who have put forward the thesis that Edgar's coronation was delayed for fourteen years do not seem to have faced. The traditional place of coronation was already, before his accession, Kingston[2]: that the ceremony of 973 should take place at Bath in itself suggests that it was not a coronation in the ordinary modern sense of the word, one that inaugurated a reign, without which a king was not *christus Domini*, not a king *consecratus a Deo*, a king that the Church could recognise. There is a further difficulty which seems fatal to the hypothesis of a delayed coronation. If the source lying behind the 'Vita Oswaldi' which described Edgar's marriage ceremony referred to Ælfthryth as queen—and it is difficult to suppose the contrary— and if Nicholas of Worcester was warranted in his statement that she 'sacram unctionem cum corona suscepit',[3] then the hypothesis requires us to believe that Ælfthryth was anointed and crowned queen nine years before Edgar was anointed and crowned king. This is quite incredible. But if we reject as late and unreliable this evidence for Ælfthryth's coronation, then we must conclude that she was not queen before 973. This conclusion would, however, be incompatible with the contemporary statement that Ælfthryth was associated with Edgar in the task of reforming the monasteries, her special care being the nuns.[4] Are we to suppose that this association was possible though Ælfthryth was not the acknowledged queen? And there was only one way in which Edgar could acknowledge her as queen: she must be anointed and crowned. On this point, at least, our sources are consistent and serve to confirm one another. We conclude, and we submit that the conclusion is inevitable, that Edgar was at least twice anointed: at the beginning of his reign over Mercia in 957 and quite possibly also in 959 at his *ordinatio* as king of England and again in 973 at what could quite properly be called a *coronatio*.[5] How

---

[1] *The Chronicle of Æthelweard* (ed. Campbell), p. 55.

[2] If we can trust Ralf de Diceto (*Historical Works*, i.140), from Edward the Elder onward. For Athelstan, Eadred and Eadwig see Plummer, *op. cit.*, ii.133, 145, 149. For Edmund we apparently have to rely upon Diceto, i.146. Again, Ethelred was crowned at Kingston.   [3] Above, p. 405, n. 6.   [4] Cockayne, *Leechdoms*, iii.438-40.

[5] It seems improbable that he would not have been anointed at his *ordinatio* as king of Mercia in 957. We know too little of contemporary conceptions to dismiss as improbable a second anointing at his *ordinatio* in 959. On repeated anointings see further below, p. 411.

ordinatio and *coronatio* were distinguished we will shortly explain. Here let us note that, though *coronationes* were, we believe, frequent, that of 973 was exceptional. This we must infer not only from the notices of it in the Chronicles, but from phrases that occur in two of Edgar's charters which purport to come from 973. One of these charters makes the king speak of the first year of his *consecratio*,[1] the other of the first year of his *dedicatio*.[2] The text of neither, in the form in which it has come down to us, is acceptable, but it is difficult to believe that the dating clauses they embody were a complete invention at some later time.

Since our conclusions in this matter run directly contrary to current teaching, which not only has postponed Edgar's coronation but has suggested a romantic explanation for the postponement,[3] it may be well if we emphasise that this romance derives, not from any contemporary witness, but from twelfth-century legends. There is no obvious reason why we should prefer late legends to the authority of one who must have known the king well and who must be identified, if not with that reforming prelate, Bishop Æthelwold, then with a writer in his immediate circle, who has left us a vernacular account of Edgar's dealings with the monasteries.[4] This narrative was apparently intended for the instruction of nuns and it may be stigmatised as a work of edification; and since Edgar is in a sense the hero of the story, we should not expect to find anything to his dispraise. Surely enough there is not a word of his misspent youth, as the later legend runs, but much that seems incompatible with the legend. As a boy, it would seem, Edgar appeared to Æthelwold, whose standards were strict, suited to the monastic life, and though Edgar felt that he had no vocation, even then he resolved that the conditions he found at Abingdon must be improved when he was given the opportunity. Not only did he carry out this boyish resolution, but immediately upon becoming king—and we must remember that he was no more than fourteen at the time of his accession to the throne of Mercia— having taken counsel, he proceeded to his task of establishing reformed monasteries over the country. We are told that in the latter years of his short life he supervised the monasteries personally, while his queen Ælfthryth supervised the nunneries. What we are not told is that this devotion to religion was the fruit of repentance, that a wicked man had turned away from his wickedness and had saved his soul alive. If the writer could conceivably have said these things, surely he would have said them in a work of edification. Your homilist does not usually miss such an opportunity, nor was this particular homilist squeamish in his denunciation of the fleshly sins of the canons whom Edgar had cast out in favour of monks. Must we not conclude that nothing was said of Edgar's sins and repentance for

---

[1] Kemble, no. 584; Birch, no. 1301.   [2] Kemble, no. 595; Birch, no. 1307.
[3] Cf. Stenton, *Anglo-Saxon England*, p. 363.   [4] Cokayne, *op. cit.*, iii.432-44.

the simple reason that there was nothing to say? And then, again, the writer says nothing about any scruples on Edgar's part in submitting to anointing and crowning because he felt unworthy. Is this another opportunity lost by the homilist or another example of an idle invention of which he knew nothing? Need we supply the answer? But we may add that of the gossip that has been repeated, and indeed elaborated, by modern historians other contemporaries appear equally ignorant. Edgar to them is a hero king—and, indeed, we know enough of him to know that he was of heroic proportions— but we should expect them at least to refute malicious gossip if it were current.

We have referred somewhat lengthily to this contemporary narrative because it lends support to conclusions we have drawn independently of it and because its testimony does not seem to have been given adequate consideration. We turn now to explain the difference between *ordinatio* and *coronatio*. When Bishop Gilbert of Limerick, in the early years of the twelfth century, was describing, for the benefit of the Irish episcopate, a model church organisation, such as he had seen in France and England, he was at pains to explain the distinction between a primate and other archbishops. A primate, he says, is so superior that it falls upon him alone to ordain the king and to crown him on the three solemn festivals: 'solus ex eis qui regem ordinat et in tribus solemnitatibus coronat'.[1] We have already seen that *ordinatio* is the word used in the canons of 786-7 for the inaugural consecration of a king. What then is a *coronatio*? As many later texts will tell us, it is the ceremony we find it convenient to distinguish as a crown-wearing.[2] It is a commonplace of English history that William the Conqueror wore his crown on the three great festivals at Winchester, Westminster and Gloucester,[3] and it has been suggested, on the evidence of Edward the Confessor's charters, that he was but continuing the practice of his predecessor.[4] It would appear to have escaped notice that this suggestion is confirmed by the Ramsey Abbey chronicler, who states that Edward wore his crown at Westminster on the Christmas day before his death. It may be well to give the chronicler's words in full:

rex Edwardus in die Natalis Domini, facto Londoniae generali totius fere nobilitatis conventu, cum gloria et honore regio coronatus est.[5]

The chronicler was, it is true, writing a century or so after the event, but he was using contemporary documents. There is no reason why he should invent this story, and since he adheres elsewhere as closely

---

[1] *Patrologia Latina*, clix.1003. The bishop's Irish name was Gilla-easpuic, latinised as Gillebertus. [2] See *E.II.R.*, lxi.309-10 and p. 411, n. 5, below.
[3] Peterborough Chronicle, *s.a.* 1086 (Thorpe, i.355; Plummer, i.219).
[4] Larson, *The King's Household in England before the Norman Conquest*, pp. 200-1.
[5] *Chronicon Abbatiae Rameseiensis*, p. 178. See also William of Malmesbury, *Gesta Regum*, i.280: In Natale Domini apud Lundoniam coronatus est.

as possible to the originals before him, there are no grounds for rejecting this part of his account of the last days of Edward's life, which otherwise accords with the differently phrased account in the Saxon Chronicles.[1] It would, in fact, have been remarkable if the Conqueror had not, in crown-wearing as in so much else, followed the precedent of the king whose heir he claimed to be. Nor must we regard the Confessor as an innovator. The 'Vita Oswaldi' points to a similar practice in the tenth century. At Whitsuntide, we are told, it was customary for the king to summon the archbishops, bishops, abbots, abbesses, ealdormen, sheriffs and judges.[2] Previously the author had described a similar assembly at Easter, when all the leading prelates, ealdormen and thegns were royally entertained by the king.[3] The inference from these passages, that already in the tenth century there were crown-wearings at the principal feasts, is supported by the Northern annals which Roger of Wendover has embodied and, it is to be feared, embellished in his 'Flores Historiarum'.[4] Since there is in other Northern annals confirmation for much of what he says,[5] we need have little hesitation in accepting as historical the substance, if not every detail, of his relation.[6] He tells us that, when Edgar granted Lothian to Kenneth II of Scotland, he made it a condition that every year at the principal feasts, when the king of England wore his crown, the king of Scots should come and celebrate the feast with the other great men of the realm. We suggest that, in the light of these two independent sources, we can accept crown-wearings, at least as early as Edgar's reign, as an established fact, and we shall shortly find that there is reason to believe that the ceremony had been instituted yet earlier.

Now at the Conqueror's crown-wearings the *laudes* were sung and this undoubtedly was a custom to be found in Normandy as well as among the Franks[7]; but it does not follow that the custom was not to be found equally among the English. What other meaning are we to give to the words of the Ramsey chronicler: King Edward wore his crown *cum gloria et honore regio*? It has been said that 'there were no pre-Norman *laudes*' and that the Normans introduced the *laudes* into England[8]; but while it is true that no English pre-Conquest text

---

[1] Chronicles, *s.a.* 1065 (Thorpe, i.332, 334; Plummer, i.192-3).

[2] *Vita Oswaldi*, p. 436: 'Instabat eo tempore sacrum tempus quo more solito archiepiscopi et alii omnes advenirent sacerdotes praeclari et conspicui abbates et religiosae abbatissae ac cuncti duces, praefecti et judices. . . .' *Praefectus* translates *gerefa* (Liebermann, *Gesetze der Angelsachsen*, i.138-9): it is a synonym for the usual *praepositus*. The equivalent for *judex* here is uncertain.

[3] *Vita Oswaldi*, p. 425 (corrected by Nero E.1, fo. 9*b*): 'veneruntque omnes primates aegregii et duces eximii, prepotentes milites ex omnibus castellis et oppidis atque civitatibus et territoriis populusque infinitus ad regem . . . quos omnes suscepit regaliter . . . in illo Pascali.' *Miles* translates *thegn*.

[4] Wendover, *Flores*, i.416.   [5] Simeon of Durham, *Opera*, ii.382.

[6] Wendover has plainly adapted his source to support the claim of kings of England to feudal superiority over Scottish kings. The reference (p. 417) to Henry II is proof of this.

[7] Kantorowicz, *Laudes Regiae*, pp. 53-64, 85-101; Schramm, *Der König von Frankreich*, i.120-4.   [8] Kantorowicz, *op. cit.*, pp. 80, 97 *n*, 110, 178.

has come down to us, it would be rash, in face of the evidence, to assert that laudatory chants were never sung, as was the contemporary Frankish practice, in honour of the Old English kings. We suggest, indeed, that the 'Vita Oswaldi' has preserved fragments of one such chant in honour of King Edgar. We extract some lines from the description of Easter festivities which merges very curiously into a panegyric of Edgar.[1]

> Erat bellicosus ut aegregius
> [P] saltes filius Iesse,
> sapiens ut Iustus,
> [fidelis] ut Paulus,
> misericors [ut] Moyses,
> audax ut Iosue,
> terribilis ut castrorum
> acies ordinata.

Let us compare them with lines taken from a chant in honour of the Frankish king Eude (888-98)[2]:

> Sis Deo dignus ut Abel,
> Sis fidelis ut Samuel,
> Sic judices ut Daniel,
> Et credas ut Nataniel.
> Vivendo vivas ut Enohc
> Pacificus uti Sadoc,
> Sis benedictus ut Iacob,
> Sanctissimus ut fuit Iob.

We have but to change *erat* into *sis* and, as we have done, put the praises of Edgar into metrical form and the resemblance is too close to the earlier chant for there to be any doubt of the nature of the text before the author of the 'Vita Oswaldi'. The two chants in honour of Eude and in honour of Edgar were from a common mould, but apart from their general sentiment they had little else in common. The author of the Edgar chant, if we may so describe it, adapted the first six lines from a passage in the consecratory prayer *Omnipotens sempiterne Deus*,[3] the last two lines we have given being lifted from the Song of Songs.[4] We have presented the more obvious similarities between the panegyric and the Frankish chant, but the

---

[1] *Vita Oswaldi*, p. 425 (corrected by Nero E, 1, fo. 10). Over *saltes* is the gloss *citharedus* and over *Iesse* 'id est Dauid'. *Iustus* (required for the purpose of rhyme) appears to be Solomon: no saint or biblical character named Justus was distinguished for wisdom. The missing adjective in the third line is probably *fidelis*, but there can be no certainty.

[2] For the text and the circumstances in which the chant was sung see Favre, *Eudes comte de Paris et roi de France*, pp. 89, 235-6; *M.G.H., Poetae Latini,*, IV.i.137-8 (reprinted by Schramm, *Zeitschrift der Savigny-Stiftung*, Kan. Abt. xxiii.200-1).

[3] This prayer appears in the Second Recension and is derived from a continental (West Frankish) source, which Bouman would date early in the tenth century (*op. cit.*, pp. 112 21). The relevant passage reads: Abrahae fideliter firmatus, Moysi mansuetudine fretus-Iosue fortitudine munitus, David humilitate exaltatus, Salomonis sapientia decoratus.

[4] Cant. Canticorum, v.3.

opening words of the panegyric may also derive from the Edgar chant, though it is more difficult to put them into metrical form.

Rex autem armipotens Eadgar, sceptris et diadematibus pollens et iura regni bellica potestate regaliter protegens, cuncta inimicorum superba collas pedibus suis stravit . . .

The rhymes in *ens* are suggestive,[1] and we may compare the first stanza of the chant in honour of Eude:

> Odo princebs altissime
> Regumque potentissime,
> Regale ceptrum suscipe
> Longo regendum tempore.

These chants were not based upon the imperial *laudes* or any similar model,[2] but they have the same spirit and the same purpose and were no less fit to be sung at a religious ceremony.

But though we conclude that such verses were chanted in honour of Edgar, this need not mean that there were not also sung *laudes* resembling those which were later sung before the Norman kings of England. Let us take two lines from the poem in which his panegyrist tells of Athelstan's coronation:

> Some play the harp; some contest with praises;
> Together they sing 'Tibi laus, tibi gloria, Christe'.[3]

And next let us turn to the *laudes* sung in honour of the Conqueror's queen and particularly to the second part, where the soloists cease to chant their many verses beginning 'Christus vincit'.[4] The choir echoes the soloists' last words,

> Ipsi soli decus, potestas et imperium
> per infinita secula seculorum,

and, after a pause, begin their own full-voiced chorus,

> Ipsi soli gloria, laus et iubilatio
> per infinita secula seculorum . . .

Then, after an Alleluia, they begin again,

> Gloria victori sit Christo laude perhenni,

---

[1] The chant may well have begun: Eadgar rex armipotens. But the other lines of the stanza are too conjectural to permit of a reconstruction. To the last clause we have cited there is a striking parallel in the Metz chant in honour of the Emperor Charles [?the Bald]: 'Colla gentium tibi sternantur' (Kantorowicz, *op. cit.*, pp. 73-5).

[2] For these see *ibid.*, pp. 15-16, 105-6.

[3] William of Malmesbury, *Gesta Regum*, i.146.
> Ille strepit cithara, decertat plausibus iste,
> In commune sonat 'Tibi laus, tibi gloria, Christe'.
The obscurities of the poet's style do not make for easy understanding, but our translation does, we think, give the sense. The *certamen* is presumably the antiphonal chanting of the first part of the *laudes*, which was accompanied by harps.

[4] Maskell, *Monumenta Ritualia*, ii.85-8.

and so, after repeated Glorias, with a last triumphant 'Gloria victori', they are still. Is it not such a chorus as this, to the praise and glory of the victorious Christ, that the poet recalls? What other chant could he have in mind? Now we may think that a poem written after Athelstan's death, perhaps a good many years after,[1] is not the best of evidence for the year (924 or 925) when he was crowned; but do we need better proof that *laudes* were sung in honour of English kings a century before the Conquest? And if these *laudes* were sung at coronations in the tenth century, there can be little doubt that, as later custom demanded, they were sung also at crown-wearings.

We venture the conclusion that the ceremony of crown-wearing was not only observed in pre-Conquest England but that the ceremony resembled generally that customary among the Franks. The evidence is fragmentary, but so also is the continental evidence. The next point we seek to establish is that crown-wearings were suitable occasions for other ceremonies as well or, conversely, might be arranged to coincide with such ceremonies at which a large attendance of dignitaries would be expected. In the first place we are concerned with the marriage and the coronation of queens. Let us give some continental examples. In 862 Lothaire II married his mistress Waldrade and had her crowned by the bishops who supported him, apparently at a single ceremony: we are not told that Lothaire wore his crown, but the presumption is that he did.[2] In 865, when he was compelled to take back his legitimate wife, Theutberge, to make the fact public they wore their crowns ceremonially together at a mass celebrated by the papal legate.[3] Again, in 866 Charles the Bald had his wife Ermentrude crowned in the church of St. Médard at Soissons and appears to have been crowned with her.[4] With one exception, English parallels are post-Conquest. Adeliza of Louvain was married to Henry I on 29 January 1121 and crowned on the following day. We have particularly good reason for knowing that the king wore his crown on this occasion, because the archbishop forcibly asserted his right to crown him.[5] Again, John's 'second coronation' was combined with the coronation of Isabelle of Angoulême,[6] and Henry III wore his crown when Eleanor of Provence was crowned in 1236.[7] The one pre-Conquest example we have passed over is the marriage of Ælfthryth to King Edgar and to this we now return, for it must be considered in the light of earlier continental and later English parallels.

We have already remarked that the author of the 'Vita Oswaldi', in contriving his fictitious account of Edgar's coronation, thrust ele-

---

[1] Malmesbury has not preserved sufficient of the text to enable a close estimate of its date to be made, but there is general agreement that it comes from the tenth century.
[2] *Annales de St. Bertin*, p. 115.   [3] *Ibid.*, p. 149.   [4] *Ibid.*, p. 158.
[5] *Chronicle of John of Worcester*, p. 16; Eadmer, *Historia Novorum*, pp. 292-3.
[6] *Rotuli de Liberate*, p. 1; *Rotuli Normanniae*, p. 34.   [7] *Cal. of Liberate Rolls*, i.255.

ments of a coronation office into an incongruous setting. If we remove
those elements we should be able to recover, though doubtless mutilated and deformed, something of the document before the writer,
a document contemporary, or more nearly contemporary, with the
events it described. The conclusion of that document seems to have
been rephrased, but little changed in substance. It described, as we
have seen, a marriage feast or rather two feasts, one for the bishops
and nobles over which King Edgar presided and one for the abbots
and abbesses and noble matrons over which Queen Ælfthryth presided. The commencement of the document, on the other hand,
appears to have been more extensively rewritten in the hagiographer's inflated style. Nevertheless we can recover the purport of
the original document. It described a large assembly of prelates and
magnates summoned by the king to meet at Whitsuntide. The company proceed to church to which the king goes crowned.[1] It is at
this point that the extracts from the coronation office are introduced,
so that we can but conjecture what was said in the original document, but presumably it described briefly a religious ceremony,
which was followed by the feasts described in the concluding sentences which we have summarised. Now these happenings in this
sequence—the assembly on one of the principal festivals, the procession of the crowned king to church, the concluding feast—are
characteristic elements of a crown-wearing when we get to know
something of the details of the ceremony in the twelfth century.[2] The
inference we draw is that the original document described a crown-
wearing at Whitsuntide in 964 or 965, at which there was also celebrated the marriage of Edgar and Ælfthryth, and that, not only did
the king wear his crown, but the queen was anointed and crowned.[3]
There were therefore both a *coronatio* and a *consecratio*. The mistake
of the writer of the 'Vita Oswaldi' was to confuse these ceremonies
with an *ordinatio regis* and to assign a part to Oswald as archbishop
of York. If Oswald took part in the consecration and coronation of
Ælfthryth, it was as bishop of Worcester; but we should expect
Archbishop Osketel of York to have been present and Oswald's part
to have been inconspicuous. Let us repeat that the marriage and
coronation of a queen would, if analogies are any guide, be an
obvious occasion for the king to wear his crown. It is true that we
cannot adduce any parallel where a marriage was arranged for one
of the principal feasts when the king would in any case wear his
crown, but we can adduce a parallel where such a crown-wearing
was combined with another outstanding ceremony. This was at
Christmas 1065 when a crown-wearing preceded by three days the
dedication of Westminster Abbey, to which the Confessor attached

[1] See p. 401, n. 4, above.
[2] Richardson in *Traditio*, xvi.128-31.
[3] See p. 401, n. 6, above.

the greatest importance.[1] The difficulty in assembling a large company of prelates and magnates obviously made it convenient to take advantage of a crown-wearing to perform other ceremonies. It was for this reason that great councils were held on the principal feasts, not only after the Conquest but before.[2]

Some final words may now be said on the ceremony of 973. This also took place at Whitsuntide and therefore, it must be assumed, on the occasion of a crown-wearing. The anointing of the king made the ceremony, as we have said, exceptional, although a repetition of the unction is not altogether unknown in the case of other kings.[3] Edward II would have been anointed a second time, if he could have obtained the pope's approval,[4] and it is possible that John was anointed at his mysterious 'second coronation' when Isabelle of Angoulême was anointed and crowned.[5] Other kings who felt the need for rehabilitation, as Stephen and Richard I did after their captivity, were satisfied with a specially solemn crown-wearing.[6] Without desiring to add to conjectures, we might suppose either that Edgar, for reasons we are never likely to know, felt the need for rehabilitation or, more probably, that the ceremony marked the recognition of his sovereignty over Britain, to which the story of the submission of the eight kings bears witness, and that he dedicated himself anew to the task. That he was a deeply religious man can hardly be questioned. Long after the event mediaeval writers alleged that the ceremony marked the conclusion of a long period of penance for a fleshly sin. Such stories seem to be palpable fictions, but they show how difficult it has always been, in the absence of contemporary evidence, to explain Edgar's motive.[7]

[1] *Chronicon Abbatiae Rameseiensis*, p. 178. We have already cited the beginning of the entry from this chronicle (above, p. 405). It continues: ibidemque . . . ecclesiam Westmonasterii quam ipse, largis sumptibus aedificatam, possessionibus ampliaverat et donis, in Natali Sanctorum Innocentium cum gaudio celebri et apparatu solemni fecit dedicari. . . . For other authorities see Freeman, *Norman Conquest*, ii.521.

[2] Larson, *The King's Household*, pp. 200-1; Liebermann, *The National Assembly in the Anglo-Saxon Period*, pp. 48-9.

[3] Pepin himself was anointed twice, first in 751 and then in 754 by Pope Stephen II.

[4] L. G. W. Legg, *English Coronation Records*, pp. 69-76.

[5] There are duplicate entries on the Liberate and Norman Rolls (p. 409, n. 6, above) for the customary rewards to royal clerks for chanting the *laudes*. The former reads: 'ad secundam coronationem nostram et ad unctionem nostram et coronationem Isabelle regine uxoris nostre': the latter reads: 'ad secundam coronationem nostram et ad unctionem et coronationem Isabelle regine uxoris nostre'. The second *nostram* in the former entry appears to be a mistake; but this does not dispose of the matter. To begin with, there are further references to the king's *second* coronation, so that there is no doubt of its special importance (*Rot. de Liberate*, pp. 4-5; *Rot. Normanniae*, p. 36). But the king had already worn his crown and the *laudes* had been chanted at Whitsuntide 1200 (*Memoranda Roll, 1 John*, p. 90), while at Easter 1201 the king and queen wore their crowns at what was afterwards called his *first* coronation at Canterbury (*E.H.R.*, lxi.309-10). Clearly the ceremony of 8 October was a different kind of coronation from a crown-wearing on one of the principal feasts. [6] Richardson in *Traditio*, xvi.129-30.

[7] The evidence is examined by Stubbs, (*Memorials of St. Dunstan*, pp. xciv-ci), who rejects the legends, but believes the fact of Edgar's vicious youth to be established beyond question. This would seem to put out of court any suggestion that Edgar delayed his coronation on grounds of piety, a suggestion first made by Nicholas of Worcester (*ibid.*, p. 423), quite apart from the evidence that he was crowned at the beginning of his reign. But the belief in Edgar's vicious youth depends upon some ambiguous words in the Anglo-

The consecrations and crown-wearings of King Edgar have occupied a great space in our discussions. This has been inevitable, because his reign is the only one before the Conquest that can be said to be even partially documented for our purpose, with the sole exception of the reign of Edward the Confessor. Between these reigns there is a great gap in our evidence, and while there would seem obviously to have been a continuous tradition of royal ceremonial, there may well have been lapses in practice, especially under the Danish kings. What, however, we are concerned to stress is that the Conquest marked no breach in this tradition. Whatever innovations there may have been were in minor details.

Saxon Chronicle and may have no other basis than his apparently irregular unions, first with Æthelflæd and then with the mysterious Wulfthryth, who is variously described as a saint and as a concubine. He had issue by both women as well as by Ælfthryth, but how the first two unions ended we are not told. It may well be that the circumstances were not such as to offend contemporary moral standards: they must have been known to the Abingdon writer, who nevertheless regards Edgar as a model of piety and virtue. Since there is no suggestion that Edward, Edgar's son by Æthelflæd, was illegitimate, the inference is that he was born in wedlock (see above, p. 401, n. 6). We can but suggest that the union was subsequently dissolved.

GERVASE OF BLOIS, ABBOT OF WESTMINSTER

FOR several reasons it seems desirable to say more of Gervase of Blois than can be compressed into a footnote. The received story of his career is manifestly false and, when the story is told as accurately as the sources permit, we learn a good deal worth knowing of the history of the Church in the twelfth century and in especial of the relations of Stephen and Henry II to royal abbeys, as well as something of Henry's attitude towards his predecessor.

Gervase was the fruit of a liaison between Stephen and an obscure Norman woman known as Damette,[1] 'the Little Lady', and he must have been born in Stephen's youth, some years before his marriage in 1125 to the count of Boulogne's daughter, Maud. At the time of Stephen's accession Gervase was apparently still a young man. The abbacy at Westminster was then either vacant or shortly to be vacated by Abbot Herbert, who seems to have died at an advanced age in September 1136,[2] whether in office or not is uncertain.[3] The king took the opportunity to make provision for his natural son but, presumably on account of his youth, Gervase was not appointed abbot until the end of 1138. We must assume that he was canonically dispensed from the disability occasioned by his illegitimate birth, for he was 'ordained' as abbot by the papal legate, Alberic of Ostia, on 17 December.[4] This fact is sufficient guarantee against any suspicion that his appointment was irregular, though it is possible that, if the monks had had a free choice, it would have fallen upon the prior, Osbert of Clare, who felt that he had a good claim to the succession.[5] But we have no real reason to suppose that Osbert would have commended himself, for, whatever his merits, he had a knack of making himself disliked,[6] and it may well be that the monks were not ill-disposed towards a king's son or to one outside their number as their head. They had, as we shall see, little reason to regret their late

---

[1] Flete, *History of Westminster Abbey*, p. 8: 'Gervasius dictus de Bleys, filius regis Anglie Stephani de domina Dameta genitus et de Normannia similiter oriundus.' Dameta can hardly be a baptismal name and is presumably the latinised form of the diminutive of *dame*. Gervase's brothers, Amalric and Ralf, were doubtless also her sons (Pearce, *Monks of Westminster*, p. 42). [2] *Ibid.*, p. 41; Flete, *op. cit.*, p. 142.
[3] No abbot was present at Stephen's coronation (William of Malmesbury, *Historia Novella*, p. 16). Abbot Herbert may either have been too ill to attend or have resigned on the ground of infirmity.
[4] *The Chronicle of John of Worcester*, p. 53: regis filius Gervasius abbas Westmonasterii ordinatur a legato.
[5] *Letters of Osbert of Clare*: Introduction by J. A. Robinson, pp. 2-4.
[6] As his own letters show (*ibid.*, pp. 4-9, 49-61).

abbot who, if not professed at Westminster, had long been a monk there before his appointment by Henry I.[1]

It must be recognised that ever since the twelfth century Gervase has had a dubious reputation,[2] a reputation that has grown worse as the centuries have advanced. In Dean Armitage Robinson's words, 'he was a thoroughly bad abbot'[3]; but this is a mere echo of the eighteenth-century historians of the abbey, who, in turn, echo a historian of the fifteenth century.[4] The evidence for this conclusion has yet to be produced, and evidence regarding Gervase is as abundant as we can reasonably expect in the case of a twelfth-century abbot of no particular distinction. Let us begin at the beginning. When Gervase was consecrated, Westminster Abbey had for years been torn by dissension, and there is the best of reasons for believing that under the late abbot the possessions of the abbey had been dilapidated; for not only does Osbert of Clare say so in a very forcible letter to Abbot Herbert,[5] but in 1129 or 1130 the monks had been authorised by the king to recover the lands that had been dispersed and had been prepared to pay the enormous sum of 1000 marks for this authority. Abbot Herbert had, moreover, become involved with Jewish money-lenders.[6] If the abbot had been an imprudent administrator, the fomenter of dissension had been the prior, Osbert of Clare, who had, in consequence, been banished to Ely.[7] It will be apparent that at this juncture the abbacy was an unenviable office for a youth; but if Gervase had been obviously unsuited to the task of reform, it would have been strange if the papal legate had connived at his appointment. And it speaks well for the young abbot that at first he lived in amity with his formidable prior who, after many years' absence, had returned to Westminster.[8]

Osbert of Clare was a restless man of ideas, and one of his projects was to obtain from the pope the canonisation of Edward the Confessor. He proceeded forthwith to enlist the support of the new abbot. This led to the support of the king and the king's brother, the powerful bishop of Winchester, for their support must surely be attributed in no small measure to Abbot Gervase. Stephen did not stand to gain by Edward's canonisation, rather the reverse; for if it had any political implications, the advantage would accrue to the Empress and her son, who could claim that they were of the blood of the Confessor, while Stephen certainly could make no such claim.[9]

[1] Pearce, *op. cit.*, p. 41.

[2] For John of Hexham and the Life of Robert of Gorham see below, pp. 420-1.

[3] *Letters of Osbert of Clare*, p. 17.

[4] Dart, *Westmonasterium* (1742), ii, pp. xiv-xv; Widmore, *History of the Church of St. Peter Westminster* (1751), pp. 24-6. Both rely upon Flete. Later writers have followed Dean Armitage Robinson unquestioningly: e.g. Holzmann, *Papsturkunden in England*, i.244, 249; Scholz in *Speculum*, xxxvi.44; Chaplais in *Medieval Miscellany*, pp. 91-6.

[5] *Letters of Osbert of Clare*, no. 2, p. 51.

[6] *Pipe Roll, 31 Henry I*, p. 150: 800 marks were remitted.

[7] *Letters of Osbert of Clare*, pp. 2-11.   [8] *Ibid.*, p. 16.

[9] This has been demonstrated by Scholz, 'The Canonization of Edward the Confessor', in *Speculum*, xxxvi.42-4.

Armed with letters of recommendation from the king and Bishop Henry, who had now become legate, Osbert set out for Rome, it would seem in the late summer of 1139.[1] He failed to obtain the agreement of the pope to the immediate canonisation of Edward; but, it has been supposed, he took the opportunity of his visit to give the Curia an unfavourable account of the youthful abbot's conduct. The result of Osbert's machinations, it is alleged, was a bull that has been interpreted as a severe rebuke to Gervase 'for wasting the abbey properties and keeping armed retainers in the abbey'.[2] Why Osbert should besmirch his abbot and why his testimony should, in this matter, be preferred to that of Cardinal Alberic, who had so recently consecrated Gervase, has not been explained. No explanation is, in fact, possible, for this reconstruction of events, which Dean Armitage Robinson adopted from earlier historians of the abbey, rests upon a misunderstanding of a singularly instructive series of papal letters, all bearing the same date, 9 December, in a year which there is every reason to believe is 1139.[3]

It is obvious that, in the few months between Gervase's consecration and Osbert's departure for Rome, the new abbot—even if he had not been absent for much of the time, which, as we shall see, is highly likely—could have had few opportunities for dilapidating the possessions of the abbey, which is the particular charge laid against him by mediaeval writers.[4] It is, however, possible that he had already arranged for the lease to his mother of the manor of Chelsea and that the transaction was more in his mother's interest than in that of the monks. But that the annual rent of £4 charged in the lease was greatly disproportionate to the value of the property is far from certain.[5] No doubt it is, in general, highly scandalous for an abbot to lodge the king's mistress in a pleasant monastic manor accessible over a short stretch of river from the royal palace, and it was presumably the scandal occasioned by this transaction that was

[1] Bishop Henry seems not to have made his legation known until 29 August (William of Malmesbury, *Historia Novella*, p. 29). It follows that Osbert of Clare's letter to him and his letter to the pope recommending Osbert must be after that date (*Letters of Osbert of Clare*, pp. 83-7).   [2] *Ibid.*, p. 18.

[3] Two are included in the *Letters of Osbert of Clare*, nos. 19, 20; two others are printed by Holzmann, *Papsturkunden in England*, i, nos. 24, 25 (the text of no. 24 being already accessible in Flete's *History*, pp. 90-1). As Scholz shows, Holzmann's dating 1139-42 is too wide (*Speculum*, xxxvi.43 n). We exclude 1140 as quite improbable, not least because Osbert's letter to Bishop Henry referring to the fourth year of Stephen seems manifestly to refer to the current year (*Letters of Osbert of Clare*, p. 84).

[4] By Flete, p. 89, as well as by John of Hexham and the St. Alban's writer.

[5] The history of the manor is far from clear. In the Middlesex hidage, which appears to date from the early twelfth century, it is shown as belonging to the abbey (Weinbaum, *London unter Eduard I und II*, bd. ii, texte, p. 85); but in D.B., i.130 b 1 it is shown as belonging to Edward of Salisbury. The monks alleged that their title dated from Edward the Confessor and supported their claim with a spurious charter of William I (*Regesta*, i.120-1 (no. 89)). The manor must be that later known as the Neyte: the suggestion that it lay in Kingsbury appears to be based upon a misapprehension (*ibid.*, ii.392). The Domesday value is £9, but in comparing this valuation with the rent of £4, it must be noted that Damette gave in addition 40 shillings and a pall worth 100 shillings (*Dart, op. cit.*, i.23-4).

remembered against Gervase in later years.[1] If, however, this was folly, it was a youthful folly, and we are more likely than a monastic disciplinarian to view with indulgence the desire of Gervase to have his mother housed within easy reach of the abbey. But was it improvident of him to enter into the other leases cited by John Flete, the fifteenth-century historian of the abbey, who is followed, without further enquiry or explanation, by later writers? These leases could hardly have been arranged in the early months of Gervase's abbacy, while the terms granted do not seem to be particularly generous to the lessees or disadvantageous to the convent. Annual rents, for example, of £9 for the manor of Moulsham in Essex, of £20 for the manor of Hendon in Middlesex and of £30 for the distant manor of Deerhurst in Gloucestershire may well be reasonable in terms of twelfth-century monetary standards, however low these rents may have seemed three centuries later.[2] Without a far-reaching investigation one could hardly pronounce upon these transactions[3]; but they are evidently on a different plane, at least as regards their motive, from the lease of the manor of Chelsea.

If Osbert of Clare knew of this lease—and it may not yet have been within his knowledge—he certainly made no complaint at the Curia of this or any similar transactions, for of the burden of Osbert's complaint we have the testimony of Pope Innocent II himself. On the same day that the pope wrote to Abbot Gervase the supposed letter of reproof, he wrote to Bishop Henry of Winchester. And what did the pope say to his legate? 'We have learnt by the complaint made by our dear son Osbert, on behalf of our sons the monks of St. Peter's, Westminster, that the possessions of the church and the goods of the monastery have been taken away and forcibly detained by many people of those parts.' And what is the legate to do? He is to hear the monks' complaints and to see that they have justice.[4] Here then we are back to the depredations committed in the time of Abbot Herbert. It is Abbot Gervase who, mindful of the promise he had given at his consecration,[5] is seeking to retrieve the dispersed and dilapidated property of his house. If this is not testimony to his fitness for office, to his desire to do his duty, language has no meaning.

It is in the light of the pope's plain instructions to the legate that we must read the more rhetorical letter addressed to Gervase and the

---

[1] We may so interpret John of Hexham's words (p. 330): qui res loci illius juveniliter dissipavit. As we explain later, this information was given by Gervase's successor at Westminster, Abbot Laurence.

[2] The value of Moulsham in Domesday Book is £12 (£9 T.R.E.), of Hendon £9 (£12 T.R.E.) and of the demesne of Deerhurst £26 (D.B., i.128 b 2; 166 a 2; ii.15).

[3] Hale, *The Domesday of St. Paul's* (Camden Soc.), affords the most convenient material for comparison: with the table at p. xx compare the leases for money rents at pp. 125-32. There is nothing here to suggest that the Westminster leases were abnormal.

[4] *Letters of Osbert of Clare*, no. 20.

[5] The words 'secundum professionem a te factam canonice satage dispersa congregare' in the letter we next discuss refer to the promise all bishops and abbots made: see *Traditio*, xvi.151-3.

convent.[1] Much of the letter is commonplace. The abbot is to maintain due discipline: the monks are to give him canonical obedience.
Knights[2] and lay folk are not to be admitted within the monastic
precincts. Ironically enough, the incursion of lay folk into the
cloister had been encouraged by the supposed traducer of Abbot
Gervase, for Osbert of Clare had plumed himself upon the numbers
of women and citizens who had come to the chapter house to listen
to his preaching in the time of Abbot Herbert.[3] And the third Norman abbot, the great Gilbert Crispin, had admitted even Jews into
the precincts of the monastery.[4] But it is not to be supposed that
these happenings were known at the Curia, and Westminster was
not singular in such lax practices. As for matters more directly applying to Westminster, Gervase is enjoined to reassemble the lands and
rents that had been distributed among individual monks and, with
the advice of the chapter, to manage both the internal and external
property of the abbey. He is also to recover the churches and tithes
which had been dispersed without the consent of the brethren.
These injunctions clearly have reference to the position as it stood at
Gervase's entry upon his office: again we are back to the irregularities in the administration of Abbot Herbert which the new abbot is
required to correct. A more personal note might perhaps be read into
the injunction to Gervase to make the monks professed in the abbey
his collaborators and colleagues and not to take counsel of strange
monks or confide his secrets to them; but this is far more likely to be
a warning to Gervase not to follow in the footsteps of Abbot Herbert.
It is not, of course, impossible that, in the distracted state of the
convent, the young man had sought counsel outside the abbey. We
cannot say. If he had done so, it was surely a venial fault. But read
into the letter what we may, we cannot find in it any direct charge
against Gervase. The advice might have been given to almost any
convent of monks in England, for the pattern did not vary greatly
throughout the land. But of 'armed retainers' or of 'waste' committed by Gervase there is not a word: these are no more than the
misunderstandings of eighteenth-century writers, who had little skill
in dating or comprehending papal documents of the twelfth century.[5]

[1] Holzmann, *Papsturkunden*, no. 24.

[2] As we learn from Domesday Book (D.B., i.128 a 2), some of the abbot's knights had
been lodged in houses close to the abbey and may still have been there half a century
later: see above, p. 69.

[3] *Letters of Osbert of Clare*, no. 3, p. 56.

[4] This is clear from the prologue to his *Disputatio Iudei et Christiani* (ed. Blumenkranz),
p. 27.

[5] We may perhaps point out a more recent error. Mr Scholz, who follows Armitage
Robinson in disparaging Gervase, says that Pope Innocent 'forbade the abbot in this
letter' to sell 'Edward's royal insignia' (*Speculum*, xxxvi.44). The direction is addressed to
the monks, as the use of the plural shows, and not to the abbot, who did not have personal
custody of the regalia. Nor is it a prohibition of the sale of the regalia, but a direction that
any transaction regarding them should have the assent of the whole convent. What lies
behind this direction is presumably a claim by the king's treasurer to the custody of
regalia: the dispute continued for centuries (*Traditio*, xvi.192-4). This has no bearing,
as Mr Scholz supposes, upon either the cult of St. Edward or the canonisation.

Before we outline Abbot Gervase's later history, so far as we are able from sources easily accessible, it will be well to look at another statement of Dean Armitage Robinson's. 'Abbot Gervase seems to have been deposed by the Pope in 1146. But he still held on till he was ejected by King Henry II in the third or fourth year of his reign.'[1] For the first of these sentences no authority is cited and we have failed to find it.[2] No chronicler seems to have noticed an event which, if it had occurred, would have been a scandal of the first order. All the facts available to us are, on the other hand, inconsistent with any idea of Gervase's deposition, whether by the pope or by any authority delegated by him. Indeed, the general impression left by the evidence is that he enjoyed the respect due to the head of one of the greater Benedictine abbeys, enhanced doubtless by his royal birth.

To begin with, it has been plausibly argued that Abbot Gervase was one of the four abbots from the province of Canterbury who attended the Lateran Council which opened on 3 April 1139.[3] Certainly, if he were not in Rome at the time, the abbey had an efficient agent there who secured from the pope a confirmation of the privileges of the abbey,[4] and the balance of probability points to Gervase. It would follow that he set out within a month or two of his consecration and was back at Westminster by about Midsummer.[5] This would explain why it was left to Prior Osbert to make the journey to Rome later in the year, with two objects: the first, to arm the abbot with sufficient authority to reform the abuses that had grown up in the monastery and to recover alienated property, and, the second, to secure the canonisation of Edward the Confessor. In the second undertaking Osbert was unsuccessful; but in the first he succeeded abundantly, so far as letters from the pope could ensure success. Dean Armitage Robinson took the view that Osbert returned in disgrace because of his failure in the second purpose of his mission[6]; but there seems no ground for this conclusion. The reform of the monastery was a more pressing matter, and it is quite unlikely that anyone took the postponement of canonisation tragically, unless it was Osbert himself. It is true that Osbert seems very soon after to have disappeared from Westminster, but the reason is quite obscure and there is no evidence that he was replaced in the office of

---

[1] *Letters of Osbert of Clare*, p. 19.
[2] Perhaps there was a misunderstanding of Gilbert Foliot's letter of 1148, saying that Eugenius III had rejected Gervase as a candidate for the see of Lincoln (*Epistolae*, i.92, no. 76).
[3] Saltman, *Theobald Archbishop of Canterbury*, p. 139.
[4] The argument is based upon the fact that bishops and abbots attending the council took the opportunity to obtain privileges. The abbot of Westminster obtained at least two, dated 22 April 1139 (Holzmann, *Papsturkunden*, nos. 20, 21), one of importance.
[5] The council which opened on 3 April lasted until nearly the end of the month: for dates see Jaffé-Loewenfeld, *Regesta*, i.885-9. We must allow a full month and probably a week or two longer, since there was no hurry, for the journey in either direction.
[6] *Letters of Osbert of Clare*, p. 19.

prior for a good many years.[1] Even if he were exiled by Gervase, it by no means follows that the rupture was the fault of the abbot. The internal history of the abbey is, however, very dark in these years.

Gervase is found with other prelates in the legatine council held by Cardinal Imar in 1145,[2] and in 1148 he was one of three candidates put forward by Bishop Henry of Winchester for the vacant see of Lincoln. Though he, like the others, was rejected by Eugenius III, the fact does not cast any slur upon him.[3] So far as the surviving evidence goes, it indicates that Gervase was active in prosecuting the interests of the abbey, in recovering advowsons and manors,[4] and notably in repelling the attempt of Malvern Priory to assert its independence.[5] One minor act, but one that may commend Gervase to us, was the setting aside of a sum of money annually for the repair of books in the ambry: if this was not done at the abbot's instance, it was done with his authority.[6] Seemingly the death of Stephen made no immediate difference to Gervase's position. At the coronation of Henry II the abbot of Westminster would have much to do and he would be brought into intimate contact with the new king.[7] We have no direct statement that Gervase was present, but his absence would certainly have caused remark. Thereafter he paid at least one visit to the court, shortly before Henry embarked at Dover in January 1156 to remain overseas until April 1157.[8] In the spring of 1157 Gervase's representative was busy at the Curia obtaining from Adrian IV privileges and confirmations for the abbey,[9] and we catch some other glimpses of him at this period. Together with other prelates and members of the *familia* of Archbishop Theobald, he attends a session of judges delegate, where he witnesses an agreement between the monks of Belvoir and of Thetford.[10] About the same time, apparently early in 1157, we get from Archbishop Theobald a tribute to his handling of the dispute with the monks of Malvern. Moved by Gervase, whom they had grievously wronged, they fell at his feet, asking his pardon and promising to satisfy him, which they did by surrendering the privilege they had surreptitiously obtained from Adrian IV, exempting them from the authority of the abbot of Westminster.[11]

[1] Everything connected with Osbert's second exile is extremely speculative: see the notes by the editor to letters assigned to this period (*ibid.*, pp. 215-9). After his visit to Rome in 1139 information is extremely scanty. Hugh appears as prior before 1157 and Elias towards the end of Gervase's abbacy. Osbert reappears at Westminster as a simple monk in 1157-8 (Pearce, *Monks of Westminster*, pp. 42-4).
[2] Thorpe, *Registrum Roffense*, p. 41; Holzmann, *Papsturkunden*, ii.193.
[3] Gilbert Foliot, *Epistolae*, i.92, no. 76.
[4] Saltman, *Theobald Archbishop of Canterbury*, pp. 507-8.
[5] John of Salisbury, *Letters*, i.80-1.
[6] Robinson and James, *Manuscripts of Westminster Abbey*, p. 1: pro reparandis libris armarii.   [7] For the abbot's duties see *Traditio*, xvi.191, 198-202.
[8] Flete, *op. cit.*, p. 143. For Henry's movements see Robert of Torigni, pp. 186, 192.
[9] Holzmann, *Papsturkunden*, i, nos. 68-70.
[10] Historical MSS. Commission, *MSS. of Duke of Rutland*, iv.159-60. For the mandate under which Archbishop Theobald and the bishop of London acted see Holzmann, *Papsturkunden*, i, no. 60.   [11] John of Salisbury, *Letters*, i.80-1.

We cannot, of course, on the strength of this evidence affirm that Gervase was a model, or even a prudent, abbot. We do not know how the brethren fared under him, for there were no twelfth-century Westminster monks who wrote the lives of their abbots as did some of their contemporaries at Battle, Bury, St. Alban's and Walden. We cannot perhaps regard as testimony in his favour the silence of Osbert of Clare: yet it is noteworthy that Osbert, who had not failed, when exiled from Westminster for the first time,[1] to reprove Abbot Herbert, did not in his second exile add to his collection of letters a reproof addressed to Abbot Gervase. We can, however, affirm that the evidence is incompatible with the picture Dean Armitage Robinson would leave with us of a worthless abbot, deprived by the pope, clinging to office, thanks presumably to the favour of his royal father, until a new and upright king ejected him. There is, however, one testimony against Gervase, that of his successor, Abbot Laurence; for the accusation that he dissipated the possessions of the abbey, which is found both in the chronicle of John of Hexham, the continuator of Simeon of Durham, and in the life of Robert of Gorham, abbot of St. Alban's, written by a contemporary in that house, can have come only from Laurence.[2] Laurence had been a monk at both Durham and St. Alban's, and evidently kept in touch with both communities.[3] The Durham writer has little to say of him and hardly explains why he left there to become a monk at St. Alban's. The St. Alban's writer accuses him of black ingratitude for the benefits that Robert of Gorham heaped upon him after Laurence had been appointed by the king abbot of Westminster.[4] Years before, it is to be remarked, he had ingratiated himself with the Empress and through her he had found favour with Henry II[5]; and his appointment to Westminster was political. Laurence seems, in fact, to have been an ambitious and rather unscrupulous man, anxious to excuse his intrusion into an abbacy rendered vacant by the removal of an abbot against whom no canonical proceedings had been taken. He does not look like a witness of credit.[6]

The stories Abbot Laurence told of Gervase or, at least, as his hearers related them, do not hang together. John of Hexham says no more than that Gervase dissipated the possessions of the abbey in his

---

[1] *Letters of Osbert of Clare*, no. 2: see especially p. 51.

[2] John of Hexham, *Chronicle*, in Simeon of Durham, *Opera*, vol. ii: his reference to Gervase is at p. 330. The most accessible edition of the life of Abbot Robert of Gorham, one of the *Vita Abbatum*, attributed to Matthew Paris but written about the end of Henry II's reign, is in vol. i of the badly edited *Gesta Abbatum* of Walsingham in the Rolls Series.

[3] He is termed *magister* Laurentius to distinguish him from the prior of the same name, with whom he has been frequently confused. His name is entered in the Durham martyrologium (*Liber Vitae Ecclesiae Dunelmensis* (Surtees Soc.), p. 142). The references to him by the St. Alban's writer show his continued relations with that house: a deposed prior of St. Alban's migrated to Westminster while he was abbot (Walsingham, *Gesta Abbatum*, i.108: this passage is inserted out of chronological order).

[4] *Ibid.*, pp. 133-4.   [5] Flete, *op. cit.*, p. 92.

[6] Nevertheless he was a learned and able abbot: see his notice in *Dict. Nat. Biog.* and Scholz in *Speculum*, xxxvi.51-3.

youth (*juveniliter*). The story recorded at St. Alban's was that Gervase had dissipated nearly all the property of the abbey, converting it to secular purposes, so that nothing was left for the food or clothing of the convent. It was this tale, so the chronicler affirms, that moved Abbot Robert to let Abbot Laurence have horses, silver cups and spoons and clothing to the value of nearly two hundred marks. It is odd that hungry and ragged mouths should want horses and table silver, though their abbot might, and it is odd to read in a variant account that this gift enabled Abbot Laurence to restore speedily the prosperity of the abbey.[1] The fifteenth-century chronicler of Westminster, John Flete, unwittingly casts further doubts upon Laurence's stories, and Flete was a conscientious writer, who sought contemporary authority for his statements. We can accept his word for it that many of the abbey buildings were ruinous when Laurence entered upon his office; but this was because they had been destroyed by fire. We can accept his word for it that the manors owned by the abbey in Oxfordshire, Gloucestershire and Worcestershire had been devastated or alienated; but this had been the work of Robert earl of Gloucester, and his followers.[2] Since Earl Robert had died in 1147 we can put a date to these happenings: they certainly occurred in Abbot Gervase's time, but they were hardly his fault, though doubtless the possessions of an abbey ruled by Stephen's son inevitably invited the attacks of the adherents of the Empress. It is difficult to know what Gervase could have done to ameliorate the position while the country was divided into two hostile parts, and Westminster was not the only religious house to suffer disastrously in the years when Christ and His saints slept. Doubtless Abbot Laurence deserves credit for restoring the abbey buildings and recovering the abbey's possessions in time of peace; but he was able to do so through the favour of his patron, Henry II, favour Abbot Gervase had lacked.[3]

When, therefore, we have sifted the allegations against Gervase, we seem to arrive at this result. He has been, in the first place, blamed for the imprudence and incapacity of his predecessor, Abbot Herbert. In the second place, he has been blamed for the consequences to his house of the civil war. His removal from office cannot then be imputed to misconduct, but must be ascribed to Henry II's hatred of Stephen and all his works. Gervase was inevitably a marked man and he was replaced by an old supporter of the Angevins. His case is exactly parallel to that of Abbot Reginald of Reading, another marked man.[4] In neither case was there any question of ecclesiastical shortcomings. In both cases there was political animosity. But the removal of the two abbots would not have been possible had not the king possessed undisputed control over appointments to royal abbeys if he chose to exercise it. That is a lesson worth remembering.

[1] Walsingham, *Gesta Abbatum*, i.112.
[3] Flete, *loc. cit.*
[2] Flete, *op. cit.*, p. 92.
[4] Above, pp. 256-7.

THE CHAMBERLAINS OF THE EXCHEQUER

THE first question we should perhaps put is 'What did the title of chamberlain mean in the twelfth century?' As we have already indicated,[1] a man might be entitled 'chamberlain' who held, so far as we can tell, no office, at least no permanent office, at court. Since there are signs that the title might descend from father to son, we guess that it might be honorific and connote no more than a certain status at court and that a chamberlain of this kind might be entitled to perform certain ceremonial duties but have no real duties. And then the title might be conferred upon men with very differing real duties, such as serving the king in a domestic capacity on one hand or on the other acting as tutor to one of the king's sons.[2] There must be some connexion with the chamber, but this covered a wide range of duties, for by the twelfth century the king's chamber meant much more than the king's private apartments. The chamber had become the department that controlled the royal finances, and since the king's possessions and resources had grown vastly, accommodation for much of his valuables and money had to be found in a separate treasury with chamberlains of its own. These considerations suggest that we must be very cautious in drawing inferences from the title unless we have positive evidence of the duties that a particular chamberlain performed. Again, we must face the difficulty that a man might be entitled chamberlain for more than one reason. He might have a hereditary claim to an honorific chamberlainship, and he might hold a quite distinct chamberlainship to which real duties attached. Thus A might have held an ancient chamberlainship that had become honorific, while B, an heir of his, might have been appointed to a later chamberlainship which entailed real duties. Obviously we cannot argue that because B is found discharging certain duties, therefore his ancestor A had discharged them in the remote past. Yet arguments of this kind have plunged the history of the chamberlains of the exchequer into seemingly inextricable confusion, a confusion from which it is our purpose to extricate the history of the office.

It is not open to dispute that in the thirteenth century the chamberlains of the exchequer were deemed to hold their offices by serjeanty, that is, the right to hold office was in each case regarded as inhering in the tenure of certain lands, the Mauduit chamberlainship being

---

[1] Above, p. 222.　　[2] Below, p. 428.

associated with Hartley Mauditt and the Fitz Gerold chamberlainship with Sevenhampton and Cricklade. If this doctrine had any
firm basis in law we should expect to find it stated, or at least implied, in the charters granted by Henry II to the two chamberlains
who held office in the treasury at the beginning of his reign. These
two charters, the one in favour of William Mauduit II granted at
Whitsuntide 1153 and the other in favour of Warin fitz Gerold
granted (it would seem) at Michaelmas 1155, are printed below for
the first time. It is quite clear that both charters grant the chamberlainship of the treasury in gross, in other words, whether the office
was held for life or whether it descended by inheritance, it did not
run with the tenure of lands. In William Mauduit's case the office
is obviously additional to the chamberlainship he had held in 1135.
'Insuper eciam', says Duke Henry, 'reddidi eidem camerariam
mei thesauri cum liberacione et cum omnibus pertinenciis.' Nor is the
chamberlainship of the treasury granted to him in fee and inheritance as his other chamberlainship is. On the other hand the
companion chamberlainship of the treasury granted to Warin fitz
Gerold is in inheritance. But the office, though heritable, does not
run with, nor is it related in any way to, the honour of Eudes *dapifer*,
a large part of which is also granted by the same charter to Warin
to be held by knight service,[1] not, be it noted, by serjeanty. These
two charters should dispose, once and for all, of the doctrine that
these chamberlainships were originally serjeanties, a doctrine for
which J. H. Round was largely responsible.[2] That they were claimed
and recognised as serjeanties in the thirteenth century may be true
enough but, like the coronation serjeanties which were also recognised in that century,[3] these are among a number of fictions that
were then accepted by the exchequer. That other exchequer serjeanties were supposed to have been created by Henry II doubtless
made it easier to believe that the two chamberlains held their office
by serjeanty, though scrutiny of their charters should dissipate any
such notion. But since a critic of Round's eminence not only knew
of one of the charters, but actually cited it in support of the thesis
that the chamberlainships were serjeanties, and since this thesis has
hitherto passed unchallenged, some further explanation seems desirable, especially since one fallacy inevitably breeds another. For if
the chamberlains of the exchequer held their office by serjeanty and
if one of the serjeanties could be traced back to a Domesday tenant,
as Round argued, then the organisation of the exchequer, in fact, if
not in name, could be traced back to the eleventh century.

To put the issue clearly, it will be well to have before us examples
of charters that actually did create a serjeanty. A well-authenticated

---

[1] If corroboration of the charter were required, this is supplied by *Red Book of the Exchequer*, pp. 354-5, and *Pipe Roll, 14 Henry II*, p. 39.
[2] *Commune of London*, pp. 81-5.   [3] *Traditio*, xvi.131-6.

serjeanty is that granted by Henry I to Eustace of Barrington. The king's charter gives to Eustace, his serjeant,

terram illam que fuit Gaufridi Forestarii in Hatfelda solutam et quietam pro custodia forestae meae.[1]

Here, it will be seen, certain land is given on condition that a specific service is performed. All forms of tenure demanded some form of service. What distinguishes serjeanty from military tenure is that knight service is not required and, although the distinction is not clear cut, what distinguishes serjeanty from socage is that a money payment is not required.[2] Of course, the nature of the service could be changed and that change could convert another tenure into serjeanty. Authenticated cases of this kind are rare, and the following brief charter of Henry II's is therefore of special interest.

Henricus rex Anglorum *etc*. Sciatis me dedisse et quietum clamasse in perpetuum de me et heredibus meis Auchero et heredibus suis xxvi. solidos quos ipse Aucherus michi reddere solebat singulis annis de firma de Waltham de terra que fuit patris sui et Orgari fratris sui tali condicione quod Aucherus vel heredes sui accingent quando ego vel heredes mei bersabimus. Testibus rege Henrico filio meo, comite Willelmo de Mandeuile et aliis. Apud Westmonasterium.[3]

These two charters relate to forest serjeanties. Another charter of Henry II's is perhaps of more direct interest because, though it did not in set terms convert some other tenure into serjeanty, this was its effect, and also because what was created was a 'chamberlain' serjeanty. The beneficiary was Richard le Roux (*Ruffus, le Rus*), a chamberlain to whom the king granted land at Immeden (Melksham) in Wiltshire at Michaelmas 1166.[4] The king seems also to have granted him land at Imber in the same county, though it formed part of the estates of the bishop of Salisbury.[5] After Richard had possessed these lands for some years they were granted to him in inheritance, together with the wood of Seende and his houses at Devizes, which presumably he already held. The terms of the grant should be noted:

Sciatis me concessisse et dedisse et presenti carta confirmasse Ricardo Ruffo camerario meo pro servicio suo Immedmere et Immedon et bosculum de Sende et domus quas idem Ricardus habebat apud Divisas sibi et heredibus suis habenda et tenenda de me et heredibus meis per servicium camerarie mee.[6]

---

[1] British Museum Additional Charter 28313; *Facsimiles of Royal Charters*, no. 8. The date is 1126-7.

[2] We simplify. Maitland's description can hardly be bettered (*History of English Law*, i.282-90).

[3] Harleian MS. 391, fo. 67*b*. The extreme limits of date are the young king's coronation on 14 June 1170 and his death on 11 June 1183; but since he left England for the last time on April 1180, it must be earlier than this.

[4] *Pipe Roll, 14 Henry II*, p. 157.   [5] *Ibid.*, p. 160.

[6] *Foedera*, i.41. The charter is ascribed to 1177 by Eyton, *Itinerary of Henry II*, p. 218. For the later history of the serjeanty see *Book of Fees*, pp. 12, 341, 380, 586, 738, 1177.

Here we have three charters, using different language but each creating a serjeanty in the recognised meaning of the word, the meaning that it certainly had before the end of the twelfth century. We have but to contrast these charters with a charter granting an exchequer 'serjeanty' to see how different the latter was. This charter was in favour of Roger of Wallingford and was granted by Henry II at or about Michaelmas 1156. It has been supposed that 'the post of Usher of the Exchequer was a serjeanty attached to the manor of Aston Rowant in Oxfordshire, part of the land assigned in Domesday Book to Richard and other of the King's servants'[1]: but what does Roger's charter say?

Sciatis quod ego dedi Rogero de Warenguefort servienti meo ministerium de hosteria de scaccario meo pro servicio suo cum omnibus pertinenciis eidem ministerio. Quare volo et firmiter precipio quod idem Rogerus et heredes sui habeant et teneant predictum ministerium de magistratu hostierie de scaccario meo bene et in pace et honorifice et libere et quiete sicut aliquis illud melius habuit tempore Henrici regis avi mei quod nullus de eodem ministerio se intromittat nisi per eum. . . .[2]

Plainly the office is granted in gross: its tenure does not run with any land. Roger is already one of the king's serjeants, but that does not make the office a serjeanty. Who held the office under Henry I we do not know, but there is nothing to suggest that it was some predecessor in title of Roger's in Aston Rowant or any other land.

It is alleged, too, that Gervase, the weigher of the exchequer at the beginning of Henry II's reign, held his land at Broad Windsor

per servitium moram faciendi ad scaccarium domini regis ad denarios dicti regis ibidem ponderandos, et qualibet die pro servitio illo accipiet xii. denarios de bursa domini regis.[3]

This language is not of the mid-twelfth century and there is no reason to suppose that it corresponds closely to the terms of Gervase's charter, if he had one. The land which Gervase is alleged to have held in serjeanty was held by his father and grandfather before him, and there is no shadow of evidence that the Domesday tenant, Hunger,[4] for all that he was one of the king's serjeants, occupied the office that his grandson occupied or any corresponding office. Round believed that, because he had traced the descent of the land, he had traced the descent of the office: 'by the help of the genealogical and topographical research', he said 'one is now enabled to carry back this exchequer serjeanty to the days of the Conqueror himself'.[5] This is the same fallacious reasoning that enabled him to carry back

---

[1] *Dialogus de Scaccario*, p. xxx. The claim that the land was held in serjeanty was made under Henry III (*Book of Fees*, pp. 1376, 1395).
[2] Madox, *History of the Exchequer*, ii.272 n. *m*; *Foedera*, i.42.
[3] Coker, *Survey of Dorsetshire* (1732), p. 15. We have not traced the original document: compare a *Book of Fees*, pp. 260, 1182, 1239, 1387.
[4] D.B., i.851.   [5] *E.H.R.*, xxvi.726.

the Mauduit exchequer serjeanty to the days of the Conqueror.[1] It is possible that Gervase, who seems to have been nephew by marriage of Herbert the Chamberlain,[2] was the weigher of the exchequer (or rather of the treasury[3]) under Henry I, but we cannot carry conjecture beyond this. Just as Roger of Wallingford was granted the office of usher as recompense for his services, so presumably Gervase, whom we may safely suppose to have been also one of the king's serjeants, was rewarded with the office of weigher.

In the absence of evidence and in the presence of authentic charters in a very different sense, the doctrine that the exchequer (or treasury) serjeanties, whether the chamberlainship or some other office, originated in the twelfth century falls to the ground. That they were of eleventh-century origin is mere myth, irreconcilable with any evidence we have for the origin of the exchequer or the early history of the treasury, and unworthy of further discussion. A late twelfth-century origin—or rather the conversion of one form of tenure into another—is not perhaps inherently impossible, but no proof has been adduced that will stand scrutiny. No charter corresponding to those granting forest serjeanties or the 'chamberlain' serjeanty of Richard le Roux can be produced as evidence of the creation or transformation of the chamberlainships of the exchequer. No charter converted into a serjeanty the knights' fees that had belonged to the honour of Eudes *dapifer* and that Henry II granted to Warin fitz Gerold. Whether the chamberlainship to which William Mauduit II laid claim, to which the castle of Porchester and lands in England and Normandy were appurtenant, was a serjeanty is a quite irrelevant question, for this chamberlainship was distinct from the chamberlainship of the treasury. A reference to the *cartae* of 1166 will show Henry fitz Gerold, brother and heir of Warin, acknowledging that he owes knight service for the honour of Eudes *dapifer* and for the lands that the king had given him in Sparsholt and Sevenhampton.[4] William Mauduit III, the son of the chamberlain of the grant of 1153, owes knight service for the lands that had formerly belonged to Michael of Hanslope, but he is silent regarding the rest of the barony that he held of the king.[5]

We can test in another way the doctrine that these chamberlainships were serjeanties. It can hardly be disputed that Herbert the Chamberlain, who served as treasurer under Henry I, had previously been a chamberlain of the treasury. It would appear also that, when he finally retired from duty in the treasury, he retained the title of chamberlain, which descended to his son, who is found in Winchester, as Herbert the king's chamberlain, in 1148.[6] There is, how-

---

[1] *Commune of London*, p. 83; *Ancestor*, v.207.   [2] *E.H.R.*, xxvi.725.
[3] He was known as Gervase *de Thesauro* under Henry II (*ibid.*, p. 726). We thus have an exact parallel with the chamberlains of the treasury, who became known subsequently as chamberlains of the exchequer.   [4] *Red Book of the Exchequer*, pp. 354-6.
[5] *Ibid.*, p. 313.   [6] *Winton Domesday* (D.B. iv), pp. 542, 558.

ever, nothing to connect Herbert fitz Herbert or his descendants with the treasury.[1] Two other generally recognised early chamberlains of the treasury are Geoffrey de Clinton and William of Pont de l'Arche. Geoffrey was dead in 1132,[2] leaving as his heir another Geoffrey, who was also entitled king's chamberlain but has no known connexion with either the treasury or the exchequer.[3] William was dead by 1148.[4] He appears to have left an heir, Robert of Pont de l'Arche, who, however, seems never to have been termed chamberlain.[5] It should be evident that the failure of all attempts to establish the descent of the offices from holder to heir[6] has been inevitable: the offices did not descend in this fashion at all. There has, in fact, been no problem to solve, only a misapprehension to disperse.

Before we take leave of Herbert fitz Herbert, we may perhaps make use of the well-documented history of the family to illustrate the manner in which the idea of serjeanty attached itself to land held by hereditary ministers. Herbert fitz Herbert succeeded to the land that his father had held in chief in Berkshire and Wiltshire and to more extensive lands that he had held as a mesne tenant.[7] He seems to have died between 1148 and 1154, for early in 1155 his son Robert obtained a charter from Henry II recognising his right to his father's land and office.[8] It runs:

Sciatis me reddidisse Roberto filio Hereberti Camerarii totam terram patris sui et ministerium patris sui de cameraria mea.

It will be seen that this charter does not countenance any notion that tenure of the chamberlainship depended upon tenure of any part of the land. Shortly after the issue of this charter Robert died and was succeeded by his brother Herbert.[9] It was Herbert who, in 1166, claimed that he held his Berkshire fee

---

[1] For Herbert fitz Herbert's sons, Robert and Herbert, see below, pp. 427-8.

[2] Farrer, *Itinerary of Henry I*, p. 143 n.

[3] *Cartulary of Oseney Abbey*, i.3, 5, 6, 425; Salter, *Early Oxford Charters*, no. 69; *Hatton's Book of Seals*, nos. 194, 508.

[4] Winton Domesday (D.B. iv), p. 558. See also Stephen's charter, which must be before the queen's death in May 1152, in *Monasticon*, vi.172, no. xi.

[5] For Robert's lands see *Red Book of the Exchequer*, pp. 206-8, 209, and for his descent from William see *V.C.H., Hants*, iv.387. There are a number of references to Robert in the Pipe Rolls from 7 Henry II (p. 57) onwards. Most will be found abstracted in the *Red Book of the Exchequer*. The later references apparently refer to a son of the same name.

[6] *Dialogus de Scaccario*, Oxford ed., pp. 20-1; ed. Johnson, pp. xxv-xxvii.

[7] The extent of his possessions is indicated by the *cartae* of 1166, though these, of course, refer to his son (*Red Book of the Exchequer*, pp. 205, 207, 246, 305, 307). The Hampshire lands which the Domesday Herbert had acquired by marriage with Hunger's daughter reverted to Gervase the weigher in 1130 on Herbert's death (*E.H.R.*, xxvi.724-726). They were the basis of a claim in the thirteenth century by Thomas of Windsor to hold the office of melter by serjeanty (*Book of Fees*, pp. 76, 703, 1418-9).

[8] Eyton, *Antiquities of Shropshire*, vii.150.

[9] This is the inference from the references under Berkshire and Hampshire to Herbert fitz Herbert in *Pipe Roll, 2 Henry II*, pp. 35, 56, and its silence regarding Robert.

in capite . . . per servitium unius militis et per serjantiam suam et illud servitium debet facere per corpus suum.[1]

Since Herbert's predecessors had enfeoffed a number of knights, it is clear that we must identify this serjeanty, and the service that Hubert admitted he was bound to perform in person, with the chamberlainship that his brother, his father and his grandfather had held before him. In just the same way as this chamberlainship became associated with the tenure of certain lands, so, at a later date, by steps which are not so clear, the exchequer chamberlainships became associated with the tenure of certain lands. In neither case was there a historical or legal foundation for the claim.

If we thus dispose of one fallacy, we can, with the aid of the charters granted to William Mauduit and Warin fitz Gerold, dispose of another, equally pernicious, namely that these chamberlains were deputies, in the exchequer, of the master chamberlain. Aubrey de Vere was created master chamberlain in 1133 after an interval of twenty-seven years during which there had been no such office in England, that is during the whole of the proved existence of the exchequer up to that date.[2] This creation was, like the chamberlainships of the treasury, in gross[3]: it was not a serjeanty,[4] it carried no specific duties, and there is nothing in the charter to suggest that the master chamberlain had any duties in the exchequer or that he had to find deputies in the treasury. The office was honorific, one that carried status and certain emoluments at court and nothing more.[5] Whether upon Aubrey's death in 1141 his son, another Aubrey, was recognised as master chamberlain by Stephen is unknown. In any case he speedily deserted the king and, though he was recognised as master chamberlain by the Empress and by her son, this was an empty honour. Aubrey's subsequent return to the king's allegiance earned for him recognition as earl of Oxford and perhaps (though this can be only conjectural) as master chamberlain.[6] But his vacillations cannot have commended him to Henry, and he had to pay 500 marks in 1155 to obtain the new king's recognition of his claim to the office.[7] But already William Mauduit, if not Warin fitz Gerold, was occupying the chamberlainship of the treasury. How a relationship of principal and deputy can be read into these appointments it is difficult to conceive. Chamberlains were many and various in the twelfth century—one chamberlain was tutor to the king's son[8]—and there is no reason to suppose that one chamberlain with a specialised

---

[1] *Red Book of the Exchequer*, p. 307.
[2] For the history of the office see G.E.C. *Complete Peerage*, x, Appendix F.
[3] For the charter see *Hatton's Book of Seals*, no. 39: it was previously printed by Madox.
[4] As Round pointed out (*King's Serjeants and Officers of State*, pp. 121-2).
[5] 'Constitutio Domus Regis' in *Dialogus de Scaccario*), p. 133.
[6] *Complete Peerage*, x.202-3.
[7] *Red Book of the Exchequer*, p. 651.
[8] *Pipe Roll, 2 Henry II*, p. 65, 'Mainardo camerario'; p. 66, 'Mainardo magistro filii regis': and so *Pipe Roll, 3 Henry II*, p. 101; *4 Henry II*, p. 180.

office deputised for some other chamberlain, even though that chamberlain was called the master chamberlain.

THE MAUDUIT CHAMBERLAINSHIP

Though the essential document for the history of the chamberlainship of the exchequer held by the Mauduit family is the charter granted by Henry duke of Normandy to William Mauduit II, it will clear up many obscurities and settle a number of doubts if we examine in some detail six documents in all, which illustrate the early history of the family. The three earliest documents are a writ and two charters of Henry I which have been printed in the *Regesta Regum Anglo-Normannorum*: the three others are a charter of the Empress, the charter of Duke Henry mentioned above, and finally a charter of Henry as king, all of which we print below. The texts are all derived from the Beauchamp Cartulary (British Museum Additional MS. 28024), a very imperfect rendering of the originals: in three cases some assistance is derived from abstracts in the King's Bench roll for the Michaelmas term 1253 (KB 26/151). It may be helpful if we first supply notes on these six documents (which we distinguish as A, B, C, D, E and F) and thereafter give a general commentary explaining their significance.

A. A writ,[1] addressed to William (Giffard), bishop of Winchester, and Henry de Port (the sheriff), notifying the grant to Hawise, widow of William Mauduit I, of her dower and all that William gave her in his lifetime, namely Shalden and Hartley Mauditt (both near Alton, Hants), with the demesne mansion and other land and houses in Winchester. This writ can be dated within narrow limits. It is not later than the election of William of Warelwast as bishop of Exeter, shortly before his consecration on 11 August 1107,[2] nor can it be earlier than the 'Winton Domesday' which shows Robert Mauduit I in possession of the houses in Winchester that had belonged to William Mauduit I.[3] This survey cannot itself be earlier than 1102, when Roger bishop of Salisbury, who is mentioned in it, was elected to that see.[4] The extreme dates for the writ are therefore 1102-7, but since the king was absent in Normandy from July 1106 to some time in Lent 1107[5] and since William of Warelwast did not return to England until Whitsuntide,[6] it is not likely to have been issued as late as 1107. It appears to have followed an action by Hawise to recover her dower, presumably not very long after her husband's death, which may have happened before Henry I's accession; for it will be noticed that the writ does not suggest that William Mauduit I

---

[1] *Regesta*, no. 729: text printed at p. 311, no. xxviii.
[2] Eadmer, *Historia Novorum*, pp. 185, 187.
[3] *Domesday Book*, iv.533, 534.
[4] Eadmer, *op. cit.*, p. 141; *Domesday Book*, iv.535a: Round's dating in *V.C.H. Hants* i.527-8, cannot be sustained.
[5] For particulars see Farrer, *Itinerary of Henry I*, pp. 38-9.
[6] Eadmer, *op. cit.*, p. 185.

was alive after the reign of Rufus. There seems no reason why the writ should not be as early as 1103 and no objection can be taken to placing it *circa* 1105.[1]

B. A charter[2] addressed to William (Giffard) bishop of Winchester, the sheriff of Hampshire and the reeve of Winchester, notifying the grant to William Mauduit II of his mother's dower upon her death, together with Fyfield, which his father held. This charter, and a companion charter in similar but abbreviated terms addressed generally,[3] cannot be later than the creation of Robert, Henry I's son, earl of Gloucester, before the end of 1122.[4] A related charter of Robert's shows that Fyfield had been held by Robert Mauduit I,[5] and the inference is that the king's charter gives effect to a family arrangement, presumably following the death of Robert Mauduit II in the White Ship on 25 November 1120.[6]

C. A charter,[7] addressed generally, granting to William Mauduit II the daughter and land of Michael of Hanslope. If the occurrence of Rabel of Tancarville among the witnesses indicates that he is chamberlain, the date cannot be earlier than 1129 when he succeeded his father.[8]

D. A charter, addressed generally, granting to William Mauduit II Barrowden (Rutland), with the soke that Michael of Hanslope had there. This charter was issued after the Empress had assumed the title of lady of the English in April 1141, but before the creation of Miles of Gloucester as earl of Hereford on 25 July 1141. It may therefore be safely assigned to May 1141 when the Empress is known to have been at Reading.[9]

E. A charter, addressed generally, granting to William Mauduit II (i) the chamberlainship as he held it in 1135 and the land appurtenant thereto in England and Normandy, in particular the castle of Porchester, (ii) the land of Michael of Hanslope which Henry I granted him, together with Barrowden and the whole soke which Queen Maud granted to Michael and the Empress granted to William, (iii) the chamberlainship of the treasury, (iv) Harborough and Bowden (Leicestershire) with the constableship of Rockingham Castle and, prospectively, (v) a hundred pounds' worth of lands in

---

[1] Farrer, no. 98, dated it 1101-6; the editors of the *Regesta*, 1102-5. The place of issue, Lega, appears more likely to be East Leigh, near Havant, than Bessels Leigh, as Farrer suggested.   [2] *Regesta*, ii, no. 1255: text at p. 340, no. cxxxi.

[3] Additional MS. 28024, p. 28b: it omits any reference to Fyfield.

[4] Round, *Geoffrey de Mandeville*, p. 433. The more precise dating, June-September 1122, cannot be sustained by the evidence cited in the *Complete Peerage*, v.683.

[5] Additional MS. 28024, p. 28b: printed *Regesta*, ii.340.

[6] Ordericus Vitalis, *Historia Ecclesiastica*, iv.419.

[7] *Regesta*, ii, no. 1719: text at p. 375. Some better readings will be found in the abstract in KB 26/151, m. 46d.

[8] *Histoire Littéraire de France*, xxxii.204. William of Tancarville presumably died before Michaelmas, since he is not mentioned as a holder of land in the pipe roll of 1130, while Rabel is (*Pipe Roll, 31 Henry I*, pp. 22, 80, 108). Rabel witnesses as *camerarius* in 1131 (Haskins, *Norman Institutions*, pp. 299-302; *Regesta*, no. 1688). The date, 1129, assigned to another charter witnessed by Rabel the chamberlain (*ibid.*, no. 1587) seems to us very dubious.   [9] Florence of Worcester, *Continuatio*, p. 130.

the royal demesne and from lands to be acquired by Henry. This charter may be ascribed, with great probability, to Whitsuntide 1153.[1]

F. A charter confirming to William Mauduit III the barony that his father held in England and Normandy, namely Hanslope with its appurtenances, Barrowden with (Wrangdike) Hundred and other appurtenances, Manton (Rutland), Shalden and Hartley Mauditt, his land at Rouen and his other Norman possessions. It must be dated before the king's departure from England in August 1158, perhaps, as Eyton suggested, early in that year.[2]

The information in these charters can be supplemented by the information contained in the pipe roll of 1130. This shows that William Mauduit II had in some previous year fined with the king to have his mother's dower in England and his father's land in Normandy.[3] Document B is one outcome of this fine: presumably another charter dealt with the Norman land, but this seems not to have survived. The pipe roll also shows that William of Pont de l'Arche agreed to pay 1000 marks for the office and daughter of Robert Mauduit.[4] As we have already explained, this 'office' cannot have been the hereditary chamberlainship.[5] Assuming that William married the daughter, it seems practically certain that this must have been a second marriage. For he can hardly have been born later than 1080,[6] and we may see the not uncommon outcome of a marriage between an elderly man and a young woman in the domestic tragedy recounted in the *Gesta Stephani*.[7] For the young wife took a lover, and they imprisoned the unfortunate husband. There is another piece of corroborative evidence. William's heir, Robert of Pont de l'Arche,[8] did not inherit the lands of Robert Mauduit and was presumably the son of an earlier marriage. It seems probable, too, that the Robert Mauduit who perished in the White Ship was the son of the elder Robert Mauduit and that his death explains why a daughter was left sole heiress. We may have here the explanation of the recognition of William Mauduit II as chamberlain before his brother's death— of which document C is convincing proof—and how it was that, after the death of William of Pont de l'Arche (and presumably of his wife), William Mauduit II was able to reassemble the inheritance of William Mauduit I, as document E shows him achieving. Doubtless the favour evidently accorded to him by Henry I, and the Empress and Henry II as well, helped him greatly; but his path seems to have been cleared by successive deaths in the senior branch of his family.

It may be well to bring together our facts and inferences in the

---

[1] Henry was then at Leicester and is not known to have been there at any other time in 1153-4: see *E.H.R.*, lxi.86-7.   [2] *Itinerary of Henry II*, p. 34.
[3] *Pipe Roll, 31 Henry I*, p. 38.   [4] *Ibid.*, p. 37.   [5] Above, p. 221.
[6] The many references to him in the 'Winton Domesday' (D.B. iv), 521, 534, 535, 537 indicate that he was then at his maturity.
[7] *Gesta Stephani* (ed. Potter), pp. 100-1. The incident is placed *s.a.* 1143.
[8] Above, p. 427.

form of a pedigree, which will help to make the early history of family plain. We have ventured to assume that Hawise was the second wife of William Mauduit I. This assumption seems to be warranted by a number of facts. Hawise survived her husband for many years, probably more than twenty. Her undoubted son, William Mauduit II, survived his brother, Robert Mauduit I, by nearly thirty years. Hawise established her right to her dower lands against Robert and these lands were secured to the younger son, who also, as a further special favour, obtained from the king the grant of his father's Norman lands, which can only have been done at the expense of Robert. These facts plainly call for an explanation. But we do not press the interpretation we have adopted, and the pedigree is easily amended, if it is assumed that Hawise was the mother of both of the sons of William Mauduit I.

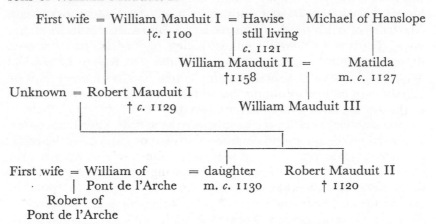

First wife = William Mauduit I = Hawise   Michael of Hanslope
               †c. 1100   still living
                                  c. 1121
                    William Mauduit II =   Matilda
                          †1158   m. c. 1127
Unknown = Robert Mauduit I
            † c. 1129   William Mauduit III

First wife = William of   = daughter   Robert Mauduit II
         | Pont de l'Arche   m. c. 1130   † 1120
      Robert of
    Pont de l'Arche

Of the men here shown in this pedigree all three William Mauduits and Robert Mauduit I are termed chamberlain, or are stated, in contemporary or sub-contemporary documents, to have held the office, and it is evident that the chamberlainship in question was not one specifically connected with the treasury. William of Pont de l'Arche is described as a chamberlain, but it is doubtful whether his title was at all affected by his second marriage. Robert Mauduit I, William Mauduit II, William Mauduit III and William of Pont de l'Arche seem all to have served as chamberlains of the treasury, but there is no suggestion in any of the documents here printed or other contemporary source that this office was hereditary or in any way associated with the tenure of any part of the Mauduit inheritance. Documents A and B are, in fact, irreconcilable with the claim that Hartley Mauduit was held 'per camerariam ad scaccarium', a claim for which the evidence goes back no farther than 1212.[1] Further, the documents suggest that the office of chamberlain, while passing from

---

[1] *Book of Fees*, p. 74. For later claims to the same effect see *ibid.*, p. 1364, *Inquisitions Post Mortem*, i.105 (no. 387).

father to son in the Mauduit family, was not strictly hereditary in the early period. It does not seem open to doubt, in the light of document C, that William Mauduit II was a chamberlain before the death of Robert Mauduit I and he certainly continued to hold office after the marriage of Robert's daughter. Nor did Henry II grant a chamberlainship in fee and inheritance to William Mauduit III, though he was certainly recognised as chamberlain shortly after Henry's charter confirming him in his father's barony.[1] Incidentally this charter shows that the possessions of William Mauduit II had been very much reduced from those lavishly granted when Henry was not yet king and was bidding for support.

A few words may be added regarding William of Pont de l'Arche. It is evident from document B that the relations between him and the Mauduit family did not begin with his marriage to a daughter of the house. The arrangement by which he paid £10 a year to William Mauduit II suggests that Hawise had granted him a lease of her dower lands (which would not, of course, extend beyond her own life) and that by a family arrangement the rent was to be paid to William Mauduit. But there is no indication that William of Pont de l'Arche had any other connexion with the Mauduit family or owed to them any claim to a chamberlainship.

D

Add. MS. 28024, fo. 49
KB 26/151, m. 46d

Matildis imperatrix, regis Henrici filia, Anglorum domina, archiepiscopis, episcopis, abbatibus, comitibus, baronibus, iusticiis, vicecomitibus, ministris et omnibus fidelibus suis Francis et Anglis tocius Anglie, salutem. Sciant omnes tam presentes quam futuri quod reddi et concessi in feodo et hereditate Willelmo Maledocto camerario meo Bergedunam[2] cum soca[3] quam ibi Michael de Hameslapa[4] antecessor suus habuit ad tenendum in capite sibi et heredibus suis de me et heredibus meis ita bene et honorifice sicut Matildis regina mater mea dedit eam Michaeli de Hameslapa antecessori[5] quam Willelmus de Albini tenebat de rege Henrico per xx. libras ad firmam, et pro hac reddicione dedit michi c. marcas argenti de releuamine. Quare volo et[6] firmiter precipio quod bene et in pace et honorifice et libere et quiete teneat in bosco et plano, in pratis et pascuis, in viis[7] et semitis,

---

[1] He is termed chamberlain in the Constitutions of Clarendon (*Select Charters*, p. 164).
[2] Berwedonam, KB.   [3] socha, Add. MS.   [4] Hamslepe, KB.
[5] Queen Maud's charter is given in abstract on the same folio of Additional MS.: the lands granted were in Barrowden, Luffenham, Seaton and Thorp by Water.
[6] From this point onwards *et* is in most instances omitted in the transcript: many words are put in more modern form or blundered.   [7] via, Add. MS.

in aquis et molendinis, infra burgum et extra in omnibus locis, cum soca et saca, tol et team et infangenetheof, cum omnibus libertatibus et quietacionibus et consuetudinibus cum quibus antecessor suus predictus Michael melius et liberius tenuit. Testibus Theobaldo archiepiscopo Cantuariensi, Willelmo episcopo sancti Dauidis, Roberto comite Gloucestrie, comite Reginaldo Cornubie, Milone Gloucestrie constabulario, Gaufrido Boterello, Willelmo de Feblato,[1] Iohanne mariscallo, Willelmo cancellario, Radulfo Painello, Willelmo Painello, Roberto filio Martini. Apud Radingas.[2]

E

Add. MS. 28024, fo. 21b

Henricus dux Normannorum et Aquitanorum et comes Andegauorum omnibus archiepiscopis, episcopis, consulibus et baronibus, vice-comitibus, iusticiis et omnibus amicis et fidelibus suis Normannis et Anglis, salutem. Sciatis me reddisse et concessisse Willelmo Male-docto camerario meo in feodo et hereditate sibi et heredibus suis ministerium camerarie mee sicut ipse habuit in anno et die quo rex Henricus fuit viuus et mortuus et totam terram que ad camerariam pertinet et in Normannia et in Anglia, et nominatim castellum de Porcestria cum toto honore, et totam terram Michaelis de Hamslape, sicut rex Henricus eam illi dedit, et Bergedonam cum tota soca quam regina Matillis dedit Michaeli et mater mea illam Willelmo reddidit. Insuper eciam reddidi eidem camerariam mei thesauri cum libera-cione et cum omnibus pertinenciis[3]
castellum scilicet de Porcestria, ut supradiximus, et omnes terras ad predictam camerariam et ad predictum castellum pertinentes, siue sint in Anglia siue Normannia, sicut pater suus illam camerariam cum pertinenciis melius habuit et sicut Robertus Maledoctus frater suus eam habebat die quo viuus fuit et mortuus et totam terram patris sui sicut pater suus eam melius et liberius unquam tenuit, tali condicione quod dum ego vixero non mittam eum vel heredem suum de terra illa in placitum et si aliquis heredum meorum illum vel heredem suum in placitum[4] vellet mittere priusquam illum in placitum mitteret excangium equiualens de dominio suo ei inde daret. Preterea eidem dedi in augmentum sui feodi pro bono seruicio Hauerbergam et Bugedonam cum tota soca et constabulariam de Rochingeham[5] in feodo et hereditate sibi et heredibus suis ad

[1] diffubulato, Add. MS.   [2] Radinam, Add. MS.
[3] A line or more has been omitted in the transcript.   [4] MS. inserts non.
[5] Richegeam, MS. That William Mauduit II was constable of Rockingham Castle is shown by a writ on fo. 53b ordering those owing castle-guard to obey his summons: this writ which is witnessed by Thomas the chancellor at St. Edmund's cannot be later than August 1158 when the king left England and was probably issued at Whitsuntide 1157 when he wore his crown at St. Edmund's.

tenendum de me et de meis heredibus et centum libratas terre in dominio meo et de terris michi accidentibus de primis meis conquisicionibus. Quare volo et firmiter precipio ut idem Willelmus omnia ista predicta bene et libere et quiete et honorifice teneat in bosco et in plano, in pratis et pascuis, in aquis et [molendinis, in viuariis et piscariis, infra burgum et][1] extra, in viis et semitis et in omnibus locis, cum tol et team, cum soca et saca et infangenthef et cum omnibus libertatibus et cum liberis consuetudinibus predictis terris et honoribus pertinentibus. Testibus Willelmo cancellario, Willelmo Cumin, Roberto comite Legerecestrie, Rogero comite Herefordie, Ricardo de Humez constabulario, Manessero Biset dapifero, Walchelino Maminot, Hugone de Bello Campo, Iohanne de Eid', Halenallo fratre suo, Radulfo de Chahainiis et Willelmo Grenocer, Iohanne Maledocto, Henrico filio Geroldi. Apud Legerecestriam.

F

Add. MS. 28024, fo. 22a
KB 26/151, m. 46d

Henricus rex Anglorum, dux Normannorum et Aquitanorum, comes Andegauorum, archiepiscopis, episcopis, abbatibus, comitibus, iusticiis, vicecomitibus, ministris et omnibus fidelibus suis tocius Anglie et Normannie, Francis et Anglis, salutem. Sciatis me concessisse et confirmasse Willelmo Malduit filio Willelmi Malduit camerarii mei baroniam totam quam pater suus de me tenuit tam in Anglia quam in Normannia die qua homo meus deuenit apud Wodestoc predictus Willelmus camerarii filius videlicet Hameslapam cum pertinenciis suis et terram suam de Bergedona cum hundredo et aliis pertinenciis et Manetonam et alias terras quas dedi patri suo apud Notingham et Scaldedenam et Herlegam cum pertinenciis suis et terram suam de Rothomago et omnes alias terras et tenuras suas de Normannia. Quare volo et firmiter precipio quod ipse post mortem patris sui et heredes sui post ipsum in feodo et hereditate de me et heredibus meis predictam baroniam et terram habeat et teneat bene et in pace, libere, quiete et honorifice, cum omnibus pertinenciis suis, in bosco et plano, in pratis et pascuis, in viis et semitis, in aquis et molendinis, in viuariis et piscariis, infra burgum et extra in omnibus rebus et locis, cum tol et theam et infangenthef et soca et saca et cum omnibus libertatibus et liberis consuetudinibus cum quibus pater suus melius et liberius tenuit tempore regis Henrici aui mei vel meo. Testibus Roberto episcopo Lincolniensi, Thoma cancellario, Ricardo de Haia, Roberto de Monteforti,[2] Willelmo de sancto Iohanne, Willelmo de

---

[1] Words within crotchets omitted in MS.
[2] Mounteford, MS.

Caisneto, Hugone de Piris, Willelmo de Lanualeio, Roberto de Wateuilla. Apud Wudestocam.

THE FITZ GEROLD CHAMBERLAINSHIP

A single charter suffices to illustrate the history of this chamberlainship, a confirmation issued by Henry II early in his reign in favour of Warin fitz Gerold. In the course of the thirteenth century the chamberlainship passed to Isabelle de Forz, countess of Aumale, and was with other property granted by her to Adam of Stratton in 1276.[1] A writ of *quo warranto* was brought against Adam in the King's Bench in the Michaelmas term 1283 in respect of the Hundred of Highworth (Wilts.), and in the course of the proceedings he produced this charter, the text of which is entered on the rolls for the term. There is nothing in the charter that connects the chamberlainship with Sevenhampton (in Highworth), as claimed by a later Warin fitz Gerold under King John,[2] or with Cricklade and Sevenhampton, as claimed subsequently by his daughter, Margery de Reviers, Isabelle's grandmother.[3]

There is no evidence that Warin fitz Gerold had a hereditary claim to a chamberlainship of any sort, such as William Mauduit had. Of his career before he became chamberlain of the treasury little is known. In Stephen's reign he seems to have had some connexion with the elder Aubrey de Vere, probably through Aubrey's daughter, Roesia, the wife of Geoffrey de Mandeville. It was their son, Geoffrey de Mandeville III, who granted Sawbridgeworth to Warin.[4] By 1153 Warin was chamberlain to Duke Henry,[5] and though he is found witnessing a charter of Stephen's at Dunstable early in 1154, the charter is one in which the king confirms a charter of the duke's,[6] and there is no ground for supposing that, like the younger Aubrey de Vere, he vacillated in his allegiance, for he is found with the duke in Normandy later in the year.[7] After Henry's accession to the throne he may have served the office of chamberlain of the treasury by deputy, for he was active in the chamber until his death in 1158, when he was succeeded in the treasury, and apparently in the chamber also, by his brother and heir Henry fitz Gerold.[8]

The date of the charter must lie between Henry II's coronation on 19 December 1154 and his departure for the Continent in August

[1] *Cal. Charter Rolls*, ii.200.   [2] *Red Book of the Exchequer*, p. 486.

[3] *Book of Fees*, pp. 737, 1420.

[4] For the grant see *Red Book of the Exchequer*, p. 356; Sloane Charter xxxii.64 (*B.M. Facsimiles*, no. 43); Douglas, *Feudal Documents from the Abbey of Bury St. Edmund's*, pp. 164-6 (misdated). It seems probable that the grant of this manor, upon which Eudes *dapifer* had had a lien, was connected with the grant to Warin of Eudes' honor: cf. Round, *Geoffrey de Mandeville*, pp. 236, 241.   [5] Delisle-Berger, *Actes de Henri II*, nos. 33-57*.

[6] *Cal. Charter Rolls*, iii.378.   [7] Delisle-Berger, no. 76*.

[8] The replacement of Warin by Henry in *Pipe Roll, 4 Henry II*, pp. 123-4 (cf. *Pipe Roll, 3 Henry II*, pp. 80-1) shows that he was dead before Michaelmas. Many references in the pipe rolls show that Warin was active in the chamber: for Henry's activities there see *Pipe Roll, 4 Henry II*, p. 179; *6 Henry II*, p. 47; *10 Henry II*, p. 21; *13 Henry II*, p. 207; *14 Henry II*, p. 199.

1158. Since the pipe roll of 1156 shows claims by sheriffs for allowances in respect of lands granted to Warin at Sparsholt, Cricklade and Highworth,[1] it is probable that the charter was issued at Michaelmas 1155, when the king was at Winchester.[2]

KB 27/79, m. 25
KB 27/80, m. 7

Henricus rex Anglorum et dux Normannorum et Aquitanorum et comes Andegauorum archiepiscopis, episcopis, abbatibus, comitibus, iusticiis, baronibus, vicecomitibus, ministris et omnibus fidelibus suis tocius Anglie et Normannie, salutem. Sciatis me dedisse et concessisse et confirmasse Warino filio Geroldi pro seruicio suo sibi et heredibus suis ad tenendum de me et de heredibus meis camerariam meam de thesauro meo et totum feodum militum quod habebam in meo dominio de honore Eudonis dapiferi, excepto feodo decem militum quod Ricardus de Lucy tunc habebat de feodo Willelmi de Saucheuilla. Et nominatim ei do et concedo totam terram quam idem Eudo dapifer habuit in Londonia die qua fuit viuus et mortuus, et manerium de Kemsinges, cum omnibus pertinenciis suis, et in Crykelada quicquid erat in dominio meo, et Seuehamtonam, cum toto hundredo de Worthe, et Sparsholte, cum omnibus pertinenciis suis. Quare volo et firmiter precipio quod ipse et heredes sui habeant et teneant de me et heredibus meis camerariam predictam et omnia prenominata in pace et libere et quiete et honorifice, cum soka et saka et tol et theam et infangenethef, et cum omnibus aliis libertatibus et liberis consuetudinibus predicte camerarie et terris et tenementis prenominatis pertinentibus in bosco et plano, in pratis et pascuis, in aquis et molendinis, et in omnibus locis et in omnibus rebus sicut ego ipse ea melius et honorificencius tenui in manu mea et sicut aliquis ante me ea liberius et quietius habuit et hec omnia predicta ei do et concedo in expectacione guarisonis sue quam ei dabo. Testibus Alienora regina Anglorum et Theobaldo Cantuariensi archiepiscopo et Thoma cancellario et comite Raginaldo et Roberto comite Legercestrie et Hugone comite de Norffolcia et Henrico de Essexa constabulario et Ricardo de Humez constabulario et Ricardo de Lucy et Manassero Biset dapifero et Roberto de Dunestanuilla. Apud Wyntoniam.

[1] *Pipe Roll, 2 Henry II*, pp. 34, 35, 57.
[2] Cf. Eyton, *Itinerary of Henry II*, pp. 12-13.

THE ASSIZES OF HENRY II

Iᴺ the *Select Charters* Stubbs printed, without any indication that they might not be authentic, texts that he entitled the Assize of Clarendon of 1166 and the Assize of the Forest of 1184.[1] He seems to have had no suspicion that they might be fabrications: indeed, in 1867, when he appears first to have come across them in a manuscript of Howden's *Chronica*, he had spoken of their 'immense value . . . as to our constitutional history',[2] and this opinion he never revised. These texts have been generally accepted by historians with no more misgivings than Stubbs had and certainly without challenge, presumably in the belief that their acceptance by Stubbs was sufficient warranty. They stand, it might be thought, rather in a class apart, for, as a rule, Stubbs did not pretend to present critical texts of the documents and excerpts he gathered together for his collection: he took them, without disguise, as they stood in printed sources available at the time of compilation in 1870. But these two, with a few others, he edited himself.

The *Select Charters* passed through eight editions during Stubbs's lifetime. The changes he thought fit to make in successive editions were slight. It was not until after his death that substantial eliminations, revisions and additions were made by H. W. C. Davis for the ninth edition, which appeared in 1913. Davis's work seems to have been at times somewhat perfunctory, and the revision he considered necessary did not meet what was required if all the texts were to stand scrutiny. It is hardly an exaggeration to say that the most unsatisfactory among them remained unaltered. We may take as an example the text of the Provisions of Oxford, which Stubbs borrowed from the *Annals of Burton*, edited in the Rolls Series by Luard, who had made no attempt to collate the single manuscript of the annals with parallel texts.[3] Consequently the scribe's obviously unsatisfactory text, accompanied by a wooden translation, has been printed and reprinted to the mystification of generations of students for nearly a century. Even an easily filled lacuna has remained a blank.[4] The critical

---

[1] First edition (1870), pp. 134-9, 149-52; ninth edition (1913), pp. 167-73, 185-8.

[2] 'Benedict of Peterborough', i.lxi.

[3] *Annales Monastici*, i.446-53; *Select Charters* (1st ed.), pp. 378-87. The sole text of the annals is in B.M., Cotton MS. Vespasian E, iii. For other texts of the Provisions see Richardson and Sayles, 'The Provisions of Oxford' in *Bulletin John Rylands Library*, vol. xvii, and separately. Luard (p. xxxvi) states his belief that no other copies existed.

[4] Ninth edition, pp. 378-87. Some slight revision has been made in the translation, but it remains a deplorable specimen of translator's English: e.g. 'and that in the year he give

standard of the *Select Charters* was then the critical standard of the mid-Victorians, and, for the most part, it remains at that level, except in those cases where an edition excerpted by Stubbs has been superseded.

The legislative texts from the period between the reign of Stephen and the appearance of the statute roll under Edward I have never been systematically collected or critically examined. There is a large gap between the *Gesetze der Angelsachsen* of Liebermann, which ends with the 'Leges Edwardi Confessoris',[1] and the *Statutes of the Realm*, and, even so, the editing of the 'Vetera Statuta', those, that is, before the reign of Edward III, is in many ways unsatisfactory.[2] Consequently it is not to be expected that the legislative texts in the *Select Charters*, purporting to represent the legislation of Henry II, should be satisfactory, though historians have not been deterred from drawing hazardous, and sometimes astonishing, conclusions from these texts of very questionable authenticity. We do not propose to examine all of them.[3] But it is very material to our study of the judicature under Henry II to determine the value of the texts that have passed for the Assize of Clarendon and the related Assize of Northampton, and we have extended our enquiry to cover the text that Stubbs put forward as the Assize of the Forest, which derives from the same sources. The results of this enquiry may put students on their guard and may, at the same time, give an apt illustration of Stubbs's critical standards.

We turn first to the Assize of Clarendon. Of this we have three purported texts, two of them preserved by Roger of Howden, while the third is included in a legal collection in the Bodleian, Rawlinson C. 641.[4] The text which should command the greatest respect is that

---

up (*rende*) his accounts at the exchequer' (p. 386); 'Be it remembered to amend the hostelry (*hostel*) of the king and the queen' (p. 387).

[1] *Gesetze der Angelsachsen*, i.627-72: followed by the brief 'Libertas Londoniensis' (pp. 673-5), which, however, is a document of a different kind.

[2] Richardson and Sayles, *The Early Statutes*, pp. 46-7.

[3] We may note, however, that the Assize of Arms (*Select Charters*, (1st ed.), pp. 146-9; (9th ed.), pp. 183-4), which is also one of Howden's texts, is very questionable. As to date, it would seem evident from the many directions to the justices (paragraphs 9-12) that it was issued in the year of a general eyre: it could not therefore be 1181, to which Howden assigns it ('Benedict', i.278), for there was no eyre in that year (*E.H.R.*, xlviii.170). As to the text, it is incredible that an official enactment would refer to the king as 'domino regi Henrico, scilicet filio Matildis imperatricis' ('Benedict', i.279; *Select Charters* (9th ed.), p. 183). The intention was to distinguish Henry II from his son, the young king, but this was not the official way of doing it. There are, it is true, contemporary texts in which Henry II is so distinguished (Delisle, *Actes de Henri II*, Introduction, p. 206), but this was never his official style and is not to be found in original official documents, though it occurs in purported copies. Howden, for example, introduces the qualification into the headnote to the treaty of 1175 with the king of Scots ('Benedict', i.96). Here the evident purpose is to distinguish the father from the son. Such a distinction cannot have been necessary subsequent to 11 June 1183 when the young king died. On the other hand, the exaction of an oath of fealty to the king suggests a date soon after the revolt of 1173-4. The parallel with the similar requirement in the Assize of Northampton, which deals with some of the consequences of the revolt, is obvious. The language as a whole is, however, nearer to the official style than we would expect in a private compilation. The inference is that it is a garbled version of an authentic assize. An obvious emendation is called for in paragraph 2 where 'xvi. marcis' should read 'xv. marcis', as later texts show (above, p. 95, n. 4).

[4] We cite the texts known to us, but it is not impossible that there are other texts in manuscript that have not been brought to light.

which appears in the *Select Charters* as the Assize of Northampton. It was incorporated by Roger of Howden in what seems to be its right place under the year 1176 in the *Gesta Regis Henrici Secundi* with the title 'the assizes made at Clarendon which were afterwards rehearsed at Northampton'. The text stands unaltered, with the same title, in Howden's revised version of his chronicle, the *Chronica*.[1] The other two texts,[2] which derive from a common original, differ radically from the text of 1176. Clearly, if the latter text is authentic, the parent of the other texts cannot have been authentic, and conversely, if we accept these other texts as derivatives of the authentic text, we must reject the text of 1176, and with that rejection we call into question the only record we have, apart from the pipe rolls, of the proceedings at the council of Northampton in that year. The text given by Howden in the *Gesta* may not be free from corruptions, but if we accept it as representing the original authentic text, then we must suppose that, when it purports to recite the text of the Assize of Clarendon, it does not depart widely from the actual text of 1166, which we must presume the draftsman had before him.

The text of 1176, let us emphasise, is described not as an 'assize' but as 'assizes', and it obviously deals with three matters: the repression of crime; the land law; the chapters of the eyre. As it stands, the text is unsatisfactory, for paragraphs 10 and 12 seem obviously misplaced and it is possible that they had no place in the original. Leaving these paragraphs aside, the remaining eleven are easily divisible: the repression of crime is the subject of paragraphs 1-3; the land law, paragraphs 4 and 5; the chapters of the eyre, paragraphs 6-9, 11, 13. The second and third sections are not complete in themselves. The third section does not purport to give the whole of the chapters of the eyre, but certain additional chapters. The second section, similarly, merely amends the existing law: for example, it alters the period of limitation in the Assize of Novel Disseisin, but it does not repeat the text of the assize, which we have good reason to suppose had been promulgated at Clarendon ten years before. By contrast the first section is drafted on a different plan: it gives, or appears to give, a composite text, the provisions of 1166 as amended in 1176. Two of these amendments are clearly distinguished in the text: one increasing the penalties inflicted on those who failed in the ordeal, the other extending the application of the assize from its inception at Clarendon to its rehearsal at Northampton and thenceforward during the king's pleasure. Although the third paragraph is not distinguished as an addition made at Northampton, we are in no

---

[1] 'Benedict of Peterborough', i.108-11; Howden, *Chronica*, ii.89-91.

[2] Howden's text, i.e. that in the 'Liber de legibus Anglie', was printed by Stubbs in 'Benedict', ii, app. 2, and again in Howden, ii.248-52. It had previously been printed by Palgrave, *Rise and Progress of the English Commonwealth* (1832), ii.clxxviii-clxxxi. The somewhat superior text in Rawlinson C. 641 was preferred for the *Select Charters* (1st ed., pp. 138-9).

doubt that it was added then. In 1166 there could have been no question of an admission of crime before the hundred reeve or town reeve and a subsequent denial before the justices, since, as we have shown,[1] there were no itinerant justices before whom this denial could be made. The paragraph is clearly an amendment devised to deal with a problem that had arisen since 1166. Similarly it seems impossible that a text drafted early in 1166 (perhaps in 1165) could have spoken of men accused *coram iustitiariis domini regis*, words that appear in the first line of paragraph 1: if these words are omitted the sense is still complete and we have little doubt that they have been interpolated in the course of revising the text.

When we have excised what appear to be the additions of the draftsman of 1176, we get a short enactment of three succinct paragraphs suited to the circumstances of 1166. It will make for clarity if we present the original text as we would restore it, while emphasising that, in the absence of an independent parallel text, we cannot hope to obtain more than an approximation.

(i)   Si quis retatus fuerit de murdro vel latrocinio vel roberia vel receptatione hominum talia facientium vel de falsonaria vel iniqua combustione per sacramentum duodecim militum de hundredo (et si milites non adfuerint, per sacramentum duodecim liberorum legalium hominum) et per sacramentum quatuor hominum de unaquaque villa hundredi, eat ad iudicium aque, et si perierit alterum pedem amittat.

(ii) Et si ad aquam mundus fuerit inueniat plegios et remaneat in regno, nisi retatus fuerit de murdro vel alia turpi felonia per commune comitatus et legalium militum patrie, de quo, si predicto modo retatus fuerit, quamuis ad aquam saluus fuerit, nihilominus infra quadraginta dies a regno exeat et catalla sua secum asportet, saluo iure dominorum suorum, et regnum abiuret in misericordia domini regis.

(iii) Item nulli liceat in burgo neque in villa hospitatari aliquem extraneum ultra unam noctem in domo sua quem ad rectum habere noluerit, nisi hospitatus ille essonium rationabile habuerit quod hospes domus monstret vicinis suis. Et cum recesserit coram vicinis recedat et per diem.[2]

Certain comments may be desirable before we pass on. The three sections of the text of 1176 are, as we have remarked, different in character, the first being fuller than the other two. What is the

---

[1] Above, pp. 196-205, especially p. 199.

[2] It may be remarked that the effect of this provision is to modify the customary law as it is found in the 'Leges Edwardi Confessoris'. The host had been responsible for his guest after two nights: the new provision made him responsible after one night. If this was enforced for a time, it had no lasting effect. Bracton knows only the older rule (*Traditio*, vi.78).

explanation of the difference? More than one explanation seems possible. It may be that what Howden obtained was an imperfect draft and not the final text of the assizes as they were revised at Northampton. Alternatively we may suppose that the first section was fuller than the other sections because it was intended for transmission to the counties, while the second and third needed no elaboration because they were drafted primarily for the information of the itinerant justices and, in a sense, by them, for the justiciar and the more prominent among them must assuredly have been largely responsible for putting into writing the changes in the law. Even so, the first section may seem to need further elucidation, but the opportunity for this would be afforded by the writ which, we must suppose, transmitted the legislation to the counties, very much as, forty years later, an explanatory writ conveyed the Great Charter to the sheriffs.[1] The procedure in 1166 must have followed the same lines. The assize for the repression of crime was transmitted to the counties. It sufficed if the assize amending the land law and any additional chapters of the eyre were conveyed to the justices, who would make them known at their sessions in the counties.

Now, if we turn to the other texts which purport to give the Assize of Clarendon, we are confronted with a document of a very different sort, diffuse and rambling, which is as unlike an enactment prepared by an official draftsman as we can well imagine. It is unnecessary to reproduce this pseudo-assize, though, by a collation of the two available texts, it would not be difficult to improve upon that in the *Select Charters*.[2] The version given there will suffice for the purpose of comparison. It should be evident at a glance that the text rehearsed at Northampton in 1176 could not possibly be this supposititious text of 1166. Whatever the precise relationship between the two texts— and they are similar in substance, if not in form—there can be no doubt that the pseudo-assize draws upon the Northampton text or, rather, upon the first section of it. Let us remark, to begin with, that the pseudo-assize (except perhaps in the first paragraph) assumes the existence of the system of itinerant justices which, as we have shown, is not earlier than 1168. Thus in paragraph 4 it is contemplated that those accused of crime will be held in custody until the itinerant justices, before whom they are to make their law, arrive from some other county. Again, in paragraph 19 it is evident that the author has in mind the fully developed system of eyres of the later years of Henry II. He assumes that the justices will issue a summons to the sheriff, ordering him to assemble the county court. On receiving this summons the sheriff, as a preliminary to the eyre, makes enquiry in the county court to ascertain who have come into the county 'since

---

[1] *Rot. Litt. Pat.*, p. 180b; *Bulletin John Rylands Library*, xxviii.426-9.

[2] For example, in paragraph 6 in *Select Charters* (9th ed.), p. 171, for *justitiam* in line 1 *justitias* should be substituted and for *cum* in line 2 *omnes*. As it stands this paragraph is, and has always been, unintelligible.

this assize': these strangers are either to find sureties for their appearance before the justices or are to be taken into custody. We cannot be certain that this procedure is not an invention of the author's or, it may be, describes the practice of some particular sheriff: there seems to be no corroborative text. But, however that may be, it is certain that the procedure could not have been envisaged in 1166. It is hardly necessary, however, to continue a minute examination of the pseudo-assize since sufficient indication of its date and its relation to the text of 1176 is contained in its final paragraph.

Et vult dominus rex quod hec assisa teneatur in regno suo quamdiu ei placuerit.

We have a parallel in the text of 1176:

Hec assisa attenebit a tempore quo assisa facta fuit apud Clarendonam continue usque ad hoc tempus et amodo quamdiu domino regi placuerit. . . .

If these words mean anything, they mean that originally the assize was limited to one specific investigation, that ordered in 1166, and that it was not until 1176 that the procedure was ordered to be continued indefinitely during the king's pleasure. Obviously the compiler of the pseudo-assize has adapted this sentence for his own purpose. He was at work therefore after 1176.

There is no avoiding the conclusion that the pseudo-assize is a private composition, without authority, on a smaller scale but of the same kind as the 'Leges Henrici' and the 'Leges Edwardi Confessoris'. It is one of the apocrypha of the twelfth century. This does not mean that it is valueless, though in the absence of corroboration any statement it contains must be under suspicion. But a great deal is corroborated in substance, if not in detail. Thus the statement in paragraph 7 that, where gaols were lacking, they were to be built is borne out by the pipe rolls.[1] There is no reason to suppose that a provision of this kind was in the original assize and may have dropped out of the text *per incuriam*; but it may be deduced that an instruction to this effect was issued early in 1166, perhaps in the covering writ to the sheriffs, which has not come down to us. With some reserves, then, the compilation may be accepted as a statement of the procedure in the latter part of Henry II's reign. Two paragraphs, however, stand apart from the rest of the text, those numbered 20 and 21. The former prohibits the reception into religious houses of any of the lower classes whose good repute is not assured. The latter prohibits the sheltering of heretics who had been excommunicated and branded at Oxford[2]

---

[1] This was noticed by Stubbs ('Benedict', ii.cli), who thought that it was 'a confirmation of the date ascribed to this assize in the foregoing preface' (i.e. at pp. lix–lxiii).

[2] Despite Stubbs's elaborate argument ('Benedict', xlii–lxi), the date of the council of Oxford at which the heretics were condemned remains uncertain. The unreliable Ralf de Diceto (*Opera*, i.318) gives no date, but notices it before he mentions Henry's departure for the Continent in Lent 1166. The annals of Tewkesbury have a brief notice in the same year (*Annales Monastici*, i.49). But William of Newburgh who gives the most de-

and orders the burning of the houses of those who receive them. Neither of these paragraphs is *in pari materia* and neither appears to be corroborated by other sources. That they are entirely inventions we dare not say; but what grains of truth may lie behind them we can only speculate.

We turn next to the Assize of the Forest, and once more we propose to show that a brief text incorporated by Howden in the *Gesta* is authentic, while a longer text accepted by Stubbs must be rejected. There can be little doubt that, when Alan de Neville went on eyre in 1166 and 1167,[1] the forest law he was required to administer was set down in writing: in other words, there was an assize of the forest. This can hardly be anything else than the *prima assisa Henrici regis* which Howden introduces into the *Gesta* under the year 1184. He does not say that the assize was made then, but that, after the death of Thomas fitz Bernard in that year, the administration of the forests was reorganised and the four new justices of the forest and their serjeants were required to swear that they would enforce the assize.[2] There is consequently no reason to suppose that the assize was newly enacted. The purpose of the assize was to check the laxity that had prevailed in enforcing the forest law, and it re-imposes the severity of Henry I's forest administration. It is quite unlikely that Henry II had waited for thirty years before doing this or that the administration of the forest law had been lax under Alan de Neville or Thomas fitz Bernard, rather the contrary, and the inference must be that the assize was drawn up not many years after Henry II's accession. The probabilities seem to be that it formed part of the legislative output of 1165-6, which included the Assize of Clarendon and the Assize of Novel Disseisin.[3] The Assize of the Forest is a typical succinct official text, consisting of five articles only: there is no reason to doubt its authenticity.

When, however, Howden came to revise and expand his chronicle, he inserted under the year 1198 a composite document consisting of an assize of the forest and certain additional *precepta*.[4] The first twelve paragraphs appear to represent the assize and the last five the *precepta*: the significance and origin of the latter are obscure, but the assize is evidently an expansion of the five articles of Henry II's assize. At a later stage in his revision Howden came across and incorporated in—or, rather, thrust into—his revised chronicle an apocryphal 'Liber de legibus Anglie'. This he ascribed to Ranulf

tailed and, apparently generally reliable, account seems to place this *episcopale concilium* in 1160-1 (*Historia*, i.131). No other contemporary writer who notices the event appears to indicate the date. It is difficult to suppose that the king held two great councils at Oxford and Clarendon about the same time in 1166.

[1] Above, p. 199. [2] 'Benedict of Peterborough', i.323-4.

[3] We cannot, however, exclude the possibility that the assize was drawn up early in the reign since entries relating to pleas of the forest in Wiltshire and Dorset appear in the pipe roll for 1160 (*Pipe Roll, 6 Henry II*, pp. 20, 42): but these *placita* do not seem to relate to ordinary forest offences and the first regular forest eyre appears to have been that of Alan de Neville in 1166-7. [4] Howden, iv.63-4.

Glanville—apparently in the sense that the items there collected represented the law as it was administered while Glanville was justiciar—and inserted, inappropriately enough, under the year 1180.[1] This collection contains an 'assize of the forest' which is a variant, and perhaps an earlier version, of the text Howden had ascribed to 1198, but again apparently only in the sense that this was the law that the justices on eyre in that year administered. Howden's next step was to turn back to the annal for 1184, expunge the text of the assize given there and substitute (without warrant) a reference to the text in the 'Liber de legibus Anglie'.[2] Howden therefore came gradually to acquire three texts of an 'assize of the forest':

A. The text inserted in the *Gesta* under 1184, which seems manifestly to belong to the early years of Henry II's reign.

B. The text in the 'Liber de legibus Anglie', which Howden seems to have thought came from a date before 1184, but of which he seems to have had no knowledge before the end of the twelfth century.

C. The text he inserted under the year 1198, which appears to be an expansion of B.

Stubbs edited all three texts; but in his belief A was of independent authority, since he attributed the *Gesta*, not to Howden, but to a different and earlier writer.[3] Nevertheless he came to give primary authority to B, which, however, he garbled by adding to the text four articles for which there was no authority in any manuscript of Howden or, so far as he knew, in any mediaeval manuscript at all.[4] It is true that he placed these articles between crotchets, but the implication is that they are of the twelfth century. It is noteworthy that he made no use of the additional articles in the text Howden ascribed to 1198. The conflate text Stubbs thus constructed, on principles known only to himself, he saw fit to include in the apparatus of his edition of the *Gesta*[5] and afterwards borrowed for the *Select Charters*.[6] In the explanatory paragraph he prefixed to this reprint he made the astonishing statement (unaltered in the ninth edition) that 'this, the Assize of Woodstock [for Stubbs had now given his garbled text this title], is the first formal act concerning them [the justices of the forest] that is now in existence'.[7] Here we have an example of Stubbs at his hastiest and most careless: less kindly adjectives might perhaps be used. Not only did he mislead others, but he misled himself. Let us recall the commentary he makes upon

---

[1] *Ibid.*, ii.215-52. Royal MS.14. C.2 appears to be the only one containing the full text of the 'Liber' (*ibid.*, i.lxxv-lxxvi, lxxx-lxxxii).

[2] *Ibid.*, ii.290.   [3] Above, p. 13.

[4] His sources were two divergent texts in Vespasian F. iv and in Manwood's *Treatise and Discourse of the Laws of the Forest* (1598), all Elizabethan.

[5] 'Benedict of Peterborough', ii.clix-clxiv. Stubbs excluded from this text the articles concerning the 'regard' of the forest prefixed to the 'assize' (Howden, ii.243-4).

[6] *Select Charters* (1st ed.), pp. 150-2; and in later editions.

[7] *Ibid.*, pp. 149-50; ninth ed., p. 186.

Henry II's forest law in the *Constitutional History*. 'In 1184 he promulgated the Assize of Woodstock, a code of forest ordinances, which were very stringent, but somewhat less inhuman than the customs of his grandfather.'[1] It is a relatively small matter that he should term the document the 'Assize of Woodstock' and attribute it to 1184, for Stubbs gave 'Benedict' as his first authority for his assertion that Henry II had ameliorated the forest law. And if any of his readers had verified the reference, they would have found in the place cited the true assize promulgated by Henry, which begins with these words:

In the first place the king forbids any man to offend in any way against his hunting or against his forests, nor have offenders any assurance that they will be shown mercy in return for the sacrifice of their goods, as has been the practice hitherto. For if anyone from henceforth commits an offence and is rightfully convicted, it is the king's will that justice shall be dealt to him fully, in such manner as had been done in the time of Henry his grandfather, namely that he shall lose his eyes and his testicles.

If Stubbs believed that this early assize had been repealed by Henry thirty years after his accession, it is not unreasonable to suggest that he should have stated so explicitly and have disclosed the grounds for his belief. Had he not stated that the supposititious assize of 1184, now entitled the Assize of Woodstock, was of 'immense value . . . as to our constitutional history'? We do not question that the forest laws of the twelfth century are, having regard to the future, of considerable significance for the constitutional historian, just as they testify to the selfishness and barbarism that still clung even to so enlightened a ruler as Henry II.[2] Of course, to understand the forest law, like any other branch of law, we must go beyond the enactment to its administration, and abundant entries in the pipe rolls make it plain that the law can rarely have been enforced in all its rigour, though the menace of mutilation lay everlastingly in the background. Did we not know the assize, we should, on the evidence of the pipe rolls,

---

[1] *Constitutional History*, i.527. Stubbs's favourable view of Henry II's forest law appears to be based upon the omission from the text, as it stands in the *Select Charters*, of the words 'ut amittat oculos et testiculos'. But this omission seems to be *per incuriam*, since the words are found in the variant text in Howden, *s.a.* 1198 (*Chronica*, iv.63-6), as Stubbs himself noted ('Benedict', ii.clxi, n. 2). They are quite inconsistent with the scheme of penalties in paragraph 12 of Stubbs's text, which is alleged to have been introduced by some unnamed king 'at Woodstock'. It seems certain, however, that the law remained unchanged under Henry II and his sons; otherwise it is impossible to explain the twelfth clause of the 'Unknown Charter', 'Et concedo ne homo perdat pro pecude vitam neque membra', or the tenth chapter of the Charter of the Forest of 1217, 'Nullus de cetero amittat vitam vel membra pro venatione nostra'. In the assize attributed by Howden to 1198 there are two references to mutilation, in articles i and xiv (Howden, iv.63, 65). Such inconsistencies seem fatal to the 'Assize of Woodstock'.

[2] For what it is worth, the testimony of William of Newburgh is that Henry II was more lenient in punishing forest offences than his grandfather, who 'homicidarum et fericidarum in publicis animadversionibus nullam vel parvam esse distanciam voluit' (*Historia*, i.280). Since we have only one pipe roll of Henry I, which contains few references to forest offences, there is no means of comparing the administration in the two reigns; but it is clear that by 1130 pecuniary penalties were already being exacted.

regard the forest law and forest eyres primarily as a source of revenue in the twelfth century, and it is hard to escape the conclusion that within a very few years the motive of gain came to outweigh any other consideration. But the complexity and importance of the subject are all the more reason why we should be scrupulously accurate in recording the evidence and scrupulously critical in treating it. Stubbs was neither accurate nor critical; he was muddled, and the more we know, the more irrelevant and mistaken his comments upon the forest law seem.

When Charles Petit-Dutaillis came to write a study of the mediaeval forest to supplement its treatment in the *Constitutional History*, he had occasion to examine the texts that Stubbs had edited.[1] He was so far misled that he regarded the text in the *Gesta* as a mere fragment of the apocryphal 'Assize of Woodstock', though Stubbs had himself suggested in 1867 that the earlier articles might be those 'of some more ancient assize'.[2] Stubbs, however, seems later to have overlooked or abandoned this suggestion, and Petit-Dutaillis certainly failed to recognise in the shorter text an authentic enactment of an early date in Henry II's reign which was in large part incorporated in the later compilation, though a comparison of the first article in the two texts should alone have convinced him of the priority of the shorter text.[3] When he remarked that the Assize of Woodstock looked as if it were a stringing together of articles of various dates[4] he had doubtless seized upon a clue to its origin; but it was no part of his purpose to establish a critical text and we cannot reproach him if his comments on the text which Stubbs finally adopted are not always happily inspired. We can, indeed, hardly hope for a satisfactory edition until all the legislative texts of the period, authentic and apocryphal, have been collected and critically examined, with a firm grasp upon the elementary principles of diplomatic. It should not be necessary to emphasise that all official enactments may be expected to follow a common pattern and that the very heterogeneity of the texts collected by Stubbs should have carried its own warning.

It may be instructive if, to conclude, we say something more of the two collections of legislative texts in which the apocryphal Assize of Clarendon and the apocryphal Assize of the Forest are to be found. The 'Liber de legibus Anglie' preserved by Howden consists of four items, besides the law-book that passes under Glanville's name. These four items are:

---

[1] Petit-Dutaillis, *Studies and Notes supplementary to Stubbs' Constitutional History* (1923), pp. 147-251: the immediately relevant sections are at pp. 166-86.

[2] *Ibid.*, p. 175; 'Benedict', ii.clxii, n. 8.

[3] His own hypothesis is that the assize of the forest had been the work of Henry I, which he endeavoured to reconstruct (*op. cit.*, pp. 175-6). Petit-Dutaillis was misled by his disbelief that assize 'can simply mean custom' (*ibid.*, p. 174, n. 6). That assize could mean, and for long did mean, the established law, whether customary or written, is amply shown by the use of the phrase 'assize of the Jewry' (Richardson, *English Jewry under Angevin Kings*, pp. 176-7).   [4] *Op. cit.*, p. 175.

The 'Articuli' of William I.
The 'Leges Edwardi Confessoris'.
The Assize of the Forest.
The Assize of Clarendon.[1]

The third and fourth items we have described above. All four are apocryphal, but they are not all by the same compiler. The first is dated by Liebermann about 1110[2]; the second appears to belong to Stephen's reign[3]; the third may have been written under Richard I or late in Henry II's reign; the fourth is certainly of a date after 1176 but may not be so late as Richard I. Rawlinson C. 641 is a more extensive and miscellaneous collection of the late twelfth and early thirteenth centuries.[4] Among some authentic items it includes the 'Leges Edwardi Confessoris' in the original version, written apparently in the closing years of Henry I's reign,[5] the apocryphal Assize of Clarendon, the 'Instituta Cnuti', ascribed by Liebermann to the reign of Henry I,[6] and the 'Articuli' of William I: it does not contain any version of the Assize of the Forest. Evidently this collection, though similar in composition, was made quite independently of that which came into the hands of Roger of Howden.

Such collections, of which these two are specimens, raise interesting questions. The compilation of apocryphal texts was active throughout the twelfth century, and the texts were so often collected that it is evident that they were highly esteemed. There are so many of them that it is hard to believe that the authors intended or hoped to deceive or that lawyers, at least, would be deceived, though Howden seems to have been incapable of distinguishing between authentic legislative instruments and apocryphal enactments. These apocrypha may sometimes contain wild fictions, but on the whole they appear to be sober statements of contemporary law as it was understood by the authors or perhaps as they thought it should be. They therefore have considerable value, although the modern historian would have rated the compilers more highly if they had confined themselves to the collection of authentic documents or the plain statement of custom. The vogue for this form of legal literature passed as the law became more professional, but there are later examples of apocryphal lawbooks in the 'Mirror of Justices' and 'Britton', the former a work of fiction whose import is still uncertain, the latter a serious compilation based largely upon Bracton and *Fleta*, which is given a quite

---

[1] For a description of Royal MS. 14 C 2, see Stubbs's Introduction, pp. lxxiv–lxxviii, to Howden, vol. i, and British Museum, *Catalogue of . . . Old Royal and King's Collections*, ii.133. The four tracts are printed in Howden, ii.215-52.

[2] *Gesetze der Angelsachsen*, i.486-8; iii.279.

[3] *Ibid.*, i.627. The text is that of the 'retractatio', which is found only in association with the 'Articuli' (Lieberman, *Über die Leges Edwardi Confessoris*, p. 119).

[4] For the contents of this manuscript see the *Catalogue of Rawlinson Manuscripts* by Macray, ii.329-30. It is to be noted, however, that what is called the Constitutions of Clarendon in French rhyme is, in fact, a disorderly series of stanzas from *La Vie de Saint Thomas le Martyr* by Guernes de Pont-Sainte-Maxence: see the edition by E. Walberg, pp. cxvi–cxvii.   [5] *Gesetze*, i.627; iii.341.   [6] *Ibid.*, i.612; iii.330.

unnecessary fictional aspect by recasting the matter as an enactment of Edward I. If we are surprised that any of the twelfth-century apocrypha should have deceived Stubbs, we may reflect that Sir Edward Coke accepted the 'Mirror of Justices' as a reliable authority and that it is even now difficult to convince some historians that the 'Modus Tenendi Parliamentum' is a work of fiction.

CALENDAR OF EVENTS IN 1214-15

THE purpose of this calendar[1] is explained in the text. The chief difficulty to meet is that of dating events in England when we have only the date of a happening in Italy, that is a decision in the Curia at Rome or Anagni or Ferentino, from which must be inferred the precedent and consequent events in England. We start with the generally accepted fact that a journey between England and Rome took about thirty days: it might be much more leisurely and it might be expedited to some small extent.[2] The further journey to Anagni, which lies some thirty-five miles to the south-east of Rome, would have required at least another day's travelling. Ferentino is yet another six miles distant from Anagni, and could hardly have been reached by nightfall, even by a speedy messenger who set out from Rome in the early morning. We can scarcely allow less than two extra days for the longer journey. Other considerations are: the point in England from which the messenger started; the possibility of a delayed Channel crossing; and, if the business at the Curia involved negotiations or litigation, the delay occasioned thereby. We must in any case assume that mere office routine, the process of settling, preparing and sealing a papal instrument, would itself normally occupy some days. So far as the return journey is concerned, there are fewer conjectures to be made. But a messenger returning from Rome could not, in most cases, be certain where to find the recipient, or rather the impetrant, of the letters he carried. We distinguish between recipient and impetrant because papal letters were as a rule addressed to another person than to him who sought them. If, for example, a plaintiff desired an action to be tried before judges delegate, the mandate would be addressed to the three persons he had selected to act in that capacity, but the execution of the mandate depended upon himself: he had to secure that the judges delegate received it. Similarly, if the king wished the archbishop of Canterbury to do something in his ecclesiastical capacity, he might obtain a letter from the pope addressed to the archbishop, but the letter would be handed at the Curia to the king's

---

[1] Not every possibly relevant document is included, since there must be some selection, but none that seems to be material has been omitted. Since the calendar was originally compiled, two papers have appeared covering much the same ground up to June 1215: 'The Eve of Magna Carta' by Cheney in *Bulletin John Rylands Library*, xxxviii.311-41, and 'The Making of Magna Carta' by Holt in *E.H.R.*, lxxii.401-22.

[2] Landon, *Itinerary of Richard I* (Pipe Roll Soc.), pp. 184-91.

agent and the king might delay using it or decide not to use it at all.

These considerations are of fundamental importance when we seek to draw inferences from a papal instrument. Apart from its terms and date, we can be sure of the normal time for the journey either way and of the nature of the case put before the Curia, for the instrument must represent substantially the assumed facts put forward by the impetrant and the remedy he desired: but we cannot be sure of more than this. We cannot be certain, in cases of gravity, that the instrument represents all that the impetrant desired, and not merely the utmost he could obtain. If the case were contentious and both parties were represented, the impetrant might get considerably less than he wanted. Even if the impetrant alone were represented, we are not to suppose that his wishes were automatically gratified. The Curia did not act with ostentatious levity or partiality. Consequently, although we may well believe that Innocent III lent a ready ear to King John's requests, we are not to suppose that they were gratified instantly and to the full, without argument or consideration. A case in point is the bull *Etsi karissimus* of 24 August 1215 which annulled the Great Charter.[1] It has been suggested that King John's request for the bull might have been despatched a bare thirty days previously.[2] This suggestion defies probability, particularly so since the bull is dated at Anagni. Even if it be conceded that the barons were not at the time represented at the Curia, it must yet be supposed, on this hypothesis, that the king's request was accorded without careful scrutiny of the relevant documents, notably the text of the charter, and that the terms of the lengthy instruments consequently necessary were settled out-of-hand. This was not the method of conducting business in the papal chancery or in any chancery.

Etsi karissimus itself supplies a good deal of information that historians appear to have undervalued. It gives us John's final account of his negotiations with the barons: this account may have been distorted a little by the paraphrasing necessary to fit it into the bull and it needs careful scrutiny, but substantially it is a reliable, although *ex parte*, narrative. When it is combined with the information in Walter Mauclerc's account of the proceedings at the Curia in February and March 1215, the resulting papal letters of 19 March, and John's letter to the pope of 29 May,[3] we get a fairly adequate account of the transactions between the king and the barons from January onwards. For our present purpose the importance of these documents lies in the fact that they tell us how long it took in a particular instance to obtain a decision from the Curia and to make the decision known in England. We begin with a meeting between the king and the barons at Epiphany which resulted in no agreement, except to

[1] *Selected Letters of Innocent III*, pp. 212-9.
[2] Painter, *The Reign of King John*, p. 341.
[3] For these documents see the calendar below.

refer the dispute to the pope and to observe a truce meantime until
Low Sunday (26 April). Both the king and the barons, of course, put
their case in writing. The king's letter was entrusted to Walter Mauclerc, who was delayed by severe illness, but reached Rome on
19 February. The barons' representatives were a clerk of Eustace de
Vesci and a chaplain of Richard de Percy: they seem to have started
well after Mauclerc and did not arrive in Rome until 1 March. Some
days later, although the barons' letter had been studied in the Curia,
it had not been read by the pope. Thereafter the pope, as he said, had
a careful discussion with the barons' representatives[1] and he announced his decision in their presence on 19 March. The letters of
this date, embodying the decision, were handed to the messengers
and taken by them to England. Presumably that addressed to the
barons was handed to their representatives, while, without doubt,
that addressed to the king would be handed to the king's messenger.
The letter addressed to the archbishop and his suffragans was handed
to the barons' messengers,[2] but we may assume that a copy of it
would be available to the king's messenger.[3]

When did these letters arrive? According to John, the barons took
up arms before the messengers returned with the mandate addressed
to them. But though this statement appears in the pope's letter of
18 June and again in *Etsi karissimus*, the point is not made in John's
letter to the pope of 29 May and we may be sure that it was a
technicality, a quibble, not worth pursuing. But when could it be
said that the barons took up arms? Let us remark parenthetically
that it is futile to search the narratives of the equally unreliable Roger
of Wendover and the Canon of Barnwell for an answer. There are,
however, better indications. Since the barons are never charged by
the king with breaking the truce, we may be sure that they were not
in arms before Low Sunday. A London chronicler has the circumstantial story that the barons defied the king by a black (that is an
Austin) canon on 5 May at Reading.[4] Since the king was at Reading
between the third and the sixth of the month,[5] it seems that we may
accept the chronicler's statement. The king himself says that it was
after the messengers returned that he made his offer to submit the
dispute to the arbitration of four representatives on either side, with
final reference to the pope, and we know that this offer was made on
9 May. Then again the king refers to a previous offer of his—also
after the messengers had returned—to do full justice to the barons
before the pope—an offer that was refused. Obviously the indications
are that the messengers delivered their letters early in May or in the

---

[1] *Etsi karissimus*: 'cum quibus habito diligenti tractatu'.
[2] *Etsi karissimus*: 'scripsimus per eosdem'.
[3] Hence the existence of a copy in the royal treasury.
[4] *Liber de Antiquis Legibus*, p. 201: also in related annals.
[5] Except where otherwise noted, we take the particulars of the king's movements
from Hardy's *Itinerary*.

last days of April, that is, at best, a little more than five weeks or, it may be, just over six weeks from the date of the papal letters. That does not necessarily mean that the actual journey exceeded the normal thirty days by more than a day or two, if at all; but it does indicate that we must in every case allow an interval between the date of an instrument and the day on which the messengers were able to set out on their journey homewards. It is to be noted, too, that in this instance the interval between the date of the king's original letter and the receipt of the pope's decision could hardly have been less than a hundred days and may have been more. Since the issue was highly contentious and the barons' case was not presented until nearly a fortnight after the king's case, the time occupied was perhaps unusually lengthy, but nevertheless we have here an illustration of the need for making adequate allowance for the conduct of business at the Curia.

What is an adequate allowance must depend upon the circumstances of the case. This is perhaps a platitude, and it is certainly a principle easier to enunciate than to apply. But let us return to *Etsi karissimus*, the date of which is 24 August; this we take to be the day upon which the pope gave his decision. The terms of the bull show that, in his petition, the king furnished a detailed account of the dispute with the barons; he presumably annexed a transcript of the Great Charter, which obviously required to be submitted.[1] If the petition itself was, in view of the previous hearing in March, easy to understand, the charter demanded explanation, not least the fact that Pandulf, the pope's familiar, had been a party to it. Nor is it to be supposed that Pandulf himself had neglected to furnish the pope with his own comments and justification. Again, we cannot suppose that a decision was reached without anxious questioning of the messenger on matters of fact and the terms of the charter. And even if we suppose that Innocent was free from other engrossing business and treated the king of England's affairs with the most urgent consideration, we cannot imagine that the preliminary examination of the case and the audience by the pope could be easily fitted into a week. The Curia was not a fast-moving machine. Even granted that the messenger was unusually swift, we can hardly allow less than five full weeks between the date of the king's petition and the decision. It might reasonably be objected that such expedition is altogether unlikely, and an alternative suggestion might be made that the king despatched his messenger almost immediately after the ratification of the charter on 19 June. This might give a period of about six weeks for the consideration of the affair at the Curia, and we must agree that, in normal circumstances, six weeks might not be excessive

---

[1] Roger of Wendover seems to imply that only extracts from the charter were transmitted (*Flores Historiarum*, iii.323). This would seem improbable, although doubtless attention would be drawn to those clauses particularly affecting the king. In any case our argument is not affected.

for so grave a matter. But this alternative involves the unlikely supposition that the king did not await the council at Oxford, which opened on 16 July and which he joined on the 17th. Reckoning five full weeks back from 24 August, we arrive at 20 July, when the council was in progress. The probabilities then seem to point to the conclusion that it was the way the proceedings at the council were tending that decided the king and his advisers to ask the pope to quash the charter. It must be admitted, on the other hand, that in *Etsi karissimus* no mention is made of any events subsequent to the charter. Possibly the king did not desire to weaken his case by an admission that he was still in treaty with the barons, though the suppression of material facts might invalidate the resultant bull.

However, the point we wish to make at the moment is that, allowing for the utmost expedition, it is extremely difficult to suppose that the interval between the king's request and the pope's decision was less than five weeks. The same conclusion emerges, we suggest, from the papal mandate of 7 July, dated at Ferentino, which appears to be related to the king's letter to the pope of 29 May, though this letter must have been supplemented by another, now missing, or more probably by instructions to the messenger. The interval between the two dates is thirty-nine days. This allows perhaps a week for argument and negotiation in the Curia, a period obviously not excessive when what was contemplated was the suspension of a cardinal-archbishop on the eve of the Lateran Council.

Another example is afforded by the pope's confirmation on 30 March of the king's charter granting freedom of election to cathedral and conventual churches. If we are right in supposing that the decision to seek papal confirmation was taken on 15 January and that the messenger left shortly afterward, we must allow for an interval of about seventy days between his departure and the decision at the Curia. The situation was perhaps embarrassing, for the confirmation of the charter meant what, in later times, would be called a concordat that reserved to the king the right to influence and, in practice, control elections at his pleasure, for the nominal freedom of election was conditioned by the necessity to obtain, firstly, the king's licence to elect and, secondly, his approval of the elected prelate. Whatever the reason, the matter would seem to have been under consideration for six weeks or so before the pope decided to give his assent.

Plainly it is impossible to generalise from the four cases we have discussed, but we think that, for the reasons we have indicated, given the date of a papal instrument, it is unsafe to assume that the petition out of which it originated was despatched from England less than five weeks earlier or that the instrument itself was received in England less than five weeks later. Further, while the normal time for the journey one way might be thirty days, in any particular case it is unsafe to assume that this was not exceeded. Consequently, for the purpose of the following calendar, we have allowed thirty to thirty-five days for the journey and thirty-five to forty days before and after the date of a papal instrument to cover both the period necessary for the decision on a petition and the period necessary for delivering the bull or letter in England. In any particular case these periods may be inadequate: occasionally they may be a little excessive. To indicate that the limits we have assigned for the commencement or completion of a journey are conjectural, we have placed them in square brackets. Rarely will the addition or subtraction of a few days affect any deductions to be drawn from the suggested sequence of events.

1214

[26 September- 1 October]   The king writes to the pope complaining of the attitude of Eustace de Vesci (Papal letter of 5 November, below).

13 October   The king returns to England from his campaign in Poitou. He lands at Dartmouth ('Electio Hugonis', *Memorials of St. Edmund's Abbey*, ii.92: Hardy's *Itinerary* shows the king at Dartmouth on 15 October).

4 November   The king visits Bury St. Edmund's. Several chroniclers indicate that there was a meeting of dissident barons here about this time, and it is to be noted that two days earlier Robert fitz Walter, Geoffrey de Mandeville and William d'Aubigny were with the king and may have continued in his company (*Rot. Chartarum*, p. 202). 'These barons, although they were from various parts of the kingdom of England, were all, however, called Northerners' (*Liber de Antiquis Legibus*, p. 201).

5 November   The pope writes to Eustace de Vesci. He recalls his previous order to the earls, barons, and other nobles that they should continue in fealty to the king. So that this mandate may have greater effect, he orders Eustace not to put any obstacle in the way by confederacies and plots nor to impede or allow others, so far as he can prevent it, to impede the king's ministers (*Foedera*, i. 126).

21-22 November   The king is at the New Temple, London, from 16 to 23 November. There is a numerous attendance of bishops and earls. Among the barons present on the 22nd are the Northerners,

Robert fitz Walter, Geoffrey de Mandeville, Richard of Montfichet and William d'Aubigny. On the 21st, 'with the common consent of our barons', the king accords free elections to cathedral and conventual churches: to this charter Geoffrey de Mandeville is a witness (Wilkins, *Concilia*, i.545; *Statutes of the Realm*, i, *Charters of Liberties*, p. 5; *Rot. Chartarum*, pp. 202-3: one charter is wrongly dated 22 *December*).

[10-15 December]   The pope's letter to Eustace de Vesci is received.

25 December   The king keeps Christmas at Worcester.

1215

6 January   On the Feast of Epiphany or shortly afterwards, the king arrives at the New Temple. There is an exceptionally large attendance, including eleven bishops and abbots. The Northerners present include Robert de Ros, besides the four present on 22 November (*Rot. Chartarum*, pp. 203-4: one charter is wrongly dated 21 January). No list of witnesses includes Eustace de Vesci. The meeting lasts several days, but the king and the barons separate without reaching agreement. According to the barons' account they asked the king to confirm their ancient and accustomed liberties, but he refused and, in turn, asked them to give a written undertaking on behalf of themselves and their successors never in future to demand such liberties. According to the king the barons made their demands disrespectfully and with a threat of force (*Foedera*, i.120; papal letter of 19 March to bishops, below). A truce is arranged with the Northerners until Low Sunday (26 April), for which date a meeting at Northampton is projected (*Rot. Litt. Pat.*, p. 126*b*; *Curia Regis Rolls*, vii.215). Both sides meanwhile appeal to the pope.

8 January   The abbot of Beaulieu is supplied with letters of credit for his journey to the Curia on the king's affairs (*Rot. Litt. Pat.*, p. 126*b*). It is doubtful whether the abbot went: his place seems to have been taken by Walter Mauclerc.

15 January	It appears that in the course of the meeting it was agreed that the charter according free elections to cathedral and conventual churches, granted at the New Temple on 21 November, should be transmitted to the pope for confirmation. Although dated 15 January, the copy made for this purpose was in all other respects identical with the original (*Foedera*, i.126-8; Cheney and Semple, *Selected Letters of Innocent III*, pp. 198-201). On this day the king leaves the New Temple for Guildford.
[15-20 January]	Probably a little earlier than this the king writes to the pope and sends Walter Mauclerc as his agent (*Foedera*, i.20). The king's letter has not survived, but its purport can be gathered from two papal letters of 19 March (below).
[25-30 January]	The barons write to the pope and despatch as their agents John of Ferriby, a clerk of Eustace de Vesci, and John of St. Osbert, a chaplain of Richard de Percy (*Foedera*, i.120; corrected by Cheney in *E.H.R.*, lxvi.266 n).
19 February	Walter Mauclerc, who has been detained by grievous illness, arrives in Rome (*Foedera*, i.120).
	A safe-conduct is given to the Northerners to enable them to meet the archbishop, bishops and William Marshal at Oxford on 22 February (*Rot. Litt. Pat.*, p. 129).
[20-25 February]	The king complains to the pope that 'nobles, magnates, barons and knights' refuse to pay scutage in respect of the Poitou campaign (*Foedera*, i. 128).
1 March	The barons' representatives arrive in Rome (*Foedera*, i.120).
19 March	In their presence the pope delivers his judgement (*E.H.R.*, xliv.92). Its substance appears from two letters of this date addressed to the archbishop of Canterbury and his suffragans and to the barons. The pope reproaches the archbishop and bishops for not intervening in the quarrels between the king and the barons: they are charged by some with aiding the barons because at no time before peace was made between the king and the clergy had such issues arisen. They are to endeavour to restore peace and to persuade the nobles to make their requests respectfully. The pope also writes to the

magnates and nobles to this effect and condemns all conspiracies and plotting against the
king (*Foedera*, i.127; Cheney and Semple, *op.
cit.*, pp. 194-7). At the same time the pope
writes to the king: this letter has not survived,
but it is clear from the pope's other letters that
its purport was to urge the king to grant the
barons' just requests.

30 March   The pope confirms the king's charter granting freedom of election (Cheney and Semple,
op. cit., pp. 198-201, and references given above).

1 April   The pope writes to the nobles, magnates,
barons and knights, directing them to pay
scutage in respect of the Poitou campaign
(*Foedera*, i.128; Cheney and Semple, *op. cit.*,
p. 202).

13 April   A council takes place at Oxford attended by
the archbishop and certain bishops and barons:
no mention is made of the Northerners (*Electio
Hugonis*, p. 124).

23 April   Safe-conduct up to 28 May for those accompanying the archbishop or bearing his letters
patent who wish to speak with the king (*Rot.
Litt. Pat.*, p. 134).

26 April   The truce between the king and the barons
(Low Sunday)   expires. The barons may, as arranged, have
assembled at Northampton.

27 April   According to Roger of Wendover, a meeting
takes place at Brackley between the barons and
the archbishop, the Earl Marshal and others,
on behalf of the king. The barons present a
schedule of their demands (*Flores Historiarum*,
iii.298).

[27 April-4 May]   The pope's letters of 19 March are received.
For the limits of date, see above, pp. 452-3.

5 May   The barons 'defy' the king at Reading (*Liber
de Antiquis Legibus*, p. 201, and related annals;
Surrey Archaeological Collections, xxxvi.49). According to the Dunstable annalist (but erroneously) the *diffidatio* was at Wallingford (*Annales
Monastici*, iii.43).

6 May   The king offers to reform the evil customs
introduced by himself, Richard I and Henry II,
saving his right to appeal to the pope (king's
letter of 29 May and the bull *Etsi karissimus*
below).

[6-11 May]   The pope's letter of 1 April is received (obviously it could not be used).

[8 May]   The king asks the archbishop and his suffragans to excommunicate the barons: the archbishop refuses, although in the opinion of Pandulf and the bishop of Exeter (Simon of Apulia) excommunication was legally justifiable (king's letter of 29 May, below).

9 May   By the hands of the archbishop and two or three of his suffragans the king proposes that the differences between himself and his barons should be submitted to the arbitration of four men chosen by each side with the pope as 'superior' (king's letter of 29 May; *Rot. Chartarum*, p. 209*b*).

10 May   As a corollary, the king issues a notification that any proceedings taken against the barons will be by the law of the land or by judgement of their peers in his court (*Rot. Litt. Pat.*, p. 141). According to the king's statement to the pope, he offered the barons judgement of their peers on all their petitions (letter of 29 May).

12 May   The king orders the sheriffs to seize the lands and chattels of his enemies (*Rot. Litt. Claus.*, i.204).

[9-14 May]   The king writes to the pope complaining that the barons have taken up arms with the intention of expelling him from the kingdom and asks that the archbishop and bishops may be directed to excommunicate them and lay their lands under interdict (papal letter of 18 June, below).

16 May   The king is negotiating a truce with the barons, with the archbishop as an intermediary (*Rot. Litt. Pat.*, p. 136*b*). A truce has been established by 27 May (*ibid.*, p. 142).

17 May   The barons occupy London (*Rot. Litt. Pat.*, p. 137*b*; *Liber de Antiquis Legibus*, p. 201).

25 May   Safe-conduct to Saer de Quency up to 31 May to treat of peace between the king and the barons (*Rot. Litt. Pat.*, p. 138*b*).

27 May   Safe-conduct to the archbishop and his company to Staines to treat of peace with the barons (*Rot. Litt. Pat.*, p. 142).

29 May   In the presence of Brother William of the apostolic chamber and the bishops of Worcester

and Coventry, at Odiham, the king offers to submit to the pope's decision all the petitions of the barons. On the same day the king writes to the pope, narrating the steps he had taken to come to an accord with the barons (*Foedera*, i.129). Apparently the messenger bearing this letter received supplementary instructions which resulted in the papal letters of 7 July (below).

8 June

The king, who is at Merton, issues a safe-conduct from 9 to 11 June to those who come to Staines on the part of the barons (*Rot. Litt. Pat.*, pp. 142-3).

10 June

The truce is prolonged to 15 June. The king is at Windsor (*Rot. Litt. Pat.*, p. 143a).

[10-15 June]

From Windsor the king goes over to Runnymede, where presumably negotiations had already begun on 10 June (*Electio Hugonis*, pp. 128-9: the date is confirmed by the date of the grant of temporalities on 11 June, *Rot. Litt. Pat.*, p. 142b).

15 June

At Runnymede the king and barons agree on terms of peace. (The Great Charter therefore bears this date, although final peace was not made until the 19th: see McKechnie, *Magna Carta*, pp. 36-40.)

18 June

In a letter addressed generally to the people of England the pope requires them to give the king their aid and favour against the barons. The archbishop and his suffragans have been directed to excommunicate the barons and lay their lands under interdict if, after eight days' warning, they do not accept and observe the procedure laid down in the pope's letters of 19 March, namely, if they cannot come to a settlement (*concordia*), to let their differences with the king be determined in his court by their peers according to the customs and laws of the realm (*Magna Carta Commemoration Essays*, pp. 43-5; reprinted Adams, *Council and Courts in Anglo-Norman England*, pp. 367-71).

19 June

Peace is concluded and the king receives the homage of the barons (*Rot. Litt. Pat.*, pp. 143b, 180b; *Rot. Litt. Claus.*, i.215a).

7 July

The pope sends a mandate addressed to the bishop of Winchester (Peter des Roches), the abbot of Reading and Pandulf. All disturbers of the king and kingdom, their accomplices and accessories are excommunicate and their lands are placed under interdict. The archbishop and his suffragans are to be enjoined, on pain of suspension, to cause both sentences to be published every Sunday and festival until the offenders make satisfaction to the king and return humbly to his service (*E.H.R.*, xliv.91-2; Cheney and Semple, *op. cit.*, pp. 207-9).

16 July
A council opens at Oxford to arrange for the execution of the Great Charter. The king, who has been delayed by illness, arrives on 17 July. The council continues until 24 July and is adjourned to 20 August (Richardson, *The Morrow of the Great Charter*, pp. 4-10, and references there given).

[16-21 July]
The king writes to the pope requesting him to quash the Great Charter.

[23-28 July]
The pope's letters of 18 June are received. Apparently the king makes no immediate use of them, but they are before the judges delegate, who use similar phraseology when drafting their letter of 5 September (below).

[11-16 August]
The papal mandate of 7 July is received.

19 August
The king notifies the barons that he will not attend the council meeting arranged for 20 August and is sending representatives (*Rot. Litt. Pat.*, p. 153).

20 August
The barons meet the king's representatives who appear to have disclosed the terms of the mandate of 7 July (Walter of Coventry, *Memoriale*, ii.223).

[c. 22 August]
The barons again defy the king. This must have been before John embarked at a port on the Hampshire coast for Sandwich, which he reached by 28 August (*Bulletin John Rylands Library*, xxix.192-4). He was at Wareham on the 22nd.

24 August
Under this date the pope issues the bull *Etsi karissimus*, reciting the history of the dissensions between the king and the barons and quashing the Great Charter. In a concurrent letter addressed to the barons, the pope advises them to ask the king to grant graciously what ought lawfully to be conceded: he also invites them to send proctors to the General Council, when

he will order affairs to the satisfaction of the king and the peace and freedom of clergy and people (*Foedera*, i.135-6; Cheney and Semple, *op. cit.*, pp. 212-9).

5 September   The barons being now in arms, the judges delegate named in the mandate of 7 July call upon the archbishop of Canterbury and his suffragans to excommunicate them (*E.H.R.*, xliv.90-3).

13 September   The king informs the pope that he is sending as his representatives the archbishops of Bordeaux and Dublin, the chancellor, the abbot of Beaulieu and others, who will inform him of all things pertaining to the king and the kingdom (*Rot. Litt. Pat.*, p. 182).

[*c.* 15 September]   Stephen Langton (who has been suspended by the judges delegate) leaves for Rome. Pandulf also leaves (*Rot. Litt. Pat.*, p. 182*b*).

[28 September-   The bull and papal letter of 24 August are
3 October]   received. They are disregarded by the barons.

[15-20 October]   Langton arrives in Rome and appeals against his suspension. The king is represented by the abbot of Beaulieu, Thomas of Hardington and Geoffrey of Crawcombe (Wendover, *Flores Historiarum*, iii.344-5).

4 November   The pope confirms the sentence passed upon Langton (*Foedera*, i.139; Cheney and Semple, *op. cit.*, p. 220; Wendover, *Flores Historiarum*, iii.345).

CONTRACTS OF SERVICE

THE relative paucity of original deeds, other than those relating to land, from the twelfth and thirteenth centuries is liable to give many false impressions. It has, for example, led to the hypothesis that contracts for military service first appeared under Edward I.[1] We can see no ground for any other conclusion than that such contracts have had a continuous history at least from the eleventh century onwards, though the forms with which such contracts were clothed underwent change. There can be no doubt that the knights employed by the Norman and Angevin kings, whether they came from England, from Normandy or Poitou, Flanders or some other foreign country, were engaged under contract. Such contracts may originally have been parol, but in course of time they were naturally committed to writing as men became more literate and instruments multiplied. When in his conflicts with his barons Henry III engaged foreign mercenaries,[2] it is impossible to conceive their agreement to serve him except under precise conditions of service.

The importance of the document we print below lies in its date, 20 July 1270, for it disposes at once of any idea that written contracts were first devised after Edward I came to the throne. Under this contract Adam of Jesmond agreed to serve Edward, at that time bearing no other title than the eldest son of Henry III, with four knights for one year. These knights were to accompany the prince on his crusade. The contract does not look in the least like a novelty but, on the contrary, it has every appearance of being in common form, and we can hardly doubt that other troops of knights who accompanied Edward entered into similar contracts. The fact, too, that the contract is for service on a crusade suggests that it had had many predecessors reaching back a great many years; for a mercenary could not, like a landed knight, afford to give his services, even in a holy war, merely for spiritual benefits.[3] A man must live. There was much matter-of-fact business and hard bargaining about a crusade.

It is more than likely that other and earlier examples of such con-

[1] Morris, *Welsh Wars of Edward I*, pp. 68-9; cf. Lyon, *From Fief to Indenture*, p. 251.
[2] For Flemish mercenaries in England in 1233 see Powicke, *King Henry III and the Lord Edward*, i.124-32, especially p. 124 *n*. Little is known of the force raised by Eleanor of Provence in 1264: that the rank and file were 'volunteers' (*ibid.*, ii.476) would be more than surprising.
[3] We do not suggest that Adam of Jesmond was himself a landless knight: he had, in fact, recently been sheriff of Northumberland.

tracts as the present will come to light, for we do not believe that it is in any way remarkable, except that it is the earliest that has been found. Forms doubtless changed over the centuries. A contract in French of, let us say, the year 1100 would be a rare find, but more from the philological than from the historical standpoint. A contract of that date, or of any date prior to the reign of Henry II, would in all probability be in Latin.

Next we would remark that there is nothing remotely 'feudal', bastard or otherwise, about the present contract. In others, where property is conveyed, there may be stipulations which recall the principles of 'feudal' law, but any such similarities are illusory. For example, on 15 May 1319, an indenture was entered into by William Latimer whereby he undertook to serve Thomas, earl of Lancaster, in peace and war, with a troop of horse and to be of his council for the duration of his life. Certain property was conveyed to him for life and provision was made for surrender in the event of his default. On the other hand, he was protected by a stipulation that he was not required to serve against the king in person.[1] This clause, it is true, resembles a saving of liege homage; but there is no word of homage in the indenture, and the meaning of the clause is that Latimer shall not be required to surrender the property if he refuses to commit a felony, which is a very different legal concept. However strange the terms of the indenture might seem to-day. the relations between Latimer and the earl were, in fact, contractual and not feudal, just as the relations between Adam of Jesmond and Edward were contractual and not feudal.

CONTRACT BETWEEN EDWARD, ELDEST SON OF HENRY III, AND ADAM OF JESMOND

Cotton Charter, xxix.65

A tuz ceus ke ceste escrit verrunt u orrunt Adam de Gesemue saluz en nostre Seignur. Sachez ke jo su demoré ov my sire Edward, eyné fiz le rays de Engletere, pur aler ov li en la Tere Sainte, may cynkime de chevaler, à demorer en sun service un an enter, e dait le an comencer au prochain passage de Septembre. E pur ceste chose fere il me a doné pur totes choses sys sent mars en deners e passage, co est à dire luage de la nef e ew à taunt de personis e de chevaus cum il afert de chevalers. E si il avenist ky jo demorase pur maladye u pur autre achesun, ke Dew defende, un chevaler pur may e mes chevalers devaunt dys enterement li parferrunt sun servise al anée u li lerray taunt de le aver cum il aferra a parfere le terme ke arere serra de le anée, e co serra à l'elexion de may. E si il avenist par aventure ke Dew faist sun comaundement de le avaunt dist mun seignur sir Edward, jo serray tenu à cely ke il lerra u enverra pur li ausi cum à li memis, solum la furme avaunt escrite. E en temoynage de ceste

---

[1] Holmes, *The Estates of the Higher Nobility*, pp. 122-3.

chose ay fet ceste escrit seler de mun sel. Donez a Weymuster le vintime jur de Joile de la an de le encorunement nostre seignur le rays Henri le fiz le rays Johan cynkauntime quarte.

TRANSLATION

To all those who shall see or hear this writing Adam of Jesmond wishes salvation in Our Lord. Know that I have agreed with my lord Edward, the eldest son of the king of England, to go with him to the Holy Land, accompanied by four knights, and to remain in his service for a whole year to commence at the coming voyage of September. And in return he has given me, to cover all expenses, six hundred marks in money and transport, that is to say the hire of a ship and water for as many persons and horses as are appropriate for knights. And should it happen that I am detained by sickness or any other accident, which God forbid, a knight in my place and my knights aforesaid will undertake his service fully for the year or else I will return to him so much money as shall be necessary to complete the period which is lacking from the year, and this shall be at my option. And if it should by chance happen that God's will shall be that my aforesaid lord, sir Edward, shall die, I shall be bound to him, whom my lord shall leave or send in his place, as to himself, according to the form above written. And in witness hereof I have caused my seal to be set to this writing.

Given at Westminster the twentieth day of July in the fifty-fourth year from the coronation of our lord King Henry, son of King John.

THE ALLEGED ARTICLES OF 1308

W E print below, from the only manuscript in which the text is to be found, the articles against Gavaston, alleged to have been presented by the earl of Lincoln in the Easter parliament of 1308. This document will be discussed when we come to deal with the constitutional crises of the reign of Edward II, but in the meantime it is given here in order that the criticism, in chapter one, of Stubb's editing of the *Chronicles of the Reigns of Edward I and Edward II* may be fully intelligible.

The British Museum manuscript with the press-mark Burney 277 is a miscellaneous collection of scraps. Folios 5 to 8 are part of a small pamphlet containing documents connected with the Ordinances of 1311. The Ordinances are not now to be found there, but it is highly probable that leaves containing them have been lost. In its present state this section of the manuscript is composed as follows:

Folio 5*a* Blank

Folio 5*b* (A) Coronation Oath in Latin and French.

          (B) 'La primer enprise e l'ordenaunce mustré par le cunte de Nicole au roy' (printed below). This continues to folio 6*a*.

Folio 6*a* (C) Letters patent of 18 May 1308, notifying the exile of Gavaston (printed: *Annales Londonienses*, p. 154; *Foedera*, ii.i.44). This entry is preceded by the explanatory note: E le roy graunta l'ordenaunce par ceste chartre.

Folio 6*b* (D) 'La seconde emprise e l'ordenaunce mustré par le cunte de Lancastre' (printed: *Liber Custumarum*, pp. 198-9; *Annales Londonienses*, pp. 168-9; *Chronicon de Lanercost*, pp. 525-6).

          (E) Letters patent of 16 March 1310, notifying the king's assent to the appointment of the Ordainers (printed: *Foedera*, ii.i.105; *Annales Londonienses*, pp. 169-70).

(An unnumbered folio follows, formerly an outside wrapper, blank.)

Folio 7*a* (F) Declaration by bishops, earls and barons of 17 March 1310 (printed: *Rotuli Parliamentorum*, i.443; *Parliamentary Writs*, ii.ii, App. 26-7; *Liber Custumarum*, pp. 200-2; *Annales Londonienses*, pp. 170-1; *Registrum Roberti Winchelsey*, pp. 1065-6).

Folio 7b (G) Names of the Ordainers and their oath (printed: *Parliamentary Writs*, ii.ii, App. 27).

Folio 8   An outside wrapper: on fo. 8b there is a portion of a commentary on the *Song of Songs*.

As already indicated, it seems probable that after folio 7 some leaves have been lost that contained the Ordinances, which are, of course, found in similar collections, such as that in Cotton MS. Claudius D.ii, and in MS. K.ii in the library of the Dean and Chapter of Canterbury, and in the London *Liber Custumarum*. No other surviving collection has come to light which contains the document alleged to have been presented to the king in 1308.

The text, as printed below, has been punctuated and accents have been supplied where necessary to make the sense clear: to the same end j and v have been substituted for i and u in accordance with modern usage. In the footnotes will be found variant readings, where

B = Burney MS.277;

L = Annales Londonienses (*Chronicles of the reigns of Edward I and Edward II*, i.153-4);

St. R. = Process against the Despensers (*Statutes of the Realm*, i.182).

The Latin version of the articles in the *Gesta Edwardi de Carnarvon* by a Bridlington writer (*Chronicles of the reigns of Edward I and Edward II*, ii.33-4) is too loose to justify full collation, but some significant variants are noted.

LA PRIMER ENPRISE E L'ORDENAUNCE MUSTRÉ PAR LE CUNTE DE NICOLE AU ROY

Homage e serment de ligeaunce est plus par reson de la coroune qe par reson de la person le roy e plus alié[1] à la coroune qe à la person, e ceo apert qar[2] avaunt ceo[3] qe l'estat de la coroune soit descendu nule ligeaunce est à la persone regardaunt,[4] dount, si le roy en[5] cas ne soi[6] meyne[7] mie par reson, en droit de l'estat[8] de la coroune ly[9] liges sount lietz par[10] serment fete à la coroune de remenir le rey en[11] l'estat de la coroune par reson,[12] autrement ne serroit point lur[13] serment tenu. Outre[14] ceo dounc fet à demaunder coment home doit[15] menir le roy, ou par sute de lay ou par aspreté. Par sute solom[16] lay ne poet home pas[17] redrescer qar il n'averoit[18] pas juges, si ceo ne fust de par le roy, en queu cas,[19] si la volunté le roy ne soit acordaunt à la reson, si[20] n'averoit il fors qe errur meintenuz e confermez. Dount il covent, pur[21] le serment sauver, qe qaunt le roy ne volt la[22] chose

[1] *se lie* L, St. R.   [2] *qe* St. R.   [3] *ceo* om. St. R.   [4] *regardé* L.
[5] *par* St. R.   [6] *se* L, St. R.   [7] *demeyne* L.   [8] *de l'estat* om. St. R.
[9] *si* L.   [10] L inserts *lur*.   [11] *et* St. R.   [12] L, St. R. add *et*.   [13] *le* St. R.
[14] *Entre* B : St. R. substitutes *Ore* for *Outre ceo dounc*.   [15] L inserts *donques*.
[16] *de* L, St. R.   [17] L inserts *le*.   [18] *avera* L.   [19] L inserts *qe se soit*.
[20] L substitutes *et ensi il n'averoit mie*.   [21] *par* L.   [22] *la* om. St. R.

redrescer e[1] ouster ceo[2] q'est pur le comun pople mauvais e damageous[3] pur la coroune, e[4] par[5] le pople ajugé est[6] que la chose soit ousté par aspreté, qar[7] il est par soun serment lié[8] de governer son[9] pople e ses[10] liges[11] sount[12] lietz de governer ové ly e[13] en eide de luy.[14]

En droit de la persone dount home parle[15] le pople le doit juger noun suffrable par la reson q'il desherite la coroune e la fait poure à son poer. Il, par son cunsail, ouste le roy du consail de sa realme e mette descord entre le roy e son pople, e il atrete a luy liaunces des genz par serment ausi haust cum le roy, en fesaunt luy meimis pier au roy, en enfeblisement[16] de la coroune, qar par les bens de la coroune il ad tret à luy e à son poer la force de la coroune, issi q'en luy n'est remis qe la coroune ne fust destruit e il meismes soverain du realme par ses mauvaitez, en traison de son lige seingnur e de la coroune e encuntre sa fay.

Par ceo qe le seingnur ad empris de maintenir le,[17] countre chechun home en touz pointz, saunz aver regard a nuli reson come aferoit au roy, il ne poet estre jugé ne ateint par sute liveré en la lay, par quai le pople,[18] come celi q'est robbeour du pople e treitre à son lige seingnur e au realme, le agard come home ateint e jugé, en priaunt au roy qe, come il soit lié par serment à tenir les leyes qe le pople eslira[19] par le serment de son encorounement, q'il accepte le agard le pople e le face.

Translation

THE FIRST UNDERTAKING AND THE ORDINANCE
PRESENTED BY THE EARL OF LINCOLN TO THE KING

Homage and the oath of allegiance are more in respect of the Crown than in respect of the king's person and are more closely related to the Crown than to the king's person; and this is evident because, before the right to the Crown has descended to the person, no allegiance is due to him. And, therefore, if it should befall that the king is not guided by reason, then, in order that the dignity of the Crown may be preserved, the lieges are bound by the oath made to the Crown to reinstate the king in the dignity of the Crown or else they would not have kept their oath. The next question is how the king should be reinstated, whether by an action at law or by constraint. It is not, however, possible by recourse to the law to obtain redress, because there would be no other judges than the royal judges, in which case, if the king's will was not accordant with right

---

[1] *ne* L, St. R. [2] *ceo* om. L, St. R. [3] St. R. adds *et.*
[4] *en* L: St. R. om. *e par le pople.* [5] *pur* B. [6] *est* om. L. [7] *qil* St. R.
[8] *lié par son serment,* L, St. R. [9] *le* St. R. [10] *les* L.
[11] St. R. repeats *et ses liges.* [12] *sount* om. L. [13] *e* om. L.
[14] After *governer* St. R. reads *en eide de lui et en defaute de lui.*
[15] The Bridlington writer reads 'quantum ad personam domini Petri de Gavastone'.
[16] *enfebisement* B. [17] 'predictum Petrum', Bridlington.
[18] 'comites', Bridlington. [19] 'populum regere', Bridlington.

reason, the only result would be that error would be maintained and confirmed. Hence, in order that the oath may be saved, when the king will not right a wrong and remove that which is hurtful to the people at large and prejudicial to the Crown, and it so adjudged by the people, it behoves that the evil must be removed by constraint, for the king is bound by his oath to govern his people, and his lieges are bound to govern with him and in support of him.

As regards the person who is talked about, the people ought to judge him as one not to be suffered because he disinherits the Crown and, as far as he is able, impoverishes it. By his counsel he withdraws the king from the counsel of his realm and puts discord between the king and his people, and he draws to himself the allegiance of men by as stringent an oath as does the king, thereby making himself the peer of the king and so enfeebling the Crown, for by means of the property of the Crown he has gathered to himself and put under his control the power of the Crown, so that by his evil deeds it lies solely with him to determine whether the Crown should be destroyed and he himself made sovereign of the realm, in treason towards his liege lord and the Crown, contrary to his fealty.

Since the lord king has undertaken to maintain him against all men on every point, entirely without regard to right reason, as behoves the king, he cannot be judged or attainted by an action brought according to law, and therefore, seeing that he is a robber of the people and a traitor to his liege lord and his realm, the people rate him as a man attainted and judged, and pray the king that, since he is bound by his coronation oath to keep the laws that the people shall choose, he will accept and execute the award of the people.

BIBLIOGRAPHY

Standard works of reference are not included. Articles and separate volumes are cited under the name of the author or the title, and titles of Journals or Series are included only in special cases.

Acta Stephani Langton. Ed. K. Major (Cant. and York Soc., Oxford, 1950).
Actes des Comtes de Flandres, 1071-1128. Ed. Fernand Vercauteren (Brussels, 1938).
Actes de Henri II. See *Recueil.*
Actes de Philippe Auguste. See *Recueil.*
Acts of the Parliaments of Scotland. Ed. T. Thomson and C. Innes (Record Commission, London, 1844-75).
ADAM OF EYNSHAM, *Magna Vita Sancti Hugonis Episcopi Lincolniensis.* Ed. J. F. Dimock (Rolls Series, London, 1864).
   [Another edition by D. L. Douie and H. Farmer (London, 1961)].
ADAMS, G. B. *Council and Courts in Anglo-Norman England* (New Haven, 1926).
— *Origin of the English Constitution* (New York, 1912; enlarged ed., 1920).
— *Political History of England, 1066-1216* (London, 1905).
ÆLFRIC. *Colloquy.* Ed. G. N. Garmonsway (London, 1939).
— *Lives of the Saints.* Ed. W. W. Skeat (E.E.T.S., London, 1881-1900).
— 'On the Old and the New Testament' in *The Old English Version of the Heptateuch,* ed. S. J. Crawford (E.E.T.S., London, 1922), 15-75. See *Bibliothek.*
AELRED OF RIEVAULX. 'Relatio de Standardo' in *Chronicles, Stephen,* etc. (*q.v.*), vol. iii, 181-99.
ÆTHELWEARD. *Chronicle.* Ed. A. Campbell (London, 1962).
Ancient Charters. Ed. J. H. Round (Pipe Roll Soc., London, 1888).
ANDERSON, A. O. See *Early Sources.*
Anglia Sacra. Ed. Henry Wharton (London, 1691).
Anglo-Saxon and Old English Vocabularies. Ed. T. Wright and R. P. Wülcker (London, 1884).
Anglo-Saxon Charters. Ed. A. J. Robertson (Cambridge, 1939).
Anglo-Saxon Chronicle. Ed. B. Thorpe (Rolls Ser., London, 1861). See *Two of the Saxon Chronicles.*
Anglo-Saxon Dictionary. Ed. J. Bosworth and T. N. Toller (Oxford, 1898, 1921).
Anglo-Saxon Wills. Ed. D. Whitelock (Cambridge, 1930).
Anglo-Saxon Writs. Ed. F. E. Harmer (Manchester, 1952).
'Annales Acquicinctensis Monasterii' in *Historiens de la France,* xviii, 534-53.
Annales de St. Bertin. Ed. C. Dehaimes (Société de l'Hist. de France, Paris, 1871).
Annals of Anchin. See 'Annales Acquicinctensis Monasterii'.
Annals of Burton. See *Annales Monastici.*

'Annales Londonienses', in *Chronicles of the Reigns of Edward I and Edward II* (*q.v.*).

Annales Monastici. Ed. H. R. Luard (Rolls Ser., London, 1864-69). [Vol. I: 'Tewkesbury', 'Burton'; vol. II: 'Winchester', 'Waverley'; vol. III: 'Dunstable', 'Bermondsey'; vol. IV: 'Osney', 'Chronicon' [of Thomas Wykes], 'Worcester'.]

Annals of Tewkesbury. See *Annales Monastici*.

ANSELM. *Opera Omnia*. Ed. F. S. Schmitt (Edinburgh, 1946-61).

Archaeologia. Soc. Antiquaries (London, 1770-   ).

Archives de Normandie et de la Seine-Inférieure. Ed. Paul E. Chevreux and Jules Joseph Vernier (Rouen, 1911).

'Articuli X', *in* Liebermann, *Gesetze* (*q.v.*), i, 488-9.

ASHDOWN, M. See *English and Norse Documents*.

ASSER. *Life of King Alfred*. Ed. W. H. Stevenson (Oxford, 1904). [Reprinted 1959 with introduction by D. Whitelock.]

BALLARD, A. *British Borough Charters, 1042-1216* (Cambridge, 1913).

BARKER, E. 'Maitland as a Sociologist' in *Sociological Review* (London), xxix (1937), 121-35.

BARLOW, F. *Feudal Kingdom of England, 1042-1216* (London, 1955).

BATESON, MARY. 'The Laws of Breteuil' in *E.H.R.*, xv, 73-8, 302-18, 496-523, 754-7; xvi, 92-110, 332-45.

Battle of Maldon. Ed. E. V. Gordon (London, 1937).

Bayeux Tapestry. Of the many reproductions with commentary, the following may be mentioned: by F. R. Fowke (London, 1898); ed. F. M. Stenton (London, 1957), and in *English Historical Documents*, vol. ii (*q.v.*).

BECKET. See *Materials*.

BELL, H. E. *Court of Wards and Liveries* (Cambridge, 1953).

'Benedict of Peterborough'. *See* Roger of Howden.

Berkeley Charters. See *Descriptive catalogue*.

Bibliothek der Angelsächsischen Prosa. Ed. W. M. Grein (Cassel and Göttingen, 1872). [This contains Ælfric's 'Be Hester'.]

BIGELOW, M. M. *Placita Anglo-Normannica* (London, 1879).

BIRCH, W. DE G. See *Cartularium*.

BLAIR, P. H. *Introduction to Anglo-Saxon England* (Cambridge, 1956).

BLIEMETZRIEDER, FRANZ J. P. *Adelhard von Bath* (Munich, 1935).

BLOCH, M. *Les rois thaumaturges* (Strassburg, 1924).

— *La Société Féodale: la formation des liens de dépendance* (Paris, 1939).

— *La Société Féodale: les classes et le gouvernement des hommes* (Paris, 1940).

BLOIS. *See* Peter.

BLOMEFIELD, F. *Topographical History of the County of Norfolk* (London, 1805-10).

BOEHMER, H. *Kirche und Staat in England und in der Normandie im xi und xii. Jahrhundert* (Leipzig, 1899).

— 'Das Eigenkirchentum in England' in *Texte und Forschungen: Festgabe für Felix Liebermann* (Halle, 1921).

BONGERT, YVONNE. *Recherches sur les cours laïques au xiii* siècle (Paris, 1949).

Book of Fees. Ed. H. C. Maxwell Lyte (London, 1921-31).

BORN, BERTRAN OF. *Poésies Complètes*. Ed. Antoine Thomas (Toulouse, 1888).
— *Gedichte*. Ed. A. Stimming (Halle, 1892).
BORRELLI DE SERRES, L. L. *Recherches sur divers services publics du xiiie au xviie siècle* (Paris, 1895-1909).
BOUARD, M. DE. 'De la Neustrie Carolingienne à la Normandie féodale: continuité ou discontinuité', in *B.I.H.R.*, xxviii (1955), 1-14.
BOUMAN, C. A. *Sacring and Crowning* (Groningen, 1957).
BOUSSARD, J. *Le Comté d'Anjou sous Henri Plantagenêt* (Paris, 1938).
— 'Henri II Plantagenêt et les origines de l'armée de métier' in *Bibliothèque de l'Ecole des Chartes*, cvi (1947), 189-224.
BRACTON, HENRY. *De legibus et consuetudinibus Angliae*. Ed. G. E. Woodbine (New Haven, 1915-42).
— *Bracton's Note Book*. Ed. F. W. Maitland (London, 1887).
BRETON. See *Oeuvres*.
Britton. Ed. F. M. Nichols (Oxford, 1865).
BROOKE, Z. N. *The English Church and the Papacy* (Cambridge, 1931).
— 'The Effect of Becket's Murder on Papal Authority in England' in *Camb. Hist. Journal*, ii (1926-28), 213-28.
BROOKE, Z. N. and BROOKE, C. N. L. 'Henry II, Duke of Normandy and Aquitaine' in *E.H.R.*, lxi (1946), 81-9.
BROWN, R. A. 'The Treasury of the later Twelfth Century' in *Jenkinson Studies*, pp. 35-49.
See *Memoranda Roll*.
BRUNNER, H. *Die Entstehung der Schwurgerichte* (Berlin, 1871).

CAENEGEM, R. C. VAN. See *Royal Writs*.
Calendar of Charter Rolls. (London, 1903-27).
Calendar of Documents preserved in France [918-1206]. Ed. J. H. Round (London, 1899).
Calendar of Inquisitions Post Mortem (London, 1904-   ).
Calendar of Miscellaneous Inquisitions (London, 1916-   ).
CAM, H. M. *Studies in the Hundred Rolls* (Oxford, 1921).
— *The Hundred and the Hundred Rolls* (London, 1930).
— *Liberties and Communities in Mediaeval England* (Cambridge, 1944).
— 'An East Anglian Shire-Moot of Stephen's Reign, 1148-53' in *E.H.R.*, xxxix (1924), 568-71.
— 'Stubbs seventy years afterwards' in *Cambridge Hist. Journal*, ix (1948), 129-47.
— 'Early Groups of Hundreds' in *Tait Essays*, pp. 13-25.
Camden Society Publications: *continued as* Camden Series, Royal Hist. Soc. (London, 1838-   ).
CANTERBURY. *See* Gervase.
Cartae Antiquae. Ed. L. Landon and J. Conway Davies (Pipe Roll Soc., London, 1939, 1960).
Cartularium Monasterii de Rameseia. Ed. W. H. Hart and P. A. Lyons (Rolls Ser., London, 1884-94).
Cartularium Monasterii Sancti Iohannis Baptiste de Colecestria. Ed. S. A. Moore (Roxburghe Club, London, 1897).
Cartularium Rievallense (Surtees Soc., Durham, 1889).
Cartularium Saxonicum. Ed. W. de G. Birch (London, 1885-93).

Cartulary of Darley Abbey. Ed. R. R. Darlington (Derbs. Arch. and Nat. Hist. Soc., 1945).

Cartulary of Oseney Abbey. Ed. H. E. Salter (Oxford, 1929-36).

'Catalogue of Rawlinson Manuscripts' (W. D. Macray) in *Catalogus Codicum Manuscriptorum Bibliothecae Bodleianae*, Part V (Oxford, 1862, 1878).

Catalogue of Western Manuscripts in the Old Royal and King's Collections [British Museum]. By G. F. Warner and J. P. Gilson (London, 1921).

CHADWICK, H. M. *Studies in Anglo-Saxon Institutions* (Cambridge, 1905).

— *Origin of the English Nation* (Cambridge, 1907).

Chancellor's Roll, 8 Richard I. Ed. D. M. Stenton (Pipe Roll Soc., London, 1930).

CHAPLAIS, P. 'Seals and Original Charters of Henry I' in *E.H.R.*, lxxv (1960), 260-75.

— 'The Chancery of Guienne' in *Jenkinson Studies* (*q.v.*), pp. 61-80.

— 'The Original Charters of Herbert and Gervase, Abbots of Westminster' in *Medieval Miscellany* (*q.v.*), pp. 89-110.

CHARTROU, JOSEPHE, *L'Anjou de 1109 à 1151* (Paris, 1928).

CHENEY, C. R. 'The Punishment of Felonous Clerks' in *E.H.R.*, li (1936), 215-36.

— 'King John and the Papal Interdict' in *B.J.R. L.*, xxxi (1948), 295-317.

— 'The Eve of Magna Carta' in *B.J.R. L.*, xxxviii (1956), 311-41.

— 'King John's Reaction to the Interdict on England' in *Trans. R.H. Soc.*, 4th Ser., xxxi (1949), 129-50.

— 'The Alleged Deposition of King John' in *Powicke Essays* (*q.v.*), 100-16. *See* Innocent III.

CHENEY, MARY. 'The Compromise of Avranches, 1172, and the spread of Canon Law in England' in *E.H.R.*, lvi (1941), 188-95.

CHEW, H. M. *The English Ecclesiastical Tenants in Chief and Knight Service* (Oxford, 1932).

Christopher Hatton's Book of Seals. Ed. L. C. Loyd and D. M. Stenton. (Oxford, 1950).

Chronica Monasterii de Melsa. Ed. E. A. Bond (Rolls Ser., London, 1866-68).

Chronicles and Memorials, Richard I. Ed. W. Stubbs (Rolls Ser., London, 1864-65).

Chronicles of the Reigns of Edward I and Edward II. Ed. W. Stubbs (Rolls Ser., London, 1882-83).

Chronicles of the Reigns of Stephen, Henry II and Richard I. Ed. R. Howlett (Rolls Ser., London, 1885-90).

Chronicon Abbatiae Rameseiensis. Ed. W. D. Macray (Rolls Ser., London, 1886).

Chronicon de Lanercost. Ed. J. Stevenson (Bannatyne Club, Edinburgh, 1839).

Chronicon Monasterii de Abingdon. Ed. J. Stevenson (Rolls Ser., London, 1958).

Chronicon Monasterii de Bello. Ed. J. S. Brewer (Anglia Christiana Soc., London, 1846).

Chroniques des comtes d'Anjou et des seigneurs d'Amboise. Ed. Louis Halphen and René Poupardin (Paris, 1913).

Chroniques de Saint-Martial de Limoges. Ed. H. Duplès Agier (Société de l'Hist. de France: Paris, 1874).

CHURCHILL, I. J. *Canterbury Administration* (London, 1933).

CLARE. See *Epistolae.*

CLAY, C. T. 'Notes on the early Archdeacons in the Church of York' in *Yorkshire Archaeological Journal,* xxxvi (1944-47), 269-87, 409-34. See *Early Yorkshire Charters.*

Close Rolls, 1227-1272 (London, 1902-1938).

Cockayne. See *Leechdoms.*

Codex Diplomaticus Aevi Saxonici. Ed. J. M. Kemble (English Historical Society, London, 1839-48).

COGGESHALL. *See* Ralph.

COKE, EDWARD. *Institutes of the Laws of England* (London, 1628-44). (Part I: commentary on Littleton.)

COKER, JOHN. *Survey of Dorsetshire* (London, 1732).

COLE, H. See *Documents.*

Complete Peerage of England, Scotland, Ireland, Great Britain and United Kingdom. Rev. ed. Vicary Gibbs (London, 1910-59).

Concilia Magnae Britanniae et Hiberniae, 446-1718. Ed. D. Wilkins (London, 1737).

CONSTABLE. See *Prerogativa Regis.*

'Constitutio Domus Regis' in *Dialogus de Scaccario,* ed. C. Johnson *(q.v.),* 129-35.

CORBETT, W. J. 'Development of the Duchy of Normandy and the Norman Conquest of England' in *Cambridge Medieval History,* v (1926), 481-520.

Corpus Iuris Canonici. Ed. E. Friedberg (Leipzig, 1876-82).

Councils and Ecclesiastical Documents relating to Great Britain and Ireland. Ed. A. W. Haddan and W. Stubbs (Oxford, 1869-78).

Coventry. *See* Walter.

Crawford Collection of Early Charters and Documents. Ed. A. S. Napier and W. H. Stevenson (Anecdota Oxoniensa, Mediaeval and Modern Series, part 7: Oxford, 1905).

CRISPIN, GILBERT. *Disputatio Iudei et Christiani.* Ed. B. Blumenkranz (Utrecht, Antwerp, 1956).

'Cronica de Electione Hugonis Abbatis' in *Memorials of St. Edmund's Abbey (q.v.),* ii, 29-130.

CRONNE, H. A. 'The Office of Local Justiciar in England under the Norman kings' in *Univ. Birmingham Hist. Journal,* vi (1957-58), 18-38.

Crown Pleas of the Wiltshire Eyre, 1249. Ed. C. A. F. Meekings (Wiltshire Arch. and Nat. Hist. Soc., 1961).

Curia Regis Rolls (London, 1923-   ).

DANIEL OF MORLEY. 'Philosophia' in *Archiv für die Geschichte der Naturwissenschaften,* viii (1917), 6-40, ix, 50-1.

DARLINGTON, R. R. *See* Cartulary of Darley Abbey; William of Malmesbury.

DART, JOHN. *Westmonasterium* (London, 1742).

DAVIS, H. W. C. *England under the Normans and Angevins* (London, 1905).

— 'Henry of Blois and Brian Fitz-Count' in *E.H.R.,* xxv (1910), 297-303.

Davis, H. W. C. *Historical Papers*. Ed. J. R. H. Weaver and A. L. Poole (London, 1933).
See *Regesta*.

Delisle, Léopold V. 'Chroniques et Annales Diverses' in *Histoire Littéraire de France*, xxxii, 182-264.

— 'Des Revenus publics en Normandie au xii⁰ siècle' in *Bibliothèque de l'École des Chartes*, x (1848-49), 173-210, 257-89 etc.
[See the further particulars in P. Lacombe, *Bibliographie des travaux de L. Delisle* (Paris, 1902), p. 5.]
See *Recueil des Actes de Henri II*.

Denholm-Young, N. *Collected Papers on Medieval Subjects* (Oxford, 1946).

Dept, G. G. *Les influences anglaise et française dans le comté de Flandre* (Ghent, 1928).

Descriptive catalogue of the charters and muniments in the possession of Lord Fitzhardinge at Berkeley Castle. Ed. I. H. Jeayes (Bristol, 1892).

De necessariis observantiis scaccarii dialogus. Ed. A. Hughes, C. G. Crump and C. Johnson (Oxford, 1902).
[Cited as *Dialogus de Scaccario* (Oxford).]

Dialogus de Scaccario. Ed. and trans. C. Johnson (Edinburgh, 1950).
[References are to this edition unless otherwise stated.]

Dibdin, L. T. 'Roman Canon Law in England' in *Quarterly Rev.*, ccxvii (1912), 413-36.

Diceto. *See* Ralf.

Dickens, Bruce. See *Early Middle English Texts*.

Dimitresco, Marin. *Pierre de Gavaston, comte de Cornuailles* (Paris, 1898).

Diplomatarium Anglicum. Ed. B. Thorpe (London, 1865).

Documents Illustrative of English History in the Thirteenth and Fourteenth Centuries. Ed. H. Cole (Record Comm., London, 1844).

Dodsworth. *See* Dugdale.

Domesday Book. (London, 1783-1816).

Domesday Monachorum of Christchurch, Canterbury. Ed. D. Douglas (London 1944).

Domesday of St. Paul's. Ed. W. H. Hale (Camden Soc., London, 1858).

Domesday Studies. Ed. P. E. Dove (London, 1888-91).

Douglas, D. 'Some early surveys from the abbey of Abingdon' in *E.H.R.*, xliv (1929), 618.
See *Domesday Monachorum; Feudal Documents*.

Drogheda. *See* William.

Drummond, J. Douglas. *Studien zur Kriegesgeschichte Englands im* xii *Jahrhundert* (Berlin, 1905),

Ducoudray, Gustave. *Les origines du parlement de Paris et la justice aux* xiii⁰ *et* xiv⁰ *siècles* (Paris, 1902).

Dugdale, William. *Origines Juridiciales* (London, 1666; 3rd ed. 1680).

— and Dodsworth, R. *Monasticon Anglicanum.* Ed. J. Caley, H. Ellis and B. Badinell (London, 1846).

Dunham, W. H. *Lord Hastings' Indentured Retainers, 1461-83.* [Trans. Connecticut Academy of Arts and Sciences, xxxix (1955).]

Dunning, P. J. 'The Arroasian Order in medieval Ireland' in *Irish Historical Studies*, iv (1945), 297-315.

Durham. *See* Simeon.

EADMER. *Historia Novorum*. Ed. M. Rule (Rolls Ser., London, 1884).
— 'Vita Anselmi' in *ibid.*, 305-440.

EARLE, J. *Handbook of the Land-Charters and other Saxonic Documents* (Oxford, 1888).

Early Middle English Texts. Ed. Bruce Dickins and R. M. Wilson (Cambridge, 1950).

Early Oxford Charters. See *Facsimiles*.

Early Sources of Scottish History, 800-1286. Collected and trans. A. O. Anderson (Edinburgh, 1922).

Early Yorkshire Charters. Ed. W. Farrer and C. T. Clay (Yorkshire Arch. Soc., 1914-).

Ecclesiastical Courts. See *Report*.

EDWARDS, J. G. *William Stubbs* (Hist. Assoc. Pamphlet, London, 1952).
— " 'The Itinerarium Regis Ricardi' and the 'Histoire de la Guerre Sainte' " in *Tait Essays* (*q.v.*), pp. 59-77.

EKWALL, E. *Street-names of the city of London* (Oxford, 1954).

ELECTIO HUGONIS. See *Cronica*.

ELLIS, H. *General Introduction to Domesday Book* (Record Comm., London, 1833).

Elmham. *See* Thomas.

ELTON, O. *F. T. Powell* (Oxford, 1906).

English Coronation Records. Ed. L. G. W. Legg (London, 1901).

English and Norse Documents. Ed. M. Ashdown (Cambridge, 1930).

English Historical Documents. Ed. D. C. Douglas (London, 1953-).
    Vol. I (*c.* 500-1042): ed. D. Whitelock (1955).
    (Vol. II (1042-1189): ed. D. C. Douglas and G. W. Greenaway (1953).

'Epistolae Cantuarienses, 1187-1199' in *Chronicles . . . Richard I* (*q.v.*), vol. ii.

Epistolae Herberti de Losinga, Osberti de Clara et Elmeri prioris Cantuariensis. Ed. R. Anstruther (Caxton Soc., London, 1846).

Essays in History presented to R. L. Poole. Ed. H. W. C. Davis (Oxford, 1927).

EYTON, R. W. *Antiquities of Shropshire* (London, 1854-60).
— *Court, Household and Itinerary of King Henry II* (London, 1878).

Facsimiles of Early Charters in Oxford Muniment Rooms. Ed. H. E. Salter (Oxford, 1929).

Facsimiles of Royal Charters. See Warner.

FARAL, EDMOND. *La Légende Arthurienne* (Paris, 1929).
— *Les Arts Poétiques du xiie et du xiiie siècle* (Paris, 1924).
— *La vie quotidienne au temps de Saint Louis* (Paris, 1956).

FARRER, W. *An Outline Itinerary of King Henry the First* (Oxford, 1920). See *Early Yorkshire Charters*.

FAVRE, EDOUARD. *Eudes, comte de Paris et roi de France*, 882-98 (Paris, 1893).

Feet of Fines: Henry II and Richard I (Pipe Roll Soc.,, 1884, 1898).

Feet of Fines for the County of Lincoln, 1199-1216. Ed. M. S. Walker (Pipe Roll Soc., London, 1954).

Feet of Fines for the County of Norfolk, 1201-1215; for the County of Suffolk, 1199-1214. Ed. B. Dodwell (Pipe Roll Soc., London, 1958).

Feudal Documents from the Abbey of Bury St. Edmunds. Ed. D. C. Douglas (London, 1932).

Fines, sive Pedes Finium, 1195-1214. Ed. J. Hunter (Record Comm., London, 1835, 1844).

FIRTH, C. H. *Modern History in Oxford, 841-1918* (Oxford, 1920).

FISHER, D. J. V. 'The Anti-Monastic Reaction in the Reign of Edward the Martyr' in *Cambridge Hist. Journal*, x (1952), 254-70.

FISHER, H. A. L. *F. W. Maitland* (Cambridge, 1910).

FLACH, JACQUES. *Les Origines de l'ancienne France* (Paris, 1886-1917).

Fleta. Ed. H. G. Richardson and G. O. Sayles (Selden Soc., London, 1953-).

FLETE, JOHN. *History of Westminster Abbey.* Ed. J. Armitage Robinson (Cambridge, 1909).

FLORENCE OF WORCESTER. *Chronicon* [450-1117: with two Continuations to 1141 and 1295]. Ed. B. Thorpe (Eng. Hist. Soc., London, 1848-49). *See* John of Worcester.

Foedera, Conventiones, Litterae et Cujuscunque Generis Acta Publica. Ed. T. Rymer (Record Comm., London, 1816-69).

FOLIOT. *See* Gilbert.

FORTESCUE, JOHN. *Governance of England.* Ed. C. Plummer (Oxford, 1885).

FOSS, EDWARD. *The Judges of England* (London, 1848-64).

FREEMAN, E. A. *The History of the Norman Conquest* (latest editions: Oxford, 1877-79).

— *The Reign of William Rufus* (Oxford, 1882).

— *Methods of Historical Study* (London, 1886).

GABEL, LEONA C. *Benefit of Clergy in England in the Later Middle Ages* (Northampton, Mass., 1929).

GALBRAITH, V. H. *The Making of Domesday Book* (Oxford, 1961).

— *Studies in the Public Records* (London, 1948).

— 'An Episcopal Land-Grant of 1085' in *E.H.R.*, xliv (1929), 353-72.

GANSHOF, F. L. *Qu'est-ce que la féodalité* (Brussels, 1944).

GÉNESTAL, R. *Le Privilegium Fori en France* (Paris, 1924).

GEOFFREY OF MONMOUTH, *Historia Regum Britanniae.* Ed. A. Griscom (London, 1929).

GEOFFREY DE VIGEOIS. 'Chronica' in *Nova bibliotheca* (*q.v.*), ii, 279-342.

— 'Ex Chronico' in *Historiens de la France*, xii, 421-51.

GERALD THE WELSHMAN. *Opera.* Ed. J. S. Brewer (Rolls Ser., London, 1861-91).

— 'De Iure et Statu Menevensis Ecclesiae' in *Opera*, iii, 101-373.

— 'De Principis Instructione Liber' in *Opera*, viii, 3-329.

— 'De rebus a se gestis' in *Opera*, i, 1-122.

— 'Symbolum Electorum' in *Opera*, i, 197-387.

— 'De Vita Galfridi Archiepiscopi Eboracensis' in *Opera*, iv, 357-431.

— 'Vita Sancti Hugonis' in *Opera*, vii, 87-147.

— 'Gemma Ecclesiastica' in *Opera*, ii, 1-364.

— 'Topographica Hibernica' in *Opera*, v, 3-204.

GERVASE OF CANTERBURY. *Historical Works.* Ed. W. Stubbs (Rolls Ser., London, 1879-80).

GERVASE OF TILBURY. *Otia Imperialia*. Ed. R. Pauli (Mon. Germ. Hist., *Scriptores*, xxxvii (1885), 359-94).

Gesta Regis Henrici Secundi. *See* Roger of Howden.

Gesta Ricardi. *See* Roger of Howden.

Gesta Stephani. Ed. K. R. Potter (London, 1955).

GHELLINCK, JOSEPH DE. *L'essor de la littérature latine au xiie siècle* (Paris, 1946).

GILBERT FOLIOT. *Epistolae*. Ed. J. A. Giles (Patres Eccl. Angl., Oxford, 1845).

GILBERT OF NOGENT. *See* Guibert.

GIRALDUS CAMBRENSIS. *See* Gerald.

GLANVILLE. *De Legibus et Consuetudinibus Regni Angliae*. Ed. G. E. Woodbine (New Haven, 1932).
See Southern.

GLOVER, R. 'English Warfare in 1066' in *E.H.R.*, lxvii (1952), 1-18.

GODEFROY, L. 'Interdit' in *Dictionnaire de théologie catholique* (ed. Vacant), vii, 2280-90.

GOOCH, G. P. *History and Historians in the Nineteenth Century* (London, revised ed. 1952).

GOULBURN, E. M. and H. SYMONDS. *Life, Letters and Sermons of Bishop Herbert de Losinga* (London, 1878).

GREIN, W. M. See *Bibliothek*.

GROSS, C. *The Gild Merchant* (Oxford, 1890).

GRUNDY, G. B. *Fifty-five years at Oxford* (London, 1945).

GUERNES DE PONT-SAINTE-MAXENCE. *La Vie de Saint Thomas le Martyr*. Ed. Emmanuel Walberg (Lund, 1922).

GUIBERT DE NOGENT. *Histoire de sa vie*. Ed. G. Bourgin (Paris, 1907).

GUILHIERMOZ, PAUL. *Essai sur l'origine de la noblesse en France au moyen âge* (Paris, 1902).

GUILLAUME LE BRETON. See *Oeuvres*.

GUIRAUD, PAUL. *Fustel de Coulanges* (Paris, 1896).

GÜTSCHOW, ELSE. *Innocenz III und England* (Munich, 1904).

GUY OF AMIENS. 'De Bello Hastingensi carmen' in *Monumenta Historica Britannica*, ed. H. Petrie, 856-72.

Gwynn Studies. See *Medieval Studies*.

HADDAN, A. W. See *Councils*.

HALE, W. H. See *Domesday*.

HALL, H. *Introduction to the Study of the Pipe Rolls* (Pipe Roll Soc., London, 1884).

— *Formula Book of English Official Historical Documents*. Part II: *Ministerial and Judicial Documents* (Cambridge, 1909).

HALPHEN, LOUIS. *Le comté d'Anjou au xie siècle* (Paris, 1906).

HARCOURT, VERNON. *His Grace the Steward and Trial by Peers* (London, 1907).

HARDY, T. D. *Itinerary of King John* (prefixed to *Rotuli Litterarum Patentium*, *q.v.*).

HARMER. See *Anglo-Saxon Writs*.

HARTRIDGE, R. A. R. *History of Vicarages in the Middle Ages* (Cambridge, 1930).

HASKINS, C. H. *Norman Institutions* (Cambridge, Mass., 1918).

HASKINS, C. H. *Studies in the History of Mediaeval Science* (Cambridge, Mass., 1924).

— 'The Abacus and the King's Curia' in *E.H.R.*, xxvii (1912), 101-6.

HASTINGS, M. 'High History or Hack History: England in the Later Middle Ages' in *Speculum*, xxxvi (1961), 225-53.

HATTON. *See* Christopher.

Heimskringla af Snorre Sturlasson. Ed. Finnur Jónsson (Copenhagen, 1893-1901).

— Trans. Eriling Monsen and A. H. Smith (Cambridge, 1932).

HEMING. *Chartularium Ecclesie Wigornensis.* Ed. T. Hearne (Oxford, 1723).

HENRY OF HUNTINGDON. *Historia Anglorum.* Ed. T. Arnold (Rolls Ser., London, 1879).

HERBERT DE LOSINGA. See *Epistolae.*

HERMANN OF TOURNAI. 'De Miraculis Sancte Mariae Laudunensis' *in* Migne, *Patrologia Latina*, clvi (1853), 987-1018.

HEXHAM. *See* John.

Histoire des ducs de Normandie et les rois d'Angleterre. Ed. F. Michel (Soc. de l'Hist. de France, Paris, 1840).

Histoire de Guillaume le Maréchal, Comte de Striguil et Pembroke, Régent d'Angleterre. Ed. Paul Meyer (Soc. de l'Hist. de France, Paris, 1891-1901).

Historia Eliensis. Ed. E. O. Blake (Camden Soc., Third Series, London, 1962).

Historia et Cartularium Monasterii Gloucestrie. Ed. W. H. Hart (Rolls Ser., London, 1863-67).

Historiae Anglicanae Scriptores Decem. Ed. Roger Twysden (London, 1652).

Historiae Dunolmensis Scriptores Tres. Ed. James Raine (Surtees Soc., 1839).

Historians of the Church of York. Ed. James Raine (Rolls Ser., London, 1879-94).

Historical Essays in Honour of James Tait. Ed. J. G. Edwards, V. H. Galbraith and E. F. Jacob (Manchester, 1933).

Historiens de la France. Vol. xxiii (Paris, 1876), 605-723: Scripta de Feodis ad Regem spectantibus.

HITTORP, M. *De divinis catholicae ecclesiae officiis* (Paris, 1610).

HOLDSWORTH, W. S. *History of English Law* (London, 1922-52).

HOLLINGS, M. 'The Survival of the Five Hide Unit in the Western Midlands' in *E.H.R.*, lxiii (1948), 453-87.

HOLMES, G. A. *The Estates of the Higher Nobility in Fourteenth-Century England* (Cambridge, 1957).

HOLT, J. C. *The Northerners* (Oxford, 1961).

— 'The Making of Magna Carta' in *E.H.R.*, lxxii (1957), 401-22.

HOLTZMANN, WALTHER. *Papsturkunden in England* (Berlin, 1930-52).

HOWDEN. *See* Roger.

HOYT, R. S. *The Royal Demesne in English Constitutional History, 1066-1272* (New York, 1950).

HUNNISETT, R. F. *The Medieval Coroner* (Cambridge, 1961).

— 'The Origins of the office of Coroner' in *Trans. R.H. Soc.*, 5th Ser., viii (1958), 85-104.

HUNT, R. W. 'The Disputation of Peter of Cornwall against Symon the Jew' in *Powicke Studies (q.v.)*, 143-56.

HUNTINGDON. *See* Henry.

HURNARD, N. D. 'The Jury of Presentment and the Assize of Clarendon' in *E.H.R.*, lvi (1941), 374-410.
— 'Magna Carta, Clause 34' in *Powicke Studies* (*q.v.*), 157-79.
HURSTFIELD, J. *The Queen's Wards* (London, 1958).
HUTTON, W. H. *William Stubbs, Bishop of Oxford* (London, 1906).

INMAN, A. H. *Domesday and Feudal Statistics* (London, 1900).
INNOCENT III. 'Epistolae' in *Patrologia Latina*, vols. 214-217.
— *Selected Letters of Pope Innocent III concerning England, 1178-1216*. Ed. C. R. Cheney and W. H. Semple (London, 1953).
'Instituta Cnuti' *in* Liebermann, *Gesetze* (*q.v.*), i, 612-16.
Inquisitions Post Mortem. See *Calendar*.
Itinerary of King John. See Hardy.

JAFFÉ-LOEWENFELD. See *Regesta*.
JAMES, M. R. *See* Map; Thomas of Monmouth.
JENKINSON, H. 'Medieval Tallies' in *Archaeologia*, lxxi (1925), 289-351.
— 'William Cade, a Financier of the Twelfth Century' in *E.H.R.*, xxviii (1913), 209-27.
— 'A Money-Lender's Bonds of the Twelfth Century' in *Poole Essays* (*q.v.*), 190-210.
— *Domesday Rebound* (London, 1954).
See *Studies*.
JOHN, ERIC. *Land Tenure in Early England* (Leicester, 1960).
JOHN OF HEXHAM. 'Chronicle' *in* Simeon of Durham, *Historical Works* (*q.v.*), ii, 284-332.
JOHN OF SALISBURY. *Letters*. Ed. W. J. Millor, H. E. Butler and C. N. L. Brooke (London, 1955).
— *Policraticus*. Ed. C. C. J. Webb (Oxford, 1909).
JOHN OF WORCESTER. *Chronicle*. Ed. J. R. H. Weaver (Oxford, 1908).
JOHNSON, C. 'Some Charters of Henry I' in *Tait Essays* (*q.v.*). 137-42. See *Dialogus*.
JOLLIFFE, J. E. A. 'The Chamber and the Castle Treasuries under King John' in *Powicke Studies* (*q.v.*), 115-42.
JOSEPH NOEL DE WAILLY. *Récits d'un ménéstral de Reims au treizième siècle*. Ed. Natalis de Wailly (Soc. de l'Hist. de France, Paris, 1876).
'Judicia Civitatis Lundoniae' *in* Liebermann, *Gesetze* (*q.v.*), 1, 173-83.
JUSTINIAN. See *Les Institutes*.

KANTOROWICZ, E. H. *Laudes Regiae* (Berkeley, 1946).
KELLY, AMY. *Eleanor of Aquitaine and the Four Kings* (London, 1952).
KEMBLE, J. M. See *Codex Diplomaticus*.
King Alfred's Version of the Consolations of Boethius. Ed. W. J. Sedgefield (Oxford, 1900).
KNOWLES, D. *The Monastic Order in England* (Cambridge, 1940).
— *The Episcopal Colleagues of Archbishop Thomas Becket* (Cambridge, 1951).
— 'The Canterbury Election of 1205-6' in *E.H.R.*, liii (1938), 211-20.
KREHBIEL, E. B. *The Interdict* (Washington, 1909).
KUTTNER, S. and RATHBONE, E. 'Anglo-Norman Canonists of the Twelfth Century' in *Traditio*, vii (1949-51), 279-358.

LACOMBE, G. 'An unpublished document on The Great Interdict' (Stephen Langton's 'Sermo ad populum') in *Catholic Hist. Review* (Washington), xv (1930), 408-20.

Landferth, 'Translatio et Miracula sancti Swithini' in *Acta Sanctorum*, July, vol. i (1867), pp. 294-9, supplemented in *Analecta Bollandiana*, vol. iv (1885), pp. 367-410.

LANDON, L. *Itinerary of King Richard I* (Pipe Roll Soc., London, 1935).

LARSON, L. M. *The King's Household in England before the Norman Conquest* (Madison, 1904, reprinted 1959).

LANGTON. See *Acta*; Lacombe.

Layettes du Tresor des Chartes. Ed. Alexandre Teulet (Paris, 1863-1909).

LEA, J. W. *The Bishop's Oath of Homage* (London, 1875).

LEACH, A. F. *Educational Charters and Documents, 598-1909* (Cambridge, 1911).

See *Rescriptum*.

LECLERCQ, H. 'Chevalerie' *in* Cabriol-Leclerq, *Dictionnaire d'archéologie chrétienne*, iii (1914), 1305-7.

Leechdoms, Wortcunning and Starcraft of Early England. Ed. Oswald Cockayne (London, 1864-66).

'Leges Edwardi Confessoris' in Liebermann, *Gesetze* (*q.v.*), i, 627-72.

'Leges Henrici' *in* Liebermann, *Gesetze* (*q.v.*), i. 547-611.

LEGG, J. WICKHAM. See *Three Coronation Orders*.

LEGG, L. G. W. See *English Coronation Records*.

LEHMANN, W. C. 'John Millar, Professor of Civil Law at Glasgow' in *Juridical Review* (Edinburgh) N.S., vol. vi (1961), 218-33.

'Leis Willelme' *in* Liebermann, *Gesetze* (*q.v.*), i, 492-520.

LELAND. *Itinerary*. See William de Vere.

Les Institutes de Justinien en français. Ed. F. Olivier-Martin (Paris, 1935).

Letters of William Stubbs. Ed. W. H. Hutton (London, 1904).

Letters. See John of Salisbury.

'Liber Custumarum' in *Munimenta Gildhallae Londoniensis*. Ed. H. T. Riley (Rolls Ser., London, 1859-62).

Liber de Antiquis Legibus. Ed. T. Stapleton (Camden Soc., London, 1846).

Liber de Miraculis Sanctae Osithae. See William de Vere.

Liber Vitae Ecclesiae Dunolmensis (Surtees Soc., London, 1841; facsimile, ed. A. Hamilton Thompson, 1923).

'Liber Winton' in *Domesday Book* (*q.v.*), iv, 529-62.

'Libertas Londoniensis' *in* Liebermann, *Gesetze* (*q.v.*); i, 673-5.

LIEBERMANN, F. *Die Gesetze der Angelsachsen* (Halle, 1903-16).

— *Über die Leges Anglorum saeculo xiii ineunte Londoniis collectae* (Halle, 1894).

— *Über die Leges Edwardi Confessoris* (Halle, 1896).

— *Ungedruckte anglo-normannische geschichtsquellen* (Strassburg, 1879).

— *The National Assembly in the Anglo-Saxon Period* (Halle, 1913).

— 'Einleitung zum Statut der Londoner Friedensgilde unter Aethelstan' in *Mélanges Fitting* (Montpellier, 1908), vol. ii.

— 'The Text of Henry I's Coronation Charter' in *Trans. R.H. Soc.*, New Ser., viii (1894), 21-48.

— 'Drei nordhumbrische Urkunden um 1100' in *Archiv für das Studium der neueren Sprachen*, cxi, 275-84.

Life of Christina de Markyate. Ed. C. H. Talbot (Oxford, 1959).

Lincoln. See *Registrum Antiquissimum.*

List of Sheriffs. See *Public Record Office.*

Literae Cantuarienses. Ed. J. B. Sheppard (Rolls Ser., London, 1887-89).

LITTLETON, THOMAS. *Tenures. See* Coke.

Lives of Edward the Confessor. Ed. H. R. Luard (Rolls Ser., London, 1858). *See* Southern.

LLOYD, J. E. *History of Wales to the Edwardian Conquest* (London, 1911, 3rd ed., 1939).

LOSINGA. See *Epistolae;* Goulburn and Symonds.

LOT, F. *L'Art militaire et les armées au moyen âge en Europe et dans le Proche Orient* (Paris, 1946).

LUCHAIRE, ACHILLE. *Les communes françaises à l'époque des Capétiens directs* (Paris, 1911).

Lupus (Sermo Lupi). See Wulfstan.

LYNDWOOD, WILLIAM. *Provinciale* (Oxford, 1679).

LYON, B. D. *From Fief to Indenture* (Cambridge, Mass., 1957).

— 'The Money Fief under the English Kings, 1066-1485' in *E.H.R.,* lxvi (1951), 161-93.

McKECHNIE, W. S. *Magna Carta* (Glasgow, 1905; 2nd ed. 1914).

McKISACK, M. 'London and the Succession to the Crown during the Middle Ages' in *Powicke Essays (q.v.),* pp. 86-89.

MADOX, T. *History and Antiquities of the Exchequer of England* (London, 2nd ed., 1769).

— *Formulare Anglicanum* (London, 1702).

Magna Carta Commemoration Essays. Ed. H. E. Maldon (Royal Hist. Soc., London, 1917).

Magna Vita sancti Hugonis. See Adam of Eynsham.

Magni Rotuli Scaccarii Normanniae sub Regibus Angliae. Ed. T. Stapleton (Soc. Antiquaries, London, 1840-44).

Magnus Rotulus Scaccarii, 31 Henry I. Ed. J. Hunter (Record Comm., London, 1833).

[Cited as Pipe Roll.]

Magnus Rotulus Pipae, 1155-58. Ed. J. Hunter (Record Comm., London, 1844).

[Cited as Pipe Roll.]

Magnus Rotulus Pipae, 1189-90. Ed. J. Hunter (Record Comm., London, 1844).

[Cited as Pipe Roll.]

MAITLAND, F. W. *Domesday Book and Beyond* (Cambridge, 1897).

— *Roman Canon Law in the Church of England* (London, 1898; in this volume there is reprinted, *inter alia,* 'Canon Law in England' from *E.H.R.,* xi (1896), 446-78).

— 'William Stubbs, Bishop of Oxford' in *E.H.R.,* xvi (1901), 417-26. *See* Bracton; Pollock; *Select Pleas of the Crown; Select Pleas in Manorial Courts; Three Rolls of the King's Court.*

MAJOR. See *Acta*

MALMESBURY. *See* William.

Manuscripts of Westminster Abbey. Ed. J. A. Robinson and M. R. James (Cambridge, 1909).

MANWOOD, JOHN. *Treatise and Discourse of the Laws of the Forest* (London, 1598).

MAP, WALTER. *De Nugis Curialium*. Ed. M. R. James (Oxford, 1914).

MARKYATE, CHRISTINA. See *Life*.

MASKELL, W. *Monumenta ritualia ecclesiae anglicanae* (Oxford, 1882).

Materials for the History of Thomas Becket. Ed. J. C. Robertson and J. B. Sheppard (Rolls Ser., London, 1875-85).

MATTHEW PARIS. *Chronica Majora*. Ed. H. R. Luard (Rolls Ser., London, 1872-84).

— *Chronica Majora*. Ed. William Wats (London, 1640).

— *Historia Anglorum sive Historia Minor*. Ed. F. H. Madden (Rolls Ser., London, 1866-69).

— 'Vita Viginti trium Abbatum' in *Chronica Majora*, ed. Wats and in Walsingham, *Gesta Abbatum* (*q.v.*).

'Matthew of Westminster', *Florés Historiarum*. Ed. H. R. Luard (Rolls Ser., London, 1890).

Medieval Miscellany for D. M. Stenton. Ed. P. M. Barnes and C. F. Slade (Pipe Roll Soc., 1962).

Medieval Studies presented to Aubrey Gwynn, S.J. Ed. J. A. Watt, J. B. Morrall and F. X. Martin (Dublin, 1961).

Memoranda Roll, 1 John. Introd. H. G. Richardson (Pipe Roll Soc., London, 1943).

— *10 John*. Ed. R. A. Brown (Pipe Roll Soc., 1957).

Memorials of St. Dunstan. Ed. W. Stubbs (Rolls Ser., London, 1874).

Memorials of St. Edmund's Abbey. Ed. T. Arnold (Rolls Ser., London, 1890-96).

MERCATI, A. 'La Prima Relazione del Cardinale Nicolò de Romanis sulla sua Legazione in Inghilterra' in *Poole Essays* (*q.v.*), 274-89.

MEYER, P. See *Histoire*.

Mirror of Justices. Ed. W. J. Whittaker, with Introd. by F. W. Maitland (Selden Soc., London, 1893).

Misae Roll. See *Rotuli de Liberate*.

MITCHELL, S. K. *Studies in Taxation under John and Henry III* (New Haven, 1914).

Modus Tenendi Parliamentum. Ed. T. D. Hardy (Record Comm., London, 1846). Reprinted in Stubbs, *Select Charters*.

[also ed. M. V. Clarke, *Medieval Representation and Consent* (London, 1936), 373-84].

Monasticon Anglicanum. See Dugdale.

MONMOUTH. See Geoffrey, Thomas.

MONTESQUIEU, CH. DE SECONDAT, BARON DE. *De l'esprit des Lois*. Ed. G. Truc (Paris, 1944-45).

Monumenta Germaniae Historica: Leges, Poetae, Scriptores. Ed. G. H. Pertz, G. Waitz and others.

[Cited as M.G.H.]

MOREY, ADRIAN. *Bartholomew of Exeter* (Cambridge, 1937).

MORLEY, DANIEL OF. See Daniel.

MORRIS, J. E. *The Welsh Wars of Edward I* (Oxford, 1901).

MORRIS, W. A. *The Mediaeval English Sheriff to 1300* (Manchester, 1927).

Morris, W. A. *The Early English County Court* (Berkeley, 1926).

— 'A Mention of Scutage in the Year 1110' in *E.H.R.*, xxxvi (1921), 45-6.

Napier, A. S. See *Crawford Charters*.

Navel, H. 'L'enquête de 1133 sur les fiefs de l'évêché de Bayeux' in *Bull. Soc. Antiquaires de Normandie*, xlii (1935), 5-80.

Neilson, G. 'Chivalry' in *Encyclopaedia of Religion*, iii (1910), 565-7.

Newburgh. *See* William.

Nichols, F. M. 'Feudal and Obligatory Knighthood' in *Archaeologia*, xxxix (1863), 189-244.

Nogent, Gilbert of. *See* Guibert.

Norgate, Kate. *England under the Angevin Kings* (London, 1887).

— *John Lackland* (London, 1902).

— *Minority of Henry III* (London, 1912).

— *Richard the Lion Heart* (London, 1924).

Nova Bibliotheca. Ed. Philippe Labbe (Paris, 1657).

Oeuvres de Rigord et de Guillaume le Breton. Ed. H. F. Delaborde (Soc. de l'Hist. de France, Paris, 1882).

Offler, H. S. 'The Tractate De Iniusta Vexacione Willelmi Episcopi Primi' in *E.H.R.*, lxvi (1951), 321-41.

Ogle, A. *The Canon Law in Mediaeval England* (London, 1912).

Olivier-Martin, F. *Les régences et la majorité des rois* (Paris, 1931).

— 'Les chapes de plomb' in *Mélanges Mandonnet* (Paris, 1930), tom. ii, pp. 283-7.

See *Les Institutes.*

Oman, C. W. C. *Memories of Victorian Oxford* (London, 1941).

Ordericus Vitalis. *Historia Ecclesiastica.* Ed. A. le Prévost (Soc. de l'Hist. de France, Paris, 1838-55).

Orpen, G. H. *Ireland under the Normans* (Oxford, 1911-20).

Osbert of Clare. *Letters.* Ed. E. W. Williamson. Introd. by J. Armitage Robinson (London, 1929).

See *Epistolae.*

Packard, S. R. *Miscellaneous Records of the Norman Exchequer* (Smith Coll. Studies, Northampton, Mass., 1926-27).

— 'King John and the Norman Church' in *Harvard Theological Review* (Cambridge, Mass.), xv. (1922), 15-40.

Page, William. *London: its origin and early development* (London, 1923).

Painter, S. *The Reign of King John* (Baltimore, 1949).

— *French Chivalry: Chivalric Ideas and Practices in Mediaeval France* (Baltimore, 1940).

— 'The Houses of Lusignan and Chatellerault, 1150-1250' in *Speculum*, xxx (1955), 374-84.

Palgrave, F. *The Rise and Progress of the English Commonwealth* (London, 1832).

See *Rotuli Curiae Regis; Parliamentary Writs.*

Parliamentary Writs and Writs of Military Summons. Ed. F. Palgrave (Record Comm., London, 1827-34).

Paris. *See* Matthew.

Patent Rolls of Reign of Henry III [1216-32] (London, 1901-3).

Patres ecclesiae Anglicanae. Ed. J. A. Giles (Oxford, 1843-48).

Patrologiae cursus completus: Series Latina. Ed. J. P. Migne (Paris, 1844-   ).

PAYNE-GALLWEY, RALPH. *The Crossbow* (London, 1903).

PEARCE, E. H. *The Monks of Westminster* (Cambridge, 1916).

PETER OF BLOIS. *Opera.* Ed. J. A. Giles ['Epistolae' in vols. i, ii (1847), reprinted in Migne, *Patrologia,* ccvii (1895), 1-560].

— 'Dialogus inter Regem Henricum II et Abbatem Bonaevallensem' in *Opera (q.v.),* iii, 302.

Peterborough. *See* Benedict.

PETIT-DUTAILLIS, CHARLES. *Studies and Notes Supplementary to Stubbs's Constitutional History* (Manchester, 1908-29: reprinted 1930).

— *Le Désheritement de Jean sans Terre* (Paris, 1925).

Pipe Rolls, 5 Henry II to 16 John (Pipe Roll Soc., London, 1884-1959). For earlier rolls see *Magnus Rotulus.*

Place Names of Surrey [English Place Name Society, xi (1934)].

Placita de Quo Warranto. Ed. W. Illingworth and J. Caley (Record Comm., London, 1818).

Pleas before the King or his Justices. Ed. D. M. Stenton (Selden Soc., London, 1949, 1953).

Pleas of the Crown for the County of Gloucester. Ed. F. W. Maitland (London, 1884).

PLUCKNETT, T. F. T. *Concise History of the Common Law* (5th ed., London, 1956).

PLUMMER, C. See *Two of the Saxon Chronicles.*

POLLOCK, F. and MAITLAND, F. W. *History of English Law before the Time of Edward I* (Second edition: Cambridge, 1898, reprinted 1911, 1923, 1952).

Pont-Sainte-Maxence. *See* Guernes.

POOLE, A. L. *From Domesday Book to Magna Carta* (Oxford, 1955).

— *Obligations of Society in the Twelfth and Thirteenth Centuries* (Oxford, 1946).

— 'Outlawry as a Punishment of Criminous Clerks' in *Tait Essays (q.v.),* 239-46.

POOLE, R. L. *The Exchequer in the Twelfth Century* (Oxford, 1912).

— *Lectures on the History of the Papal Chancery* (Cambridge, 1915). See *Essays*

POTTER, K. R. See *Gesta Stephani;* William of Malmesbury.

POWELL, F. Y. *See* Elton.

POWICKE, F. M. *Loss of Normandy* (Manchester, 1913, revised ed. 1960).

— *Stephen Langton* (Oxford, 1928).

— *King Henry III and the Lord Edward* (Oxford, 1947).

— *The Thirteenth Century* (Oxford, 1953).

— 'Per Iudicium Parium vel per Legem Terrae' in *Magna Carta Commemoration Essays (q.v.),* 96-179.

— 'Roger of Wendover and the Coggeshall Chronicle' in *E.H.R.,* xxi (1906), 286-96.

— 'The Bull *Miramur plurimum* and a Letter to Archbishop Stephen Langton, 5 September 1215' in *E.H.R.,* xliv (1929), 86-93.

— 'The Oath of Bromholm' in *E.H.R.,* lvi (1941), 529-48. See *Studies.*

Prerogativa Regis: Tertia Lectura Roberti Constable. Ed. S. E. Thorne (New Haven, 1949).

PRESTWICH, J. O. 'War and Finance in the Anglo-Norman State' in
  T.R.H.S., 5th Series, iv (1954), 19-43.
PSICHARI, HENRIETTE. *Renan d'après lui-même* (Paris, 1937).
Public Record Office, List of Sheriffs (*Lists and Indexes*, no. ix: London, 1898).

'Quadripartitus' *in* Liebermann, *Gesetze* (*q.v.*), i, 529-46.

RALF DE DICETO. *Opera Historica*. Ed. W. Stubbs (Rolls Ser., London,
  1876).
— 'Abbreviationes Chronicarum' in *Opera* (*q.v.*), i, 3-263.
RALPH OF COGGESHALL. *Chronicon Anglicanum*. Ed. J. Stevenson (Rolls
  Ser., London, 1875).
RAMSAY, J. H. *The Foundations of England*, B.C. 55-A.D. *1154* (London,
  1898).
— *The Angevin Empire, 1154-1216* (London, 1903).
— *The Dawn of the Constitution* (London, 1908).
— *History of the Revenues of the Kings of England* (Oxford, 1925).
Ramsey Abbey. See *Cartularium*.
Records of St. Bartholomew's, Smithfield. Ed. E. A. Webb (London, 1900).
Recueil des Actes de Henri II, roi d'Angleterre et duc de Normandie. Ed. L.
  Delisle and É. Berger (Paris, 1909-27).
Recueil des Actes de Philippe-Auguste, roi de France. Ed. H. F. Delaborde,
  Ch. Petit-Dutaillis and J. Monicat (Paris, 1916-   ).
Recueil des chartes de l'abbaye de Cluny. Ed. Alexandre Bruel (Paris, 1876-
  1903).
Red Book of the Exchequer. Ed. H. Hall (Rolls Ser., London, 1896).
Regesta Pontificum Romanorum. Ed. Phillipp Jaffé (Berlin, 1851, 2nd ed.
  S. Loewenfeld, F. Kaltenbrunner and P. Ewald, Leipzig, 1881-88).
Regesta Regum Anglo-Normannorum. Ed. H. W. C. Davis: vol. i; C. Johnson
  and H. A. Cronne: vol. ii (Oxford, 1913, 1956).
Regiam Majestatem and Quoniam Attachiamenta. Ed. T. M. Cooper (Stair
  Soc., Edinburgh, 1947).
Registrum Antiquissimum of the Cathedral Church of Lincoln. Ed. C. W. Forster
  and K. Major (Lincoln Rec. Soc., 1931-   ).
Registrum Henrici Woodlock. Ed. A. W. Goodman (Cant. and York Soc.,
  Oxford, 1940-41).
Registrum Roberti Winchelsey. Ed. Rose Graham (Cant. and York Soc.
  Oxford, 1917-53).
Registrum Roffense. Ed. John Thorpe (London, 1769).
Registrum Sacrum Anglicanum. Ed. W. Stubbs (Oxford, 1858; rev. ed. 1897).
Registrum Simonis de Gandavo. Ed. C. T. Flower and M. C. B. Dawes
  (Cant. and York Soc., Oxford, 1934).
*Report of the Commissioners appointed to inquire into the Constitution and Working
  of the Ecclesiastical Courts* [Historical Appendix (1) by W. Stubbs]
  (London, 1883).
Rescriptum pro Monachis. Ed. T. E. Holland *in* Collectanea, 2nd series,
  (Oxford Hist. Soc., 1890) 156-59; A. F. Leach, *Educational Charters*
  (*q.v.*), 104-7.
RICHARD, A. *Histoire des comtes de Poitou* (Paris, 1903).
RICHARD OF DEVIZES. 'De rebus gestis Ricardi I' in *Chronicles of the Reigns
  of Stephen etc.* (*q.v.*), vol. iii.

RICHARD OF HEXHAM. 'Chronicle' in *Chronicles, Stephen,* etc. (*q.v.*), vol. iii, 139-78.

RICHARDSON [SUGGETT], HELEN. 'A Twelfth-Century Anglo-Norman Charter' in *B.J.R.L.,* xxiv (1940), 168-72.

— 'An Anglo-Norman Return to the Inquest of Sheriffs' in *B.J.R.L.,* xxvii (1942-43), 179-81.

RICHARDSON, H. G. *The English Jewry under the Angevin Kings* (London, 1960).

— 'The Morrow of the Great Charter' in *B.J.R.L.,* xxviii (1944), 422-43, xxix (1945-46), 185-200.

— 'Henry I's Charter to London' in *E.H.R.,* xlii (1927), 80-87.

— 'Richard fitz Neal and the Dialogus de Scaccario' in *E.H.R.,* xliii (1928), 161-71, 321-40.

— 'Letters of the Legate Guala' in *E.H.R.,* xlviii (1933), 250-59.

— 'The Marriage and Coronation of Isabelle of Angoulême' in *E.H.R.,* lxi (1946), 289-314.

— 'King John and Isabelle of Angoulême' in *E.H.R.,* lxv (1950), 360-71.

— 'The Chamber under Henry II' in *E.H.R.,* lxix (1954), 596-611.

— 'The Letters and Charters of Eleanor of Aquitaine' in *E.H.R.,* lxxiv (1959), 193-213.

— 'Gervase of Tilbury' in *History,* xlvi (1961), 102-14.

— 'Roman Law in the Regiam Majestatem' in *Juridical Review,* lxvii (1958), 155-87.

— 'An Early Fine: Its Causes and Consequences' in *L.Q.R.,* xlviii (1932), 415-24.

— 'Glanville Continued' in *L.Q.R.,* liv (1938), 381-99.

— 'The Annales Paulini' in *Speculum,* xxiii (1948), 630-40.

— 'The English Coronation Oath' in *Speculum,* xxiv (1949), 44-75.

— 'The Origins of Parliament' in *Trans. R.H. Soc.,* 4th Ser., xi (1928), 137-83.

— 'William of Ely, the King's Treasurer (?1195-1215)' in *Trans. R.H. Soc.,* 4th ser., xv (1932), 45-90.

— 'The English Coronation Oath' in *Trans. R.H. Soc.,* 4th ser., xxiii (1941), 129-58.

— 'The Commons and Medieval Politics' in *Trans. R.H. Soc.,* 4th ser., xxviii (1946), 21-45.

— 'Studies in Bracton' in *Traditio,* vi (1948), 61-104.

— 'The Coronation in Medieval England' in *Traditio,* xvi (1960), 111-202.

RICHARDSON, H. G. and SAYLES, G. O. *The Administration of Ireland, 1172-1377* (Dublin, 1963).

— *The Early Statutes* (London, 1934).

— *The Irish Parliament in the Middle Ages* (Philadelphia, 1952).

— *Parliaments and Great Councils in Medieval England* (London, 1961).

— 'The Provisions of Oxford' in *B.J.R. L.,* xvii (1933), 291-321 [and published separately].

— 'Early Coronation Records' in *B.I.H.R.,* xiii (1936), 129-45, xiv (1937), 1-9.

See *Rotuli Parliamentorum; Select Cases of Procedure without Writ.*

Rigord. See *Oeuvres.*

ROBERT OF TORIGNI. 'Chronica' in *Chronicles, Stephen . . . (q.v.)*, iv, 81-315.
ROBERTSON, A. J. See *Anglo-Saxon Charters.*
ROBERTSON, E. W. *Historical Essays* (Edinburgh, 1872).
ROBINSON, J. ARMITAGE. *Gilbert Crispin, Abbot of Westminster* (Cambridge, 1911).
— 'The Coronation Order in the Tenth Century' in *Journal of Theological Studies*, xix (1918), 56-72.
  See Flete; Osbert; *Manuscripts of Westminster Abbey.*
ROGER OF HOWDEN. *Gesta Regis Henrici Secundi et Ricardi I.* Ed. W. Stubbs (Rolls Ser., London, 1867). [formerly attributed erroneously to Benedict (abbot) of Peterborough].
— *Chronica.* Ed. W. Stubbs (Rolls Ser., London, 1868-71).
ROGER OF WENDOVER. *Chronica.* Ed. H. G. Hewlett (Rolls Ser., London, 1886-89). [An inferior edition of the text from 1154 to that of Coxe.]
— *Flores Historiarum.* Ed. H. O. Coxe (Eng. Hist. Soc., London, 1841-44).
Rolls of the Justices in Eyre for Gloucestershire, Warwickshire and Staffordshire, 1221-22. Ed. D. M. Stenton (Selden Society, London, 1940).
ROTH, CECIL. *History of the Jews in England* (Oxford, 1941).
Rotuli Chartarum, 1199-1216. Ed. T. D. Hardy (Record Comm., London, 1837).
Rotuli Curiae Regis: 6 Richard I-1 John. Ed. F. Palgrave (Record Comm., London, 1835).
Rotuli de Dominabus. Ed. J. H. Round (Pipe Roll Society, 1913).
Rotuli de Liberate ac de Misis et Praestitis, regnante Iohanne. Ed. T. D. Hardy (Record Comm., London, 1844).
Rotuli de Oblatis et Finibus. Ed. T. D. Hardy (Record Comm., London, 1835).
Rotuli Litterarum Clausarum, 1204-1227. Ed. T. D. Hardy (Record Comm., London, 1833-44).
Rotuli Litterarum Patentium, 1201-1216. Ed. T. D. Hardy (Record Comm., London, 1835).
Rotuli Normanniae. Ed. T. D. Hardy (Record Comm., London, 1835).
Rotuli Parliamentorum [1278-1503]. (London, 1783).
Rotuli Parliamentorum Anglie hactenus Inediti. Ed. H. G. Richardson and G. O. Sayles (Camden Ser., London, 1935).
Rotulus Cancellarii, 3 John. Ed. J. Hunter (Record Comm., London, 1833).
ROUND, J. H. *Commune of London* (Westminster, 1899).
— *Family Origins and other Studies.* Ed. W. Page (London, 1930).
— 'Domesday Survey' in *V.C.H.*, Worcester, i, 235-80.
— *Feudal England* (London, 1895, reprinted 1909).
— *Geoffrey de Mandeville* (London, 1892).
— *The King's Serjeants and Officers of State with their Coronation services* (London, 1911).
— *Peerage and Pedigree* (London, 1910).
— *Studies in Peerage and Family History* (Westminster, 1901).
— *Studies in the Red Book of the Exchequer* (London, 1898).
— 'The Weigher of the Exchequer' in *E.H.R.*, xxvi (1911), 724-27.
— 'Military Tenure before the Conquest' in *E.H.R.*, xii (1897), 492-94.
— 'The Officers of Edward the Confessor' in *E.H.R.*, xix (1904), 90-2.
  See *Ancient Charters; Calendar de Documents; Rotuli de Dominabus.*
ROWSE, A. L. *The Use of History* (London, 1946).

Royal Writs in England from the Conquest to Glanvill. Ed. R. C. van Caenegem (Selden Soc., London, 1959).

Salisbury. *See* John.
SALTER, H. E. 'A Dated Charter of Henry I' in *E.H.R.*, xxvi (1911), 487-91.
See *Cartulary of Oseney Abbey; Facsimiles; Thame Cartulary*.
SALTMAN, A. *Theobald Archbishop of Canterbury* (London, 1956).
SANDERS, I. J. *Feudal Military Service in England* (London, 1956).
Sarum Charters and Documents. Ed. W. D. Macray (Rolls Ser., London, 1891).
Sarum Missal. Ed. J. Wickham Legg (Oxford, 1916).
SAYLES, G. O. *Medieval Foundations of England* (London, 1948; 2nd ed. 1950).
See Richardson; *Select Cases in Court of King's Bench*.
SCHOLZ, B. W. 'The Canonisation of Edward the Confessor' in *Speculum*, xxxvi (1961), 38-60.
SCHRAMM, P. E. *History of the English Coronation* (Oxford, 1937).
— *Der König von Frankreich* (Weimar, 1939).
— 'Die krönung bei den Westfranken und Angelsachen von 878 bis um 1000' in *Zeitschrift der Savigny-Stiftung für Rechtsgeschichte*, liv (1935), *Kanonistische Abteilung*, xxxiii, 117-242.
— 'Die Krönung in Deutschland bis zum Beginn des Salischen Hauses' in *Z.S.S. lv, Kan. Abt.*, xxiv, 184-332.
Scriptores Rerum Gestarum Willelmi Conquestoris. Ed. J. A. Giles (London, 1845).
Select Cases in the Court of King's Bench. Ed. G. O. Sayles (Selden Soc., London, 1936-   ).
Select Cases of Procedure without Writ. Ed. H. G. Richardson and G. O. Sayles (Selden Soc., London, 1941).
Select Charters. *See* Stubbs.
Select Pleas of the Crown. Ed. F. W. Maitland (Selden Soc., London, 1888).
Select Pleas in Manorial and other Seignorial Courts. Ed. F. W. Maitland (Selden Soc., London, 1889).
SEMPLE, W. H. *See* Innocent III.
SIGEBERT OF GEMBLOUX. *Chronica* (with continuations). M.H.G., *Scriptores*, vi, 300-91.
SIMEON OF DURHAM. *Historical Works*. Ed. T. Arnold (Rolls Ser., London, 1882-85).
[*Historia Ecclesiae Dunholmensis*. vol. i; *Historia Regum*. vol ii].
— 'De Iniusta Vexacione Willelmi episcopi' in *Historical Works*, i, 170-95.
Social England. Ed. H. D. Traill (London, 1894-97; rev. ed., 1901-04).
SOMNER, W. *The Antiquities of Canterbury* (London, 1703).
SOUTHERN, R. W. 'The First Life of Edward the Confessor' in *E.H.R.*, lviii (1943), 385-400.
— 'A Note on the Text of "Glanvill, De Legibus et Consuetudinibus Regni Angliae" ' in *E.H.R.*, lxv (1950), 81-9.
Statutes of the Realm, vol. i (Record Comm., London, 1810).
STEENSTRUP, J. C. H. K. 'Kong David' in *Historisk Tidsskrift*, 10th Ser. ii (1933), 290-2.

STENTON, D. M. 'Roger of Howden and "Benedict" ' in *E.H.R.*, lxviii (1953), 574-82.
— 'King John and the Courts of Justice' in *Procs. Brit. Acad.*, xliv (1958), 103-28.
See *Rolls of Justices; Pleas before the King*.
STENTON, F. M. *Anglo-Saxon England* (Oxford, 1943; 2nd ed. 1947).
— *The First Century of English Feudalism* (Oxford, 1932; 2nd ed. 1961).
— *William the Conqueror* (London, 1908).
— 'An Early Inquest relating to St. Peter's, Derby' in *E.H.R.*, xxxii (1917), 47-8.
STEPHENSON, CARL. 'Feudalism and its Antecedents in England' in *Amer. H. Rev.*, xlviii (1942-43), 245-65.
STEVENSON, W. H. 'The Great Commendation to King Edgar in 973' in *E.H.R.*, xiii (1898), 505-7.
See Asser; *Crawford Collection*.
STILLINGFLEET, EDWARD. *Ecclesiastical Cases relating to the Duties and Rights of the Parochial Clergy* (London, 1698-1704).
STIMMING, ALBERT. See Born, Bertran of.
STRAYER, J. R. 'The Development of Feudal Institutions' in *Twelfth-Century Europe and the Foundations of Modern Society*. Ed. M. Glagett, G. Post and R. Reynolds (Madison, 1961).
STUBBS, WILLIAM. *Constitutional History of England* (Oxford, 1896-97). [vol. i: 6th ed., 1897; vol. ii: 4th ed., 1896; vol. iii: 5th ed., 1896].
— *French translation: Histoire Constitutionelle de l'Angleterre*. Ed. Ch. Petit-Dutaillis (Paris, 1907-27).
— *Lectures on Early English History*. Ed. A. Hassall (Oxford, 1906).
— *Select Charters and Other Illustrations of English Constitutional History to the Reign of Edward I.* (1st ed., 1870, 9th ed. by H. W. C. Davis, 1921).
— *Seventeen lectures on the study of Medieval and Modern History* (Oxford, 3rd ed., 1900).
See *Charters*; *Chronicles and Memorials*; *Chronicles of Reigns*; *Councils*; Gervase of Canterbury; *Letters*; *Memorials of St. Dunstan*; Ralf de Diceto; *Registrum Sacrum*; Roger of Howden.
Student's Dictionary of Anglo-Saxon. Ed. Henry Sweet (Oxford, 1897).
Studies in Medieval History presented to F. M. Powicke. Ed. R. W. Hunt, W. A. Pantin and R. W. Southern (Oxford, 1948).
Studies presented to Sir Hilary Jenkinson. Ed. J. Conway Davies (London, 1957).
Suggett. See Richardson.

TAIT, James. *The Medieval English Borough* (Manchester, 1936).
See *Historical Essays*.
TANCRED. 'Ordo Judiciarius' in *Pillii, Tancredi, Gratiae Libri de Iudiciorum Ordine*. Ed. Friedrich C. Bergmann (Göttingen, 1842).
TANNER, J. R. 'The Teaching of Constitutional History' in *The Teaching of History*, ed. W. A. J. Archbold (Cambridge, 1901).
TAYLOR, ISAAC. 'Wapentakes and Hundreds' in *Domesday Studies* (*q.v.*), 67-76.
Teulet. See *Layettes*.
Textus Roffensis. Ed. T. Hearne (Oxford, 1730).

Thame Cartulary. Ed. H. E. Salter (Oxfordshire Record Soc., 1947-48).

THOMAS OF ELMHAM. *Historia Monasterii Sancti Augustini Cantuariensis.* Ed. C. Hardwick (Rolls Ser., London, 1858).

THOMAS OF MONMOUTH. *The Life and Miracles of St. William of Norwich.* Ed. A. Jessopp and M. R. James (Cambridge, 1896).

THOMAS OF WALSINGHAM. *Gesta Abbatum Monasterii Sancti Albani.* Ed. H. T. Riley (Rolls Ser., London, 1867-69).

THOMAS, PAUL. *Le droit de propriété des laïques sur les églises et le patronage au moyen âge* (Paris, 1906).

THOMPSON, J. WESTFALL. *The Literacy of the Laity in the Middle Ages* (Berkeley, 1939).

THORNE, S. E. See *Prerogativa.*

Thorne. *See* William.

THORPE, B. See *Anglo-Saxon Chronicle; Diplomatarium.*

THORPE, J. See *Registrum Roffense.*

Three Coronation Orders. Ed. J. Wickham Legg (Henry Bradshaw Soc., vol. 19, 1900).

Three Rolls of the King's Court. Ed. F. W. Maitland (Pipe Roll Soc., vol. xiv, London, 1891).

Tilbury. *See* Gervase.

TOMLINSON, JOHN. T. *The 'Legal History' by Canon Stubbs . . . Reviewed.* (London, 1884).

Torigni. *See* Robert.

Tournai. *See* Herman.

TOUT, T. F. *Chapters in the Administrative History of Mediaeval England* (Manchester, 1920-33).

— 'Robert Fitz Walter' in *Dict. Nat. Biog., s.v.* Fitzwalter.

TURNER, G. J. 'The Sheriff's Farm' in *Trans. R.H.Soc.,* New Ser., xii (1898), 117-49.

Two of the Saxon Chronicles Parallel. Ed. C. Plummer (Oxford, 1892-99). [Translated page for page by G. N. Garmonsway, *The Anglo-Saxon Chronicle* (London, 1939; rev. ed. 1960).]

TWYSDEN, ROGER. See *Historiae Anglicanae.*

M. TYSON. 'The Annals of Southwark and Merton' in *Surrey Archaeological Collections,* xxxvi (1925), 24-57.

VACARIUS. *Liber Pauperum.* Ed. F. de Zulueta (Selden Soc., London, 1927).

VAN CAENEGEM. See *Royal Writs.*

VERCAUTEREN, F. See *Actes des Comtes de Flandres.*

Vere. *See* William.

VINCENT, A. *Discoverie of Brook's Errors* (London, 1622).

VINOGRADOFF, P. *English Society in the Eleventh Century* (Oxford, 1908).

Vita Ædwardi Regis. Ed. F. Barlow (London, 1962).

'Vita Oswaldi Archiepiscopi Eboracensis' in *Historians of the Church of York (q.v.),* i, 399-475.

Vita Wulfstani. See William of Malmesbury.

VOSS, LENA. *Heinrich von Blois, Bischof von Winchester, 1129-71* (Berlin, 1932).

Wailly. *See* Joseph.

Walberg. *See* Guernes.

Walsingham. *See* Thomas.

WALTER OF COVENTRY. *Memoriale.* Ed. W. Stubbs (Rolls Ser., London, 1872-73).

WARNER, G. F. and ELLIS, H. J. *Facsimiles of Royal and other Charters in the British Museum* (London, 1903).

WARREN, W. L. *King John* (London, 1961).

WEBB, E. A. See *Records.*

WEINBAUM, MARTIN. *London unter Eduard I und II* (Stuttgart, 1933).

Wendover. *See* Roger.

WEST, J. R. *St. Benet of Holme, 1020-1210* (Norfolk Record Soc., 1932).

Westminster. *See* Matthew.

WHARTON. See *Anglia Sacra.*

WHITE, G. H. 'Financial Administration under Henry I' in *Trans. R.H.Soc.,* 4th series, viii (1925), 56-78.

WHITELOCK, D. 'Wulfstan and the Laws of Cnut' in *E.H.R.,* lxiii (1948), 433-52.

See *Anglo-Saxon Wills; English Historical Documents;* Wulfstan.

WIDMORE, RICHARD. *History of the Church of St. Peter, Westminster, commonly called Westminster Abbey* (London, 1751).

WILLIAM OF DROGHEDA. *Summa Aurea.* Ed. L. Wahrmund in *Quellen zur Geschichte des römisch-kanonischen Processes im Mittelalter* (Bd. II, heft 2, 1914).

WILLIAM OF MALMESBURY. *Gesta Pontificum.* Ed. N. E. S. A. Hamilton (Rolls Ser., London, 1870).

— *Gesta Regum.* Ed. W. Stubbs (Rolls Ser., London, 1887-89).

— *Historia Novella.* Ed. K. R. Potter (London, 1955).

— *Vita Wulfstani.* Ed. R. R. Darlington (Camden Ser., London, 1928).

WILLIAM OF NEWBURGH. 'Historia Rerum Anglicarum' in *Chronicles, Stephen etc. (q.v.),* vols. i-ii.

WILLIAM OF POITIERS. *Histoire de Guillaume le Conquérant.* Ed. R. Foreville (Paris, 1952).

WILLIAM THORNE. 'Chronica de rebus gestis abbatum Sancti Augustini Cantuariae' in *Historiae Anglicanae Scriptores Decem (q.v.),* cols. 1753-2202.

WILLIAM DE VERE. 'Liber de Miraculis Sanctae Osithae' *in* John Leland, *Itinerary.* Ed. Toulmin Smith (London, 1906-10), vol. v, 167-72.

WILMART, ANDRÉ. 'Les Mélanges de Mathieu préchantre de Rievaulx au debut du xiiie siècle in *Revue Benedictine* (Maredsous), lii (1940), 15-84.

WILSON, R. M. See *Early Middle English Texts.*

Winton Domesday. See *Liber Winton.*

Worcester. *See* Florence; John.

WÜLCKER-WRIGHT. See *Anglo-Saxon and Old English Vocabularies.*

WULFSTAN. *Sermo Lupi ad Anglos.* Ed. D. Whitelock (London, 1939).

Abbreviations

B.I.H.R.	*Bulletin of Institute of Historical Research*
B.J.R.L.	*Bulletin of John Rylands Library*
E.E.T.S.	*Early English Text Society*
E.H.R.	*English Historical Review*
L.Q.R.	*Law Quarterly Review*

Manuscripts

Bodleian Library
    Rawlinson C. 641

British Museum
    Additional MSS.
        14252
        28024
    Additional Charters
        1046
        20420
        28313
    Arundel 29 (Walden Abbey Chronicle)
    Burney 277
    Cotton:
        Claudius D. II
        Cleopatra D. III (Hailes Abbey Chronicle)
        Julius D. II
        Nero C. III
        Nero E. I (Vita Oswaldi)
        Titus A. I
        Vespasian
            E. III
            E. V
            E. VI (Walden Abbey Chronicle)
            E. XXI (Historia Roffensis)
            F. IV
    Cotton Charter xxix. 65
    Egerton MS. 3031
    Harleian MSS.
        391
        458
        1708
        3656 (Newnham Priory Cartulary)
    Harleian Roll A. 3
    Royal MS. 14. C. 2
    Sloane Charter xxxii. 64

Cambridge University Library
    Dd. vii. 14

Canterbury, Dean and Chapter Library
    K. 11

Public Record Office, London
    Ancient Deeds
        A (E. 40), 2383
          5937
        14404
        L (D. L. 25) 110

Public Record Office, London (cont.)
Coram Rege Rolls
K. B. 27/79, 80
Curia Regis Rolls
K. B. 26/151
Pipe Roll, no. 61

St. Paul's Cathedral Library
MS. 15/839

INDEX OF PERSONS AND PLACES

INDEX OF SUBJECTS